THE DEVELOPMENT OF

ANIMAL BEHAVIOR

A READER

EDITED BY

JOHAN J. BOLHUIS AND
JERRY A. HOGAN

FOREWORD BY

PATRICK BATESON

Copyright © Blackwell Publishers Ltd 1999
Selection and editorial matter copyright © Johan J. Bolhuis and Jerry A. Hogan 1999

First published 1999

2 4 6 8 10 9 7 5 3 1

Blackwell Publishers Ltd
108 Cowley Road
Oxford OX4 1JF
UK

Blackwell Publishers Inc.
350 Main Street
Malden, Massachusetts 02148
USA

British Library Cataloguing in Publication Data

A CIP catalogue record for this book is available from the British Library.

Library of Congress Cataloging-in-Publication Data

The development of animal behavior / edited by Johan J. Bolhuis and Jerry A. Hogan.
p.   cm.
Includes bibliographical references and index.
ISBN 0–631–20707–4 (hbk.: alk. paper). – ISBN 0–631–20708–2 (pbk.: alk. paper)
1. Animal behavior.   2. Developmental psychobiology.   I. Bolhuis, Johan J.   II. Hogan, Jerry A.
QL763.D465 1999 591.5 – dc21   98–16168 CIP

Typeset in 9$^1/_2$ on 11$^1/_2$ pt Ehrhardt
by Best-set Typesetter Ltd, Hong Kong
Printed in Great Britain by T.J. International, Padstow, Cornwall

This book is printed on acid-free paper

Contents

List of Contributors

Patrick Bateson
Sub-Department of Animal Behaviour, University of Cambridge, Madingley, Cambridge CB3 8AA, England

Johan J. Bolhuis
Institute of Evolutionary and Ecological Sciences, Behavioural Biology, Leiden University, P.O. Box 9516, 2300 RA Leiden, The Netherlands

John C. Fentress
Department of Psychology, Dalhousie University, Halifax, NS, Canada B3H 4J1

Gilbert Gottlieb
Center for Developmental Science, University of North Carolina, 521 South Greensboro Street, Campus Box 8115, Chapel Hill, NC 27599-8115, USA

William G. Hall
Department of Psychology, Duke University, Durham, NC 27706, USA

Harry F. Harlow*
Primate Center, Madison, Wisconsin, USA

Margaret K. Harlow*
Primate Center, Madison, Wisconsin, USA

Donald O. Hebb*
McGill University, Montreal, Canada

*Deceased

Robert A. Hinde
St John's College, Cambridge, CB2 1TP, England

Jerry A. Hogan
Department of Psychology, University of Toronto, Toronto, Canada M5S 1A1

Donald E. Kroodsma
Department of Biology, University of Massachusetts, Amherst, MA 01003-0027, USA

Jaap P. Kruijt
Zoological Laboratory, University of Groningen, PO Box 14, 9750 AA Haren, The Netherlands

Zing-Yang Kuo*

Daniel S. Lehrman*
Institute of Animal Behavior, Rutgers University, Newark, NJ, USA

Konrad Lorenz*
Max Planck Institut für Verhaltensforschung, Seewiesen, Germany

Peter J. McLeod
Department of Psychology, Dalhousie University, Halifax, NS, Canada B3H 4J1

Peter Marler
Animal Communication Laboratory, University of California, Davis, CA 95616-8761, USA

Robert W. Oppenheim
Department of Neurobiology, Wake Forest University, The Bowman Gray School of Medicine, Medical Center Boulevard, Winston-Salem, NC 27157-1010, USA

Carla J. Shatz
Department of Neurobiology, University of California, Berkeley, USA

Carel ten Cate
Institute of Evolutionary and Ecological Sciences, Behavioural Biology, Leiden University, P.O. Box 9516, 2300 RA Leiden, The Netherlands

Conrad H. Waddington*
University of Edinburgh, Scotland, UK

Christina L. Williams
Department of Psychology, Duke University, Durham, NC 27706, USA

* Deceased

Foreword

Patrick Bateson

A witty author of garden books, Christopher Lloyd, wrote something that has relevance to this collection of readings. He described how people who have bought hydrangeas with blue flowers, may plant them in their gardens and the following year find to their consternation that the flowers have become pink. Lime in the soil is responsible for the colour change. "People either find this easy to understand or quite impossible, so I shall not labour the reasoning" (Lloyd, 1987, pp. 400–1). Those of us who work on behavioral development will recognize the observation. Some people have found it easy to understand that the developing individual's behavior is a product of many things, some of which are inside the body and some outside. Others wanted to know *the* cause of behavior. If this second group got their minds round the possibility of more than one cause, then they wanted to analyse the effect in terms of the proportional contributions of the genes and the environment.

Possibly the division of the world into those who thought in terms of interacting systems and those who didn't really boiled down to a matter of pragmatism. The systems thinkers wanted to describe processes as they found them, whereas the linear thinkers were simply concerned with the most effective method of unraveling behavioral development. The notion that everything interacts seamlessly with everything else might have been all right for holistic philosophers, but it seems downright obscurantist to the experimentally minded. Whether or not it was simply a matter of how to get on with empirical research that divided the two camps – and I suspect it wasn't – I have noticed a change in recent years. The modern generation of young scientists seem to be able to think in terms of systems and also do good experiments. Is this because they have been reared on computers since they were very young? When you meet, in the dungeon of the dark castle, a dragon that can only be killed with a special sword which you had to pick up on the top of a mountain, you have started to accustom yourself to the conditional character of the world. The change in scientific style brought about by a particular type of early experience may itself be an interesting topic for developmental analysis.

For whatever reason, experimentalists are less likely these days to hold all but one variable constant and, when a single independent variable is found to produce an effect, it is not immediately taken to be *the* cause; nor is everything else deemed unimportant. The nature of the feedback in free-running systems is such that the experimentalist's sharp distinction between independence and dependence evaporates. The dependent variable of a moment ago becomes the independent variable of the present. The current state of the individual will influence which of its genes are expressed, and also affect its social and physical world. Individuals both choose and change the conditions to which they are exposed. Even for the most analytically minded, the development of individuals is readily perceived as an interplay between them and their environment.

The merging of what were previously two streams of thought suggests that even the dichotomy of thinkers into those who liked dichotomies and those that didn't has been breaking down. In this context, it is appropriate to mention a perennial bug-bear of writers about behavioral development (many of whom have essays in this set of readings), namely the division of behaviour into learning and instinct. The critics of the criticism saw the attack on the ancient dichotomy as an attempt to explain all behavioral development in the same terms. That was not the point. The problem was that a whole series of different aspects of behavior had been identified. The word 'innate' has at least seven separate meanings attached to it: present at birth; being a behavioral difference caused by a genetic difference; adapted over the course of evolution; unchanging throughout development; shared by all members of a species; present before the behavior serves any function; and not learned. 'Instinctive' had been deployed in similar ways to innate. A further and special meaning was also attached to instinct, namely a distinctly organized system of behavior driven from within the body. It does not take a great deal of thought to appreciate that when one of the supposed features of a particular pattern of behavior has been justified, work still needs to be done before attributing any other feature to that pattern – and further work may fail to provide the justification. For instance, a blind baby may start to smile in the same way as a normal baby, justifying the view that smiling is not learned. Nevertheless, later on in their lives, sighted people will modify their smiles to facial expressions that are characteristic of their own culture, evidence that fails to confirm the view that this pattern of behavior cannot be changed by experience.

The argument is, then, that we should be explicit about what we mean. When we are explicit, it becomes obvious that numerous factors affect the outcome of developmental processes. As in the case of the human smile, dispositions to respond strongly to some features of the environment often develop without direct experience of those features, and stereotyped motor patterns often develop without obvious opportunities for practice. These aspects of a behavioral repertoire, once developed, may be modified by experience. Similarly, learning processes are rule-governed and have an organization that may develop without obvious practice, but may also change with experience. Several different developmental processes may lead to the adaptive complexity of behaviour, but any given behaviour pattern may be affected by all or several of them. Since biological processes tend to be non-linear and highly conditional in their operation, the chances are that the various influences do not add together and, that being the case, small changes in certain factors may sometimes make big differences to the outcome and large changes in others will have no effect whatsoever. Even when expressed like this it is obvious why the old either/or oppositions applied to behavior have evaporated as knowledge has advanced.

Developmental processes may be remarkably well buffered against fluctuations in the environment. Moreover, if an individual is prevented from developing in one way, the same behavior pattern may sometimes develop in another way. Given their dispositions and proclivities, individuals may choose environments to which their characteristics are well adapted. Individuals are also equipped with conditional rules so that their behavioral development is directed down one of several different routes with different end-points, depending on the prevailing conditions. Without a strong set of binding ideas, it isn't easy to think about all aspects of the various strands of evidence, which often seem to point in opposite directions. Many mathematical techniques, such as catastrophe theory and "chaos," have been developed to deal analytically with the complexities of dynamical systems. For all that, it is questionable whether the descriptive use of mathematics brings with it any explanatory power. Enhanced computer literacy has certainly made it possible for biologists and psychologists to think about the interplay between many different influences with comparative ease. It is not difficult to construct simple working models (Elman et al., 1996). When the rules of operation are non-linear, the behavior of these models may change in complicated ways that are difficult to predict when the parameters are altered.

In my own theoretical work with Gabriel Horn, we have taken from behavioral development the specific example of imprinting (Bateson and Horn, 1994; see chapter 13 of the present volume for a brief discussion). Our model builds on a proposal that the behavior of experienced animals relies on three sub-processes that sequentially analyze the features of stimuli, recognize those feature combinations that are familiar and organize appropriate responses. We tried to ensure that most of the sub-processes are as plausible in neural terms as current knowledge allows and that the whole system has the behavioral structure of an intact animal. The model exhibited features of behavioral development seen in animals, tending to settle into familiar habits, while also able to build with increasing elaboration on the basis of previous perceptual experience. We were pleased with the result because these two features are sometimes seen as contradictory. So the model helped to resolve a general dispute over evidence for sensitive periods in development.

The case for some theory of mechanism is that it spawns explicit working models which bring with them mental discipline and expose weaknesses in a verbal argument that are all too easily missed. They can show how we are easily misled by the dynamics of development into supposing that the processes are so complicated that they are beyond comprehension. From the point of view of future empirical research, they can suggest profitable new lines of enquiry. They bring understanding of how real systems generate the seemingly elaborate things that we observe. Their predictions may be false, but they are worth testing just because the assumptions are rooted in psychological and biological reality.

Many powerful voices have urged the behavioral and social sciences to model themselves on the success stories of classical physics or molecular biology. The obvious attractions of producing simple, easily understood explanations has meant that crucial distinctions have been fudged in the name of

being straightforward and analysis has been focused on single factors in the name of clarity. This has been particularly obvious in studies of development. Nobody likes to think that their pet principles are constrained. Indeed, a common feature of bolder writers has been to drive their speculations all over the place as though these were the attractive and necessary simplifications for which everybody craves. It is not difficult to see why the mismatch between theory and reality generated irritation in those who had to deal with the complications of behavioral development. Explanations are worthless if they do not bear some relation to real phenomena.

While premature generalizations may be readily criticized, focusing on complexity, almost for its own sake, has no merit either. So how do we move forward? Understanding how the parts relate to each other is a precondition to understanding process and understanding process is the precursor to uncovering principles. Inevitably, tension still exists between ideas that emphasize differences and celebrate complexity and those that unify and simplify. I think that the overall message of the readings found in this book is this. We should value the search for coherence as well as the intuitions of those who really know what happens when an individual develops.

References

Bateson, P. and Horn, G. (1994) Imprinting and recognition memory: a neural net model, *Animal Behaviour*, **48**, 695–715.

Elman, J. L., Bates, E. A., Johnson, M. H., Karmiloff-Smith, A., Parisi, D. and Plunkett, K. (1996) *Rethinking Innateness*, Cambridge, Mass.: MIT Press.

Lloyd, C. (1987) *The Well-tempered Garden*, Harmondsworth, Middlesex: Penguin.

Preface

After a period of intense research efforts studying functional aspects of behavior, there is now a shift in animal behavior research towards a renewed emphasis on causal and developmental questions. Previously we have made an effort to capture this changing focus in a volume of contemporary essays on behavioral development (Hogan, J.A. and Bolhuis, J.J., *Causal Mechanisms of Behavioural Development*, Cambridge University Press, 1994). However, in both teaching and research we felt a need for a collection of classic theoretical and empirical papers that have shaped the field of behavioral development. The present volume is the result of our attempts to produce such a Reader. As we would want the book to play a role in student courses on development, we did not want to limit ourselves to a collection of classics from the past, but have also included some recent updates of various key topics in development. We hope that this blend has made this a more complete book that covers the whole field of contemporary research into the development of animal behavior. Obviously, different researchers will have different views on which papers to include in such a book, and the present collection reflects our personal preferences. For instance, just as with our previous volume of contemporary papers, we have concentrated on causal analyses of development. We believe that a causal analysis is currently the most appropriate way to approach developmental problems, and we hope that by concentrating on causal approaches we have succeeded in producing a balanced and coherent Reader.

We are grateful to the various contributors for allowing us to reprint their papers, to Pat Bateson for writing the Foreword, and to him, Robert Hinde and Mark Johnson for advice. Thanks are also due to a succession of editors at Blackwell Publishers who have helped us in organizing this Reader: Alison Mudditt, Nathalie Manners, Martin Davies and their assistants.

Cambridge,   J.J.B.
Toronto,   J.A.H.
December 1997

Acknowledgments

Chapter 1, "Principles of Development and Differentiation" by Conrad H. Waddington, first appeared in C. H. Waddington, *Principles of Development and Differentiation* (New York: Macmillan, 1966), pp. 1–9, 14–15, 44–63, 70–9.

Chapter 2, "Ontogenetic Adaptations and Retrogressive Processes in the Development of the Nervous System and Behaviour: A Neuroembryological Perspective" by Robert W. Oppenheim, first appeared in K. J. Connolly and H. F. R. Prechtl (eds), *Maturation and Development: Biological and Psychological Perspectives* (Philadelphia, PA: Lippincott, 1981), pp. 73–109.

Chapter 3, "From Watsonian Behaviorism to Behavior Epigenetics" by Zing-Yang Kuo, first appeared in Zing-Yang Kuo, *The Dynamics of Behavior Development* (New York: Plenum Press, 1967), pp. 3–26.

Chapter 4, "Developmental Changes in Sensitivity to Experience" by Patrick Bateson and Robert A. Hinde, first appeared in M. H. Bornstein (ed.), *Sensitive Periods in Development* (Hillsdale, NJ: Lawrence Erlbaum, 1987), pp. 19–34.

Chapter 5, "Behavioral Development: Toward Understanding Processes" by Carel ten Cate, first appeared in P. P. G. Bateson and P. Klopfer (eds), *Perspectives in Ethology*, vol. 8 (New York: Plenum Press, 1989), pp. 243–69.

Chapter 6, "A Critique of Konrad Lorenz's Theory of Instinctive Behavior" by Daniel S. Lehrman, first appeared in *Quarterly Review of Biology*, **28** (1953), pp. 337–63.

Chapter 7, "Heredity and Environment in Mammalian Behaviour" by Donald O. Hebb, first appeared in *British Journal of Animal Behaviour*, **1** (1953), pp. 43–7. Reprinted by permission of Academic Press Ltd, London.

Chapter 8, "Evolution and Modification of Behavior" by Konrad Lorenz, first appeared in K. Z. Lorenz, *Evolution and Modification of Behavior* (Chicago: University of Chicago Press, 1965), pp. 1–27, 79–82.

Chapter 9, "Semantic and Conceptual Issues in the Nature–Nurture Problem" by Daniel S. Lehrman, first appeared in L. R. Aronson, E. Tobach, D. S. Lehrman and J. S. Rosenblatt (eds), *Development and Evolution of Behavior* (San Francisco, CA: Freeman, 1970), pp. 17–52.

Chapter 10, "The Developing Brain" by Carla J. Shatz, first appeared in *Scientific American*, **267**, September 1992, pp. 60–7. Reprinted with permission. Copyright © 1992 by Scientific American, Inc. All rights reserved.

Chapter 11, "Development of Species Identification in Ducklings – VI: Specific Embryonic Experience Required to Maintain Species-Typical Perception in Peking Ducklings" by Gilbert Gottlieb, first appeared in *Journal of Comparative and Physiological Psychology*, **94**(4), August 1980, pp. 579–87. Copyright © 1980 by the American Psychological Association, Inc. Reprinted by permission.

Chapter 12, "The Companion in the Bird's World" by Konrad Lorenz, first appeared in Konrad Lorenz, *Studies in Animal and Human Behaviour* (London: Methuen, 1935; 2nd edn 1970), pp. 124–33.

Chapter 13, "Development of Perceptual Mechanisms in Birds: Predispositions and Imprinting" by Johan J. Bolhuis, first appeared in C.F. Moss and S.J. Shettleworth (eds), *Neuroethological Studies of Cognitive and Perceptual Processes* (Boulder, CO: Westview Press, 1996), pp. 158–84. Copyright © 1996 by Westview Press. Reprinted by permission of Westview Press.

Chapter 14, "Sensory Templates in Species-Specific Behavior" by Peter Marler, first appeared in J. C. Fentress (ed.), *Simpler Networks and Behavior* (Sunderland, MA: Sinauer, 1976), pp. 314–29.

Chapter 15, "Aspects of Learning in the Ontogeny of Bird Song: Where, from Whom, When, How Many, Which, and How Accurately?" by Donald E. Kroodsma, first appeared in G.M. Burghardt and M. Berkoff (eds), *The Development of Behavior* (New York: Garland STPM Press, 1978), pp. 215–30.

Chapter 16, "Motor Patterns in Development" by John C. Fentress and Peter J. McLeod, first appeared in E. M. Blass (ed.), *Handbook of Behavioral Neurobiology*, vol. 8: *Developmental Processes in Psychobiology and Neurobiology* (New York: Plenum Press, 1986), pp. 35–60.

Chapter 17, "Suckling Isn't Feeding, or Is It? A Search for Developmental Continuities" by William G. Hall and Christina L. Williams, first appeared in *Advances in the Study of Behavior*, vol. 13 (1983), pp. 219–54.

Chapter 18, "Ontogeny of Social Behaviour in Burmese Red Junglefowl (*Gallus gallus spadiceus*)" by Jaap P. Kruijt, first appeared in *Behaviour*, Supplement 9 (1964), pp. 2–5, 172–5, 177–9.

Chapter 19, "Social Deprivation in Monkeys" by Harry F. Harlow and Margaret K. Harlow, first appeared in *Scientific American*, **207**(5), November 1962, pp. 136–46. Copyright © 1962 by *Scientific American*, Inc. All rights reserved.

Chapter 20, "Mother–Infant Separation and the Nature of Inter-Individual Relationships: Experiments with Rhesus Monkeys" by Robert A. Hinde, first appeared in *Proceedings of the Royal Society of London B*, **196** (1977), pp. 29–50.

Chapter 21, "Structure and Development of Behavior Systems" by Jerry A. Hogan, first appeared in *Psychonomic Bulletin and Review*, 1(4) (1994), pp. 439–50. Copyright © 1994 Psychonomic Society, Inc.

PART I

General Principles of Development

Introduction

Development can be considered to begin with the fertilized egg, and we begin our Reader with an excerpt from an introductory chapter by the great Scottish embryologist C. H. Waddington. This excerpt explains many of the basic concepts and facts of experimental embryology, such as canalization and induction, which provide a necessary foundation for understanding later behavioral development. Although this chapter was written more than 30 years ago, Waddington was far ahead of his time in realizing the importance of molecular genetics for understanding developmental processes. His framework still reflects that of contemporary studies of embryology (e.g., Slack, 1991).

The next chapter, by Robert Oppenheim, examines the common belief that animal development consists of "a gradual and continuous epigenetic progression in which the organism takes on more and more of the features of the adult, and in which each step in the progression is thought to constitute an integral antecedent (causal mechanism) for some subsequent event." Oppenheim discusses evidence at both the neurological and the behavioral level that calls this belief into question. He shows that states are reached in early development that appear to be adaptations to that stage of development: ontogenetic adaptations. An example is some of the behavior a chick shows when hatching: once the chick has hatched, that behavior is never seen again. Chapter 17, which analyzes the relation of the suckling behavior of young rats to later feeding behavior, provides another excellent example of the same phenomenon.

The chapter by Zing-Yang Kuo, a Chinese psychologist who worked in the United States during the 1920s and 1930s, presents a classical statement of the concept of epigenesis in behavior. He also discusses the question of the relation between early and later behavior. Kuo's ideas had an important influence on later workers. He was also well known for his colorful and provocative language, and those qualities are clearly in evidence in this excerpt: "in ontogenesis, no movement is a preparatory act to serve a future purpose of the animal."

The last two chapters in this section show how embryological principles translate into behavioral ones. Patrick Bateson and Robert Hinde discuss the concept of sensitive periods in development, and show what kinds of evidence are necessary to demonstrate the existence of a sensitive period. Their article is especially important because it clearly describes the different kinds of explanations for the phenomenon (which are not mutually exclusive) and also distinguishes between explanations of the same type (which are mutually exclusive). Carel ten Cate presents a process-oriented approach to development. His chapter emphasizes that development involves the interaction of many different factors, a point that is also made in all the preceding chapters. But he then goes on to show how it is possible to study the ways in which these factors actually exert their effects.

Reference

Slack, J. M. W. (1991) *From Egg to Embryo*, Cambridge: Cambridge University Press.

CHAPTER 1

Principles of Development and Differentiation (*excerpt*)

Conrad H. Waddington

The Problems of Development

Embryology, like all sciences, begins with the observation of processes going on in nature, which it then tries to understand and explain. Before we can propose theories we need to know the problems they are intended to deal with. There are, of course, an enormous variety of different types of embryonic development in the animal world, corresponding to the great range of types of adult that are finally produced. However, one can get a good idea of the general problems we have to deal with by considering only one or two cases.

The basic facts

We will select two of the kinds of eggs that have been most studied experimentally – those of sea urchins and of newts. Figures 1.1 and 1.2 show a series of steps in the early development of these two types of eggs. Neither figure covers the whole of development. We shall not, in this book, discuss the preliminary processes of egg maturation in the ovary; and we shall take for granted the occurrence of meiotic divisions, by which the chromosome complement is reduced from the diploid to the hap-

From C. H. Waddington, *Principles of Development and Differentiation* (New York: Macmillan, 1966), pp. 1–9, 14–15, 44–63, 70–9.

loid number, and of fertilization, by which the number is restored again. These are subjects for genetics rather than for embryology. The diagrams also do not illustrate development right up to the adult condition, but they trace it far enough to show the main kinds of process that occur during differentiation and thus to indicate the types of problem with which embryologists are faced.

It is obvious that there are certain similarities between the two kinds of eggs. For instance, in both cases, in the first phase of development immediately after fertilization the original egg cell becomes divided into a larger number of small cells. This process, known as cleavage, takes place in eggs of all types. The processes at work are fundamentally those which are always concerned with cell division. They belong as much to the field of cell biology as to that of embryology, and we shall not discuss them in detail here for lack of space.

At the end of the period of cleavage we see that the little embryo forms a collection of cells which is not a solid mass but is hollow in the center. This hollow sphere of cells is known as the blastula stage, and again it is one that can be found, in some form or other, in nearly all animal embryos. It is quite a transient stage and is immediately followed by a period characterized by a number of foldings and movements of cell masses from one place to another. These foldings are known as the process of gastrulation, and again they occur, though in a

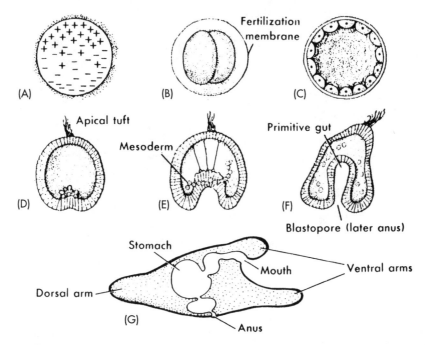

Figure 1.1 Early development of sea urchin. (**A**) The fertilized egg as seen from the side. It floats with the animal pole upward and the vegetative pole downward. It is characterized by two gradients, one strongest at the animal pole falling off toward the vegetative pole, and the other running in the opposite direction. These are indicated by + for the first and by − for the second. (**B**) The egg, after fertilization, has thrown off a membrane ("the fertilization membrane") and by this stage has divided into two. (**C**) The egg is seen in vertical section. It has divided into a large number of cells which adhere to the fertilization membrane and leave a large hollow space in the center: this is the blastula stage. By the stage shown in (**D**) a group of cilia (the apical tuft) has appeared at the animal pole while the vegetative pole is beginning to become flattened and some cells are breaking free and moving into the interior of the blastula cavity. By the stage shown in (**E**) there are more of these cells, and some of them have put out processes that reach across the blastula cavity and attach to cells in the animal half of the egg. By the contraction of these attachment cells the vegetative end of the blastula is pulled gradually inward, forming a pocket which is the primitive gut. By the stage shown in (**F**) this has become a deep finger-shaped cavity reaching right across the blastula. Its top end is just beginning to be bent toward the right, which will become the ventral side of the larva. (**G**) This end of the primitive gut has joined onto the ventral surface, and a hole has appeared at the point of junction: this is the mouth. Meanwhile, the four corners of the ventral side have been pulled out into arms and another pointed arm appears on the dorsal side, so that the whole larva has acquired the shape of a sharp pyramid lying on its side.

variety of different ways, in the embryos of all classes of animals. They result in the production of an embryonic form that contains three layers. The outer layer forms the skin and the nervous system and is known as the ectoderm. The layer that lies deepest in the center of the embryo forms the intestine and its derivatives and is known as the endoderm. Between these two lies a middle layer, the mesoderm, which forms the muscles, skeleton, kidneys, and many other organs.

The processes by which these three layers are brought into being differ in different types of em-

bryo (figure 1.3), depending largely on the particular shape of the blastula from which the development starts. For instance, in the embryos of reptiles and birds the shape of the embryo is altered by the enormous supplies of nutritive material that have to be provided to keep the embryo alive within the egg shell until it is sufficiently developed to come out and feed for itself. The blastulae of these forms have been accommodated to the vast amount of yolk by becoming flat circular plates instead of hollow spherical balls. Clearly the foldings necessary to produce three layers from a plate are quite different

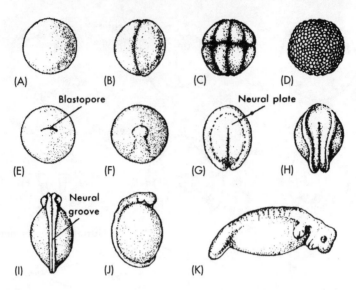

Figure 1.2   The development of an amphibian such as a newt or salamander. The egg first divides into a number of smaller cells and by the stage shown in (**D**) consists of a hollow ball of numerous cells. By the stage (**E**) the cells have become too small to be marked on the later drawings. In (**E**) the egg is seen from below (that is, from the vegetative pole). One can see a small crescent-shaped groove, the blastopore, which is actually the entrance into a narrow cavity that pushes into the interior of the hollow ball of cells. The crescent gradually grows round into a more circular shape (**F**). Shortly after this, if one looks at the egg from the opposite (animal) end (**G**), one can see a horseshoe-shaped area marked off on the surface by a ridge. This is the rudiment – the neural plate – from which the whole nervous system will develop. A little later (**H**) the boundary ridges (known as the "neural crest") have moved closer together. By the stage shown from on top in (**I**) and from the side in (**J**) the ridges have come together in the mid-dorsal lines, so that the whole neural area has been folded beneath the surface, where it forms a separate tube. The anterior end of this tube, toward the top in the diagrams, is already beginning to form the brain and nervous system of the head. By the stage shown in (**K**) the embryo is becoming elongated. In the head region, the eyes can be recognized, and somewhat behind this are two swellings, which are the rudiments of the gills. The tail is beginning to grow out at the posterior end.

from those required to produce a similar set of layers from a hollow sphere. However, in both cases the end result of the foldings of gastrulation is the production of the three major layers – the ectoderm, mesoderm, and endoderm.

Once the three layers are formed they begin to develop into definite organs corresponding to those of the adult. For instance, in the sea urchin the endoderm soon begins to form a recognizable mouth, behind which is a stomach and an intestine leading to the anus. In the early stages of the embryo of the newt a very obvious and striking event is the formation of the nervous system. Part of the external ectoderm is first marked off from the rest by slightly elevated folds and is then folded inward to form a groove, and finally a tube, which gives rise to the brain and spinal cord and from which the rest of the nerves grow out. Meanwhile, the endoderm

of the newt is also developing into the definitive regions of the intestine; and the mesoderm forms the first element of the skeleton, known as the notochord, along the center of the back, while on each side of it the tissue becomes divided up into a sequence of squarish blocks, the somites, which give rise to the muscles and bony skeleton of the backbone.

Embryology and evolution

This book is mainly concerned with principles, and we shall not pursue further here a detailed discussion of the changes in anatomy which go on in various types of embryo. In the early history of embryology, up to about the end of the nineteenth century, these changes in morphology took the center of the stage. It was, of course, necessary for them

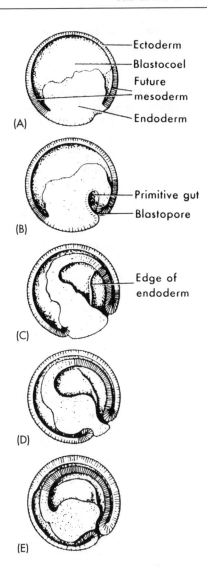

(A)
Ectoderm
Blastocoel
Future
mesoderm
Endoderm

(B)
Primitive gut
Blastopore

(C)
Edge of
endoderm

(D)

(E)

Figure 1.3 Newt gastrulation. The drawings show what is going on in the interior of the egg between the stages (E) and (G) in figure 1.2. We are looking at the right halves of embryos that have been cut in half down their dorso–ventral plane. (A) is the blastula stage, a hollow ball in which the lower part is made of much larger cells than the upper regions. In (B) (corresponding to figure 1.2 (E)) the blastopore has begun to appear at the bottom right. After this the primitive gut becomes deeper and larger as the mesoderm moves round the edge of the blastopore into the interior and the endoderm swings round along with it.

to be described in detail first, before one could consider further how they were brought about. Even the mere description of them raised a number of apparently interesting problems. For instance, why is it that all embryos pass through a stage corresponding to the blastula, and then through a process of gastrulation to reach a three-layered condition? There was no apparent answer until Darwin's theory of evolution became accepted about the middle of the nineteenth century. Then it seemed clear that this similarity in the embryos of different forms must be related in some way to the fact that animals are evolved one from the other. Even before this time von Baer had formulated one general "law" about such morphological comparisons between embryos, stating that the more general features of an animal, which are common to all members of a large group, appear earlier during embryonic development than the specialized features that characterize any particular species. With the coming of evolution theory this idea was reformulated by Haeckel into the rule that the stages in the embryonic development of an animal in some way repeat the stages of the evolution of its ancestors. The main reason for mentioning these old ideas here is that this "law" has become very widely known, and is often repeated in the phrase that during its development an animal "climbs up its family tree."

This is a memorable and catchy expression, but it is actually quite misleading. The embryonic stages of any highly evolved animal are never at all closely similar to the adult stages of its ancestors. They do, however, sometimes look like embryonic stages of the evolutionary ancestors. For instance, it is generally accepted that the mammals, including man, evolved from fishlike forms. These ancestral fish had gills provided with gill slits through which the water could circulate. Human embryos at a certain stage have slits in the same position as gill slits. However, they do not look like the gill slits of adult fish, though they have some resemblance to the gill slits of embryonic fish. But there is nothing very profound in this, it is just what we would have expected. If a fish or any other type of animal is to change during evolution, it is almost inevitable that these changes will take place gradually, by slight modifications of the existing pattern of organization. Now, if an early embryonic stage is changed, for instance, by a gene mutation, this will probably cause alterations in many subsequent stages, and it is only to be expected that the final result on the adult will be considerable, and therefore almost certainly harmful and most unlikely to survive the rigors of natural selection. The changes that will be preserved to form part of the evolutionary sequence are most likely to be relatively small ones occurring in the later stages of development when they do not have such drastic consequences. Thus we should expect that most of the changes involved in the evolution from fish to man will have affected relatively late stages of embryonic development, so that the early stages, when the gill slits first appear, are likely to remain almost unaltered throughout the whole evolutionary process; and this is just what we find.

It is, moreover, quite inappropriate to try to use evolutionary arguments to provide a causal explanation of embryo development, as some of the early evolutionists did. It is not at all sufficient, to our present way of thinking, to say that a human embryo possesses gill slits because it was evolved from a fish which also possesses gill slits. This is true enough as far as it goes, but we want to be able to go much further and to state what processes and reactions going on within this particular egg, which we see in front of us, cause it to develop the structures that we see appearing. We want to understand the immediate causes, as well as the historical derivation, of the changes that we see proceeding in any given instance of embryonic development.

The meaning of differentiation

The rest of this book will be concerned with trying to discover at least the general nature of these causal processes. Before starting on this task it is necessary to emphasize again something of the complexity of the problems that have to be solved. Perhaps the best way to clarify the issues is to distinguish three types of process that we shall have to deal with. They are often lumped together under the name "differentiation," but one can distinguish three major categories of change: differentiation in time, differentiation in space, and differentiation in shape.

Differentiation in time   If one watches any particular small region of an egg it will be found gradually to change in character as time goes on. First it is a part of the general substance of the egg. As the egg undergoes cleavage into many cells the region will become provided with its own nuclei and cell membranes and become a mass of cells, but at first these cells are of a very general kind. A little later the cells will begin to form some particular tissue of the adult – for instance, part of a muscle, of a bone, of a kidney, and so on. In doing so, the cells must change in chemical composition; a muscle cell must develop the contractile proteins of the muscle fibers, and bone cell must lay down the bone substances, and so on. There is, therefore, a sequence of changes as time passes, by which this region of the egg gradually acquires the characteristics of some specialized tissue of the adult. Since this process results in the production of an adult tissue, it is technically referred to as *histogenesis*.

Differentiation in space   The egg, at the time of fertilization, is more or less similar (though never exactly the same) in all its parts. It is still usually pretty uniform when it is divided into a number of cells and becomes a blastula. Gradually, however, one part of it will become a brain, another part an intestine, and each of these will become subdivided again into a forebrain, midbrain, hindbrain, and so on; into the esophagus, stomach, gut, and the rest of it. There is an obvious production of many more different regions of the embryo than there were to start with. As a matter of fact, as we shall see, eggs at the time of fertilization are not entirely uniform throughout their whole mass. They always start with some regional differences between one part and another, but at first there are very few differences and these are usually slight and difficult to detect. Later there are many more regional differences, and they are more striking and well marked. The process by which the egg becomes divided into many distinct different regions is known as *regionalization*.

Differentiation in shape   Eggs usually have a very simple shape, often spherical. The organisms into which they develop have, of course, complicated shapes. Not only is their overall external surface molded into a structure of trunk, legs, head, tail, and what have you, but internally they contain many different organs, each with a rather constant and particular shape. The processes by which these changes in shape occur are known as *morphogenesis*.

The integration of development

In any ordinary embryo all these three processes – of histogenesis, regionalization, and morphogenesis – are going on simultaneously and in intimate connection with one another. The reason for separating them is that it is clear that they call for different types of explanation. Histogenesis, for instance, is a change in the nature of the substance in a particular region; that is to say, it could be explained in purely chemical terms. Regionalization is also a chemical process, involving the production of different substances in different regions of the embryo. Again it demands a chemical explanation, but one that can show how different chemical processes will occur in the different places that become regionally distinct. Morphogenesis is quite different. It involves masses of material becoming changed in shape; that is to say, it demands an explanation in terms of processes that will give rise to forces, which can push the material out of its original shape into another. These processes, of course, are certain to involve chemical reactions, but the causes of the morphogenesis will not be the chemical reactions themselves but the forces to which they give rise.

It is important to remember that all these three types of process can go on both at the cell level and at the tissue level. For instance, when a cell of the early mesoderm gradually changes into a muscle cell we have histogenesis at the cell level. In many cases, however, it does not seem to be possible to persuade single cells to undergo certain types of histogenesis. They only do so when forming part of a larger group of cells, and in that case we have histogenesis at the tissue level. Similarly the example of regionalization quoted – that is, the division of the nervous system into later parts of the brain and the spinal cord – is at the tissue level; but we can find it at the cell level also, for instance, in the formation of the central body, dendrites, and axon of a single nerve cell. Again we quoted examples of morphogenesis at the tissue level, but we can find single cells or groups of very small numbers of cells in which morphogenesis and the formation of a definite shape also occur. Thus we have to look for explanations of processes of

different kinds taking place at different levels of biological organization.

. . .

Preformation and epigenesis

Right at the beginning of the history of embryology in the fourth century BC, Aristotle formulated a major problem that has haunted the subject ever since. He distinguished between two ideas, which have become known as "preformation" and "epigenesis." Preformation is the notion that the egg at the time of fertilization already contains something corresponding to every feature that will eventually be present in the fully formed adult. Certain eighteenth-century anatomists, shortly after the microscope was invented, thought in fact that they could see a complete little man located in the head of the sperm, or a shadowy figure of the final animal embedded in the egg. This was, of course, mere imagination, dependent on the inadequacy of their instruments. However, the basic idea of preformation is not that every feature of the adult is already present as such in the fertilized egg; it is rather that in the egg every feature is represented by *something*, though this may be quite different from the adult form of the feature. The idea complementary to this is epigenesis, which supposes that many features of the adult are not represented at all in the fertilized egg; which contains only a smaller number of elements, and that during development these react together to produce the much larger number of adult features.

A discussion of the merits of these opposing views was carried on vigorously for many centuries. Nowadays, the issue *ought* to be finally settled and understood. We know that a fertilized egg contains *some* preformed elements – namely, the genes and a certain number of different regions of cytoplasm – and we know that during development these interact in epigenetic processes to produce final adult characters and features that are not individually represented in the egg. We see, therefore, that both preformation and epigenesis are involved in embryonic development.

In the present stage of biology, the study of the preformed element in the fertilized eggs, taken in hand by the geneticists, has made such enormous progress that nobody is likely to be able to overlook it for long. Embryologists certainly have to accept it as part of the basic groundwork from which they start. Their attention is more immediately concentrated on trying to understand the causal processes by which the genes interact with one another and with the cytoplasm of the egg. The focus of their interest is in the processes that we have referred to as epigenesis. In fact, the word "epigenetics" is a quite appropriate name for the whole causal study of development, emphasizing, as it does, its fundamental dependence on genetics and its interest in causes and processes.

.   .   .

The development of cells, tissues, and organs

The discussion so far has dealt only with development at the simplest level relevant to biology, that of biochemical substances. This is really the province more of geneticists than of embryologists. The student of embryos is faced with the need to understand how a part of the egg turns into the liver, another part into the brain, a third part into a forearm, and so on. These developments are, of course, based on chemical changes, but they amount to something much more complicated than that. They are alterations in elaborately organized complex systems, and mere conventional chemistry is not enough to give an account of them, any more than it could account for the evolution of a Model "T" Ford (an "embryonic" motor vehicle) into a Thunderbird roadster on the one side or a rocket transporter on the other (to give two examples of specialized motor vehicles corresponding to adult cells).

In approaching the problems of the development of cells and organs we have still to base ourselves on the fundamental postulate that the nature of the changes that occur will be ultimately dependent on genes. The new point we have to consider is that we shall be dealing with parts of the developing body which are affected by very many genes. Nobody knows exactly how many genes are active in the development of any type of cell, but it is probably several hundred. Presumably even more would be involved in the development of any fairly complicated organ, but nobody has recently made a serious attempt to find out. The fullest description we have

of the large range of genes affecting the development of an organ is a study made about a quarter of a century ago on the wings of the fruit fly Drosophila, which has been very extensively studied by geneticists. The developmental effects of about forty genes were described. It is worth summarizing briefly the main outlines of the story because some principles of general importance emerge from it (figure 1.4).

The wing of a fly like Drosophila develops from a small bunch of cells, known as the imaginal bud, which lies in the body of the larva or grub. This begins to grow out into the wing at the time the larva turns into a pupa. When it begins the imaginal bud is in the form of a hollow bag, one side of which is thicker than the other. The thick side becomes folded in toward the center of the bag and begins to grow rapidly, so that it soon bursts through the other thin side, which disappears. The folded area then flattens out into a leaflike blade, somewhat similar in shape to the final wing, though very much smaller in area. This blade begins to grow, at different rates along its length and across its width. During this period its base becomes attached to the surface of the body, so that the wing begins to stick out to the side of the animal. After a time the wing blade begins to become inflated: the body fluid (or blood) of the animal seems to be pumped into it, forcing the two surfaces apart and expanding the whole thing like an inflated rubber bag. This goes on until the wing blade becomes a thin-walled inflated sack. After that the internal pressure drops again, and the wing begins to contract, so that eventually it once more forms a flat blade. It is during this contraction that the wing acquires its final outline. As the internal fluid drains away, and the two surfaces of the wing blade come together, they come into complete contact with one another everywhere except for a few channels, which are arranged in a definite pattern. These are the so-called veins, which remain filled with blood and with a thickened surface even in the adult wing. The final stage of development is characterized by a great expansion in area of each of the cells. This expansion is so great that the wing is at first crumpled up into complicated folds. It is only after the final insect emerges from the pupa that body fluid is again pumped into the wings through the veins, and this expands the folds and stretches out the wing to its final flattened shape. Finally the wing dries out,

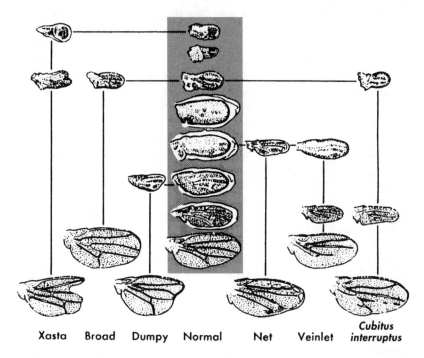

Xasta　Broad　Dumpy　Normal　Net　Veinlet　**Cubitus interruptus**

Figure 1.4　Genetic control of the development of the Drosophila wing. Stages in the normal development of the wing are shown in the eight drawings down the center of the figure. From the imaginal bud of the top, through stages of enlargement by cell division (next two figures), expansion by the internal pressure of body fluid (fourth figure), then renewed contraction during which the final veins appear (next three figures), leading to the formation of the final adult wing (shown on a smaller scale). On the left are shown the effects of three genes that affect the general shape of the wing. *Xasta* affects the first formation of the wing in the imaginal bud. *Broad* affects the first expansion by cell-division. Dumpy causes an increased contraction. On the right are three genes affecting the vein. In *net* there is less contraction than usual and some extra veins appear. In *veinlet* the veins first appear in their normal form but the tips of them are later obliterated. In *cubitus interruptus* there is an abnormality in the first signs of the veins that appear during the growth phase.

presumably by simple evaporation of moisture from its surface. Its cells die and the wing is then in its final form.

Now we know genes that affect every one of these stages of development. In fact, for most stages we know several genes that are active. For instance, in the first stage of expansion and growth at the very beginning of the pupal period, there are some genes that increase the growth in length, others that increase the growth in width. Again at the time of inflation and contraction there are some genes that increase the inflation, others that increase the contraction. Throughout the whole of the development all these genes are interacting with one another in complicated ways. It is particularly important to notice that we can find many examples of genes that seem to act antagonistically to each other. The final

shape of the wing is a compromise between genes that, for instance, tend to increase the inflation and genes that tend to increase the contraction; between genes that tend to cause an increase in length and those that cause an increase in width, and so on. The end result is a balance between many opposing forces.

The canalization of development

The Drosophila wing serves as an example to illustrate this point, but the principle is a very general one. Any organ such as a wing, a leg, or an eye must always be regarded as expressing some sort of compromise or balance between the conflicting or competing activities of very many genes.

It is particularly important to discover that these

balances show a certain degree of stability, in the sense that it is quite difficult to persuade the developing system *not* to finish up by producing its normal end result. If something occurs that would tend to strengthen one of the factors (say, a tendency toward elongation), its effectiveness will be opposed by the conflicting tendencies (toward broadening and shortening) which will also be present in the system, and the net result will be less than we might have expected. In fact, unless the elongating tendency is very strong, the forces opposing it may swamp it out altogether, so that the final wing appears completely normal. This is the explanation, in developmental terms, of the phenomenon of dominance and recessivity which is so well known to geneticists. If, by producing a heterozygous individual, we reduce the dose of a gene from its usual level of two normal alleles to the lower level of one normal plus one mutant allele, we often find that this makes no difference to the appearance of the animal at the end of development. The whole developing system, involving interaction between many genes, has reacted so as to absorb the comparatively slight degree of abnormality produced by the single dose of the mutant allele. The balance is stable enough not to be disturbed. The system is to some extent "self-righting," like a well-designed automobile which has a tendency to straighten itself out after being put into a slight curve.

This self-righting tendency of development is seen in many contexts and at many levels of organization. It is, in fact, much more widely known and better recognized in embryological connections than in the field of genetics. Here are a few examples. As we shall see later, many eggs contain particular types of cytoplasm arranged at definite places within them. When such an egg is centrifuged the different types of cytoplasm may be displaced; but if such a centrifuged egg is left to itself it is usually found that there is a strong tendency for the cytoplasms to move back again to their original pattern. Exactly how this is done is still obscure. It seems usually to depend in some way on patterns of difference within the cell surface; possibly there are local regions of the cell surface with particular attraction for particular types of cytoplasm; but however it is done, the net result is a tendency for the egg to right itself after disturbance.

Again, if a piece is removed from an early egg, or even if the egg is cut in half, it is frequently found that the system rights itself, and a completely normal embryo is produced (see figure 1.9). This happens in the human being, when two identical twins may be produced by one egg which in some way becomes effectively divided in two, so that each twin arises from what should have been only half the normal system. In many types of animal this kind of self-righting or "regulation" persists into much later stages long after the first few cell divisions. Even when it begins to be lost, lesser but still quite extensive regulation continues to occur. For instance, a half brain or a half limb may produce a whole organ, and even a quite small part of the embryo will often show some tendency to increase itself and form more than would have been expected.

The genetic basis for the regulatory processes seen in very early embryos has never been fully investigated, and it would be difficult to do so. However, it is quite possible to study the less impressive examples of resistance to disturbance that can be found in the later stages of development and to show that they depend on the properties of the genes contained in the organism. For instance, if we subject a developing embryo to some external agent (for example, temperature) that tends to make it produce an abnormal end result, we find that the degree to which it shows an effect of the treatment can be either increased or decreased by selective breeding. This is a proof that it is its genes that control its ability to absorb the abnormal treatment – that is, to right itself.

The general phrase for the property we have been discussing is "the canalization of development." The region of an early egg that develops into a brain or into a limb or any other organ follows some particular pathway of change. What we have found now is that these pathways are "canalized," in the sense that the developing system has an inbuilt tendency to stick to the path, and is quite difficult to divert from it by any influence, whether an external one like an abnormal temperature or an internal one like the presence of a few abnormal genes. Even if the developing system is forcibly made abnormal – for instance, by cutting part of it away – it still tends to get itself back onto the canalized pathway and finish up as a normal adult. The canalization is, of course, not complete. Developing systems do not always reach the fully normal adult state. The point is that they have a tendency to do so, and are not entirely at the mercy of any temporary abnormalities. It is easy to see why this may be a valuable property for animals developing in a very changeable world, and why natural selection should have built up systems of genes that interact in this self-stabilizing way which partly buffers out the effect of potentially harmful circumstances.

One can make a mental picture of the situation by thinking of the development of a particular part of an egg as a ball running down a valley. It will, of course, tend to run down to the bottom of the valley, and if something temporarily pushes it up to one side, it will again have a tendency to run down to the bottom and finally finish up in its normal place. If one thinks of all the different parts of the egg, developing into wings, eyes, legs, and so on, one would have to represent the whole system by a series of different valleys, all starting out from the fertilized egg but gradually diverging and finishing up at a number of different adult organs. Such a mental picture has been called the "epigenetic landscape" (figure 1.5).

This "landscape" presents, in the form of a visual model, a description of the general properties of a complicated developing system in which the course of events is controlled by many different processes that interact in such a way that they tend to balance each other. If, for instance, process A for some reason becomes stronger than usual, this will have repercussions that will eventually cause some opposing process B to become stronger also, so that

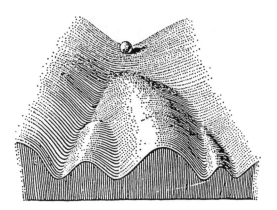

Figure 1.5 The epigenetic landscape. The various regions of a developing embryo have in front of them a number of possible pathways of development, and any particular part will be switched into one or other of these potential paths.

the overall balance remains much the same. Regulatory interactions of this kind are often spoken of nowadays as examples of "feedback," but that word actually has many senses. It is most properly used in situations such that, when process A tends to go faster than usual, secondary effects are produced that slow A down again. But this is by no means the only kind of regulation that occurs in embryonic systems. For instance, a mutant gene may genuinely produce an inefficient enzyme, and this does not produce any secondary effects that cause the enzyme to become more efficient; what happens is that the slack gets taken up somewhere else in the cell's biochemical system, and the overall result on the cell's total activity is minimized or even completely "buffered out."

Is differentiation reversible?

The epigenetic landscape immediately suggests several very important questions. First of all, how do the various parts of the egg get into the various valleys? How is it decided that one part of a Drosophila will develop into a wing, another part into a leg, and so on? This is the problem of "switch mechanisms" – that is, processes that switch development into one channel or another, or, to put the same thing in a different way, processes that switch on one group of gene activities rather than another group. This is the subject of the next section.

But there is another question we might discuss now. Once a part of the egg has got into a channel and traveled some distance along it toward becoming an adult organ like a limb or an eye, can it reverse its direction and go back again toward an embryonic condition? Or can it suddenly change out of this path of development and start becoming something quite different without going back on its tracks to an earlier condition? Is developmental change reversible or not? Do adult cells of one type (such as muscle cells or skin cells) still contain the potentialities that are needed to form cells of a different type (such as bone cells or nerve cells)?

If a group of partially differentiated cells are cut out from a late embryo and placed in a drop of a suitable nutritive medium, they often start growing much more rapidly than they had done in the body. The mass of cells gradually becomes looser, and individual cells creep out into the medium along the surface of the vessel in which they are placed. Such masses of cells, kept alive outside the body, are known as tissue cultures.

Under such conditions many early embryonic cells will continue their development and eventually become more differentiated (but see p. 23). On the other hand, already differentiated cells usually lose many of the obvious signs of differentiation and appear to become much simpler (figure 1.6). They take on one or another of three basic appearances, and look as if they had gone back toward an embryonic condition. This is, however, often somewhat deceptive. If after a period in tissue culture in which the cells appear to have lost many of their signs of differentiation, they are put back again into the body of an animal, or into other conditions in which the group becomes tightly coherent once more, it is often found that the cells have in fact retained their differentiated character, and can soon begin to exhibit again all the signs of specialization

they had had in the first place. There is still a good deal of argument whether they ever do become really de-differentiated or not. Some authors maintain that cells that are caused to grow rapidly, so that they undergo many cell divisions quickly one after the other, do actually lose their differentiation and regress to an embryonic condition, from which they can then be persuaded to differentiate once more into something quite different from what they had originally been.

There are other situations in which there is better evidence that at least some differentiated cells can be caused to lose their initial differentiation and then to develop along some other pathway. Some of the best cases of this occur during regeneration. In many animals, though unfortunately not in man, if a part of the body is removed, various processes go on by which a new part is grown to replace it. All these processes are known as regeneration, but the

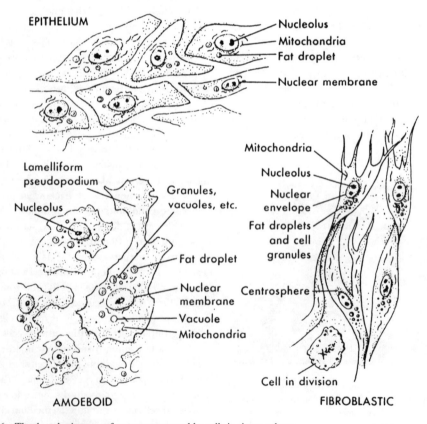

Figure 1.6 The three basic types of structure assumed by cells in tissue culture.

end result may be attained in a number of rather different ways. For instance, if the lens is removed from the eye of a frog or newt a small growth may appear in some other part of the eye and eventually develop into a new lens (figure 1.7); sometimes it is formed from the retina, which is the layer of very specialized cells that actually receive the visual image in the eye, in other cases from the cornea, which is the transparent covering over the outer surface of the pupil. In both instances the lens is formed from cells that are originally highly differentiated, and they have to lose their initial differentiation and then develop again along a new pathway that leads to the formation of lens cells.

In most other instances of regeneration the first sign of the process is the accumulation at the surface

of the wound of a small bundle of embryonic-looking cells. This little group of cells, known as a blastema, then begins to grow and gives rise to all the necessary parts to replace whatever has been amputated (see figure 1.8). For instance, if the hand and forearm of a newt's front leg are cut off, a blastema will form at the cut surface and eventually grow into just these parts of the forearm and hand that have been removed, neither more nor less. This is a very remarkable performance.

The question we have to ask now is, where do the cells of the blastema come from? Many people have argued that in animals that can regenerate, the body contains a reserve supply of embryonic cells, which are scattered through the more differentiated cells but which retain their embryonic condition. When a wound is made these reserve cells are supposed to accumulate and form the blastema and then begin to differentiate. This does in fact occur in the regeneration of some invertebrates, such as flatworms, but in the vertebrates that can regenerate well, such as newts and salamanders, something more interesting is involved. In these animals, irradiation with x-rays, even if carried out some months before a limb is amputated, entirely prevents any regeneration (the reasons for this are still quite obscure). We can take an x-rayed animal, cut off its forelimb, wait long enough to be sure that no regen-

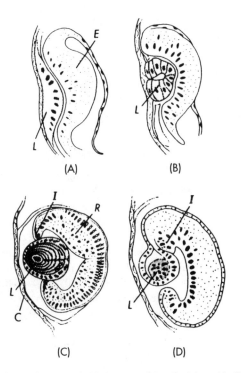

(A)   (B)

(C)   (D)

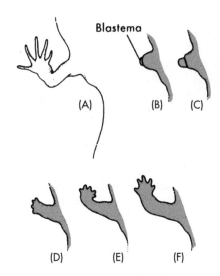

Blastema

(A)   (B)   (C)

(D)   (E)   (F)

Figure 1.7 Lens development and regeneration. (**A–C**) Three stages in the normal development of the eye in amphibians. The eyecup, *E*, grows out from the brain, and where it touches the ectoderm induces the latter to form a vesicle which becomes the lens, *L*. In (**C**) *R* is the retina, derived from the eyecup, the edges of this being the iris, *I*; (*C*) is the cornea, developed from the ectoderm. If the lens is removed from such an eye, a new one may be regenerated from the retina or iris, as seen in (**D**), it may also be produced from the cornea.

Figure 1.8 Regeneration. (**A**) Outline of the hind limb of the crested newt. (**B–F**) The first stages in the regeneration of the limb when it is amputated through the thigh region.

eration is going to occur, and then graft onto the stump an arm from another, nonirradiated newt. This grafted limb can heal on quite satisfactorily. After it had done so, it can be amputated in its turn, leaving only a small disc of unirradiated material attached to the stump on the x-rayed animal. At this stage, regeneration happens. This is very good evidence that the cells of the blastema, which grow into the new limb, are derived locally. It seems, in fact, that already differentiated skin cells, and probably muscle cells, at the site of the wound lose their differentiation and then constitute the blastema.

Moreover, in other experiments it has been shown that if the upper arm bone (humerus) is removed from a newt forelimb, it is not regenerated; but if this boneless arm is amputated, a regenerate grows out from the stump, and does contain a new humerus, although no normal bone-forming cells were present at the cut surface. This shows that the cells that form the blastema do really return, to some extent at least, to an embryonic condition, and differentiate again in other pathways. However, they do not seem to become completely embryonic so that they could develop into something quite foreign to their nature; for instance, attempts to persuade blastema produced on limbs to develop into tails have had very little success.

There is, then, rather good evidence that differentiation, at least along certain pathways, can under some circumstances be reversed. However, it is usually not at all easy to reverse it, although the less definite differentiation of plant cells is much more flexible. But it is only in rather few cases that we know experimental methods of persuading animal cells that have once differentiated to go back to a more embryonic condition. It may be that certain types of differentiation – for instance, in nerve cells – are pretty well irreversible.

As we have been arguing all through this chapter, the changes of differentiation are caused by gene activities. Development along a particular pathway is brought about when certain particular genes are active. The cases in which we can show that differentiated cells can regress to an earlier condition, and then develop again in a different direction, demonstrate that, in these cases at least, the genes required for the second course of differentiation must still be present, even if they are not operating in first-course differentiation. In types of differentiation that are not reversible – or, at least,

in which we cannot prove reversibility – it is possible that some of the genes whose activities are not required become completely inactivated, or even possibly lost from the cell altogether. This certainly occurs in some cases. For instance, during the development of the red blood cells of mammals the whole nucleus disappears after setting going the processes leading to the manufacture of hemoglobin. The final cell does not even contain the genes for doing this, let alone those necessary to differentiate into anything else. However, this is rather a special situation. There is very little evidence that genes are often lost from differentiated cells; it is much more probable that usually the difficulty in reversing differentiation is not that other genes have been lost but rather that the development involves such a complicated network of processes that it would be an extremely long and tricky process to unravel them. One could, in theory, take an automobile, dismantle it, and build the pieces up again with a little modification into two motorcycles, but it wouldn't be easy; and it is something like this that we are asking a differentiated cell to do when we try to persuade it to lose its present differentiation and develop into something else.

Nuclear transplantation

From this point of view, it seems reasonable to expect that the developmental changes in the nucleus, which contains the genes but not much else, may be more easily reversed than the changes undergone by the cell as a whole. It would be easy to test this if the nucleus from one sort of differentiated cell could be transferred into the cytoplasm of another more embryonic cell, and one watched to see whether the nucleus could still carry out all the functions necessary for some other type of differentiation.

In practice this is not an easy result to achieve. The early embryologists were able, by a variety of methods, to introduce a nucleus into one of the specialized regions of cytoplasm contained in some eggs where it would not have been in normal development. For instance, if a newt's egg is constricted by a loop of hair, after fertilization but before it has divided into the first two cells, the nucleus will be confined to one of the two ends of the cell. It is only this end that divides in the first few cell divisions (figure 1.9). Later, when the cells and the nuclei

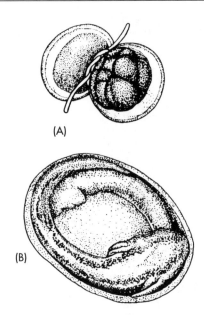

(A)

(B)

Figure 1.9 Spemann's constriction experiment.

have become smaller, one of the nuclei may pass across the bridge into the other end, which then begins dividing in turn. Spemann found that if this passage across the bridge took place as late as the 16-cell stage, the region that at first had no nucleus might develop normally into all the organs of an adult. Since the arrangement of the cleavage nuclei is quite random, he drew the conclusion that any of the first 16 nuclei is as good as any other, and that they all have the capacity to control every type of differentiation.

This is not a very surprising conclusion when it applies only to the early nuclei formed by the first few cleavages. The real question arises about the potentialities of the later nuclei, taken from cells that have really started to differentiate. In recent years several embryologists have been successful in transferring the nuclei from some differentiated cells into more embryonic cytoplasm. So far this has been successfully done only on the embryos of frogs and toads. Surprisingly, the results in the two types of animals are rather different.

The method used has been to inject a nucleus sucked out of a late differentiated cell into an early uncleaved egg of the same species. One has, of course, to be sure that any differentiation that then takes place is under the control of the injected

nucleus, and not under that of the egg's own nucleus. This nucleus can, however, be eliminated, either by physically removing it or by killing it with ultraviolet. Actually, in toads this is not necessary, since if the injected nucleus is put into an unfertilized egg, the egg's own nucleus plays no part in subsequent events, while the stimulus of pricking the egg to inject the nucleus is sufficient to make development start. In both frogs and toads it has been found that a nucleus taken from the early embryonic cells, up to the stage of the blastula, is usually capable of making possible complete development into a normal larva. But it has been found in frogs that the nuclei begin to lose their capacity to allow complete differentiation soon after the blastula stage. It appears that they undergo some change that cannot be reversed merely by placing the nucleus in the early egg cytoplasm.

These changes are, in fact, rather stable. A typical experimental result is shown in figure 1.10. The first step is to take a number of nuclei from the endoderm of a late blastula and inject them into a series of enucleated eggs (only two are shown in the drawing, for simplicity, but actually many more were used). These recipient eggs are allowed to develop to the young blastula stage, and then from each egg another series of nuclear transplantations is made. The nuclei from each blastula should be exactly the same, since they were derived from one original transplanted nucleus. The animals into which they develop therefore form a "clone" – that is, a group of genetically identical individuals. It is found that the clones may differ, some giving full normal development, some producing mainly, or entirely, misshapen and badly developed tadpoles. This shows that in the initial late blastula with which the experiment started, some nuclei had already lost some of the capacity to allow normal development to proceed. If one of the eggs in each clone is allowed to proceed only as far as the blastula stage, and is then used as a source for more nuclei for transplantation, one can get a second transplant generation. It is found that the character of the clone – whether it consists of normal or malformed tadpoles is repeated in this generation. The change in nuclear properties is therefore fairly stable, and has actually been followed through quite a large number of generations.

In frogs the loss by the nuclei of their full capac-

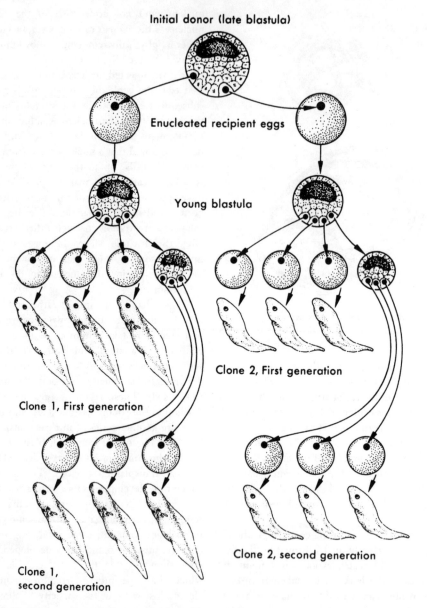

Initial donor (late blastula)

Enucleated recipient eggs

Young blastula

Clone 2, First generation

Clone 1, First generation

Clone 2, second generation

Clone 1,
second generation

Figure 1.10   Nuclear transplantation (see text for explanation).

ity proceeds fairly rapidly after the blastula stage, and while the embryo is still at an early stage of differentiation there seem to be no nuclei left that can support the complete development of all types of tissue when tested in this way. However, in toads, of the genus Xenopus, the loss of capacity goes much more slowly. Even when the tissues are fully differentiated and functional, some of their nuclei, after transplantation, will allow a complete new animal to develop. This has been demonstrated, for instance, for a nucleus from a fully differentiated cell from the lining of the intestine. This shows that it is possible for a nucleus to control the production of cell-specific proteins while still retaining the genetic capacities required for the differentiation of other cell types.

We still do not understand the nature of the changes that have occurred in those nuclei that fail to support complete differentiation. Possibly all differentiation involves some degree of inactivation of the nonfunctioning genes, which becomes progressively more difficult to reverse so that these genes can operate again. Or possibly the alterations are in some more general characteristics, such as the nature of the nuclear envelope, and do not directly affect the genes themselves. The subject is one of the most important in the present phase of experimental embryology, and is being very actively studied.

Regionalization and the Control of Gene Activity

The problem of how the various parts of an egg get directed into different paths of development, so that they produce the whole range of organs of the adult, has always been a central interest for embryologists. Fairly recently geneticists have also begun to ask themselves how the activities of the genes are controlled, so that some of them are switched on to produce their corresponding protein, while others are switched off. There are two types of situation in which the switching on or off of genes may occur. First, there is the regionalization problem; different genes may be switched on in different cells – for instance, the hemoglobin gene in a blood cell, the insulin gene in a pancreas cell, and so on. Second, in one and the same type of cell, different genes may be switched on at different times; for instance, a cell becomes definitely a blood cell, presumably by the switching on of some of its genes, a considerable time before it actually begins to produce hemoglobin, the gene for which is probably switched on some time later. The two types of switching may, of course, operate in exactly the same way. It is beginning to look, however, as though most of the studies of gene switching that have started from a genetic angle have actually been dealing with genes that come into play one after another during the gradual development of a cell, and that the switching which brings about the differentiation between different types of cells may involve another kind of mechanism.

Another difficulty in interpreting data about when proteins are produced is that this may result from "translation" control at the ribosomes and not from "transcription" control of gene activity.

The control of single genes in bacteria

It will be logical to start with the genetic investigation of fairly simple systems, even though these studies were carried out more recently than most of the embryological work.

The product of a sequence of enzymes may inhibit the activity of some early enzyme in the series. But there is another, and even more radical, influence that such substances may exert on the enzyme makeup of the cell. Many instances are known in which substances produced by enzymes influence not merely enzyme activity, but the actual production of the enzyme in question. This is known as enzyme repression, and should be clearly distinguished from enzyme inhibition.

In some cases the presence in the medium of a particular molecule leads to the new production of an enzyme capable of metabolizing that molecule. For instance, if the sugar lactose is added to a culture of the bacterium *Escherichia coli* there is a very rapid production of an enzyme *beta galactosidase* which can break down lactose. This is enzyme induction, and an enzyme that can be produced in this way is said to be inducible. The molecules that act as inducers of it are mostly substances with which it can react, like lactose, although a few other substances, with molecules with some similarity to lactose but not reactive with the enzyme, will also act in this way. Reactions of this kind may be of great practical importance. For instance, when an antibiotic such as penicillin is present in the medium it can, in some strains of bacteria, induce the production of a penicillinase which destroys it, and thus reduces its efficiency.

Since bacteria can be grown in enormous numbers, it is practical with them, as it is not in most higher organs, to induce a lot of mutations with x-rays or ultraviolet and to look through these to find the particular mutations in which one is interested. In this way it has been possible to analyze in genetic terms the system that brings about enzyme induction or repression. It has been found that the inducing or repressing molecules do not react directly with the gene for the enzyme. Instead, they react

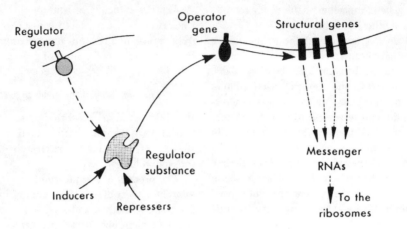

Figure 1.11   The regulation of gene activities in bacteria.

first with a regulator substance which is present in the cytoplasm (or at least is not on the chromosomes, although it might be in nuclear sap). This regulator substance is produced by a particular gene, known as the *regulator gene* for that system. The enzyme whose production is controlled is produced by another gene, referred to as the "structural gene," because it controls the structure of the enzyme protein. In some cases the regulator substance controls the activities not of a single gene producing one enzyme, but of a small group of genes controlling several enzymes. The genes in the group lie side by side along the chromosome, and the activity of the whole group is controlled by one particular member. This controlling gene is known as the *operator*, and the whole group it controls is the *operon*, consisting of several enzyme–producing structural genes (figure 1.11).

The property of the regulator substance is to react not only with the external inducer molecule but also with the operator gene. When one is dealing with an inducible enzyme, the regular substance is normally combined with the operator gene, and represses its activities so that no structural genes are active and none of the protein is made; but when the regulator substance is combined with the inducer molecule it can no longer react with the operator gene, and the whole operon then becomes active and produces its various enzymes. In the case of a repressible enzyme, the regulator substance is present but is not able to react with the operator

gene until it is combined with the external repressing substance; when it is so combined, it reacts with the operator and represses its activities. It is noteworthy that in both cases the combination of the regulator substance with the operator gene represses the activity of the operator. The regulator substances are therefore sometimes called repressor substances.

If the regulator gene is put out of action by mutating to an inoperative form, there is no repressor substance produced, and the corresponding enzymes then become "constitutive" – that is, they appear in all cells, irrespective of the presence or absence of any external inducer substance.

The chemical nature of the regulator substances is still not entirely certain. Most of the evidence points to them being proteins. In fact they are probably allosteric proteins, with two active sites, one able to react with the operator, and one to react with the inducing or repressing external molecule. If one supposes that the properties of the operator site are altered according to whether the other site is or is not combined with an inducing or repressing molecule, then the whole system becomes easy to understand.

The control of single genes in higher organisms

This system of inducible enzymes in bacteria provides one clear-cut mechanism by which gene activities can be controlled. It is quite likely that similar systems operate in more highly evolved organisms also. However, so far we do not know of any absolutely clear-cut example in a higher organism that can be analyzed so precisely. Moreover there are some reasons why one should be a little cautious in supposing that the control of gene activities in higher organisms is always carried out just in this way. For instance, the DNA in bacteria is normally combined with very little or no protein, whereas in higher organisms the DNA normally exists in the form of chromosomes which contain a large proportion of protein. Higher organism DNA might therefore be less easily controlled by allosteric protein regulator substances. Only time will tell how far this is so.

It is probably significant that in higher organisms, few if any examples are known of enzymes or other proteins becoming "constitutive" and appearing in every cell of the body. Such embryos would probably die at a fairly early stage; but so many young embryos have been looked at that if it ever happened that, for instance, the repressor of the hemoglobin gene was absent and this substance appeared in every cell, this should have been detected by now. The absence, or rarity, of such cases suggests that the control of single genes, by the mechanisms found in bacteria, is not the whole story, at least in the early stages of development. It seems rather likely that the control mechanisms that operate in early development act in some other way, to affect whole batteries of genes, whereas, perhaps, control systems for single genes may come into play later. In any case, we have to remember that gene activity can be controlled not only by affecting transcription from DNA to RNA, as in the bacterial example just described, but also by affecting the translation of messenger RNA into protein.

.   .   .

The amphibian egg

It is now time to turn to the studies on switch mechanisms that have been made by embryological rather than genetic methods. The most thorough and far-reaching studies have been carried out in amphibia – frogs and, particularly, newts and salamanders. The eggs of these animals are fairly large, about two millimeters in diameter. They contain a

fair amount of yolk in the form of granules scattered through the cytoplasm, and this enables them to live in dilute salt solutions, using their yolk as a source of energy until the embryo develops into a complicated tadpole able to feed for itself. Even small groups of cells, cut out from an embryo and isolated in salt solution, will continue to live and develop. Moreover, the embryos are very good at healing wounds, and this makes it possible to graft small pieces taken from one place into some other location, either in the same or in a different embryo. The eggs are, therefore, very suitable for experimental manipulation, and they have been as much the favorite objects of embryologists as the fruit fly Drosophila was for so long the favorite of geneticists.

The essential structure of the egg at the time of fertilization is simple. The yolk platelets, although scattered throughout the whole, are more concentrated at the lower, vegetative, end, and the nucleus tends to lie toward the other, animal, pole, which is also more deeply pigmented in the surface layer. Soon after fertilization a further regional difference puts in an appearance. One can detect a special cytoplasmic region, lying slightly below the equator of the egg and concentrated on one side of the main axis. This side will eventually develop into the structures of the backbone of the animal, and all through early development the region formed by this special cytoplasm plays an extremely important role.

The first question to be asked, therefore, is how does this region of cytoplasm – often spoken of as "the gray crescent," which describes its appearance in the eggs of some species – come to be located on one particular side of the egg? The localization is quite a complicated process, depending on the interaction of several factors. For one thing, the crescent always appears just above the main concentration of yolk at the vegetative pole. If the egg is turned upside down and held that way, so that the yolk falls to the bottom of it in its new position, then the crescent will form above this displaced mass (figure 1.12).

This factor, however, is only sufficient to locate the crescent somewhere just below the equator, and does not specify on which side of the egg it will appear. Experiments have shown that two factors are involved in this. One is some sort of built-in structural characteristic of the egg at the time

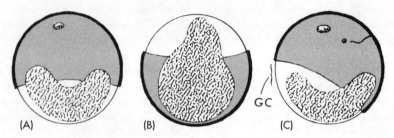

Figure 1.12 Formation of the gray crescent. (**A**) section through a frog egg before fertilization. The upper two-thirds of the egg is covered by a heavily pigmented layer, and the heaviest yolk forms a rather cup-shaped mass at the lower vegetative end. When a fertilized egg is held upside down, the yolk gradually pours down from the upper region to the lower (**B**); and the gray crescent, and later the blastopore, will be formed somewhere just above this – that is, within the pigmented layer. (**C**) Normal fertilization. The sperm has entered in the upper right and is moving off toward the egg nucleus. The whole pigmented cap is rotated toward the point of sperm penetration. It is the region on the other side of the egg, from which the pigmented coat has moved away, that becomes the gray crescent (GC).

it is laid. This may be a feature of the outer surface, or cortex, of the egg, but it is not fully understood. Its effect is that, from the time of laying, one side of the egg has a certain tendency to be the position at which the crescent will form and the dorsal organs develop. However, this tendency is not very firmly fixed, and can be overcome. For instance, if the fertilizing sperm is led into an egg along a thread and therefore forced to penetrate it at the point where the thread touches the egg surface, then it is often found that the crescent appears at the side of the egg opposite the point of penetration, even though that may not be the side predisposed for it.

The importance of the crescent for future development was proved many years ago. If a newt's egg is pinched in two by a loop of thread, both halves may produce a complete normal adult (p. 17). However, a portion of an egg will only develop fully if it contains a sufficient quantity of the crescent. If the plane of the constriction happens to put the whole crescent in one half, leaving the other half without any, the second half may undergo cell division if it contains a nucleus, but never produces any of the characteristic adult tissues; its cells remain embryonic and without any special features. It is, therefore, the cytoplasm of the crescent that first switches on the gene activities that control the synthesis of the proteins characteristic of adult cell types. Cells lacking the crescent material can, presumably, synthesize the proteins required for the mitotic spindles used at cell division, but they do not seem able to synthesize anything else.

With modern methods we have recently been able to see signs of the switching on of gene activity, beginning quite early in development. After the usual period of cleavage into a large number of cells, the amphibian egg forms a hollow blastula in which the layer of animal cells, with little yolk, is much thinner than the mass of vegetative cells, which are very yolky. It then starts its process of gastrulation, by which the hollow ball is converted into a three-layered embryo (see p. 6). In these eggs, gastrulation involves part of the upper animal region of the egg being folded into the interior through a fairly narrow hole, which pushes from the outside inward, making a finger-shaped cavity, which is called the primitive gut and eventually turns into the intestine. This hole, known as the blastopore, appears just at the bottom of the crescent. If an egg at this stage is offered the raw materials of proteins or nucleic acids – amino acids or nucleotides – labeled with radioactive isotopes, most of the cells absorb very little of them, which is evidence that little synthesis is going on. However, just in the cells derived from the crescent, which are now beginning to move into the blastopore, there is a rapid uptake of these substances, and they become built into proteins and nucleic acids.

The newly synthesized materials of both these types are at first located mainly in the cell nucleus. In fact we can locate them more precisely, in the nucleolus inside the nucleus. This organelle is lacking in the very early embryonic cells of most amphibians, and begins to put in an appearance in the blastopore cells about the time gastrulation begins.

The exact function of the nucleolus of these cells is still somewhat uncertain, but the evidence suggests it is concerned with the synthesis of the machinery that will be required for protein synthesis, in particular the synthesis of the soluble RNA and of the ribosome particles to which messenger RNA will later become attached. It is, of course, reasonable to assume that the first genes that it would be necessary to switch would be those controlling the synthesis of ribosomes, which are an essential part of the machinery which other genes can use later to produce their specific proteins.

The crescent material makes up only a small fraction of the whole egg, perhaps a tenth of it. How do the genes get switched on in other regions? One of the main reasons why the amphibian egg has been so fascinating to embryologists is that we can prove that the switching in other parts of the egg is strongly affected by influences that originate within the crescent region and then move out from it.

The original demonstrations of this effect were made some forty years ago, long before anyone seriously tried to interpret development in genetic terms. The experiments used straightforward embryological techniques, of cutting out one part of an egg and grafting it on some other egg at a different place, or simply excising a portion of the egg and isolating it in a salt solution.

If any small fragment of the animal part of the gastrula, lying above the crescent, is cut out and isolated, it fails to develop into any of the more specialized adult cell types, and forms instead only a rather rudimentary type of skinlike tissue. Probably this involves the operation of some genes, but surely not of very many. Now in normal development the cells in the blastopore region are folded into the interior of the egg and come to lie underneath a large part of the animal half. It is just the part of the exterior that becomes underlain that develops into the main ectodermal organs of the dorsal axis or backbone – namely, the brain and neural tube. Meanwhile the cells from the blastopore region continue their own development, turning into the muscles, kidneys, and so on. They will, in fact, do this when isolated as small groups in salt solution. It certainly looks as though the development of the brain and nervous system might be influenced by something coming from the underlying cells of the blastopore as they develop into the mesodermal organs.

A definite proof of this can be made by putting together in a salt solution two fragments, one taken from the animal pole and the other from the crescent region. In these circumstances the animal pole fragment, which if isolated would develop only into a simple type of skin, is now found to develop into nerve cells characteristic of the brain and neural system. Or one can take a piece of the crescent region from one embryo and graft it into another so that it comes to underlie a part that would normally develop into the skin; it is then found that these "prospective" skin cells now develop into a brain or other part of the nervous system (figure 1.13).

The process by which one part of an embryo, in this case the crescent region, influences some neighboring part, such as the prospective skin cells, making that part develop into an organ which it would not otherwise have done, is spoken of as "embryonic induction." It is a very common process in embryonic development. In vertebrates such as newts, birds, and mammals, very many types of induction have been described. For instance, shortly after the crescent cells have induced the formation of the brain and nervous system, about the time of gastrulation, these organs begin to induce other things in their turn. The very front tip of the brain induces the formation of the nose organs; slightly behind this, two outgrowths from the brain, which later develop into the eyes, induce the overlying skin to form the lenses; still further posteriorly the hindbrain induces the ears; and so on. Similar processes have also been found in the embryos of various invertebrate groups, but there is no space to describe these here.

Nearly all the experiments that have been carried out up to date on embryonic induction have used small fragments of embryonic tissue, containing perhaps a hundred or more cells. It is only in the last few years that work has been begun in which individual cells have been studied. In many embryos it is possible to disaggregate the tissues, during early stages at least, and thus to obtain single cells which can be isolated or combined in various ways. It is general experience that single cells which have been isolated from tissues that normally contain many hundreds of cells will not differentiate. There is a minimum number – different for different species and stages and types of tissue – that must be put fairly close together before it is possible

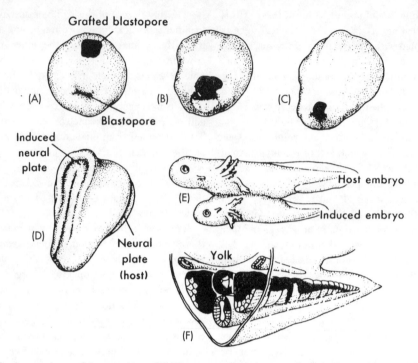

Figure 1.13 An organizer graft in a newt's egg. (A) The egg seen from the vegetative pole. Its own blastopore is lying at the lower side of the drawing, while at the other side there has been grafted a fragment from the blastopore region of another egg (which was stained with a vital dye to make it more visible). In (B) and (C) this grafted material moves into the interior of the egg just as does the tissue around the host blastopore. In (D) one can see at the lower side the edge of the neural plate (that is, neural fold) of the host embryo, and on the upper side a second neural plate formed in connection with the graft. (These four figures are taken from a cinema film.) (E) A diagrammatic drawing of a similar embryo at a later stage. In (F) we have a section and perspective drawing of part of the yolk of the host embryo and the structure of the secondary embryo. Dark cells are derived from the graft; light cells are host material that has been induced to undergo these types of differentiation.

for differentiation to go forward. This minimum number is larger if the cultures have a greater volume, lesser if it has a smaller, which suggests that the isolated cells tend to lose some essential components by diffusion into the medium. Processes of induction can also be observed. For instance, separated ectoderm cells from the amphibian gastrula do not develop into nerve cells unless they come into contact, or near contact, with cells from the mesoderm. One very active subject of debate at the present time is whether the substances presumed to be acting during induction are the same as those whose loss into the medium by diffusion prevents further differentiation. There are hints, at least, that both types of substances may be ribonucleoproteins, but there is not yet much firm evidence about them.

At present our insight into these processes is still based mainly on experiments with tissue masses – that is, groups of cells – rather than with single cells.

Induction processes as they occur in living embryos are quite complicated and involve several different types of reaction. Their study has unfortunately been somewhat bedeviled by the rather unfortunate terminology introduced by the original German workers on the subject. They used words which, when translated into English, or American, seem to some biologists to have a rather mystical flavor. But this is really beside the point. The facts, though complicated, are quite definite facts, and deserve a proper scientific explanation.

One of the main complexities is this. In a living embryo the crescent cells do not merely switch the neighboring cells into a new line of synthesis so that they produce the proteins characteristic of nerve cells. The induction gives rise to a well-organized brain and nervous system, with an elaborate morphological structure and pattern (figure 1.13). This, of course, involves a much higher level of complexity or biological organization than a mere collection of cells containing specific nerve proteins. The original German words seem to imply that induction always involves these complex levels of organization, since the word chosen to refer to what we have called the crescent cells was "the organization center" or, for short, "the organizer." Now this really confuses two issues. It is perfectly possible to switch a mass of embryonic cells, from becoming a disorderly group of skin cells into becoming an equally disorderly collection of nerve cells, with no or minimal organization (figure 1.14). This is, in some sense, "an induction." But something that brings this about is scarcely entitled to be called an organizer. It is better to refer to it instead as an "evocator." When morphological organization occurs as well, as it often does, then we are obviously dealing with something more, and we require another word to refer to it. Since "organization" has already been used in a loose sense to refer to the whole process, it is better to use for this purpose the word "individuation." It is still reasonable to go on using the expression "embryonic induction" when we want to refer to the whole process, without specifying precisely any particular aspect of it.

There is another important aspect to induction for which we also require a word. The induction of a particular organ can only be carried out on the cells from a particular part of an embryo at a particular stage in their development. For instance, the cells of an early amphibian embryo do not begin to respond to the evocators of nervous tissue until about the time of gastrulation, and they lose this responsiveness again fairly soon after gastrulation ends. The word "competence" is used to describe their state during the period when they can respond; or we can speak of them at that time as "competent with respect to neural induction." A little later they will become competent with respect to other types of induction, for instance that of a lens. Interpreted in genetic terms this must mean that there is only a certain period during which the particular genes for these types of tissues

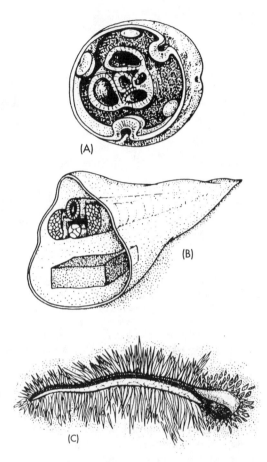

(A)

(B)

(C)

Figure 1.14 Individuation in tissue explants from newt's eggs. (**A**) A fragment of gastrula ectoderm that has been cultured in an evocating substrate and has developed into a very disorderly mass of neural tissue covered by a thin layer of skin in which some nasal placodes have appeared; there is a minimum of individuation. (**B**) A sheet of gastrula ectoderm was wrapped round a fragment of dead adult liver, which has evocated in it a well-formed embryonic axis (neural tube, notochord, and somites.) Since the dead liver can hardly have played a part in specifying the details of this pattern, the mass of induced tissue must have individuated itself. (**C**) A fragment from the blastopore region of a gastrula has been cultured and has developed into a number of tissues (dark neural tube, light notochord, muscle cells, head mesenchyme) showing some orderliness in arrangement, which must again be due to self-individuation.

are susceptible to being switched on or off (figure 1.15).

One of the important general questions about development is the nature of this susceptibility to

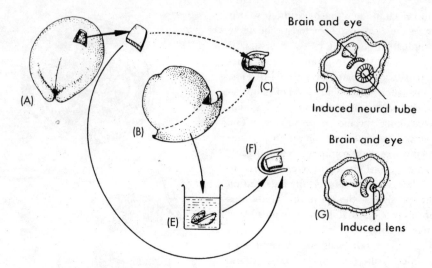

Figure 1.15   Competence. (**B**) An early newt gastrula seen from above with the blastapore just out of sight at top left. The ectodermal region above the dotted line is removed and its competence tested by wrapping it round a fragment taken from the brain–eye region of an open neural plate stage embryo (**A**) which is capable of induction. If this inducer is combined with the gastrula ectoderm immediately after the latter is isolated (**C**) the inducer develops into brain and eye, and induces from the ectoderm part of the neural tube (**D**). If, however, the gastrula ectoderm is kept for 36 hours in salt solution (**E**) before the inducer is added to it (**F**), its competence has changed, and now in response to the same inducer it forms a lens (**G**).

switching. Are the genes in the very early embryonic cells perhaps combined with something else, which puts them out of reach of the usual regulator substances? Does this something have to be removed before the normal switch mechanisms can come into operation? Unfortunately we still know hardly anything about this, and it is a problem that it has not yet been possible to tackle with the more modern molecular biological methods of approach.

CHAPTER 2

Ontogenetic Adaptations and Retrogressive Processes in the Development of the Nervous System and Behaviour: A Neuroembryological Perspective

ROBERT W. OPPENHEIM

To each part of our life there is something specially seasonable, so that the feebleness of children, as well as the high spirit of youth, the soberness of maturer years, and the ripe wisdom of old age – all have a certain advantage which should be secured in its proper season.

(Cicero)

Introduction

The causal mechanisms underlying the development of cells, tissues, organs and their function are seldom simple or straightforward. This should surprise no-one who studies developing animals, for as the pioneer embryologist Roux was fond of saying, only with the greatest reluctance and after judicious questioning does the embryo reveal its secrets. However, admitting this complexity should not divert attention from the fact that animal development is generally held to consist of a gradual and continuous epigenetic progression in which the organism takes on more and more of the features of the adult, and in which each 'step' in the progres-

From K. J. Connolly and H. F. R. Prechtl (eds), *Maturation and Development: Biological and Psychological Perspectives* (Philadelphia, PA: Lippincott, 1981), pp. 73–109.

sion is thought to constitute an integral antecedent (causal mechanism) for some subsequent event. Consequently, the unravelling of the events responsible for the *transitions* in ontogeny represents the central focus of a developmental approach. Understanding the characteristics of the stages themselves, though important, is a subordinate consideration. Insofar as such views merely reflect prevailing epigenetic interpretations of development (as against *performationism*), one cannot quarrel with their correctness. However, it is often implicitly assumed that the exclusive goal of development is the formation of a reproductively mature organism. Almost half a century ago, Shumway expressed this when he said: 'It is the function of the embryo to become an adult . . .' (Shumway, 1932, p. 98). Similarly, the biologist Bonner has argued that: 'the goal . . . of development is the final form and function of the adult' (Bonner, 1958, p. 1). By assuming that the only perspective for understanding ontogeny is with reference to what is to come, or that ontogeny is only an anticipation, antecedent or incipient form of an adult characteristic, such views are unduly narrow, and probably wrong.

Life histories are often complex and frequently involve dramatic transitions, deletions, regressions, and apparent discontinuities in which the stages are often only fully comprehended when considered as adaptations in their own right and not solely as preparations for adulthood (Williams, 1966; Stearns, 1976). Development is not always progressive and constructive. For example, immature animals (embryos, fetuses, larvae, neonates) frequently inhabit environments that are markedly different from those of the adult. Consequently, each of these stages may have required the evolution of specific morphological, biochemical, physiological, and behavioural mechanisms which are different from the adult, and which may require modification, suppression or even destruction before the adult stage can be obtained. Although this observation is not original (see Gould, 1977), I do believe that, with some notable exceptions, the significance of *ontogenetic adaptations*[1] in higher vertebrates has been consistently ignored, especially as regards neurobehavioural development.

I emphasize neurobehavioural development here because although embryologists have to some extent neglected ontogenetic adaptations, on the whole they have achieved a balance in viewing development as representing adaptations *and* as a preparation for maturity. For instance, the embryologist Harrison has commented that: 'We must in fact consider the embryo not merely as a developing organism, in which the parts are important potentially, but also as an organism which in each stage of development has functions to perform that are of importance for that particular stage' (Harrison, 1904, p. 217).

Furthermore, I do not mean to imply that all developmental psychobiologists or child psychologists have neglected ontogenetic adaptations. For instance, Werner clearly demonstrated an awareness of transient behaviour patterns when he wrote: 'each higher level (of development) represents a new entity . . . and is understandable in terms of itself. The more primitive level is not to be derived by the subtraction of single qualities from the higher level. Any level, however primitive it may be, represents a relatively closed, *self-subsisting to-*

tality. Conversely, each higher level is fundamentally an innovation and cannot be gained by merely adding certain characteristics to those determining the preceding level' (Werner, 1948, p. 22).

In addition, there have been recent debates in developmental psychology concerning the related question of the stability *vs* the reversibility of early behavioural characteristics. In contrast to the focus of the present essay, however, these debates largely revolve around the issue of the extent to which one can predict how an animal will respond or behave at a given age, based either on its earlier behaviour and/or on the situations it has or has not experienced at some earlier period.[2]

Despite their differences over the issue of the continuity *vs* discontinuity, or the stability *vs* reversibility of development, most of the participants in this debate have viewed development as a preparation for maturity. Indeed, this concern is often so deep-seated that it has sometimes led to a neglect of the adaptive features of behavioural stages in ontogeny. For instance, Hooker, who studied human fetuses, once commented that: 'each form of activity shown by any fetal organism . . . is a step in preparation for postnatal behavioral capabilities' (Hooker, 1952, p. 120).

Schneirla (1965), in the developmental aspects of his approach-withdrawal theory, has made an effort to account for the specificity of certain neonatal responses to visual stimuli by the prior 'experience' of the fetus with tactile-proprioceptive stimuli. Although Schneirla is necessarily vague about how this ontogenetic 'cross-modal' transfer of sensory information occurs, nevertheless he attempts to apply a type of developmental continuity to events that typically do not fit this conceptual scheme. In other words, since the embryo or fetus is not exposed to patterned visual stimulation *in utero* – yet in most precocial animals, the eyes are functional at birth – Schneirla proposes that prenatal experience with non-visual stimuli may represent a necessary antecedent to later visually guided behaviour. In this way he is able to rescue the continuity hypothesis from a potentially serious objection, and thereby argue that, in principle at least, all behavioural events in ontogeny may have an *experiential* history or continuity. Lipsitt (1976), in discussing the significance of transient infantile reflexes in humans, has expressed the belief that these reflexes 'must have some possible later function' (p. 115), thereby apparently ignoring the possibility of an immediate or even previous (fetal) function for such behaviour. Finally, Piaget (1976), despite his recognition of qualitative differences in the intellectual mechanisms of children and adults, has steadfastly adhered to a view in which each stage of cognitive development is held to be a necessary antecedent of subsequent stages but which largely ignores the possible ontogenetic adaptations represented by each stage. As one supporter of Piaget has recently put it: '. . . the cognitive skills of the child are not . . . adaptive. The child's skills are preparatory for the successful strategies . . . of adults' (Marshack, 1979, p. 394).

These few examples are representative of what I believe has been a rather pervasive and longstanding tradition in developmental psychology of ignoring ontogenetic adaptations. While I recognize that there are signs of change (Galef, 1979; Mason, 1979), these are recent and do not lessen the present need to draw a conceptual distinction between the various requirements of development. To avoid any misinterpretation, I should also point out that I am not denying that at some level of organization, from the genome to the organism, all stages in ontogeny can be considered as a preparation for adulthood. However, my use of the term ontogenetic adaptation is not meant to imply a mutually exclusive process independent of antecedent events. I recognize that in many cases ontogenetic events may serve immediate needs, as well as influence future goals. Furthermore, I do not want to leave the impression that the development of an ontogenetic adaptation – even of completely transient traits – is fundamentally different from the development of an adult trait. At some level of organization, both represent the end product of a previous, gradual epigenetic process. The only major difference is at which stage in the life cycle the adaptiveness is expressed. If ontogenetic adaptations constitute an important feature of behavioural development, then a major goal of this essay must be to document such cases. A subsidiary goal is to relate such adaptations to neurobiological mechanisms, in an attempt to demonstrate transient structures and functions in neurogenesis that could either mediate behavioural adaptations or subserve transient *neurogenetic* functions.

Thus in this essay I hope to show:

(i) that there are continuities and discontinuities in development; that there are losses as well as gains and that development is both destructive (regressive) and constructive (progressive);

(ii) that neurobehavioural characteristics of immature animals are often functional and adaptive, and not merely imperfect anticipations of adult traits;

(iii) that the immediate function of behavioural and neural characteristics in ontogeny may sometimes be the major factor in their adoption by natural selection.

The theme running throughout the essay is not only that epigenetic mechanisms characterize embryonic development but that epigenesis is a valuable conceptual *leitmotiv* for understanding behavioural changes over the whole life cycle. Because I believe that these changes have some neurogenetic basis and are subject to embryonic-like regulatory mechanisms, I have chosen the term *neuroembryological* to describe this perspective. The term has been used by Trevarthen (1973, 1979) in a similar vein to describe the mechanisms controlling the postnatal development of perception and cognition in humans. The major novelty of such an approach is the attempt to apply the principles, concepts and findings of developmental biology to both the prenatal and postnatal development of behaviour. (For a more detailed discussion of the neuroembryological approach to behavioural development, see Oppenheim, 1981a).

Metamorphic Development as a Model of Ontogenetic Adaptations

Animals that undergo striking life-history changes, in which the larval stages may differ so much from the adult that sometimes they have been mistaken for entirely different species (Barrington, 1968), exhibit the most unequivocal examples of ontogenetic adaptations. It is commonly assumed that because of the dramatic nature of the transformation which these animals undergo during their development, they are fundamentally different from most vertebrates. And for this reason it is widely believed that, at least with regard to their metamorphic nature, they have little to tell us about development in higher vertebrates in which metamorphosis does not occur. In contrast, I would argue that such forms merely represent an exaggeration of events that are characteristic of most developing animals.

Hence, ontogenetic modifications of structures, functions and behaviours in larval animals represent useful models of related phenomena in non-metamorphosing animals in which the changes are not clearly revealed. For this reason it is pertinent to review briefly some of the neural and behavioural changes that occur during the development of animals exhibiting dramatic (metamorphic) life-history changes. What is especially remarkable in the case of amphibian metamorphosis is that all the changes, whether they involve cell death, growth, reorganization or differentiation, are apparently orchestrated by a single hormone, thyroxine. (This represents a striking example of the embryological principle that the *type* of response of developing cells to extrinsic stimuli is determined not by the stimulus but rather by the intrinsic competence of each cell type at a particular stage. The stimulus is merely permissive).[3] Equally dramatic changes occur during the metamorphosis of other vertebrates such as cyclostomes and fishes; and, of course, many invertebrates, especially higher insects, also undergo striking transformations from embryo to pupa to adult (see Etkin and Gilbert, 1968).

In general, virtually all of the changes that occur during amphibian metamorphosis reflect the transformation from an aquatic to a terrestrial existence. The loss of the tail, the appearance of legs, permeability changes in the skin, the formation of a new gut, the modification of respiratory mechanisms (e.g. the loss of gills) are all adaptations for terrestrial life. In some amphibians, and in lampreys and eels, a secondary metamorphosis also occurs during the time of spawning, when they return to the environment of their birth. This secondary metamorphosis, which is largely under the control of a prolactin-like hormone, represents a partial reversal of the original metamorphic changes. In the case of the red-spotted newt of the eastern United States, after a terrestrial existence lasting for two to three years, it returns to water, assumes the larval colour and smooth larval skin and develops a laterally flattened tail for swimming. Secondary metamor-phosis in these forms is somewhat analogous to the changes that occur during sexual maturation and puberty in higher verbetrates.

Neural and Behavioural Changes in Animals Showing Metamorphic Development

Transient neural mechanisms which mediate behavioural activities that are lost or reorganized during metamorphosis have been most extensively studied in amphibians. However, before reviewing this evidence, it is important to point out that in amphibians, as well as in most other animals showing metamorphosis, the entire larval nervous system is never discarded wholly. Only specific cell types, neural regions, muscles or sensory receptors are lost or reorganized.

Rohon-Beard (R-B) cells are a primitive type of sensory cell derived from the neural crest and located within the dorsal spinal cord of amphibian tadpoles (Coghill, 1929; Hughes, 1957). These cells mediate tactile and muscle sensitivity in the embryo and tadpole. During metamorphosis the R-B cells regress and disappear entirely and are replaced by the typical vertebrate dorsal root ganglion cells, located *outside* the spinal cord, which mediate somato-sensory sensation in the trunk and appendages of the adult form. The R-B sensory system also appears to mediate sensitivity to a specific type of stimulation (i.e. light touch), a capacity not present during the very earliest larval stages when the tadpole responds only to stronger stimulation. The early responsiveness to more intense stimulation apparently is mediated by another transient type of mechanism involving non-neural skin excitability (Roberts and Smith, 1974).

Here, then, is a case where a fundamental adaptation – sensitivity to environmental stimulation – is mediated by entirely different structures in tadpole and adult. Hence, it is difficult to argue that the R-B cells are in any sense an antecedent of dorsal root ganglion cells or that larval somato-sensory activity represents an incomplete or incipient form of adult somato-sensory activity. It is plausible, however, that the development of normal adult somato-sensory mechanisms beyond the level of the ganglion cells (e.g. in the dorsal column nuclei or brain) is somehow dependent upon the prior activity or presence of the R-B cells. However, this possibility has not been examined.

Many amphibian larvae have a pair of large interneurons in the hindbrain known as Mauthners cells, or M-cells, which regress or disappear following metamorphosis. These cells send axons to the caudal-most spinal cord and collaterals from these axons synapse with motoneurons at many different spinal levels. Functionally, these cells appear to mediate startle responses and they also are involved in the sinusoid swimming activity of the tadpole (Detwiler, 1936; Kimmel and Eaton, 1976). Since a number of studies have shown that exogenous thyroxine hastens the regression of these cells, it is believed that normally their loss is under direct control of endogenous levels of thyroxine (see Jacobson, 1978). Presumably, these cells are transient adaptations for an aquatic environment. Fish retain the M-cells into maturity, when they are primarily involved in mediating startle responses (Kimmel and Eaton, 1976). Thyroxine is also responsible for inducing tail resorption, including the loss of tail motoneurons in amphibian tadpoles (Kaltenbach, 1968; Hadorn, 1974). The massive loss of lumbar motoneurons by cell death during limb development (Prestige, 1971; Blight, 1978) is also partially controlled by thyroxine levels (Kollros, 1968).

The pineal eye in *Xenopus* tadpoles contains photoreceptors and appears to be involved in eliciting swimming behaviour in response to changes in illumination (Roberts, 1978). This capacity is transient, however, only being effective for about one day just prior to and following hatching. After this, the lateral eyes begin to influence swimming and the pineal mechanism is either inhibited or lost.

Young larvae of many amphibians have a cement gland in the mouth region which secretes a mucus that serves to attach the tadpole to objects. The cement gland is also innervated, and tactile stimulation of the cement gland inhibits swimming (Roberts and Blight, 1975). The gland and its inhibitory role are also transient in nature: by about one week after hatching when the tadpole begins to feed, the gland degenerates and touching the mouth no longer inhibits swimming.

Many amphibians exhibit changes in retinal photoreceptor pigments following metamorphosis, and these changes have been related to changes in ecologically relevant phototactic behavioural pref-

erences (Muntz, 1963; Jaeger and Hailman, 1976). The outer segments of retinal rods decrease in length during amphibian metamorphosis, an event which also may have profound effects on the animal's visual physiology (Kinney and Fisher, 1978). Changes occur in the visual pigments and other retinal elements of larval marine fish, which are probably related to the different visual environments inhabited by the larvae and adults (Barrington, 1968).

It has also been reported that, during amphibian development, transient retino-tectal synapses are continuously being formed, only to be lost and then reformed at a new site, a process thought to be either related to differential growth rates in the retina and tectum or for the maintenance of appropriate retino-tectal projections for vision, during stages when the eyes are shifting their position in the head (Gaze et al., 1974; Longley, 1978; Ewert and Burghagen, 1979).

Behaviourally, *Xenopus* tadpoles have a strong tendency to form social aggregations, whereas after metamorphosis they tend to be solitary (Wassersug, 1973). Similarly, spiders which are solitary as adults live communally for a week or so after hatching (Burch, 1979). Early communal living apparently is adaptive, since experimentally isolated spiderlings have a lower survival rate. Juvenile snails show an escape response to the odour of predatory turtles, which they subsequently lose when they attain a size at which they are no longer preyed upon (Berg, 1978). When lobsters grow claws large enough to defend themselves they switch their behavioural response to predators from escape to defence. However, claw removal in the adult reinstates the earlier escape behaviour, indicating that claw development merely inhibits the neural mechanism mediating escape responses (Lang et al., 1977). Although this list of examples is by no means exhaustive (e.g. see Edwards, 1969; Eibl-Eibesfeldt, 1975; Pipa, 1978), it is adequate for showing that the occurrence of transient and provisional neural and behavioural mechanisms is unquestionably a common theme during the development of animals undergoing complex life-history changes. Based on the striking changes in gross morphology that occur from the tadpole, larval or pupal stage to the adult in these forms (as well as the marked ecological changes between stages), this comes as no surprise. However, it does raise an obvious question: are such changes restricted to these forms or do similar neural and behavioural adaptations exist in the development of animals that do not undergo metamorphosis?

Transient Mechanisms during the Neurogenesis of Non-metamorphic Vertebrates

From fertilization to primary induction and throughout early embryogenesis, there are a multitude of general developmental mechanisms, processes and structures which are transient in nature and which, strictly speaking, are not direct antecedents or precursors of any adult structure. Their main role appears to be to induce, regulate or otherwise control the orderly construction of the embryo. Some examples are the specializations of the egg which aid in fertilization, the massive cell movements leading to invagination during gastrulation, induction of the neural plate by the transient chordomesoderm, the formation of neural folds, and the presence of pharyngeal pouces (gill slits) in the embryos of higher vertebrates. None of these features are found in the adult and their transient presence in the embryo apparently reflects their role as necessary aspects of developmental mechanics. That is to say, there may be no alternative way to construct an adult organism other than by the occurrence of these transient processes.

In contrast, other transient features such as the yolk-sac, extra-embryonic membranes, extra-embryonic circulation and embryonic excretory mechanisms are clearly temporary adaptations to the specific needs of the embryonic or fetal environment. Apart from these obvious and more general examples of transient features and ontogenetic adaptations, however, one may ask whether there is evidence for similar provisional adaptations in neural development.

In a series of elegant anatomical studies, Rakic (1971, 1975) has presented evidence suggesting that an early-appearing type of glial cell in the cerebellum serves as a mechanical 'guide' for migrating granule cells en route from the external to the internal granular layer. Later, following the cessation of granule cell migration, these glial cells differentiate into astrocytes and subserve an entirely different function. Glial cells appear to subserve a similar

transient function in other brain areas (Rakic, 1972).

Neuronal cell-death is now recognized as a fundamentally significant aspect of normal neurogenesis in many parts of the central and peripheral nervous system (see Oppenheim, 1981b). Thousands of cells begin differentiation, including axonal growth and synapse formation, only to undergo complete degeneration subsequently. Although the adaptive significance of neuronal cell-death is still not entirely clear, it appears to be a redundancy mechanism for ensuring the adequate innervation of post-synaptic targets. Competition for a limited number of targets results in the elimination of those cells which fail to form a stable synaptic contact. Indirect evidence suggests that the cells that die have formed functional synaptic connections and that the functional interaction between pre- and post-synaptic cells in involved in the regulation of cell survival (Pittman and Oppenheim, 1979). Other provisional functions for the initial overproduction of neurons followed by cell death have also been suggested (Oppenheim, 1981b).

In a recent electron microscopic study, Knyihar et al. (1978) have found that there is a transient population of neurons in the dorsal horn of the fetal monkey's spinal cord, which receive afferent synapses from the dorsal root ganglia. Following the loss of these cells, the afferent projections appear to shift to another cell type. The transient synapses first appear on about the 31st day of gestation and begin to disappear on day 50. Although it is not known whether these synapses are functional, Bodian (1968) has shown independently that the fetal monkey's spinal cord exhibits reflex activity on about the 46th day of gestation.

In two related studies which generally have been overlooked, Humphrey (1944, 1950) reported the presence of two different types of transient motoneurons and two different types of transient 'sensory' neurons in the human fetal spinal cord (see also Youngstrom, 1944). One of each type of neuron (motor and sensory) disappears during very early stages, prior to the onset of any behavioural activity in the fetus. Humphrey suggests that the transient sensory cells are homologous to the amphibian Rohon-Beard cells and that the motoneurons are homologous to the primary motor neurons in the salamander spinal cord, as described by Coghill (1929) and Blight (1978). The second type of transient motor and sensory cells are present at later stages, when reflex activity begins, but they also disappear by nine to ten weeks of gestation. Humphrey speculates that the later-disappearing sensory cells may mediate early fetal proprioceptive function until the dorsal root ganglion cells are sufficiently mature to take over this role. It is also conceivable that the transient synapses and cells in the monkey and human spinal cord serve a *trophic* neurogenetic role in regulating differentiation (see below).

Another type of apparent transient cell found in higher mammals is the so-called Cajal-Retzius (C-R) neurons. These are the first cells to differentiate in all layers of the cerebral cortex. In humans they seem to disappear during the latter part of gestation, whereas in the dog they persist until about two weeks after birth. It is not clear, however, whether the C-R cells actually degenerate, merely become transformed morphologically from their early appearance, or simply shift their position in the cortex (Noback and Purpura, 1961; Fox et al., 1966; Molliver and Van der Loos, 1970). Although it is conceivable that the C-R cells mediate some aspects of prenatal neural or behavioural activity, it is considerably more likely that they subserve a transient neurogenetic trophic function.

The possibility that contacts between neurons early in development may serve a trophic function independent of their later role in mediating neural transmission is not a new idea. But until recently, trophic interactions between motoneurons and muscles were the only well-documented example of such a relationship (Jacobson, 1978). However, there is increasing evidence that similar interactions may occur in the central nervous system. Early developing mono-aminergic neurons may influence the proliferation, migration and differentiation of other cells prior to the onset of synaptic transmission (Lewis, 1978; Lauder and Krebs, 1978). The early appearance of inhibitory neurotransmitters in the embryo may have a similar function (Wolff et al., 1978). In none of these cases involving putative trophic interactions is it known whether the original early cellular contacts are transient or whether they persist, forming functional synapses later in development. However, transient axo-glial synapses do occur in the embryonic brain and spinal cord of chicks and mammals (Hendrickson and Vaughn,

1974; Oppenheim et al., 1978; Wolff et al., 1978) and although these may only reflect developmental errors, they may also serve a transient neurotrophic role.

Although cell death is the most extreme case of a retrogressive phenomenon in neurogenesis, other kinds of synaptic changes involving axonal or dendritic 'remodelling' and synaptic regression also occur during normal development (Weiss and Pysh, 1978; Barker and Ip, 1966; Sotelo and Palay, 1971; Møller, 1978; Booth et al., 1979). The most thoroughly studied type of synaptic remodelling is the phenomenon of polyneuronal innervation, in which cells or subcellular synaptic targets are innervated by more neurons in developing stages than in the adult. Polyneuronal innervation was first observed to occur in the neuromuscular junction but has now also been found to occur on spinal motoneurons, in autonomic ganglia, on Purkinje cells and on cerebral cortical cells (see Purves and Lichtman, 1980, for review).

In the case of polyneuronal innervation of the neuromuscular junction, the excess axons later appear to be retracted back into the parent axon, leaving only a single axon in contact with the muscle (Korneliussen and Jansen, 1976; O'Brien et al., 1978); no actual degeneration either of the entire motoneuron or of the axon branch is involved. Blocking neuromuscular activity with curare retards or inhibits the transition from polyneuronal to singly innervated synapses (Srihari and Vrbova, 1978), suggesting that functional interactions are involved.

The function of polyneuronal innervation is still unclear. It may be a subsidiary mechanism to cell death for regulating the innervation density of a synaptic target, or it may be a necessary condition for a specific type of early neuromuscular activity (e.g. Lewis, 1976); other possible functions have also been suggested (Purves and Lichtman, 1980). Neuronal cell-death is largely an embryonic or prenatal phenomenon, whereas the loss of polyneuronal innervation is restricted mainly to postnatal stages. It is to be expected, however, that future studies may uncover important exceptions to these trends, especially when such studies are extended to a wider variety of cell types and species.

Hormones may also subserve transient functions during development. For instance, whereas the pituitary hormone ACTH regulates adrenal cortical function in adult mammals, the melanocyte-stimulating hormone (MSH) apparently serves this function in the fetus (Challis and Torosis, 1977; Silman et al., 1979).[4] This functional neuro-endocrine transformation may be related to the fact that in human development the fetal zone of the adrenal cortex atrophies, while the cortex hypertrophies. Thyroxine and sex hormones also control certain aspects of neurogenesis and behavioural development during specific developmental stages in mammals (Eayrs, 1971; Nicholson and Altman, 1972; McEwen, 1978). Furthermore, Seyfried et al. (1979) reported that thyroxine may be involved in the changing susceptibility to audiogenic seizures in certain strains of mice during development. It has also been suggested that the presence of large amounts of α-fetoprotein in the blood of developing mammals serves to protect the developing brain against circulating estradiol by binding the estradiol and thereby preventing its entry into the wrong cells (McEwen et al., 1975). Since oestrogen is also thought to have a general organizing role in the development of some parts of the brain, it is of related interest that there are transient oestrogen receptors in rat neocortex which disappear by the third postnatal week (Sheridan, 1979).

Certain types of neurons (e.g. neural-crest cells) may express entirely different neurochemical phenotypes in the embryo or developing animal compared with the adult (Cochard et al., 1978), but the function of such transitions is unknown. The biochemical synthetic pathways for some neurotransmitters may also differ between the embryo and adult. In the chick embryo, for instance, the neurotransmitter γ-amino-butyric acid (GABA) is formed primarily via a pathway using putrescine, whereas in the adult GABA is formed by L-glutamic acid (DeMello et al., 1976). Finally, there are several reports of higher levels of certain neurotransmitters, receptors and transmitter-related enzymes in the CNS of developing vs mature animals (Coyle, 1977; Candy and Martin, 1979; Uzbekov et al., 1979). It has been suggested that such differences may reflect transient developmental functions (e.g. trophic actions) which require higher amounts of these molecules.

Much of the evidence for the existence of transient neurobiological mechanisms is restricted to embryonic, fetal or early postnatal stages: it is not known to what extent these phenomena may also characterize later stages of development. The tradition in all branches of neuroscience, including psychology, has been to consider the mature nervous system as a relatively static entity. It has long been held that once the major growth period is over, the nervous system remains immutable, with the possible exception of subtle, submicroscopic changes in synapses related to learning and memory. Over the last 10 to 15 years, however, this view has gradually shifted in order to accommodate the increasing evidence for previously unsuspected modifications in neural development (e.g. cell death, synaptic remodelling, axonal sprouting, dendritic growth, functional reorganization). It is important to consider whether similar dynamic processes may continue into maturity.

It is known that in some mammals certain parts of the nervous system continue to undergo major neurogenetic changes long after birth. New neurons are produced in the cerebellum, olfactory system and hippocampus postnatally (Altman, 1967; Hinds, 1968; Bayer and Altman, 1974) and in some instances this may even continue into adulthood (Kaplan and Hinds, 1977; Kaplan, 1979). Sensory receptors in the gustatory and olfactory system are renewed on a regular basis throughout life (Jacobson, 1978). As suggested by Altman (1967), these postnatally acquired neurons may represent cell types which require specific postnatal environmental (i.e. experiential) interactions for expressing their adaptive contributions to behavioural development. Neural, endocrine and neurochemical changes may accompany the onset of puberty (Grumbach, 1978; Meyer et al., 1978; Silman et al., 1979; Wilkinson et al., 1979). Cerebral cortical changes of a rather gross nature continue in humans at least up to six years of age (Conel, 1939–67; Yakovlev and Lecours, 1967; Rabinowicz, 1979), and it seems likely that more subtle changes also occur both before and after this period in humans as well as in other animals (Epstein, 1974; Reynolds and Jeeves, 1978; Booth et al., 1979; Buell and Coleman, 1979; Squire and Cohen, 1979).

The considerable evidence for experiential or functionally mediated modifications of neural structure and physiology is also consistent with the notion that some parts of the nervous system retain a capacity for adaptive modification during the entire developmental period, and perhaps even throughout life (see Globus, 1975; Rosenzweig and

Bennett, 1976; Misretta and Bradley, 1978, for reviews).

The occurrence of transient EEG and other electrophysiological patterns during ontogeny (Corner et al., 1973; Dreyfus-Brisac, 1979), the differential effects of drugs on young *vs* mature animals (Shaywitz et al., 1976; File, 1978), and the re-representation of function in different neural structures during development (Humphrey, 1969; Kolb and Noneman, 1976; Alexander and Goldman, 1978), also appear to reflect the presence of different neural mechanisms at different developmental stages. Although it is perhaps too early to predict just how far one can carry the idea of transient or provisional mechanisms in neural development, taken together these various lines of evidence suggest that such phenomena may be a common feature of normal development.

The Behaviour of Embryos

It has long been recognized that the embryos and fetuses of most animals are behaviourally active, and from ancient times to the present the significance of this activity for biological and psychological development has been studied, discussed and debated[5] (see Preyer, 1885, for a review of the early literature and Hooker, 1952; Gottlieb, 1973; Oppenheim, 1981a, for reviews of the more recent literature). Despite this historical tradition, however, it is still not possible to provide any definite answers to the question of why embryos are behaviourally active.

Some suggestions have been offered. One is that embryonic activity is an epiphenomenon and thus is merely an overt manifestation of neural maturation, with no special adaptive function. In fact, it is a cardinal principle of most developing systems that cells, tissues and organs develop and become functional before they are actually needed for survival (e.g. human infants born prematurely have the capacity for vision and for pulmonary respiration). A second suggestion is that embryonic behaviour represents the first necessary steps in the development of adult behaviour. According to this view, each step in behavioural ontogeny is critically dependent on previous steps, and embryonic behaviour is viewed as a fundamental link in the emergence of postnatal behaviour patterns. Although this is an

exceedingly appealing proposition, our understanding of such a progression in even simple types of behaviour in non-humans is so vague – except on a descriptive level – that for the present there is no compelling reason to accept this view of embryonic behaviour as being more plausible than any other. Its major appeal, of course, is that it fits our present preconceptions about developmental continuity.

There are two primary variants or sub-classes of this 'continuity' view of embryonic behaviour. One focuses on the overt activity itself and argues that the manifestation of embryonic motor behaviour represents a kind of necessary practice or use for the organization of later behaviour of all kinds (i.e. motor, sensory, cognitive). The other view tends to focus on the sensory environment and contends that the sensory experiences of the developing embryo are necessary for moulding adult behaviour patterns. These views are not mutually exclusive: often both have been used by adherents of a strict continuity view of embryonic behaviour (e.g. Kuo, 1967). My reason for dealing with them separately is to help sharpen conceptual clarity over these issues, for in practice it is always exceedingly difficult – if not impossible – to manipulate sensory input without also influencing motor activity.

A third conceptualization of embryonic behaviour views the prenatal period as qualitatively unique and thus considers embryonic behaviour to be an ontogenetic adaptation for meeting the special requirements of the *in ovo* or *in utero* environment. I include here anything that cannot be considered solely as a precursor of some adult feature.

Most embryos are relatively well protected in the egg or uterus, and their nutritional and other physiological requirements are usually taken care of – either wholly or in large part – by 'passive' mechanisms requiring little if any active behavioural regulation on the part of the embryo itself. Of course, environmental changes involving light, sound, movement, mechanical, temperature and chemical factors are potential sources of stimulation to the developing embryo. But since the embryo is physically constrained by the closed system of the egg or uterus there is very little that it can do behaviourally to modify the presence (or absence) of potentially deleterious (or desirable) environmental stimuli. It is conceivable, however, that in some instances embryos or fetuses may actively use behavioural mechanisms for adaptively regulating their relationship to the environment. For instance, it has been suggested that the movements of fish and amphibian embryos may aid respiration (Tracy, 1926). Also, of course, external (or endogenous) stimulation may influence embryonic neural and behavioural development in the absence of any immediate overt response by the embryo (see Kammer and Kinnamon, 1979).

All avian embryos use overt behavioural activity involving postural and vestibular reflexes to attain the appropriate position in the egg for hatching. Indeed, hatching mechanisms in all egg-laying animals represent a clear case of an ontogenetic adaptation involving behavioural, neural and other special features which are used only once in the life of the individual and which are not antecedents of any adult behaviour or adaptation (see Oppenheim, 1973, for a review of hatching). Moreover, many of the morphological devices used for hatching, such as the avian egg-tooth, the insect egg-burster and the amphibian hatching gland, are also entirely provisional structures. This is not to deny, however, that certain aspects of hatching, such as the alternating leg-movements of birds (Hamburger and Oppenheim, 1967), may also be used in other, later types of behaviour, such as locomotion (Bekoff, 1979).

In human fetuses the attainment of the normal vertex position for birth may require active behavioural mechanisms. Many fetuses in a breech position two to three months prior to birth are found to have shifted spontaneously to the normal vertex position before birth (Prechtl, 1965; Braun et al., 1975). Langreder (1949) has suggested that reflex stepping and crawling movements, which continue for a short while after birth, may serve to position the fetus in a vertex position. He pointed out that babies born with motor defects, such as limb paralysis, were more likely to be in an abnormal position at birth. Similarly, the dramatic *decrease* in spontaneous activity observed in avian and mammalian embryos just before birth or hatching (Oppenheim, 1974) may serve to preserve the normal hatching or birth position from disruption. Fetal swallowing may serve to reduce the amount of amniotic fluid in preparation for birth, as well as to provide supplementary nutrients to the fetus (Goodlin, 1979).

Spontaneous embryonic activity may also prevent the occurrence of adhesions between the embryo and extra-embryonic membranes, or between different parts of the embryo (e.g. between the appendages and the trunk) (Oppenheim, unpublished observations). The contractions of the amnion in avian embryos, which results in passive embryonic activity, may also aid in the prevention of such adhesions (Hamilton, 1956; New, 1957). In avian and mammalian embryos, spontaneous neuromuscular activity is known to be important for the normal differentiation of muscle and for the prevention of muscular atrophy (Drachman, 1968; Giacobini et al., 1973; Pittman and Oppenheim, 1979). Similarly, embryonic activity is also necessary for the normal development of joints: immobilization leads to serious joint and bone defects, such as ankylosis and clubfoot (Drachman and Sokoloff, 1966; Oppenheim et al., 1978). Despite the effects of embryonic immobilization on joint and muscle development, however, the resulting behavioural inactivity (and sensory deprivation) does not affect certain aspects of later behavioural development following the cessation of drug-induced paralysis (Carmichael, 1926, 1927; Oppenheim et al., 1978; Pittman and Oppenheim, 1979). This lends support to the idea that embryonic activity is an adaptation for the regulation of joint and muscle morphogenesis and not (at least not solely) a necessary antecedent of later behaviour.

It has been suggested that endogenous neural activity in the embryo is necessary at certain stages of development (as a form of *intrinsic* stimulation) for normal neurogenesis (Roffwarg et al., 1966; Oppenheim, 1974; Gottlieb, 1976a). Although there is considerable evidence against this argument (Harrison, 1904; Carmichael, 1926; Crain et al., 1968; Model et al., 1971; Obata, 1977; Oppenheim et al., 1978), since so many aspects of neurogenesis (and behaviour) remain to be examined under conditions of embryonic functional deprivation, it would be premature to dismiss this idea. At some stages of development, pharmacologically induced dysfunction can drastically alter neural maturation in tissue culture (Bergey et al., 1978), as well as in the intact embryo (Pittman and Oppenheim, 1979).

Finally, there is considerable evidence that, in birds, embryonic auditory function or experience may regulate certain aspects of behaviour, such as hatching (Vince, 1973), post-hatching species recognition (Gottlieb, 1976b) and individual recognition (Tschanz, 1968), as well as other kinds of responses to auditory signals after hatching (Impekoven, 1976). I mention these phenomena because the behaviours in question all appear to be primarily transient in nature, in that they involve provisional or ontogenetic adaptations such as hatching, approach and attachment responses to the parents, and defence against predators.

It is clear from the foregoing discussion that there are many different ways in which embryonic behaviour may serve as ontogenetic adaptations. Nonetheless, it would be misleading to conclude that all embryonic behaviour is an adaptation, or to argue that embryonic behaviour cannot be both an adaptation *and* a necessary antecedent for later behaviour. Critical analytical studies are the only satisfactory approach to these questions and at present such studies are still few in number.

Postnatal Behaviour

It can be argued that, in view of the obvious 'ecological' differences between the prenatal and postnatal periods, the demonstration of transient or provisional behaviour and neural mechanisms in the embryo is hardly surprising, and indeed is to be expected. After birth or hatching, however, ecological changes for most non-metamorphic animals are either minimal or non-existent. Virtually all mammals are born into and continue to exist in a terrestrial environment which requires many general adaptations which are similar in the newborn and adult (e.g. pulmonary respiration, independent excretory mechanisms, digestion).

If this argument is valid for most neural and behavioural mechanisms, then one would expect there either to be relatively few ontogenetic adaptations after birth or hatching, or, if present, that they would be restricted to the period before weaning, sexual maturation or the establishment of an independent existence. Such a view in fact seems to have predominated in most previous investigations and discussions of postnatal behavioural development. Even in those instances where behaviours are obviously qualitatively different in the neonate and adult (e.g. different modes of mammalian ingestive behaviour such as suckling *vs* adult feeding), often there has been an implicit belief that the neonatal behaviour is a necessary antecedent of the adult

pattern. In view of these traditional preconceptions, it is not surprising that there are few convincing examples of postnatal ontogenetic adaptations, or that the vast majority of these are restricted to the *early* postnatal period.

Consequently, what I wish to do in the remainder of this section is to delineate behaviours which either exist or predominate in the young animal but which change, disappear or become less frequent in the adult. It will become evident that in many cases the evidence that a particular postnatal behaviour is either an ontogenetic adaptation or an antecedent is weak, circumstantial or entirely conjectural. I have included such cases, nonetheless, in the hope that by virtue of their vagueness they will serve to stimulate more research into the nature and significance of these phenomena in development.

Newborn human infants exhibit a number of reflexes or reflex-like behaviours, known as infantile or primary reflexes, which typically disappear within the first year or so of life (McGraw, 1935, 1942; Peiper, 1963; Touwen, 1976). These include sucking, rooting, stepping, grasping, reaching, crawling, swimming and the Moro reflex.[6] For a long time the consensus has been that many of these behaviours represent phylogenetic vestiges or remnants, lacking any adaptive function for the infant (McGraw, 1942). However, as I pointed out in the previous section there is evidence that certain of these reflexes, such as stepping and crawling, may in fact serve to position the human fetus in the normal vertex position for birth.

Since, later in development, several of these infantile reflexes are superseded by grossly similar behaviours which are under voluntary control, it has also been thought that the reflexes represent primitive antecedents of their voluntary counterparts. However, early attempts to maintain some of these behaviours, such as reflex stepping, by exercise, did not prevent their disappearance or lead to the early appearance of voluntary walking (McGraw, 1935; Peiper, 1963), thus supporting the view that they represent atavisms or ancestral vestiges. In contrast, more recent attempts at preserving reflex stepping and reflex reaching by daily exercise apparently have been successful (Bower, 1976; Super, 1976; Zelazo, 1976). Moreover, it has been reported that the exercise of these reflexes can hasten the appearance of later voluntary walking and reaching. Consequently, it is now argued that the early reflexes in fact do represent antecedents of their voluntary counterparts. Without wishing to dispute the claim that exercise can retard the disappearance of reflex stepping or reaching, nonetheless it seems premature to conclude that the early and later behaviour are isomorphic. Furthermore, considerably more work is needed before it can be concluded that early exercise can hasten the appearance of voluntary walking or reaching: the existing reports are only preliminary in nature (Zelazo and Kolb, 1972; Bower, 1976). Even should the reports be confirmed, however, it still would not be clear what relevance this has for normal development. In most Western societies these reflexes are not deliberately exercised and they disappear long before the appearance of their voluntary counterparts; nevertheless, voluntary walking and reaching develop normally in the vast majority of infants.[7]

The early appearance and later disappearance of neonatal reflexes and other similar stereotyped behaviour has also been reported in animals such as rats, rabbits, dogs and monkeys (Kennard, 1938; Hines, 1942; Fox, 1965, 1971; Fox and Appelbaum, 1969; Stelzner et al., 1975; Teitelbaum et al., 1976; Vanderwolf et al., 1978). In one case an infantile reflex apparently serves one function in the young and an entirely different function in the adult. The African meercat has a reflex which is triggered when the young are picked up by the scruff of the neck by the mother. This apparently serves to prevent injury to the young by the mother's teeth. For adult meercats, copulation is facilitated when the male grabs the female by the neck, thereby stopping her struggling by triggering the relaxation reflex (Ewer, 1968; also see Brewster and Leon, 1980).

Despite our ignorance about the functional or adaptive aspects of many transient behaviours, such as reflex walking, their existence raises the question of what happens to the neural substrate when the overt behaviour disappears. The most extreme alternative is that the neurons mediating the behaviour simply degenerate or regress. Although this appears to be unlikely, it should not be dismissed entirely. It seems more plausible that the neurons do not degenerate but merely modify their anatomical connectivity; as noted earlier, there is ample evidence for such synaptic remodelling, both prenatally and postnatally. Finally, there is the possibility that there are no anatomical changes at all, but rather that the behaviours either become suppressed by active physiological inhibition or become *physiologically* re-organized or re-integrated into more mature behaviour patterns (e.g. reflex stepping and voluntary walking may share some of the same neural mechanisms).

Support for the last alternative rests largely on the pathological evidence of various types of infantile-like behaviours reappearing in adult animals following brain damage (Kennard, 1938; Peiper, 1963; Teitelbaum 1967,[8] Paulson and Gottlieb, 1968) or of early brain damage delaying the normal loss of infantile behaviour (Smith et al., 1974; Stelzner et al., 1975).

Since it is not central to my argument that the neural mechanisms for essential ontogenetic behavioural adaptations either regress or become modified anatomically when the behaviour disappears, the possibility that many such adaptations in fact do disappear due to encephalization or physiological inhibition is by no means inconsistent with the proposition that the behaviours are transient adaptations. The maternally evoked micturition reflex of many altricial neonatal mammals, for instance, which is an ontogenetic adaptation for emptying the bladder, disappears during normal development but can be later reinstated by spinal transection, indicating that descending inhibitory circuits are responsible for suppressing this reflex during ontogeny (DeGroat et al., 1975). Sucking behaviour in mammals represents another particularly good illustration of a similar phenomenon.

In virtually all mammals, sucking represents the major pattern of ingestive behaviour from birth until weaning. Notwithstanding the recent interesting demonstration that in the appropriate circumstances neonatal rats can also ingest liquids by adult-like 'lapping' (Hall, 1979), suckling remains the sole means of food intake in the natural situation during most of the pre-weaning period. Therefore suckling is clearly an ontogenetic adaptation which later disappears and is replaced by a qualitatively different form of ingestive behaviour. In adult humans, reflex-like rooting and sucking occurs in certain neuropathological conditions (Paulson and Gottlieb, 1968) and in juvenile or mature rats neonatal-like suckling behaviour can be reinstated by treatment with certain drugs (Williams et al., 1979; Brake and Williams, 1979). Consequently, it seems likely that in most mammals the neural mechanisms for suckling do not regress anatomically, but rather become actively suppressed during normal development. This being the case, one can ask whether, in addition to being an ontogenetic adaptation, suckling is also a necessary antecedent for mature ingestive behaviour. Using an ingenious technique for artificially rearing rats from birth to weaning – thereby depriving them of normal suckling experience – Hall (1975) has shown that the absence of suckling produces no apparent deficits in later adult ingestive behaviour, including appetitive learning for food (also see Thoman and Arnold, 1968; Scott, 1973). Although it is possible that suckling deprivation may affect more subtle aspects of later ingestive behaviour, this finding nonetheless is consistent with my argument that there are transient and largely provisional adaptations in postnatal behaviour.

The evidence showing that the neural basis for reflex sucking persists in the adult may mean either that the same mechanism used in neonatal suckling is also used later in other adult behaviours – but that the deprivation of early suckling does not impair the development or maintenance of this mechanism – or that the neonatal neural mechanism is also entirely provisional, being suppressed (by encephalization?) but not destroyed once its usefulness has been outlived. Although at present it is impossible to decide between these two alternatives, the issue is amenable to analysis. For this reason, suckling may be an especially favourable model for examining the nature and developmental history of postnatal ontogenetic adaptations, as well as their neural basis.

Although the development of behaviour in the postnatal period has not been studied as extensively in non-mammalian animals, transient behaviour patterns are probably as common in birds and reptiles as in mammals. For example, many altricial birds elicit feeding from the parents by a stereotyped and transient behaviour pattern known as gaping. This striking behaviour gradually disappears during the nestling and fledgling periods, when independent feeding by pecking or other means develops (Prechtl, 1953; Nice, 1962; Berger, 1968; Horwich, 1969). Often gaping is accompanied by a specific vocalization (the begging call), which later disappears.

The hatchlings of the parasitic European cuckoo have a special behaviour pattern, used for ejecting the eggs or young of the host species from the nest (Jourdain, 1925). Similarly, the newly-hatched young of parasitic African honeyguides have transient hooks on the beak which they use to kill their nestmates (Southern, 1964). In cuckoos, the ejection behaviour is present shortly after hatching and disappears about five days later (Eibl-Eibesfeldt, 1975). These peculiar ontogenetic adaptations serve to ensure that the young of parasitic birds will receive all of the food from the foster parents.

In several species of snakes (vipers), the young use a particular behaviour pattern for luring prey which is not found in the adults (Burghardt, 1978). Young crocodilians emit an alarm vocalization to predators which apparently serves to attract adults, but which is seldom, if ever, emitted by adult crocodilians (Burghardt, 1978; Staton, 1978).

Play, Prolonged 'Infancy' and Early Learning

In many species of mammals, the young exhibit high levels of what has been called play behaviour. Later in development, such behaviour subsides or disappears entirely (see Bekoff, 1972, 1976). The extent to which play is an ontogenetic adaptation, as well as an antecedent of later behaviour, is a topic that is now being debated (e.g. see Bekoff and Byers, 1981). There is evidence that short-term play deprivation produces no immediate deleterious effects (Fagan, 1977), but attempts to deprive animals of play for longer periods of time have resulted in severe, long-lasting behavioural deficits. However, since virtually all such studies have used various isolation techniques, which inevitably deprive the animal of far more than just play, the findings are equivocal (Bekoff and Byers, 1981). Although it seems entirely plausible that play is an essential developmental antecedent of later behaviour, which, in the words of one investigator, serves 'to allow the developing organism to realize behavioural potentialities essential for normal behavioural development and adult life' (Bekoff, 1972, p. 424), at present such a belief rests more on faith than fact. For instance, the widespread assumption that social play in juvenile primates is necessary for the emergence of social interactions in the adult appears to have been refuted. In field observations, Baldwin and Baldwin (1973) found that play behaviour by juveniles was virtually non-existent in some troops of squirrel monkeys. Yet many later social interactions developed normally. Although subtle differences in some aspects of later social behaviour were also found, it is a moot point as to whether these differences have any adaptive significance. Play-like behaviour in juvenile rats has been proposed as an ontogenetic adaptation for inhibiting aggression by adults (Galef, 1979). Adult rats are more tolerant of and less aggressive toward young animals compared with other unfamiliar conspecifics. This may aid the young rat in learning important aspects of its environment by allowing social interactions with adults. In both kittens and human infants, play itself undergoes qualitative changes which may be associated with specific developmental requirements at different stages (Barrett and Bateson, 1978; Largo and Howard, 1979a, b).

Regardless of the present uncertainty about the specific role or roles of play behaviour, the fact that play is largely restricted to specific developmental periods argues for its inclusion as an ontogenetic adaptation. It is not simply an imperfect or immature form of an adult behaviour, in the way that the first uncertain steps of an infant are an incipient form of adult walking. The propensity for play may have evolved as an ontogenetic adaptation for facilitating the acquisition of behaviour which becomes adaptive only later in life. From this perspective, play could be considered to be *both* an ontogenetic adaptation and a developmental antecedent (Bekoff and Byers, 1981).

Like play, the prolonged period of infancy or immaturity that is characteristic of some animals, especially humans, is also both an ontogenetic adaptation *and* a period of preparation for maturity. Arguments for the significance of delayed development or neoteny in man are old and have generally focused on the extended period of postnatal development as being important for learning and for establishing close social interactions with parents and other adults (Butler, 1984; Lovejoy, 1904; Armstrong, 1906). Fiske, one of the early champions of the view that prolonged infancy is important in human evolution and ontogeny, put it this way: 'Instead of being born with a few simple capacities thoroughly organized, man came at last to be born with the germs of many complex capacities which were reserved to be unfolded and enhanced or checked and stifled by the incidents of personal

experience in each individual' (Fiske, 1899, p. 315). And commenting on the significance of human neoteny for brain development, Fiske argued that: 'The prolonging of the plastic period of infancy, entailing a vast increase in teachableness and versatility, has contributed to the . . . enlargement of the cerebral surface' (Fiske, 1884, p. 36).[9]

Despite the presence of a prolonged infancy in humans, it has become increasingly clear in the last 10 to 15 years that human infants (and the young of many other species as well) are not the totally helpless, incompetent creatures we once imagined. It is now recognized that in some respects young animals, even neonates, are exceedingly competent, often surpassing the adults in certain capacities. The Czech paediatrician Papousek (1969) has asked: 'Are neonates in some ways more perfect, and their capacities in some functions greater than later on?' (p. 266). Many of the sensory, perceptual and motor capacities of newborn and young animals represent special adaptations or competencies for interacting with adults (Bower, 1976; Konner, 1977; Macfarlane, 1977; Trevarthen, 1979). For instance, newborn infants can both respond to and produce certain vocalizations which are not typically present in the language of their culture, sounds which older children and adults find difficult to produce or discern (Eimas, 1975; Harnad et al., 1976; Trehub, 1976). This ability of the newborn apparently represents an adaptation for ensuring the acquisition of even the most acoustically arcane of human languages. It has also been suggested that the specific stages of human language and intellectual development may represent adaptations to particular needs of the child (Lamedella, 1976; Parker and Gibson, 1979): those authors also argue that the stages of language and intellectual development in modern man may represent phylogenetically earlier modes of these functions and thus constitute examples of recapitulation. I hasten to point out that the theory of recapitulation, as applied to either neurobehavioural or embryological development, has a long history of confusion and controversy (e.g. Gould, 1977) and this must be reckoned with in any modern attempts at resuscitation. Even if correct in a limited number of cases, however, modern recapitulation theory does not necessarily imply that the ancestral repetitions that are present in the ontogenetic stages of a descendant are either merely non-functional (i.e.

non-adaptive) vestiges, or preparations for adulthood. The retention of ancestral traits in the ontogeny of a descendant in fact may reflect ontogenetic adaptations.

The possibility that even the absence of adult capacities may be developmentally adaptive also should be considered in any comprehensive theory of ontogeny. For instance, the absence of homeothermy in most newborn altricial animals may be an adaptation for limiting energy loss and thus contribute to rapid growth (Galef, 1979). The relative immobility of immature altricial animals may serve a similar energy-conserving function. The well-known phenomenon of infantile amnesia, i.e. deficits in long-term memory for certain kinds of learning in young animals (Campbell and Coulter, 1976), may not only reflect an immature nervous system but may also be adaptive in preventing the retention of many irrelevant environmental changes. Exceptions to the infantile amnesia phenomenon, such as learned taste aversions (e.g. Gregg et al., 1978; Campbell and Alberts, 1979), may also represent ontogenetic adaptations. Alternatively, they may be only another example of the development of a physiological mechanism prior to its need by the organism for survival.

Although it has long been believed that the learning capacities of immature animals were uniformly inferior to the adult, evidence now indicates that for certain tasks, especially those that are ecologically relevant, the young animal may equal or even surpass the adult. Newborn kittens readily learn the position of specific maternal nipples, as well as how to orientate to the nest site (Rosenblatt, 1971, 1979). Young shrikes are much more proficient at learning to use thorns to impale prey when given practice at 20 to 30 days after hatching compared with 45 days post-hatching (Smith, 1972). Rats 4 to 6 weeks old learn an avoidance task faster than adult animals (Myslivecek, 1976). And five-week-old puppies also learn an avoidance task faster than puppies eight to ten weeks old (Fox, 1971). Juvenile great-tits learn certain complex tasks faster than adult birds (Vince, 1960, 1961) and the problem-solving ability of newly-hatched ducklings may be as good or better than it is later in life (Heaton, 1978).

Behaviours that are more easily influenced or acquired during certain developmental periods, such as social attachments in birds (Hess, 1973;

Immelmann, 1975; Bateson, 1979), and in mammals (Scott, 1962), food preferences in reptiles (Burghardt and Hess, 1966) and rats (Galef, 1977), the effects of infant handling on later stress reactions (Levine and Lewis, 1959), song learning in birds (Marler and Mundinger, 1971) and language acquisition in humans (Lenneberg, 1969) can also be viewed as ontogenetic adaptations. Similar to the previous examples of play and the prolonged immaturity of primates, these phenomena represent the evolution of acquisition mechanisms which are relatively restricted to particular stages of ontogeny and which may be related to some of the underlying neurobiological (and neuro-endocrinological) changes described above.

All of these various lines of evidence regarding learning or learning-like processes suggest that it may be considerably more profitable in the future to consider such phenomena within an ecological framework, in which the major focus is on what an animal has to learn at each stage of development in order to increase its chance of survival rather than viewing learning as a progressive unitary process that gets better and better (or more and more mature-like) as the animal develops.

Behavioural Changes Later in Life

Until quite recently, most studies of behavioural development have focused on the period prior to the attainment of sexual maturity; the assumption being that although changes may occur following this period, puberty or adolescence nevertheless represents the last real ontogenetic stage before adulthood. The attitude seems to have been that, following the watershed of sexual maturity, any subsequent changes in behaviour merely represent minor quantitative variations on a pattern already fundamentally established in the adolescent or juvenile period (or even earlier).[10] Consequently, any later changes are not thought to be subject to the same developmental controls or regulatory mechanisms characteristic of earlier periods. The behavioural changes that often accompany old age are considered to be an exception to this conceptual view, but even here the differences have been largely attributed to a process of organic dissolution, in which the neural and behavioural changes are considered a by-product of illness or pathology and thus of no real adaptive significance in their own right.

Recently, however, the trend in developmental psychology, sociology and psychiatry has been to challenge the older notion that development, growth and change ceases at puberty or late adolescence (Gould, 1976; Baltes and Schaie, 1973; Sheehy, 1976; Valliant, 1977; Levinson, 1978). It is becoming increasingly clear that, following infancy, there continue to be fundamental qualitative changes in virtually all aspects of human behaviour. Although there are undoubtedly many important continuities, interactions and antecedent relationships between the behavioural characteristics expressed at different periods of the life cycle beyond infancy, it seems unlikely that the early stages merely represent important preparations for some ultimate adaptations later in life. Rather, I propose as a working hypothesis that even the changes that occur in adulthood, including aging, may represent adaptations for specific periods of life.[11] The task for future research will be to show that, like embryonic development, later stages of the life cycle are also controlled and regulated by epigenetic regulatory mechanisms which affect both structure and function, including neurobiological characteristics. Although by definition I include differential gene activity in such epigenetic regulatory mechanisms, this is not meant to imply that changes in the life cycle, either before or after puberty, are predetermined, fixed or inevitable. Rather, like all other ontogenetic processes they merely represent potentials that always require environmental factors, ranging from embryonic cellular interactions all the way to social influences, for their expression. I realize that at present the attribution of embryonic-like developmental processes to later stages of the life cycle may appear to be a rather unorthodox position, since the contemporary consensus seems to be that *epigenetic* development ceases at the very latest after puberty (e.g. see Bower, 1979).[12] As discussed below, however, our current understanding of differential gene activity at any stage in the life cycle is still so sketchy that strong conventional views on this issue largely reflect preconceptions which can only stifle future progress.

One notable contribution from the life-span perspective is the work of Levinson (1978), who has identified four major stages or eras, each with its own distinctive and unifying psychosocial qualities, in his study of the human male life cycle. These are: childhood and adolescence (0 to 22 years), early adulthood (17 to 45), middle adulthood (40 to 65), and late adulthood (60 to death). Each era is made up of periods: a transition period leading to a new era and lasting for about five years, and a stable period lasting for most of the remainder of the era. Regarding the distinctness of these eras and periods, Levinson has said: 'As our study progressed our findings led us from the idea of a steady, continuous process of development to the idea of qualitatively different periods in development' (p. 40). Concerning the relationship of each era and period to chronological age, Levinson points out that: 'we did not begin this study with preformed hypotheses about developmental periods unfolding in an age-linked sequence. We were as surprised as everyone else by (*the discovery that*) there is a single, most frequent age at which each period begins. There is a range of variation, usually about two years above and below the average' (pp. 52–3). And in apparent agreement with Piaget's views on the sequence of cognitive development, Levinson and his colleagues also argue that these periods occur in a fixed sequence. Finally, regarding the ultimate nature of the eras and periods, Levinson offers the following tentative hypothesis: 'The eras and periods are grounded in the nature of man as a biological, psychological and social organism. . . . They represent the life cycle of the species. Individuals go through the periods in infinitely varied ways, but the periods themselves are universal' (p. 322).

The conclusions and interpretations cited by Levinson, and indeed the facts themselves, must be viewed with great caution since they are based on a relatively small sample size (40) and because the data represent only a relatively limited sample of the potential information that could have been collected from the subjects. Many of the data come from interviews, without any apparent attempt at standardized testing. And to suggest that the findings are universal and species typical, in the absence of data from women or from other cultures, strikes one as the height of presumption and chauvinism.

Most of the periods, eras or stages described by Levinson and other 'life-span' developmental theorists can be viewed as plausible adaptations to changing social requirements and cultural expectations. Aging and senescence, however, appear to be enigmatic when considered from this perspective.

Aging has long been considered to represent a progressive accumulation of deleterious changes, leading ultimately to death (Finch and Hayflick, 1977). In considering the evolution of aging and death, it has generally been held that these phenomena serve either to limit the life-span and hence population size – as George Bernard Shaw once noted: 'Death is nothing but making room' (1930, p. 75) – or that aging results from the selection of genes which produce slight increases in fitness in youth, but which produce markedly deleterious effects later on, after the reproductive period (Williams, 1957; Kirkwood and Holliday, 1979). In other words, it is often argued that aging is the price an organism must pay for the retention of certain adaptations earlier in the life cycle. The assumption in either case is that senescence itself has no function – indeed that it is the antithesis of adaptation.

In contrast, it has also been suggested that there may be selection pressures for maintaining old age as a distinct stage in the life cycle of many animals (Sacher, 1978). Older, non-reproductive individuals may confer some advantage to younger members of the population (Hamilton, 1966; Rockstein et al., 1977; Young, 1978). Some of the behavioural changes that often accompany aging (Birren and Schaie, 1976; Timiras, 1978) may be adaptive for this period of life, and the characteristics of old organisms could thus be the result of evolutionary selection. For instance, Barnes (1979) has suggested that the memory deficits associated with aging in rats may in fact be an adaptation for reducing the amount of information that can be stored in order to maintain some optimal signal-to-noise ratio.

The biochemical, physiological, morphological and behavioural changes that occur during aging are not random, nor do they uniformly affect all characteristics (Birren and Schaie, 1967; Finch and Hayflick, 1977; Lamb, 1977). The same holds true for the neurobiological and neuro-endocrinological changes that accompany aging. Although it was once thought that there was a general deterioration (i.e. cell loss or regression) in most parts of the nervous system, this no longer appears to be true. In some brain regions or cell types there may be substantial cell loss with aging (Nandy, 1973; Brody and Vijayashankar, 1977), whereas in other regions or cell types little or no loss may occur (Konigsmark and Murphy, 1970, 1972; Brody, 1973; Howard, 1973; Klein and Michel, 1977). Less severe regres-

sive changes involving axonal, dendritic and synaptic modifications also occur with aging and these may be selective for certain cell types or brain regions (Scheibel et al., 1975, 1977; Vaughn, 1977; Scheff et al., 1978; Geinesman, 1979; Hinds and McNelly, 1979; Machado-Salas and Scheibel, 1979). I find it especially interesting that recent evidence indicates a continuation of dendritic growth in some parts of the normal human brain into the seventh decade of life (Buell and Coleman, 1979). Thus, there is reason to believe that *constructive* changes may also occur in the brain, even very late in life.

Evidence from several different lines of work have led to the recent proposal that aging in animals, including neurobiological changes, are the result of a programme for aging involving brain-endocrine relationships (Finch, 1976; Timiras, 1978). During each stage of the life-span, the brain-endocrine system is thought to function differently, leading to changes in neurotransmission, brain function and behaviour. As in all other neuroendocrine functions, the environment is also presumed to play an integral role in regulating the expression of specific characteristics controlled by this mechanism.

Although the evidence supporting such a 'brain-endocrine master plan' for aging is still tentative, there are experimental data showing that alterations in neuro-endocrine relationships can modify the aging process (Everitt and Burgess, 1976; Finch and Hayflick, 1977; Landfield et al., 1978). I mention this hypothesis in the present context mainly to illustrate that there are potential mechanisms for controlling the age-dependent expression of the neurobiological and behavioural changes which characterize ontogenetic adaptations throughout the life cycle.

The Evolution and Genetics of Ontogenetic Adaptations

Recapitulation theory, as enunciated and developed by Ernst Haeckel in the last half of the nineteenth century, rested on the fundamental belief that evolutionary novelties generally were added to the final stages of ontogeny and that, by and large, the earlier stages of individual development represented a retracing of an animal's ancestry. According to this view, ontogenetic adaptations (e.g. frog tadpoles) are considered a rare exception to the general rule that new adaptations only occur at the terminal stages of ontogeny (see Gould, 1977). In contrast, Darwin (1868), in his theory of natural selection and in his theory of heredity ('Pangenesis'), clearly recognized that selection may act at all stages of ontogeny, leading in some instances to the evolution of ontogenetic adaptations.

Subsequently, a number of biologists, most notably Garstang (1922), Haldane (1932), and DeBeer (1958), have also argued that ontogeny can be altered at virtually any stage, that ontogenetic adaptations are common features of development, and that the order with which characters appear in phylogeny is not necessarily faithfully reproduced in ontogeny. As Haldane (1932) noted: 'It would seem that within limits natural selection will tend to make life-cycles more and more variegated, as every increase in complexity will increase the possibility of fixing the time of action of genes. In general, the more limited is the period of action of a gene, the more unalloyed will be its benefits if it is useful at a certain period' (p. 22). What this means for my present argument is that as long as the same genes control behaviour and neurobiological mechanisms at different stages of development, behavioural adaptations at one stage will always be subordinated to those of the other stages. Thus, ontogenetic adaptations are much more likely to occur when genetic mechanisms at different stages in the life cycle become relatively emancipated from one another. Apparently most evolutionary biologists now accept this view, in that they recognize the existence of ontogenetic adaptations, that in principle such adaptations can occur at any stage in the life cycle, and that ontogenetic novelties, often being based on specific genetic changes, may provide unique opportunities for evolution (e.g. see Dobzhansky, 1956; DeBeer, 1958; Williams, 1966; Frazzetta, 1975; Gould, 1977).

Although often it may be true – especially in metamorphic animals – that different structural genes control different stages of development, other possible genetic mechanisms also exist. As Goldschmidt (1938) recognized, by altering the rate of expression of structural genes (by regulatory genes and by extrinsic controls) it is possible to produce qualitatively new or different characteristics during ontogeny. For instance, it has been suggested recently that virtually all of the striking differences between chimpanzees and humans only reflect the differential timing of expression of the same structural genes (King and Wilson, 1975; Bruce and Ayala, 1978). Explicit genetic models have been presented, showing how changes in the timing and regulating of gene activity could be involved in evolutionary and ontogenetic novelties (Britten and Davidson, 1969; Holliday and Pugh, 1975; Soll, 1979). The most detailed attempt to conceptualize ontogenetic adaptations within an integrated framework of modern embryology, molecular genetics and evolution is that of Zuckerkandl (1976). It is worth noting that it is now widely recognized that developmental changes can occur by selective gene expression (or activity), or by gene suppression (inactivity). In fact, there is increasing evidence that selective and progressive gene *inactivity* may be the more common feature in the development of higher organisms (Caplan and Ordahl, 1978), including brain development (e.g. Omnen, 1975).

Perhaps the most direct evidence for the role of differential gene activity in regulating major ontogenetic transformations comes from the studies of chromosome 'puffing' in certain invertebrates. It has been observed that the giant chromosomes of some flies exhibit swollen regions (puffs) that reflect areas of high RNA synthetic activity. And it has now been shown that the puffs represent differential gene activity associated with specific metamorphic events (Ashburner, 1980). The pattern of chromosomal puffing changes systematically during development and differential puffing and protein synthesis can be induced by hormones known to regulate metamorphosis (Kroeger, 1968).

DNA–RNA hybridization studies, by which one can determine which RNAs are active at different stages of development (Omnen, 1975; Berrill and Karp, 1976), and recombinant DNA studies (Dawid and Wahli, 1979), have the potential to reveal a great deal about the role of genes in ontogeny, but at present the evidence provided by these techniques concerning the regulation of development and ontogenetic adaptations by differential gene activity in most higher animals is practically non-existent. Although it seems likely that many of the changes that occur during prenatal *and* postnatal development will eventually be shown to be mediated in part by differential gene activity, our present knowledge of the genes involved, their mode of action and their epigenetic control is minimal, even for relatively simple cytochemical processes. Hence, it is no surprise that our understanding of the genetic and epigenetic mechanisms controlling the complex behavioural and neurobiological changes associated with ontogenetic adaptations at most stages of development has barely advanced beyond the stage of informed speculation.

Although there is evidence from humans and other animals suggesting a time-dependent penetrance for a number of genetic disorders and normal traits involving the nervous system and behaviour (Crow and Smouse, 1977; Knudson and Meadows, 1978; McKusik, 1978; Hegmann, 1979; Marzetta and Nash, 1979), at present this information provides little insight into the role of genes in the expression of ontogenetic adaptations during normal development. And considering the present nascent state of behavioural, developmental and neural genetics (e.g. Ehrman and Parsons, 1976; Garn and Bailey, 1978; Breakefield, 1979), this situation is not likely to change for a very long time. In particular, the relative absence of information on genetic variance and on the norms of reaction of genotypes for most species, especially with regard to neural and behavioural traits, underlines the enormous obstacles that must be overcome if we are ever to understand the genetic and epigenetic nature of ontogenetic adaptations.

Conclusions

In this essay I have summarized the evidence for the existence of transient and provisional adaptations in behavioural development, and have tried to show that there are also apparent transient features and regressive changes in neurobiological development. In attempting to present an argument which runs counter to much past and contemporary thought about developmental processes – and which in many instances lacks crucial experimental support – I have sought to avoid either overstating my case or engaging in idle speculation. It is unlikely that I have been entirely successful on either score.

As one moves away from the embryonic and early neonatai periods, the evidence for qualitative changes in either behavioural or neurobiological characteristics becomes progressively weaker. Simi-

larly, the putative adaptive role of such changes also becomes increasingly uncertain and problematic when dealing with stages beyond infancy and early childhood. Although there are cases, especially in metamorphic animals, in which structures and functions appear to be entirely transient and provisional, neither serving as a necessary antecedent for some later characteristic nor being retained for some later, albeit different, function, this is unlikely to be true of most ontogenetic adaptations. As has been repeatedly pointed out with regard to both ontogeny and evolution, when environments change and new adaptations are required, it is intuitively more simple and genetically more likely that organisms will remodel or reorganize existing mechanisms rather than discard the old and develop an entirely novel one. However, such an admission is not an argument against ontogenetic adaptations, but merely a concession that in most instances ontogenetic adaptations may serve both immediate *and* future needs.

In that eighteenth-century milestone of developmental psychology, *Emile; Or Concerning Education*, Rousseau (1762) said about puberty: 'We are born, so to speak, twice over, born into existence and born into life, born a human being and born a man (p. 172). If, as I have argued, ontogenetic adaptations are a recurring event throughout the life cycle from embryo to adult, then perhaps we are born again, so to speak, many times over. Recently, abrupt and discontinuous changes, as against gradualism and continuity, have been invoked once again as being characteristic of evolution or phylogeny (Eldredge and Gould, 1972). Perhaps it is time to reconsider some of our deeply held beliefs about similar events in ontogeny.

Acknowledgements

Some of the ideas in this essay were first presented in 1973 at a symposium on embryonic behaviour at the XIIIth International Congress of Ethology in Washington, DC. Their present state of 'differentiation' has been aided immeasurably by countless discussions and debates with many friends and colleagues. The central idea that ontogenetic adaptations represent an important but neglected feature of ontogeny stems from a suggestion made to me by Viktor Hamburger that hatching in birds may illus-

trate a more general feature of behavioural development (i.e. transient adaptations) than is commonly
recognized. Others who were especially helpful in
sharpening my thoughts on this issue as well as in
saving me from some grievous errors were Ted
Hall, Tim Johnston and Pat Bateson.

I owe a special debt of gratitude to my namesake,
the paediatrician Nathan Oppenheim, who, in his
writings at the turn of the present century on child
development, helped me to recognize the broader
implications of ontogenetic adaptations in the life
cycle.

Notes

1 Delage and Goldsmith (1912) have previously introduced the term *ontogenetic adaptations*; but they have
   defined the concept in an entirely different way from
   that used here (also, see Baldwin, 1902). As they explain:
   'We know that, in the course of its life, every living thing
   adapts itself continuously to its environment and acquires thereby some useful structure. This constitutes
   the so-called *ontogenetic adaptation*, taking the word
   ontogenetic in its broader sense, and applying it not only
   to embryonic life but to the entire span of individual
   existence' (p. 276). What they are calling ontogenetic
   adaptations might be more properly called *functional
   adaptations* in the neo-Lamarckian terminology of Roux
   (1881) (i.e. developmental modifications in structure,
   physiology and behaviour brought about by use). My
   definition of *ontogenetic adaptations* could include such
   functional adaptations but it is much more broadly
   conceived.

2 For a detailed discussion of the issue of continuity *vs*
   discontinuity in behavioural development, see Sameroff,
   1975; Clarke and Clarke, 1976; Bateson, 1978; Brainerd,
   1978; Kagan et al., 1978; Cairns, 1979.

3 I use the term 'permissive' rather loosely here. Strictly
   speaking, in developmental biology, 'permissive refers
   to the role of cell–environment interactions in the *expressive* or differentiation phase of development. In contrast, *instructive* interactions affect the *determination*
   process leading to the choice of a particular phenotype
   (Wessells, 1977).

4 Silman et al. (1978) have also made the interesting suggestion that the presence of higher levels of the endogenous opiate, β-endorphin, in the fetus at birth may
   serve to mitigate pain or stress associated with parturi-
   tion. (β-endorphin binds to morphine receptors and
   thus may have pain-killing effects.) Furthermore,
   Panksepp (1979) has suggested that failure of specific
   brain systems to exhibit the normal maturational transition from high β-endorphin levels to high levels of the

less potent opiate peptides (e.g. the enkephalins) may be
involved in the etiology of human infantile autism.

5 By behaviourally active I refer to the fact that the embryo or fetus exhibits neuromuscular activity (either
   spontaneous or reflexive) as well as to the fact that many
   of the sensory modalities also become functional (i.e.
   responsive to stimulation) during the prenatal period.

6 There are also other motor activities which are not reflexes, but which show similar increases and decreases
   during early development. Most vertebrate embryos exhibit a peak of spontaneous motility around the mid-
   point of incubation or gestation, with lower levels before
   and after this period (Oppenheim, 1974). Human infants display a remarkable variety of spontaneous and
   rhythmical motor stereotypes during the first year of
   life, which subsequently decrease or disappear altogether (Thelen, 1979).

7 Pontius (1973) has pointed out that the early exercise of
   behaviour such as reflex stepping may have deleterious
   effects on later behaviour. She cites the case of infants
   who have been placed in baby walkers or bouncers and
   who develop exaggerated bilateral extensor thrust of the
   legs and poor balance, both of which interfere with the
   emergence of voluntary walking (see Simpkiss and
   Raikes, 1972).

8 There is some fragmentary evidence suggesting that
   considerably more complex behaviours may also be subject to similar controls. Intellectual mechanisms characteristic of developing children have been reported to
   reappear in adults following brain damage (Inhelder,
   1956; Rozin, 1976).

9 Prolonged immaturity, delayed development, neoteny,
   etc. are important and exceedingly complex evolutionary processes. The quotes provided here are not intended to imply that increased learning is the sole
   benefit of these processes. Mason (1979) has provided a
   useful discussion of the myriad questions that arise
   when one examines these phenomena within the framework of modern evolutionary and psychobiological
   theory (also, see Gould, 1977).

10 One of the reasons for this stems from the old but
   still widely held belief that early experiences, that is
   those occurring during the so-called formative years
   of from one to three or from one to five in humans,
   establish basic behavioural tendencies, propensities or
   characteristics which determine or influence all subsequent development. According to this view, to quote
   from a modern proponent: '. . . the educational developments that take place in the year or so that begins when
   a child is about eight months old are the most important
   and the most in need of attention of any that occur in
   human life' (White, 1975, p. 130). This view has recently come under attack and has led to debates over
   the issue of continuity *vs* discontinuity in behavioural
   development (e.g. see note 2). It is probably also true
   that studies of physical development showing that
   little growth occurs after puberty (Tanner, 1978;

Katchadourian, 1977) have fostered the belief that significant neurobiological and behavioural changes also virtually stop at this time.

11 I am aware of the dangers and weaknesses of adopting what Lewontin (1979) and Gould and Lewontin (1979) have called the 'adaptationist' approach to evolutionary problems, in which, without further proof, most aspects of the morphology, physiology and behaviour of organisms are viewed as adaptive optimal solutions with a heritable basis (also see the critique of Clutton-Brock and Harvey, 1979). Although I admit to occasional lapses of 'just-so' story telling, I have no desire to add to the crass sociobiological literature which Lewontin cites as typifying the adaptationist approach. Indeed, my present thesis, which is largely motivated by ontogenetic considerations, differs fundamentally from this approach, which by and large tends to ignore or eschew ontogenetic issues. My major aim is to draw attention to certain neglected features of developing organisms and to emphasize the need for experimental analysis in order to determine the epigenetic nature of these characteristics. Moreover, as there are important alternatives to the occurrence of adaptations by natural selection, it has not been my intention to imply that the ontogenetic adaptations I discuss here necessarily must have been the central focus of selection. I am in full agreement with Gould and Lewontin that a pluralistic approach to problems of adaptation is more desirable than an exclusive concern with adaptation by natural selection.

12 Although the adherents of this view do not dispute the obvious fact that gene products continue to be transcribed throughout the life cycle, it seems to be a widely held belief that the expression of qualitatively 'new' genes virtually ceases at puberty, or even earlier. Hence it is often assumed that all behavioural and other changes after this time are mediated by fundamentally different (i.e. non-epigenetic) mechanisms.

References

Alexander, G. E., Goldman, P. S. (1978) Functional development of the dorsolateral prefrontal cortex: An analysis utilizing reversible cryogenic depression, *Brain Research*, 143, 233–49.

Altman, J. (1967) Postnatal growth and differentiation of the mammalian brain, with implications for a morphological theory of memory. In Quarton, G., Melnechuk, T. (eds), *The Neurosciences: A Study Program*, New York: Rockefeller University Press.

Armstrong, A. C. (1906) Herder and Fiske on the prolongation of infancy, *Philosophical Review*, 15, 59–67.

Ashburner, M. (1980) Chromosomal action of ecdysone, *Nature*, 285, 435–6.

Baldwin, J. M. (1902) *Development and Evolution*, New York: Macmillan.

Baldwin, J. D., Baldwin, J. I. (1973) The role of play in social organization: Comparative observations on squirrel monkeys, *Primates*, 14, 369–81.

Baltes, P. S., Schaie, K. W. (1973) *Life-Span Developmental Psychology*, New York: Academic Press.

Barker, D., Ip, M. C. (1966) Sprouting and degeneration of mammalian motor axons in normal and deafferented skeletal muscle, *Proceedings of the Royal Society of London, B*, 163, 538–54.

Barnes, C. A. (1979) Memory deficits associated with senescence: A neurophysiological and behavioral study in the rat, *Journal of Comparative and Physiological Psychology*, 93, 74–104.

Barrett, P. B., Bateson, P. P. G. (1978) The development of play in cats, *Behaviour*, 66, 106–20.

Barrington, E. J. W. (1968) Metamorphosis in lower chordates. In Etkin, W., Gilbert, L. I. (eds), *Metamorphosis*, New York: Appleton-Century-Crofts.

Bateson, P. P. G. (1978) How does behavior develop? In Bateson, P. P. G., Klopfer, P. H. (eds), *Perspectives in Ethology*, New York: Plenum Press.

—— (1979) How do sensitive periods arise and what are they for? *Animal Behaviour*, 27, 470–86.

Bayer, S. A., Altman, J. (1974) Hippocampal development in the rat: Cytogenesis and morphogenesis examined with autoradiography and low-level x-irradiation, *Journal of Comparative Neurology*, 158, 55–80.

Bekoff, A. (1979) A neuroethological study of walking in the chicken and its prenatal origins. *Paper presented at the XVI International Ethological Conference, Vancouver.*

Bekoff, M. (1972) The development of social interaction, play and metacommunication in mammals: An ethological perspective, *Quarterly Review of Biology*, 47, 412–34.

—— (1976) Animal play: Problems and perspectives. In Bateson, P. P. G., Klopfer, P. H. (eds), *Perspectives in Ethology*, New York: Plenum Press.

—— Byers, J. A. (1981) A critical reanalysis of the ontogeny and phylogeny of mammalian social and locomotor play: An ethological hornets' nest. In Immelmann, K., Barlow, G. W., Main, M., Petrinovich, L. (eds), *Issues in Behavioural Development*, London: Cambridge University Press (in press).

Berg, C. J. (1978) Development and evolution of behavior in mollusks, with emphasis on changes in stereotypy. In Burghardt, G. M., Bekoff, M. (eds), *The Development of Behavior: Comparative and Evolutionary Aspects*, New York: Garland Press.

Berger, A. J. (1968) Behavior of hand-raised Kirtlands warblers, *The Living Bird*, 3, 103–16.

Bergey, G. K., MacDonald, R. L., Nelson, P. G. (1978) Adverse effects of tetrodotoxin on early development and survival of postsynaptic cells in spinal cord cultures, *Neuroscience Abstracts*, 4, 601.

Berrill, N., Karp, G. (1977) *Development*, New York: McGraw-Hill.

Birren, J. W., Schaie, K. W. (eds) (1976) *Handbook of the Psychology of Aging*, New York: Van Nostrand Reinhold.

Blight, A. R. (1978) Golgi-staining of 'primary' and 'secondary' motoneurons in the developing spinal cord of an amphibian, *Journal of Comparative Neurology*, 180, 679–90.

Bodian, D. (1968) Development of fine structure of spinal cord in monkey fetuses, II: Pre-reflex period to period of long intersegmental reflexes, *Journal of Comparative Neurology*, 133, 133–66.

Bonner, J. T. (1958) *The Evolution of Development*, Cambridge: Cambridge University Press.

Booth, R. G., Greenough, W. T., Lund, J. S., Wrege, K. (1979) A quantitative investigation of spine and dendrite development of neurons in visual cortex (area 17) of *Macaca nemstrina* monkeys, *Journal of Comparative Neurology*, 186, 473–90.

Bower, T. G. R. (1976) Repetitive processes in child development, *Scientific American*, 255 (5), 38–47.

——(1979) *Human Development*, San Francisco: W. H. Freeman.

Brainerd, C. J. (1978) The stage question in cognitive-developmental theory, *Behavioral and Brain Sciences*, 2, 173–213.

Brake, S. C., Williams, C. L. (1979) Methysergide stimulates rhythmic and arrhythmic EMG-recorded sucking in 20-day old rats, *Neuroscience Abstracts*, 5, 214.

Braun, F. H. T., Jones, K. L., Smith, D. W. (1975) Breech presentation as an indicator of fetal abnormality, *Journal of Pediatrics*, 86, 419–21.

Breakefield, X. O. (1979) *Neurogenetics: Genetic Approaches to the Nervous System*, New York: Elsevier.

Brewster, J., Leon, M. (1980) Facilitation of maternal transport by Norway rat pups, *Journal of Comparative and Physiological Psychology*, 94, 80–88.

Britten, R. J., Davidson, E. H. (1969) Gene regulation for higher cells: A theory, *Science*, 165, 349–57.

Brody, H. (1973) Aging of the vertebrate brain. In Rockstein, M., Sussman, M. L. (eds), *Development and Aging in the Nervous System*, New York: Academic Press.

Brody, J., Vijayashankar, N. (1977) Anatomical changes in the nervous system. In Finch, C. E., Hayflick, L. (eds), *Handbook of the Biology of Aging*, New York: Van Nostrand Reinhold.

Bruce, E. J., Ayala, F. J. (1978) Humans and apes are genetically very similar, *Nature*, 276, 264–5.

Buell, S. J., Coleman, P. D. (1979) Dendritic growth in the aged human brain and failure of growth in senile dementia, *Science*, 206, 854–6.

Burch, T. L. (1979) The importance of communal experience to survival for spiderlings of *Araneus diadematus*, *Journal of Arachnology*, 7, 1–18.

Burghardt, G. M. (1978) Behavioral ontogeny in reptiles: Whence, whither and why? In Burghardt, G. M., Bekoff, M. (eds), *The Development of Behavior: Comparative and Evolutionary Aspects*, New York: Garland Press.

——Hess, E. H. (1966) Food imprinting in the snapping turtle, *Chelydra serpentina*, *Science*, 151, 383–4.

Butler, N. M. (1894) Anaximander on the prolongation of infancy in man. In *Classical Studies in Honour of Henry Drisler*, New York: Macmillan.

Cairns, R. B. (1979) *Social Development: The Origins and Plasticity of Interchanges*, San Francisco: W. H. Freeman.

Campbell, B. A., Alberts, J. R. (1979) Ontogeny of long-term memory for learned taste aversions, *Behavioral and Neural Biology*, 25, 139–56.

——Coulter, X. (1976) The ontogenesis of learning and memory. In Rosenzweig, M. R., Bennett, E. L. (eds), *Neural Mechanisms in Learning and Memory*, Cambridge, Mass.: MIT Press.

Candy, J. M., Martin, I. L. (1979) The postnatal development of the benzodiazepine receptor in the cerebral cortex and cerebellum of the rat, *Journal of Neurochemistry*, 32, 655–8.

Caplan, A. I., Ordahl, C. P. (1978) Irreversible gene repression model for control of development, *Science*, 201, 120–30.

Carmichael, L. (1926) The development of behavior in vertebrates experimentally removed from the influence of external stimulation, *Psychological Review*, 33, 51–68.

——(1927) A further study of the development of behavior in vertebrates experimentally removed from the influence of external stimulation, *Psychological Review*, 34, 34–47.

Challis, J. R. G., Torosis, J. D. (1977) Is α-MSH a trophic hormone to adrenal function in the foetus? *Nature*, 269, 818–19.

Clarke, A. M., Clarke, A. D. B. (1976) *Early Experience: Myth and Evidence*, London: Open Books.

Clutton-Brock, T. H., Harvey, P. H. (1979) Comparison and adaptation, *Proceedings of the Royal Society of London*, 205, 547–66.

Cochard, P., Goldstein, M., Black, I. B. (1978) Ontogenetic appearance and disappearance of tyrosine hydroxylase and catecholamines in the rat embryo, *Proceedings of the National Academy of Sciences*, 75, 2986–90.

Coghill, G. E. (1929) *Anatomy and the Problem of Behaviour*, Cambridge: Cambridge University Press.

Conel, J. L. (1939–67) *The Postnatal Development of the Human Cerebral Cortex*, Vols 1–8, Cambridge, Mass.: Harvard University Press.

Corner, M. A., Bakhuis, W. A., Van Wingerden, C. (1973) Sleep and wakefulness during early life in the domestic chicken, and their relationship to hatching and embryonic motility. In Gottlieb, G. (ed.), *Studies on the Development of Behavior and the Nervous System, Vol. I: Behavioral Embryology*, New York: Academic Press.

Coyle, J. T. (1977) Biochemical aspects of neurotransmission in the developing brain, *International Review of Neurobiology*, 20, 65–103.

Crain, S. M., Bornstein, M. B., Petersen, E. R. (1968) Maturation of cultured embryonic CNS tissues during chronic exposure to agents which prevent bioelectric activity, *Brain Research*, 8, 363–72.

Crowe, R. R., Smouse, P. E. (1977) The genetic implications of age-dependent penetrance in manic-depressive illness, *Journal of Psychiatric Research*, 13, 273–85.

Darwin, C. (1868) *The Variation of Animals and Plants Under Domestication*, New York: Appleton; (Reprinted, 1920).

Dawid, I. B., Wahli, W. (1979) Application of recombinant DNA technology to questions of developmental biology: A review, *Developmental Biology*, 69, 305–28.

DeBeer, G. (1958) *Embryos and Ancestors*, Oxford: Clarendon Press.

DeGroat, W. J., Douglas, J. W., Glass, J., Simonds, W., Weimer, B., Werner, P. (1975) Changes in somatovesical reflexes during postnatal development in the kitten, *Brain Research*, 94, 150–54.

Delage, Y., Goldsmith, M. (1912) *The Theories of Evolution*, New York: Huebsch.

DeMello, F. G., Bachrack, U., Nirenberg, M. (1976) Ornithine and glutamic acid decarboxylase activity in the developing chick retina, *Journal of Neurochemistry*, 27, 847–51.

Detwiler, S. R. (1936) *Neuroembryology*, New York: Macmillan; (Reprinted, New York: Hafner, 1964).

Dobzhansky, T. (1956) What is an adaptive trait? *American Naturalist*, 90, 337–47.

Drachman, D. B. (1968) The role of acetylcholine as a trophic neuromuscular transmitter. In Wolstenholme, G. E. W., O'Connor, M. (eds), *Ciba Foundation Symposium on Growth of the Nervous System*, Boston: Little, Brown.

——Sokoloff, L. (1966) The role of movement in embryonic joint development, *Developmental Biology*, 14, 401–20.

Dreyfus-Brisac, F. (1979) Ontogenesis of brain bioelectric activity and sleep organization in neonates and infants. In Falkner, F., Tanner, J. M. (eds), *Growth, Vol. 3: Neurobiology and Nutrition*, New York: Plenum Press.

Eayrs, J. T. (1971) Thyroid and the developing brain: Anatomical and behavioral effects. In Hamburgh, M., Barrington, E. J. W. (eds), *Hormones in Development*, New York: Appleton-Century-Crofts.

Edwards, J. S. (1969) Postembryonic development and regeneration of the insect nervous system, *Advances in Insect Physiology*, 6, 97–137.

Ehrman, L., Parsons, P. A. (1976) *The Genetics of Behavior*, Sunderland, Mass.: Sinauer Associates.

Eibl-Eibesfeldt, I. (1975) *Ethology: The Biology of Behavior*, New York: Holt, Rinehart & Winston.

Eimas, P. D. (1975) Developmental studies in speech perception. In Cohen, L. B., Salapatek, P. (eds), *Infant Perception: From Sensation to Cognition, Vol. II: Perception of Space, Speech, and Sound*, New York: Academic Press.

Eldredge, N., Gould, S. J. (1972) Punctuated equilibria: An alternative to phyletic gradualism. In Schopf, T. J. M. (ed.), *Models in Paleobiology*, San Francisco: Freeman & Cooper.

Epstein, H. T. (1974) Phrenoblysis: Special brain and mind growth periods, *Developmental Psychobiology*, 7, 217–24.

Etkin, W., Gilbert, L. I. (eds) (1968) *Metamorphosis*, New York: Appleton-Century-Crofts.

Everitt, A. V., Burgess, J. A. (1976) *Hypothalamus, Pituitary and Aging*, Springfield, Ill.: C. C. Thomas.

Ewer, R. F. (1968) *Ethology of Mammals*, London: Logos.

Ewert, J. P., Burghagen, H. (1979) Ontogenetic aspects of visual size-constancy phenomena in the midwife toad *Alytes obstetricians, Brain, Behavior and Evolution*, 16, 99–112.

Fagan, R. M. (1977) Selection for optimal age-dependent schedules of play behavior, *American Naturalist*, 111, 395–414.

File, S. E. (1978) Exploration in immature rats: Effects of drugs, *Developmental Psychobiology*, 11, 405–12.

Finch, C. E. (1976) The regulation of physiological changes during mammalian aging, *Quarterly Review of Biology*, 51, 45–83.

——Hayflick, L. (eds) (1977) *Handbook of the Biology of Aging*, New York: Van Nostrand Reinhold.

Fiske, J. (1884) *The Destiny of Man Viewed in Light of His Origin*, Boston: Houghton-Mifflin.

——(1899) *Excursions of an Evolutionist*, Boston: Houghton-Mifflin.

Fox, M. W. (1965) Reflex-ontogeny and behavioural development in the mouse, *Animal Behaviour*, 13, 234–41.

——(1971) *Integrative Development of Brain and Behavior in the Dog*, Chicago: University of Chicago Press.

——Applebaum, J. (1969) Ontogeny of the orienting-jump response of the rabbit, *Behaviour*, 25, 77–83.

——Inman, O. R., Himwich, W. A. (1966) The postnatal development of neocortical neurons in the dog, *Journal of Comparative Neurology*, 127, 199–206.

Frazetta, T. H. (1975) *Complex Adaptations in Evolving Populations*, Sunderland, Mass.: Sinauer.

Galef, B. G. (1977) Social transmission of food preferences: An adaptation for weaning in rats, *Journal of Comparative and Physiological Psychology*, 91, 1136–40.

——(1979) The ecology of weaning: Parasitism and the achievement of independency by altricial mammals. In Klopfer, P. H., Gubernick, D. J. (eds), *Parental Care*, New York: Plenum Press.

Garn, S. M., Bailey, S. M. (1978) The genetics of maturational processes. In Faulkner, F., Tanner, J. M. (eds), *Human Growth, Vol. 1: Principles of Prenatal Growth*, New York: Plenum Press.

Garstang, W. (1922) The theory of recapitulation: A critical restatement of the biogenetic law, *Journal of the Linnean Society of Zoology*, 35, 81–101.

Gaze, R. M., Keating, M. J., Chung, S. H. (1974) The evolution of the retinotectal map during development in *Xenopus, Proceedings of the Royal Society of London, B*, 185, 301–30.

Geinesman, Y. (1979) Loss of axosomatic synapses in the dentate gyrus of aged rats, *Brain Research*, 168, 485–92.

Giacobini, G., Filogamo, G., Weber, M., Bouquet, p., Changeux, J. P. (1973) Effects of a snake α-neurotoxin on the development of innervated skeletal muscles in the chick embryo, *Proceedings of the National Academy of Sciences*, 70, 1708–12.

Globus, A. (1975) Brain morphology as a function of presynaptic morphology and activity. In Riesen, A. H.

(ed.), *The Developmental Neuropsychology of Sensory Deprivation*, New York: Academic Press.

Goldschmidt, R. (1938) *Physiological Genetics*, New York: McGraw-Hill.

Goodlin, R. C. (1979) *Care of the Fetus*, New York: Masson.

Gottlieb, G. (ed.) (1973) *Studies in the Development of Behavior and the Nervous System, Vol. I: Behavioral Embryology*, New York: Academic Press.

——(1976a) Conceptions of prenatal development: Behavioral embryology, *Psychological Review*, 83, 215–34.

——(1976b) Early development of species-specific auditory perception in birds. In Gottlieb, G. (ed.), *Studies on the Development of Behavior and the Nervous System, Vol. III: Development of Neural and Behavioral Specificity*, New York: Academic Press.

Gould, R. L. (1976) The phases of adult life: A study in developmental psychology, *American Journal of Psychiatry*, 129, 521–31.

Gould, S. J. (1977) *Ontogeny and Phylogeny*, Cambridge, Mass.: Belknap Press.

——Lewontin, R. C. (1979) The spandrels of San Marco and the Panglossian paradigm: A critique of the adaptationist program, *Proceedings of the Royal Society of London*, 205, 581–98.

Gregg, B., Kittrell, E., Domjan, M., Amsel, A. (1978) Ingestional aversion learning in preweanling rats, *Journal of Comparative and Physiological Psychology*, 92, 785–95.

Grumbach, M. M. (1978) The central nervous system and the onset of puberty. In Faulkner, F., Tanner, J. M. (eds), *Human Growth, Vol. 2: Postnatal Growth*, New York: Plenum Press.

Hadorn, E. (1974) *Experimental Studies of Amphibian Development*, New York: Springer-Verlag.

Haldane, J. B. S. (1932) The time of action of genes and its bearing on some evolutionary problems, *American Naturalist*, 66, 5–24.

Hall, W. G. (1975) Weaning and growth of artificially reared rats, *Science*, 190, 1313–15.

——(1979) Feeding in infant rats: Special conditions for an unexpected response, *Science*, 209, 206–9.

Hamburger, V., Oppenheim, R. W. (1967) Prehatching motility and hatching behavior in the chick, *Journal of Experimental Zoology*, 166, 191–204.

Hamilton, H. L. (1956) *Lillie's Development of the Chick*, New York: Holt, Rinehart & Winston.

Hamilton, W. D. (1966) The moulding of senescence by natural selection, *Journal of Theoretical Biology*, 12, 12–45.

Harnad, S. R., Steklis, H. D., Lancaster, J. (eds) (1976) Origins and evolution of language and speech, *Annals New York Academy of Sciences*, 280.

Harrison, R. G. (1904) An experimental study of the relation of the nervous system to the developing musculature of the frog, *American Journal of Anatomy*, 3, 197–220.

Heaton, M. B. (1978) Development of problem-solving abilities in the neonatal Peking duck. *Journal of Comparative and Physiological Psychology*, 92, 246–54.

Hegmann, J. P. (1979) Gene influences timing the develop-

ment of size and nervous system functional differences, *Behavioral Neural Biology*, 25, 510–22.

Hendrikson, C. K., Vaughn, J. E. (1974) Fine structural relationship between neurites and radial glial processes in developing mouse spinal cord, *Journal of Neurocytology*, 3, 659–75.

Hess, E. (1973) *Imprinting: Early Experience and the Developmental Psychobiology of Attachment*, New York: Van Nostrand Reinhold.

Hinds, J. W. (1968) An autoradiographic study of histogenesis in the mouse olfactory bulb, 1: Time of origin of neurons and neuroglia, *Journal of Comparative Neurology*, 134, 287–304.

——McNelly, N. A. (1979) Aging in the rat olfactory bulb: Quantitative changes in mitral cell organelles and somatodendritic synapses, *Journal of Comparative Neurology*, 184, 811–20.

Hines, M. (1942) The development and regression of reflexes, postures and progression in the young macaque, *Carnegie Institute of Washington, Contributions to Embryology*, no. 196, 155–209.

Holliday, R., Pugh, J. E. (1975) DNA modification mechanisms and gene activity during development, *Science*, 187, 226–32.

Hooker, D. (1952) *The Prenatal Origin of Behavior*, Lawrence, Kansas: University of Kansas Press.

Horwich, R. H. (1969) Behavioral ontogeny of the mockingbird, *The Wilson Bulletin*, 81, 87–93.

Howard, E. (1973) DNA content of rodent brains during maturation and aging, and autoradiography of postnatal DNA synthesis in monkey brain, *Progress in Brain Research*, 40, 91–114.

Hughes, A. F. (1957) The development of the primary sensory system in *Xenopus laevis*, *Journal of Embryology and Experimental Morphology*, 9, 269–84.

Humphrey, T. (1944) Primitive neurons in the embryonic central nervous system, *Journal of Comparative Neurology*, 81, 1–45.

——(1950) Intramedullary sensory ganglion cells in the roof plate of the embryonic human spinal cord, *Journal of Comparative Neurology*, 92, 333–80.

——(1969) Postnatal repetition of human prenatal activity sequences with some suggestions of their neuroanatomical basis. In Robinson, R. J. (ed.), *Brain and Early Behavior Development in the Fetus and Infant*, New York: Academic Press.

Immelmann, K. (1975) The evolutionary significance of early experience. In Baerends, G., Beer, C., Manning, A. (eds), *Function and Evolution in Behavior*, Oxford: Clarendon Press.

Impekoven, M. (1976) Prenatal parent–young interactions in birds and their long-term effects. In Rosenblatt, J. S., Hinde, R. A., Shaw, E., Beer, C. (eds), *Advances in the Study of Behavior*, Vol. 7, New York: Academic Press.

Inhelder, B. (1956) In Tanner, J. M., Inhelder, B. (eds), *Discussions on Child Development*, New York: Universities Press.

Jacobson, M. (1978) *Developmental Neurobiology*, 2nd edn, New York: Plenum Press.

Jaeger, R. G., Hailman, J. P. (1976) Ontogenetic shift of spectral phototactic preferences in anuran tadpoles, *Journal of Comparative and Physiological Psychology*, 90, 930–45.

Jourdain, F. C. R. (1925) A study on parasitism in the cuckoos, *Proceedings of the Zoological Society of London*, 95, 639–67.

Kagan, J., Kearsley, R. B., Zelazo, P. R. (1978) *Infancy: Its Place in Human Development*, Cambridge, Mass.: Harvard University Press.

Kaltenbach, J. C. (1968) Nature of hormone action in amphibian metamorphosis. In Etkin, W., Gilbert, L. I. (eds), *Metamorphosis*, New York: Appleton-Century-Crofts.

Kammer, A. E., Kinnamon, S. C. (1979) Maturation of the flight motor pattern without movement in *Manduca sexta*, *Journal of Comparative Physiology*, 130, 29–37.

Kaplan, M. S. (1979) Neurogenesis in the adult rat visual cortex, *Neuroscience Abstracts*, 5, 629.

——Hinds, J. W. (1977) Neurogenesis in the adult rat: Electron microscopic analysis of light radio-autographs, *Science*, 197, 1092–4.

Katchadourian, H. (1977) *The Biology of Adolescence*, San Francisco: W. H. Freeman.

Kennard, M. A. (1938) Reorganization of motor function in the cerebral cortex of monkeys deprived of motor and premotor areas in infancy, *Journal of Neurophysiology*, 1, 477–96.

Kimmel, C. B., Eaton, R. C. (1976) Development of the Mauthner cell. In Fentress, J. C. (ed.), *Simpler Networks and Behavior*, Sunderland, Mass.: Sinauer.

King, M. C., Wilson, A. C. (1975) Evolution at two levels in humans and chimpanzees, *Science*, 188, 107–16.

Kinney, M. S., Fisher, S. K. (1978) Changes in length and disk shedding rate of *Xenopus* rod outer segments associated with metamorphosis, *Proceedings of the Royal Society of London*, 201, 169–77.

Kirkwood, T. B. L., Holliday, R. (1979) The evolution of aging and longevity, *Proceedings of the Royal Society of London*, 205, 531–46.

Klein, A. E., Michel, M. E. (1977) A morphometric study of the neocortex of young adult and old maze-differentiated rats, *Mechanisms of Aging and Development*, 6, 441–452.

Knudson, A. G., Meadows, A. T. (1978) Developmental genetics of neural tumors in man. In Saunders, G. F. (ed.), *Cell Differentiation and Neoplasia*, New York: Raven Press.

Knyihar, E., Csillik, B., Rakic, P. (1978) Transient synapses in the embryonic primate spinal cord, *Science*, 202, 1206–9.

Kolb, B., Noneman, A. J. (1976) Functional development of prefrontal cortex in rats continues into adolescence, *Science*, 193, 33–6.

Kollros, J. J. (1968) Endocrine influences in neural development. In Wolstenholme, G. E. W., O'Connor, M. (eds), *Ciba Foundation Symposium on Growth of the Nervous System*, Boston: Little Brown.

Konigsmark, B. W., Murphy, E. A. (1970) Neuronal populations in the human brain, *Nature*, 228, 1335–6.

——(1972) Volume of the ventral cochlear nucleus in man – its relationship to neuronal population and age, *Journal of Neuropathology and Experimental Neurology*, 31, 304–6.

Konner, M. (1977) Evolution of human behavior development. In Leiderman, P. H. (ed.), *Culture and Infancy; Variations in the Human Experience*, New York: Academic Press.

Korneliussen, A., Jansen, J. K. S. (1976) Morphological aspects of the elimination of polyneuronal innervation of skeletal muscle fibres in newborn rats, *Journal of Neurocytology*, 5, 591–604.

Kroeger, H. (1968) Gene activities during insect metamorphosis and their control by hormones. In Etkin, W., Gilbert, L. I. (eds), *Metamorphosis*, New York: Appleton-Century-Crofts.

Kuo, Z.-Y. (1967) *The Dynamics of Behavior Development: An Epigenetic View*, New York: Random House.

Lamb, M. J. (1977) *Biology of Aging*, New York: John Wiley.

Lamedella, J. T. (1976) Relations between the ontogeny and phylogeny of language: A neorecapitulationist view, *Annals of the New York Academy of Sciences*, 280, 396–412.

Landfield, P. W., Waymire, J. C., Lynch, G. (1978) Hippocampal aging and adrenocorticoids: Quantitative correlations, *Science*, 202, 1098–1102.

Lang, F., Govind, C. K., Costello, W. J., Greene, S. I. (1977) Developmental neuroethology: Changes in escape and defensive behavior during growth of the lobster, *Science*, 197, 682–5.

Langreder, W. (1949) Über Foetalreflexe und deren intrauterine Bedeutung, *Zeitschrift für Geburtshilfe und Gynäkologie*, 131, 237–45.

Largo, R. H., Howard, J. H. (1979a) Developmental progression in play behavior of children between nine and thirty months, 1: Spontaneous play and imitiation, *Developmental Medicine and Child Neurology*, 21, 299–310.

——(1979b) Developmental progression in play behavior of children between nine and thirty months, 2: Spontaneous play and language development, *Developmental Medicine and Child Neurology*, 21, 492–503.

Lauder, J. M., Krebs, H. (1978) Serotonin as a differentiation signal in early neurogenesis, *Developmental Neuroscience*, 1, 15–30.

Lenneberg, E. H. (1969) On explaining language, *Science*, 164, 635–43.

Levine, S., Lewis, G. W. (1959) Critical periods for effects of infantile experience on maturation of stress response, *Science*, 129, 42–3.

Levinson, D. J. (1978) *The Seasons of a Man's Life*, New York: Ballantine.

Lewis, D. M. (1976) The contraction of polyneuronally innervated fibers of kitten muscles, *Journal of Physiology*, 263, 179–80.

Lewis, P. D. (1978) Neurohumoral influences on cell proliferation in brain development, *Trends in Neurosciences*, 1, 158–9.

Lewontin, R. C. (1979) Sociobiology as an adaptationist program, *Behavioral Science*, 24, 5–14.

Lipsitt, L. P. (1976) Developmental psychobiology comes of age: A discussion. In Lipsitt, L. P. (ed.), *Developmental Psychobiology: The Significance of Infancy*, New York: John Wiley.

Longley, A. (1978) Anatomical mapping of retino-tectal connections in developing and metamorphosed *Xenopus*: Evidence for changing connections, *Journal of Embryology and Experimental Morphology*, 45, 249–70.

Lovejoy, A. O. (1904) Some eighteenth century evolutionists, *Popular Science Monthly*, 65, 323–40.

Machado-Salas, J. P., Scheibel, A. B. (1979) Limbic system of the aged mouse, *Experimental Neurology*, 63, 347–55.

Macfarlane, A. (1977) *The Psychology of Childbirth*, London: Fontana/Open Books.

Marler, P., Mundinger, P. (1971) Vocal learning in birds. In Moltz, H. (ed.), *The Ontogeny of Vertebrate Behavior*, New York: Academic Press.

Marschack, A. (1979) Data for a theory of language origins, *Brain and Behavioral Sciences*, 2, 394–6.

Marzetta, C. A., Nash, D. J. (1979) Ontogenetic study of the Mi^{wh} gene in mice, *Developmental Psychobiology*, 12, 527–32.

Mason, S. (1979) Ontogeny of social behavior. In Marler, P., Vandenbergh, J. G. (eds), *Handbook of Behavioral Neurobiology, Vol. 3: Social Behavior and Communication*, New York: Plenum.

McEwen, B. S. (1978) Sexual maturation and differentiation: The role of gonadal steroids, *Progress in Brain Research*, 48, 291–307.

——Plapinger, L., Chaptal, C., Gerlach, C., Wallach, G. (1975) Role of fetoneonatal estrogen binding proteins in the association of estrogen with neonatal brain cell nuclear receptors, *Brain Research*, 96, 300–406.

McGraw, M. B. (1935) *Growth: A study of Johnny and Jimmy*, New York: Appleton.

——(1942) *The Neuromuscular Maturation of the Human Infant*, New York: Appleton; reprinted, 1963, New York: Hafner.

McKusik, V. A. (1978) *Mendelian Inheritance in Man*, 5th edn, Baltimore: Johns Hopkins Press.

Meyer, G., Ferres-Torres, R., Mas, M. (1978) The effects of puberty and castration on hippocampal dendritic spines of mice: A Golgi study, *Brain Research*, 155, 108–12.

Misretta, C. M., Bradley, R. M. (1978) Effect of early sensory experience on brain and behavioral development. In Gottlieb, G. (ed.), *Studies on the Development of Behavior and the Nervous System, Vol. IV: Early Influences*, New York: Academic Press.

Model, P., Bornstein, M. B., Crain, S. A., Pappas, G. D. (1971) An electron microscopic study of the development of synapses in cultured fetal mouse cerebrum continuously exposed to xylocaine, *Journal of Cell Biology*, 49, 363–71.

Møller, M. (1978) Presence of a pineal nerve in the human fetus: A light and electron microscopical study of the innervation of the pineal gland, *Brain Research*, 154, 1–12.

Molliver, M. E., Van der Loos, H. (1970) The ontogenesis of cortical circuitry: The spatial distribution of synapses in somesthetic cortex of newborn dog, *Ergebnisse Anatomie und Entwicklungsgeschichte*, 42, 7–53.

Muntz, W. R. A. (1963) The development of phototaxis in the frog, *Rana temporaria*, *Journal of Experimental Biology*, 40, 371–9.

Myslivecek, J. (1976) Ontogeny of active avoidance learning and memory, *Activitas Nervosa Superior*, 18, 291–301.

Nandy, K. (1973) Neuronal degeneration in aging mammals. In Rockstein, M. (ed.), *Development and Aging in the Nervous System*, New York: Academic Press.

New, D. A. T. (1957) A critical period for the turning of hen's eggs, *Journal of Embryology and Experimental Morphology*, 5, 293–9.

Nice, M. M. (1962) Development of behavior in precocial birds, *Transactions of the Linnaean Society of New York*, 8, 1–211.

Nicholson, J. L., Altman, J. (1972) The effects of early hypo- and hyperthyroidism on the development of rat cerebellar cortex, 1: Cell proliferation and differentiation, *Brain Research*, 44, 13–23.

Noback, C. R., Purpura, D. P. (1961) Postural ontogenesis of neurons in cat neurocortex, *Journal of Comparative Neurology*, 117, 291–308.

Obata, K. (1977) Development of neuromuscular transmission in culture with a variety of neurons and in the presence of cholinergic substances and tetrodotoxin, *Brain Research*, 119, 141–53.

O'Brien, R. A. D., Ostberg, A. L., Vrbova, G. (1978) Observations on the elimination of polyneuronal innervation in developing mammalian skeletal muscle, *Journal of Physiology*, 282, 571–628.

Omnen, G. A. (1975) Genetic mechanisms in human behavioral development. In Schaie, K. W., Anderson, V., McClearn, G., Money, J. (eds), *Developmental Human Behavior Genetics: Nature–Nurture Redefined*, Lexington, Mass.: Lexington Books.

Oppenheim, R. W. (1973) Prehatching and hatching behavior: A comparative and physiological consideration. In Gottlieb, G. (ed.), *Studies on Development of Behavior and the Nervous System, Vol. I: Behavioral Embryology*, New York: Academic Press.

——(1974) The ontogeny of behavior in the chick embryo. In Lehrman, D. S., Rosenblatt, J. C., Hinde, R. A., Shaw, E. (eds), *Advances in the Study of Behavior*, Vol. 5, New York: Academic Press.

——(1981a) The neuroembryological study of behavior: Progress, principles, perspectives. In Hurt, R. K. (ed.), *Current Topics in Developmental Biology, Vol. 17: Neural Development*, New York: Academic Press (in press).

——(1981b) Cell death and related regressive phenomena in neurogenesis: A selective historical review and progress report. In Cowan, W. M. (ed.), *Studies in Developmental*

Neurobiology: Essays in Honor of Viktor Hamburger, London; Oxford University Press (in press).

——Pittman, R., Gray, M., Maderdrut, J. L. (1978) Embryonic behavior, hatching and neuromuscular development in the chick following a transient reduction of spontaneous motility and sensory input by neuromuscular blocking agents, *Journal of Comparative Neurology*, 179, 619–40.

Panksepp, J. (1979) A neurochemical theory of autism, *Trends in Neuroscience*, 2, 178–80.

Papousek, H. (1969) Individual variability in learned responses in human infants. In Robinson, R. J. (ed.), *Brain and Early Behaviour*, New York: Academic Press.

Parker, S. T., Gibson, K. R. (1979) A developmental model of the evolution of language and intelligence in early hominids, *Behavioral and Brain Sciences*, 2, 367–408.

Paulson, G., Gottlieb, G. (1968) Developmental reflexes: The reappearance of foetal and neonatal reflexes in aged patients, *Brain*, 91, 37–52.

Peiper, A. (1963) *Cerebral Function in Infancy and Childhood*, New York: Consultants Bureau.

Piaget, J. (1976) Piaget's Theory. In Inhelder, B., Chipman, H. S. (eds) *Piaget and His School*, New York: Springer-Verlag.

Pipa, R. L. (1978) Patterns of neural reorganization during the postembryonic development of insects, *International Review of Cytology*, Supplement 7, 403–38.

Pittman, R., Oppenheim, R. W. (1979) Cell death of motoneurons in the chick embryo spinal cord, IV: Evidence that a functional neuromuscular interaction is involved in the regulation of naturally occurring cell death and the stabilization of synapses, *Journal of Comparative Neurology*, 187, 427–46.

Pontius, A. A. (1973) Neuro-ethics of 'walking' in the newborn, *Perceptual and Motor Skills*, 37, 235–45.

Prechtl, H. F. R. (1953) Zur Physiologie des Angeborenen auslösenden Mechanismen, 1: Quantitative Untersuchungen über die Sperrbewegung junger Singvögel, *Behaviour*, 5, 32–50.

——(1965) Problems of behavioral studies in the newborn infant. In Lehrman, D. S., Rosenblatt, J. S., Hinde, R. A., Shaw, E. (eds), *Advances in the Study of Behavior*, Vol. I, New York: Academic Press.

Prestige, M. (1971) Differentiation, degeneration and the role of the periphery: Quantitative considerations. In Schmitt, F. O. (ed.), *The Neurosciences, Second Study Program*, New York: Rockefeller University Press.

Preyer, W. (1885) *Specielle Physiologie des Embryo*, Leipzig: Grieben.

Purves, D., Lichtman, J. W. (1980) Elimination of synapses in the developing nervous system, *Science*, 210, 153–7.

Rabinowicz, T. (1979) The differentiate maturation of the human cerebral cortex. In Falkner, F., Tanner, J. M. (eds), *Human Growth, Vol. 3: Neurobiology and Nutrition*, New York: Plenum Press.

Rakic, P. (1971) Neuro-glia relationship during granule cell migration in developing cerebellar cortex: A Golgi and electromicroscipic study of *Macacus rhesus*, *Journal of Comparative Neurology*, 141, 283–312.

——(1972) Mode of cell migration in the superficial layers of fetal monkey neocortex, *Journal of Comparative Neurology*, 145, 61–84.

——(1975) Cell migration and neuronal ectopias in the brain, *Birth Defects*, 11, 95–129.

Reynolds, D. M., Jeeves, M. S. (1978) A developmental study of hemisphere specialization for recognition of faces in normal subjects, *Cortex*, 14, 511–20.

Roberts, A. (1978) Pineal eye and behaviour in *Xenopus* tadpoles, *Nature*, 273, 774–5.

——Blight, A. R. (1975) Anatomy, physiology and behavioural role of sensory nerve endings in the cement gland of embryonic *Xenopus*, *Proceedings of the Royal Society of London, B*, 192, 111–27.

——Smith, D. (1974) The development of a dual touch sensory system in embryos of the amphibian *Xenopus laevis*, *Journal of comparative Physiology*, 88, 31–42.

Rockstein, M., Chesky, J., Sussman, M. (1977) Comparative biology and evolution of aging. In Finch, C. E., Hayflick, L. (eds), *Handbook of the Biology of Aging*, New York: Van Nostrand Reinhold.

Roffwarg, H. P. Muzio, J. N., Dement, W. C. (1966) Ontogenetic development of the human sleep–dream cycle, *Science*, 152, 604–19.

Rosenblatt, J. S. (1971) Suckling and home orientation in the kitten: A comparative, developmental study. In Tobach, E., Aronson, L. R., Shaw, E. (eds), *The Biopsychology of Development*, New York: Academic Press.

——(1979) The sensorimotor and motivational bases of early behavioral development of selected altricial mammals. In Spear, N. E., Campbell, B. A. (eds), *Ontogeny of Learning and Memory*, Hillsdale, N.J.: Earlbaum.

Rosenzweig, M. R., Bennett, E. L. (eds) (1976) *Neural Mechanisms in Learning and Memory*, Cambridge, Mass.: MIT Press.

Rousseau, J-J. (1762) *Emile; Or Concerning Education* (English translation by E. Worthington, 1888), Boston: Heath.

Roux, W. (1881) *Der Kampf der Theile im Organismus*, Leipzig: Englemann.

Rozin, P. (1976) The evolution of intelligence and access to the cognitive unconscious. In Sprague, J. M., Epstein, A. N. (eds), *Progress in Psychobiology and Physiological Psychology*, New York: Academic Press.

Sacher, G. A. (1978) Evolution of longevity and survival characteristics in Mammals. In Schneider, E. L. (ed.), *The Genetics of Aging*, New York: Plenum Press.

Sameroff, A. J. (1975) Early influences on development: Fact or fancy, *Merrill-Palmer Quarterly*, 21, 267–94.

Scheff, S. W., Benardo, L. S., Cotman, C. W. (1978) Decrease in adrenergic axon sprouting in the senescent rat. *Science*, 202, 775–8.

Scheibel, M. E., Lindsay, R. D., Tomiyasu, U., Scheibel, A. B. (1975) Progressive dendritic changes in aging human cortex, *Experimental Neurology*, 47, 392–403.

————————(1977) The aging human Betz cell, *Experimental Neurology*, **56**, 598–609.

Schneirla, T. C. (1965) Aspects of stimulation and organization in approach–withdrawal processes underlying vertebrate behavioral development. In Lehrman, D. S., Hinde, R. A., Shaw, E. (eds), *Advances in the Study of Behavior*, Vol. I, New York: Academic Press.

Scott, J. P. (1962) Critical periods in behavioral development, *Science*, **138**, 949–58.

——(1973) The organization of comparative psychology, *Annals of the New York Academy of Sciences*, **223**, 7–40.

Shaw, G. B. (1930) *Back to Methuselah*, New York: W. H. Wise.

Shaywitz, B. A., Klopper, J. H., Yage, R. D., Gordon, J. D. (1976) Paradoxical response to amphetamine in developing rats treated with 6-hydroxy-dopamine, *Nature*, **261**, 153–5.

Sheehy, G. (1976) *Passages: Predictable Crises of Adult Life*, New York: Dutton.

Sheridan, P. J. (1979) Estrogen binding in neonatal neocortex, *Brain Research*, **178**, 201–6.

Shumway, W. (1932) The recapitulation theory, *Quarterly Review of Biology*, **7**, 93–9.

Silman, R. E., Leone, R. M., Hooper, R. J. L. (1979) Melatonin, the pineal gland and human puberty, *Nature*, **282**, 301–3.

Simpkiss, M. J., Raikes, A. S. (1972) Problems resulting from excessive use of baby walkers an baby bouncers, *Lancet*, **1**, 747.

Smith, R. L., Parks, T., Lynch, G. (1974) A comparison of the role of the motor cortex in recovery from cerebellar damage in young and adult rats, *Behavioral Biology*, **12**, 177–98.

Smith, S. M. (1972) The ontogeny of impaling behavior in the loggerhead shrike, *Lanius ludovicianus*, *Behaviour*, **42**, 232–47.

Soll, D. R. (1979) Timers in developing systems, *Science*, **203**, 841–9.

Sotelo, C., Palay, S. L. (1971) Altered axons and axon terminals in the lateral vestibular nucleus of the rat: Possible examples of axonal remodelling, *Laboratory Investigation*, **25**, 653–71.

Southern, H. N. (1964) Parasitism. In Thomson, A. L. (ed.), *A New Dictionary of Birds*, New York: McGraw Hill.

Squire, L. R., Cohen, N. (1979) Memory and amnesia: Resistance to disruption develops for years after learning, *Behavioral and Neural Biology*, **25**, 115–25.

Srihari T., Vrbova, G. (1978) The role of muscle activity in the differentiation of neuromuscular junctions in slow and fast chick muscles, *Journal of Neurocytology*, **7**, 529–40.

Staton, M. S. (1978) Distress calls of crocodilians – whom do they benefit? *American Naturalist*, **112**, 327–32.

Stearns, S. C. (1976) Life-history tactics: A review of the ideas, *Quarterly Review of Biology*, **51**, 3–47.

Stelzner, D. J., Ershler, W. B., Weber, E. D. (1975) Effects of spinal transection in neonatal and weanling rats: Survival of function, *Experimental Neurology*, **46**, 156–77.

Super, C. M. (1976) Environmental effects on motor development: The case of 'African infant precocity', *Developmental Medicine and Child Neurology*, **18**, 561–7.

Tanner, J. M. (1978) *Foetus into Man: Physical Growth from Conception of Maturity*, Cambridge, Mass.: Harvard University Press.

Teitelbaum, P. (1967) The biology of drive. In Quarton, G. C., Melnechuk, T., Schmitt, F. O. (eds), *The Neurosciences, A Study Program*, New York: Rockefeller University Press.

——Wolgin, D. L., DeRyck, M., Marin, O. S. M. (1976) Bandage-backfall reaction: Occurs in infancy, hypothalamic damage and catalepsy, *Proceedings of the National Academy of Sciences*, **73**, 3311–14.

Thelen, E. (1979) Rhythmical stereotypies in normal human infants, *Animal Behaviour*, **27**, 699–715.

Thoman, E. B., Arnold, W. J. (1968) Incubator rearing of infant rats without the mother: Effects on adult emotionality and learning, *Developmental Psychobiology*, **1**, 219–22.

Timiras, P. S. (1978) Biological perspectives on aging, *American Scientist*, **66**, 605–13.

Touwen, B. C. L. (1976) *Neurological Development in Infancy: Clinics in Developmental Medicine*, No. 58, London: S.I.M.P. with Heinemann; Philadelphia: Lippincott.

Tracy, H. C. (1926) The development of motility and behavior reactions in the toadfish, *Journal of Comparative Neurology*, **40**, 253–369.

Trehub, S. E. (1976) The discrimination of foreign speech sounds by infants and adults, *Child Development*, **47**, 466–72.

Trevarthen, C. (1973) Behavioral embryology. In Carterette, E. C., Friedman, M. P. (eds), *The Handbook of Perception*, New York: Plenum Press.

——(1979) Neuroembryology and the development of perception. In Falkner, F., Tanner, J. M. (eds), *Human Growth, Vol. 3: Neurobiology and Nutrition*, New York: Plenum Press.

Tschanz, B. (1968) Trottellummen: Die Entstehung der persönlichen Beziehung, zwischen Jungvogel und Eltern, *Zeitschrift für Tierpsychologie*, **4**, 1–103.

Uzbekov, N. G., Murphey, S., Rose, S. P. R. (1979) Ontogenesis of serotonin receptors in different regions of rat brain, *Brain Research*, **168**, 195–9.

Valliant, G. E. (1977) *Adaptation to Life*, Boston: Little, Brown.

Vanderwolf, C. H., Kolb, B., Cooley, R. K. (1978) Behavior of the rat after removal of the neocortex and hippocampal formation, *Journal of Comparative and Physiological Psychology*, **92**, 156–75.

Vaughn, D. W. (1977) Age-related deterioration of pyramidal cell basal dendrites in rat auditory cortex, *Journal of Comparative Neurology*, **171**, 501–16.

Vince, M. A. (1960) Developmental changes in responsiveness in the great tit (*Parus major*), *Behaviour*, **15**, 219–43.

——(1961) Developmental changes in learning capacity. In Thorpe, W. H., Zangwill, O. L. (eds), *Current Problems in*

Animal Behaviour, Cambridge: Cambridge University Press.

——(1973) Some environmental effects on the activity and development of the avian embryo. In Gottlieb, G. (ed.), *Studies on the Development of Behavior and the Nervous System, Vol. I: Behavioral Embryology*, New York: Academic Press.

Wassersug, R. J. (1973) Aspects of social behavior in anuran larvae. In Vial, J. L. (ed.), *Evolutionary Biology of the Anurans: Contemporary Research on Major Problems*, Columbia: University of Missouri Press.

Weiss, G. M., Pysh, J. J. (1978) Evidence for loss of Purkinje cell dendrites during late development: A morphometric Golgi analysis in the mouse, *Brain Research*, **154**, 219–30.

Werner, H. (1948) *Comparative Psychology of Mental Development*, Chicago: Follett.

Wessells, N. K. (1977) *Tissue Interactions and Development*, Menlo Park, Cal.: Benjamin.

White, B. L. (1975) *The First Three Years of Life*, Englewood Cliffs, N.J.: Prentice-Hall.

Wilkinson, M., Herdon, H., Pearch, M., Wilson, C. (1979) Precocious puberty and changes in α-β-adrenergic receptors in the hypothalamus and cerebral cortex of immature female rats, *Brain Research*, **167**, 195–9.

Williams, C. L., Rosenblatt, J. S., Hall, W. G. (1979) Inhibition of suckling in weanling-age rats: A possible serotonergic mechanism, *Journal of Comparative and Physiological Psychology*, **93**, 414–29.

Williams, G. (1957) Pleiotropy, natural selection and the evolution of senescence, *Evolution*, **11**, 398–411.

——(1966) *Adaptation and Natural Selection*, Princeton, N.J.: Princeton University Press.

Wolff, J. R., Rickmann, N., Chronwall, B. M. (1978) Axo-glial synapses and GABA-accumulating glial cells in the embryonic neocortex of the rat, *Cell Tissue Research*, **201**, 239–48.

Yakovlev, P. I., Lecours, A.-R. (1967) The myelogenetic cycles of regional maturation of the brain, In Minkowski, A. (ed.), *Regional Development of the Brain in Early Life*, Oxford: Blackwell.

Young, J. Z. (1978) *Programs of the Brain*, Oxford: Oxford University Press.

Youngstrom, K. S. (1944) Intramedullary sensory type ganglion cells in the spinal cord of human embryos, *Journal of Comparative Neurology*, **81**, 47–53.

Zelazo, P. (1976) From reflexive to instrumental behavior. In Lipsitt, L. P. (ed.), *Developmental Psychobiology: The Significance of Infancy*, Hillsdale, N.J.: Erlbaum.

Zelazo, N., Kolb, S. (1972) 'Walking' in the newborn, *Science*, **176**, 1058–9.

Zukerhandl, E. (1976) Programs of gene action and progressive evolution. In Goodman, M., Tashian, R. E., Tashian, J. H. (eds), *Molecular Anthropology*, New York: Plenum.

CHAPTER 3

From Watsonian Behaviorism to Behavior Epigenetics

ZING-YANG KUO

If we accept mechanistic and non-Darwinian concepts of behavior as basic to behaviorism, we must consider both Jacques Loeb (Loeb, 1889, 1918) and John B. Watson as the pioneer behaviorists. The word "behaviorism" was coined by Watson (1913, 1914), and the movement was, at first, a methodological revolt rather than an attempt to build a new system of psychology. At that time, psychology was still the handmaiden of philosophy, and Watson himself had been trained by philosophically-oriented psychologists, although his own researches were mainly on animal behavior. (In this respect, Loeb, as an experimental biologist, was freer from the bondage of philosophy.) Soon such philosophers as Bertrand Russell and Ralph Barton Perry became interested in behaviorism, and psychologists like Tolman, Weiss, Lashley, and even Watson himself attempted to give behavioristic interpretations of the mental entities – thinking, memory, and the like – losing sight of the original aim of the behavioristic movement. To call thought processes subvocal speech (Watson, 1914, 1919); to give behavioristic interpretations of consciousness, ideas, memory, and the like (e.g., Tolman, 1951); to sub-

stitute for mental faculties various new names of "hypothetical constructs"; to devise ingenious and elaborate schema of cerebral structures, applying the principles of electronic computers or information processing; to explain reasoning, intelligence, memory, etc., or to rename "volition" or "will" as drive or motivation (with physiological implications): all these are philosophical speculations at best. They hardly help us solve any basic problems in behavior. Instead, the behaviorist should concentrate his efforts on behavioral problems, leaving all the problems of mental concepts alone; these, as a matter of fact, should be imperceptibly and ultimately absorbed, never to reappear, as our knowledge of behavior advances and broadens and as our experimental techniques, especially the biophysical and biochemical ones, are improved.

The fundamental error of the behaviorists, therefore, was that they paid too much attention to the claims of philosophers and philosophically-oriented psychologists and tried to use objective or physiological constructs as replacements for the names of the old mental entities. Watson's greatest contribution to the behavioristic movement was not his hypothetical constructs, but his repudiation of introspection as a scientific method, his pioneer work in the study of the behavior of newborn infants, and this statement in the forceful and courageous preface to his 1919 book *Psychology from the Standpoint of a Behaviorist:*

From Zing-Yang Kuo, *The Dynamics of Behavior Development* (New York: Plenum Press, 1967), pp. 3–26.

The key which will unlock the door of any other scientific structure will unlock the door of psychology. The differences among the various sciences now are only those necessitated by the division of labor. Until psychology recognizes this and discards everything which cannot be stated in the universal terms of science, she does not deserve her place in the sun . . . nor does the author claim behavior psychology as a creation of his own. It has had rapid development and is a direct outgrowth of the work on animal behavior. It is purely an American production. . . .

On the other hand, the concepts of tropism (taxis) reflex and of instinct and learning and the stimulus and response (S-R) formula, which may appear to us now as extreme oversimplifications or as obsolete, refer to real behavioral problems and, as such, must be carefully examined and investigated by the behaviorists before they can be discarded and replaced by newer and broader concepts of behavior.

The Descendants of Watsonian Behaviorism

Watson's S-R formula and his almost unquestioning acceptance of the concept of conditioned reflex as the key to the study of behavior were rather unfortunate because of their oversimplification of the phenomena of behavior. However, with some minor variations such as Tolman's "purposive behaviorism," the S-R formula and conditioned reflex concept have become the standard-bearer of behaviorism and the keynote of American animal psychology for the last fifty years. Its main thesis is animal learning. Its basic principle is conditioning – Pavlovian or Skinnerian. And the animal used in learning experiments has been mainly, if not exclusively, the albino rat. Theories of learning may vary, but none has been diverted from Watson's original S-R formula.

Whether or not one agrees with the fundamental views of the psychologists of learning, one must admit that the descendants of Watsonian behaviorism have evolved what has now become an American tradition in psychology. There are two aspects of this tradition: (1) The strictly experimental attitude which has resulted in the development of laboratory techniques with rigid standards and elaborate procedures, and (2) mathematical-mindedness. The statistical requirements for any animal experiment have become so rigid and so sophisticated that no editor of an American technical periodical will accept any paper on animal behavior without adequate statistical data. These research techniques constitute a very commendable contribution, and no coming student of behavior, whatever his scientific outlook, can afford not to master them before he begins his research on animals. And many younger European workers on animal behavior have just begun to appreciate this scientific achievement of the American animal psychologists.

However, it must be admitted that much American experimental work, especially the learning research on rats, has been carried out in a very narrowly confined environment so that conclusions from the results of such experiments may not be accepted without a great many reservations. Moreover, the stress on mathematics has gone beyond the bounds of scientific proportion. Although recent progress in mathematical physics and computer engineering has been rapid, the phenomena of behavior are far more complex than physical events, and the science of behavior is still in its infancy in comparison with the very advanced stage of the physical sciences. For these reasons, I feel strongly that it is premature to devise "mathematical models" for the prediction of behavior. If many learning theorists have apparently succeeded in their mathematical predictions, that can be explained by the fact that they have ignored the great complexity and variability of behavior and have reduced behavioral phenomena to an extremely few simple parameters. For example, the behavior of a fly would be a very complicated affair if we took into account the complexity, variability, and interplay of such determining factors as morphology, biophysics, biochemistry, developmental history, environmental context and the various characteristics of the stimulating objects. However, if we simply put a fly in a very small blackened box with two small openings both penetrated by outside light and send a stream of cold air through one opening and a stream of warm air through the other, we could predict with almost mathematical accuracy by which of the two openings the fly would escape from the box and in how many trials. But, in so doing, we must ignore other details of the fly's activities inside the black box. In other words, the success of such an experimental prediction is due not to the accuracy of mathematical theories or models, but rather to the oversimplification of the experimental situation in animal learning.

The Unsolved Problem of Behaviorism

Because the behaviorists have confined themselves to methodological approaches without broadening their outlook on behavior and raising their scientific horizon beyond the simple S–R formula and the concept of conditioned reflex, they have been forced to fall back on the problem of the "psyche." If even learning cannot be explained without postulating motivation, learning set, or modification of cerebral structures, no behaviorist can avoid the problem of intervening variables. To call them physiological counterparts of behavior neither explains behavior nor satisfies the demands of the mentalists. Or to admit the existence of neural processes, while denying the relevance of the neural connection between stimulus and response, as does the operant behaviorist, is a scientific evasion at best. The protestation against behaviorism from philosophers, mentalistic psychologists, or even social scientists (cf. the symposium on "The Limits of Behaviorism in Political Science," American Academy of Political and Social Science, Philadelphia, 1962) may be ignored. But when a physiologist like Adrian complains that he cannot understand "thought" without reference to the mind or when the psychologist of animal learning insists that he, too, needs some such concepts as motivation or learning set in order to explain the learning process, it seems that the time has come for us to re-examine the current scientific outlook of physiology and reassess the basic scientific value of the behaviorists' S–R formula. Perhaps the merger of physiology with the science of behavior, with a much more broadened prospectus, may lead to the eventual dissolution of the problem of intervening variables.

Gestalt Psychology as a Protest Against Behaviorism

In reviewing the history of behaviorism it may be fitting to say a few words about Gestalt psychology

as a countermovement against it before World War II. The Gestalt psychologists' criticism of the oversimplification of the S–R formula and the concepts of reflex and chain reflexes was valid. Nevertheless, I feel compelled to part company with them in practically every phase of their treatment of animal behavior. This, even though my concepts of behavioral gradients and environmental context may appear to some as another holistic approach. As a matter of fact, both concepts are not only experimentally analyzable, but can be analyzed only by the atomistic methods that have been anathematized by the Gestalt psychologists.

It should also be noted that, besides being predeterministic concerning development, the Gestalt concept of behavior is not free from vitalistic implications.

The Protest of Ethology

Although C. O. Whitman and O. Heinroth and various others have been credited as pioneers in the field, it was Konrad Z. Lorenz and Niko Tinbergen who systematically conceptualized ethology. Ethology was unknown in America before World War II, yet its impact on the thinking and research of American behavioral scientists was no less dramatic than Gestalt psychology had been in the late 1920s and the 1930s. Like the Gestalt psychologists, the ethologists' chief target was American behaviorism in the current sense. The main principles of ethology consist of revival of the concept of instinct and an emphasis on (1) naturalistic observation, (2) social aspects of behavior, (3) species-specificity, (4) the adaptive value of behavior for the survival of the species, and (5) the need for a diversification of animal species in behavior studies. These are all aimed at American learning psychologists and perhaps rightly so, especially at those who had confined themselves to running rats in mazes.

Behaviorism Reconsidered

In reviewing the history of the behavioristic movement one most important aspect has been long overlooked: the ontogenetic implications. These were clear to me in the basic tenets of behaviorism, in Watson's own later interest in the behavior of human neonates, in the vigorous anti-instinct campaign in the 1920s, and in Watson's effort (1924) to catch up with the anti-instinct trend. An objective and unbiased historian of science should have been able in the late 1920s to forecast the future trend of development of the original Watsonian behaviorism, namely, the ontogenetic approach to the study of animal behavior. Despite theoretical differences that were an inevitable historical outcome, the great proliferation of studies of prenatal behavior of various vertebrates and of newborn infants in the 1930s was not merely a coincidence. The studies of various aspects of the ontogeny of postnatal behavior after World War II must be regarded partly as a continuation of the 1930s trend and partly as silent (in most cases) protest against the rat-learning psychologists from Tolman to Hull, Skinner, and their followers, who seem to have deviated from the original tenets of Watsonian behaviorism.

"The basic aim of this book is to present the epigenetic point of view as a logical crystallization of the continuous and truly behavioristic trends initiated by Loeb and Watson; it is an attempt to replace the versions of Tolman, Hull, Skinner, and the learning theorists on the one hand and the main concepts of behavior advocated by the ethologists on the other." In what follows we shall discuss the various aspects of this viewpoint, illustrated, whenever possible, with experimental or observational evidence; at the same time, we shall suggest a new orientation for future behavioral studies.

The Meaning of Epigenesis in Behavior

We shall define behavioral epigenesis as a continuous developmental process from fertilization through birth to death, involving proliferation, diversification, and modification of behavior patterns both in space and in time, as a result of the continuous dynamic exchange of energy between the developing organism and its environment, endogenous and exogenous. The ontogenesis of behavior is a continuous stream of activities whose patterns vary or are modified in response to changes in the effective stimulation by the environment. In these epigenetic processes, at every point of energy exchange, a new relationship between the organism and the environment is established; the organism is no longer

the same organism and the environment no longer the same environment as they were at the previous moment. Thus, in ontogenesis, both patterns of behavior and patterns of the environment affect each other and are therefore in a constant state of flux; that is, changes in the environmental patterns produce changes in behavior patterns which in turn modify the patterns of environment. The epigenetic view of behavior is bidirectionalistic (Gottlieb, 1970) rather than environmentalistic, as it considers every behavior pattern as a *functional product* of the dynamic relationship between the organism and its environment, rather than as a passive result of environmental stimulation. In other words, the epigenesis of behavior is a continuum of the dynamic process of interlocking reactions between the organism and the environment, resulting in the reorganization or modification of the existing patterns of both the behavioral gradients and the environmental context. At the same time, it does not violate the current views of heredity held by physiological geneticists and experimental morphologists, according to whom ". . . the phenotype is more and more considered not as a mosaic of individual gene-controlled characters but as the joint product of a complex interacting system, the total epigenotype" (Mayr, 1963, p. 6). The epigenetic behaviorist accepts the morphological structures and their functional capabilities at a given stage as the end result of development in the preceding stages, but considers them merely as one of the five groups of determiners of behavior. The higher the phyletic level (especially, when there is a complex social life) and the more advanced the morphogenesis, the more important are the other determining factors in shaping or modifying behavior patterns. In vertebrates, and in birds and mammals in particular, as ontogenesis progresses and as the developing animal widens its environmental contacts, especially through sensory inputs from the distance receptors, more new patterns of behavior are required from time to time to meet the new demands of the continuing changes of the environment. Such new patterns are determined mainly by the developmental history or historical antecedents of the animal, the existing pattern of behavioral gradients, and the environmental context; morphological structures and their functional capabilities act as determining factors of behavior only in a negative way, that is, they merely set a limit to certain body movements (for example, a dog can only snarl at or bite its enemy but cannot throw a stone at him).

Some Salient Points on Behavioral Epigenesis

The following comments should help to clarify the epigenetic view of behavior and serve as a guide for future investigations of behavior:

1.   The behavior of animal and man is a continuous stream of activity from fertilization to death. In such a continuous process of energy exchange between the organism and the environment, behavior never comes to an end. If there is an end in behavior, that end must be death for death is the end of all ends. However, in this continuum, behavior patterns are in a process of perpetual change – from moment to moment, from sleep to wakening, from eating and drinking to defecation and micturition, from combat to copulation, from laying eggs to brooding and feeding the young, and so on. But for the sake of scientific convenience, we often take only a very small fraction of such ceaselessly changing events for investigation. We are justified in doing so only if we are fully aware that we are not reading any teleological meaning into such a small fraction of ever-changing behavioral events. Neither courtship, threat, fighting, hoarding, nor learning a T-maze to discriminate visual patterns is an "intended," "driven," or "motivated" behavior, for no behavior pattern or series of patterns is an entity, nor does it have any "goal" to reach. When we say that the animal has reached its "goal" (e.g., the food box or copulation), it is an anthropomorphic statement of the fact that the sequence of behavioral events under observation has undergone a shift. In this situation, the behaving organism itself has no purpose, but its stream of activities is arbitrarily sectionalized or fractionalized to serve the purpose or the observer or experimenter. Furthermore, in ontogenesis, no movement is a preparatory act to serve a future purpose of the animal. Thus the beak movements of the chick embryo are no more a preparatory action for postnatal food getting than for crying in fright or pain, crowing, grooming, or fighting, etc. The epigeneticist does not entertain any concept of finalism in behavior. In short, behavior begins with heartbeats and ends when all cardiac movement stops; this is the true and only finalism of behavior.

2.   Both the American animal psychologists and the European ethologists have made two basic assumptions: the uniformity of nature (environment) and the uniformity of behavior. Both assumptions are based on inadequate observation.

As far as environment is concerned, light, sound, temperature, humidity, wind force, and the chemical composition of the air are in a state of constant change, except in an elaborately and mechanically controlled laboratory room. When social environment is added, the variation is far greater. Even the effectiveness of the stimulating object varies from moment to moment. If we include intraorganic or endogenous stimulation as part of the animal's environment, the environmental variability becomes far more complex. And when we come to the animal's environment in nature or in the field, environmental changes are far beyond the manipulation of the observer. I have been a bird-watcher since childhood, yet I have not seen two birds in the same nest grow up under the same natural conditions; as a result, no two birds react to the same stimulating object in an identical manner. But biased by an a priori assumption of uniformity, students of behavior are often apt to overlook or ignore the variability of environment and its effects on behavior.

To emphasize the significance of the variability of behavior let us illustrate it somewhat in detail with a single case from our unpublished records on fighting behavior in the dog.

The dog in question was a smooth-haired Shan Chow named Bobby who was selected for training as a fighter. He had all the anatomical qualities of a good fighter. After training, Bobby would always attack any dog in sight, regardless of sex. However, his fighting behavior manifested the following variations:

• If the dog attacked offered no resistance, Bobby would grab him by the back of the neck, shake him for a minute or less, and then let him loose.
• If the victim happened to fall to the ground on his back, Bobby would grab his throat and shake him until the dog was motionless or dead.
• If the other dog offered resistance, fighting would be very fierce. Bobby would never stop until the other dog was either killed or so injured

that he became almost motionless, or until the fighting was interrupted by the trainer.

- If the other dog's resistance was not easily overcome, fighting became furious and continued until the victim was killed or both dogs were seriously wounded and exhausted, or until they were stopped by the trainer.

- If the first fight did not end decisively, Bobby and his opponent would fight so ferociously on the second encounter that the trainer and his assistant would be unable to separate them except by ducking both dogs into a pond. Climbing up from the pond, both would rush to fight again until Bobby finally succeeded in killing or subduing his enemy.

- When Bobby was attacking another dog and some other dogs who were his friendly companions came to his assistance, he would give up his victim and walk away.

- When Bobby was a small pup, he had been attacked by another fierce dog. Later, after he had grown up to be the strongest dog in the laboratory, Bobby would always walk away from his old attacker whenever he saw him in the distance. However, on one occasion, he was too close to avoid him; the other dog then attacked Bobby but proved to be no match for him. Fighting was ended by the trainer's intervention. From this time on, Bobby would rush after his old enemy whenever he was in sight.

- Bobby was trained to attack any female on sight. But, on one occasion, he rushed to attack a female in heat, and he was changed into a totally different dog. After several faulty attempts, Bobby succeeded in his first copulation. From that time on, Bobby never attacked any bitch whether in heat or not.

- When feeding was two to three hours overdue, Bobby was very reluctant to engage in any fighting.

- After two or three copulations in a day, Bobby would not initiate any fighting unless he was attacked.

- His tendency to attack other dogs was reduced by about a third during extremely cold or hot days.

- If Bobby was five or more pounds heavier than his usual weight, he was much less aggressive, his fighting was much less fierce, and it did not last as long as usual.

- When Bobby was between ten and twenty days old, the trainer used the sound of a Chinese rattle to frighten him. After he grew up to be a fighter, the sound of the rattle would always stop him when he was rushing after another dog. However, once his attack was already in progress, the rattle became ineffective.

- Soon after a heavy engagement in fighting, Bobby was reluctant to get involved in another battle.

This account of the variation in the fighting patterns of this dog has been confined to the level of gross activities. We have not touched upon variations in the biophysical and biochemical components of the patterns. These would make our description of the fighting behavior even more complex.

In fact, this description of Bobby's fighting patterns is an extreme oversimplification of the variability of behavior. Bobby never attacked the same dog twice in the same manner. He might make a frontal attack, leap on the other's back, grab its neck, or ear, or push it to the ground and grab and seize any part of the victim's body, etc. Furthermore, his attack varied with the reaction of his victim. A really stereotyped response pattern, especially in the higher vertebrates, hardly exists.

The seemingly uniform responses we may sometimes observe are more apparent than real. Not only does the same organism not make two identical responses to an identical stimulating object, but even in such a seemingly simple movement as the lifting of the head of a four or five day old chick embryo, its amplitude and extent are never twice the same. The number of muscle fibers and their neural connections involved in the head lifting, the extent of the muscular contractions, the energy consumption, and other physical and chemical changes vary from moment to moment. We must take all these variations into consideration if the science of behavior is not to remain on the crude descriptive level of gross bodily movement.

3. The developmental history of the animal is of utmost importance.

4. In view of the variability of behavior and of environment and the diversification of historical antecedents among individuals of the same species,

we believe that no two individuals of the same species acquire in their life history the same behavioral repertoire, except those motor activities which are the direct results of morphological structures and their functional capabilities. In animals of lower phyletic levels and in embryos or fetuses, in which environmental variations within the shell or uterus are more or less standardized and anatomical and chemical factors play a comparatively more important role in determining behavior, there are greater similarities in behavior among the growing animals of the same species. In such instances there may be some justification in calling such prenatal behavior or behaviors of lower organisms, *species-typical* or *species-characteristic* (both are better terms than "species-specific," as used by many ethologists and American animal psychologists with the implication of predeterminism).

On the other hand, when we come to postnatal development, except for certain movements, such as modes of locomotion or eating or drinking which are directly determined by anatomical structures or their functional differences, the organization of behavior patterns is so varied and so diversified that we can hardly group them into categories and call them species-specific unless we project our subjective, purpose-directed aims into the end results of the patterns, ignoring the variables of such patterns. In other words, unless we project human ends into the classification of animal behavior and disregard all the variables in environment and developmental history, it does not seem possible for students of behavior to arrive at a behavioral inventory or repertoire common to all vertebrate animals of the same species. Our objective should be to discover the behavioral repertoire of the individual animal and its causal factors rather than that of the species. On the same grounds we shall raise questions with regard to behavioral genetics.

5. In methodology, the behavioral epigeneticist insists on strict laboratory procedure and, at the same time, makes use of field or naturalistic observations as a means of discovering problems of behavior to be solved in the laboratory. However, we must point out emphatically that it is a dangerous procedure to arrive at any scientific generalizations from naturalistic observations, especially when such observations are of short duration, because the observer may not have seen enough of the variability of behavior and environment in the field.

Lorenz's observations on the fighting behavior of wolves and chow dogs is a case in point. He reports that fighting within either of these species almost always ends harmlessly for both combatants. Whenever two animals are engaged in combat, the weaker one soon lies on the ground and exposes its throat while the stronger one climbs over it, and both bark. The victor then walks away with an appearance of dignity and makes no further attack on the vanquished. Lorenz concludes that these behavior patterns result from an evolutionary process and are of great value for the preservation of the species. I have never observed wolves fighting. However, since my childhood I have been observing the fighting behavior of chows, and since 1928 I have conducted a large number of controlled experiments on the fighting behavior of these animals. Apart from such experimental fights, I have kept no record, but I have undoubtedly seen over one thousand of these fights. Therefore, on the basis of observations and experiments on these animals as well as on other species, I have concluded that animal fighting is so complex and variable, and involves the interwoven reactions of so many factors, that it would be most unscientific to follow Lorenz and single out one pattern of fighting and chivalry and explain it in Darwinian terms while ignoring many other fighting patterns. The case of Bobby previously described is evidence enough. Suffice it to state here that there are indeed certain situations in which the weaker dog saves itself from injury by lying on its back, a truly successful application of Gandhi's philosophy of nonresistance or Russell's pacifism through submission: "Better Red than dead." However, there are also many circumstances in which such a response is an invitation to certain death, as it gives the top dog an opportunity to grab the underdog's throat and shake it until the underdog is dead or at least shows no sign of bodily movement. I have seen many cases in the field and in my laboratory of truly pacifist and nonresistant chow dogs dying after they had behaved in the fashion Lorenz described. A remarkable product of adaptive behavior through evolution and natural selection, indeed!

As far as my own observations are concerned, when dogs fight in the manner Lorenz describes, both combatants belong to the class of what I used to call the Gandhi variety. Both the top dog and the underdog lack the anatomical elements to be good fighters. As a matter of fact, the top dog of this type has never engaged in a real fight in its life and is disqualified for training in fighting. Whenever it meets a stronger and more aggressive dog, it immediately becomes submissive and readily accepts the role of the underdog, although it will reverse its role when confronted with a still weaker and more submissive one. Chow dogs of this type in the Chinese villages are mostly underfed, look unhealthy, and have a great variety of skin diseases and verminous infestation. All such dogs are true to the type observed and reported by Lorenz. The chow dogs he observed are probably family pets; unlike the Chinese peasants, no Western dog lover will allow his pup to fight with his neighbors' dogs to the finish. One who was familiar with the developmental history and the anatomical make-up of the dogs Lorenz observed would probably have arrived at a different conclusion. Personally, I have witnessed scores of dog fights which, unless forcibly interrupted by men, would always end in either death or severe injury to one or both combatants. These cases do not include the dogs with special training for fighting in my laboratory.

Let me illustrate my point with another naturalistic observation. For some decades I have been observing the behavioral relationship between the common magpie and common eagle in South China. The magpie is much less than one-half the size of the eagle, and its wing span is hardly more than one-third of the eagle's. Moreover, its beak and claws lack the sharpness of the eagles' hook-like beak and talons. Nonetheless, every time I hear an eagle cry in pain, I am sure, even without looking up in the sky, that the eagle must be flying low and that a magpie must be making diving attacks on the back of its head or neck. The eagle is absolutely defenseless until it climbs up in the air beyond the reach of the magpie. On the other hand, when an eagle is resting on a roof top or the top of a tree, a magpie might come along, hopping back and forth on its long legs in front of the eagle, making typical magpie noises, and often coming within one foot of the eagle. However, neither bird appears to be concerned about the presence of the other. There is no sign of territorial dispute, neither threat nor hostility, nor friendliness. Each simply "ignores" the presence of the other. In both cases, the behavior of the two birds appears stereotyped and species-specific as far as my observation is concerned; the ethologists would, therefore, say that this behavior must be taken as genetically determined through natural selection. However, the type of behavior pattern on the roof or tree top and the type in the air seen incompatible. One favors the notion of interspecies coexistence, the other interspecies struggle. But why have both types been preserved? Have they survival value at different moments? To me this is not a question of natural selection, nor does it have anything to do with the question of survival value for either species. It is a question of the ontogeny of behavior during which different environmental complexes have brought about both types of rather incompatible patterns. This is an experimental problem to be tested in the laboratory so as to determine the actual environmental–ontogenetic factors responsible for the development of such incompatible patterns. If contradictory patterns of behavior exist in two species even in nature as is the case between the magpie and the eagle, it at least indicates that animal life in nature is far more complex and variable than the naturalists have thought.

In sum, naturalistic observations are valuable only insofar as they help the student of behavior broaden his outlook so that in devising experimental programs he will look beyond the narrow confines of his laboratory animal.

Five Groups of Determining Factors

Despite the great variability and complexity of behavior, for the convenience of investigation and description we may classify the determining factors of behavior into the following five categories:

- Morphological factors
- Biophysical and biochemical factors
- Stimulating objects
- Developmental history
- Environmental context

Every response of the animal is the *functional product* of the combined effects of the interwoven reactions of these five factoral groups through inputs and feedbacks and their organic trace effects (Schneirla, 1965). Our present knowledge concerning any of these factors and their interrelations is not adequate to devise any useful mathematical formula for the prediction of behavior. The behavioral epigeneticist hopes for the day when he will be able, like the theoretical physicist, to arrive at such a formula even though he may have to wait for some decades. His hope is based on the fact that, notwithstanding such great variability and complexity, there are to be found some common factors in behavior such as those due to some common morphological characteristics of the species. For example, morphological structures of the limbs determine the modes of locomotion; the oral structure determines the modes of eating and drinking, the vocal apparatus determines the characteristics of voice and singing. Moreover, there are certain common characteristics both in the developmental history (e.g., in prenatal life most animals develop under a more or less standardized environment) and in the environmental context. We can use such common characteristics as the base upon which we should be able to build our correlations with the biochemical and biophysical factors as well as with the varying characteristics of the stimulating objects (all of which also have certain constant characteristics) in order to arrive at a tentative formula. This would probably be an appropriate and relatively fast approach toward the goal of prediction and control of behavior and ultimately toward the creation of behavioral neo-phenotypes, that is, novel behavior patterns, unknown or unobserved before.

I have italicized the words *functional product*, to stress the fact that behavior is not merely an accumulated or arithmetical sum of these five categories of determinants. Thus, if we were to designate Beh to represent behavior; A to represent biophysical and biochemical factors; B, morphological factors; C, developmental history; D, stimulating objects; and E, environmental context, this would be the formula for behavior: Beh = (A + B + C + D + E). But this formula would be much too simple to make any scientific sense. We must bear in mind that each category of the determining factors comprises an enormous number of variables. The interwoven reactions among these variables themselves are complex enough. But when those reactions of the variables of all five categories are brought together, it may be far beyond the capability of ordinary statistical methods to arrive at an adequate formula. Unless we deal with the behavior of uni-

cellular animals or animals without social life, it may require many years, even decades – especially when we deal with the species known as *Homo sapiens* with its complicated language capacities and social cultures – before any attempt at a mathematical formula for the prediction of behavior or even aspects of behavior would be justified.

While it is fully justifiable for the behavioral scientist to limit his investigations to one level, or even to certain aspects of one level, of behavior (for example, various aspects of learning or conditioning; effects of early experiences on later life; "imprinting"; effects of cortical lesions on learning; so-called critical periods, etc.), we must not forget the fact that our knowledge of behavior based on the results of such investigations is negligible. Any attempt to draw conclusions from such studies and to use them as principles of behavior in general or as the basis for theories of behavior is bound to be hampered immediately by a large number of problems that may be insoluble, unless we broaden and reorient the outlook of behavioral studies.

Conclusion

Thus, from the standpoint of the epigenetic behaviorist, the relationship between the behaving organism and its environment is an extremely complex and variable dynamic process. It goes deeper and beyond the molar level. As we shall see more clearly in the following chapters, *behavior* is far more than the visible muscular movements. Besides such movements, the morphological aspect, the physiological (biophysical and biochemical) changes, the developmental history of the animal, and the ever-changing environmental context are interwoven events which are essential and integral parts of behavior. In our study of behavior all such events must be investigated in a coordinated way. The behavioral process is not just a stimulus–response relationship, a conditioning process, nor just a revelation of innate actions in the form of "courtship," "threat," food-begging, egg-rolling in the nest, and the like. In other words, *the study of behavior is a synthetic science*. It includes comparative anatomy, comparative embryology, comparative physiology (in the biophysical and biochemical sense), experimental morphology, and the qualitative and quantitative analysis of the dynamic relationship between the organism and the external physical and social environment.

The chief objective of the epigenetic behaviorist is to seek order out of such complex behavioral phenomena in order to formulate laws of behavior without resorting to vitalism, either explicitly or implicitly. He or she has two main tasks: to obtain a comprehensive picture of the behavioral repertoire of the individual and its causal factors from stage to stage during development; and to explore the potentials and limitations of new behavior patterns ("behavioral neo-phenotypes") that are not commonly observed or do not exist in "nature" so as to predict or control the evolution of behavior in the future.

This is the main theme of radical behaviorism from the epigenetic standpoint. In the light of this theme, facts derived from experiments and observations are presented and interpreted, and certain more or less unconventional concepts of behavior are developed and discussed in the following chapters.

References

Gottlieb, G. (1970) Conceptions of prenatal behavior. In L. R. Aronson et al. (eds), *Development and Evolution of Behavior*. San Francisco: Freeman.

Loeb, J. (1889) *Der Heliotropismus der Tiere und seine Uebereinstimmung mit dern Heliotropismus der Pflanzen*. Würzburg: Hertz.

Loeb, J. (1918) *Tropisms, Forced Movements, and Animal Conduct*. Philadelphia: Lippincott.

Mayr, E. (1963) *Animal Species and Evolution*. Cambridge, Mass.: Harvard Univ. Press.

Schneirla, T. C. (1965) Aspects of stimulation and organization in approach–withdrawal processes underlying vertebrate behavioral development. In D. S. Lehrman, R. A. Hinde, and E. Shaw (eds), *Advances in the Study of Behavior*, vol. 1, New York: Academic Press.

Watson, J. B. (1913) Psychology as the behaviorist views it. *Psychol. Rev.* **20**: 158–77.

Watson, J. B. (1914) *Behavior: An Introduction to Comparative Psychology*. New York: Holt.

Watson, J. B. (1919) *Psychology from the Standpoint of a Behaviorist*. Philadelphia: Lippincott.

Watson, J. B. (1924) *Behaviorism*. New York: Norton.

CHAPTER 4

Developmental Changes in Sensitivity to Experience

PATRICK BATESON and ROBERT A. HINDE

Introduction

Sensitivity to certain types of experience changes throughout life. It is not surprising, then, that particular experiences should sometimes produce long-term effects on behavior more readily at certain stages of the life-cycle than at others. A classical example is imprinting in birds; a young duckling quickly learns to direct its filial behavior toward a particular moving object when it is exposed to that object within a period of time that starts soon after hatching and finishes some days later (Lorenz, 1935; see also Hoffman, 1987). Another good example is provided by the song-learning of many birds; details of the species-characteristic song are acquired by example only if the male Chaffinch has heard that song during an early period in its life (Thorpe, 1961). Similar examples occur in human development. Learning a language and, particularly, learning to articulate its distinctive sounds is much easier in childhood than in later life (Lenneberg, 1967; see also Snow, 1987). Such phenomena are clearly important for those interested in the study of behavioral development. However, they have been undervalued in recent years as a consequence of the wide-ranging attacks on the

From M. H. Bornstein (ed.), *Sensitive Periods in Development* (Hillsdale, NJ: Lawrence Erlbaum, 1987), pp. 19–34.

notion of continuity and connectedness in development and the suggestions that the effects of early experience are obliterated later in life (e.g., Clarke and Clarke, 1976; Kagan, 1984; see also Hinde and Bateson, 1984, for further discussion of the issue).

This controversy should be seen in historical perspective. Periods of susceptibility to long-term effects of current experience were originally termed "critical periods" by ethologists. This term, previously used in embryological studies, was first applied in the English language to behavioral examples by Lorenz (1937) when he published a translation of his famous Kumpan paper. "Critical period" implies a sharply defined phase of susceptibility preceded and followed by lack of susceptibility; if the relevant experience is provided before or after the period, no long-term effects are supposedly detectable. Experimental work on imprinting in the 1950s and 1960s showed, however, that the period was not so sharply defined as had been previously supposed and the term "sensitive period" was substituted by many ethologists (e.g., Hinde 1961; see also Bateson, 1979, and Immelmann and Suomi, 1981, for discussions of terminology). The sensitive period concept implies a phase of greater susceptibility preceded and followed by lower sensitivity, with relatively gradual transitions.

Despite this revision by the ethologists, the earlier concept of "critical period" persisted, particularly in the secondary literature, and was generalized to studies of human children. Clarke and Clarke (1976) sharply attacked the critical period concept, largely on the basis of evidence that children reared under conditions of extreme social deprivation could be rehabilitated later in life. Rutter (1980) agreed that the notion of fixed and absolute critical periods no longer warranted serious consideration with respect to human behavioral development. However, he also pointed out that periods of heightened responsiveness during development had obvious validity in certain cases. If a child is too old, rehabilitation of certain deficits could be difficult. Rutter's position was, therefore, substantially the same as that of those ethologists who had used the less rigid notion of sensitive period. Nonetheless, differences of opinion remained between the biologists and those developmental psychologists who were sceptical about the importance of early experience.

In this chapter we therefore begin by stressing the nature of the evidence for sensitive periods. How is the evidence collected? What operations are required to demonstrate the existence of a sensitive period? After dealing with these questions we go on to consider how the evidence is interpreted. We argue that different explanations for a particular case may refer to different levels of analysis or to events occurring at different moments back in time from the observed alteration in sensitivity; therefore, they need not be mutually exclusive. We classify these explanations according to whether behavioral, physiological, or molecular events are postulated as the cause of the change in sensitivity and whether or not they are supposed to occur immediately before the change.

However, some explanations are at the same level and refer to events that are believed to occur at the same time with respect to the change in sensitivity. Such rival interpretations are mutually exclusive and it may be possible to distinguish between them. As an example, we consider the relative merits of a clock model and a competitive exclusion model both of which have been used as physiological explanations for what happens prior to a reduction in sensitivity. In the final part of the chapter we emphasize that, even when variability in behavior can normally be attributed to differences in experience within a finite part of the life-cycle, it does not follow that such differences remain stable under all

conditions. Indeed, some evidence suggests that, in special circumstances, a seemingly unmodifiable preference arising from early experience may be changed in adulthood. When this is realized, it becomes possible to perceive how the concept of the sensitive period remains valid within limits but how, under particular conditions, the long-term effects of early experience may be overlain or modified by the effects of events occurring later in life. Therefore, the view that the characteristics of certain forms of behavior are *normally* dependent on experience obtained early in life can be reconciled with the view that *sometimes* they can be changed later.

The Nature of the Evidence

Even though the attacks on the "myth" of early experience were in our view somewhat misplaced (see Hinde and Bateson, 1984), it remains true that if the concept of sensitive period is to be useful, it is necessary to be precise about what has to be done in order to demonstrate that a particular aspect of behavior is more strongly affected by an experience at one stage of development than at others. The operations needed to establish the existence of a sensitive period are shown in figure 4.1. The time when ex-

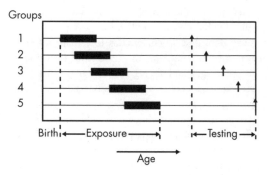

Figure 4.1 The operations required to demonstrate the existence of a sensitive period in development. Exposure is denoted by the thick bars. The number of groups is obviously arbitrary. Note that if the length of time from exposure to testing is kept constant (as shown by the arrows), the age of onset of exposure is confounded with the age of testing; but if the age of testing is kept constant, then the age of onset of exposure is confounded with the time from exposure to testing.

posure to a given agent takes place is shown by the heavy lines. If the duration of exposure is merely started at different times and ended at the same time, then the evidence that is taken to support an age-specific effect is ambiguous; it could arise because the individuals that were exposed at an earlier age were also exposed for longer. Similarly, if the time from the end of exposure to testing is not kept constant, differences between the groups could arise because the effects of exposure could have attenuated more in Group 1 than in Group 5. A more subtle point is that, if the length of time from exposure to testing is kept constant (as shown by the arrows), the age of onset of exposure is confounded with the age of testing; but if the age of testing is kept constant, then the age of onset of exposure is confounded with the time from exposure to testing. Strictly, the only way to be sure that neither of the confounded variables is responsible for the differences between the groups is to run two separate experiments. In one experiment the time from the end of exposure to testing is kept constant and in the other the age of testing is kept constant. However, in many cases the plausibility of one or other of the alternative explanations for the results would be low and the extra work unjustified.

These points about the ambiguity of findings that purport to have demonstrated a sensitive period are not hypothetical. In some well-known studies of sexual imprinting in zebra finches, Immelmann (1969) fostered the nestlings with another species, the Bengalese finch. When adult, the zebra finch males fostered in this way preferred to court Bengalese finch females to females of their own species. Immelmann started the fostering at different ages and found that when the nestlings were above a certain age at the onset of fostering, their subsequent sexual preferences were for members of their own species. He attributed the lack of effectiveness of exposure to the Bengalese finches in the older birds to the existence of a sensitive period (Immelmann, 1972). However, an alternative explanation was not excluded. The birds first exposed to Bengalese finches at a later age also received less exposure overall. So the differences in outcome could have been ascribed to differences in length of exposure to the Bengalese finch foster parents.

Another example of potentially misleading conclusions being drawn from an inadequate demon-

stration of a sensitive period was Shepher's (1971) famous study of Israeli kibbutzniks. Most preferred not to marry a person they had known from early life. However, a few did and these people had usually entered the kibbutz after their sixth birthday. On the basis of this evidence, Shepher (1971) suggested that humans have a sensitive period for "negative imprinting" which ends by the age of 6 years. However, the people concerned did not withdraw from the kibbutz at a fixed period of time after entry, so age of entry into the kibbutz is confounded with length of exposure to class mates. Possibly the process that eventually influences mate choice has to be initiated before the age of 6, but even this conclusion is equivocal since many other variables might have been confounded with late entry into the kibbutz. Such difficulties can be overcome by properly controlled experiments, although these are admittedly much easier to do with animals than with people. A good example of an animal study is Landsberg's (1976) work on the sensitive period for imprinting in ducklings.

The influence of initial contact with her new born on the human mother's subsequent affection for her child provides yet another area of research where the claims for a sharply defined sensitive period have far outrun the evidence. In an excellent and well-balanced review, Goldberg (1983) notes that, among other shortcomings, the majority of the studies confound timing with amount of contact – the mothers having contact with their babies closer to birth also have more exposure to them. She also notes that even the relatively unambiguous evidence suggests that the contact is mildly beneficial rather than essential. Its effects can easily be overridden by subsequent experience. These points draw attention to the general limitations of much of the evidence for sensitive periods. Nonetheless, experimental demonstration of a sensitive period for a given type of stimulation can (and should) involve adequate controls for the length of exposure and the length of the interval between the stimulation and testing.

Limitations of the Evidence

Even when the evidence for a sensitive period satisfies the requirements which we have outlined above, the conclusions that can be drawn from the findings are often limited in extent. It is well worth bearing in mind the following cautions before generalizing too widely:

(1) Even the most perfect demonstration of a sensitive period does not mean that the length of the period will be constant when the conditions are altered. In the case of filial imprinting in birds, social isolation lengthens the period (see Bateson, 1979).

(2) Sensitive periods relate to specific types of input; other types of experience may exert effects at quite different times in the life-cycle. While several types of behavior may be affected by experience during a given period of development, it does not follow that this is the only sensitive period in the life-cycle (contrast this view with Scott, 1962).

(3) Evidence for the existence of a sensitive period is not an explanation for the ineffectiveness of stimulation outside that period. Nothing new is added by stating that something has to occur "within the sensitive period" in order to be effective, since the operations used to define the period are precisely those that generate the evidence to be explained.

(4) The explanation for the onset of sensitivity need not necessarily be the same as the explanation for the end. The end of the sensitive period for filial imprinting is almost certainly brought about by different processes from those responsible for the onset, a point we consider in greater detail later.

(5) The grouping of phenomena under the descriptive heading of "sensitive periods" does not imply that they can all be explained in the same way. For instance, processes that regulate the stage in childhood when language development can begin must surely be different from those controlling when an attachment is most readily formed to an adult.

(6) Many descriptively defined sensitive periods may have no biological function whatsoever. They may merely represent a time of rapid reorganization when a given system is more easily disrupted by deprivation or insult. Even the implication that filial and sexual imprinting in a given individual have the same biological function is probably false (see Bateson, 1979).

Table 4.1 The variety of ways in which evidence for a sensitive period might be explained

Level	Immediate	Preceding
Organismic	Type 1	Type 2
Physiological	Type 3	Type 4
Molecular	Type 5	Type 6

Types and Levels of Explanation

Distinct types of explanations for sensitive periods are easily confused. This is partly because the difference between an immediate cause and one that operated further back in time is, as always, a matter of degree and, therefore, not always obvious. The problem is compounded because explanations are offered at a number of distinct levels of analysis ranging from the organismic to the molecular. In an attempt to bring some order into the tangle, we have classified six types of explanation in table 4.1. Our aim is both to distinguish between these separate types of explanation for the sake of clarity and also to relate them. The classification arbitrarily separates explanations in terms of events that accompany or immediately precede a change in sensitivity from those that postulate causes that lie further back in time. It also only considers three of the levels at which the change might be explained.

(1) *Immediate organismic* A striking correlate of the end of the sensitive period for imprinting in birds is the increase in avoidance of novel objects. The end of sensitivity was therefore attributed to neophobia or the fear of novelty (Hess, 1959; Hinde, Thorpe, and Vince, 1956).

(2) *Preceding organismic* One commonly invoked explanation for the growth of avoidance of novel objects was that prior experience with another object had led to the establishment of a preference for the familiar and rejection of anything that the animal could detect as being different (Bateson, 1979; Bindra, 1959). As another example, in the cognitive development of the child, Vygotsky (1962) pointed

out that experiences influencing a child's cognitive development must lie within the "zone of proximal development." Many kinds of information processing are only possible when they have been preceded by experiences that set up the necessary cognitive capacities.

(3) *Immediate physiological* Irrespective of how they are generated, alterations in the abilities to perceive and deal with the external world could play an important role in determining when a sensitive period starts. In the case of filial imprinting some evidence suggests that the onset of the sensitive period is associated with an increase in visual efficiency (Paulson, 1965) and an increase in motor ability (Hess, 1959). In birds that are hatched naked and helpless, the onset occurs much later than in precocious birds such as Mallard and domestic chicks (e.g., Burtt, 1977). In addition, an increase in the state of general "arousal" has often been thought to be important in imprinting (e.g., Kovach, 1970; Martin and Schutz, 1974; Rajecki, 1973).

Some sensitive periods can be fruitfully explained in terms of increased vulnerability to external influences at times of rapid change, as Bloom (1964) and Scott (1978) have argued. This usage seems particularly apt in the case of physical growth. Starvation or illness reduce rates of growth but the individual can subsequently catch up if it has not been held back too much. The physiological threshold for less than full recovery is much more likely to be exceeded during the stages of development when growth is normally rapid (see Bateson, 1976).

(4) *Preceding physiological* Onsets and ends of sensitivity have often been explained in terms of changes governed by a postulated physiological clock. Alternatively, when prior experience prevents or permits sensitivity to the long-term effects of novel input, it may pre-empt other types of experience from having the same impact (e.g., Sluckin and Salzen, 1961). The phenomenon may then be explained in terms of competitive exclusion (e.g., Bateson, 1981). The essence of this view is that a particular member of a class of inputs from the environment gains access to the systems responsible for executing the relevant behavior and thereby excludes access to others.

(5) *Immediate molecular* Some changes in sensitivity to experience may spring from gene expression at that particular moment in development. Although no clear examples are well known to us, we presume that when the onset or end of a sensitive period is attributed to "genetic programming" (e.g., Hess, 1973), the author of such an explanation believes that activation of particular genes exerts an immediate influence on sensitivity at the behavioral level.

(6) *Preceding molecular* Gene expression, if involved in the onset of a sensitive period, will usually precede it, since many intermediate steps will probably intervene before sensitivity is altered. It seems likely for instance that the onset of sexual maturity in humans involves expression of genes that were previously latent, since many structural changes requiring protein synthesis occur at the time. Furthermore, it is probable that many stable preferences and habits are established when sexual behavior is first performed. Inasmuch as both these possibilities are real, gene expression at an earlier moment in time is responsible for the onset of some sensitive periods.

It must be stressed that a link between a behaviorally defined sensitive period and preceding gene expression would not imply that further explanation at higher levels was no longer required. Apart from the need to know the processes that mediate between molecules and behaviour, gene expression is itself regulated and dependent on the characteristics of larger systems. Both the individual's state and its social environment can be important factors in influencing the onset of sexual maturity in mice (e.g., Drickhamer, 1982). In Western countries the age of puberty in humans has been dropping steadily in recent decades and, even though the extent of the change may have been exaggerated (see Bullough, 1981), considerable evidence suggests that the prior nutritional plane of the individual is important in the timing of puberty (e.g., Frisch, 1978). So descending to Type 6 explanations in our table 4.1 might well be followed by ascent to Type 2 explanations.

In summary, our major point here is that the various types of explanation listed in table 4.1 are not necessarily incompatible with each other. However, we believe it is essential to be clear about the type of explanation under discussion.

Distinguishing between Explanations of the Same Type

While the various types of explanation listed in table 4.1 need not be incompatible, two explanations of the same type for the same phenomenon may well be in competition with each other. Particularly clear examples of opposed explanations are the two of Type 4 (i.e., Preceding Physiological) mentioned above as being used to account for the end of the sensitive period for imprinting. The first suggests that an internal clock determines when sensitivity declines, as well as when it initially increases. The second suggests that, while the onset of sensitivity is dependent on developmental state (and in that sense is determined by an internal timekeeper), the end is a result of competitive exclusion, resulting from induced neural growth.

Support for a clock model was provided by data which seemed to show that the sensitive period for filial imprinting is better calculated in terms of age from the beginning of embryonic development rather than in terms of age from hatching (Gottlieb, 1961; but see Landsberg, 1976). Although preceding events at the behavioral level might influence a clock in non-specific ways (see Aslin, 1981), the postulation of such mechanisms implies the proposal of a strong degree of autonomy from preceding external experience.

A number of possible physiological mechanisms could be suggested for the alternative model of competitive exclusion. For instance, suppose that gaining access involves growth of neural connections and that the area available for connections has finite size. When growth has proceeded beyond the halfway point and cannot be reversed easily, the input experienced first will be better able to control the behavior than other forms of input. The outcome of such a process is illustrated in figure 4.2, which shows the proportion of access captured by first one (A) and then a second stimulus (B), assuming that the growth curves have an exponential character. This view of what happens was initially developed by Bateson (1981). It was dubbed the "capacity model" by Boakes and Panter (1985) and underlies the modeling attempts of Bischof (1985).

On the model of neural growth, an influence of the input on the rate of growth will also affect

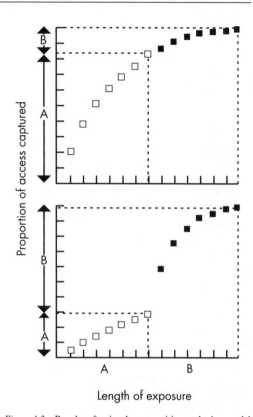

Figure 4.2 Results of a simple competitive exclusion model when access to an executive system is captured at a particular stage in development. The amount of access captured by a stimulus equals $1 - e^{-K.t.r}$ where e is the base of the natural logarithm, K is a constant set at 0.5 in these simulations, t is the length of exposure to the stimulus, and r is the initial responsiveness to the stimulus. In the top simulation the initial responsiveness (r) is 0.25 to stimulus A and 0.5 to stimulus B. In the bottom simulation the values of r are 0.05 to A and 0.5 to B.

whether or not the input experienced first is subsequently more or less effective than input experienced later. For instance, a weak and impoverished stimulus might be reasonably expected to promote much slower growth than a strong and rich one. This point is illustrated in figure 4.2. When birds such as mallard ducklings or domestic chicks are reared in the dark or have their visual experience attenuated by being reared in patternless environments, the sensitive period for filial imprinting can be extended (e.g., Moltz and Stettner, 1961). This result is readily explained by the competitive exclusion model on the hypothesis that the rate of growth is slower when the intensity and quality of the input is low. However, the result can also be explained by the clock model if the supposition is that the running speed of the clock is partly dependent on external stimulation. Does this mean that no evidence can help us to distinguish between the two rival explanations? Not quite, since the experience is portrayed as having a non-specific stimulatory effect in the clock model, whereas it is thought to have a specific pre-emptive effect in the competitive exclusion model. In the second case some specific memory of the experience is required, otherwise it cannot have a pre-emptive effect.

When domestic chicks or mallard ducklings are reared in isolation in a static but patterned environment, the sensitive period for imprinting is extended (e.g., Bateson, 1964). However, when the sensitive period comes to an end, it can be shown that the birds have a memory for the environment which they had experienced. The birds are more likely to respond socially to a moving object if it bears the same pattern as the walls of the cages in which they were previously isolated. This means that it would be incorrect to argue that rearing the animals in isolation merely delays a postulated clock bringing the sensitive period to a close. So, at least in the case of the end of the sensitive period for filial imprinting, the competitive exclusion model seems preferable to the clock one.

Recovering the Capacity for Change

The concept of sensitive period implies sensitivity of a particular type of behavior to a given form of stimulation during a limited phase in development. The concept does not necessarily imply that the behavior patterns in question cannot be influenced later in life under any circumstances. However, some proponents of the "critical period" concept believed that, at crucial moments in development, "decisions" are made and cannot be repeated or reversed later in development (e.g., Scott, 1978, p. 5). Sometimes a decisive event early in development can indeed set in train a set of changes that are so great and inter-related that virtually nothing can be done to alter the outcome later in life. The determination of gender by ambient temperature early in the development of turtles is a striking example (Bull, 1980).

Furthermore, at the purely behavioral level, a biologist would expect adaptations that protect certain well-developed preferences and habits from alteration. If knowledge of kin acquired in early life plays an important role in mate choice, as seems to be the case in many species (see Bateson, 1983a), such knowledge ought not to be easily disrupted by later experience, since opportunities for encountering kin will be limited in later-life. Immelmann (1984) gives many other cases where preservation of information acquired early in life is likely to be of great importance to the animal.

However, Clarke and Clarke (1976), taking such claims for immutability to be the major proposition about "critical periods," attacked it vigorously. At the end of their book devoted to examining the available evidence, they claimed that virtually no behavioral deficit induced by early experience was irreversible. They overstated their case. Forms of behaviour that are normally well buffered from change later in life may, nevertheless, be altered under special conditions.

Sargant (1957), drawing on a wide variety of examples ranging from military "brain-washing" and police interrogation to religious conversions and psychotherapy, noted that attempts to change adult minds were especially likely to be successful if the person had been made extremely frightened or upset. Once such a state of stress has been induced, Sargant argued, humans are enormously suggestible. The common element in the various military, political, religious, and therapeutic attempts to change the way human adults think and behave is a *combination* of stress and suggestion. Similarly, cases where trauma has renewed the plasticity of behavior have been observed in animals (see Bateson, 1983b).

High levels of stress are associated with rapid synthesis and turnover of noradrenalin (see Anisman, 1978; Ursin et al., 1978). Strikingly, noradrenalin (or norepinephrine) is implicated as a factor by the neurophysiological work on brain plasticity (see Pettigrew, 1982). These studies are especially relevant because they were carried out on a form of neural plasticity that characteristically occurs at a particular stage early in the life-cycle.

The influence of early experience on the development of human binocular vision is well known (see Banks et al., 1975; Hohmann and Creutzfeldt, 1975). The physiology of what probably happens is now largely understood from studies of the domestic cat's visual system (e.g., Horn, 1985; Rauschecker, 1984). The capacity of an eye to drive neurones in the cat's visual cortex depends on whether that eye received visual input from about 1 to 3 months after birth (e.g., Hubel and Wiesel, 1970; Rauschecker and Singer, 1981). If an eye is visually deprived during this period, it virtually loses its capacity subsequently to excite cortical neurones. Once established, it is exceedingly difficult, on the one hand, to reverse the dominance of one eye over the other or, on the other hand, to impair binocular vision in normally reared subjects. The phenomenon looks like and, indeed, has become one of the classic examples of sensitive periods in development. Even so, infusion of noradrenalin into the visual cortex of older cats can re-establish plasticity (reviewed in Pettigrew, 1982). If normally reared animals are monocularly deprived during the period of noradrenalin infusion, binocular control of the neurones is lost in the visual cortex of the hemisphere that was infused. No such change occurs in the visual cortex of the other hemisphere. The neural sites that are known to be affected by monocular deprivation are innervated by the diffuse projections of the locus coeruleus, a structure in the mid-brain that actively synthesizes noradrenalin (e.g., Amaral and Sinnamon, 1977; Redmond and Huang, 1979).

It would be wrong to suppose that noradrenalin is a sufficient condition for all forms of neural plasticity and it may well be too simple an idea to suppose that this neurotransmitter alone puts a particular set of neuronal connections in a state where they can be changed by a new input. Sites of neural plasticity in the visual cortex of the cat are innervated by many different fibers coming from other parts of the brain. The enabling condition for change could, therefore, be a particular cocktail of neurotransmitters rather than the presence of just one. The attraction of this possibility is that a particular site could be differentially prepared for change, giving much greater specificity to the influence of afferent input at a particular stage in development. Although a lot remains to be done, the work pioneered by Pettigrew and his colleagues starts to point to neural mechanisms by which behavioral systems, normally stable once formed, can be changed again later in life.

Conclusions

It is clear that sensitivity to those types of stimulation that influence the development of behavior can change with time. In this chapter we have been concerned with what generalizations may be drawn from such examples. We noted that the processes that augment the sensitivity of particular systems to particular events at particular stages are not necessarily the same as those that subsequently reduce the sensitivity. Nor are the sets of processes that give rise to one sensitive period necessarily the same as those that give rise to another. This lack of generality raises a difficulty for the use of a common term, like "sensitive period," which can easily be taken to imply a common underlying mechanism. If the term has little explanatory power, why use it? The answer, we believe, is simply that it draws attention to the fact that all forms of stimulation are not equally important at all stages in development. Descriptions of sensitive periods are an important first step towards understanding an aspect of development. The description of regularity invites analysis of the *processes* that generate such regularity. Such analysis is the kind of research which will eventually unlock the mysteries of neural and behavioral development.

We suggest that much of the argument over sensitive periods has been at cross-purposes. In part, confusion has arisen because different types of explanation have been treated as though they were the same. In order to bring some sharpness of focus to the debate, we have suggested a classification that draws attention to the ways in which they differ and, having made the distinctions, shows how the explanations may then be related. It also enables the relative merits of genuinely rival explanations, such as the physiological clock and competitive exclusion models, to be examined more closely.

Another difficulty about the way in which the concept of sensitive periods has been used was that the greater effectiveness of a stimulus at a particular stage in development was taken to mean irreversibility of its effects. Admittedly, in some cases the presence (or absence) of the appropriate form of stimulation within a sensitive period sets in train changes in structure that are so great that virtually nothing can be done to alter them later in life. However, many behavioral outcomes of early experience can be changed, even though sometimes only under rather special conditions. When that point is appreciated, the views of the enthusiastic proponents of the sensitive period concept and those of their critics can be reconciled.

In summary, we consider the operations required to demonstrate the existence of a sensitive period in development. However, we emphasize that in many cases the times of onset and ending of sensitivity are dependent on conditions. Having noted that the causal and functional explanations for sensitive periods vary widely from case to case, we then classify the varieties of levels and moments back in time at which explanations may be offered. Once distinguished, many of these may be usefully related to each other. Two rival explanations of the same type for the end of the sensitive period for imprinting are considered: a physiological clock and competitive exclusion resulting from induced neural growth. The competitive exclusion model seems the more satisfactory of the two. Finally, we discuss how, under certain conditions such as those that generate high stress, behavior that is influenced by early experience in early life can sometimes be changed once again in adulthood.

References

Amaral, D. G., and Sinnamon, H. M. (1977) The locus coeruleus: Neurobiology of a central noradrenergic nucleus, *Progress in Neurobiology*, 9, 147–96.

Anisman, H. (1978) Neurochemical changes elicited by stress: Behavioral correlates. In H. Anisman and G. Bignami (eds), *Psychopharmacology of Aversively Motivated Behavior*, New York: Plenum.

Aslin, R. N. (1981) Experiential influences and sensitive periods in perceptual development: A unified model. In R. N. Aslin, J. R. Alberts and M. R. Petersen (eds), *Development of Perception: Psychobiological Perspectives, Vol. 2: The Visual System*, New York: Academic Press.

Banks, M. S., Aslin, R. N., and Letson, R. D. (1975) Sensitive period for the development of human binocular vision, *Science*, 190, 675–77.

Bateson, P. P. G. (1964) Effect of similarity between rearing and testing conditions on chicks' following and avoidance responses, *Journal of Comparative and Physiological Psychology*, 57, 100–103.

Bateson, P. P. G. (1976) Rules and reciprocity in behavioural development. In P. P. G. Bateson and R. A. Hinde (eds), *Growing Points in Ethology*, Cambridge: Cambridge University Press.

Bateson, P. [P. G.] (1979) How do sensitive periods arise and what are they for? *Animal Behaviour*, 27, 470–86.

Bateson, P. [P. G.] (1981) Control of sensitivity to the environment during development. In K. Immelmann, G. W. Barlow, L. Petrinovich and M. Main (eds), *Behavioral Development*, Cambridge: Cambridge University Press.

Bateson, P. [P. G.] (ed.) (1983a) *Mate Choice*, Cambridge: Cambridge University Press.

Bateson, P. [P. G.] The interpretation of sensitive periods. In A. Oliverio and M. Zappella (eds) (1983b) *The Behavior of human infants*, New York: Plenum.

Bindra, D. (1959) *Motivation: A systematic Reinterpretation*, New York: Ronald Press.

Bischof, H. J. (1985) Environmental influences on early development: A comparison of imprinting and cortical plasticity. In P. P. G. Bateson and P. H. Klopfer (eds), *Perspectives in Ethology, Vol. 6: Mechanisms*, New York: Plenum.

Bloom, B. S. (1964) *Stability and change in human characteristics*, New York: Wiley.

Boakes, R., and Panter, D. (1985) Secondary imprinting in the domestic chick blocked by previous exposure to a live hen, *Animal Behaviour*, 33, 353–65.

Bull, J. J. (1980) Sex determination in reptiles, *Quarterly Review of Biology*, 55, 3–21.

Bullough, V. L. (1981) Age at menarche: A misunderstanding, *Science*, 213, 365–6.

Burtt, E. H. (1977) Some factors in the timing of parent–chick recognition in swallows, *Animal Behaviour*, 25, 231–9.

Clarke, A. M., and Clarke, A. D. B. (1976) *Early Experience: Myth and Evidence*, London: Open books.

Drickhamer, L. C. (1982) Delay and acceleration of puberty in female mice by urinary chemosignals from other females, *Developmental Psychobiology*, 15, 433–45.

Frisch, R. E. (1978) Population, food intake and fertility, *Science*, 199, 22–30.

Goldberg, S. (1983) Parent–infant bonding: Another look, *Child Development*, 54, 1355–82.

Gottlieb, G. (1961) Developmental age as a baseline for determination of the critical period in imprinting, *Journal of Comparative and Physiological Psychology*, 54, 422–7.

Hess, E. H. (1959) Two conditions limiting critical age for imprinting, *Journal of Comparative and Physiological Psychology*, 52, 513–18.

Hess, E. H. (1973) *Imprinting*, New York: Van Nostrand Reinhold.

Hinde, R. A. (1961) The establishment of the parent–offspring relation in birds with some mammalian analogies. In W. H. Thorpe and O. L. Zangwill (eds), *Current Problems in Animal Behaviour*, Cambridge: Cambridge University Press.

Hinde, R. A., and Bateson, P. (1984) Discontinuities versus continuities in behavioral development and the neglect of process, *International Journal of Behavioral Development*, 7, 129–43.

Hinde, R. A., Thorpe, W. H., and Vince, M. A. (1956) The following response of young Coots and Moorhens, *Behaviour*, **9**, 214–42.

Hoffman, H. S. (1987) Imprinting and the critical period for social attachments: some laboratory investigations. In M. H. Bornstein, *Sensitive Periods in Development*, Hillsdale, NJ: Lawrence Erlbaum.

Hohmann, A., and Creutzfeldt, O. D. (1975) Squint and the development of binocularity in humans, *Nature*, **254**, 613–14.

Horn, G. (1985) *Memory, Imprinting, and the Brain*, Oxford: Oxford University Press.

Hubel, D. H., and Wiesel, T. N. (1970) The period of susceptibility to the physiological effects of unilateral eye closure in kittens, *Journal of Physiology*, **206**, 419–36.

Immelmann, K. (1969) Über den Einfluss frühkindlicher Erfahrungen auf die geschlechtliche Objekt-fixierung bei Estrildiden, *Zeitschrift für Tierpsychologie*, **26**, 677–91.

Immelmann, K. (1972) Sexual and other long-term aspects of imprinting in birds and other species, *Advances in the Study of Behavior*, **4**, 147–74.

Immelmann, K. (1984) The natural history of bird learning. In P. Marler and H. S. Terrace (eds), *The Biology of Learning*, Berlin: Springer-Verlag.

Immelmann, K., and Suomi, S. J. (1981) Sensitive phases in development. In K. Immelmann, G. W. Barlow, L. Petrinovich and M. Main (eds), *Behavioral Development*, Cambridge: Cambridge University Press.

Kagan, J. (1984) *The Nature of the Child*, New York: Basic Books.

Kovach, J. K. (1970) Critical period or optimal arousal? Early approach behavior as a function of stimulus, age and breed variables, *Developmental Psychology*, **3**, 73–7.

Landsberg, J. W. (1976) Posthatch age and developmental age as a baseline for determination of the sensitive period for imprinting. *Journal of Comparative and Physiological Psychology*, **90**, 47–52.

Lenneberg, E. H. (1967) *Biological Foundations of Language*, New York: Wiley.

Lorenz, K. (1935) Der Kumpan in der Umwelt des Vogels, *Journal für Ornithologie*, **83**, 137–213, 289–413.

Lorenz, K. (1937) The companion in the bird's world, *Auk*, **54**, 245–73.

Martin, J. T., and Schutz F. (1974) Arousal and temporal factors in imprinting in Mallards, *Developmental Psychobiology*, **7**, 69–78.

Moltz, H., and Stettner, L. J. (1961) The influence of patterned light deprivation on the critical period for imprinting, *Journal of Comparative and Physiological Psychology*, **54**, 279–83.

Paulson, G. W. (1965) Maturation of evoked responses in the duckling, *Experimental Neurology*, **11**, 324–33.

Pettigrew, J. D. (1982) Pharmacologic control of cortical plasticity, *Retina*, **2**, 360–72.

Rajecki D. W. (1973) Imprinting in precocial birds: interpretation, evidence and evaluation, *Psychological Bulletin*, **79**, 48–58.

Rauschecker, J. (1984) Neuronal mechanisms of developmental plasticity in the cat's visual system, *Human Neurobiology*, **3**, 109–14.

Rauschecker, J. P., and Singer, W. (1981) The effects of early visual experience on the cat's visual cortex and their possible explanation by Hebb synapses, *Journal of Physiology*, **310**, 215–39.

Redmond, D. E., and Huang, Y. H. (1979) Current concepts, II: New evidence for a locus coeruleus-norepinephrine connection with anxiety, *Life Sciences*, **25**, 2149–62.

Rutter, M. (1980) The long-term effects of early experience, *Developmental Medicine and Child Neurology*, **22**, 800–15.

Sargant, W. (1957) *Battle for the Mind*, London: Heinemann.

Scott, J. P. (1962) Critical periods in behavioral development, *Science*, **138**, 949–58.

Scott, J. P. (1978) *Critical Periods*, Stroudsberg, Pa: Dowden, Hutchinson & Ross.

Shepher, J. (1971) Mate selection among second generation kibbutz adolescents and adults: Incest avoidance and negative imprinting, *Archives of Sexual Behavior*, **1**, 293–307.

Sluckin, W., and Salzen, E. A. (1961) Imprinting and perceptual learning, *Quarterly Journal of Experimental Psychology*, **13**, 65–77.

Snow, C. (1987) Relevance of the notion of a critical period to language acquisition. In M. H. Bornstein, *Sensitive Periods in Development*, Hillsdale, NJ: Lawrence Erlbaum.

Thorpe, W. H. (1961) *Bird-song*, London: Cambridge University Press.

Ursin, H., Baade, E., and Levine, S. (eds) (1978) *Psychology of Stress*, New York: Academic Press.

Vygotsky, L. S. (1962) *Thought and Language*, Cambridge, Mass.: M.I.T. Press.

CHAPTER 5

Behavioral Development: Toward Understanding Processes

CAREL TEN CATE

Introduction

If we took some bird eggs, from a domestic chicken for instance, and put half of them in an incubator, leaving the other half out, it would not be a surprise to discover that only the eggs put in the incubator will hatch. From this simple experiment we could correctly conclude that "warmth" is necessary for the transformation of eggs into chicks. However, the experiment tells us no more than that we have identified only one of the participants in a complex process. Of course, we all know that the warmth interacts with other factors outside and inside the egg. And although we can trace these factors, such as genes, yolk, etc., in the same way as the effect of warmth is assessed, a full understanding of how they assemble a chick is only obtained by studying their interactions: the embryological process.

The trivial example above illustrates two principles which are just as important in the study of behavioral development as they are in the study of physical development. The first principle is that identifying (or failure to identify) one factor con-

tributing to the multifactorial and interactive process of development does not allow a conclusion about the importance of other factors: If it is shown that a particular environmental factor has an influence on the development of a specific behavior pattern, it does not exclude contributions of other factors. On the other hand, if this environmental factor was shown to have no influence on the emergence of the behavior, it would be wrong to accept this as proof of the influence of some other specific factor like, for instance, genes. A direct, positive assessment of the contribution of each of these factors is needed for such acceptance.

The second principle arising from the "egg and chick" example is the distinction between *identifying* the various factors influencing behavioral development and studying *how* these factors exert their effect. An experiment in which a change in adult behavior occurs as a consequence of a manipulation earlier in life need not tell us something about the process by which this manipulation produced the change.

The aim of this paper is to demonstrate the implications of these principles for understanding behavioral development. This enterprise is not a new one. Other people have put forward similar ideas and contributed to their empirical foundation (e.g., Lehrman, 1953, 1970; Kruijt, 1964, 1966; Bateson, 1976, 1983). Recently, Oyama (1985) has provided

From P. P. G. Bateson and P. Klopfer (eds), *Perspectives in Ethology*, vol. 8 (New York: Plenum Press, 1989), pp. 243–69.

a powerful conceptual reassessment of these principles. The present paper should be seen as a case study, illustrating the use of these principles in developmental research. To this end, I will focus mainly on two subjects deeply rooted in traditional ethology: the phenomenon of "imprinting," and in particular "sexual imprinting," and that of song learning in birds. Basically, what I want to advocate is a change in attitude toward the study of behavioral development and, in particular, toward imprinting and related processes, like song learning. This change in attitude parallels the one which has occurred among learning theorists (Dickinson, 1980). The traditional behaviorist focused on the behavioral change per se, brought about by some manipulation. The limitations of the explanatory value of this approach gave rise to modern learning theory, in which the conditioning experiment is used as an analytical tool for studying *how* animals acquire knowledge through experience (see Dickinson, 1980).

After a short introduction to the subject of imprinting, I shall discuss some studies showing how application of the above-mentioned principles leads to a number of new questions and interpretations of this well-examined phenomenon. This will lead me to discuss research on another traditional topic among developmental ethologists: that of song learning, which shows many resemblances to imprinting. Finally, a short paragraph will give some attention to the "so what?" question: What, if any, is the importance of these ideas in a broader context, for instance for understanding evolutionary processes?

Imprinting as a Phenomenon

The young of many precocial birds, such as goslings or chicks, have a strong tendency to form a social preference for the first moving, conspicuous object they encounter after hatching. In doing so, they are fairly unselective, and thus exposure to human beings or artificial stimuli such as a rotating light can lead to a preference for these objects over conspecifics. This preference develops without the presence of any obvious external reinforcement, it may be achieved within a couple of hours (which gave rise to the notion of a so-called "sensitive phase"), and it usually shows great stability. These special characteristics gave the process its name: *filial imprinting*. The publication and translation of Lorenz's paper *Der Kumpan in der Umwelt des Vogels* (Lorenz, 1935, 1937), and his claim for the uniqueness of the process (Lorenz, 1935), are especially seen as the source of inspiration for many further studies. These studies focused on the characteristics of imprinting, its relation with other learning processes, and also on the attractiveness of different stimuli (for reviews, see Bateson, 1966; Sluckin, 1972). Lorenz also pointed to a long-term effect of early experience: Some birds that he had hand-raised, or that were reared by a foster species, later showed a sexual preference for humans or the foster species, respectively (Lorenz, 1935). This so-called "sexual imprinting" has since been shown to occur not only in precocial birds such as ducks (Schutz, 1965), snow geese (Cooke and McNally, 1975), and quail (Gallagher, 1976), but also in altricial birds such as doves and pigeons (Warriner et al., 1963; Brosset, 1971) and zebra finches (Immelmann, 1969a; Kruijt et al., 1983).

At present, the evidence suggests that filial imprinting and sexual imprinting are more likely to be two separate (though partially overlapping) processes, rather than, as Lorenz (1935) thought, two expressions of one underlying process (Bateson, 1979, 1981). For instance, in a number of species showing filial imprinting during the first days of life, the sensitive period for sexual imprinting is known to occur at a later age and may involve a different stimulus object (see Bateson, 1979). The questions that guided research on sexual imprinting have been very similar to those concerning filial imprinting. The important pioneering work of Immelmann on the zebra finch, for instance, addressed questions such as the timing of the sensitive period and the stability of the preference (Immelmann, 1972a, b; Immelmann and Suomi, 1981). He also addressed the question of whether a preference for an individual's own species was more easily obtained than one for a foster species. One such study involved the rearing of zebra finch males by mixed pairs consisting of one zebra finch parent and one Bengalese finch parent (Immelmann, 1972a, b). Males raised in this way usually preferred conspecific females over Bengalese finch females (table 5.1), a finding which I have confirmed (ten Cate, 1982, 1984; table 5.1).

Table 5.1 Mating preference of zebra finch males raised by mixed pairs[a]

	Zebra finch males raised by mixed pairs	
Preference[b]	Immelmann (1972a)	ten Cate (1984)
Z	17	30
B	4	1

[a] Mixed pairs: Male zebra finch and female Bengalese finch or vice versa.
[b] Z, conspecific females; B, Bengalese finch females.

Imprinting as a Developmental Process

At first sight, the extensive studies on sexual imprinting may suggest it to be one of the best-understood developmental processes. They have shown that sexual preferences in zebra finch males are influenced by experience with the parents, that imprinting occurs within a limited time span, that the preference is relatively stable, and also that a preference for one's own species is established more easily than one for another species. But, however important in their own right, what do these findings say about the development of species recognition in zebra finches viewed as a developmental *process*? That we can make further progress here, using the principles outlined in the Introduction, becomes clear after a closer examination of the interpretation of the data in table 5.1. These data have been interpreted as showing that zebra finches not only *learn* about parental characteristics, but also possess an *unlearned* preference for characteristics of their own species (e.g., Immelmann, 1972a; Bischof, 1979). To hypothesize the presence of such a preference is certainly valid, and initial preferences for specific stimuli have been shown for filial imprinting (e.g., Bateson and Jaeckel, 1976; Bateson, 1978a). However, in the present case, it should be noted that the evidence is obtained indirectly. The finding that the final preference of zebra finch males seems incompletely explained by imprinting is taken as evidence

for the influence of another specific factor. But there could be many ways by which an adult male might become biased toward its own species. It has, for instance, been shown that in cross-fostered zebra finch males not only parents, but also the conspecific siblings, may exert an influence (Kruijt et al., 1983). Another potential source for the learning of conspecific characteristics is a bird's own body. Evidence for such autoimprinting is present from fowl (Kruijt, 1962, 1985; Vidal, 1975, 1982). So, insofar as external participants in the process are concerned, there may be more than just parental influence. If we could control these alternative ways of learning conspecific characteristics, and a preference for the individual's own species persisted, that finding would of course be of interest. However, the question would still remain: Who are the participants in that process, and, for that matter, what is the nature of the process itself?

The point I have raised above supports the view that the influence of parents cannot, on its own, provide a satisfactory explanation for data such as those in table 5.1. But can it? This brings me to the developmental questions about the process of sexual imprinting. Identifying the importance of parental influence or the time of exposure, for instance, was an important step toward understanding the acquisition of a sexual preference by zebra finch males. The next step is to examine the processes bringing about these characteristics: *How* does exposure to a stimulus influence the acquisition? *How* is the timing achieved? *What* is the nature of the stored information, i.e., the "internal representation," resulting from the process? *How* does this representation exert its control over the behavioral output?, and so on.

In the following, I shall discuss in some detail three issues illustrating some of the progress that has been, or could be, made on these questions. First, I address the question of how exposure to one's parents may lead an individual to build up a representation of their appearance or their song. The second problem concerns the timing of the sensitive period, and, in particular, the mechanism underlying the ending of the sensitivity. The third issue is whether a developing individual can itself exert some influence on the progress of the acquisition process. The connection between these issues will, I hope, become clear later on.

The acquisition process

Immelmann (1972a) showed that young zebra finches developed a preference for the parental species, even if they were surrounded by a majority of birds of other species. This pointed to the importance of the social bond between parents and young for the imprinting process. Therefore, to tackle the first question, a logical start seemed to be the examination of what actually goes on between (foster) parents and young. To this aim, I carried out observations on various types of pairs (zebra finch, Bengalese finch, and mixed) from hatching until some 55 days of age [an extensive report of these studies is given in ten Cate (1982, 1984)]. Over this period, the relationships between young zebra finches and conspecific parents changed quite dramatically. Initially, the main interactions consisted of the young begging and the parents feeding them and brooding. After fledging, begging and feeding continued until about 35 days of age. Young and parents also spent considerable time clumping together, during which mutual preening (allopreening) occurred. A decrease in feeding coincided with the emergence of, and a steady increase in, aggression from both parents toward the juveniles. Although roughly similar changes in interactions between Bengalese parents and zebra finch young occurred, some of these interactions differed systematically in their timing and intensity from those with conspecific parents. This was examined in more detail in the mixed pairs. It appeared that in this situation parental care (feeding and brooding the young) and aggression were shown significantly more by zebra finch than by Bengalese finch parents (an example – feeding in male zebra finch/female Bengalese finch pairs – is given in figure 5.1. Toward the end of the exposure, more clumping and allopreening was shown with the Bengalese finch parent, but most clumping occurred with the (conspecific) sibling. These differences were independent of the type of mixed pair used (male zebra finch/female Bengalese finch or vice versa), which led to the conclusion that overall, young zebra finches had been exposed to more interactions with conspecifics (parents and/or siblings), than with Bengalese finches. So, could it be that the quantity of such interactions was linked with the learning process, i.e., did males raised by mixed pairs be-

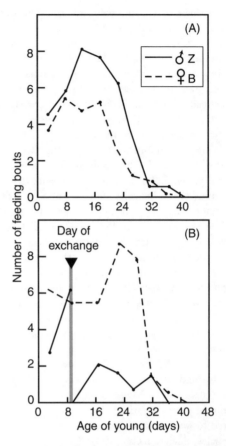

Figure 5.1 (A) Feeding frequency in mixed pairs in relation to age of young. Indicated is the mean number of feeding bouts/4-h observation period per 5-day interval received by individual male juveniles. The zebra finch parent fed significantly more frequently than the Bengalese finch parent ($p < 0.05$: Wilcoxon matched-pairs signed-rank test (WMP); N = 8). (B) Feeding frequency in mixed pairs in which the zebra finch parent was replaced by a nonbreeding zebra finch at around day 10. After exchange most feeding was done by the Bengalese finch parent ($p < 0.01$): WMP; N = 8).

come biased toward the zebra finch (table 5.1) as a consequence of more interactions with their conspecifics earlier on?

To test this hypothesis, two separate sets of experiments were set up in which young zebra finches remained visually exposed to conspecifics and Bengalese finches, but in which the interactions with these species were manipulated. The first set of experiments consisted of a *successive* exposure to each species (ten Cate et al., 1984). After being reared by their own parents for 1 month, young males were transferred to a group of Bengalese finches for another month. For one series of males, the interactions between the Bengalese finches and the males were recorded. The later preference of these males showed a highly significant correlation with the amount of interactions with the Bengalese finches earlier on: The more aggressive was the behavior and clumping shown by the Bengalese finches, the more Bengalese-finch-directed was the later preference. The tentative conclusion, that the initiatives of the Bengalese finches caused the shift in preference toward them, was supported by the finding that exposure to Bengalese finches behind a wire screen (which limited the behavior of the Bengalese finches toward the young, but main-tained visual exposure to them) led to a smaller shift (figure 5.2). A further reduction of the preference for Bengalese finches was obtained by exposure to stuffed Bengalese finches. This occurred in spite of the fact that the young males themselves showed a variety of social behavior, including precocial sexual behavior, toward the stuffed models.

A second set of experiments was carried out by manipulating the behavior of the zebra finch parent in mixed pairs, i.e., with young zebra finches sub-jected to *simultaneous* exposure to zebra finch and Bengalese finch (ten Cate, 1984). One such manipu-lation was, for instance, to replace the zebra finch parent by a bird of the same sex from a nonbreeding group when the young were around 10 days of age. This new zebra finch only occasionally fed the young (and if this increased it was replaced). The Bengalese finch parent usually responded with an increase in its feeding so that, in contrast to the situation in nonmanipulated pairs (figure 5.1A), most feeding was now done by the Bengalese finch parent (figure 5.1B). None of the other behavioral interactions between the new zebra finch parent or the Bengalese finch parent and the young showed any significant change compared with the non-manipulated pairs. So, any difference in later pref-erence of the young must be due to this reversal of parental feeding. The effect of this and other ma-nipulations is presented in figure 5.3. A significant decrease in preference for zebra finch occurred as a consequence of manipulating feeding behavior of the male zebra finch parent. Figure 5.3 also shows the effect on the preference of other manipulations,

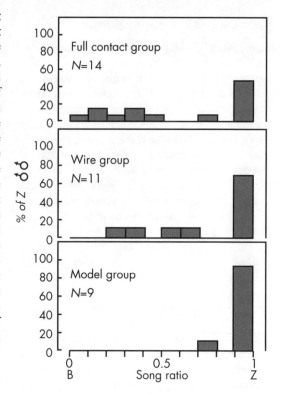

Figure 5.2 Sexual preferences shown by zebra finch males that have individually been placed in a group of Bengalese finches (full contact group); in a group of Bengalese finches but separated from them by a wire screen (wire group); and in a cage containing a number of stuffed Bengalese finches (model group). The number of zebra finches raised in each condition is indicated. Sexual preference is measured by the relative frequency of singing to zebra finch and Bengalese finch females in a choice test (see ten Cate, 1985c, for details of this method and its validation); a song ratio of 1.0 indicates an exclusive preference for the zebra finch female, a ratio of 0.0 indicates an exclusive preference for the Bengalese finch female.

in which the possibility of the young males to inter-act with the zebra finch parent was further de-creased. This resulted in a shift in preference from zebra finch to Bengalese finch. Since in all experi-ments the visual exposure to zebra finches was maintained, these results also strongly suggest that social interactions are necessary to build up a repre-sentation of the appearance of the individual with which a young male interacts.

So the above-mentioned experiments bring us a step closer to the mechanism underlying the acqui-sition of a preference. Nevertheless, it could be that

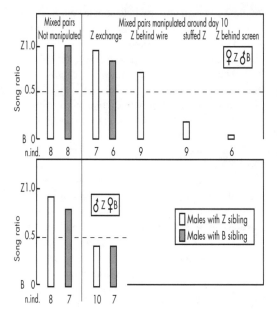

Figure 5.3 Influence of various manipulations of parental behavior on the later sexual preference of zebra finch males raised by mixed pairs. Columns indicate the mean preference (measured as the song ratio – see figure 5.2) over the indicated number of males. *Z exchange*, replacement of the zebra finch parent by a same-sexed nonbreeding bird; *Z behind wire*, the new bird was placed behind a wire screen; *stuffed Z*, a stuffed zebra finch was placed in the cage; *Z behind screen*, the new zebra finch was placed behind an opaque screen (thus it could be heard, but not seen). See ten Cate (1984) for further details.

the larger amount of interactions with conspecific parents in normal mixed pairs arose because the young zebra finches showed more responsiveness toward the conspecific parent. This may have induced the parent to show more feeding or aggression toward them. However, a more detailed study, on the difference between the parental species in mixed pairs raising mixed broods of both species, suggested the opposite (ten Cate, 1985a). Parents of both species preferentially fed conspecific young and some observations suggested that this initially arose from a greater reactivity of the parents to conspecific stimuli. This seems to add another step to the process outlined above: Parents are more responsive to conspecific young, this leads to more interactions with these young, and this in turn results in a stronger preference of these young for conspecifics later on.

The bias toward the individual's own species in table 5.1 can now be interpreted as being a consequence of the way in which the imprinting process operates. If those birds with which most interactions take place are acting as imprinting stimuli, then young zebra finch males should indeed be more likely to prefer conspecific females later on. No "unlearned" preference for species-specific characteristics has to be assumed to explain these data: *It is the way a stimulus bird behaves, rather than its appearance, which makes it a suitable imprinting object.*

Of course, this raises a new question: What gives behavioral interactions their impact? It is as though the initiatives of parents or other birds somehow act as an unconditioned stimulus, making parental appearance become the conditioned one. One way to obtain this effect could be that each behavioral initiative that brings a parent very close to a young, or makes it touch it (aggression, feeding, clumping, and allopreening all produce this effect), leaves an impact. The cumulative effect of these experiences would be the development of an internal representation. In addition to the mechanism above, an interesting possibility is that a contingency between a bird's own behavior and that of others may have an impact. This hypothesis originates from work by Watson (1972, 1981) and Watson and Ramey (1972). Experiments with human babies suggested that a guiding factor for directing social behavior might be the contingency between the baby's behavior and some response to it. When movement of a mobile was linked with head movements of the baby, this not only stimulated the baby to show these movements, but the baby also started to direct social behavior to it. So, translated to the imprinting situation, a bird might become imprinted on the individual that responds to its behavior. An attempt to test this hypothesis in a filial imprinting experiment (ten Cate, 1986a) has been undertaken, but although it showed that for filial imprinting, as well, the learning process was indeed most enhanced when chicks were exposed to a contingent moving ("behaving") stimulus, the question of whether or not this enhancement was due to a contingency effect could not be answered conclusively.

A developmental process very similar to the one suggested here may also be important in song learning. Here, too, the learning process seems enhanced by giving a young bird the opportunity to interact with a tutor, as compared with a situation in which such interaction is absent, or where recorded songs are played to an isolated individual [e.g., in zebra finches (Immelmann, 1969b; Price, 1979; Böhner, 1983), in canaries (Waser and Marler, 1977), in nightingales (Todt et al., 1979), in Bengalese finches (Dietrich, 1980), in indigo buntings (Payne, 1981), in chaffinches (Slater, 1983), and in white-crowned sparrows (Baptista and Petrinovich, 1984)]. In addition, when two potential live tutors are available, zebra finches seem to choose the one with which most aggressive interactions occur (Clayton, 1987). Pepperberg (1985), reviewing the enhancement of song learning by social interactions, draws attention to what might be a human analog of the stimulating effect of social interactions on achieving behavioral modifications: Live, social interactions with other humans are necessary to overcome existing strong inhibitions toward specific learning tasks.

It must be noted that demonstrating the enhancement of filial and sexual imprinting and song learning by interaction with the stimulus object (or by exposure to a moving rather than a nonmoving stimulus), does not exclude the possibility that some stimuli possess physical characteristics (e.g., color, shape, sound) that make them more attractive than others. Social interaction and physical characteristics should be seen as two factors which both may influence the outcome of the learning process. I will discuss the interactive effects of these two factors in more detail later on.

The timing process

An important feature of both the imprinting and the song-learning process is that learning seems limited to a specific period early in life. For sexual imprinting, a number of studies have concentrated on the delineation of the sensitive phase, e.g., in quail (Gallagher, 1977, 1978), mallard (Schutz, 1965), domestic cockerels (Vidal, 1975), and also in the zebra finch (Immelmann, 1972a, b; Immelmann and Suomi, 1981). However, such delineations need to be treated carefully, not because of the methodological difficulties facing the experimenter (although they are often underestimated: see Bateson, 1987b), but because their application is necessarily restricted until we know the process that underlies them. Are onset and offset of a phase simply a con-

sequence of some internal clock (such as the physiological state at different ages), or are they influenced by rearing conditions, and if so, how are they influenced? If the latter were the case, any delineation would only be valid within the conditions of the experiment showing it. Only knowledge about the process would allow a prediction concerning the outcome of subjecting an animal to various treatments at different ages.

That delineation of a sensitive phase is a problem quite different from examining its cause is well demonstrated by work of Eales (1985) on song learning in zebra finches. Zebra finch song consists of one phrase, composed of smaller elements, which is repeated several times to form a song bout. The characteristics of this phrase are highly constant for a given individual, but phrases of different males may vary considerably. Young males usually copy the song of their (foster) father, even if this is a Bengalese finch male (Immelmann, 1969b). Since young males become independent of their parents at around 35 days of age (Immelmann, 1962; ten Cate, 1982), Eales (1985) was interested in whether song acquisition occurred before or after this age. To examine this, she carried out a number of experiments (see Eales, 1985, for details). In a first series, young males were removed from their parents and denied further interaction with adult males when they were either 35, 50, 65, or 120 days old. It appeared that the songs of males removed at 35 days of age shared no characteristics with those of their father, whereas those removed at 65 or 120 days were nearly identical to those of their fathers (see figure 5.4 for an example), with intermediate copying from males removed at 50 days. In another experiment, males were transferred from their own father to a different male at, again, 35, 50, or 65 days. As shown in figure 5.5, these males, too, seem to have learned their song after day 35 and before day 65. It should be noted that, strictly speaking, such an experiment varies two factors – not only age but also the length of the exposure, which also may influence from whom song is copied. Nevertheless, the data suggest a sensitive phase for song learning somewhere between 35 and 65 days of age. This was confirmed by later experiments of Clayton (1987), in which the length of exposure to successive tutors was kept constant. In addition, Clayton (1987) showed that introduction to a new tutor after 80 days of age did not alter the song acquired from

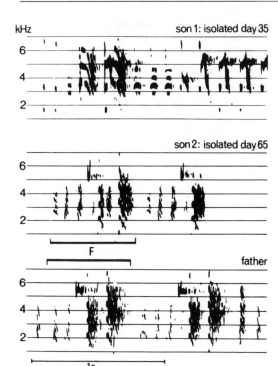

Figure 5.4 Sonagrams of the song of one zebra finch father and two of its sons, which were removed from the father at different ages. Son 2 copied its father's phrase (**F**), while the song of son 1 showed no resemblance to its father's song (Eales, 1985).

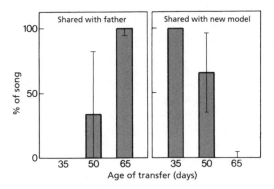

Figure 5.5 Percentage of song elements shared by zebra finch males with either their father or a new model, in relation to the age of transfer from father to the new model (modified from Eales, 1985). Median value and interquartile ranges are given.

previous tutors. Thus a sensitive phase was neatly delineated. But it should be noticed that the experiments do not demonstrate *how* the sensitive phase is brought to an end, a question that will be central to the remainder of this section.

A number of hypotheses have been proposed to explain how sensitive phases may come to an end (see Bateson 1979, 1987a, b). One possible hypothesis is the traditional "clock" model, which assumes that some physiological factor, intrinsic to the animal but extrinsic to the learning system, ends the receptivity to external stimulation, i.e., stops the learning process. So, for song learning in zebra finches, physiological changes at about 65 days of age might make further learning impossible. Another hypothesis is the "self-termination" model, which assumes that learning stops when a certain specified amount of input has been received. So, the cumulative input of 65 days of exposure to adult song may have been enough to reach the limits of the zebra finches' capacity to store or process information about songs. Further stimulation would then be incapable of getting access to the song-learning system, and thus no further learning would occur. To make a black and white distinction between these hypotheses: The clock model assumes an infinite capacity of the learning system but a limited time span available for learning; the self-termination model assumes a limited capacity of the learning system but an infinite time span available for learning. Formulated in this way, the models lead to different predictions. A testable difference is that in the absence of relevant stimulation (e.g., singing males) until well after the age of 65 days, the clock model predicts that no learning of tutor songs will take place later on, whereas the self-termination model predicts that, since little or no learning could have occurred previously, the capacity for song learning will be extended to later ages. For the zebra finch, relevant information with respect to both models emerged when Eales (1985) had a closer look at males that were removed from their parents at 35 days of age and thereafter not exposed to other males. As mentioned, their song shared no characteristic with their father's song. Most of these males developed highly abnormal and unpatterned songs, showing no phrase structure (figure 5.6A). The interesting finding occurred when these males were placed with adult males at the age of 6 months. All males then modified their songs into the character-

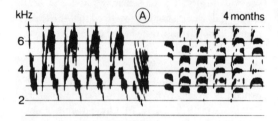

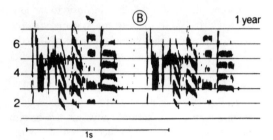

Figure 5.6 Sonagrams of a zebra finch male removed from its father at 35 days of age. (**A**) Sonagram at 4 months of age, i.e., when adult, showing an abnormal, unpatterned song. (**B**) Sonagram of the same male at 1 year of age. The male had been placed in a group of adult males at 6 months of age, after which the characteristic phrase structure developed (Eales, 1985).

istic phrase structure, and thus apparently learned their song well after the assumed sensitive phase (figure 5.6B). This indicates that, lacking adequate tutoring, sensitivity is maintained until such a tutor becomes available. This supports the model that song learning is, at least to some degree, *self-terminating*; i.e., *the progress of the learning process itself may influence the ending of the sensitive phase.*

The notion of self-terminating sensitivity has also been put forward for filial imprinting. Bateson (1987a, b) showed that the puzzling variation in the timing of sensitivity among studies of filial imprinting becomes understandable if here, too, the termination of the learning process is dependent on its progress.

Although similar detailed experiments on the timing underlying the process of sexual imprinting are lacking, some of the present findings would fit in well with the self-termination mechanism. For instance, Immelmann (1972a; Immelmann and Suomi, 1981) reported that the preference of zebra finch males could be more easily altered when they had been exposed first to Bengalese finches and next

to zebra finches than when the transfer occurred in the opposite direction. As we have seen in the previous section, the acquisition of a preference is enhanced by interactions between (foster) parents and young. The quantity of these interactions is lower between Bengalese finch parents and zebra finch young than between zebra finch parents and young. Given this, the learning process may proceed more slowly with Bengalese finch parents. If imprinting is self-terminating, i.e., the learning stops after a specific amount of experience, then an earlier ending of sensitivity should be expected with conspecific parents (but see ten Cate et al., 1984, for alternative explanations).

As mentioned above, the concept of self-termination requires that there be a limited capacity somewhere in the imprinting (or song-learning) system. This might be a limitation in memory space, or in access from the memory to some behavioral system responsible for the later behavioral output. The plausibility of this assumption, as well as an extensive overview of the evidence and full implications of the various models for the termination of sensitive phases, are given by Bateson (1979, 1981, 1987a, and, in particular, 1987b). The notion of a self-terminating developmental process is not unique to imprinting and song learning. In a recent paper, Chalmers (1987) discusses several "rules" that may underlie the predictable, characteristic changes that are often seen in behavior during development. He argues that one of the ways such changes are brought about is that the behavioral performance reaches a set point that is independent of age, but dependent on quality or quantity of the performance; in other words, the progress of the developmental process brings itself to an end.

An interactive model for imprinting and song learning   The data of Eales (1985, 1987) indicate another phenomenon, mentioned in the previous section: Exposure to the juvenile songs of age-mates only or to the vocalizations (calls) of females produces very slow, if any, song learning in zebra finch males. This in spite of opportunities to interact with age-mates or females. It indicates that, although female calls can be used as song elements (Eales, 1987), the physical qualities of the acoustic stimulation may influence song learning: Male song is of higher quality (leads to more rapid learning, hence earlier termination of sensitivity) than female vocalizations or the juvenile songs of age-mates. A similar preference to copy some song types rather than others was obtained by Marler (1970), who showed that tape-tutored white-crowned sparrows were more likely to accept conspecific than heterospecific songs as models. Marler postulated "a sensory 'template', somewhere in the auditory pathway, which focuses attention on sound patterns of a certain type" (Marler, 1970). Conclusive evidence for such phenomena for sexual imprinting is still lacking (see previous section and ten Cate, 1984, 1985b, 1988; ten Cate and Mug, 1984), although the possibility is still open. For filial imprinting, ample evidence is available that naive chicks prefer some physical characteristics over others (see Sluckin, 1972). As mentioned in the previous section, these findings show that imprinting and song-learning processes can be influenced in two ways. Frequent interactions with a stimulus (or exposure to a moving one) will enhance the acquisition of knowledge of its appearance or song type. At the same time, the physical qualities (e.g., appearance or sound) of the stimulus are important.

The next step is to relate these findings to the self-terminating character of imprinting and song-learning processes. Since ending of the learning process, i.e., ending of the sensitive phase, seems dependent on the progress of the process, which in turn depends on both physical qualities and behavior of the stimulus, the developmental process is an *interactive* one. A descriptive model showing these interactive relationships is given in figure 5.7. The two factors influencing the learning process are indicated along the two axes. As we have seen, learning speed increases with increasing amount of social interaction (or stimulus behavior), which is indicated along the y-axis. The zero level of social interactions would be exposure to a taped tutor in song learning, or a nonmoving stimulus such as a stuffed bird in sexual or filial imprinting. Intermediate stimulation might be provided by a stimulus bird behind a wire screen, and optimal stimulation might involve tutor and young bird in the same cage. The x-axis indicates that learning is also enhanced by physical characteristics of the stimulus: the color of the light used for filial imprinting, the acoustic qualities of conspecific songs over other song types or female calls, etc. It is the combination of both factors which influences the progress of the learning process: It will proceed slowly with a stimulus of

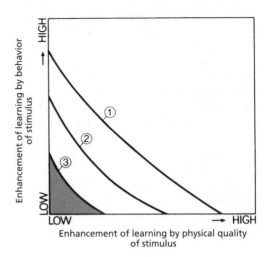

Figure 5.7 Graphical representation of the dependence of sensitive-phase duration on both physical quality of a stimulus and the enhancement of its attraction by movement or behavior shown by this stimulus. 1, 2, and 3 are isoclines, each connecting points of equal learning speed, i.e., giving sensitive phases of equal length. Line 1 connects points at which the combination of stimulus quality and behavior leads to a rapid learning (a short sensitive phase). The shaded area below line 3 indicates the condition in which learning proceeds too slowly to produce a noticeable effect (the sensitive phase never ends). Line 2 represents an intermediate learning speed (a sensitive phase of intermediate length).

poor physical quality and limited possibilities of enhancing its attraction due to constraints on its behavior. The notion of self-termination brings an important extra dimension in the model. It suggests that the cumulative effects of experience are asymptotic. As a result, novel experience exerts a smaller and smaller influence on the bird's behavior. The model implies in the top right part of the figure that this state can be reached very quickly, and in the bottom left part that it will only be reached very slowly. In fact, it can well be imagined that in the bottom left corner a threshold occurs, below which the stimulation is so limited that learning is never complete; i.e., even an infinite exposure to that condition never leads to the end of the sensitivity. Also, the model implies that an equally long sensitive phase (i.e., identical learning speed) can be obtained by a rearing condition involving limited possibilities of interacting with a high-quality stimulus, and by a condition involving excellent opportunities to interact with a stimulus of poor physical quality. Now some hypothetical isoclines can be drawn, connecting points for which the combination of both factors requires identical periods of exposure to produce self-termination. The completed figure now captures the connections between the main influences on imprinting and song learning. The shaded area indicates the threshold at which learning only occurs after infinite exposure. The different lines indicate the different levels of learning speed, with high learning speed implying a rapid learning and thus a shorter period of sensitivity.

Does this model have any use, in the sense that it can clarify findings for which other hypotheses could not account? There is no better way of illustrating this than with an example, which is provided by some at-first-sight paradoxical findings in studies of song learning in the white-crowned sparrow.

Marler (1970) demonstrated two things: that tape-tutored white-crowned males would copy conspecific songs only, and that these songs were learned before 50 days of age. More recently, Baptista and colleagues (Baptista and Morton, 1981; Baptista and Petrinovich, 1984, 1986; Baptista, 1985; Petrinovich and Baptista, 1987) demonstrated that hand-reared birds could learn after 50 days of age when exposed to a live tutor, but not when exposed to a taped one. Also, not only conspecific songs could be learned from a live tutor, but heterospecific songs could be learned when birds were exposed to members of these species or to conspecifics singing heterospecific songs. That some filtering occurs in tape-tutored birds, similar to Marler's findings, is not disputed. But in addition, Baptista and Petrinovich (1986) state that "social interaction can override any auditory gating mechanism that would prevent white crowned sparrows from learning allospecific songs" (see also Baptista, 1985; Pepperberg, 1985). About the observation of learning occurring after the 50-day limit observed by Marler (1970), Baptista and Petrinovich (1986) state: "Perhaps there is no sensitive phase at all when a live tutor is presented after a period of isolation from song as existed in the present study: the lack of acoustic stimulation could delay the period of sensitivity." They continue by saying:

Two facts mediate against this interpretation. First, tape-tutored birds do not learn after 50 days of age. If isolation merely delays the onset of the

sensitive phase these birds should learn also. Second, two male and two female students were held in group isolation until they were 100 days old and then exposed to a live tutor. None of the birds copied the tutor song. . . . Both of the male students were singing an isolate song prior to tutoring, and this isolate song persisted. (Baptista and Petrinovich, 1986)

The quotations above illustrate that although the traditional clock-model approach of sensitivity ending at around 50 days of age is not capable of explaining the data, Baptista and Petrinovich also reject the possibility of delayed sensitivity resulting from isolation. In a recent paper (Petrinovich and Baptista, 1987), a modified clock-model is proposed, with the suggestion that sensitivity to strong stimulation (i.e., to live tutors) is maintained for a longer period than is sensitivity to weaker forms of stimulation. Although indeed the findings can be interpreted in this way, I suggest that they also fit a self-termination model if the effects of social stimulation or sensitivity to certain song types over others are not seen as independent, dichotomous categories but as interactive ones, as presented in figure 5.7. Using this model, the results obtained by Marler (1970) and Baptista and Petrinovich (1984, 1986; Petrinovich and Baptista, 1987) fit very well together, and the findings which are presented as anomalies with respect to the possibility of delayed sensitivity in fact support the interactive model.

So, how can we fit the various findings in the model outlined in figure 5.7? Marler exposed his birds to a high-quality stimulus (conspecific song). Baptista and Petrinovich first isolated white-crowned sparrows for 50 days. This condition does not exclude all learning: As has been demonstrated by deafening males, males may learn from their own auditory feedback (Marler, 1970). However, it seems plausible that a bird's own juvenile isolate song is a lower-quality stimulus than full adult song (surprisingly, no experiments have been reported to examine whether isolate song is indeed the less attractive stimulus of the two). Assuming that the learning proceeds very slowly with the bird having feedback from its own vocalizations only, both anomalies observed by Baptista and Petrinovich become understandable. First, the learning may proceed so slowly that at 50 days of isolation the process is not even halfway to the required amount of stimulation. When the birds are next subjected to full contact with heterospecific stimulus birds, this creates exposure to a better acoustical stimulus, the effect of which can be enhanced by interaction with it. This experience may be in time to override the pre-emptive effect that a bird's own isolate song had, thus explaining why isolate birds may learn from a live tutor after 50 days.

Assuming that conspecific song provides a higher-quality stimulation than isolate songs, the pre-emptive effect of conspecific song may have been sufficient to prevent an effect of exposure to a live tutor in birds that were exposed to taped, conspecific tutor song for the first 50 days. Thus the self-termination model explains the first observation with which Baptista and Petrinovich have difficulties.

Another thing the interactive model would predict is that *given enough time* a bird's own isolate song, although of poor quality, may eventually produce enough cumulative stimulation to terminate the learning process. This state may have been reached in the white-crowned sparrows that were isolated (i.e., exposed to their own song and that of age-mates, since the birds were reported to be group-isolated) for 100 days, before they were introduced to the live tutor. So again the interactive model explains a seeming anomaly in the data obtained by Baptista and Petrinovich. Thus, at the moment, the interactive self-termination model seems a possible alternative to the clock model for understanding song learning in the white-crowned sparrow.

The framework presented here might also be of use to examine interspecific differences. Zebra finches, for instance, seem not to be capable of learning from a taped tutor, whether or not a conspecific song is played (Price, 1979). This suggests that the enhancement of learning the characteristics of a stimulus by some more intensive exposure to it is essential for learning to occur. This is in contrast with a species like the white-crowned sparrow. It means that figure 5.7 would look different for the zebra finch – the shaded area representing no learning would extend along the *x*-axis, as shown in figure 5.8.

An active role for the developing individual?

As shown above, the developmental process underlying imprinting and song learning is an interactive

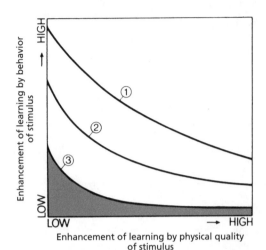

Figure 5.8 Like figure 5.7, but representing a situation in which, even for a stimulus of high physical quality, enhancement of the stimulation by some form of behavior (or movement) of the stimulus is essential for learning to occur.

one, in which progress of learning is influenced by several factors. Presumably, further research will show that the process is more complex. For instance, the amount of experience required to reach self-termination might vary to some degree with developmental age, so reality may be in between the clock and self-termination models.

In this section I want to point to an implicit assumption made in previous sections, which is that the developing bird itself is supposed to be passively "waiting" for the moment that the cumulative experience terminates the learning process. But why should it do so? It would be most adaptive if, in conditions leading to very slow learning, the young bird itself could to some extent compensate for this. This would prevent it, for instance, from being forced toward independence without sufficient knowledge of what its mates should look like, or what its song should sound like. The example I will use to illustrate this point is, I admit, a speculative one. However, its aim is to stimulate research on, rather than to prove, this possibility.

A number of estrildid finch species (the group of species to which the zebra finch belongs) have been reported to show "listening" or, as it sometimes has been called, "peering" behavior (Morris, 1958; Immelmann, 1962; Immelmann and Immelmann, 1967). Immelmann (1962) describes listening as

Table 5.2   Occurrence of listening behavior in juvenile zebra finch males, with respect to the species of their foster fathers

	Number of juvenile zebra finch males	
Species of foster father	Observed	Listening
Zebra finch	38	–
Bengalese finch	56	14

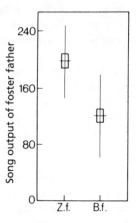

Figure 5.9   Song output by Bengalese and zebra finch fathers raising zebra finch offspring. Song output was measured when the offspring were between 30 and 55 days of age. The numbers refer to the frequency of scores indicating that a father sang within a 1.5 min period during a total of 20 hr of observation/father. Mean, S.D., and S.E.M. are given; zebra finch fathers have a significantly higher song output than do Bengalese finch fathers ($p < 0.001$; Mann–Whitney U-test).

follows: "during the singing of one male, another male perches beside him, stretches his neck until his head is close to the bill of the singing male and freezes in this posture." Although studies on the singing and song learning of zebra finches never reported its occurrence, the behavior can be shown by this species (ten Cate, 1986b). However, the conditions under which this occurs seem quite special. It was observed predominantly in juvenile males, and in particular in juvenile males having a Bengalese finch foster father, rather than a zebra finch father (table 5.2). The age at which the behavior was observed corresponded with the period for which, under similar conditions, the data of Eales (1985) suggested that young males learn their father's song, i.e., after day 35 of age. This coincidence suggests a link between listening and song learning, as has also been suggested for listening behavior shown by juvenile Bengalese finches (Dietrich, 1980). But if such a link exists, why should listening be shown with Bengalese finch fathers only, and not with conspecific ones? One possible suggestion (see ten Cate, 1986b) arises when the singing behavior of the Bengalese and zebra finch fathers is compared. Bengalese finch fathers sing less than do zebra finch fathers (figure 5.9). Also, the song of Bengalese finches is usually longer, more variable, softer, and has different acoustic features as compared with zebra finch song. Some, or the combination, of these factors might mean that the stimulation offered by a singing Bengalese finch male drops below a certain threshold needed by a young zebra finch male to enable accurate copying. By listening behavior, the young male may actively increase its exposure to Bengalese finch songs, thus enabling adequate copying. So, it

seems plausible that, *in case of low stimulation either in quantity or in quality, a developing individual might behave in such a way that it actively increases the exposure to that stimulation.*

For imprinting processes, too, there is some evidence suggesting an active role of the young bird in acquiring information. In a filial imprinting experiment, chicks and ducklings will actively work (e.g., by pressing a pedal) to present themselves with the most effective form of stimulation (Bateson, 1971).

The example of the listening behavior also illustrates another point. Had only the outcome of the learning process been studied, i.e., whether zebra finch males copied the song of either species, we might well have concluded that young zebra finches are just as capable of copying Bengalese finch song as they are of copying conspecific song. The observation of listening to Bengalese finch fathers suggests that such a conclusion might well have been wrong. Only observation of the behavior of the young birds during their development can bring to light whether active acquisition of knowledge by a juvenile bird contributes to the learning process.

Discussion

The examples discussed above illustrate a number of things. The sexual-imprinting studies demonstrate that awareness of behavioral development as a multifactorial process leads to new questions about how observed behavioral phenomena arise and how such questions can be tackled. The song-learning studies show how the interaction of several factors may operate to produce a unifying explanation for phenomena previously treated as being independent and only partially explainable. Finally, the examples emphasize a methodological point: the importance of observing the actual course of development in an individual and the experience to which it is subjected, not only to get a handle on the processes underlying behavioral change, but also, as the listening example illustrates, as the only way to discover a process.

Of course, the examples were selectively chosen to illustrate various points. Other questions about certain aspects of song-learning and imprinting processes can be asked. An important one concerns the way in which information about a stimulus is stored: What is the way in which a stimulus is internally represented? What determines the apparently limited capacity of a "memory store"? Can previously acquired knowledge of a stimulus be "erased" by a later one? Can previously acquired knowledge be overridden but still maintain an influence over behavioral output, or can such existing knowledge be "updated" under certain conditions, thus modifying a previously acquired representation and resulting in "mixed" songs or preferences? There is, for instance, some evidence that successive exposure of young zebra finch males to conspecific parents and next to Bengalese finches may produce not only males singing songs consisting of elements of both species (Clayton, 1987), but also males with a sexual preference for individuals combining elements of both species in their appearance (ten Cate, 1986c, 1987). This suggests that these males possess an internal representation consisting of a mixture of characteristics of both species. Knowledge of such phenomena is at present very limited, but nevertheless necessary to predict when and how experience terminates the learning process.

Better knowledge of the processes of song learning and imprinting raises other questions. First,

whether the way in which both processes operate makes sense against the context in which they occur in nature. Second, whether the better knowledge does tell more about what these processes are for, i.e., about the function of song learning and imprinting.

The experiments discussed above have shown that both physical qualities of, and interaction with, a stimulus may enhance the learning of its characteristics. Under the conditions occurring in nature, it seems likely that these factors will in particular promote the learning of characteristics of parents and siblings. Other individuals may lack the appropriate stimulus qualities (e.g., by singing heterospecific songs) or may have no interactions with the juveniles. In addition to this, the learning processes are highly flexible; rapid progress is made when the conditions for learning are "right," e.g., when parents are nearby and active, and learning is very limited when the conditions are "wrong," e.g., when parents are absent. The ending of learning after a specific amount of experiences has been received, rather than after a specific time period has elapsed, also seems a mechanism to produce effective learning. At the same time, an active role of the juvenile bird may prevent the sensitivity getting extended to situations in which no additional adequate learning may occur. So, the combination of the different factors suggests that, under normal circumstances, they will promote learning of a particular type of stimuli.

This conclusion highlights that, apparently, it is very important to limit learning to the characteristics of specific individuals. Why should this be so? For sexual imprinting, the coincidence in the timing of imprinting and the development of adult plumage characteristics in young birds led Bateson (1979) to suggest that imprinting is primarily a mechanism to learn the characteristics of close kin. As shown above, the "design" of the process fits with this suggestion. Learning the characteristics of kin may enable an individual to achieve a balance between inbreeding and outbreeding (Bateson, 1987b, 1980, 1982). Better knowledge of how the imprinting process operates also enabled a better assessment of how sex-related differences in mate choice arise (ten Cate, 1985b, 1988).

As for the function of song learning, this is at the moment a subject of discussion. Three different hypotheses have been suggested: Song learning may primarily have evolved as a mechanism to transfer a complex behavior pattern (a specific song type) to the next generation, to allow individuals to match their song to that of neighbors, which may have a number of advantages, or to allow identification of birds from genetically different populations, which may have an advantage in choosing mates (see Baker and Cunningham, 1985, and accompanying commentaries, for the various views on this subject). A species on which the discussion focuses is the white-crowned sparrow, and the timing of song learning in this species is used as a way to discriminate between the various hypotheses. As we have seen, the timing of the sensitivity in the white-crowned sparrow is probably more dependent on rearing conditions than was previously realized. It can therefore be doubted whether present knowledge allows a firm conclusion about when songs are learned in nature, and from what tutor. This leaves the question about the function of song learning in the white-crowned sparrow still open. Nevertheless, study of the song-learning process has helped to identify the factors which may, under natural circumstances, contribute to song learning and its timing. Measuring parameters such as exposure to song and interactions with other individuals in free-living birds seems necessary for translating the existing findings to natural conditions.

To conclude, the aim of this chapter has been to demonstrate that, however interesting and useful it is to identify participants in the developmental process, it must be seen as a fist step in studying behavioral development. Phenomena such as an own-species bias in imprinting, or a sensitive phase for song learning, may at first seem self-explanatory and well understood; they are, in fact, descriptions of the end product of dynamic processes and open to further investigation. Finally, I hope to have demonstrated that an interactive approach to development is more than just stating that life is complicated, and that it does lead to testable hypotheses and unifying explanations concerning behavioral development.

Acknowledgments

This chapter has been awarded the first Niko Tinbergen-Förderpreis by the German Ethologische Gesellschaft e.V. (the association of German ethologists). The text arose out of a talk given at the Association for the Study of Animal Behaviour 50th Anniversary meeting (June 1986). I am very grateful to Pat Bateson and Joan Stevenson-Hinde for inviting me to present that talk.

An important influence on my own development as an ethologist was exerted by Jaap Kruijt and Pat Bateson, and the ideas presented here owe much to their guidance and support over the years. They, as well as Lucy Eales, Karen Hollis, and Peter Slater, commented on the manuscript. Lucy Eales also kindly provided photographs of the sonagrams. Dick Visser prepared the figures. Writing was done while I held a Science and Engineering Research Council fellowship at the Sub-Department of Animal Behaviour at Madingley. Preparation of the final manuscript has been made possible by a fellowship of the Royal Netherlands Academy of Arts and Sciences. Hil Lochorn-Hulsebos typed the final version of the manuscript.

References

Baker, M. C., and Cunningham, M. A. (1985) The biology of bird-song dialects, *Behav. Brain Sci.*, **8**: 85–133.

Baptista, L. F. (1985) The functional significance of song sharing in the white crowned sparrow, *Can. J. Zool.*, **63**: 1741–52.

Baptista, L. F., and Morton, M. L. (1981) Interspecific song acquisition by a white crowned sparrow, *Auk*, **98**: 383–5.

Baptista, L. F., and Petrinovich, L. (1984) Social interaction, sensitive phases and the song template hypothesis in the white crowned sparrow, *Anim. Behav.*, **32**: 172–81.

Baptista, L. F., and Petrinovich, L. (1986) Song development in the white-crowned sparrow: Social factors and sex differences, *Anim. Behav.*, **34**: 1359–71.

Bateson, P. P. G. (1966) The characteristics and context of imprinting, *Biol. Rev.*, **41**: 177–220.

Bateson, P. P. G. (1971) Imprinting. In Moltz, H. (ed.), *Ontogeny of Vertebrate Behavior*, New York: Academic Press, pp. 369–78.

Bateson, P. P. G. (1976) Specificity and the origins of behavior, *Adv. Stud. Behav.*, **6**: 1–20.

Bateson, P. P. G. (1978a) Early experience and sexual preferences. In Hutchison, J. B. (ed.), *Biological Determinants of Sexual Behaviour*, London: Wiley, pp. 29–53.

Bateson, P. (1978b) Sexual imprinting and optimal outbreeding, *Nature*, **273**: 659–60.

Bateson, P. (1979) How do sensitive periods arise and what are they for? *Anim. Behav.*, **27**: 470–86.

Bateson, P. (1980) Optimal outbreeding and the development

of sexual preferences in Japanese quail, *Z. Tierpsychol.*, **53**: 231–44.

Bateson, P. (1981) Control of sensitivity to the environment during development. In Immelmann, K., Barlow, G. W., Petrinovich, L., and Main, M. (eds), *Behavioral Development*, Cambridge: Cambridge University Press, pp. 432–53.

Bateson, P. (1982) Preferences for cousins in Japanese quail, *Nature*, **295**: 236–7.

Bateson, P. (1983) Genes, environment and the development of behavior. In Halliday, T. R., and Slater, P. J. B. (eds), *Genes, Development and Learning*, Oxford: Blackwell Scientific, pp. 52–81.

Bateson, P. (1987a) Biological approaches to the study of behavioral development, *Int. J. Behav. Devel.*, **10**: 1–22.

Bateson, P. (1987b) Imprinting as a process of competitive exclusion. In Rauschecker, J. P., and Marler, P. (eds), *Imprinting and Cortical Plasticity*, New York: John Wiley, pp. 151–68.

Bateson, P. P. G., and Jaeckel, J. B. (1976) Chicks' preference for familiar and novel conspicuous objects after different periods of exposure, *Anim. Behav.*, **24**: 386–90.

Bischof, H. J. (1979) A model of imprinting evolved from neurophysiological concepts, *Z. Tierpsychol.*, **51**: 126–37.

Böhner, J. (1983) Song learning in the zebra finch (*Taeniopygia guttata*): Selectivity in the choice of a tutor and accuracy of song copies, *Anim. Behav.*, **31**: 231–7.

Brosset, A. (1971) L' "Imprinting", chez les Columbidés – Etude des modifications comportementales au cours du vieillissement, *Z. Tierpsychol.*, **29**: 279–300.

Chalmers, N. R. (1987) Developmental pathways in behavior, *Anim. Behav.*, **35**: 659–74.

Clayton, N. S. (1987) Song tutor choice in zebra finches, *Anim. Behav.*, **35**: 714–21.

Cooke, F., and McNally, C. M. (1975) Mate selection and colour preferences in lesser snow geese, *Behaviour*, **53**: 151–70.

Dickinson, A. (1980) *Contemporary Animal Learning Theory*, Cambridge: Cambridge University Press.

Dietrich, K. (1980) Vorbildwahl in der Gesangentwicklung beim Japanischen Mövchen (*Lonchura striata* var. *domestica*, Estrildidae), *Z. Tierpsychol.*, **52**: 57–76.

Eales, L. A. (1985) Song learning in zebra finches: Some effects of song model availability on what is learned and when, *Anim. Behav.*, **33**: 1293–1300.

Eales, L. A. (1987) Song learning in female-raised zebra finches: Another look at the sensitive phase, *Anim. Behav.*, **35**: 1356–65.

Gallagher, J. (1976) Sexual imprinting: Effects of various regimens of social experience on mate preference in Japanese quail (*Coturnix coturnix japonica*), *Behaviour*, **57**: 91–115.

Gallagher, J. (1977) Sexual imprinting: A sensitive period in Japanese quail (*Coturnix coturnix japonica*), *J. Comp. Physiol. Paychol.*, **91**: 72–8.

Gallagher, J. (1978) Sexual imprinting: Variations in the per-

sistence of mate preference due to difference in stimulus quality in Japanese quail (*Coturnix coturnix japonica*), *Behav. Biol.*, **22**: 559–64.

Immelmann, K. (1962) Beiträge zu einer vergleichende Biologie australischer Prachtfinken (*Sperm.*), *Zool. Jb. Syst.*, **90**: 1–196.

Immelmann, K. (1969a) Über den Einfluss frühkindlicher Erfahrungen auf die geschlechtliche Objektfixierung bei Estrildiden, *Z. Tierpsychol.*, **26**: 677–91.

Immelmann, K. (1969b) Song development in the zebra finch and other estrildid finches. In Hinde, R. (ed.), *Bird Vocalisations*, Cambridge: Cambridge University Press, pp. 61–81.

Immelmann, K. (1972a) The influence of early experience upon the development of social behavior in estrildine finches, *Proc. XV Int. Ornithol. Congr.*, The Hague, 1970, pp. 316–38.

Immelmann, K. (1972b) Sexual and other long-term aspects of imprinting in birds and other species, *Adv. Stud. Behav.*, **4**: 147–74.

Immelmann, K., and Immelmann, G. (1967) Verhaltensökologische Studien an afrikanischen und australischen Estrildiden, *Zool. Jb. Syst*, **94**: 609–86.

Immelmann, K., and Suomi, J. (1981) Sensitive phases in development. In Immelmann, K., Barlow, G. W., Petrinovich, L., and Main, M. (eds), *Behavioral Development*, Cambridge: Cambridge University Press, pp. 395–421.

Kruijt, J. P. (1962) Imprinting in relation to drive interactions in Burmese red junglefowl, *Symp. Zool. Soc. London*, **8**: 219–26.

Kruijt, J. P. (1964) Ontogeny of social behavior in Burmese red junglefowl (*Gallus gallus spadiceus*) Bonnaterre, *Behaviour Suppl. XII*, 1–201.

Kruijt, J. P. (1966) The development of ritualized displays in junglefowl, *Phil. Trans. Royal Soc. London B*, **251**: 479–84.

Kruijt, J. P. (1985) On the development of social attachments in birds, *Neth. J. Zool.*, **35**: 45–62.

Kruijt, J. P., ten Cate, C. J., and Meeuwissen, G. B. (1983) The influence of siblings on the development of sexual preferences in zebra finches, *Dev. Psychobiol.*, **16**: 223–9.

Lehrman, D. S. (1953) A critique of Konrad Lorenz's theory of instinctive behavior, *Quart. Rev. Biol.*, **28**: 337–63.

Lehrman, D. S. (1970) Semantic and conceptual issues in the nature–nurture problem. In Aronson, L. R., Tobach, E., Lehrman, D. S., and Rosenblatt, J. S. (eds), *Development and Evolution of Behavior*, San Francisco: Freeman, pp. 17–52.

Lorenz, K. (1935) Der Kumpan in der Umwelt des Vogels, *J. Ornithol.*, **83**: 137–213, 289–413.

Lorenz, K. (1937) The companion in the bird's world, *Auk*, **54**: 245–73.

Marler, P. (1970) A comparative approach to vocal learning: Song development in white crowned sparrows, *J. Comp. Physiol. Psychol. Monogr.*, **71**: 1–25.

Morris, D. (1958) The comparative ethology of grassfinches

(*Erythrurae*) and Mannikins (*Amadinae*), *Proc. Zool. Soc. Lond.*, **131**: 389–439.

Oyama, S. (1985) *The Ontogeny of Information*, Cambridge: Cambridge University Press.

Payne, R. B. (1981) Song learning and social interaction in indigo buntings, *Anim. Behav.*, **29**: 688–97.

Pepperberg, J. M. (1985) Social modelling theory: A possible framework for understanding avian learning, *Auk*, **102**: 854–64.

Petrinovich, L., and Baptista, L. (1987) Song development in the white-crowned sparrow: Modification of learned song, *Anim. Behav.*, **35**: 961–74.

Price, P. H. (1979) Developmental determinants of structure in zebra finch song, *J. Comp. Physiol. Psychol.*, **93**: 260–77.

Schutz, F. (1965) Sexuelle Prägung bei Anatiden, *Z. Tierpsychol.*, **22**: 50–103.

Slater, P. J. B. (1983) Chaffinch imitates canary song elements and aspects of organization, *Auk*, **100**: 493–5.

Sluckin, W. (1972) *Imprinting and Early Learning*, 2nd edn, London: Methuen.

ten Cate, C. (1982) Behavioral differences between zebra finch and Bengalese finch (foster) parents raising zebra finch offspring, *Behaviour*, **81**: 152–72.

ten Cate, C. (1984) The influence of social relations on the development of species recognition in zebra finch males, *Behaviour*, **91**: 263–85.

ten Cate, C. (1985a) Differences in the interactions between zebra finch and Bengalese finch parents with conspecific versus heterospecific young, *Z. Tierpsychol.*, **67**: 58–68.

ten Cate, C. (1985b) On sex differences in sexual imprinting, *Anim. Behav.*, **33**: 1310–17.

ten Cate, C. (1985c) Directed song of male zebra finches as a predictor of subsequent intra- and interspecific social behavior and pair formation, *Behav. Proc.*, **10**: 369–74.

ten Cate, C. (1986a) Does behavior contingent stimulus movement enhance filial imprinting in Japanese quail? *Dev. Psychobiol.*, **19**: 607–14.

ten Cate, C. (1986b) Listening behaviour and song learning in zebra finches, *Anim. Behav.*, **34**: 1267–8.

ten Cate, C. (1986c) Sexual preferences in zebra finch males raised by two species, I: A case of double imprinting, *J. Comp. Psychol.*, **100**: 248–52.

ten Cate, C. (1987) Sexual preferences in zebra finch males raised by two species, II: The internal representation resulting from double imprinting, *Anim. Behav.*, **35**: 321–30.

ten Cate, C. (1988) The causation and development of sex differences in partner preferences, *Proc. XIX Int. Ornithol. Congr.* (*1986*), Ottawa (in press).

ten Cate, C., and Mug, G. (1984) The development of mate choice in zebra finch females, *Behaviour*, **90**: 125–50.

ten Cate, C., Los, L., and Schilperoord, L. (1984) The influence of differences in social experience on the development of species recognition in zebra finch males, *Anim. Behav.*, **32**: 852–60.

Todt, D., Hultsch, H., and Heike, D. (1979) Conditions affecting song acquisition in nightingales (*Luscinia megarhynchos L.*), *Z. Tierpsychol.*, **51**: 23–35.

Vidal, J.-M. (1975) Influence de la privation sociale et de "l'autoperception" sur le comportement sexuel du coq domestique, *Behaviour*, **52**: 57–83.

Vidal, J.-M. (1982) "Auto-imprinting": Effects of prolonged isolation on domestic cocks, *J. Comp. Physiol. Psychol.*, **96**: 256–67.

Warriner, C. C., Lemon, W. B., and Ray, T. S. (1963) Early experience as a variable in mate selection, *Anim. Behav.*, **11**: 221–4.

Waser, M. S., and Marler, P. (1977) Song learning in canaries, *J. Comp. Physiol. Psychol.*, **91**: 1–7.

Watson, J. S. (1972) Smiling, cooing, and "the Game," *Merrill-Palmer Quart.*, **18**: 323–39.

Watson, J. S. (1981) Contingency experience in behavioral development. In Immelmann, K., Barlow, G. W., Petrinovich, L., and Main, M. (eds), *Behavioral Development*, Cambridge: Cambridge University Press, pp. 83–9.

Watson, J. S., and Ramey, C. T. (1972) Reactions to response-contingent stimulation in early infancy, *Merrill-Palmer Quart.*, **18**: 217–27.

PART II

Theoretical Debates –
Nature/Nurture and Beyond

Introduction

The nature/nurture debate, which pervades many areas of behavioral investigation, took front and centre stage in the field of animal behavior shortly after the Second World War. The influence of European ethology was then beginning to be felt more generally in North America, and many American psychologists reacted against what they saw as a strong nativistic bias among the ethologists. The most vociferous proponent of the European side of the debate was Konrad Lorenz, one of the founding fathers of ethology, who in 1973 shared the Nobel prize for physiology with fellow ethologists Niko Tinbergen and Karl von Frisch. A quite moderate response to this debate was given by Hebb, who quietly pointed out that it is theoretically impossible to separate the effects of genes and experience on behavior. A much stronger response was given by Daniel S. Lehrman, an American psychologist, who attacked the theories of Lorenz quite vigorously on many fronts. Because of space limitations, we have included only the first part of Lehrman's critique, but these pages include his views on development.

Lorenz, not surprisingly, reacted very negatively to Lehrman's criticisms, and we include parts of his rebuttal contained in a small book published 12 years after Lehrman's critique. A significant feature of Lorenz's arguments is his point that learning itself is a phylogenetically adapted mechanism, an 'innate schoolmarm' that directs what an animal does or does not learn. We end this section with the paper Lehrman published as a reaction to Lorenz's book, Lehrman's last major paper before his untimely death. In this important paper, Lehrman notes that both he and Lorenz agree on the facts, which means that their disagreements must depend on their differing interpretations of those facts, the different meanings they give to the same words, and on the questions they find most important to ask. This analysis served to calm the debate, and most workers in the field now accept an interactionist or epigenetic view of development. A more recent exposition of this point of view has been published by Oyama (1985).

Apart from highlighting many of the issues that the nature/nurture debate has entailed, the chapters by Lehrman and Lorenz also exemplify the fact that many scientific debates are not purely scientific. Human emotions and personal animosities play an important role in the way points of view are expressed and defended.

Reference

Oyama, S. (1985) *The Ontogeny of Information*, Cambridge: Cambridge University Press.

CHAPTER 6

A Critique of Konrad Lorenz's Theory of Instinctive Behavior (*excerpt*)

Daniel S. Lehrman

Beginning about 1931, Konrad Lorenz, with his students and collaborators (notably N. Tinbergen), has published numerous behavioral and theoretical papers on problems of instinct and innate behavior which have had a widespread influence on many groups of scientific workers (Lorenz, 1931, 1932, 1935, 1937a; Lorenz and Tinbergen, 1938; Lorenz, 1939; Tinbergen, 1939; Lorenz, 1940, 1941; Tinbergen, 1942, 1948a, 1950; Lorenz, 1950; Tinbergen, 1951). Lorenz's influence is indicated in the founding of the *Zeitschrift für Tierpsychologie* in 1937 and in its subsequent development, and also in the journal *Behaviour*, established in 1948 under the editorship of an international board headed by Tinbergen.

Lorenz's theory of instinctive and innate behavior has attracted the interest of many investigators, partly because of its diagrammatic simplicity, partly because of its extensive use of neurophysiological concepts, and partly because Lorenz deals with behavior patterns drawn from the life cycle of the animals discussed, rather than with the laboratory situations most often found in American comparative psychology. These factors go far toward accounting for the great attention paid to the theory in Europe, where most students of animal behavior are

Originally published in *Quarterly Review of Biology*, **28** (1953), pp. 337–63.

zoologists, physiologists, zoo curators or naturalists, unlike the psychologists who constitute the majority of American students of animal behavior Schneirla, 1945).

In recent years Lorenz's theories have attracted more and more attention in the United States as well, partly because of a developing interest in animal behavior among American zoologists and ecologists, and partly through the receptive audience provided for Lorenz and his colleague, Tinbergen, by American ornithologists. The ornithologists were interested from the start, especially because a great part of the material on which Lorenz based his system came from studies of bird behavior, but the range of interest in America has widened considerably. Lorenz and his theories were recently the subject of some discussion at a conference in New York at which zoologists and comparative psychologists were both represented (Riess, 1949a,b), and are prominently represented in the recent symposium on animal behavior of the Society of Experimental Biologists (Armstrong, 1950; Baerends, 1950; Hartley, 1950; Koehler, 1950; Lorenz, 1950; Tinbergen, 1950), and extensively used in several chapters of a recent American handbook of experimental psychology which will be a standard sourcebook for some years to come (Beach, 1951a; Miller, 1951; Nissen, 1951).

Because Lorenz's ideas have gained wide attention, and in particular because a critical discussion of these matters should bring usefully into review Lorenz's manner of dealing with basic problems in the comparative study of behavior, a reconsideration of Lorenz's system and school seems very desirable at this time.

Lorenz's Instinct Theory

We may best represent the general characteristics of the theory under discussion in terms of a case analyzed by Lorenz and Tinbergen (1938). The many subsequent references to this case and the proffered analysis by these authors and their colleagues leave no doubt that the case and its treatment may stand as representative.

Egg-rolling in the gray goose

When a gray goose, sitting on its nest, sees an egg that has rolled out of the nest, it reacts in a characteristic fashion. It extends its head toward the egg and then, keeping its head and neck pointed toward the egg and its eyes fixed upon it, stands up and slowly steps forward to stand on the rim of the nest. Next the goose bends its neck downward and forward so that the egg rests against the underside of the bill. It then proceeds to roll the egg back into the nest by shoving it back between its legs, using the underside of the bill. At the same time that this movement of the head and neck is taking place in the sagittal plane, the goose performs side-to-side movements of the head which have the effect of balancing the egg against the under-side of the bill.

The instinctive act

The egg-rolling movement in the sagittal plane may be considered first, without reference to whatever side-to-side movements may occur, since these two types of movement are distinguished very sharply in the theory.

Lorenz and Tinbergen found that the goose's tendency to perform the sagittal movement can be "exhausted" by repeated elicitation, even though observations indicated that the muscles involved evidently are not themselves fatigued. The authors therefore concluded that what is exhausted is a central neural mechanism.

The form of the sagittal movement is always much the same, regardless of variations in the shape of the egg-object or irregularities in the path over which the egg is rolled. Furthermore, when the egg rolls away from its bill, the goose, instead of stopping the sagittal movement and reaching out toward the egg, frequently continues the sagittal movement to completion much as though an egg were present. The longer one waits after "exhaustion," the easier it is to re-elicit the act.

In connection with certain other behavior patterns, Lorenz (1937b) has noted that, after long resting intervals, the animal may perform a complete act without any external stimulus. This performance "in a vacuum" is regarded by Lorenz as the extreme case of the lowering of the threshold of elicitation after long non-exercise of the act. He calls it "Leerlaufreaktion," or "going off in a vacuum" [translated by Tinbergen (1942) as "vacuum activities"].

The sagittal movement thus has the following characteristics: (1) it displays a reaction-specific exhaustibility; (2) although released by stimuli coming from the egg, once released it remains constant in form regardless of variations in stimulation from the environment and even of the presence or absence of the original releasing stimulus; and (3) the threshold for elicitation falls continuously during non-exercise of the act.

The movement in the sagittal plane, distinguished from lateral deviations, is a typical "instinctive act" (Erbkoordination) in Lorenz's system. This "instinctive act," of course, is only a part of the total behavior pattern of egg-rolling. However, Lorenz maintains that every "instinctive" behavior pattern has as its focus such an "instinctive act" or "consummatory act" (Craig, 1918), the performance of which serves as goal for much of the rest of the pattern.

To Lorenz, *the* instinctive act is a rigidly stereotyped innate movement or movement pattern, based on the activity of a specific coordinating center in the central nervous system. In this coordinating center, there is a continuous accumulation of excitation or energy specific for the act. When the animal comes into the appropriate external situation for the performance of the act, stimuli provided by that situation release the energy, the instinctive act is performed, and some or all of the excitation is used up. The center specific for the act thus is able to coordinate the instinctive act completely independently of the receptors, so that once the act is released (i.e., elicited) its performance occurs in complete form, coordinated by impulses from the center and without any chain-reflex character. The function of the stimulus is to release or elicit the act. Once released, the act no longer depends for its form on anything outside the central nervous system. When the animal happens *not* to be in the appropriate stimulus-situation, this reaction-specific energy is presumed to be accumulated, or dammed up. Also, the greater the amount of reaction-specific energy which has accumulated, the more easily may the act be elicited and the more complete will be its form when elicited.

This picture is regarded by Lorenz as a representation of the neurophysiological basis of the above-described functional characteristics of the instinctive act. In particular, accumulation of energy in a neural center capable of determining the form and order of performance of the various movements of the act, independently of the receptors (except for a trigger-like elicitation), is postulated to explain the reaction-specific exhaustibility (using up of the specific energy), the presumed independence of the form of the act from concurrent external stimulation (reaction-specificity of the energy), and the lowering of the threshold during a non-exercise interval (i.e., when an accumulation of reaction-specific excitation is presumed to occur).

The innate releasing mechanism

If energy specific for the instinctive act can accumulate continuously in the neural center specific for that act, why is the act not continuously performed? Tinbergen (1948a) concludes that each coordinating center is normally held under inhibition by another center which functions to block impulses from the coordinating center, save under specific conditions of external stimulation. This postulated inhibiting center is called the "innate releasing mechanism." The effect of an external stimulus which elicits an instinctive act is to release the instinctive center from this inhibition.

For example, the sagittal component of the goose's egg-rolling movement is not performed continuously, even though energy specific for it is being produced continuously in the central nervous system. The movement is only performed in a par-

ticular stimulus-situation: i.e., when a smooth-outlined hard object is present near the nest. (In non-experimental situations, such an object in such a place will almost always be an egg that has rolled out of the nest.) This combination of stimuli, which is considered capable of releasing the particular instinctive act from the inhibition under which it is held by the innate releasing mechanism, is called the "innate releasing pattern." According to Lorenz and Tinbergen (1938), "The innate releasing pattern . . . [is] . . . the innately-determined readiness of an animal to respond to a particular combination of external stimuli with a particular behavior. It thus consists of an innate receptoral correlate of a combination of stimuli which, despite its relative simplicity, characterizes a certain biologically-significant situation sufficiently uniquely so that the animal will not normally perform the appropriate reaction except in that situation."

The view, then, is that the innate releasing mechanism holds the instinctive act under inhibition until there appears a specific innate releasing pattern of stimuli capable of switching off the inhibition and "triggering" an outflow of impulses from the instinctive center to the peripheral effectors.

Also, the higher the level reached by the accumulation of reaction-specific energy in the center, the more difficult is presumed to be any inhibition of the act by the releasing mechanism. Consequently, the less completely does any stimulus-combination need to fit the innate releasing pattern as a whole to elicit the act. This explanation is offered by Lorenz for the fact that the instinctive act is easier to elicit, the more time has elapsed since it was last performed. The Leerlaufreaktion thus is a breaking of reaction-specific energy through the inhibiting barrier, when such energy reaches a very high level.

The taxis

Side-to-side movements of the head, by which the goose keeps the egg balanced against the underside of the bill, unlike the sagittal movement, lack the character of centrally-preformed movement patterns. The side-to-side movements are believed to be elicited independently by contact stimulation of the underside of the bill by the egg being rolled. Whenever the egg rolls off center, a bill movement toward the side of the deviation restores the egg to the path. If the egg happens to roll free so that the bird may continue the sagittal movement without any egg, there are no accompanying side-to-side movements. When the bird is permitted to roll a cylinder, there are usually no side-to-side movements, since a cylinder is unlikely to roll from side to side in its path.

Thus the side-to-side movement is not only *elicited* by external stimuli like the sagittal movement, but is also continuously *oriented* with respect to external stimuli while being performed. In this respect lateral deviations differ fundamentally from the instinctive act, the form of which is determined centrally so that the external stimulus acts as a trigger only.

Movements like the side-to-side movements, which are continuously oriented to stimuli during their performance, are called by Lorenz orienting movements, or *taxes*. A taxis may occur simultaneously with an instinctive act (as in the case of the goose's egg-rolling), or may occur interspersed with instincts in a behavior-chain.

The stimuli releasing the act (innate releasing pattern for the instinctive act), according to Tinbergen (Tinbergen and Kuenen, 1939; Tinbergen, 1942) are not necessarily the same as those guiding it (i.e., the innate receptor pattern for the taxis). In the case of egg-rolling, for example, the instinctive act is released by a combination of visual stimuli and tactual stimuli related to the hardness of the egg, as felt by the tip of the bill in tapping. The (side-to-side) taxis, on the other hand, is released by tactual stimuli on the underside of the bill.

Appetitive behavior

The first part of the goose's reaction to the egg outside the nest is a stretching of the neck forward and downward, toward the egg. This act, according to Lorenz, has a different character from the instinctive act itself. It serves the purpose of getting the animal into the particular situation in which a specific instinctive act can be released. The act thus is truly goal-directed, according to Lorenz, who terms it "appetitive behavior" (Appetenzverhalten). He regards *all* goal-directed behavior as appetitive, in the sense that such acts are directed toward getting the animal into a situation in which some in-

stinctive act can be released. For him, appetitive behavior can be of enormous complexity, involving instincts, taxes, and learned behavior of various kinds. Such behavior normally occurs when the level of excitation in the central nervous system for any instinctive act becomes high enough. This causes the animal to become restless and active. What specific kind of activity may occur depends on the kind of animal, and on which instinct is the source of the appetitive restlessness. For example, a rat set into activity by a high level of energy specific for the instinctive act of eating (i.e., he wants to eat) may turn toward a corner of the cage, walk toward it, pick up a piece of food in its paws, bite at it, and chew it. Now, the whole sequence of behavior in this hypothetical example would be regarded by Lorenz as appetitive to the instinctive act of chewing. For him, turning toward the corner is a taxis, the walking is an instinctive act, picking up the food might be an instinct, turning the head toward the food held in the paws is a taxis, and the chewing an instinct. Which corner the rat turns toward depends on his past experience – the taxis is thus partly learned. The turning of the head toward the food in the paws, however, might be innate. [Tinbergen (1942) points out that some taxes may be learned, others innate. According to Lorenz's system, however, all instinctive acts (as distinct from taxes) are innate.]

For Lorenz, the whole complex of behavior in this example, involving instincts and taxes, learned and innate elements, has at its core the act of chewing, and is motivated by the excitation set up by the neural center for chewing. The appetitive behavior continues until the instinctive act is performed, and the specific energy is thus used up. It is important to note that according to Lorenz the goal of the appetitive behavior is the *performance* of the act, not its biological result. That is to say, in our hypothetical case, the need of which the appetitive restlessness is an expression is reduced not by the introduction of food into the stomach, but by the act of chewing. This is shown more clearly in the case of instinctive acts like courtship displays of birds, which form the goal of appetitive behavior (moving toward the female, orienting to the female, etc.) and which according to Lorenz are subject to Leerlaufreaktionen even though they do not (like chewing and swallowing) result in the satisfaction of an *apparent* peripheral tissue need.

Problems Raised by Instinct Theories

Even this brief summary brings to light several questions which ought to be critically examined with reference to the theory. These are questions, furthermore, which apply to instinct theories in general. Among them are: (1) the problem of "innateness" and the maturation of behavior; (2) the problem of levels of organization in an organism; (3) the nature of evolutionary levels of behavioral organization, and the use of the comparative method in studying them; and (4) the manner in which physiological concepts may be properly used in behavior analysis. There follows an evaluation of Lorenz's theory in terms of these general problems.

"Innateness" of behavior

The problem Lorenz and Tinbergen consistently speak of behavior as being "innate" or "inherited" as though these words surely referred to a definable, definite, and delimited category of behavior. It would be impossible to overestimate the heuristic value which they imply for the concepts "innate" and "not-innate." Perhaps the most effective way to throw light on the "instinct" problem is to consider carefully just what it means to say that a mode of behavior is innate, and how much insight this kind of statement gives into the origin and nature of the behavior.

Tinbergen (1942), closely following Lorenz, speaks of instinctive acts as "highly stereotyped, coordinated movements, the neuromotor apparatus of which belongs, in its complete form, to the hereditary constitution of the animal." Lorenz (1939) speaks of characteristics of behavior which are "hereditary, individually fixed, and thus open to evolutionary analysis." Lorenz (1935) also refers to perceptual patterns ("releasers") which are presumed to be innate because they elicit "instinctive" behavior the *first time* they are presented to the animal. He also refers to those motor patterns as innate which occur for the first time when the proper stimuli are presented. Lorenz's student Grohmann (1938), as well as Tinbergen and Kuenen (1939), speak of behavior as being innately determined because it matures instead of developing through learning.

It is thus apparent that Lorenz and Tinbergen, by "innate" behavior, mean behavior which is hereditarily determined, which is part of the original constitution of the animal, which arises quite independently of the animal's experience and environment, and which is distinct from acquired or learned behavior.

It is also apparent, explicitly or implicitly, that Lorenz and Tinbergen regard as the major *criteria* of innateness that: (1) the behavior be stereotyped and constant in form; (2) it be characteristic of the species; (3) it appear in animals which have been raised in isolation from others; and (4) it develop fully-formed in animals which have been prevented from practicing it.

Undoubtedly, there are behavior patterns which meet these criteria. Even so, this does not necessarily imply that Lorenz's *interpretation* of these behavior patterns as "innate" offers genuine aid to a scientific understanding of their origin and of the mechanisms underlying them.

In order to examine the soundness of the concept of "innateness" in the analysis of behavior, it will be instructive to start with a consideration of one or two behavior patterns which have already been analyzed to some extent.

Pecking in the chick Domestic chicks characteristically begin to peck at objects, including food grains, soon after hatching (Shepard and Breed, 1913; Bird, 1925; Cruze, 1935; and others). The pecking behavior consists of at least three highly stereotyped components: head lunging, bill opening and closing, and swallowing. They are ordinarily coordinated into a single resultant act of lunging at the grain while opening the bill, followed by swallowing when the grain is picked up. This coordination is present to some extent soon after hatching, and improves later (even, to a slight extent, if the chick is prevented from practicing).

This pecking is stereotyped, characteristic of the species, appears in isolated chicks, is present at the time of hatching, and shows some improvement in the absence of specific practice. Obviously, it qualifies as an "innate" behavior, in the sense used by Lorenz and Tinbergen.

Kuo (1932a–d) has studied the embryonic development of the chick in a way which throws considerable light on the origin of this "innate" behavior. As early as three days of embryonic age, the neck is passively bent when the heartbeat causes the head (which rests on the thorax) to rise and fall. The head is stimulated tactually by the yolk sac, which is moved mechanically by amnion contractions synchronized with the heartbeats which cause head movement. Beginning about one day later, the head first bends *actively* in response to tactual stimulation. At about this time, too, the bill begins to open and close when the bird nods – according to Kuo, apparently through nervous excitation furnished by the head movements through irradiation in the still-incomplete nervous system. Bill-opening and closing become independent of head-activity only somewhat later. After about 8 or 9 days, fluid forced into the throat by the bill and head movements causes swallowing. On the twelfth day, bill-opening always follows head-movement.

In the light of Kuo's studies the "innateness" of the chick's pecking takes on a different character from that suggested by the concept of a unitary, innate item of behavior. Kuo's observations strongly suggest several interpretations of the *development* of pecking (which, of course, are subject to further clarification). For example, the head-lunge arises from the passive head-bending which occurs contiguously with tactual stimulation of the head while the nervous control of the muscles is being established. By the time of hatching, head-bending in response to tactual stimulation is very well established (in fact, it plays a major role in the hatching process).

The genesis of head-lunging to visual stimulation in the chick has not been analyzed. In *Amblystoma*, however, Coghill (1929) has shown that a closely analogous shift from tactual to visual control is a consequence of the establishment of certain anatomical relationships between the optic nerve and the brain region which earlier mediated the lunging response to tactual stimulation, so that visual stimuli come to elicit responses established during a period of purely tactual sensitivity. If a similar situation obtains in the chick, we would be dealing with a case of intersensory equivalence, in which visual stimuli, because of the anatomical relationships between the visual and tactual regions of the brain, became equivalent to tactual stimuli, which in turn became effective through an already analyzed process of development, which involved conditioning at a very early age (Maier and Schneirla, 1935).

The originally diffuse connection between head-lunge and bill-opening appears to be strengthened by the repeated elicitation of lunging and billing by tactual stimulation by the yolk sac. The repeated elicitation of swallowing by the pressure of amniotic fluid following bill-opening probably is important in the establishment of the post-hatching integration of bill-opening and swallowing.

Maternal behavior in the rat   Another example of behavior appearing to fulfil the criteria of "innateness" may be found in the maternal behavior of the rat.

Pregnant female rats build nests by piling up strips of paper or other material. Mother rats will "retrieve" their pups to the nest by picking them up in the mouth and carrying them back to the nest. Nest-building and retrieving both occur in all normal rats; they occur in rats which have been raised in isolation; and they occur with no evidence of previous practice, since both are performed well by primiparous rats (retrieving may take place for the first time only a few minutes after the birth of the first litter of a rat raised in isolation). Both behavior patterns therefore appear to satisfy the criteria of "innateness" (Wiesner and Sheard, 1933).

Riess (pers. com.), however, raised rats in isolation, at the same time preventing them from ever manipulating or carrying any objects. The floor of the living cage was of netting so that feces dropped down out of reach. All food was powdered, so that the rats never carried food pellets. When mature, these rats were placed in regular breeding cages. They bred, but did *not* build normal nests or retrieve their young normally. They scattered nesting material all over the floor of the cage, and similarly moved the young from place to place without collecting them at a nest-place.

Female rats do a great deal of licking of their own genitalia, particularly during pregnancy (Wiesner and Sheard, 1933). This increased licking during pregnancy has several probable bases, the relative importance of which is not yet known. The increased need of the pregnant rat for potassium salts (Heppel and Schmidt, 1938) probably accounts in part for the increased licking of the salty body fluids as does the increased irritability of the genital organs themselves. Birch (pers. com.) has suggested that this genital licking may play an important role in the development of licking and retrieving of the young. He is raising female rats fitted from an early age with collars made of rubber discs, so worn that the rat is effectively prevented from licking its genitalia. Present indications, based on limited data, are that rats so raised eat a high percentage of their young, that the young in the nest may be found under any part of the female instead of concentrated posteriorly as with normal mother rats, and that retrieving does not occur.

These considerations raise some questions concerning nativistic interpretations of nest-building and retrieving in the rat, and concerning the meaning of the criteria of "innateness." To begin with, it is apparent that practice in carrying food pellets is partly equivalent, for the development of nest-building and retrieving, to practice in carrying nesting-material, and in carrying the young. Kinder (1927) has shown that nest-building activity is inversely correlated with environmental temperature, and that it can be stopped by raising the temperature sufficiently. This finding, together with Riess's experiment, suggests that the nest-building activity arises from ordinary food (and other object) manipulation and collection under conditions where the accumulation of certain types of manipulated material leads to immediate satisfaction of one of the animal's needs (warmth). The fact that the rat is generally more active at lower temperatures (Browman, 1943; Morgan, 1947) also contributes to the probability that nest-building activity will develop. In addition, the rat normally tends to stay close to the walls of its cage, and thus to spend much time in corners. This facilitates the collection of nesting material into one corner of the cage, and the later retrieving of the young to that corner. Patrick and Laughlin (1934) have shown that rats raised in an environment without opaque walls do not develop this "universal" tendency of rats to walk close to the wall. Birch's experiment suggests that the rat's experience in licking its own genitalia helps to establish retrieving as a response to the young, as does its experience in carrying food and nesting material.

Maturation-vs.-learning, or development? The isolation experiment These studies suggest some second thoughts on the nature of the "isolation experiment." It is obvious that by the criteria used by Lorenz and other instinct theorists, pecking in the chick and nest-building and retrieving in the rat are

not "learned" behavior. They fulfil all criteria of "innateness," i.e., of behavior which develops without opportunity for practice or imitation. Yet, in each case, analysis of the developmental process involved shows that the behavior patterns concerned are not unitary, autonomously developing things, but rather that they emerge ontogenetically in complex ways from the previously developed organization of the organism in a given setting.

What, then is wrong with the implication of the "isolation experiment," that behavior developed in isolation may be considered "innate" if the animal did not practice it specifically?

Lorenz repeatedly refers to behavior as being innate because it is displayed by animals raised in isolation. The raising of rats in isolation, and their subsequent testing for nesting behavior, is typical of isolation experiments. The development of the chick inside the egg might be regarded as the ideal isolation experiment.

It must be realized that an animal raised in isolation from fellow-members of his species *is not necessarily isolated from the effect of processes and events which contribute to the development of any particular behavior pattern*. The important question is not "Is the animal isolated?" but "*From what* is the animal isolated?" The isolation experiment, if the conditions are well analyzed, provides at best a negative indication that certain specified environmental factors probably are not directly involved in the genesis of a particular behavior. However, the isolation experiment by its very nature does not give a positive indication that behavior is "innate" or indeed any information at all about what the process of development of the behavior really consisted of. The example of the nest-building and retrieving by rats which are isolated from other rats but not from their food pellets or from their own genitalia illustrates the danger of assuming "innateness" merely because a *particular* hypothesis about learning seems to be disproved. This is what is consistently done by Tinbergen, as, for example, when he says (1942) of certain behavior patterns of the three-spined stickleback: "The releasing mechanisms of these reactions are all innate. A male that was reared in isolation . . . was tested with models before it had ever seen another stickleback. The . . . [stimuli] . . . had the same releaser functions as in the experiments with normal males." Such isolation is by no means a final or complete control on possible effects from experience. For example, is the "isolated" fish uninfluenced by its own reflection from a water film or glass wall? Is the animal's experience with human handlers, food objects, etc., really irrelevant?

Similarly, Howells and Vine (1940) have reported that chicks raised in mixed flocks of two varieties, when tested in a Y-maze, learn to go to chicks of their own variety more readily than to those of the other variety. They concluded that the "learning is accelerated or retarded . . . because of the directive influence of innate factors." In this case, Schneirla (1946) suggests that the effect of the chick's experience with its own chirping during feeding has not been adequately considered as a source of differential learning previous to the experiment. This criticism may also be made of a similar study by Schoolland (1942) using chicks and ducklings.

Even more fundamental is the question of what is meant by "maturation." We may ask whether experiments based on the assumption of an absolute dichotomy between maturation and learning ever really tell us *what* is maturing, or how it is maturing? When the question is examined in terms of *developmental* processes and relationships, rather than in terms of preconceived categories, the maturation-versus-learning formulation of the problem is more or less dissipated. For example, in the rat nest-building probably does not mature autonomously – and it is *not* learned. It is not "nest-building" which is learned. Nest-building develops in certain situations through a developmental process in which at each stage there is an identifiable interaction between the environment and organic processes, and within the organism; this interaction is based on the preceding stage of development and gives rise to the succeeding stage. These interactions are present from the earliest (zygote) stage. Learning may emerge as a factor in the animal's behavior even at early embryonic stages, as pointed out by Carmichael (1936).

Pecking in the chick is also an emergent – an integration of head, bill, and throat components, each of which has its own developmental history. This integration is already partially established by the time of hatching, providing a clear example of "innate" behavior in which the statement "It is innate" adds nothing to an understanding of the developmental process involved. The statement that "pecking" is innate, or that it "matures," leads

us *away* from any attempt to analyze its specific origins. The assumption that pecking grows *as* a pecking *pattern* discourages examination of the embryological processes leading to pecking. The elements out of whose interaction pecking emerges are not originally a unitary pattern; they *become* related as a consequence of their positions in the organization of the embryonic chick. The understanding provided by Kuo's observations owes nothing to the "maturation-versus-learning" formulation.

Observations such as these suggest many new problems the relevance of which is not apparent when the patterns are nativistically interpreted. For example, what is the nature of the rat's temperature-sensitivity which enables its nest-building to vary with temperature? How does the animal develop its ability to handle food in specific ways? What are the physiological conditions which promote licking of the genitalia, etc.? We want to know much more about the course of establishment of the connections between the chick's head-lunge and bill-opening, and between bill-opening and swallowing. This does *not* mean that we expect to establish which of the components is learned and which matured, or "how much" each is learned and how much matured. The effects of learning and of structural factors differ, not only from component to component of the pattern, but also from developmental stage to developmental stage. What is required is a continuation of the careful analysis of the characteristics of each developmental stage, and of the transition from each stage to the next.

Our skepticism regarding the heuristic value of the concept of "maturation" should not be interpreted as ignorance or denial of the fact that the physical growth of varied structures plays an important role in the development of most of the kinds of behavior patterns under discussion in the present paper. Our objection is to the *interpretation* of the role of this growth that is implied in the notion that the *behavior* (or a *specific* physiological substrate for it) is "maturing." For example, the post-hatching improvement in pecking ability of chicks is very probably due in part to an increase in strength of the leg muscles and to an increase in balance and stability of the standing chick, which results partly from this strengthening of the legs and partly from the development of equilibrium responses (Cruze, 1935). Now, isolation or prevention-of-practice experiments would lead to the conclusion that this part of the improvement was due to "maturation." Of course it is partly due to growth processes, *but what is growing is not pecking ability*, just as, when the skin temperature receptors of the rat develop, what is growing is not nest-building activity, *or anything isomorphic with it*. The use of the categories "maturation-vs.-learning" as explanatory aids usually gives a false impression of unity and directedness in the growth of the behavior pattern, when actually the behavior pattern is not primarily unitary, nor does development proceed in a straight line toward the completion of the pattern.

It is apparent that the use of the concept of "maturation" by Lorenz and Tinbergen as well as by many other workers is not, as it at first appears, a reference to a process of development but rather to ignoring the process of development. To say of a behavior that it develops by maturation is tantamount to saying that the obvious forms of learning do not influence it, and that we therefore do not consider it necessary to investigate its ontogeny further.

Heredity-vs.-environment, or development? Much the same kind of problem arises when we consider the question of what is "inherited." It is characteristic of Lorenz, as of instinct theorists in general, that "instinctive acts" are regarded by him as "inherited." Furthermore, inherited behavior is regarded as sharply distinct from behavior acquired through "experience." Lorenz (1937a) refers to behavior which develops "entirely independent of all experience."

It has become customary, in recent discussions of the "heredity–environment" problem, to state that the "hereditary" and "environmental" contributions are both essential to the development of the organism; that the organism could not develop in the absence of either; and that the dichotomy is more or less artificial. [This formulation, however, frequently serves as an introduction to elaborate attempts to evaluate what part, or even what percentage, or behavior is genetically determined and what part acquired (Howells, 1945; Beach, 1947a; Carmichael, 1947; Stone, 1947).] Lorenz does not make even this much of a concession to the necessity of developmental analysis. He simply states that some behavior patterns are "inherited," others "acquired by individual experience." I do not know of any statement of either Lorenz or Tinbergen which

would allow the reader to conclude that they have any doubts about the correctness of referring to behavior as simply "inherited" or "genically controlled."

Now, what exactly is meant by the statement that a behavior pattern is "inherited" or "genically controlled"? Lorenz undoubtedly does not think that the zygote contains the instinctive act in miniature, or that the gene is the equivalent of an entelechy which purposefully and continuously tries to push the organisms's development in a particular direction. Yet one or both of these preformistic assumptions, or their equivalents, must underlie the notion that some behavior patterns are "inherited" as such.

The "instinct" is obviously not present in the zygote. Just as obviously, it is present in the behavior of the animal after the appropriate age. The problem for the investigator who wishes to make a causal analysis of behavior is: How did this behavior come about? The use of 'explanatory" categories such as "innate" and "genically fixed" obscures the necessity of investigating developmental *processes* in order to gain insight into the actual mechanisms of behavior and their interrelations. The problem of development is the problem of the development of new structures and activity patterns from the resolution of the interaction of *existing* structures and patterns, within the organism and its internal environment, and between the organism and its outer environment. At any stage of development, the new features emerge from the interactions within the *current* stage and between the *current* stage and the environment. The interaction out of which the organism develops is *not* one, as is so often said, between heredity and environment. It is between *organism* and environment! And the organism is different at each different stage of its development.

Modern physiological and biochemical genetics is fast destroying the conception of a straight-line relationship between gene and somatic characteristic. For example, certain strains of mice contain a mutant gene called "dwarf." Mice homozygous for "dwarf" are smaller than normal mice. It has been shown (Smith and MacDowell, 1930; Keeler, 1931) that the cause of this dwarfism is a deficiency of pituitary growth hormone secretion. Now what are we to regard as 'inherited"? Shall we change the name of the mutation from "dwarf" to "pituitary dysfunction" and say that dwarfism is not inherited as such – that what is inherited is a hypoactive pituitary gland? This would merely push the problem back to an earlier stage of development. We now have a better understanding of the origin of the dwarfism than we did when we could only say it is "genically determined." However, the pituitary function developed, in turn, in the context of the mouse as it was when the gland was developing. The problem is: What was that context and how did the gland develop out of it?

What, then, is inherited? From a somewhat similar argument, Jennings (1930) and Chein (1936) concluded that only the zygote is inherited, or that heredity is only a stage of development. There is no point here in involving ourselves in tautological arguments over the definition of heredity. It is clear, however, that to say a behavior pattern is "inherited" throws no light on its *development* except for the purely negative implication that *certain types* of learning are not directly involved. Dwarfism in the mouse, nest-building in the rat, pecking in the chick, and the "zig-zag dance" of the stickleback's courtship (Tinbergen, 1942) are all "inherited" in the sense and by the criteria used by Lorenz. But they are not by any means phenomena of a common type, nor do they arise through the same kinds of developmental processes. To lump them together under the rubric of "inherited" or "innate" characteristics serves to block the investigation of their origin just at the point where it should leap forward in meaningfulness. [Anastasi and Foley (1948), considering data from the field of human differential psychology, have been led to somewhat the same formulation of the "heredity–environment" problem as is presented here.]

Taxonomy and ontogeny

Lorenz (1939) has very ably pointed out the potential importance of behavior elements as taxonomic characteristics. He has stressed the fact that evolutionary relationships are expressed just as clearly (in many cases more clearly) by similarities and differences in behavior as by the more commonly used physical characteristics. Lorenz himself has made a taxonomic analysis of a family of birds in these terms (Lorenz, 1941), and others have been made by investigators influenced by him (Delacour and Mayr, 1945; Adriaanse, 1947; Baerends and Baerends-van Roon, 1950). This type of analysis

derives from earlier work on the taxonomic relations of behavior patterns by Whitman (1898, 1919), Heinroth (1910, 1930), Petrunkevitsch (1926), and others.

Lorenz's brilliant approach to the taxonomic analysis of behavior characteristics has had wide influence since it provides a very stimulating framework in which to study species differences and the specific characteristics of behavior. However, it does not necessarily follow from the fact that behavior patterns are species-specific that they are "innate" as patterns. We may emphasize again that the systematic stability of a characteristic does not indicate anything about its mode of development. The fact that a characteristic is a good taxonomic character does not mean that it developed autonomously. The shape of the skull bones in rodents, which is a good taxonomic character (Romer, 1945), depends in part upon the presence of attached muscles (Washburn, 1947). We cannot conclude that because a behavior pattern is taxonomically stable it must develop in a unitary, independent way.

In addition it would be well to keep in mind that the species-characteristic nature of many behavior patterns may result partly from the fact that all members of the species grow in the same environment. Smith and Guthrie (1921) call such behavior elements "coenotropes." Further, it is not at all necessary that these common features of the environment be those which seem a priori to be relevant to the behavior pattern under study. Lorenz's frequent assumption (e.g., 1935) that the effectiveness of a given stimulus on first presentation demonstrates an innate sensory mechanism specific for that stimulus is not based on analysis of the origin of the stimulus-effectiveness, but merely on the fact that Lorenz has eliminated the major alternative *he* sees to the nativistic explanation.

Thorpe and Jones (1937) have shown that the apparently innate choice of the larvae of the flour moth by the ichneumon fly *Nemerites* as an object in which to deposit its eggs is actually a consequence of the fact that the fly larva was *fed* on the larvae of the flour moth while it was developing. By raising *Nemerites* larvae upon the larvae of *other* kinds of moth Thorpe and Jones caused them, when adult, to choose preponderantly these other moths on which to lay their eggs. The choice of flour-moth larvae for oviposition is quite characteristic of *Nemerites* in nature. In view of Thorpe and Jones' work, it would obviously be improper to conclude from this fact that the choice is based on innately-determined stimuli. Yet, before their paper was published, the species-specific character of the behavior would have been just as impressive evidence for "innateness" as species-specificity *ever* is.

Taxonomic analysis, while very important, is not a substitute for concrete analysis of the ontogeny of the given behavior, as a source of information about its origin and organization.

References

Adriaanse, M. S. C. (1947) *Ammophila campestris* Latr. und *Ammophila adriaansei* Wilcke. Ein Beitrag zur vergleichenden Verhaltensforschung, *Behaviour*, 1: 1–34.

Anastasi, A., and J. P. Foley, Jr (1948) A proposed reorientation in the heredity-environment controversy, *Psychol. Rev.*, 55: 239–49.

Armstrong, E. A. (1950) The nature and function of displacement activities, *Symp. Soc. exp. Biol.*, 4: 361–84.

Baerends, G. P. (1950) Specializations in organs and movements with a releasing function, *Symp. Soc. exp. Biol.*, 4: 337–60.

——, and J. M. Baerends-van Roon (1950) An introduction to the study of the ethology of cichlid fishes, *Behaviour*, suppl. 1: 1–242.

Beach, F. A. (1947) Evolutionary changes in the physiological control of mating behavior in mammals, *Psychol. Rev.*, 54: 297–315.

——(1951) Instinctive behavior: reproductive activities. In *Handbook of Experimental Psychology*, ed. S. S. Stevens, John Wiley & Sons, New York, pp. 387–434.

Bird, C. (1925) The relative importance of maturation and habit in the development of an instinct, *Pedagog. Semin.*, 32: 68–91.

Browman, L. G. (1943) The effect of controlled temperatures upon the spontaneous activity rhythms of the albino rat, *J. exp. Zool.*, 94: 477–89.

Carmichael, L. (1936) A re-evaluation of the concepts of maturation and learning as applied to the early development of behavior, *Psychol. Rev.*, 43: 450–70.

——(1947) The growth of the sensory control of behavior before birth, *Psychol. Rev.*, 54: 316–24.

Chein, I. (1936) The problems of heredity and environment, *J. Psychol.*, 2: 229–44.

Coghill, G. E. (1929) *Anatomy and the Problem of Behavior.* London: Cambridge University Press.

Craig, W. (1918) Appetites and aversions as constituents of instincts, *Biol. Bull., Woods Hole*, 34: 91–107.

Cruze, W. W. (1935) Maturation and learning in chicks, *J. comp. Psychol.*, 19: 371–409.

Delacour, J., and E. Mayr (1945) The family Anatidae, *Wilson Bull.*, 57: 3–55.

Grohmann, J. (1938) Modifikation oder Funktionsreifung? Ein Beitrag zur Klärung der wochselseitigen Beziehungen zwischen Instinkhandlung und Erfahrung, *Z. Tierpsychol.*, 2: 132–44.

Hartley, P. H. T. (1950) An experimental analysis of interspecific recognition, *Symp. Soc. exp. Biol.*, 4: 313–36.

Heinroth, O. (1910) Beiträge zur Biologie, namentlich Ethologie und Psychologie der Anatiden, *Int. orn. Congr.*, 5 (Berlin): 589–702.

——(1930) Ueber brammte Bewegungsweisen bei Wirbeltieren, *S. Ges. naturf. Fr., Berl.*, 1929: 333–42.

Heppel, L. A., and C. L. A. Schmidt (1938) Studies on the potassium metabolism of the rat during pregnancy, lactation and growth, *Univ. Calif. Publ. Physiol.*, 8: 189–205.

Howells, T. H. (1945) The obsolete dogmas of heredity, *Psychol. Rev.*, 52: 23–34.

——, and D. O. Vine (1940) The innate differential in social learning. *J. abnorm. (soc.) Psychol.*, 35: 537–48.

Jennings, H. S. (1930) *The Biological Basis of Human Nature.* New York: Norton.

Keeler, C. (1931) *The Laboratory Mouse.* Cambridge, MA: Harvard University Press.

Kinder, E. F. (1927) A study of the nest-building activity of the albino rat, *J. exp. Zool.*, 47: 117–61.

Koehler, O. (1950) Die Analyse der Taxisanteile instinktartigen Verhaltens, *Symp. Soc. exp. Biol.*, 4: 269–303.

Kuo, Z. Y. (1932a) Ontogeny of embryonic behavior in Aves. I. The chronology and general nature of the behavior of the chick embryo, *J. exp. zool.*, 61: 395–430.

——(1932b) Ontogeny of embryonic behavior in Aves. II. The mechanical factors in the various stages leading to hatching, *J. exp. Zool.*, 62: 453–89.

——(1932c) Ontogeny of embryonic behavior in Aves. III. The structure and environmental factors in embryonic behavior, *J. comp. Psychol.*, 13: 245–72.

——(1932d) Ontogeny of embryonic behavior in Aves. IV. The influence of embryonic movements upon the behavior after hatching, *J. comp. Psychol.*, 14: 109–22.

Lorenz, K. (1931) Beiträge zur Ethologie sozialer Corviden, *J. Orn., Lpz.*, 79: 67–127.

——(1932) Betrachtungen über das Erkennen der arteigenen Triebhandlungen der Vögel. *J. Orn. Lps.*, 80: 50–98.

——(1935) Der Kumpan in der Umwelt des Vogels. *J. Orn., Lpz.*, 83: 137–213, 289–413.

——(1937a) Ueber den Begriff der Instinkthandlung, *Folia biotheor., Leiden*, 2: 17–50.

——(1937b) Ueber die Bildung des Instinktbegriffes, *Naturwissenschaften*, 25: 289–300, 307–18, 324–31.

——(1939) Vergleichende Verhalten sforschung, *Zool. Anz.*, 12 (Suppl. band): 69–102.

——(1940) Durch Domestikation verursachte Störungen arteigenen Verhaltens, *Z. angew. Psychol. Charakterkunde*, 59: 2–81.

——(1941) Vergleichende Bewegungsstudien an Anatiden. *J. Orn., Lpz.*, 89 (Sonderheft): 194–294.

——(1950) The comparative method in studying innate behavior patterns, *Symp. Soc. exp. Biol.*, **4**: 221–68.

——, and N. Tinbergen (1938) Taxis und Instinkthandlung in der Eirollbewegung der Graugans. I, *Z. Tierpsychol.*, **2**: 1–29.

Maier, N. R. F., and T. C. Schneirla (1935) *Principles of Animal Psychology*. New York: McGraw-Hill.

Miller, N. E. (1951) Learnable drives and rewards. In *Handbook of Experimental Psychology*, S. S. Stevens, ed., pp. 435–72. New York: John Wiley.

Morgan, C. T. (1947) The hoarding instinct. *Psychol. Rev.*, **54**: 335–41.

Nissen, H. W. (1951) Phylogenetic comparison. In *Handbook of Experimental Psychology*, S. S. Stevens, ed., pp. 347–86. New York: John Wiley.

Patrick, J. R., and R. M. Laughlin (1934) Is the wall-seeking tendency in the white rat an instinct? *J. genet. Psychol.*, **44**: 378–89.

Petrunkevitsch, A. (1926) The value of instinct as a taxonomic character in spiders. *Biol. Bull., Wood's Hole*, **50**: 427–32.

Riess, B. F. (1949a) A new approach to instinct, *Sci. & Soc.*, **13**: 150–4.

——(1949b) The isolation of factors of learning and native behavior in field and laboratory studies, *Ann. N. Y. Acad. Sci.*, **51**: 1093–1102.

Romer, A. S. (1945) *Vertebrate Paleontology*. Chicago: University of Chicago Press.

Schneirla, T. C. (1945) Contemporary American animal psychology in perspective. In *Twentieth Century Psychology*, P. Harriman, ed., pp. 306–16. New York: Philosophical Library.

——(1946) Problems in the biopsychology of social organization, *J. abnorm. (soc.) Psychol.*, **41**: 385–402.

Schoolland, J. B. (1942) Are there any innate behavior tendencies?, *Genet. Psychol. Monogr.*, **25**: 219–87.

Shepard, J. F., and F. S. Breed (1976) Maturation and use in the development of an instinct, *J. Anim. Behav.*, **3**: 274–85.

Smith, P. E., and E. C. MacDowell (1930) An hereditary anterior-pituitary deficiency in the mouse, *Anat. Rec.*, **46**: 249–57.

Smith, S., and E. R. Guthrie (1921) *General Psychology in Terms of Behavior*. New York: Appleton.

Stone, C. P. (1947) Methodological resources for the experimental study of innate behavior as related to environmental factors, *Psychol. Rev.*, **54**: 342–7.

Thorpe, W. H. and F. G. W. Jones (1937) Olfactory conditioning in a parasitic insect and its relation to the problem of host selection, *Proc. Roy. Soc., B*, **124**: 56–81.

Tinbergen, L. (1939) Zur Fortpflanzungsethologie von Sepia officinalis L, *Arch. néerl. Zool.*, **3**: 305–35.

Tinbergen, N. (1942) An objectivistic study of the innate behaviour of animals. *Bibl. biotheor. Leidon*, D, **1**: 39–98.

——(1948) Physiologische Instinktforschung, *Experientia*, **4**: 121–33.

——(1950) The hierarchical organization of nervous mechanisms underlying instinctive behaviour, *Symp. Soc. exp. Biol.*, **4**: 305–12.

——(1951) *The Study of Instinct*. Oxford: Oxford University Press.

——, and D. J. Kuenen (1939) Ueber die auslösenden und die richtunggebenden Reizsituationen der Sperrbewegung von jungen Drosseln (*Turdus m. merula* L. und *T. e. ericetorum* Turton), *Z. Tierpsychol.*, **3**: 37–60.

Washburn, S. L. (1947) The relation of the temporal muscle to the form of the skull, *Anat. Rec.*, **99**: 239–48.

Whitman, C. O. (1899) Animal behavior, *Biol. Lect. mar. biol. Lab. Wood's Hole*, **1898**: 285–338.

——(1919) The behavior of pigeons, *Publ. Carneg. Inst.*, **257**: 1–161.

Wiesner, B. P., and N. M. Sheard (1933) *Maternal Behaviour in the Rat*. London: Oliver & Boyd.

CHAPTER 7

Heredity and Environment in Mammalian Behaviour

Donald O. Hebb

A persistent theme in the study of behaviour, one that has dominated psychological thought since Locke and Leibnitz at least, has been the question: What is inborn, what acquired? Is the mind *tabula rasa*? If there are no innate ideas, is there not some framework prior to all experience into which experience is received and by which it must be shaped? Is intelligence inherited, or in what proportion? And so with schizophrenia, visual form and depth, maternal behaviour, gregariousness, pugnacity, even spinal reflexes – there is no aspect of behaviour with which this debate has not been concerned at one time or another.

So far as I can now see, even to ask the question, in the form in which it is usually asked, is a symptom of confusion; a confusion, it may be added, to which I have myself contributed as handsomely as I was able. My suspicion is that I am still confused, but I hope that with your criticism and discussion we may jointly make some progress in clarification of the ideas involved, not being concerned if a final agreement among us this afternoon is too much to ask.

In view of what is to follow, it should be said that here my bias is on the nativistic[1] side. If a choice had to be made, I would support – as I have in

First published in *British Journal of Animal Behaviour*, 1 (1953), pp. 43–7.

fact supported – Hobhouse and Kohler against Thorndike and Holt, Lashley against Watson, Kallman against Alexander, as a corrective against the common overemphasis by psychologists and psychiatrists on experience and learning in behaviour. This is what I would be inclined still to do, if I had to choose sides; but the fact is that we have no such choice.

We cannot dichotomize mammalian behaviour into learned and unlearned, and parcel out these acts and propensities to the nativist, those to the empiricist. My first example is from Dennis (1940): 'Rage . . . is unlearned in this sense, that when the child has developed a purposive sequence of behaviour which can be interfered with, he will exhibit "rage" on the first occasion on which this interference occurs.' The behaviour is unlearned; but it is not possible without the learning required for the development of purposive behaviour. Again, the first time a chimpanzee baby of a certain age sees a stranger approach he is terrified. The reaction is strongest on the first occasion, it does not have to be practised, and we must say that the shyness is not learned: but it is definitely a product of learning, in part, for it does not occur until the chimpanzee has learned to recognize his usual caretakers. The shyness or fear of strangers appears at about four months of age, or six months in the human baby. The chimpanzee reared in darkness to an age at which the fear is normally at its peak is not disturbed by his first sight of a stranger, but is disturbed by it as soon as he has had sufficient opportunity to learn to recognize those who care for him daily.

Fear of strangers, therefore, or a temper tantrum is not learned and yet is fully dependent on other learning. Do we then postulate three categories of behaviour, (1) unlearned, (2) unlearned but dependent on learning, (3) learned? Perhaps instead we had better re-examine the conception of unlearned versus learned behaviour.

The two examples given are not isolated phenomena. The neurotic disturbances in dog, cat, sheep or goat described first by Pavlov (1928), and studied further by Gantt (1944), Liddell (1938) and Masserman (1943), depend on a conflict between learned modes of response and yet the breakdown itself is clearly not learned. Insight in the chimpanzee, and Kohler (1927) showed, is the occurrence of an unlearned solution to a problem; but Birch (1945) has shown that other experience must precede. I shall not multiply examples, but can refer you here to the finding that mammalian perceptions in general appear to depend, not on formal training, it is true, but on a prolonged period of patterned sensory stimulation (Senden, 1932; Riesen, 1947, 1950, 1951; Nissen, Chow & Semmes, 1951). A paper of my own is on record to the contrary (Hebb, 1937), a clear case of a biased failure to observe, since the same paper included data whose significance I did not see until certain physiological considerations had suggested another point of view (Hebb, 1949, pp. 42, 113). All that a mammal does is fundamentally dependent on his perception, past or present, and this means that there is no behaviour, beyond the level of the reflex, that is not essentially dependent on learning.

It is equally clear that no behaviour can be independent of an animal's heredity: this is so obvious, logically, that it need not be spelt out. Our conclusion then is, that all behaviour is dependent both on heredity and on environment, and all non-reflex behaviour at least involves the special effects of environmental stimulation that we call learning.

Assuming that this is conceded, however, the question may still be asked, to what extent a given piece of behaviour is dependent on one of these influences. Is it fifty-per-cent environment, fifty-per-cent heredity, or ninety to ten, or what are the proportions? This is exactly like asking how much

of the area of a field is due to its length, how much to its width. The only reasonable answer is that the two proportions are one-hundred-per-cent environment, one-hundred-per-cent heredity. They are not additive; any bit of behaviour whatever is *fully* dependent on each. What proportion of an animal's behaviour would be left if there had not been, since the moment of fertilization, the highly specialized environment necessary for the growth of the embryo; or what basis is there for thinking of this environment as not causal, but only permissive, in determining the direction of embryonic growth? The newborn mammal is 'caused' by a uterine environment acting on a fertilized ovum. Contrariwise, without the fertilized ovum and its special properties no behaviour can result; learned behaviour, further, can never be thought of as something apart from the heredity that made possible a particular kind of sensory structure and nervous system.

The last alternative is to ask how much of the *variance* of behaviour is determined by heredity, how much by the environment. This is a meaningful and useful question, capable of an intelligent answer, but the limits of meaning of the answer must be recognized. If for example by inbreeding we produce a strain of dogs in which heredity is constant and all the variance of behaviour can be attributed to environment, we have not in any way reduced the importance of heredity for the behaviour in question. In other words, such an 'analysis of variance' cannot be translated into a statement of causal relations for the individual animal. This is seen best if we classify one of our hypothetical inbred dogs in two ways: (*a*) as above, treat the animal statistically as one of a group with common heredity but different environments, and (*b*) treat it as one of a group reared precisely as that one animal was, but with varying heredities (this latter set of conditions might be achieved, including a common uterine environment, by mating a group of inbred bitches to males of diverse breeds). If the proportionate variance is regarded as an estimate of the relative importance of heredity and environment for the individual animal's behaviour, then we should have to conclude (*a*) that environment is the only important determinant, and (*b*) that heredity is the only important determinant, for the same dog's behaviour. If again, eighty per cent of the variance of neuroticism in a particular district of London is due to variations of heredity (Eysenck and Prell, 1951), this does not make environment less important than heredity for the behaviour in question. It may mean only that the relevant environmental influences are much the same throughout that district, and it does not preclude finding another sample of human beings with more similar heredity and less similar experiences, such that the degree of neuroticism varies with environment rather than heredity.

Analysis of variance, in the present sense, is an excellent tool for studying the interaction of heredity and environment, but entirely misleading if it is interpreted as isolating things that are inherited and things that are acquired. We are on solid ground if we think consistently of all behaviour as 'caused by' or fully dependent on both environment and heredity, and cast our research in the form of asking how they interact: for each given heredity, asking over what range behaviour can vary, and how it can be manipulated by control of the environment (not only the postnatal environment); or what different heredities will permit survival in each given environment, and how behaviour is correlated with them. To misuse another term of the statisticians', what we want is an analysis of covariance rather than analysis of one variable while forgetting the other.

Here the significance of the theoretical analysis by Haldane (1946) is plain. We cannot generalize freely from one small part of either continuum, hereditary or environmental. The heredity that is 'good' in one part of the environmental range may be poor in another, as in Haldane's example of the beef-producing qualities of Aberdeen Angus and Galloway cattle in favourable and unfavourable environments. In the parallel case of man's intelligence and mental health, the heredity that gives best results in an optimal environment may give the worst in a poor one. We can say nothing about such possibilities (obviously of first significance for ideas about eugenics) on the basis of data obtained in a naturalistic study, with a limited sample of heredities and a limited range of environmental variation. The necessary experiments being impossible with man, we clearly need systematic animal studies in which for any given species the widest range of genetic variation is studied over the widest sample of feasible environments, from which for the mental health problem, we must cautiously extrapolate to man.

In all this, of course, we are really dealing with the question of instinct. I am considerably indebted in my discussion to a recent address by Professor Frank Beach, entitled 'The De-Scent of Instinct', in which he recants his earlier view that instinct is a scientifically useful conception. Whether his conclusions are accepted or not, some of his points must be reckoned with.

Much of Beach's emphasis is on the consistently negative definition of instinct or instinctive behaviour: instinctive behaviour is what is not learned, or not determined by the environment, and so on. There must be great doubt about the unity of the factors that are identified only by exclusion. There is also a common tendency to identify unlearned with genetically-determined behaviour, and Beach points out that the chemical environment of the mammalian embryo, and nutritive influences on the invertebrate larva, are factors in behaviour which do not fall either under the heading of learning or under that of genetic determinants. (One might cite here the significance of the 'royal jelly' in the development of the queen bee, or the fact that the temperature at which the fruit-fly larva is kept determines bodily characteristics such as the number of legs, a feature which of course must affect behaviour.) If thus 'instinctive' is to be equated with 'unlearned', it cannot also be equated with 'genetic'. Very often when behaviour is attributed to purely genetic determinants no real experimental control of environmental influence has been made; and very often learning is excluded simply on the ground that no obvious opportunity for it was observed by the experimenter.

Let us look at this last point more closely. The crucial but implicit assumption has always been made in the study of instinct that we know what learning is and how it operates. The notion is that learning, if relevant to the instinctive act, is the practice of that act or a closely related one – at the very least, observation of the act by another animal. If therefore there has been no opportunity for such observation, and no practice, and the act is performed effectively when the proper circumstances come along, we say that the behaviour is unlearned and thus instinctive. But, as I have already tried to show, to say that behaviour is unlearned does not mean that it is independent of learning.

For our present purposes, I shall use 'learning' to refer to a stable unidirectional change of neural function, resulting from sensory stimulation (including the stimulation that results from response). There is a great deal that we do not know about learning, and we cannot assume that we know what conditions determine it. The occurrence of learning may be far from obvious. There is a great deal of visual learning, in the sense of my definition, in the period when the young mammal first opens its eyes on the world, though nothing but physical growth seems to be going on, and the fact of learning can only be discovered by comparing the normal infant with one reared without pattern vision. The experiment of Nissen, Chow and Semmes (1951) makes the same point concerning somesthetic learning, in the period when the baby seems only to be thrashing about aimlessly. This experiment is very important as showing that the importance of early learning demonstrated by Senden (1932) and Riesen (1947, 1950, 1951) is not restricted to visual function. What Nissen, Chow and Semmes did was to raise an infant chimpanzee with cardboard mailing-tubes over hands and feet, thus preventing normal tactual exploration of the environment and of the chimpanzee's own body. Subsequently, somesthetic learning and localization of tactual stimulation of various points on the body were defective. The conditions of rearing could hardly produce any failure of development in primary sensory equipment of the skin, so it appears that the more or less random tactual experience of the normally reared infant is essential to the development of somesthetic perception.

Such early visual and somesthetic learning must modify all subsequent behaviour; and there are strong indications that this does not apply only to 'higher' behaviour but to instinctive and even to reflexive responses as well. The supposedly instinctive grooming of the chimpanzee was not found in Nissen, Chow and Semmes' animal, and responses to pain stimuli, usually considered reflexive, were atypical. The preliminary experiments of Riess and of Birch (cited by Beach, 1951, p. 424) on the relation of early experience to maternal behaviour in rats, Lorenz's studies of imprinting in birds and Thorpe's studies of early environmental influences on the subsequent behaviour of both birds and insects, all imply that the behaviour that ordinarily is 'species-predictable', and independent of special experience, is not independent of the experience that is ordinarily inevitable for all members of the species. It has appeared to me in the past that instinctive behaviour, especially in nonmammals, is correlated closely with unvarying genetic factors and not with the varying environment. But is this true? Is the environment so completely variable? It seems to me now that certain essentials of the environment are actually constant – just as constant as the animal's heredity; and therefore that we have no logical basis for giving the one correlation, that with heredity, any greater emphasis than the other correlation, with environment.

I propose consequently that we must study both variables together, in the nonmammalian world as well as the mammalian. My difficulty with the ethological programme as laid out by Tinbergen, in terms of first studying the innate before studying learning, is that it is logically impossible. 'Innate behaviour is behaviour that has not been changed by learning processes' (Tinbergen, 1951, p. 2) and we must know when and where learning occurs before we can say what this behaviour is; just as the 'learning theorist' must know what growth processes do to behaviour before he can certainly say what learning does in the growing infant. Evidently we cannot separate the two tasks; they must be carried out together.

It seems to me therefore that the ethologist is in fact studying learning perhaps without always intending to do so, just as the psychologist who works out the rules of learning for the laboratory rat is, again perhaps without intending it, really defining the hereditary potential of this animal's behaviour. Psychologists need the co-operation of the ethologists with their biological background and their demonstrated brilliance in experimental analysis. Psychology in North America has often been narrow, short-sighted, in its emphasis on one factor in behaviour: I should like to urge that ethology should not vie in narrowness, in another direction. Actually, North American psychologists, like their colleagues in England and elsewhere, are now generally alive to the great significance of your ethological studies (although as one might expect there are differences of opinion where it comes to interpretation) and it seems if our lines of communication can be kept open that there are great scientific benefits to be had, in the recognition that in the study of certain variabilities in behaviour (learning) and in the study of certain constancies of behaviour (instinct) it is the same problem that is being attacked. After all, ethology, defined as the scientific study of behaviour (Tinbergen, 1951), is coterminous with psychology, which has the same definition.

Much of the apparent disagreement between the two disciplines is in matters of terminology, in verbal statements of problem or conclusions, so I shall sum up my remarks by returning to this question: what sort of statement can be usefully and logically made about the relationship between environment or heredity, on the one hand, and behaviour on the other?

I would not suggest for a moment that the problems in this area are unreal; I do suggest that they have been poorly stated, inasmuch as we cannot dichotomize behaviour into learned and unlearned, environmentally determined and hereditarily determined. I urge that there are not two kinds of control of behaviour, and that the term 'instinct', implying a mechanism or neural process independent of environmental factors, and distinct from the neural processes into which learning enters, is a completely misleading term and should be abandoned. 'Instinctive behaviour' may be nearly as misleading, but it might be kept as a convenient designation for species-predictable behaviour, as long as it is thought of, not as determined by an invariant heredity alone, but also by an environment that is equally invariant in most or all important matters. Instinctive behaviour therefore is not valid as an analytical conception, though it may be useful as a rough descriptive term.

However, it is not enough to make destructive criticism alone, especially in a field where it is clear that important theoretical issues are involved. However well or ill-conceived the term instinct may be, or how well-framed the traditional question of environmental or hereditary control of behaviour, there is something here that we must deal with theoretically and about which we must be able to make positive statements.

In distinguishing hereditary from environmental influence, therefore, I conclude that it is reasonable and intelligible to say that a difference in behaviour from a group norm, or between two individuals, is caused by a difference of heredity, or a difference of environment; but not that the deviant behaviour is caused by heredity or environment alone. The fact that we speak English *instead* of French is determined by environment alone; but speaking English is not caused by environment independent of heredity, for no environment can make a dog or cat (or chimpanzee) speak either language, English or French. Making the reference to a difference or deviation really implies, *With environment held constant*, heredity has such and such effects (or vice versa, with heredity constant); it does not say that the behaviour is due to heredity alone. If this is correct, we can also quite accurately speak of the variance due to environment or heredity: variance again being a reference to deviations. We will, I believe, not only pay a proper respect to logic but also plan our experiments better if we speak and think of the effect that environmental influence has on a given heredity, or, in dealing with the differences between heredities, specify the environment in which they are manifested. The behaviour one can actually observe and experiment with is an inextricable tangle of the two influences, and one of them is nothing without the other.

Note

1 This term may need explanation. The repeated denial that Gestalt psychology is nativistic is unintelligible to me, in view of the powerful Gestalt criticism of empiricistic treatments of perception and intelligence, unless 'nativism' is considered to have its nineteenth-century meaning of innate ideas, so it should be noted that my use of the term implies only an opposition to extreme empiricism, or an emphasis on the obvious importance of hereditary factors in behaviour.

References

Beach, F. A. (1951) Instinctive behaviour: Reproductive activities. Chapter 12 in S. S. Stevens (ed.), *Handbook of Experimental Psychology*, New York: Wiley, pp. 387–434.

Birch, H. G. (1945) The relation of previous experience to insightful problem-solving, *J. Comp. Psychol.*, 38, 367–83.

Dennis, W. (1940) Infant reaction to restraint: An evaluation of Watson's theory, *Trans. N.Y. Acad. Sci.*, Ser. 2, 2, 202–18.

Eysenck, H. J., and Prell, D. B. (1951) The inheritance of neuroticism: An experimental study, *J. Ment. Sci.*, 97, 441–65.

Gantt, W. H. (1944) Experimental basis for neurotic behaviour: Origin and development of artificially produced disturbances of behaviour in dogs, *Psychosom. Med. Monog.*, 3, nos. 3 and 4.

Haldane, J. B. S. (1946) The interaction of nature and nurture, *Ann. Eugen.*, **13**, 197–205.

Hebb, D. O. (1937) The innate organization of visual activity, I: Perception of figures by rats reared in total darkness, *J. Genet. Psychol.*, **51**, 101–26.

——(1949) *Organization of Behaviour*, New York: Wiley.

Kohler, W. (1927) *The Mentality of Apes*, 2nd edn, New York: Harcourt, Brace.

Liddell, H. S. (1938) The experimental neurosis and the problem of mental disorder, *Amer. J. Psychiat.*, **94**, 1035–43.

Masserman, J. H. (1943) *Behaviour and Neurosis*, Chicago: University of Chicago Press.

Nissen, H. W., Chow, K. L., and Semmes, Josephine (1951) Effects of restricted opportunity for tactual, kinesthetic, and manipulative experience on the behaviour of a chimpanzee, *Amer. J. Psychol.*, **64**, 485–507.

Pavlov, I. P. (1928) *Lectures on Conditioned Reflexes*, New York: International.

Riesen, A. H. (1947) The development of visual perception in man and chimpanzee, *Science*, **106**, 107–8.

——(1950) Arrested vision, *Scient. Amer.*, **183**, 16–19.

——(1951) Post-partum development of behaviour, *Chicago Med. Sch. Quart.*, **13**, 17–24.

Senden, M. v. (1932) *Raum- und Gestultffassung bei operierten Blindegeborenen vor und nach der Operation*, Leipzig: Barth.

Tinbergen, N. (1951) *The Study of Instinct*, Oxford: Oxford University Press.

CHAPTER 8

Evolution and Modification of Behavior (*excerpt*)

Konrad Lorenz

Introduction

What is preformed in the genome and inherited by the individual is not any "character," such as we can see and describe in a living organism, but a limited range of possible forms in which an identical genetic blueprint can find its expression in phenogeny. The way in which this takes place has been well enough analyzed by the sciences of genetics and pheno-genetics, at least in some paradigmatic cases. The term "innate" should never, on principle, be applied to organs or behavior patterns, even if their modifiability should be negligible. N. Tinbergen and many other ethologists writing in English, have, therefore, altogether ceased to use the word innate, or, to be more exact, they continue to apply it only to differences appearing between behavioral or morphological characters developed by individuals reared under identical environmental conditions.

There are two debatable points about this way of applying the term: the first question is how we define "character," and the second is whether the conception of a "strictly identical environment" is operationally valid. Nobody, however, doubts that it is the most convincing proof of heredity when

From K. Z. Lorenz, *Evolution and Modification of Behavior* (Chicago: University of Chicago Press, 1965), pp. 1–27, 79–82.

hybrids of known parentage reared under identical conditions develop characters whose differences from each other are clearly correlated with those existing between the parent species and concur with the known laws of inheritance, as for instance, in the dabbling duck hybrids bred by von de Wall (1963). In the F_1 generation, these birds developed patterns of courtship behavior that were either roughly intermediate between those of the parental species, or showed ancestral characters existing in a large number of other ducks but in neither of the parental species. In the F_2 generation, the motor patterns of the individuals differed widely, showing many new combinations of recognizable characters found in the grandparent species.

The genetic hybridization experiment is not, however, the only occasion on which we have need of a term, and, commendable though semantic purism may be, it leaves us without a word denoting an indispensable concept. We did mean something when we spoke of an innate motor pattern or an innate releasing mechanism, and it is not just semantic carelessness if some of us tend to use the rather cumbersome expression, "what we formerly called innate." What indeed? The obvious need for a term is a sure indication that a concept which corresponds to something very real does exist. The aim of this book is to find out what this reality is and to define this concept. This attempt will imply first, a detailed critique of some widely held views concerning the concept of the "innate" and second, a discussion of the value and the limitations of the deprivation experiment, of the assertions which it enables us to make, and of the methodological rules that must be observed in its application.

Theoretical Attitudes toward the Concept of the "Innate"

Three distinct attitudes regarding the concept of "what we formerly called innate" are sufficiently important to merit discussion. I believe that I can show some serious logical and biological fallacies in the first, which is held by the majority of American psychologists. The second is the one taken by most modern English-speaking ethologists, who, in my opinion, have lost hold of an all-important concept, partly from overcaution, partly because they wished to compromise with behavioristic critique, but mostly in consequence of a rebound phenomenon on discovering some errors in the "naïve" attitude which Heinroth and other older ethologists assumed toward the concept of the innate and which must also be criticized in this book.

Most American psychologists, whom for brevity's sake and with some incorrectness, I shall here subsume under the concept of "Behaviorists," maintain, more or less unanimously, that the "dichotomy" of behavior into innate and learned elements is not "analytically valid." This statement is supported by two arguments. The first of these asserts that the dichotomy is only the result of "begging the question" as hitherto the only definition of the "innate" is that which is not learned and vice versa. Hebb (1953) writes, "The identity of factors only identified by exclusion must be strongly doubted" and "I strongly urge that there are not two kinds of factors determining animal behavior and that the term 'instinct' is completely misleading, as it implies a nervous process or mechanism which is independent of environmental factors and different from those nervous processes into which learning enters."

The second argument, emphasized by Lehrman (1953), contends that, even if the existence of behavior elements which are independent of learning cannot be entirely ruled out, the concept of innate behavior is nevertheless without heuristic value because it will never be practically possible to exclude

the participation of learning in the early ontogenetic processes in the egg or *in utero*, which are inaccessible to observation.

Clearly distinct from the behaviorist's attitude, yet superficially somewhat similar, is that taken by Tinbergen (1955, 1963) and a great number of other modern ethologists. Although they have dropped the word "innate" for the terminological reasons already mentioned, they are, of course, fully aware that there really are two entirely independent mechanisms affecting adaptation of behavior: the process of phylogeny, which evolves behavior as well as any other structural and functional organization, and the processes of adaptive modification of behavior during the individual's life. In spite of agreeing, on principle, with this "dichotomy," these scientists take the attitude that practically all behavior, down to its smallest units, owes its adaptedness to both of the above adaptive processes and that the types of behavior which we formerly described as "innate" and "learned" represent only the two extremes in a continuum of gradation in which all possible mixtures and blendings of the two sources of adaptation can be found. That these two extremes actually occur and do so with a surprising frequency is fully recognized but explained by the tentative and rather arbitrary assumption that the extremes, being of particular survival value, are favored by selection pressure more than the intermediate forms.

As a consequence of this attitude, any attempt to separate phylogenetically and individually adapted characters and properties of behavior, either conceptually or in the course of practical experiments, must necessarily be considered as hopeless and devoid of sense, as any trait of behavior, however minute, is automatically regarded, on principle, as being influenced by both factors achieving adaptation. This highly dangerous opinion is often supported by an argument based on some practical limitations inherent in the deprivation experiment (p. 83).

The third and most controversial attitude rests on the assumption that instinctive and learned behavior "come in chunks" which can be clearly separated from each other, as implied by *Instinkt-Dressur-Verschränkung* (intercalation of fixed pattern and learning), which I proposed more than thirty years ago. On the basis of this assumption, the obvious trend in the evolution of behavior in the direction of greater plasticity and increasing influence of learning and insight has to be regarded at least as much as a consequence of reduction and disintegration of innate fixed patterns as of higher development of those functions which, in the individual's life, affect adaptive modification of behavior.

Critique of the First Behavioristic Argument

It is simply not true that "what we formerly called innate" and "what we formerly called learned" can only be defined one by the exclusion of the other. Like another fundamental error, which will be criticized in the discussion of the second behavioristic argument, this fallacy arises if one forgets that it must never be regarded as a product of chance or taken as a matter of course when behavior is found to be adapted to a corresponding point of the species' environment. "Adaptation" is the process which molds the organism so that it fits its environment in a way achieving survival. Adaptedness is always the irrefutable proof that this process has taken place. Any molding of the organism to its environment is a process so closely akin to that of forming, within organic structure, an image of the environment that it is completely correct to speak of information concerning environment being acquired by the organism.

There are only two ways this can happen. The first is the interaction between the organism and its environment. In this process it is the species which, by means of mutation and selection, achieves adaptedness insuring survival. All the complicated structures and functions of the chromosomes, including mutation and sexual reproduction, are a mechanism evolved in the service of the function of acquiring and storing information on the environment. A very close functional analogy exists between trial-and-error learning and the way in which part of the progeny is risked in the "experiment" of mutation, a part which is cautiously measured by a mutation rate, which does not jeopardize the survival of the species and, therewith, the hoard of information already stored. Probably one of the chief functions of sexual reproduction is to disseminate new information quickly among a population.

Campbell (1958) has called attention to the fact that the procedure by which a species attains information about its environment is virtually identical with that of pure induction and is devoid of the deductive processes which guide human experimentation. The information thus gained is stored in the genes, which for this reason have been aptly described as "coded information" by geneticists.

The organization which achieves all this obviously must have been evolved on our planet at a very early stage in the history of life. We know that all higher animals and plants are descended from organisms which had already "invented" a nucleus with chromosomes performing these functions. With the advancement of biochemical knowledge concerning analogous processes in the very lowest organisms, in bacteria and viruses, we are seriously confronted, however, with the question whether the origin of these mechanisms for acquiring information might not be identical with the origin of life itself.

The second way by which information on the environment can be fed into the organic system is the interaction between the individual and its surroundings. Every response-eliciting stimulus impinging on the organism represents information on environment being received by the animal, even if this information only determines when and where a certain mechanism of behavior is activated without, however, affecting any adaptive change in the mechanism itself. All "reflexes," releasing processes, etc. as well as all orientation responses, or taxes, belong to this category.

Among all the mechanisms serving the gain of immediately exploited information, those achieving orientation in space stand apart insofar as they determine not only at what moment but also in what direction a motor pattern is to be discharged. These mechanisms imparting instantaneous temporal and spatial information are, in their more highly developed forms, largely identical with what is called intelligence in common parlance. Subjectively, their successful function is accompanied by the experience of "insight." They very often produce "learning" and frequently are its prerequisite. They are, however, totally independent of learning; they function even in the lowest unicellular organisms which do not learn.

Particularly on the basis of one constitutive property, these mechanisms must be conceptually distinguished from learning. This has been pointed out by Russell (1958–61). The processes that are under discussion here achieve an instantaneous adaptation of behavior to the environmental requirements of the moment; they do not cause a modification in the mechanism of the response but are themselves the function of the highly differentiated, phylogenetically adapted mechanisms, which, incidentally, are largely identical with what Pavlov called unconditioned reflexes.

Learning, on the other hand, is closely akin to the phylogenetical processes already discussed in its all-important function of not only acquiring, but also storing, information. We do not know as yet how this storing is achieved. It might be done by adaptively modifying neural structure, or, as some biochemists tentatively like to assume, by coding information in chain molecules in the way phylogenetical information is retained. But whatever the mechanism, adaptive modification of a function cannot take place without corresponding modification of the structure underlying it. The enormous difference in their respective time scales and in their physiological mechanisms notwithstanding, the functional analogies between the phylogenetical and the individual processes of acquiring and storing information are such that Russell seems well justified in creating a concept encompassing both.

Our absolute ignorance of the physiological mechanisms underlying learning makes our knowledge of the causation of phyletic adaptation seem quite considerable by comparison. Our conviction that Darwin's concepts correspond to realities is based on facts that grow more solid year by year and have lately received an unshakeable foundation from the modern results of biochemistry. Hence, when we talk of phylogenetic adaptation and the processes underlying it, we use concepts based on and defined by causal insights. When we put phylogenetic adaptation of behavior in antithesis to learning, we must bear in mind that the two concepts are arrived at in different ways. Learning, unlike phylogenetic adaptation, can be defined only descriptively and functionally and, moreover, only by what Hassenstein (1954) has termed an "injunctive" definition, that is, by an enumeration of a number of part-constitutive properties. Most biological concepts, including that of life itself, can only be defined injunctively. Every single one of its

part-constitutive properties: assimilation, metabolism, growth, and reproduction can be found in some non-organic model; all of them together make life. Hence, every injunctive concept has a hard core in which its applicability is unquestionable, although, on its margins, it merges into neighboring concepts without a strictly delineable border. A purely injunctive and, since we know nothing about its physiological causation, purely functional definition of learning must lack any sharp delineation. The core of the concept will be represented by classic conditioning and other "higher" forms of learning, and marginally it will merge imperceptibly into more lowly forms of adaptive modification of behavior.

On the receptor side, more highly specific habituation via sensory adaptation will form a gradation leading to processes that one would not call learning at all. On the motor side, acquiring skills through practice will grade into more simple forms of facilitation by exercise and further into the unspecific effect of activity which, by preventing the atrophy otherwise seizing many inactive structures, forms a simple prerequisite for the normal phenogeny of the organ. Although well aware of all this, I propose, for the purposes of this book, to define learning in a much too comprehensive way, including all adaptive modifications of behavior. Any workable definition of learning must unconditionally contain, as its most indispensable part-constitutive property, the character of survival value or adaptiveness, as Thorpe pointed out in 1956.

Whatever else learning may be, it certainly is an adaptive modification of behavior, and its adaptiveness, that is, its ability to adapt behavior, needs a causal explanation. There is an infinitesimally small chance that modification, as such, is adaptive to the particular environmental influence that happened to bring it about. Indeed, this chance is not greater than that of a mutation being adaptive. Geneticists rate this likelihood at about 10^{-8}. Whenever we do find a clearly adaptive range of modifiability, for instance, when we find that the thickness of fur is adaptively modified by influences of the climate in very many mammals or that plants stretch farther upward the less light they get, we know that these achievements of adaptation are due not exclusively to environmental influences, but just as much to a very specialized range of modifiability which has been selected for in the pre-history of the species.

The more complicated an adapted process, the less chance there is that a random change will improve its adaptedness. There are no life processes more complicated than those which take place in the central nervous system and control behavior. Random change must, with an overpowering probability, result in their disintegration. Blithely assuming that "learning" (whatever that may be) automatically achieves adaptive improvement of behavior mechanisms implies neither more nor less than the belief in a pre-stabilized harmony between organisms and environment. The amazing and never-to-be-forgotten fact is that learning does, in the majority of cases, increase the survival value of the behavior mechanisms which it modifies. The rare instances in which this survival function miscarries serve to illustrate rather than to negate this – but this fact itself demands an explanation.

I regard it as highly paradoxical that many American psychologists not only seem to forget this, but actually stigmatize as "preformationistic" the theories of ethologists who take into consideration that some information underlying an individual's behavior has indeed been "pre-formed" by the species. This type of psychologist probably finds it so very easy to forget the questions of survival function and phylogenetic origin of behavior in general and of learning in particular, because their experimental setups deviate from the natural surroundings of the species investigated to such an extent that it becomes all too easy to overlook the survival function of behavior altogether and, therewith, the selection pressure which caused its mechanisms to evolve. To anyone tolerably versed in biological thought, it is a matter of course that learning, like any function of comparably high differentiation and survival value, must necessarily be performed by a very special mechanism built into the organic system in the course of its evolution. The indubitable fact that every learning mechanism is phylogenetically evolved is in no way contradicted by the other fact that a learning mechanism is evolved to exploit individual experience. Both facts together inescapably raise the question of how this learning mechanism achieves the task of choosing among innumerable possibilities of behavior those for reinforcement which develop positive survival value and, for extinction, those which are detrimental to the individual or the species.

In the days of classic behaviorism, it was assumed that the fulfillment of primary bodily needs tended to reinforce, and that any bodily damage tended to extinguish the type of behavior which happened to precede these effects, thus directing the learning process toward survival value (Thorndike, 1911). Although still assuming that the organism, in some unexplained manner, should "know" what is good and bad for it, this theory not only bears in mind that an explanation is needed for the survival value of learning, but even tentatively offers one which is not too far from reality. There must be some neural mechanisms which, on their afferent side, are rooted in the homeostatic cycles of elementary vegetative and metabolic processes, and which report to the central nervous system any deviation from that particular steady state which is desirable for survival. In our own subjective experience, the report of such a disturbance is correlated with the diffuse feeling of illness which cannot be localized. With the mechanism of pain, obviously less elaborately organized on its receptor side, the accent lies on reporting the localization of the disturbance. The survival function of both organizations indubitably lies in the strong extinguishing and reinforcing effects produced by the waxing and waning of their reports.

The function of a very generalized "illness receptor" could perhaps furnish a tentative explanation for the amazing results which Richter (1954) obtained when he supplied his experimental animals with foodstuffs disintegrated into their component parts and left it to the subjects to resynthesize a balanced diet. Even when the amino acids of the necessary proteins were offered separately, the rats, as subsequent weighings showed, took just the right percentage of each constituent. Animals deprived of the adrenal cortex proved to be able to compensate for the disturbance which the operation caused in their salt metabolism by eating a correspondingly increased amount of NaCl.

The most intriguing question posed by these findings is: from whence does the organism obtain the information telling it what chemicals are needed in its metabolism at a given moment, and how are these to be recognized when encountered in the environment. We know of one case at least in which a special releasing mechanism achieves the recognition of a needed chemical: birds lacking calcium will peck at and eat any white, hard, and crumbling substance, regardless of its chemical composition, obviously guided by visual and tactile stimuli rather than chemical ones. I have known birds to poison themselves by eating carbide. It is, however, enormously improbable that similar phylogenetically evolved perceptual organizations are lying in readiness for each of the very special needs selectively supplied in Richter's experiments. His rats were, in all probability, the first ones in the evolutionary history of their species to synthesize protein from its component amino acids. It is a tempting, if untested, hypothesis that the animal tentatively eats just a little of each substance offered to it and forms an engram of "how it feels afterward." This provisional assumption is supported by the fact that omnivorous animals invariably at the first encounter eat very little of any unknown food. Similar considerations might apply to the compensation of salt intake by adrenalectomized rats.

Hull's (1943) important and indubitably correct assertion that all relief of tension acts as a reinforcement on the behavior which preceded it also presupposes the function of a built-in mechanism which, with a similarly wide range of applicability as the one just discussed, is able to direct learning toward survival value in the most varied environmental situations. Appetites and aversions, regarded by Craig (1918) as diametrically opposed types of behavior, have one structural property in common. In both cases, "purposive" behavior modifiable by learning is directed at a reinforcing external and internal stimulus situation which results in a marked relief of tension. The physiological difference lies only in the provenience of this tension. In the case of appetitive behavior, it is caused by the internal generation of endogenous stimuli pertaining to the instinctive movements which appetitive behavior is striving to "discharge." In the case of aversion, the tension is directly caused by a disturbing external situation. The organism tries to rid itself of this situation by "appetitive behavior directed at states of quiescence," as Meyer-Holzapfel (1940) more objectively describes aversion.

All the teaching mechanisms hitherto mentioned contain phylogenetically acquired information that tells the organism which of the consequences of its behavior must be repeatedly attained and which ought to be avoided in the interest of survival. This information is preponderantly localized in the perceptual organizations which respond selectively to certain external and/or internal configurations of stimuli and report them, with a plus or minus sign added, to the central mechanisms of learning.

As in the teaching mechanism just discussed, this information is frequently couched in very generalized, "abstract" terms. The organization of perceptual patterns is always confronted with the alternative of achieving either high selectivity or general applicability, or of compromising between these two properties which, in their higher degrees of differentiation, obviously cannot be achieved simultaneously. In perceptual patterns in which, as in the reinforcing mechanisms just discussed, a very general applicability is imperative, it can only be attained at the cost of low selectivity. In other words, the organism is unavoidably exposed to the dangers incurred by a correspondingly great probability of its perceptual reinforcing mechanisms miscarrying. In many omnivorous animals, for example, a mechanism exists that causes them to prefer food with a minimum content of fiber and a maximum of sugar, fat, and starch. In the "normal" conditions of wild life, this phylogenetically adapted releasing mechanism is of obvious survival value, but in civilized man it gives rise to a search for supernormal objects, the addiction to which actually amounts to a vice detrimental to health (e.g., white bread, chocolate, etc., which cause constipation and obesity in millions). In closely analogous manner, another important teaching mechanism can miscarry, that is, a mechanism which acts on the generally reliable "hypothesis" that a situation affording relief of tension is also one desirable in the interest of survival. As is to be expected, the mechanism also responds to all drugs causing relief of tension and thus conditions men and cats (Masserman, 1943) to become alcoholics and tranquilizer addicts.

The limited probability of a behavior mechanism thus miscarrying is no threat to the survival of the species, and it is still less of an argument against the well-based assumption that the mechanism in question is, under normal circumstances, of great survival value. Quite and contrary; the disturbance offers valuable insight into the causal structure by whose function that survival value is achieved.

It is childishly easy to construct thought models or machines which will "learn something," that is to say their functional properties will get altered by previous functioning. It is even difficult to devise any complicated electronic apparatus which is not susceptible to such changes, but it is immensely difficult to invent even a thought model of a system in which the change of function caused by functioning will always be in the direction of supporting, regulating, and repairing that system. The central problem of all reinforcing and/or extinguishing mechanisms lies in their content of innate information telling them what is "good" and what is "bad" for the organism. It is only on the assumption of a prestabilized harmony between the organism and its environment that one can dispense with an explanation for the survival value of learning and with an investigation of the innate information contained in the teaching mechanisms achieving it.

The "dichotomy" of behavior into "innate" and "learned" components is indeed misleading but in a sense directly opposed to that implied by Hebb (1953). The assumption that learning "enters into" every phylogenetically adapted behavior mechanism is neither a logical necessity nor in any way supported by observational and experimental fact. Although practically every functional unit of behavior contains individually acquired information in the form of a stimulus-input which releases and directs reflexes, taxes, etc. (p. 116) and thus determines the time and the place at and in which the behavior is performed, it is by no means a logical necessity that adaptive modification of behavioral mechanisms is invariably concerned in the survival function of these short-notice responses. These responses, in their very essence, are the opposite of "what we formerly called learned," being, indeed, as already mentioned, what Pavlov has termed "unconditioned reflexes."

On the other hand, it is, for the reasons already expounded, an inescapable logical necessity to assume that learning, like any other organic function regularly achieving survival value, is performed by organic structures evolved in the course of phylogeny under the selection pressure of just that survival value. All observational and experimental evidence goes to confirm this assumption. None contradicts it.

Besides the two channels represented (a) by the adaptive processes of evolution, and (b) by individual acquisition of information, no third possibility exists for information being "fed into" the organic system. Whenever and wherever a behavior pattern shows structure adapted to a corresponding point of environment, one or both of these processes must be assumed to have taken place; and it is, at least in principle, always possible to ascertain what part each of them has played. No biologist versed in phylogenetic and genetic thought would ever dream of dropping the two concepts of phyletic adaptation and of adaptive modification just because, in many cases, both are concerned in molding organic structure and/or function to fit environment. The fact that, in the case of the phenocopy, either of the two processes can achieve a result indistinguishable from that of the other, has never been considered a reason for dropping the conceptions of the two processes as being "not analytically valid."

Nor must the functional analogies which exist between the two types of acquiring information mislead anyone into thinking them to be physiologically the same. Indeed, we know that they are not. Not even the principle of "trial and error" is quite the same in both cases. It is only individual learning that is able to gain information from its errors. The hit-and-miss method of mutation and selection gains only by its successes and not by its failures and continues blindly to produce those mutants that have proved unsuccessful millions of years age. Still, there are sufficient reasons for uniting both under one functionally defined concept as Russell (1958–61) has done.

Physiologically, however, it is an entirely different process when, on the one hand, a species "experiments" by mutation or Mendelization and "records" results by one animal surviving and the other dying, and when, on the other hand, an animal "experiments" by doing this and that successively and "records" by forming a neural engram of what has brought about a reinforcing stimulus situation and what has not. For one thing, the amounts of time needed for each of these processes are different by quite a few powers of ten. In addition, the coded information stored in the genes, and also its decoding in ontogenetic development, is different from the information stored in the nervous system and its decoding by whatever happens in the releasing of a conditioned response. No similarity of results and no difficulty in the practical task of analysis can ever give us exemption from the scientific duty to trace back, to one or to the other of the two sources of information, any single point in which behavior can be shown to be adaptively molded to a corresponding point in the environment of the animal.

Hebb, in his criticism of ethology, says that it would be hard to exaggerate the importance attributed by ethologists to the distinction between the innate and the learned, implying, of course, that we overestimate this importance. I could not agree more with the statement and less with the implication. If, as physiologists of behavior, we intend to analyze the causality of adapted behavior at all, I do not see how we can pursue this object without ascertaining the source of information underlying adaptation. There are also practical reasons which make the distinction important. For instance, the belief that human aggression is based not on phylogenetic adaptation but on learning implies a tremendous underassessment of its dangers. Hitherto this belief has only led to the production of thousands of intolerably aggressive non-frustated children, but it may lead to much worse things.

Lastly, a very deep misunderstanding of biological ways of thinking is contained in the sentence by Hebb (1953, p. 14), expressing the opinion that "instinct [in the sense of a neural organization according to Tinbergen, 1952] implies a nervous process or mechanism ... which ... is different from those processes into which learning enters." We certainly do not believe that there is just one process into which learning does not enter. Even if we adhere to the superlatively comprehensive definition of learning which includes all adaptive modification, we still know dozens of very complicated behavior mechanisms whose adaptedness is entirely based on phylogenetically acquired information. The computing mechanism which enables a starling to deduce the points of the compass from the motion of the sun across the sky (a sun which the bird has never seen; Hoffmann, 1952), the complex feedback mechanism which enables a mantid to aim its grabbing movement unerringly at the prey (Mittelstaedt, 1957), the unvarying inherited courtship movement of a drake which releases a specific answer in a duck of the same species (Heinroth, 1910), the "internal clock" which prescribes rhythmical recurrence of activities in so many animals (Aschoff, 1962), all optomotor responses, and so on

are all "nervous processes or mechanisms which are different from those into which learning enters." They are as different from each other as a tooth is different from a bone or a kidney and exactly for the same reasons. We do not know how many more such mechanisms or processes do exist – all different from and independent of each other.

Critique of the Second Behavioristic Argument

This argument vastly overrates the amount of information that can be gained by the embryo during intrauterine life or in the egg. This error indubitably arises from the same fundamental fallacy which underlies the argument already discussed, namely, from forgetting that adaptedness to environment can never be a coincidence but must necessarily have a history explaining it. If Lehrman (1953) gives serious consideration to the assumption that a chick could learn, within the egg, considerable portions of the pecking behavior by having its head moved rhythmically up and down through the beating of its own heart, he totally fails to explain why the motor pattern thus individually acquired should fit the requirements of eating in an environmental situation which demands adaptedness to innumerable single givens as exactly as it does. It also remains unexplained why only certain birds peck after hatching, while others gape like passerines, dabble like ducks, or shove their bills into the corner of the mouth of the parents as pigeons do, although they all, when embryos, had their heads moved up and down by the heartbeat in exactly the same fashion. The more than wonderful adaptedness is passed over as a matter of course, in spite of the fact that it would require truly astronomical numbers to express the improbability of its arising by chance.

Adaptedness to environment can only be regarded as a matter of course by a man who, like von Uexküll, assumes a pre-stabilized harmony between organism and environment. Barring this assumption, anybody thinking it possible that the bird learns, within the egg, behavior which fits exigencies not encountered until later in life, automatically has to assume the existence of a teaching apparatus which contains the phylogenetically acquired information concerning those exigencies.

Neither Kuo (1932) nor Lehrman (1953) made this assumption.

Thus, paradoxically, the notion that the organism could, within the egg or *in utero*, learn behavior specifically adapted to later environment implies preformationism. An amusing double paradox lies in the fact that this preformationism is the penalty which some American psychologists incurred by trying to avoid, at all costs, the concepts of survival value and phylogenetic adaptation for no other reason than that they regarded them as "finalistic." Of course, they are not finalistic in the least. If a biologist says that the cat has crooked, pointed claws "with which to catch mice," he is not professing a belief in a mystical teleology, but succinctly stating that catching mice is the function whose selection pressure caused the evolution of that particular form of claws.

There is still a considerable element of truth contained in the second behavioristic argument. There are learning processes which can possibly take place within the egg or *in utero*. Prechtl and Knol (1958) has demonstrated some in the human fetus. The deprivation experiment permits assertions concerning the innate information about only those environmental givens with which the subject was specifically prevented from having experience. So it is practically never possible to state that all the information underlying the adaptedness of a whole functional unit is phylogenetically acquired. Still, in very many cases the fault which would be contained in such a not-quite-justifiable assertion would be very much smaller than is often assumed on the basis of the above-mentioned unintentional preformationism.

In very many cases, the adaptedness of behavior can be traced back to innate information, even without performing any deprivation experiment. A young male salticid spider which, after molting for the last time, approaches a female must neither mistake another species for his own, nor must he perform the signaling of his specific courtship dance in any other way than the one to which his female responds; otherwise, he would be eaten by her immediately. He has no opportunity in his short life to gain any information about what a female of his own species looks like, nor what movements he must perform to inhibit her feeding reactions and to stimulate her specific mating responses.

A young swift reared in a narrow cave in which it cannot extend its wings (far less beat them up and down), in which it cannot attain a sharp retinal image as the farthest point of the cave is much nearer than its shortest focusing distance, and in which it cannot gain any experience on parallactic shifting of retinal images, nevertheless proves to be perfectly able on the very moment it leaves the nest cavity to assess distances by the parallactic shift of the object's images. It can also cope, in its rapid flight, with all the intricacies of air resistance, upcurrents, turbulence, and air pockets and can "recognize" and catch prey, and finally effect a precise landing in a suitable place. The information implicitly contained in the adaptive molding of all these forms of behavior to the environmental givens to which they indubitably do fit would fill many volumes. The description of the innate distance computers alone would contain whole textbooks of stereometry and that of the responses and activities of flying, an equal number of data on aerodynamics.

If one assesses, even ever so roughly, the amount of information which quite indubitably is transmitted by way of the genome and compares it with what (even conceding the most unlikely possibilities) could have been acquired in individual life, the proportion is astounding. What the swift could have learned about stereometry is practically nil, even when we attribute quite superhuman learning powers to the bird. In its ability to fly, it could have learned even less than a human could learn about skiing on an indoor ski course. All the information it could have acquired individually could concern only its own body and a few basic and ubiquitous laws of physics. For instance, it could have learned to innervate synergistic and antagonistic muscles alternately. It could, from tactile experience, have deduced the first law of physics and know that two things cannot be in the same place simultaneously. Even overlooking the unlikelihood of simple motor coordinations being acquired – we know otherwise from the work of von Holst, Eibl-Eibesfeldt, and others – and the improbability of the bird's being able to apply what it has learned by tactile experience to its orientation while flying in the air and even if we attribute to the bird superhuman ability to learn, we know the proportion of learned information which could possibly enter into the responses and these activities is infinitesimally small. The naïve ethologist's assertion that they are "completely innate" is indeed less inexact than the statement that a steam locomotive or the Eiffel Tower are built entirely of metal. In other words, it attains an exactitude rarely reached by biological assertions.

. . .

Critique of the Earlier Ethologists' Attitude

The contrasting of the "innate" and the "learned" as mutually exclusive concepts is undoubtedly a fallacy, even without considering for the moment the error of applying the first of these two terms to behavior patterns and/or organs (see p. 116). As has been explained in the critique of both behavioristic arguments, it is perfectly possible that a particular motor sequence may owe to phylogenetic processes all the information on environment underlying its adaptedness and yet be almost wholly dependent on individual learning for the "decoding" (p. 120) of this information. This, indeed, is the important truth contained in the second behavioristic argument. The "decoding" of genome-bound information is, in such a case, achieved in two steps: first, by means of morphological ontogeny producing structure; and second, by means of trial-and-error behavior exploiting structure as a teaching apparatus. Processes of this kind are made to appear highly probable by the findings of Prechtl and Knol (1958) on motor patterns and "reflexes" of children born in abnormal positions.

The fallacy of treating the "innate" and the "learned" as mutually exclusive concepts led the old ethologists to make the same errors of which, from pp. 116–21, I have accused behaviorists. Like the behaviorists, the old ethologists took it for granted that the modification of behavior effected by learning invariably caused an increase in survival value. The fact that a phylogenetically evolved neurophysiological mechanism must lie behind this highly differentiated function obviously never occurred to them any more than it did to those of the behavioristic school.

For ethologists as well as for behaviorists, this truly atomistic attitude was a serious obstacle to the understanding of the relations between phylogenetic adaptation and adaptive modification of behavior. It was Lehrman's (1953) critique which, by a somewhat devious route, brought the full realization of these relations to me. In pp. 121–3 I have discussed the hypothesis that the passive movement imparted to the chick embryo's head by the beating of its heart might take part in teaching the bird to peck. As I have explained, this assumption neglects consideration of the necessity to explain the fact that the motor pattern fits environmental requirements only encountered later in life. In my first counter-critique I said rather satirically that this hypothesis, in order to circumvent the necessity of assuming an innate, that is, phylogenetically adapted motor pattern, unwittingly but unavoidably postulates the necessity of an "innate schoolmarm." In other words, it requires a phylogenetically adapted teaching mechanism. It soon dawned upon me, however, that this thrust against the preformationistic views on learning held by the behavioristic school recoiled with full force on the views held by the older ethologists including myself. I came to realize rather late in life that "learning" was a concept illegitimately used by us as a dump for unanalyzed residue and that, no better than our criticized critics, none of us had ever bothered to ask why learning produced adaptation of behavior. All older ethologists, with the outstanding exception of Craig, had been confining their attention to the innate, while more or less neglecting all problems of learning, without realizing that in doing so they were neglecting one of the most important functions of the majority of phylogenetically adapted behavior mechanisms: the function of teaching!

One of the worst repercussions which this complete neglect of the relations between the "innate schoolmarm" and individual learning had on the real understanding of phylogenetically adapted behavior mechanisms themselves was a one-sided and even physiologically erroneous view of the consummatory act. For a long time it was believed that the gradual rise and final critical drop of excitation typical of all consummatory acts was due to complete exhaustion of action-specific potentiality on the motor side. It has been conclusively demonstrated by experiments of Beach (1942) that in the case of the copulatory activities of the male chimpanzee, it is the effect of reafferent feedback which terminates the consummatory act. This proprio- and exteroceptor feedback is undoubtedly of enormous consequence for the reinforcing function of most or all consummatory stimulus situations. In the case of higher animals, it is hardly an exaggeration to say that the special structure of a typical consummatory act is quite as much the result of the selection pressure exerted by its function of reinforcing appetitive behavior as of the one exerted by its primary function. The lack of appreciation of this fact hindered a true understanding of the processes particularly of the manner in which important information concerning the biologically "right" situation can be contained in the motor pattern itself and can be "decoded" by the animal itself, thus creating a maximum of adaptivity and economy of behavior, as illustrated by the experiments of Eibl-Eibesfeldt. Only Craig gave, at least in his very vivid descriptions of consummatory activities and situations, a hint of the importance of these interactions between phylogenetical adaptation and adaptive modification of behavior.

If these admittedly atomistic errors committed by my teacher Heinroth and myself did comparatively little damage to the initial progress of ethology, this is due to the fact that the all-important element of behavior, the fixed motor pattern or *Erbkoordination*, is an extremely invariable skeletal element which influences the system into which it is built far more than it is, in its turn, influenced or changed by the general systemic interaction. The more a particulate element of a system bears the character of such a "relatively independent part" (Lorenz, 1950), the less damage is done by the otherwise illegitimate procedure of isolating it in conceptualization as well as in practical experiments. In any case, by discovering the fixed motor pattern, Whitman and Heinroth created the Archimedean point on which all ethological research is based. Naïvely calling the fixed motor pattern "innate" has done no serious damage to this research in the past or now. On the other hand, the assertion that even the fixed motor pattern can, at least in principle and to an infinitesimal extent, be changed by learning is not based on any observation or experimental result but exclusively on a prejudice and does do real damage, or at least it would do so, if modern ethologists really drew the last bitter consequences from it.

References

Aschoff, J. (1962) Spontane lokomotorische Aktivität, *Handbuch der Zoologie 10*, vol. 11. Berlin: De Gruyter.

Beach, F. H. (1942) Analysis of factors involved in the arousal, maintainance, and manifestation of sexual excitement in male animals, *Psychosomatic Med.*, **4**: 173.

Campbell, D. T. (1958) *Methodological Suggestions from a Comparative Psychology of Knowledge Processes*. Oslo University Press.

Craig, W. (1918) Appetites and aversions as constituents of instincts, *Biol. Bull.*, **34**: 91–107.

Hassenstein, B. (1954) Abbildende Begriffe, *Verhandl Deut. Zool. Ges. Tübingen*, 197–202.

Hebb, D. O. (1953) Heredity and environment in mammalian behavior, *Brit. J. Animal Behaviour*, **1**: 43–7.

Heinroth, O. (1910) Beiträge zur Biologie, namentlich Ethologie und Psychologie der Anatiden. *Verhandl. Ver. Intern. Ornithol. Kong. Berlin*, 589–702.

Hoffmann, K. (1952) Die Einrechnung der Sonnenwanderung bei der Richtungsweisung des sonnenlos aufgezogenen Stares, *Naturwissenschaften*, **40**: 148.

Hull, C. L. (1943) *Principles of Behavior*. New York: Appleton Century.

Kuo, Z. Y. (1932) Ontogeny of embryonic behavior in aves, *Intern. J. Exptl. Zool.*, **61**: 395–430, 453–89.

Lehrman, D. S. (1953) A critique of Konrad Lorenz' theory of instinctive behavior, *Quart. Rev. Biol.*, **28**: 337–63.

Lorenz, K. (1950) Ganzheit und Teil in der tierischen und menschlichen Gemeinschaft, *Studium Generale*, **9**: 455–99.

Massermann, J. H. (1943) *Behavior and Neurosis*. Chicago: University of Chicago Press.

Meyer-Holzapfel, M. (1940) Triebbedingte Ruhezustände als Ziel von Appetenzhandlungen, *Naturwissenschaften*, **28**: 273–80.

Mittelstaedt, H. (1957) Prey capture in Mantids, *Recent Advances in Invertebrate Physiology*. University of Oregon, pp. 51–7.

Prechtl, H. F. R. and Knol, A. R. (1958) Die Fussohlenreflexe beim neugeborenen Kind, *Arch. Psychiat. Z. Ges. Neurol.*, **196**: 542–53.

Richter, C. P. (1954) Behavioral regulators of carbohydrate homeostasis, *Acta Neurovegetative*, **9**: 247–59.

Russell, W. N. (1958–61) Evolutionary concepts in Behavioural science: I–III General systems (Year Book of the Society for General Systems Research), (1958) **3**: 18–28; (1959) **4**: 45–73; (1961) **6**: 51–92.

Tinbergen, N. (1952) *Instinktlehre*, Berlin: Paul Parey.

Tinbergen, N. (1955) Some aspects of ethology, the biological study of animal behaviour, *Advan. Sci.*, **12**: 17–27.

Tinbergen, N. (1963) On aims and methods of ethology, *Z. Tierpsychol.*, **20**: 404–33.

Thorndike, E. L. (1911) *Animal Intelligence*. New York.

Thorpe, W. H. (1956) *Learning and Instinct in Animals*. London: Methuen.

Wall. W. von de. (1963) Bewegungsstudien an Anatiden, *J. Ornithol.*, **104**: 1–14

CHAPTER 9

Semantic and Conceptual Issues in the Nature–Nurture Problem

Daniel S. Lehrman

The question of what is called "innate" and what is called "acquired" in the behavior of animals, including man, is one that appears regularly and persistently, as a problem and as a source of controversy among students of animal behavior and psychology. This is true in all areas studied by students of behavior. The question of how to formulate the roles of "heredity" and "environment" in the determination of behavior characteristics has agitated students of human intelligence (Anastasi and Foley, 1948), of the abilities for visual perception in higher animals (Hochberg, 1963), of species-typical ("instinctive") behavior in animals (Schneirla, 1956), and virtually every other area of interest to such students.

In the present essay, I propose to discuss the role of the concepts of "innate" and "acquired" in a number of discussions of animal behavior that have occurred in recent years.

Starting in the early 1930s Konrad Lorenz and his students and colleagues developed a conception of the mechanism of "instinctive" behavior which was and is very influential and which has, for a considerable period of time, stimulated a large amount of interesting and creative research.

From L. R. Aronson, E. Tobach, D. S. Lehrman and J. S. Rosenblatt (eds), *Development and Evolution of Behavior* (San Francisco, CA: Freeman, 1970), pp. 17–52.

Lorenz's theories (Lorenz, 1937, 1950), developed from work by zoologists on the behavior of lower animals (mostly birds, fish, and insects), formed the basis for a new and flourishing school of animal behavior studies, for which the name "ethology" was adopted.

The term "ethologist" is difficult to define. Insofar as it has a formal definition, it means approximately a scientist who studies the species-typical behavior patterns which constitute part of the animal's biological adaptation to its environment. During the 1940s and 1950s, the term tended to carry the additional informal connotation that a person designated by it was guided in his work primarily by Lorenz's theories of behavior. In recent years, however, it has become clear that the scientists working on the problems, and with the methods, characterized as "ethological," by no means constitute a monolithic body of opinion linked by fidelity to a particular set of theories. The term "ethologist" must therefore refer to a group of people characterized by a common interest in understanding the behavior of animals in relation to their natural environment (including fellow members of the species).

Lorenz's thinking has, from the start, depended very heavily upon the idea that it is always possible and profitable to distinguish "innate" from "acquired" elements of behavior. Lorenz (1965) agrees that "it would be hard to exaggerate the importance attributed by ethologists to the distinction between the innate and the learned." About fifteen years ago, three North American psychologists (Hebb, 1953; Lehrman, 1953; Schneirla, 1956) published discussions which, each in its own way, implied skepticism about both the heuristic value of the traditional distinction between "innate" and "acquired," and the reality of those two concepts as classes into which any given element of behavior could unambiguously be placed. Over the years since then there has been a considerable amount of discussion centering around these critiques (Eibl-Eibesfeldt, 1961; Lorenz, 1961; Thorpe, 1963a, 1963b; Tinbergen, 1963; Schneirla, 1966), culminating in Lorenz's recent (1965) book, *Evolution and Modification of Behavior.*

Since I was the author of one of the papers giving rise to this series of discussions (Lehrman, 1953) and since I have not published any further direct contribution to the discussion during the intervening fifteen years (although I naturally regard my work during that time as an illustration of my point of view), I would like to take advantage of the opportunity offered by this memorial volume, dedicated to the late T. C. Schneirla, to comment on the present status of this discussion, with particular reference to Lorenz's recent (1965) attempt at a definitive resolution. This is especially appropriate, since I regard Schneirla, who was my teacher, as the most creative, the most articulate, and the most consistent modern spokesman for the point of view that the use of dichotomies such as "innate" and "acquired" is restrictive, rather than instructive, in its effects on the analysis of behavior.

Semantics, Concepts, and Facts

When opposing groups of intelligent, highly educated, competent scientists continue over many years to disagree, and even to wrangle bitterly, about an issue which they regard as important, it must sooner or later become obvious that the disagreement is not a factual one, and that it cannot be resolved by calling to the attention of the members of one group (or even of the other!) the existence of new data which will make them see the light. Further, it becomes increasingly obvious that there are no possible crucial experiments that would cause one group of antagonists to abandon their point of view in favor of that of the other group. If this is, as I believe, the case, we ought to consider the roles played in this disagreement by semantic difficulties arising from concealed differences in the way different people use the same words, or in the way the same people use the same words at different times; by differences in the concepts used by different workers (i.e., in the ways in which they divide up facts into categories); and by differences in their conception of what is an important problem and what is a trivial one, or rather what is an interesting problem and what is an uninteresting one.

The critiques of the
heredity–environment dichotomy

Interaction of heredity and environment Hebb (1953) asserted that to make a dichotomy between "innate" and "environmentally-determined" behavior patterns, with the intention of assigning each element of behavior to one or the other of these classes, is misleading because the influences of heredity and of environment are not exerted upon different parts of the behavior (or of the organism), but are effective, in different ways, on the development of the *same* elements. This goes fairly directly to the heart of Lorenz's earlier use of the term "innate," since he has always implied that, if only behavior could be broken up into appropriately defined elements, it should be unequivocally possible to state which ones were wholly innate and which ones were influenced by "learning." In fact, Lorenz's characteristic method of dealing with the role of learning in behavioral development has been to conceive of an interlacement of innate and learned elements, making a chain, or of situations in which a clearly defined aspect of the behavior (e.g., its form) was innate, while another equally clearly defined aspect (e.g., its orientation to the environment) could be described as learned.

This argument of Hebb's is referred to by Lorenz (1956)[1] as the "first behavioristic argument."

Role of environment in the development of species-typical behavior Lehrman (1953) and Schneirla (1956) emphasized a somewhat different argument, which was also mentioned by Hebb. They point out that the ontogenetic development of species-specific behavior patterns may often depend upon influences from the environment, which interact with processes internal to the organism at all stages of development, in such a way that it is misleading to label those behavior patterns that seem to depend upon ordinary learning, and those that do not, as "learned" and "innate," with the implication that they have dichotomously different developmental origins. Schneirla (1966), in particular, has used the concept of "experience" to mean all kinds of stimulative effects from the environment, ranging from stimulus-involved biochemical and biological processes (having effects on the developing nervous system) to what we ordinarily call conditioning and learning. He speaks of maturation as "the contributions to development of growth and of tissue differentiation, together with organic and functional trace effects surviving from earlier development." Earlier I had said (Lehrman, 1953):

The "instinct" is obviously not present in the zygote. Just as obviously it is present in the behavior of the animal after the appropriate age. The problem for the investigator who wishes to make a closer analysis of behavior is: how did this behavior come about? The use of "explanatory" categories such as "innate" and "genetically fixed" obscures the necessity of investigating developmental *processes* in order to gain insight into the actual mechanisms of behavior and their interrelations. The problem of development is the problem of the development of new *structures* and activity *patterns* from the resolution of the interaction of existing ones, within the organism and its internal environment, and between the organism and its outer environment. At any stage of development, the new features emerge from the interactions within the *current* stage and between the *current* stage and the environment. The interaction out of which the organism develops is *not* one, as is so often said, between heredity and environment. It is between *organism* and environment! And the organism is different at each different stage of its development.

The section of my paper in which I made these remarks was called "Heredity-vs.-Environment, or Development?"

It should be obvious from these quotations that what Schneirla and I (and Hebb in a slightly different way) intended was *not* to say that learning was all-important, while accepting the traditional dichotomy that maturation is an unfolding of gene-determined anatomical, physiological, and behavioral patterns (Schneirla, 1966), and that influence from the environment consists solely of conditioning or trial-and-error learning; rather, we were questioning the value of the dichotomy itself, *not* stressing one side or the other of it.

Lorenz calls this type of discussion the "second behavioristic argument."

Some problems of definition

My first serious task is to examine some semantic problems: i.e., those arising from the use of words as labels, which may compound the actual problems arising from the conceptions to which the words were intended to apply.

Who is an ethologist? What is the significance of the fact that Lorenz labels the principal considerations introduced by Hebb, Schneirla, and myself as "behavioristic" arguments? The background for this labeling lies in the repeated assertions made by Lorenz and other writers to the effect that these criticisms arise from the fact that the people who wrote them are psychologists, and are therefore incapable of understanding biological problems. Lorenz refers to "American psychologists" as the source of criticism of his ideas, and repeatedly implies that these critics impute to biologists ideas which they do not hold, the implication being that as psychologists, they are not sensitive to the considerations that are important to biologists.

This type of labeling is, for several reasons, not a very constructive contribution to a discussion of the problems of heredity and development. For one thing, the views of biologists like Hinde (1966) and Tinbergen (1963) are very much like those expressed by these "American psychologists," and the implication that they have been unduly influenced by alien intrusions into their field of work is less than respectful.[2]

For another thing, this kind of labeling tends to arouse (or to reveal) a prejudice against the person being labeled which prevents (intentionally or unintentionally) a full appreciation of his contribution to the discussion. It is too easy to close one's mind to an argument by simply deciding that the source of the argument is an outsider.

Finally, the term "behaviorist" is an affront to the memory of T. C. Schneirla, whose lifelong work was a thoughtful, penetrating and broadly based analysis of the role of physiological, social, and ecological processes, and of the integrations among them, in the development and regulation of the behavior patterns by which the army ants (*Eciton*) are adapted to their environment; of the ways in which different species of these ants differ from each other; of the mechanisms that give rise to these species differences; and of evolution in this group. His work was not remotely related to the tradition of American "rat psychology" to which Lorenz refers by the term "behaviorism." As for me, the reason I chose to study with Schneirla was the same as the reason I chose to become a student of animal behavior: I was interested in understanding the behavior of birds as I had observed it in nature in my youth. If Lorenz intended to be tactful by pointing out that Schneirla and I should not be regarded as biologists, then the intention failed. I would much rather be called stupid!

I should not point out irrational, emotion-laden elements in Lorenz's reaction to criticism without acknowledging that, when I look over my 1953 critique of his theory, I perceive elements of hostility to which its target would have been bound to react. My critique does not now read to me like an analysis of a scientific problem, with an evaluation of the contribution of a particular point of view, but rather like an assault upon a theoretical point of view, the writer of which assault was not interested in pointing out what positive contributions that point of view had made. It does fail to express what, even at that time, I regarded as Lorenz's enormous contribution to the formulation of the problems of evolution and function of behavior, and his accomplishment in creating a school based upon the conception of species-specific behavior as a part of the animal's adaptation to its natural environment. (This would be an appropriate point for me to remark that I do not now disagree with any of the basic ideas expressed in my critique!)

The meanings of "innate" and the meanings of "inherited" The terms "innate" and "inherited" both have, in different contexts, at least two different meanings, which do not refer to the same processes, which are not arrived at by the same operations, and which have entirely different kinds of reference to the problem of development, but which are often confused with each other.

When a geneticist speaks of a character as inherited, what he means is that he is able to predict the distribution of the character in an offspring population from his knowledge of the distribution of the character in the parent population and of the mating patterns in that population. He is *not* necessarily making any inferences whatever about the developmental processes involved in the ontogeny of the character, or even the extent to which it is subject to change under environmental influence. Another way of saying this is that a character may be said to be "inherited" or "heritable" or "hereditary," if the variation of this character from individual to individual can be shown to arise from differences in the genetic constitution, or genome, of the different individuals, rather than from differences in the kind of environment in which they have been reared, or in the way in which they have been treated. Now, the fact that selective breeding (i.e., arranging for the offspring generations to consist only of individuals resulting from the matings of members of the parent generation which have been selected for the presence or absence of some specific characteristic or characteristics) can result in striking changes in the characteristics of the group of organisms certainly means that the characteristic is hereditary, but it by no means demonstrates that the *same* characteristic cannot be influenced by the environment. A genome arrived at by selective breeding in one environment may have quite different phenotypic characteristics in a second environment, while an environmental change that has great influence upon the phenotypic development of one genome may have no effect upon that of another (Haldane, 1946).

Geneticists have dealt with this problem by restricting the concepts of "heritability" and "environmental influence" with respect to any given character to an estimate of the amount of the actually observed variability in that character that can be attributed to variations among the different genomes *actually tested*, and to the amount that can be attributed to the variety of environments in which organisms with those genomes have *actually been raised*. They thus do not preclude the possibility that other genes than the ones tested might have an effect upon the character, or that environments other than the one tested may cause unpredictable changes in the phenotypic appearance of a given genome. In genetic usage, therefore, the fact that a character can, in a given environment (for example, the "normal" environment) be strikingly affected by selective breeding (as, for example, by hybridization experiments) does not directly deal with the question of whether variations in the environment during the development of the organism would or would not have an effect upon the manner of development of the adult phenotype.

There is, however, a *second* meaning which, implicitly or explicitly, is often attributed to the words "innate" or "hereditary" or "inherited" by students of animal behavior and by nongeneticists generally. This meaning is that of *developmental fixity*, i.e., that the organism is impervious to environmental effects during development, and so it *must* develop characteristics that are preorganized "in the genes," regardless of the environment in which it is reared. Now, I am *not*, at this point (but see below, pp. 132–3), attempting to discuss the question of whether there is such a thing as developmental fixity, or whether the term "innate," meaning unavailable to environmental influence, is a useful or meaningful term to apply to behavior characteristics. I am merely trying to point out that the concept of "innateness" as referring to developmental fixity is a *different* concept, and one that exists in a different, and not parallel, dimension, from the concept of "alterable by selective breeding," which is the same as "achievable by natural selection."

But it must be obvious to every candid observer of the literature of animal behavior that these two different, and incommensurate, concepts are very often implicitly mixed into one use of the term "innate." This is, for example, what Lorenz does when, in a discussion about the legitimacy of the use of the term "innate," he introduces as evidence both the fact that the offspring of a hybrid shares behavioral characteristics of both parent species and the fact that learning does not influence the development of the behavior patterns concerned.

Lorenz's use of "innate" Lorenz did not identify the distinction outlined in the preceding section, or the problems raised by it, because his recent discussion was couched in somewhat different terms. He has, however, proposed a very interesting resolution of the problem as he perceives it. He states that the term "innate" should "never, on principle, be applied to organs or behavior patterns, even if their modifiability should be negligible." He does, how-

ever, think it proper to describe as "innate" a distinctive *property* of a neural structure, such as its ability to select, from the range of available possible stimuli, the one which specifically elicits its activity, and thus the response seen by the observer. Presumably, the property of the neural structure in giving rise to a particular movement pattern would also be a property of this kind, which Lorenz refers to as a "character." He is thus making a distinction between organs, structures, and behavior patterns, which he says should not be called "innate," and special properties of these organs, structures, and behavior patterns, by which they fit into the appropriate environment. His conception is that, even if, for example, an animal can see nothing without previous visual experience at the appropriate time in its development, it might still be that if it had appropriate experience (i.e., experience of light, or of contours, etc.), some of its specific responses could be linked to specific visual stimulus configurations, *without* the animal having had any *specific* visual experience that would account for its reaction to those visual stimuli, rather than to others. In this context, he asserts that the "information" that the following response of a given species of fish is elicited by the characteristic color of the mother fish of that species, rather than by other colors, may legitimately be called "innate," if it can be demonstrated that a fish that can see will prefer to follow this color, without any previous experience of the color, even though it may be true that the development of visual abilities in the first place required experience of light. In this situation, he would not call the visual capacity as such innate, but only a specific property of the fish's visual system: that it was capable of selectively responding to the appropriate color when the animal was in a mood to follow.

This distinction is made in the service of a more fundamental distinction, which is the principal argument of Lorenz's book and the principal basis for his insistence that the concept of "innateness" is an objective and necessary one. Briefly, Lorenz states that, when a behavior pattern is adapted to a given aspect of its environment, the "information" which defines the properties by which the behavior pattern is adapted to the environment can have been incorporated into the behavior pattern of the animal either by "the adaptive processes of evolution" or by "individual acquisition of information." By "adaptive processes of evolution," Lorenz refers to the creation of the genome by natural selection, so that the gene-complex characteristic of an individual is the result of a history of selection for those genes that, in the natural environment, give rise to characteristics that are adaptive to that environment, including behavior characteristics. This is a sort of historical "trial and error" process, in which mutations that lead to useful (i.e., adaptive) results are retained, while those that lead to harmful (i.e., nonadaptive) ones are eliminated. By "individual acquisition of information," Lorenz means individual learning.

Lorenz's present argument is that behavior characteristics that are adaptive to particular points of the environment must be considered "innate" if their source, or provenance, is through the incorporation of genes into the genome through natural selection, and must be considered "learned" if their source is a change in the behavior of the animal as a result of its individual experience of that environment.

Up to this point, my purpose has been to outline the type of behavior about which opposing views have been expressed, to sketch, however briefly, the nature of the disagreements, and to point to some problems involved in defining the terms about which the disagreements have flowered. I should now like to turn to a consideration of some conceptual problems, with a view to pointing out some ways in which different workers disagree in their evaluation of the importance of various questions, even when they agree about the facts concerned.

Variation and Development

Genetic variation versus developmental process

If we rear two animals in the same environment, and they develop different behavior patterns, it is perfectly clear that the difference in the behavior patterns depends upon differences in the genetic constitution of the animals, and not upon differences in the environment. One might refer to these *differences* as "innate," meaning only that they depended upon differences in the genome. This use of the term "innate" would be meaningful and useful, provided it was recognized that the observations

that justified the conclusion that the difference between the two animals was a genetic difference do not necessarily imply anything, one way *or* the other, about the extent to which the development of the character concerned is, in either animal, influencible by changes in the environment.

This is the situation in which we find ourselves when we compare different species living in similar environments, and showing different behavior. The differences between the species obviously arise from genetic differences, and it is perfectly appropriate to use genetic terms, and terms deriving from considerations of evolutionary adaptation, in analyzing these differences and their evolutionary relationships, and the evolutionary origins of particular behavior patterns. None of these considerations, however, really bears on the question of ontogenetic origin, which is, to some degree, a question of a different kind.

To take a rather simple example, let us consider one aspect of the problem of the role of behavior patterns in the formation of species. An existing species becomes divided into two descendant species when two parts of the original population become geographically separated from each other and when, under conditions of geographical separation (i.e., when no genes are being exchanged between one population and the other), they become so different from each other genetically that they would not interbreed if the geographical barrier were removed. This may happen because, while they were in geographical isolation, they evolved in slightly different directions as a result of adaptation to slightly different environments, or it might occur because the populations were small enough so that rarely occurring mutations occurred, by chance, in different frequencies in the two populations, or it might come from some combination of these and similar factors. Whatever the reason, each of the two populations may eventually consist, more or less homogeneously, of individuals that will be sufficiently different from those of the other population so that they will no longer be as ready to mate with them as they would be with members of their own population. This may be because the members of the two populations prefer different habitats and thus do not meet each other, because the courtship behavior of a member of one population is no longer adequately stimulating to a member of the other, or for a variety of other reasons, behavioral, ecological, or morphological. Now, this "reproductive isolation" may not be complete at the time the geographical barrier between the two populations is removed. It may be that, at the time it becomes geographically possible for the two populations once more to become continuous, there has developed only a relative isolation, defined as a quantitative preference for mating with a member of the animal's own population, rather than a member of the other. In that case, a number of things may happen, the extremes of which might be defined by two alternative outcomes: (a) if the two populations are similar enough to each other so that hybrids between them can survive in the existing range of environments as well as can members of either population, the two populations may simply merge, as the genes of one are spread through the other through the hybrid matings at the points where the populations meet each other; and (b) the two populations may have become so different from each other, and adapted to such different environments, that hybrids between them will not be as well adapted for survival in *any* environment as each of the populations is to *some* environment. These hybrids will be at a selective disadvantage, compared with the offspring of within-population members of either population. In this case, the hybrids will be eliminated by natural selection, which means that, at least in the zone of overlap between the two populations, only those genomes will survive that ensure, in that environment, a preference against mating with a member of the other population (Mayr, 1942).

This process can be reproduced experimentally in the laboratory. For example, Koopman (1950) allowed individuals of two species of *Drosophila* to select mates in a mixed population. There was a moderate degree of preference for mating within the species, as could be seen by the characteristics of the larvae (the animals carried a marker gene, which made it possible to distinguish a hybrid animal from pure-bred animals in the larval stage). He removed all the hybrid larvae, and then allowed the remaining members of the offspring generation to choose mates again from a mixed population, now consisting only of the offspring of animals that had selected members of their own species for breeding. He repeated the process for a number of generations, thus tending to eliminate those genes that made possible the selection of a mate from the "wrong" species.

The result was that the degree of reproductive isolation (i.e., the strength of the tendency to select a mate from within one's own species) was gradually increased.

In all these examples, the characteristics that insure that the animals will mate only with members of their own population have been arrived at entirely by selection directed against those genes that made possible a maladaptive mating choice. That is, they have been arrived at by the adaptive processes of evolution. This process is very common in nature, and may probably be assumed to have taken place in almost every case where two closely related species breed in the same area. If, however, an animal is reared in association with members of another, closely related, species, it soon becomes clear that in some cases, such as the cowbird, the rearing conditions have no effect upon the mating preferences, while in other cases, such as some species of doves (Whitman, 1919), the mating preferences may be strongly affected, being shifted sharply in the direction of a willingness to mate with a member of the "foster" species (Mayr and Dobzhansky, 1945)! In both cases, the features of the animal that are, in normal circumstances, responsible for its absolute preference for mating with a member of its own species, have been incorporated by natural selection, by selective breeding, by "the adaptive processes of evolution." But in one case, these features include a role of learning, in the other case not! Nature selects for *outcomes*: it does not care whether this outcome is arrived at through the development of features of the animal that make it impossible for it to respond to stimuli offered by members of the other species, or whether it is arrived at through the development of features that make the animal prefer to mate with a member of the species that it experienced in its early life!

Now, I would not dream of implying that Lorenz, the discoverer of imprinting, does not know all that I have just said, and I am aware that his way of dealing with these facts would be to call the preference of the cowbird innate and that of the dove learned. I am merely pointing out that if a scientist is not overwhelmingly convinced that characteristics incorporated into the species by the actions of natural selection are, *by that fact*, demonstrated to be impervious to individual experience, he is not necessarily guilty of "a very deep misunderstanding of biological ways of thinking" or "a lack of acquaintance with phylogenetic and genetic thought" (Lorenz, 1965).

What I intend to indicate by the example that I have just given is that the clearest possible genetic evidence that a characteristic of an animal is genetically determined in the sense that it has been arrived at through the operation of natural selection does not settle any questions at all about the developmental processes by which the phenotypic characteristic is achieved during ontogeny.

Genetics and developmental fixity

In the crustacean *Gammarus*, the difference between the normal red eye color and a mutant with chocolate eyes depends upon a single mutation which affects the rate at which an eye pigment is deposited during a certain stage of development. If the mutant is reared below a given threshold temperature, the eyes will develop red, and at intermediate temperatures there will be intermediate eye colors (Ford and Huxley, 1927).

Variations in the wing structure of *Drosophila melanogaster* may be affected by a wide variety of genetic mutations (Morgan, Sturtevant, Muller, and Bridges, 1923). These mutations also have an effect upon the ability of the animal of fly. Different flies of a single genotype may be able to fly normally, weakly, or not at all, depending upon the temperature at which they are raised (Harnly, 1941).

These two examples (which, let me hasten to add, will not surprise any biologist) show that the same genes may lead to different phenotypic outcomes when the animal is subjected to different environmental influences during development. Suppose, however, that *Gammarus* or *Drosophila* were, for reasons having nothing to do with the mechanisms of eye development or wing development, unable to survive at any temperature outside the range 24°–26°C. In that case, we would have to say that the character was uninfluenced by the environmental temperature. But would this mean that the mechanism of eye development, or of wing development, was any different? I think not. Further, the situation would be similar if, instead of being unable to survive temperature variations, the animals possessed regulative mechanisms that maintained the temperature environment of the eye (or

of the wing) constant in spite of variations in environmental temperature. In both of these cases the outcome of the experiments would be that we had failed to show any effect of environmental temperature upon the development of eye color, or of flying ability. But this would not *necessarily* mean that considerations of temperature were irrelevant to the development of these characters. Further, it should be clear that the failure to show the effects of a particular environmental variable does not say anything positive about the processes involved in the development of any character.

There is a fundamental question of logic involved here. I am sure that Lorenz and his colleagues perceive those of us who are oriented by Schneirla's teaching as constantly engaged in an eager search for any little snippets of evidence that learning has any effect, however small, on the development of a behavior pattern, to the exclusion of any attention to the broad problems of adaptation, and that we exaggerate the relative importance of learning influences in the service of a need to see learning everywhere and heredity nowhere. Given the role played by the phenomena of adaptation, and by the concept of the "normal environment" in Lorenz's thinking, I can certainly understand how his impression could arise. But that is not at all our conception of our situation. It seems to us that an experimental manipulation that causes a change in the behavioral outcome has thrown some light on the process by which the behavior develops, while an experimental manipulation that *fails* to cause any change in the outcome has *failed* to throw light upon the nature of the processes leading to the outcome. To Lorenz, the failure of an experimental treatment to cause any change in outcome seems just as illuminating as does the success of an experimental treatment in affecting the outcome. He makes this quite explicit when he says that he disagrees with the formulation that "it is not characters but differences between characters which may be described as innate," and says that "the opposite formulation is at least as workable: calling innate the similarities of characters developing under dissimilar rearing conditions." To an *experimental* scientist, the insight gained by observing that a variety of treatments all failed to have any effect is not at all equivalent to that gained by observing that some treatments have effects, while others do not. Indeed, it is of the essence of the experimental method that an experiment cannot be regarded as making a contribution to the understanding of any problem unless the experimenter has succeeded in finding alternate treatments that have different effects upon the outcome. It is for this reason, and not because I think that any *particular* kind of developmental influence is all-important, that I regard an experiment that shows an effect, during development, of any treatment, as a contribution to the illumination of a process of development, while a study which succeeds only in showing that some types of manipulation have no effect upon the outcome seems only like a challenge to follow the problem to an earlier stage of development, or to a more intricate level of physiological analysis.

The criterion of developmental fixity is thus a negative one in the sense that it is based upon the *lack* of effect of experimental treatments. If a class of behavior patterns is defined in large part by such a criterion (lack of effect of treatment), as in Lorenz's classification of the instinctive act (*Erbkoordination*), the assumption that all members of the class have *developmental* or *physiological* features in common is not necessarily valid.

Learning, Experience, and Development

Learning and experience

One persistent difficulty is that Lorenz, and a number of other writers, use the term "learning" to refer solely to the kind of conditioning and associative learning that are traditionally described as the learning capacities of adult animals (Kimble, 1976), and they have made no effort to incorporate into their thinking Schneirla's concept of "experience," which refers to a wide range of processes, of which learning is only a relatively small part.

Let me repeat Schneirla's definition of "experience": the contribution to development of the effects of stimulation from all available sources (external and internal), including their functional trace effects surviving from earlier development (Schneirla, 1957, 1966). Contrast this with Lorenz's statement: "Not being experimental embryologists but students of behavior, we begin our query, not at the beginning of the growth, but at the beginning of the function of such innate mechanisms." By this

statement, Lorenz is asserting that he is simply not interested in the type of question to which Schneirla's conception addresses itself. Now, it is not at all necessary that the problem of development should be a central problem for every scientist interested in behavior, or that all students of behavior who are interested in problems of development should be interested in the development of the same types of behavior, or should be primarily concerned with the same stages of development. I think it is important, however, to recognize that there are differences of attitude involved in these disagreements, which do not have to do with factual matters, but with what each of the parties considers to be an interesting problem, or a heuristically significant question. As Lorenz states, he is really not interested in the origins of behavior patterns at those stages of development before they begin to exist as modes of adaptation to the environment. Since his interest starts at that point, it is quite understandable that the only kind of experience that would seem theoretically relevant for him would be the kind of conditioning and associative learning characteristic of animals whose behavioral organization is already ontogenetically well formed. In effect, Lorenz would like to consider the problems of experience solely in terms of the role of conditioning and associative learning in the behavior of animals, starting at stages of development when their species-specific behavior patterns are already functional, so that the problem becomes merely one of whether an animal can learn to use a nesting material other than the ones for which its normal movements are adapted, or whether it needs to have seen a red object in order to prefer to attract a fellow-member of the species with the red belly, or whether it will respond appropriately to the sound of a young animal of its species without ever having heard one before, etc. Problems of the sort referred to by Schneirla would then be left to "experimental embryologists."

This feeling on Lorenz's part is consistent with his assertion that the innate is what must be there before learning begins. However, there is already evidence that the development of organisms is not divided into such convenient chapters, corresponding to the divisions among the professional specialties of biologists. Conditioning can occur very early in life, even prenatally in mammals (Spelt, 1948; Prechtl, 1965), or pre-hatching in birds (Gos, 1935;

Hunt, 1949; Sedláček, 1962, 1964; Gottlieb, 1968). For a scientist who is *primarily* interested in the analysis of development, the existence of such early conditioning abilities cannot seem irrelevant to the problem of the ontogenetic origin of later-appearing behavior patterns.

Further, nonbehavioral physiological regulations and those that are of interest to a student of animal behavior cannot be sharply separated. Physiological events that are not normally or conventionally regarded as a part of "behavior," such as changes in body temperature, changes in bladder activity, changes in kidney activity, changes in tension in the mammary gland, dilation and constriction of the blood vessels, are all to some degree under neural control, and can be conditioned, both by Pavlovian techniques (Bykov, 1957) and by those of operant conditioning (Miller, 1969; Miller and di Cara, 1967). In addition, the conditioned stimuli may be either external stimuli or stimuli arising inside the body, including stimuli arising from changes in tension elsewhere in the body, which may themselves be conditioned (Razran, 1961). This means that the distinction between "animal behavior" and other kinds of physiological regulation are not as absolute in the organization of the animal's physiological mechanisms as they usually are in the perception of the student of animal behavior, and that it may be necessary for scientists interested primarily in animal behavior to pay attention to a great many things that are primarily of interest to other kinds of scientists (such as experimental embryologists, or even psychologists) in order to achieve a broadly based understanding of the origins and organization of the phenomena that attract their primary interest.

The separation of problems into those visible after the adaptive behavior patterns begin to function, and those which are relevant to early development (the former being the province of the student of animal behavior, while the latter is assumed to be of interest only to experimental embryologists), presupposes that it is possible to make a sharp distinction between learning and other contributions of experience to development, and that there are no intermediates. As Schneirla has repeatedly pointed out, however, sharp lines cannot be drawn, in early stages of development, between: the effects on neural development of nonbiological conditions (temperature, light, chemical conditions in the environment); nonspecific effects of gross stimulus input; the developmental effects of practice passively forced during ontogeny; the developmental effects of practice resulting from spontaneous activity of the nervous system; links and integrations between behavioral elements, resulting from early, nonfunctional partial performances; interoceptive conditioning resulting from inevitable tissue changes and metabolic activities; simple conditioning to stimulation resulting from spontaneous movements; and simple instances of conventional conditioning and learning.

Now, the introduction of the concept of "experience," in the sense described here, into the discussion of development is by no means equivalent to saying that all behavior patterns derive from learning. This point has been repeatedly made by Schneirla over many years, and I was quite aware of it when I wrote my first contribution to this discussion fifteen years ago. To quote a characteristic remark from that paper (Lehrman, 1953):

> . . . Analysis of the developmental process involved shows that the behavior patterns concerned are not unitary, autonomously developing things, but rather that they emerge ontogenetically in complex ways from the previously developed organization of the organism in a given setting. . . . The post-hatching improvement in pecking ability of chicks is very probably due in part to an increase in strength of leg muscles and to an increase in balance and stability of the standing chick, which results partly from this strengthening of the legs and partly from the development of equilibrium responses. . . . Now, isolation or prevention-of-practice experiments would lead to the conclusion that this part of the improvement was due to "maturation." Of course it is partly due to growth processes, *but what is growing is not pecking ability or anything isomorphic with it.* The use of the categories "maturation-vs.-learning" as explanatory aids usually gives a false impression of unity and directedness in the growth of the behavior pattern, when actually the behavior pattern is not primarily unitary, nor does development proceed in a straight line toward the completion of the pattern.

As I reread that paper, it seems clear to me that, even at that early stage, I was not insisting that all behavior is learned, but that the distinction between "innate" and "acquired" is an inadequate set of concepts for analyzing development, and that the development of behavior patterns could not be analyzed by assuming autonomously developing specific substrates for each behavior pattern, isomorphic with the behavior.

These remarks are my reaction to a recent re-reading of my 1953 paper. In the intervening years, I have heard it so often said that I believed that all species-specific behavior develops through individual learning that I almost came to believe that I *had* said it! I remember reading a discussion in which I. Eibl-Eibesfeldt and W. H. Thorpe apparently succeeded in convincing an initially incredulous Donald Hebb that I had insisted that all behavior is learned through individual experience (Eibl-Eibesfeldt, 1961)!

I believe this difficulty arose from the fact that many workers in the field of animal behavior had such a firmly fixed opinion that every element of behavior ought, on *logical* grounds, to be clearly classifiable as "innate" or as "learned," that any discussion that cast doubt upon the usefulness of the concept of "innate" must inevitably have seemed like an insistence that all behavior must belong to the other category! As I know from my own experience, this could be so even when the discussion in question was addressed, not to the thesis that all behavior is learned, but to the thesis that the dichotomy *itself* does not adequately express the necessities for developmental analysis of behavior.

Is development necessary?

The idea of a "genetic blueprint" The idea of a genome as a "blueprint," contained in the fertilized egg and representing a plan for the construction of an adult organism, is a very attractive one. Lorenz says that "what rules ontogeny . . . is obviously the hereditary blueprint contained in the genome and not the environmental circumstances indispensable to its realization. It is not the bricks and the mortar which rule the building of a cathedral but a plan which has been conceived by an architect. . . ." Further, he says that ". . . our first question concerning the ontogeny of an organism and its behavior is: 'What is blueprinted in its genome?'"

Now, it may be comforting, in the sense that it gives us the feeling that we have increased our understanding of the problem, to say that a behavior pattern (or a structure) is innate if it is "blueprinted in the genome" or, in a more modern vernacular, "encoded in the DNA." There are, of course, contexts in which such expressions are meaningful, but I believe that the comfort and satisfaction gained from disposing of the problems of ontogenetic development by the use of such concepts are misleading, and are based upon the evasion or dismissal of the most difficult and interesting problems of development.

It seems to me that there is a fundamental fallacy in the use of the analogy of the relationship between a blueprint and the structure represented by it to represent the relationship between the genome at the zygote stage and the phenotypic adult. A blueprint is isomorphic with the structure that it represents. The ratios of lengths and widths in the blueprint are the same as those in the structure; the topographical relationships among the parts of the structure are the same as those among the corresponding parts of the blueprint; each part of the structure is represented by a separate part of the blueprint, and each part of the blueprint refers only to a specific part or parts of the structure. It will be immediately obvious that this is profoundly different from the relationship between the genome and the phenotype of a higher animal. It is *not* true that each structure and character in the phenotype is "represented" in a single gene or well defined group of genes; it is *not* the case that each gene refers solely, or even primarily, to a single structure or character; and it is *not* the case that the topographical or topological relationships among the genes are isomorphic with the structural or topographical relationships among phenotypic structures to which the genes refer. It is, of course, a commonplace of modern biology to say that each gene is responsible for the production of a single enzyme. This formulation reflects the truly enormous advances that have been made in recent years in understanding the structure of the genes, primarily on the basis of research on the biochemical actions of genes in one-celled organisms. The problems of ontogeny and differentiation of structures in complex organisms, however, have hardly been touched as yet by the recent massive advances in molecular biology. A facile description of the genome as a "blueprint" gives a misleading impression of understanding a problem that is regarded by modern geneticists as one of the major unsolved problems of biology, and which ought to be regarded as a truly difficult problem by *any* biologist, even a student of animal behavior who is prepared to leave the problem to the experimental embryologist.

Another problem with the conception of the genome as a "blueprint" is, of course, that, while it poses as a contribution to the understanding of ontogeny, it is actually *irrelevant* to the question of individual development. As Lorenz himself says, ". . . it is perfectly possible that a particular motor sequence may owe to phylogenetic processes all the information on environment underlying its adaptiveness and yet be almost wholly dependent upon individual learning for the 'decoding' of this information." But it should be perfectly clear that, if a character "encoded" in the genes may or may not require individual experince for its development, then a scientist who is interested in the causal analysis of development is not helped very much by statements about the "encoding" or "blueprinting" or complex characters in higher animals. Here again, I repeat that the concept of "innate" in the sense of determination by the genome, and the concept of "innate" in the sense of imperviousness to individual experience, refer to different problems and relationships, which cut across each other, rather than making a single conceptual whole. And here again Lorenz, by inconspicuously merging these two conceptions into a single usage, is led to speak of patterns as being blueprinted in the genome, *as opposed to* beging based upon experience, while simultaneously acknowledging that patterns "blueprinted" in the genome may or may not develop through individual experience.

It seems to me, then, that although the idea that behavior patterns are "blueprinted" or "encoded" in the genome is a perfectly appropriate and instructive way of talking about certain problems of genetics and of evolution, it does not in any way deal with the kind of questions about behavioral *development* to which it is so often applied.

Provenance and ontogeny   In my 1953 critique, I referred to the work of Kuo (1932a, b, c, d), who made detailed observations of the behavioral development of the domestic chick embryo within the egg. On the basis of these observations, Kuo suggested that the pecking behavior that can be seen in chicks immediately after hatching develops through a series of stages in which the neck is first (early in embryonic life) passively bent when the heartbeat causes the head (which rests on the thorax) to rise and fall, with active bending of the head occurring later, at first in response to tactual stimulation. Kuo also suggested that the opening and closing of the bill (associated with pecking in the post-hatching animal) first occur when the bird's head is nodding during the embryonic period, apparently through nervous excitation furnished by the head movements through irradiation in the still-incomplete nervous system, while the opening and closing of the bill become independent of head activity only somewhat later. Kuo noted that fluid forced into the throat by movements of the bill and head apparently causes swallowing, beginning at a characteristic time during embryonic development. Kuo's suggestion was that the movements forced by the timing and order of development of the various structures, neural and motor, and by the conformation of the bird's body enforced by its position within the egg, provided an experiential contribution to the development of the integration of the head, bill, and throat components of the food-pecking lunge, which is already to be seen (although in incompletely integrated form) by the time of hatching. It has recently become clear that some aspects of the development of motility in the chick embryo do not depend upon sensory input (Hamburger, 1963; Hamburger, Wenger, and Oppenheim, 1966), and caution is required in interpreting Kuo's data, which have not yet been subjected to direct experimental test. However, the existence of conditioned responses several days before hatching is very well established in these birds (Gottlieb, 1968; Sedláček, 1962, 1964), and the nature of behavioral and neural development during embryonic life in birds, and the problem of the role of experience at this stage, are being actively investigated in several different laboratories (see Gottlieb, 1968, for review).

Of this discussion, Lorenz says "If Lehrman (1953) gives serious consideration to the assumption that a chick could learn, within the egg, considerable portions of the pecking behavior by having its head moved rhythmically up and down through the beating of its own heart, he totally fails to explain why the motor pattern thus individually acquired should fit the requirement of eating in an environmental situation which demands adaptedness to innumerable single givens. . . ."[3]

Here I must repeat something I said earlier in this essay. Nature selects for *outcomes*. Natural selection acts to select genomes that, in a normal environment, will guide development into organisms with the relevant adaptive characteristics. But the path of development from the zygote stage to the phenotypic adult is devious, and includes many developmental processes, including, in some cases, various aspects of experience. This is clear from many considerations, and is acknowledged by Lorenz himself. What then is the difficulty about assuming that, *whatever* the characteristics of the developing nervous system, they must be such as to give rise to the adaptive form of pecking which is seen after the bird hatches? The relationships described by Kuo, involving certain putative effects of experience that might be inevitable in the context of the developing structures in the egg, are no more mysterious a product of embryonic development than any other characteristics of the developing nervous system. It does not matter to the process of natural selection whether what is being selected for is a genome that gives rise to adaptive pecking at food through a developmental process that does not involve experience, or whether it is a genome that gives rise to adaptive pecking behavior via a course of development that *does* include effects of experience. This is another case in which the statement that a characteristic has been arrived at through selective breeding (i.e., in this case, through natural selection) says nothing at all about whether its development does or does not include an effect of experience. Natural selection can select for specific ways of being sensitive to experience, or for phenotypic structures that make experience possible, just as readily as it can for any other characteristics.[4]

In the same context, Lorenz speaks of "some American psychologists" as "trying to avoid, at all costs, the concepts of survival value and phylogenetic adaptation for no other reason than that they regarded them as 'finalistic.'" As I hope the discussion so far has made clear, however, I have not been trying to avoid the concepts of survival value and phylogenetic adaptation, but only to prevent them from being merged with the concepts of the *causal* analysis of *development*, in order that the understanding of ontogeny should not be confused by merging two different meanings of the term "innate," which are to some extent irrelevant to each other.

Lorenz's objection to the formulation that "it is not characters but differences between characters which may be described as innate" is not as clear as he implies. The concept of evolutionary adaptation is not arrived at, and is not maintained in the minds of observers, by perceiving one animal or one species in its adaptation to the environment. The concept of adaptation, both historically and in its everyday application, depends upon the fact that we observe *different* species to show elaborate adaptations to *different* environmental requirements. The adaptive elegance of the way in which a newly hatched pheasant pecks at food on the ground is fully apparent only to the observer who is on some level aware, while he watches the pheasant, that a newly hatched thrush would not peck at the ground, but would gape (beg) from its parent, who would be willing to feed it in a way of which the parent pheasant is incapable. Lorenz makes this quite explicit when he says (of Kuo): "It also remains unexplained why only certain birds peck after hatching, while others gape like passerines, dabble like ducks, or shove their bills into the corner of the mouth. . . ." Here Lorenz clearly, if inadvertently, acknowledges that it is the *differences* among the behavior patterns of different species living in similar environments that give rise to the sharp feeling, which I share, that the species have different genomes. It remains true, of course, that differences in the genome may give rise to differences between animals, at a very early stage of development, which *consist* of differences in the extent to which they are able to take advantage of information offered by the environment, or differences in what they will pay attention to in the environment. Therefore, although animals reared in the same environment that behave differently must have started with different genomes, this does not in any way tell us whether or to what extent differences in experience might have played a role in the development of the phenotypic differences between them as adults.

Normal and Abnormal

The differences in attitude and interests between scientists whose primary interest is in evolution and adaptation and those whose primary interest is in the causal analysis of development are fairly well demonstrated by Lorenz's reaction to a paper by Donald Jensen (1961). Jensen had suggested that many operations other than genetic selection or training could produce differences in behavior between animals. These operations include nutritional variations, alterations of the nervous system, hormone treatments, etc. Jensen suggested that studying the effects of a wide range of differential treatments upon the development of behavior differences, with the intention of inductively integrating the information thus acquired, would be a more fruitful and less controversial way of coping with problems of ontogeny and of causality than the prevalent attitude of treating the question "innate or learned?" as a primary and ultimate question on which all others must hinge.

This modest suggestion has aroused a special ire in Lorenz, which is noticeable even against the background of the generally indignant tone of his book. This is because, in Lorenz's opinion, the investigation of the effects of a very wide variety of treatments which can alter the behavior runs directly counter to the main task of the biologist: to understand how the genome that is arrived at by natural selection gives rise, in the *normal* environment, to the *normal* behavior pattern adapted for that environment.

Lorenz's concern that the introduction of "abnormalities" will distort and misrepresent the study of adaptive characters is shown by the following selection from his remarks:[5]

> Non-adaptive differences in structure and behavior are of but secondary interest to the biologist, while they are the primary concern of the pathologist. ... As students of behavior, we are not interested in ascertaining at random the innumerable factors that might lead to minute, just bearable differences of behavior bordering on the pathological. What we want to elucidate are the amazing facts of adaptedness. ... We need not bother about the innumerable factors which may cause "differences" in behavior as long as we are quite sure that they cannot possibly relay to the organism that particular information which we want to investigate. (Lorenz, pp. 32–3)

Now, Lorenz is quite right to point out that experimental treatments cannot be selected at random; they must be chosen with some intuitive feelings for their relevance to the normal phenomenon,

the development of which we wish to understand. I am not persuaded, however, that the distinction between "pathological" and "normal" is a very useful guide for understanding the causes of development; and I am not convinced that a biologist interested in understanding *development* is obligated to recoil from any treatment that disturbs the "very complicated and very finely balanced system" (Lorenz, 1965) which is the living organism. Indeed, a very good case can be made for the proposition that it is precisely by interfering with normal development and noting in what way the resulting abnormalities develop that we gain the most illuminating insights into the normal processes of development.

Experience and "normality"

Lorenz's tendency to regard conventional learning paradigms as the only method for defining environmental influences that are of any interest to a student of behavior expresses itself in a tendency to regard any other developmental effect of experience as simply a pathological effect of "bad rearing." This distinction is very clear, for example, in his statement that "we try to produce an individual whose genetical blueprints have been realized unscathed in the course of healthy phenogeny. Should we fail in this, we would incur the danger of mistaking some effects in our subject's behavior for the consequences of information withheld, while they really are the pathological results of stunted growth."

This is, of course, a logical extension of Lorenz's position that, with the exception of trial-and-error learning or classical conditioning in the fully developed nervous system, the effects of stimulation from the environment during development are matters of interest, not to the student of animal behavior, but to the experimental embryologist or the pathologist.

I think, however, that it is not so easy as Lorenz implies to make sharp distinctions between "learning" and "mere" pathologies of development. Let us look at some examples of the effects of rearing in abnormal conditions upon behavioral adaptations:

(1)   In many species of birds, the young characteristically follow their parents about within a very

short time after emerging from the egg. It has been clear since the early work of Lorenz (1935) that, in many ducks, geese, and other species of precocial birds, the ability of the young to follow selectively adults of their own species is dependent upon a very quick learning process which occurs during a restricted period very early in life; the birds thus learn through this "imprinting" experience to follow the models that they experience immediately after emerging from the egg. These will, in nature, usually be the birds' parents. If newly hatched ducklings are exposed to adult ducks of another species than their own, they may later prefer to mate with the members of the species on which they were imprinted, rather than with members of their own species (Schutz, 1965). This may happen either through long-term effects of the early experience, or through intervening (adolescent) experience with birds with which they associate because of the earlier experience (Hinde, 1962; Bateson, 1966). Now, a bird which, because of this early experience, wants to mate only with a member of another species, which refuses to mate with it, has certainly had its development altered in an abnormal direction; it is pathological, since the abnormal conditions of its development have led to an adult condition in which it is no longer adapted to its environment. This treatment, which is widely and correctly regarded as demonstrating, for the student of development, a form of learning, must also be regarded, for the student of evolutionary adaptation, as an example of pathological interference with an evolutionary adaptation through rearing in an abnormal environment.

(2) When Harlow reared rhesus monkeys without giving them any opportunity to interact with age-mates, they developed striking and pervasive abnormalities of behavior: as adults, they were not able to maintain social contact with other monkeys, their sexual behavior was so drastically interfered with that most of them were totally unable to copulate, and the balance between the role of fear and aggression and the role of more positive social responses in the social relationships of these monkeys was severely distorted. The deprived monkeys, in general, were incapable of normal integation into a group of monkeys. This distortion of the normal early experience apparently has widespread effects upon the emotional responsiveness of these monkeys, which are reflected both in specific distortions

of particular behavior patterns and in more general interferences with a wide range of behavior patterns (Harlow and Harlow, 1965).

(3) The rat shows a characteristic response of fear and anxiety to a strange environment. The level of this response and many details of it can be altered by selective breeding, and are therefore heritable in the geneticist's use of the term (Fuller and Thompson, 1960). The rat also shows a characteristic tendency to be curious about a novel environment, and to explore it (Berlyne, 1960). The tendency to explore a novel environment (and thus to find food and a nesting place) and the tendency to be fearful of it (and thus to avoid precipitate entry into new areas where predators might be lurking) are both adaptive, and the balance between these two tendencies is undoubtedly arrived at through natural selection. This balance is *also* arrived at through early experience, however, and the amount of fearfulness shown by adult rats introduced into a strange environment can be substantially influenced by early weaning, by handling during early life, or by preweaning experience with different types of mother (Beach and Jaynes, 1954; Levine, 1962; Denenberg and Whimbey, 1963). The "normal" amount of fearfulness shown by a rat in a strange environment is therefore in part a function of the way in which its mother treated it during its infancy. It is impossible to say that the rat has "learned" anything about the characteristics of the environment (including the predators) to which it will later respond; it is equally impossible to deny that the response to the strange environment is in part an effect of experience.

(4) The visual cortex of the cat contains cells that fire in response to the movement of a contour (a dividing line between a light and dark area) across an appropriate area of the retina, and which are differentially sensitive to contours in different orientation (Hubel and Wiesel, 1959, 1962). These units, which were first discovered in the cortex of the adult cat, are found in newborn kittens, and are already differentiated in their function at or shortly after birth, even in the absence of patterned visual experience, although the orientation of the receptive fields is not so clear-cut as in adult cats (Hubel and Wiesel, 1963). If the kittens are reared to the age of two or three months with one eye deprived of pattern vision, contours moved across the deprived retina will not activate the cortical cells (Wiesel and

Hubel, 1963). Further, this deprivation causes a partial failure of normal cell growth at a lower level in the visual system (lateral geniculate nucleus) (Wiesel and Hubel, 1963a). These observations on the electrophysiological effects of visual deprivation are compatible with the results of behavioral studies which show that some mammals reared without patterned visual experience are deficient in the ability to learn visual discrimination habits (Riesen, 1960) and in the ability to transfer visual pattern discriminations learned through one eye to the other eye (Riesen, Kurke, and Mellinger, 1953). The performance of visual discrimination behavior requires not only experience in the sense of visual patterns reaching the eye, but also some experience of the coordination between motor activities and the visual consequences of these activities (Riesen and Aarons, 1959; Held and Hein, 1963). This suggests that the effects of visual experience on behavior are not limited to the development of the electrophysiological mechanisms described by Wiesel and Hubel, but include developmental effects upon wider areas of behavior. Different kinds of experiential effects upon the development of behavior range from the degeneration of an already developed neural mechanism, as shown by Hubel and Wiesel,[6] through more and more specific effects, some of which must be interpreted as conventional learning (Riesen, 1961). Of this range of effects, Lorenz says:

It is a matter of taste whether or not one choses (*sic*) to call it learning when an activity is necessary to prevent atrophy and disintegration of a physiological mechanism, but it can be regarded as adaptive modification and it may well involve ontogenetic acquisition of information. . . . These modifications . . . must, therefore, never be forgotten or overlooked in our attempts to analyze this function. On principle, however, they are no obstacle to the solution of our fundamental question concerning the provenience of the information underlying each point of adaptedness in behavior. . . . But there is little danger, with circumspect experimentation . . . and with an experimenter knowing its pitfalls, that any process of true learning, particularly classical conditioning, might pass unnoticed.

Here again, Lorenz indicates his opinion that "true learning, particularly classical conditioning" is the only kind of effect of experience on the development of animal behavior that is of serious interest to a student of such behavior.

(5) The structure of the joints in the foot and leg of the domestic chick, and of the articulating surfaces of the foot and leg bones, depends upon the movement of these bones during their period of embryonic development. If the muscles of the embryonic limb are paralyzed either by interrupting the nerve supply or by treatment with pharmacological blocking agents, striking abnormalities develop, including complete lack of movement of the joints. The abnormalities include failure of the joint cavities to develop, distortion of the articulating surfaces, and failure of development of the cartilages and ligaments which surround the joint and bind the bones (Drachman and Sokoloff, 1966). If is thus clear that skeletal muscle contractions are essential for normal formation of the structural prerequisites for walking in these animals. Movements of embryonic muscles, which are to some extent the result of spontaneous activity of the central nervous system (Hamburger and Balaban, 1963; Hamburger, Balaban, Oppenheim, and Wenger, 1965), may also be affected during later stages by external stimuli, including stimuli arising from spontaneous movements (Carmichael, 1946). This is a borderline case in which it is not at all clear to what extent afferent inflow plays a role in determining the amount or direction of the relevant movement, but it is clear that the participation of the nervous system in the development of the normal morphological prerequisites for locomotor behavior are only illuminated by a treatment which produces a striking abnormality.

(6) If embryos of the fish *Fundulus heteroclitus* are kept in magnesium chloride solutions, a small percentage of them will develop into hatchlings with only one centrally-located eye (Stockard, 1909), and these fish will apparently be able to see (Rogers, 1957). This sort of treatment, and this result, would seem to me to be the quintessence of the production of a pathology by abnormal rearing, of the kind which Lorenz asserts is of no interest to the student of adaptation to the environment. These fish do, however, suggest a couple of questions, which might provide food for thought: first, are the number and location of the eyes an adaptive character; and second, is the information about the number and location of the eyes located in the genome or in the relationship between the genome

and the chemical environment? If we say that the information about the structure and location of the eyes is contained in the genome, rather than in the relationship between genome and environment, then we must be referring to the fact that different kinds of animals reared in the same environment will develop eyes of different structure and location. This again, however, means appealing to the fact that there are *differences* between animals reared in the same environment as proof that there are *differences* in the genomes. I do not see any way out of this apparent paradox except to acknowledge that statements about the genic origin of characters in complex multicellular animals are meaningful primarily when they refer to the differences between different animals in the same environment as evidence that there are differences in the genomes.

The preceding series of examples of different kinds of modification of development, leading to different kinds of outcomes, is not at all intended to show that anything about the structure of the eyes, or of the joints, or of the visual system, or of the adrenal glands, must be "learned." It is a series of examples of rearing in abnormal environments which lead, through mechanisms of varying degrees of specificity and generality, occurring at different developmental stages, affecting growth processes with different degrees of directness, to developmental outcomes that represent interferences with the normal adaptive characteristics of the animal. All of these outcomes, however, throw light upon the manner in which those adaptive characteristics develop, and on the extent to which environmental influences may play a role in their development. The distinction between "learning" and other forms of "experience" is not sharp, although it is possible to see characteristic differences among different examples; the differences between environmental influences involving effects upon the activity of the nervous system and those not involving such effects are also not sharp, and many intermediates are possible. This is not to say that no classifications are possible, and that no distinctions can be made, among the various kinds of environmental influence. It is to say, however, that the distinction between "morphological ontogeny producing structure" and "trial-and-error behavior" producing learning (Lorenz, 1965), is not a realistic way of surveying the actual range of developmental pro-

cesses that are involved in the ontogenetic origins of behavior, or of illuminating the varying processes that produce the phenotypic appearances of behavior.

To or from? The perception of development

Lorenz asserts that "some American psychologists" avoid the concepts of survival value and phylogenetic adaptation for no other reason than that they regard them as "finalistic." As Lorenz says, "they are not finalistic in the least. If a biologist says that the cat has crooked, pointed claws 'with which to catch mice,' he is not professing a belief in a mystical teleology, but succinctly stating that catching mice is the function whose selection pressure caused the evolution of that particular form of claws."

The concepts of adaptation and of natural selection are of course not teleological or preformationist, and Lorenz is quite wrong in asserting that Schneirla or I ever regarded them so. I believe, however, that a scientist who is interested in the analysis of development must have quite a different attitude toward some problems of causality and abnormality than that which is appropriately characteristic of a biologist who, like Lorenz, is primarily interested in the facts of adaptation and of evolutionary variation. If the observer's perception of a developmental process is wholly dominated by his pre-knowledge of the outcome (i.e., of the adaptive form of the fully developed behavior or structure), then it is very easy for an alteration of the developmental process, caused by a change in the environment, to seem like merely a "deviation" from the "normal" course of development. It would then seem quite natural for such an observer to say that any environmental treatment that led to a maladaptive outcome was of no interest to him, since it merely consisted in the production of a pathology, and not in the illumination of a normal course of development. To such an observer, the development of the normal genome in the normal environment to the normal outcome is merely the *background* for the production of what he is really intersted in: the details of structure and behavior by which the organism is intricately adapted to the details of its environment.

The investigator who wishes to understand developmental processes analytically must, however, have quite a different attitude toward the "normal." For him, the normal and the abnormal environment are simply two ways of treating the developing organism, and it is precisely by considering how the development is changed by any particular variation in the environment that he arrives at some understanding of the mechanisms of development. It would be overstating the case (but not by very much) to say that for the student of development, the normal environment and the normal path of development are no more meaningful or significant or perceptually prominent than any other environment or outcome. The reason why it would be overstating the case is that the student of development is, of course, interested in understanding the ontogenetic origin of the actual characteristics of real species, and he cannot (as Lorenz quite rightly points out) apply experimental treatments entirely at random, regardless of whether they will throw light upon the normal developmental outcome. It remains true, however, that insight into normal developmental processes comes from comparing normal and abnormal treatments and outcomes so that they are illuminated by the differences between them. From this point of view it is not at all true to say that the more abnormal a developmental outcome, the less insight it gives into the normal outcome.

One way of putting this point is that the student of adaptation and evolutionary variation often regards development as proceeding, at any stage, *toward* the functional form, since it is the functional form that is adaptive and since natural selection has acted to select genomes which, in a natural environment, produce the functional form; while for the analytic student of ontogeny, development must be seen as proceeding, at any stage, *out of* the immediately preceding stage, and as being produced by processes going on at that time, since it is *his* aim to understand the processes that create developmental change. The student of adaptation and evolution may, therefore, be talking in entirely legitimate and meaningful terms about the problem in which he is interested, while the application of the same terms and concepts to the problems in which the student of ontogeny is interested may accurately be seen as the intrusion of teleology and preformationism. It is in this sense that Lorenz's use of the concepts of adaptation in the discussion of development may be

seen as "finalistic" by writers who do not in the least lack understanding of biological concepts.

Conclusion: Some Problems of Communication among Scientists

It is clear that at least some of the difficulties in the discussions of the concept of "innateness" arise from the fact that while the various writers believe, and convey to their readers, that they are arguing about matters of fact or interpretation with respect to which one side or the other must be wrong, they are in fact talking about different problems. To some biologists interested primarily in the functions of behavior and in the nature of behavioral adaptations achieved through natural selection, many developmental effects of experience seem trivial and uninteresting, and do not appear to bear upon *their* central question, of the role of natural selection in the establishment of the specific details by which the behavior of specific species is adapted to the necessities of specific environments. To the student of development, however, experiential effects, no matter how diffuse and no matter how remote from the specific details of any particular sensory discrimination or motor act, must be seen as part of the network of causes for the development of any behavior pattern or behavioral capacity to which they are relevant. Further, the rest of the network seems, to such a biologist, definable only in terms of the outcome of experiments on individual development. It ought to be possible to agree on ways of formulating the concepts with which we work so that confusing meanings will be avoided, and so that mutual misunderstandings could be minimized.

One difficulty in the way of such harmony lies in the fact that intelligent people, like unintelligent ones, resent implications that they are illiterate or incompetent, and tend to defend themselves against them. In this essay, I have not succeeded in concealing my resentment at Lorenz's repeated implication that Schneirla and I are or were ignorant of biological concepts; and Lorenz's book repeatedly expresses his sense of outrage at being reminded, as if he did not already know them, of concepts of development which no biologist would deny. It is true, however, that in my earlier contribution to this discussion, I did not deal adequately with the conceptual problems posed by the adaptive character of species-specific behavior, and that what I have said in this essay represents what is, for me, a formulation of problems which I had not considered in detail previously. It is equally true that the formulation of the concept of "innateness" in his recent book is quite different from the concepts found in Lorenz's earlier writings, which always strongly implied developmental fixity as an essential criterion of innateness. There is, therefore, something unbecoming about my implication in this essay that I always knew what I now say, and that I am merely clarifying it for the benefit of people who could not understand it; just as there is something unbecoming in Lorenz's insistence that all criticisms of his point of view are based upon the ignorance of its critics, even while he changes some of his conceptions to meet the criticisms.

I do not think that this kind of problem can be eliminated in scientific communication, and I mention it now for no other reason than to try to make explicit something which is very often inherent in complex discussion. We do not lightly give up ideas which seem central to us, and when they are attacked, we tend to mobilize defenses against the attacks. This means restating the attacked ideas in such a form as to make them seem again convincing to an audience whose confidence in them might have been weakened by the criticism. But when we change the formulation of the ideas in such a situation, we may also be modifying the ideas themselves, in response to criticisms which really may have been leveled against weaknesses in the original formulations. The distinctions are not at all sharp or clear between restating an idea in a clearer form, modifying the idea so as to meet criticism, adding to the formulation things which were previously known but left out as unnecessary, and actually seeing new relationships and new concepts as a consequence of grappling with criticism. I think that no participant in active scholarly discussion can be absolutely sure that everything that he now says represents his long-standing knowledge, without the incorporation of any criticism, and without the inclusion of new ideas made possible only by coping with criticism. If this is a criticism of anybody's writing, it must also apply to some of my own writing in this very essay.

Lorenz believes that what students of behavior are primarily, or even solely, concerned with should be "to elucidate . . . the amazing facts of adaptedness." People interested in analytic studies of the causation and the development of adaptive behavior, however, also have other interests, which are equally legitimate, and for which the concepts derived solely from the study of function and adaptation may not be centrally useful. It is not necessary that all problems fit into the same conceptual framework. It is not required of any theory based on watching intact lower vertebrates that it explain the causes of war, the physiology of the nervous system, and *also* the mode of action of the genes; and it is not an affront to any theory to point out that there are some questions that it cannot answer because it has not asked them.

If it seems that this essay has been oriented primarily to a discussion of Lorenz's recent book, this is only because that book is the most recent attempt at a comprehensive discussion of the so-called "heredity–environment" issue in relation to animal behavior. My central aim has been, not to criticize any other point of view, but to present a positive statement of the relationships between the problems of adaptiveness and of development as seen from the point of view identified with, and best exemplified by, the late T. C. Schneirla.

Acknowledgments

The preparation of this paper was aided by a Research Career Award from the National Institute of Mental Health, which is gratefully acknowledged.

I am indebted to J. Rosenblatt and D. Dinnerstein for their helpful criticism of this paper during its preparation.

Contribution No. 58 from the Institute of Animal Behavior, Rutgers University.

Notes

1 Except as otherwise indicated, all further references to Lorenz are to Lorenz (1965).
2 Hinde (1968), in a paper published while this essay was being set in type, has expressed ideas quite similar to those presented here.

3 This is Lorenz's oversimplified version of my own description, which was a very cautious description of what I imagined to be a very complex series of events, in connection with which I did not use the word "learning." I did refer, at one point in a 500-word description of Kuo's observations, to "process of development, which involved conditioning at a very early age. . . ." Even fifteen years ago, under Schneirla's influence, I was trying to convey the idea of continuity and interpenetration between the processes of growth and those of the influence of environment, and to express a feeling of tentativeness and ambiguity about the distinction between the effects of experience on a developing organism and the effects of experience in a mature nervous system. And even today Lorenz is perfectly confident of the sharpest distinction between "morphological ontogeny producing structure" and "trial-and-error behavior" producing learning, with no sense of difficult intermediates of unsolved conceptual problems.

4 Hamburger's recent work (1970), makes it clear that Kuo's conceptions of the sources of early behavioral organization in the chick embryo are not tenable, and are based on incorrect assumptions about the embryology of the chick's nervous system. Lorenz's feeling and mine was wrong. I would not now use Kuo's work as an example of the study of behavioral development. I have, however, retained the present discussion of Lorenz's reaction to it because it still illustrates the conceptual and methodological problem I am discussing here.

5 These sentences are not consecutive in Lorenz's text but occur, with intervening text, in the space of a page or so.

6 I am embarrassed to recall that, in a review of the first edition of the book by Thorpe (1963a), I said of his attitude to this problem: "When experiment shows that some 'instinctive' act does not develop when practice is prevented, Thorpe speaks of the 'regression' of the instinct through non-use, thus preserving its 'innateness' in the face of the most direct possible evidence to the contrary" (Lehrman, 1957). The work of Hubel and Wiesel shows that I was much too abrupt in my reaction to this comment of Thorpe's. As I hope will be clear from the present discussion, at that time Thorpe and I both used the term "innate" without differentiating between different meanings that the term could have, or between the different conceptions that scientists interested in different kinds of problems could have.

References

Anastasi, A., and J. P. Foley, Jr (1948) A proposed reorientation in the heredity–environment controversy, *Psychol. Rev.*, **55**: 239–49.

Bateson, P. P. G. (1966) The characteristics and context of imprinting, *Biol. Rev.*, **41**: 177–220.

Beach, F. A., and J. Jaynes (1954) Effects of early experience upon the behavior of animals, *Psychol. Bull.*, **51**: 239–63.

Berlyne, D. E. (1960) *Conflict, Arousal and Curiosity*, New York: McGraw-Hill.

Bykov, K. M. (1957) *The Cerebral Cortex and the Internal Organs*, New York: Chemical Publishers.

Carmichael, L. (1964) The onset and early development of behavior. In L. Carmichael (ed.), *Manual of Child Psychology*, New York: Wiley, pp. 43–166.

Denenberg, V., and A. E. Whimbey (1963) Behavior of adult rats is modified by the experiences their mothers had as infants, *Science*, **142**: 1192–3.

Drachman, D. B., and L. Sokoloff (1966) The role of movement in embryonic joint development, *Develop. Biol.*, **14**: 401–20.

Eibl-Eibesfeldt, I. (1961) The interactions of unlearned behaviour patterns and learning in mammals. In J. F. Delafresnaye (ed.), *Brain Mechanisms and Learning*, Oxford: Blackwell, pp. 53–73.

Ford, E. B., and J. S. Huxley (1927) Mendelian genes and rates of development in *Gammarus chevreuxi, Brit. J. Exp. Biol.*, **5**: 112–33.

Fuller, J. L., and W. R. Thompson (1960) *Behavior Genetics*, New York: Wiley.

Gos, E. (1935) Les réflexes conditionnels chez l'embryon d'oiseau, *Bull. Soc. Sci. Liège*, **3**: 194–9; **4**: 246–50.

Gottlieb G. (1968) Prenatal behavior of birds, *Quart. Rev. Biol.*, **43**: 148–74.

Haldane, J. B. S. (1946) The interaction of nature and nurture, *Ann. Eugen.*, **13**: 197–205.

Hamburger, V. (1963) Some aspects of the embryology of behavior, *Quart. Rev. Biol.*, **38**: 342–65.

Hamburger, V. (1970) Development of embryonic motility. In E. Tobach, L. R. Aronson, and E. Shaw (eds), *Biopsychology of Development*, New York: Academic Press (in press).

Hamburger, V., and M. Balaban (1963) Observations and experiments on spontaneous rhythmical behavior in the chick embryo, *Develop. Biol.*, **7**: 533–45.

Hamburger, V., M. Balaban, R. Oppenheim, and E. Wenger (1965) Periodic motility of normal and spinal chick embryos between 8 and 17 days of incubation, *J. Exp. Zool.*, **159**: 1–14.

Hamburger, V., E. Wenger, and R. Oppenheim (1966) Motility in the chick embryo in the absence of sensory input, *J. Exp. Zool.*, **162**: 133–60.

Harlow, H. F., and M. K. Harlow (1965) The affectional systems. In A. M. Schrier, H. F. Harlow, and F. Stollnetz (eds), *Behavior of Nonhuman Primates*, vol. 2, New York: Academic Press, pp. 287–334.

Harnly, M. H. (1941) Flight capacity in relation to phenotypic and genotypic variations in the wings of *Drosophila melanogaster, J. Exp. Zool.*, **88**: 263–73.

Hebb, D. O. (1953) Heredity and environment in animal behaviour, *Brit. J. Anim. Behav.*, **1**: 43–7.

Held, R., and A. Hein (1963) Movement-produced stimulation in the development of visually guided behavior, *J. Comp. Physiol. Psychol.*, **56**: 872–6.

Hinde, R. A. (1962) Some aspects of the imprinting problem, *Symp. Zool. Soc. Lond.*, **8**: 129–38.

Hinde, R. A. (1966) *Animal Behaviour: A Synthesis of Ethology and Comparative Psychology*, New York: McGraw-Hill.

Hinde, R. A. (1968) Dichotomies in the study of development. In J. M. Thoday and A. S. Parkes (eds), *Genetic and Environmental Influences on Behaviour*, Eugenics Soc. Symp. no. 4, Edinburgh: Oliver and Boyd, pp. 3–12.

Hochberg, J. (1963) Nativism and empiricism in perception. In L. Postman (ed.), *Psychology in the Making*, New York: A. A. Knopf, pp. 255–330.

Hubel, D. H., and T. N. Wiesel (1959) Receptive fields of single neurones in the cat's striate cortex, *J. Physiol.*, **148**: 574–91.

Hubel, D. H., and T. N. Wiesel (1962) Receptive fields, binocular interaction and functional architecture in the cat's visual cortex, *J. Physiol.*, **160**: 106–54.

Hubel, D. H., and T. N. Wiesel (1963) Receptive fields of cells in striate cortex of very young, visually inexperienced kittens, *J. Neurophysiol.*, **26**: 994–1002.

Hunt, E. L. (1949) Establishment of conditioned responses in chick embryos, *J. Comp. Psychol.*, **42**: 107–17.

Jensen, D. D. (1961) Operationism and the question "Is this behaviour learned or innate?", *Behaviour*, **17**: 1–8.

Kimble, G. A. (1967) *Foundations of Conditioning and Learning*, New York: Appleton-Century-Crofts.

Koopman, K. F. (1950) Natural selection for reproductive isolation between Drosophila pseudoobscura and Drosophila persimilis, *Evolution*, **4**: 135–48.

Kuo, Z.-Y. (1932a) Ontogeny of embryonic behavior in Aves, I: The chronology and general nature of the behavior of the chick embryo, *J. Exp. Zool.*, **61**: 395–430.

Kuo, Z.-Y. (1932b) Ontogeny of embryonic behavior in Aves, II: The mechanical factors in the various stages leading to hatching, *J. Exp. Zool.*, **62**: 453–89.

Kuo, Z.-Y. (1932c) Ontogeny of embryonic behavior in Aves, III: The structure and environmental factors in embryonic behavior, *J. Comp. Psychol.*, **13**: 245–72.

Kuo, Z.-Y. (1932d) Ontogeny of embryonic behavior in Aves, IV: The influence of embryonic movements upon the behavior after hatching, *J. Comp. Psychol.*, **14**: 109–22.

Lehrman, D. S. (1953) A critique of Konrad Lorenz's theory of instinctive behavior, *Quart. Rev. Biol.*, **28**: 337–63.

Lehrman, D. S. (1957) Nurture, nature and ethology: Review of W. H. Thorpe, *Learning and Instinct in Animals*, 1st edn, *Contemp. Psychol.*, **4**: 103–4.

Levine, S. (1962) The effects of infantile experience on adult behavior. In A. J. Bachrach (ed.), *Experimental Foundations of Clinical Psychology*, New York: Basic Books, pp. 139–69.

Lorenz, K. Z. (1935) Der Kumpan in der Umwelt des Vogels, *J. Orn.*, **83**: 137–213, 289–413.

Lorenz, K. Z. (1937) Über die Bildung des Instinktbegriffes, *Naturwissenschaften*, **25**: 289–300, 307–18, 324–31.

Lorenz, K. Z. (1950) The comparative method in studying

innate behaviour patterns, *Sympos. Soc. Exp. Biol.*, **4**: 221–268.

Lorenz, K. Z. (1961) Phylogenetische Anpassung und adaptive Modifikation des Verhaltens, *Z. Tierpsychol.*, **18**: 139–87.

Lorenz, K. Z. (1965) *Evolution and modification of behavior*, Chicago: University of Chicago Press.

Mayr, E., and T. Dobzhansky (1945) Experiments on sexual isolation in Drosophila, IV: Modification of the degree of isolation between Drosophila pseudoobscura and Drosophila persimilis and of sexual preferences in Drosophila prosaltans, *Proc. Nat. Acad. Sci. US*, **31**: 75–82.

Mayr, E. (1942) *Systematics and the Origin of Species*, New York: Columbia University Press.

Miller, N. E. (1969) Psychosomatic effects of specific types of training, *Ann. N.Y. Acad. Sci.*, **159**: 1025–40.

Miller, N. E., and L. di Cara (1967) Instrumental learning of heart rate changes in curarized rats: Shaping and specificity to discriminative stimulus, *J. Comp. Physiol. Psychol.*, **63**: 12–19.

Morgan, T. H., A. H. Sturtevant, H. J. Muller, and C. B. Bridges (1923) *The Mechanism of Mendelian Heredity*, 2nd ed, New Haven: Yale University Press.

Prechtl, H. F. R. (1965) Problems of behavioral studies in the newborn infant, *Adv. Stud. Behav.*, **1**: 75–98.

Razran, G. H. S. (1961) The observable unconscious and the inferable conscious in current Soviet psychophysiology: interoceptive conditioning, semantic conditioning and the orienting reflex, *Psychol. Rev.*, **68**: 81–147.

Riesen, A. H. (1960) Effects of stimulus deprivation on the development and atrophy of the visual sensory system, *Am. J. Orthopsychiat.*, **30**: 23–36.

Riesen, A. H. (1961) Stimulation as a requirement for growth and function in behavioral development. In D. W. Fiske and S. R. Maddi (eds), *Functions of Varied Experience*, Homewood, Ill.: Dorsey Press, pp. 57–105.

Riesen, A. H., and L. Aarons (1959) Visual movement and intensity discrimination in cats after early deprivation of pattern vision, *J. Comp. Physiol. Psychol.*, **52**: 142–49.

Riesen, A. H., M. I. Kurke, and J. C. Mellinger (1953) Interocular transfer of habits learned monocularly in visually naive and visually experienced cats, *J. Comp. Physiol. Psychol.*, **46**: 166–72.

Rogers, K. T. (1957) Optokinetic testing of cyclopean and synophthalmic fish hatchlings, *Biol. Bull.*, **112**: 241–8.

Schneirla, T. C. (1956) The interrelationships of the "innate" and the "acquired" in instinctive behavior. In P.-P. Grassé (ed.), *L'Instinct dans le comportement des animaux et de l'homme*, Paris: Masson, pp. 387–452.

Schneirla, T. C. (1957) The concept of development in comparative psychology. In D. B. Harris (ed.), *The Concept of Development*, Minneapolis: University of Minnesota Press. pp. 78–108.

Schneirla, T. C. (1966) Behavioral development and comparative psychology, *Quart. Rev. Biol.*, **41**: 283–303.

Schutz, F. (1965) Sexuelle Prägung bei Anatiden, *Z. Tierpsychol.*, **22**: 50–103.

Sedláček, J. (1962) Temporary connections in chick embryos, *Physiol. Bohemoslov.*, **11**: 300–6.

Sedláček, J. (1964) Further findings on the conditions of formation of the temporary connection in chick embryos, *Physiol. Bohemoslov.*, **13**: 411–20.

Spelt, D. K. (1948) The conditioning of the human fetus *in utero*, *J. Exp. Psychol.*, **38**: 338–46.

Stockard, C. R. (1909) The development of artificially produced cyclopean fish – "the magnesium embryo," *J. Exp. Zool.*, **6**: 285–337.

Thorpe, W. H. (1963a) *Learning and Instinct in Animals*, 2nd edn, Cambridge, Mass.: Harvard University Press.

Thorpe, W. H. (1963b) Ethology and the coding problem in germ cell and brain, *Z. Tierpsychol.*, **20**: 529–51.

Tinbergen, N. (1963) On aims and methods of ethology, *Z. Tierpsychol.*, **20**: 410–33.

Whitman, C. O. (1919) The behavior of pigeons, *Publ. Carnegie Inst. Wash.*, **257** (3): 1–161.

Wiesel, T. N., and D. H. Hubel (1963) Single-cell responses in striate cortex of kittens deprived of vision in one eye, *J. Neurophysiol.*, **26**: 1003–17.

Empirical Paradigms: Development of Perceptual and Motor Mechanisms

Introduction

In Parts III and IV we have collected a mixture of classic empirical studies or reviews on behavioral development and more recent updates of a number of key fields of research. In organizing the chapters for these Parts, we broadly followed the scheme proposed by Hogan (1988), where behavioral development is seen as involving the development of various kinds of perceptual, motor and central mechanisms and the formation of connections between them. In this ethological framework, a behavior system is a functional unit consisting of perceptual, motor and central mechanisms.

The first two chapters of Part III are concerned with perceptual development in the visual and auditory modalities, respectively. Limitations of space forced us to omit any of the original papers by Hubel and Wiesel, which broke new ground in our understanding of how the visual cortex of the brain becomes organized during development (see Wiesel, 1982, for a review of this work). We have, however, included a recent paper by Carla J. Shatz, which integrates this early work with more recent developments in the field. Her paper emphasizes how neural activity and sensory experience are crucial for forming appropriate connections in the developing brain. The paper by Gilbert Gottlieb makes a similar point with regard to auditory development. We chose this particular paper because it also includes a discussion of the concepts of maintenance, induction and facilitation in development. A more detailed treatment of these concepts is provided in Gottlieb (1976).

The next two chapters discuss imprinting, a form of early learning. Imprinting was made famous by Konrad Lorenz, first in a paper in German (Lorenz, 1935) and soon thereafter in a shorter version in English (Lorenz, 1937). Here we have included an excerpt from an English translation of the original paper. This excerpt gives prominence to an often-forgotten aspect of Lorenz's early formulation of imprinting: his emphasis on species differences. The paper by Johan Bolhuis discusses Lorenz's views of learning, and provides a review of contemporary work on filial imprinting, as well as the development of filial predispositions (see also Bolhuis and Honey, 1998). Filial imprinting is now a prominent model system for the study of the neural mechanisms of learning and memory. Unfortunately we were not able to include more extensive reviews of this work here; the reader is referred to Horn (1985, 1992). Sexual imprinting is reviewed in Bolhuis (1991), and is discussed in some detail in the chapter by Carel ten Cate in the first section of this book.

Another avian learning phenomenon that has had an important influence on behavioral research is the acquisition of song in passerine birds. We have included a chapter by Peter Marler which has a classic formulation of the concept of templates for song learning. The chapter by Donald Kroodsma is a more recent review of work on this topic. Other good reviews of the song-learning literature are provided by Marler (1991) and Bottjer and Arnold (1986). Here too important advances have been made with regard to the analysis of the neural mechanisms of song learning, for which there was no room in the present volume. Excellent reviews of the neurobiological work on song learning can be found in Konishi (1985), Nottebohm (1991) and DeVoogd (1994).

The last chapter in Part III is specifically on the development of motor mechanisms. John Fentress and his colleagues have been pioneers in the analysis of motor development. We have included a large part of a paper by John Fentress and Peter McLeod that reviews the most important aspects of this work. A more recent review is by Berridge (1994), one of Fentress's former students, while an earlier excellent review of motor development in the cat is provided by Baerends-van Roon and Baerends (1979).

References

Baerends-van Roon, J. M., and Baerends, G. P. (1979) The morphogenesis of the behaviour of the domestic cat, *Verhandelingen der Koninklijke Nederlandse Akademie van Wetenschappen, afd. Natuurkunde, Tweede Reeks* (*Proceedings of the Royal Netherlands Academy of Sciences, Physics Section, Second Series*), Part 72, pp. 67–98.

Berridge, K. C. (1994) The development of action patterns. In Hogan, J. A. and Bolhuis, J. J. (eds), *Causal Mechanisms of Behavioural Development*, Cambridge: Cambridge University Press, pp. 147–80.

Bolhuis, J. J. (1991) Mechanisms of avian imprinting: a review, *Biological Reviews*, 66, 303–45.

Bolhuis, J. J. and Honey, R. C. (1998) Imprinting, learning, and development: From behaviour to brain and back, *Trends in Neurosciences*, **21**, 306–11.

Bottjer, S. W. and Arnold, A. P. (1986) The ontogeny of vocal learning in songbirds. In *Handbook of Behavioral Neurobiology*, vol. 8, E. M. Blass (ed.), New York: Plenum Press, pp. 129–61.

DeVoogd, T. J. (1994) The neural basis for the acquisition and production of bird song. In Hogan, J. A. and Bolhuis, J. J. (eds), *Causal Mechanisms of Behavioural Development*, Cambridge: Cambridge University Press, pp. 49–81.

Gottlieb, G. (1976) Conceptions of prenatal development: Behavioral embryology, *Psychological Review*, **83**, 215–34.

Hogan, J. A. (1988) Cause and function in the development of behavior systems. In: E. M. Blass (ed.), *Handbook of Behavioral Neurobiology*, vol. 9, New York: Plenum Press, pp. 63–106.

Horn, G. (1985) *Memory, Imprinting, and the Brain*, Oxford: Clarendon Press.

Horn, G. (1992) Brain mechanisms of memory and predispositions: Interactive studies of cerebral function and behavior. In M. H. Johnson (ed.), *Brain Development and Cognition: A Reader*, Oxford: Blackwell, pp. 485–513.

Konishi, M. (1985) Bird song: From behavior to neuron, *Annual Review of Neuroscience*, **8**, 125–70.

Lorenz, K. (1935) Der Kumpan in der Umwelt des Vogels, *Journal für Ornithologie*, **83**, 137–213, 289–413.

Lorenz, K. (1937) The companion in the bird's world, *Auk*, **54**, 245–73.

Marler, P. (1991) Song-learning behavior: The interface with neuroethology, *Trends in Neurosciences*, **14**, 199–206.

Nottebohm, F. (1991) Reassessing the mechanisms and origins of vocal learning in birds, *Trends in Neurosciences*, **14**, 206–11.

Wiesel, T. N. (1982) Postnatal development of the visual cortex and the influence of environment, *Nature*, **299**, 583–91.

CHAPTER 10

The Developing Brain

CARLA J. SHATZ

An adult human brain has more than 100 billion neurons. They are specifically and intricately connected with one another in ways that make possible memory, vision, learning, thought, consciousness and other properties of the mind. One of the most remarkable features of the adult nervous system is the precision of this wiring. No aspect of the complicated structure, it would appear, has been left to chance. The achievement of such complexity is even more astounding when one considers that during the first few weeks after fertilization many of the sense organs are not even connected to the embryonic processing centers of the brain. During fetal development, neurons must be generated in the right quantity and location. The axons that propagate from them must select the correct pathway to their target and finally make the right connection.

How do such precise neural links form? One idea holds that the brain wires itself as the fetus develops, in a manner analogous to the way a computer is manufactured: that is, the chips and components are assembled and connected according to a preset circuit diagram. According to this analogy, a flip of a biological switch at some point in prenatal life turns on the computer. This notion would imply that the brain's entire structure is recorded in a set

First published in *Scientific American*, **267**, September 1992, pp. 60–7.

of biological blueprints – presumably DNA – and that the organ begins to work only after the wiring is essentially complete.

Research during the past decade shows that the biology of brain development follows very different rules. The neural connections elaborate themselves from an immature pattern of wiring that only grossly approximates the adult pattern. Although humans are born with almost all the neurons they will ever have, the mass of the brain at birth is only about one fourth that of the adult brain. The brain becomes bigger because neurons grow in size, and the number of axons and dendrites as well as the extent of their connections increases.

Workers who have studied the development of the brain have found that to achieve the precision of the adult pattern, neural function is necessary: the brain must be stimulated in some fashion. Indeed, several observations during the past few decades have shown that babies who spent most of their first year of life lying in their cribs developed abnormally slowly. Some of these infants could not sit up at 21 months of age, and fewer than 15 percent could walk by about the age of three. Children must be stimulated – through touch, speech and images – to develop fully. Based in part on such observations, some people favor enriched environments for young children, in the hopes of enhancing development. Yet current studies provide no clear evidence that such extra stimulation is helpful.

Much research remains to be done before anyone can conclusively determine the types of sensory input that encourage the formation of particular neural connections in newborns. As a first step toward understanding the process, neurobiologists have focused on the development of the visual system in other animals, especially during the neonatal stages. It is easy under the conditions that prevail at that stage to control visual experience and observe behavioral response to small changes. Furthermore, the mammalian eye differs little from species to species. Another physiological fact makes the visual system a productive object of study: its neurons are essentially the same as neurons in other parts of the brain. For these reasons, the results of such studies are very likely to be applicable to the human nervous system as well.

.   .   .

But perhaps the most important advantage is that in the visual system, investigators can accurately correlate function with structure and identify the pathway from external stimulus to physiological response. The response begins when the rods and cones of the retina transform light into neural signals. These cells send the signals to the retinal interneurons, which relay them to the output neurons of the retina, called the retinal ganglion cells. The axons of the retinal ganglion cells (which make up the optic nerve) connect to a relay structure within the brain known as the lateral geniculate nucleus. The cells of the lateral geniculate nucleus then send the visual information to specific neurons located in what is called layer 4 of the (six-layer) primary visual cortex. This cortical region occupies the occipital lobe in each cerebral hemisphere (see figure 10.1).

Within the lateral geniculate nucleus, retinal ganglion cell axons from each eye are strictly segregated: the axons of one eye alternate with those from the other and thus form a series of eye-specific layers. The axons from the lateral geniculate nucleus in turn terminate in restricted patches

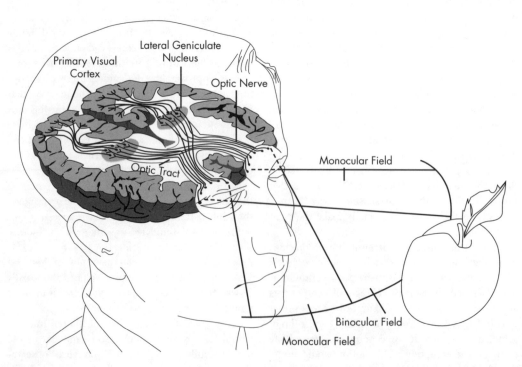

Figure 10.1   Visual pathway in the adult demonstrates the segregation of axons. Neighboring retinal ganglion cells in each eye send their axons to neighboring neurons in the lateral geniculate nucleus. Similarly, the neurons of the geniculate nucleus map their axons onto the visual cortex. The system forms a topographically orderly pattern that in part accounts for such characteristics as binocular vision.

within cortical layer 4. The patches corresponding to each eye interdigitate with one another to form structures termed ocular dominance columns.

To establish such a network during development, axons must grow long distances, because the target structures form in different regions. The retinal ganglion cells are generated within the eye. The lateral geniculate neurons take shape in an embryonic structure known as the diencephalon, which will form the thalamus and hypothalamus. The layer 4 cells are created in another protoorgan called the telencephalon, which later develops into the cerebral cortex. From the beginning of fetal development, these three structures are many cell-body diameters distant from one another. Yet after identifying one or the other of these targets, the axons reach it and array themselves in the correct topographic fashion – that is, cells located near one another in one structure map their axons to the correct neighboring cells within the target.

This developmental process can be compared with the problem of stringing telephone lines between particular homes located within specific cities. For instance, to string wires between Boston and New York, one must bypass several cities, including Providence, Hartford, New Haven and Stamford. Once in New York, the lines must be directed to the correct borough (target) and then to the correct street address (topographic location).

Corey Goodman of the University of California at Berkeley and Thomas Jessel of Columbia University have demonstrated that in most instances, axons immediately recognize and grow along the correct pathway and select the correct target in a highly precise manner. A kind of "molecular sensing" is thought to guide growing axons. The axons have specialized tips, called growth cones, that can recognize the proper pathways. They do so by sensing a variety of specific molecules laid out on the surface of, or even released from, cells located along the pathway. The target itself may also release the necessary molecular cues. Removing these cues (by genetic or surgical manipulation) can cause the axons to grow aimlessly. But once axons have arrived at their targets, they still need to select the correct address. Unlike pathway and target selection, address selection is not direct. In fact, it involves the correction of many initial errors.

. . .

The first hint that address selection is not precise came from experiments using radioactive tracers. Injections of these tracers at successively later times in fetal development outline the course and pattern of axonal projections. Such studies have also shown that structures emerge at different times in development, which can further complicate address selection.

For instance, Pasko Rakic of Yale University has shown that in the visual pathway in monkeys, the connections between the retina and the lateral geniculate nucleus appear first, followed by those between the lateral geniculate nucleus and layer 4 of the visual cortex. Other studies found that in cats and primates (including humans), the lateral geniculate nucleus layers develop during the prenatal period, before the rods and cones of the retina have formed (and thus before vision is even possible). When Simon LeVay, Michael P. Stryker and I were postdoctoral fellows at Harvard Medical School, we found that at birth, layer 4 columns in cats do not even exist in the visual cortex. I subsequently determined that even earlier, in fetal life, the cat has no layers in the lateral geniculate nucleus. These important visual structures emerge only gradually and at separate stages.

The functional properties of neurons, like their structural architecture, do not attain their specificity until later in life. Microelectrode recordings from the visual cortex of newborn cats and monkeys reveal that the majority of layer 4 neurons respond equally well to visual stimulation of either eye. In the adult, each neuron in layer 4 responds primarily if not exclusively to stimulation of one eye only. This finding implies that during the process of address selection, the axons must correct their early "mistakes" by removing the inputs from the "inappropriate" eye.

In 1983 my colleague Peter A. Kirkwood and I found further evidence that axons must fine-tune their connections. It came from our work on the brains of six-week-old cat fetuses (the gestation period of the cat is about nine weeks). We removed a significant portion of the visual pathway – from the ganglion cells in both eyes to the lateral geniculate nucleus – and placed it in vitro in a special life-support chamber. (Inserting microelectrodes in a fetus is extremely difficult.) The device kept the cells alive for about 24 hours. Next we applied electrical pulses to the two optic nerves to stimulate the ganglion cell axons and make them fire action potentials, or nerve signals. We found that neurons in the lateral geniculate nucleus responded to the ganglion cells and, indeed, received inputs from both eyes. In the adult the layers respond only to stimulation of the appropriate eye.

. . .

The eventual emergence of discretely functioning neural domains (such as the layers and ocular dominance columns) indicates that axons do manage to correct their mistakes during address selection. The selection process itself depends on the branching pattern of individual axons. In 1986 David W. Sretavan, then a doctoral student in my laboratory, was able to examine the process in some detail. Experimenting with fetal cats, he selectively labeled single retinal ganglion cell axons in their entirely – from the cell body in the retina to their tips within the lateral geniculate nucleus – at successively later stages.

He found that at the earliest times in development, when ganglion cell axons have just arrived within the lateral geniculate nucleus (after about five weeks of gestation), the axons assume a very simple sticklike shape and are tipped with a growth cone. A few days later the axons arising from both eyes acquire a "hairy" appearance: they have short side branches along their entire length.

The presence of side branches at this age implies that the inputs from both eyes mix with one another. In other words, the neural regions have yet to take on the adult structure, in which each eye has its own specific regions. As development continues, the axons sprout elaborate terminal branches and lose their side branches. Soon individual axons from each eye have highly branched terminals that are restricted to the appropriate layer. Axons from one eye that traverse territory belonging to those from the other eye are smooth and unbranched (see figure 10.2).

The sequence of developmental changes in the branching patterns shows that the adult pattern of connections emerges as axons remodel by the selective withdrawal and growth of different branches. Axons apparently grow to many different addresses within their target structures and then somehow eliminate addressing errors.

One possible explanation for axonal remodeling

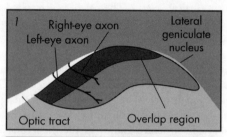
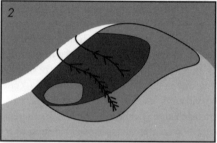
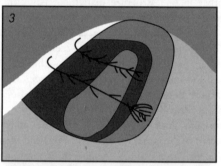
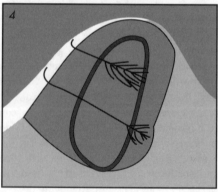

Figure 10.2 Axonal remodelling in the lateral geniculate nucleus occurs largely before birth. At the earliest times in development (1), the axons from the left eye and right eye are simple and tipped with growth cones. The shaded region represents the intermixing of inputs from both eyes. After further development (2), the axons grow many side branches. The axons soon begin to lose some side branches and start to extend elaborate terminal branches (3). Eventually these branches occupy the appropriate territory to form eye-specific layers (4).

is that specific molecular cues are arrayed on the surface of the target cells. Although this idea might seem conceptually attractive, it has very little experimental support. An alternative explanation appears to be stronger. It holds that all target neurons are fair game. Then, some kind of competition between inputs would lead to formation of specific functional areas.

An important clue concerning the nature of the competitive interactions between axons for target neurons has come from the experiments of David H. Hubel of Harvard Medical School and Torsten N. Wiesel of the Rockefeller University. In the 1970s, when both workers were at Harvard, they studied the formation of childhood cataracts. Clinical observations indicated that if the condition is not treated promptly, it can lead to permanent blindness in the obstructed eye. To emulate the effect, Hubel and Wiesel closed the eyelids of newborn cats. They discovered that even a week of sightlessness can alter the formation of ocular dominance columns. The axons from the lateral geniculate nucleus representing the closed eye occupy smaller than normal patches within layer 4 of the cortex. The axons of the open eye occupy larger than normal patches.

The workers also showed that the effects are restricted to a critical period. Cataracts, when they occur in adulthood and are subsequently corrected by surgery, do not cause lasting blindness. Apparently the critical period has ended long ago, and so the brain's wiring cannot be affected.

These observations suggest that the ocular dominance columns form as a consequence of use. The axons of the lateral geniculate nucleus from each eye somehow compete for common territory in layer 4. When use is equal, the columns in the two eyes are identical; unequal use leads to unequal allotment of territory claimed in layer 4.

.   .   .

How is use translated into these lasting anatomic consequences? In the visual system, use consists of the action potentials generated each time a visual stimulus is converted into a neural signal and is carried by the ganglion cell axons into the brain. Perhaps the effects of eye closure on the development of ocular dominance columns occur because there are fewer action potentials coming from the closed eye. If that is the case, blockage of all action potentials during the critical period of postnatal life should prevent axons from both eyes from fashioning the correct patterns and lead to abnormal development in the visual cortex. Stryker and William Harris, then a postdoctoral fellow at Harvard, obtained this result when they used the drug tetrodotoxin to block retinal ganglion cell action potentials. They found that the ocular dominance columns in layer 4 failed to appear (the layers in the lateral geniculate nucleus were unaffected because they had already formed in utero).

Nevertheless, action potentials by themselves are not sufficient to create the segregated patterns in the cortex. Neural activity cannot be random. Instead it must be defined, both temporally and spatially, and must occur in the presence of special kinds of synapses. Stryker and his associate Sheri Strickland, who are both at the University of California at San Francisco, have shown that simultaneous, artificial stimulation of all the axons in the optic nerves can prevent the segregation of axons from the lateral geniculate nucleus into ocular dominance columns within layer 4. Although this result resembles that achieved with tetrodotoxin, an important difference exists. Here ganglion cell action potentials are present – but all at the same time. Segregation to form the columns in the visual cortex, on the other hand, proceeds when the two nerves are stimulated asynchronously (see figure 10.3).

In a sense, then, cells that fire together wire together. The timing of action-potential activity is critical in determining which synaptic connections are strengthened and retained and which are weakened and eliminated. Under normal circumstances, vision itself acts to correlate the activity of neighboring retinal ganglion cells, because the cells receive inputs from the same parts of the visual world.

What is the synaptic mechanism that strengthens or weakens the connections? As long ago as 1949, Donald O. Hebb of McGill University proposed the existence of special synapses that could execute the task. The signal strength in such synapses would increase whenever activities in a presynaptic cell (the cell supplying the synaptic input) and in a postsynaptic cell (the cell receiving the input) coincide. Clear evidence showing that

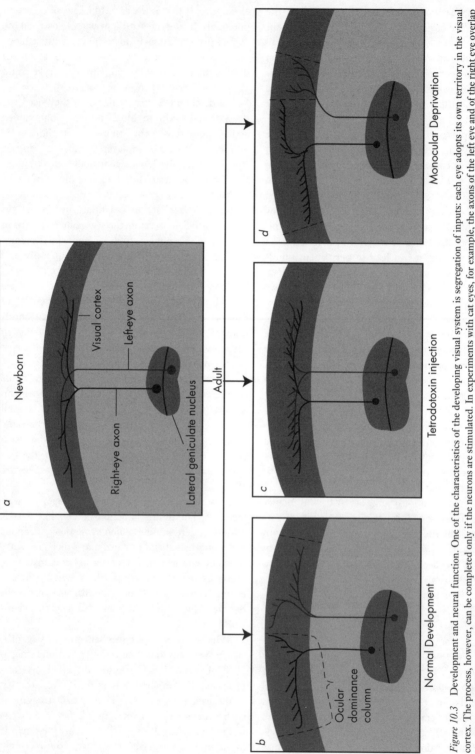

Figure 10.3 Development and neural function. One of the characteristics of the developing visual system is segregation of inputs: each eye adopts its own territory in the visual cortex. The process, however, can be completed only if the neurons are stimulated. In experiments with cat eyes, for example, the axons of the left eye and of the right eye overlap in layer 4 of the visual cortex at birth (a). Visual stimuli will cause the axons to separate and form ocular dominance columns in the cortex (b). Such normal development can be blocked with injections of tetrodotoxin; as a result, the axons never segregate, and the ocular dominance columns fail to emerge (c). Another way to perturb development is to keep one eye closed, depriving it of stimulation. The axons of the open eye then take over more than their fair share of territory in the cortex (d).

such "Hebb synapses" exist comes from studies of the phenomenon of long-term potentiation in the hippocampus. Researchers found that the pairing of presynaptic and postsynaptic activity in the hippocampus can cause incremental increases in the strength of synaptic transmission between the paired cells. The strengthened state can last from hours to days.

Such synapses are now thought to be essential in memory and learning (see "The Biological Basis of Learning and Individuality," by Eric R. Kandel and Robert D. Hawkins, p. 78). Studies by Wolf Singer and his colleagues at the Max Planck Institute for Brain Research in Frankfurt and by Yves Fregnac and his colleagues at the University of Paris also suggest that Hebb synapses are present in the visual cortex during the critical period, although their properties are not well understood.

Just how coincident activity causes long-lasting changes in transmission is not known. There is general agreement among researchers that the postsynaptic cell must somehow detect the coincidence in the incoming presynaptic activity and in turn send a signal back to all concurrently active presynaptic inputs. But this cannot be the whole story. During the formation of the ocular dominance columns, inputs that are not active at the same time are weakened and eliminated.

Consequently, one must also propose the existence of a mechanism for activity-dependent synaptic weakening. This weakening – a kind of long-term depression – would occur when presynaptic action potentials do not accompany postsynaptic activity. Synapses that have this special property (opposite to that of Hebb synapses) have been found in the hippocampus and cerebellum. The results of the Stryker and Strickland experiments suggest that such synapses are very likely to exist in the visual cortex as well.

A strongly similar process of axonal remodeling operates as motor neurons in the spinal cord connect with their target muscles. In the adult, each muscle fiber receives input from only one motor neuron. But after motor neurons make the first contacts with the muscle fibers, each muscle fiber receives inputs from many motor neurons. Then, just as in the visual system, some inputs are eliminated, giving rise to the adult pattern of connectivity. Studies have shown that the process of elimination requires specific temporal patterns of

actionpotential activity generated by the motor neurons.

The requirement for specific spatial and temporal patterns of neuronal activity might be likened to a process whereby telephone calls are placed from addresses in one city (the lateral geniculate nucleus in the visual system) to those in the next city (the visual cortex) to verify that connections have been made at the correct locations. When two near neighbors in the lateral geniculate nucleus simultaneously call neighboring addresses in the cortex, the telephones in both those homes will ring. The concurrent ringing verifies that relations between neighbors have been preserved during the wiring process.

If, however, one of the neighbors in the lateral geniculate nucleus mistakenly makes connections with very distant parts of layer 4 or with parts that receive input from the other eye, the called telephone will rarely if ever ring simultaneously with those of its neighbors. This dissonance would lead to the weakening and ultimate removal of that connection.

.   .   .

The research cited thus far has explored the remodeling of connections after the animal can move or see. But what about earlier in development? Can mechanisms of axonal remodeling operate even before the brain can respond to stimulation from the external world? My colleagues and I thought the formation of layers in the lateral geniculate nucleus in the cat might be a good place to address this question. After all, during the relevant developmental period, rods and cones have not yet emerged. Can the layers develop their specific territories for each eye even though vision cannot yet generate action-potential activity?

We reasoned that if activity is necessary at these early times, it must somehow be generated spontaneously within the retina, perhaps by the ganglion cells themselves. If so, the firing of retinal ganglion cells might be contributing to layer construction, because all the synaptic machinery necessary for competition is present. It should be possible to prevent the formation of the eyespecific layers by blocking action-potential activity from the eyes to the lateral geniculate nucleus.

To hinder activity during fetal development, Sretavan and I, in collaboration with Stryker, implanted special minipumps containing tetrodotoxin in utero just before the lateral geniculate nucleus layers normally begin to form in the cat (at about six weeks of fetal development). After two weeks of infusion, we assessed the effects on the formation of layers. Much to our satisfaction, the results of these in utero infusion experiments showed clearly that the eye-specific layers do not appear in the presence of tetrodotoxin. Moreover, by examining the branching patterns of individual ganglion cell axons after the treatment, we reassured ourselves that tetrodotoxin did not simply stunt normal growth.

In fact, the branching patterns of these axons were very striking. Unlike normal axons at the comparable age, the tetrodotoxin-treated axons did not have highly restricted terminal branches. Rather they had many branches along the entire length of the axon. It was as if, without action-potential activity, the information necessary to withdraw side branches and elaborate the terminal branches was missing.

In 1988, at about the same time these experiments were completed, Lucia Galli-Resta and Lamberto Maffei of the University of Pisa achieved the extraordinary technical feat of actually recording signals from fetal ganglion cells in utero. They demonstrated directly that retinal ganglion cells can indeed spontaneously generate bursts of action potentials in the darkness of the developing eye. This observation, taken together with our experiment, strongly suggests that action-potential activity is not only present but also necessary for the ganglion cell axons from the two eyes to segregate and form the eye-specific layers.

Still, there must be constraints on the spatial and temporal patterning of ganglion cell activity. If the cells fired randomly, the mechanism of correlation-based, activity-dependent sorting could not operate. Furthermore, neighboring ganglion cells in each eye somehow ought to fire in near synchrony with one another, and the firing of cells in the two eyes, taken together, should be asynchronous. In addition, the synapses between retinal ganglion cell axons and neurons of the lateral geniculate nucleus should resemble Hebb synapses in their function: they should be able to detect correlations in the firing of axons and strengthen accordingly.

We realized that to search for such patterns of spontaneous firing, it would be necessary to monitor simultaneously the action-potential activity of many ganglion cells in the developing retina. In addition, the observation had to take place as the eye-specific layers were developing. A major technical advance permitted us to achieve this goal. In 1988 Jerome Pine and his colleagues at the California Institute of Technology, among them doctoral student Markus Meister, invented a special multi-electrode recording device. It consisted of 61 recording electrodes arranged as a flat, hexagonal array. Each electrode can detect action potentials generated in one to several cells. When Meister arrived at Stanford University to continue postdoctoral work with Denis Baylor, we began a collaboration to see whether the electrode array could be used to detect the spontaneous firing of fetal retinal ganglion cells.

In these experiments, it was necessary to remove the entire retina from the fetal eye and place it, ganglion-cell-side down, on the array. (It is technically impossible to put the electrode array itself into the eye in utero.) Rachel Wong, a postdoctoral fellow from Australia visiting my laboratory, succeeded in carefully dissecting the retinas and in tailoring special fluids necessary to maintain the living tissue for hours in a healthy condition.

When neonatal ferret retinas were placed on the multielectrode array, we simultaneously recorded the spontaneously generated action potentials of as many as 100 cells. The work confirmed the in vivo results of Galli-Resta and Maffei. All cells on the array fired within about five seconds of one another, in a predictable and rhythmic pattern. The bursts of action potentials lasted several seconds and were followed by long silent pauses that persisted from 30 seconds to two minutes. This observation showed that the activity of ganglion cells is indeed correlated. Further analysis demonstrated that the activity of neighboring cells is more highly correlated than that of distant cells on the array.

Even more remarkable, the spatial pattern of firing resembled a wave of activity that swept across the retina at about 100 microns per second (about one tenth to one hundredth the speed of an ordinary action potential). After the silent period, another wave was generated but in a completely different and random direction. We found that these spon-

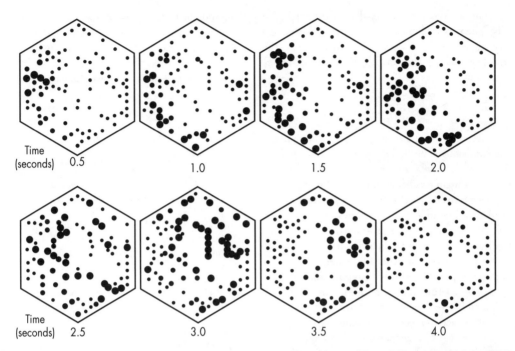

Figure 10.4 Retinal activity, recorded frame by frame every 0.5 second by a hexagonal array of microelectrodes (••••• spots), is locally synchronized. Each diagram represents the pattern and intensity of action-potential firing (●●● spots) of individual ganglion cells. The wave of retinal activity sweeps across from the lower left to the top right of the retina.

taneously generated retinal waves are present throughout the period when eye-specific layers take shape. They disappear just before the onset of visual function (see figure 10.4).

From an engineering standpoint, these waves seem beautifully designed to provide the required correlations in the firing of neighboring ganglion cells. They also ensure a sufficient time delay, so that the synchronized firing of ganglion cells remains local and does not occur across the entire retina. Such a pattern of firing could help refine the topographic map conveyed by ganglion cell axons to each eye-specific layer. Moreover, the fact that wave direction appears to be entirely random implies that ganglion cells in the two eyes are highly unlikely ever to fire synchronously – a requirement for the formation of the layers.

Future experiments will disrupt the waves in order to determine whether they are truly involved in the development of connections. In addition, it will be important to determine whether the correla-

tions in the firing of neighboring ganglion cells can be detected and used by the cells in the lateral geniculate nucleus to strengthen appropriate synapses and weaken inappropriate ones. This seems likely, since Richard D. Mooney, a postdoctoral fellow in my laboratory, in collaboration with Daniel Madison of Stanford, has shown that long-term potentiation of synaptic transmission between retinal ganglion cell axons and the lateral geniculate nucleus neurons is present during these early periods of development. Thus, at present, we can conclude that even before the onset of function, ganglion cells can spontaneously fire in the correct pattern to fashion the necessary connections.

Is the retina a special case, or might many regions of the nervous system generate their own endogenous activity patterns early in development? Preliminary studies by Michael O'Donovan of the National Institutes of Health suggest that the activity of motor neurons in the spinal cord may also be highly correlated very early in development.

It would appear that activity-dependent sorting in this system as well might use spontaneously generated signals. Like those in the visual system, the signals would refine the initially diffuse connections within targets.

.   .   .

The necessity for neuronal activity to complete the development of the brain has distinct advantages. The first is that, within limits, the maturing nervous system can be modified and fine-tuned by experience itself, thereby providing a certain degree of adaptability. In higher vertebrates, this process of refinement can occupy a protracted period. It can begin in utero and, as in the primate visual system, continue well into neonatal life, where it plays an important role in coordinating inputs from the two eyes. The coordination is necessary for binocular vision and stereoscopic depth perception.

Neural activity confers another advantage in development. It is genetically conservative. The alternative – exactly specifying each neural connection using molecular markers – would require an extraordinary number of genes, given the thousands of connections that must be formed in the brain. Using the rules of activity-dependent remodeling described here is far more economical. A major challenge for the future will be to elucidate the cellular and molecular bases for such rules.

Further Reading

Prenatal Development of the Visual System in the Rhesus Monkey. P. Rakic, in *Philosophical Transactions of the Royal Society of London*, Series B, vol. 278, no. 961, pp. 245–60; April 26, 1977.

Ocular Dominance Column Development: Analysis and Simulation. Kenneth D. Miller, Joseph B. Keller and Michael P. Stryker, in *Science*, vol. 245, pp. 605–15; August 11, 1989.

Competitive Interactions between Retinal Ganglion Cells during Prenatal Development. Carla J. Shatz, in *Journal of Neurobiology*, vol. 21, no. 1, pp. 197–211; January 1990.

Impulse Activity and the Patterning of Connections during CNS Development. C. J. Shatz, in *Neuron*, vol. 5, no. 6, pp. 745–56; December 1990.

Development. Edited by Corey S. Goodman and Thomas M. Jessell. Special issue of *Current Opinion in Neurobiology*, vol. 2, no. 1; February 1992.

CHAPTER 11

Development of Species Identification in Ducklings – VI: Specific Embryonic Experience Required to Maintain Species-Typical Perception in Peking Ducklings

Gilbert Gottlieb

The response of maternally naive Peking ducklings to the maternal call of their species (mallard) is based primarily on its repetition rate (around 4 notes/sec). That rate is species-typical in that the repetition rate of the maternal call uttered by a number of mallard hens in nature lies between 3.4 and 5 notes/sec, with an average around 4.2 notes/sec (Miller and Gottlieb, 1978). As demonstrated in a previous study in this series (Gottlieb, 1979), highly specific responsiveness to the mallard maternal call at the species-typical repetition rate develops in the Peking duck embryo in advance of auditory experience with its own or sib vocalizations. However, if the embryos are subsequently deprived of hearing their own or sib vocalizations, the lower boundary of their initial repetition-rate specificity broadens to include 2.3 notes/sec, thus transcending the species-typical range. Aurally experienced (i.e., communally incubated, vocal) embryos and ducklings are not responsive to an artificially slowed maternal call at 2.3 notes/sec when it is placed in competition with the same call

at the normal rate (3.7 notes/sec), whereas devocalized-isolated ducklings are equally responsive to both calls in such tests (Gottlieb, 1978). Since repetition rate is the key acoustic dimension guiding the Peking ducklings' response to the maternal call of its species, the devocalized-isolated duckling also responds to the maternal calls of other species if their repetition rate approximates 2.3 notes/sec (e.g., the chicken maternal call), whereas aurally experienced ducklings do not make such "mistakes."

Since the embryo develops its highly specific responsiveness to the typical repetition rate of the species maternal call in advance of auditory experience, the original responsiveness can be viewed as "innate" and thus as the outcome of primarily endogenous processes of neural maturation. As Bateson (1976) pointed out, some theorists who concern themselves with innate behavior assume that the development of such behavior is not critically linked to any specific prior experience but rather that it will exhibit and maintain itself provided only that rather general (nonspecific) life-sustaining conditions prevail during ontogeny. Thus, it becomes a question of interest to ask whether the necessary auditory experiential contribution to keep the system "fine tuned" in the present instance could be of a rather general nature, as assumed by some theories of innate behavioral development (e.g., Lorenz, 1965; Sperry, 1971), or whether the experiential requirement might be specific (i.e., the embryos having to hear their own vocalizations, which happen to be around 4 notes/sec), as is assumed by other views of the development of species-specific behavior (Gottlieb, 1971, p. 156; 1975b).

To examine the question of the requisite specificity of the embryonic auditory experience, in the present study devocalized-isolated embryos were given prior exposure to recordings of their species-

typical embryonic contact-contentment call at three different repetition rates: normal (4 notes/sec), slowed (2 notes/sec), or fast (6 notes/sec). These birds were subsequently tested after hatching for their preference in a simultaneous auditory choice test with the mallard maternal call at its normal rate (3.7 notes/sec) versus the same call at an artificially slowed rate (2.3 notes/sec). As mentioned earlier, unstimulated devocalized ducklings do not show a preference in that test, whereas vocal ducklings prefer the 3.7/sec call over the slowed 2.3/sec call. (These calls are depicted in figure 11.1.) If the embryonic auditory experiential requirement for the maintenance of the 4/sec preference is

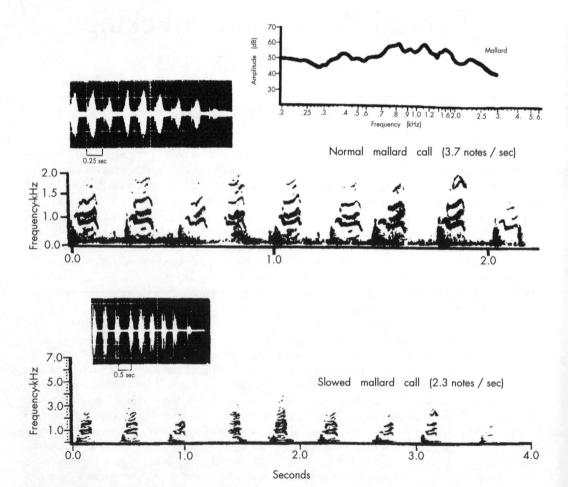

Figure 11.1 Sonagrams, oscilloscopic depiction (insets), and peak frequency bands (upper right) of mallard maternal call at 3.7 notes/sec (normal) and 2.3 notes/sec. (The frequency analysis was done acoustically in the test chamber, whereas the other analyses were made directly from test tapes. Notes in slowed mallard call appear shorter than in normal call because of the necessity of greater photographic reduction.)

specific, then the devocalized group receiving exposure to the contact-contentment call at 4 notes/sec would be the only one to show the normal preference for the species-typical rate of the maternal call. On the other hand, if the experiential requirement is not specific, then all the stimulated groups should show the normal preference for the species-typical maternal rate. A third possibility is that the embryonic auditory exposure could modify the ducklings' normal repetition-rate preference. In the present case, that would signify a shift in preference away from the normal maternal call to the one pulsed at 2.3 notes/sec in the group given previous exposure to the contact-contentment call at 2 notes/sec.

Method

Subjects

The subjects were 301 Peking ducklings, a domesticated form derived from the wild mallard duck (*Anas platyrhynchos*).

Incubation, muting, and stimulation of devocal-isolated ducklings

The embryos scheduled for devocalization were incubated in a sound-attenuating room separate from vocal-communal ducklings. Although the embryos scheduled for devocalization were not exposed to the vocalizations of more advanced embryos, they were in the same kind of incubator till Day 24, so they were exposed to the low-frequency mechanical noises of the air-conditioner and incubator-fan motors, which peak at 120 Hz at a level of 83–36 dB (linear) inside the incubator.

As described in detail in the first article of this series (Gottlieb, 1975a), during the first 6 hr of Day 24, the embryos scheduled for devocalization were removed singly from the incubator, muted, and placed in individual isolation in a soundproof incubator compartment, where they remained until they were tested at 48 hr after hatching. A small toll is associated with the devocalization procedure: 77% of the devocal-isolates hatched and survived to be tested, compared with 92% of unoperated vocal-communal ducklings during the same monthly periods of 1977, 1978, and 1979.

The embryonic auditory stimulation with one or another of the contact-contentment calls commenced on Day 24, 18 hr, for 5 min in each hour through Day 26, 18 hr. The embryos were stimulated through speakers in their individual soundproof compartments at 70 dB (B). Each of the calls was composed of a four-note burst (shown in figure 11.2) which repeated itself 16 times per minute for 5 min in each hour. Thus, the total amount of stimulation over the 2-day embryonic period was 4 hr. Each devocalized duckling was stimulated with only one of the calls, of course. Only ducklings that were completely mute were included in the study (which, as previously noted [Gottlieb, 1975a], would include around 93% of all embryos subjected to the devocalization procedure).

Age at testing

The vocal-communal and unstimulated devocal-isolated (control) ducklings were tested at a mean posthatch age of 48 hr, and the three groups of stimulated devocal-isolated (experimental) ducklings were tested at a mean of posthatch age of 48 hr, ranging from 44 to 55 hr in the former and from 43.5 to 55 hr in the latter. (The behavioral data for the vocal-communal and nonexposed devocal-isolated [control] groups are taken from a previous report in this series [Gottlieb, 1978])

Because the embryos are partially extricated from the shell for the muting procedure, devocalized ducklings usually hatch somewhat earlier than the unoperated vocal birds, which thus causes a small discrepancy in developmental age at testing. In the present case, the average developmental age at testing of the vocal-communal ducklings was Day 28, 16 hr, with a standard deviation of 12.2 hr. The averages of the unstimulated and the stimulated devocal ducklings were remarkably close: Day 28, 9 hr (unstimulated), Day 28, 10 hr (stimulated with 2.1/sec call), Day 28, 9 hr (stimulated with 4/sec call), and Day 28, 12 hr (stimulated with 5.8/sec call), with standard deviations of 9.4, 7.7, 8.4, and 9.6 hr, respectively.

Test situation

Each duckling was placed singly in a test apparatus, equidistant between two speakers, as depicted in

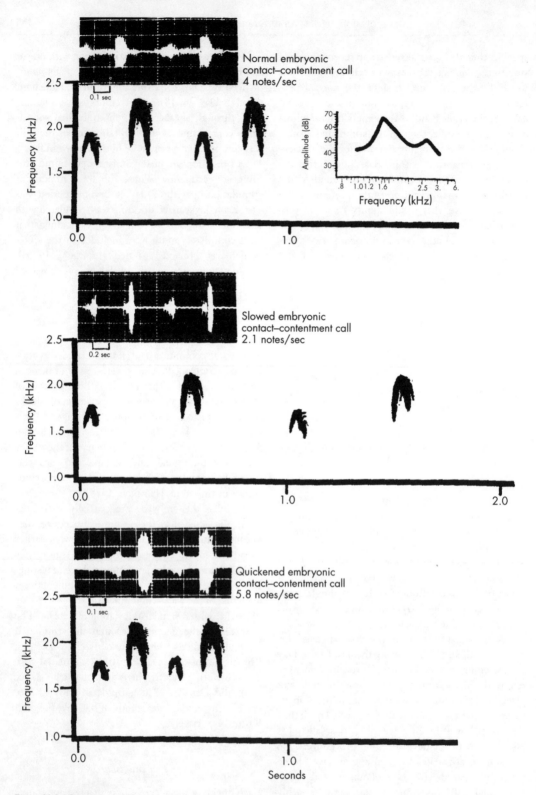

Figure 11.2 Sonagram, oscilloscopic depiction, and peak frequency bands of embryonic contact–contentment call at 4 notes/ sec (normal), 2.1 notes/sec, and 5.8 notes/sec.

figure 4 in the first article of this series (Gottlieb, 1975a).

All the birds were given a simultaneous choice test between the mallard maternal call at its normal rate (3.7 notes/sec) and the same call at an artificially slowed rate (2.3 notes/sec). Each bird was tested only once and each test lasted 5 min. After the bird entered an elliptical area painted on the floor in the immediate vicinity of each speaker, its choice and the amount of time (duration in seconds) the bird remained within the elliptically marked area were recorded. A measure of preference was derived from the duration score. When, over the course of the 5-min test, a bird stayed in one approach area more than twice the time it spent in the opposing approach area, a preference was registered. Occasionally a bird would approach both speakers and not exceed the necessary $>2\times$ ratio favoring one over the other to be accorded a preference. These birds were scored as "Both" in the tally of preference in table 11.1.

The within- and between-groups preferences of the ducklings were treated statistically by the binomial test and the chi-square test, respectively. The key question of whether the birds within a group showed a preference for the normal mallard maternal call in the choice test is answered by the binomial test (if $p \leq .05$, then the group demonstrated a preference). The chi-square test indicates whether the preferences of the groups were distributed differently. All reported p values are two-tailed.

Experimental calls

Problems associated with the measurement of repetition rate have been described elsewhere (Scoville and Gottlieb, 1978). The conventional and most appropriate method (onset of first note to onset of last note in a burst) was used here.

The normal mallard maternal call used in these experiments is composed of nine notes which make up a burst. The repetition rate of the notes in the burst is 3.7 notes/sec (see figure 11.1). As already mentioned, that call was pitted against itself at 2.3 notes/sec in the choice test (figure 11.1). The normal contact-contentment call used for stimulating the devocalized embryos was obtained from an embryo late on Day 24 of embryonic development. Its rate was 4 notes/sec (figure 11.2). This was the same two-note call used to rectify the embryos' high-frequency sensitivity in an earlier experiment (Gottlieb, 1975b). In the present experiment, the two notes were made to repeat themselves to make a four-note burst (figure 11.2).

To test the hypothesis of the study, one group of devocalized embryos was exposed to the normal

Table 11.1 Preference of vocal-communal and devocal-isolated ducklings in simultaneous auditory choice with mallard maternal call at normal and slowed repetition rates at 48 hr after hatching

			Preference		
Auditory experience	n	n responding	Normal mallard call (3.7 notes/sec)	Slowed mallard call (2.3 notes/sec)	Both
Vocal-communal					
Normal control group	50	36	30*	2	4
Devocal-isolated					
No vocal exposure	63	38	20	16	2
Exposed to slowed (2.1/sec) embryonic call	66	31	14	14	3
Exposed to normal (4/sec) embryonic call	55	34	28*	5	1
Exposed to quickened (5.8/sec) embryonic call	67	34	16	16	2

* $p < .0001$, binomial test.

contact-contentment call (4 notes/sec), one group to the same call at 2.1 notes/sec, and one group to the same call at 5.8 notes/sec. To slow the repetition rate of the contact-contentment call (and the maternal call), it was necessary only to add appropriate lengths of blank pieces of magnetic recording tape between the notes of the call. To increase the repetition rate, the blank spaces between the notes were shortened.

Results

As shown in table 11.1, according to the binomial test, only the devocalized embryos stimulated with the contact-contentment call at 4 notes/sec showed the species-typical preference for the normal maternal call over the slowed maternal call. The devocalized embryos stimulated with the contact-contentment call at either 2.1 notes/sec or 5.8 notes/sec did not show a preference in the choice test, mirroring the performance of the unstimulated control embryos. Thus, prior exposure to the contact call at 2.1 notes/sec neither maintained the preference for the normal maternal call nor induced a preference for the 2.3 notes/sec maternal call, either of which seemed possible at the outset.

Further testifying to the efficacy of the 4/sec embryonic stimulation, according to the chi-square test, the proportionate preference for the normal maternal call over the slowed maternal call was greater in the devocalized embryos stimulated with the 4/sec contact-contentment call than in all the other devocalized groups: unstimulated control embryos ($p = .02$), those stimulated with the 2.1/sec contact-contentment call ($p = .009$), and those stimulated with the 5.8/sec contact-contentment call ($p = .008$).

Testifying still further to the normalizing influence of the 4/sec embryonic stimulation in maintaining the species-typical rate preference, the preference of those devocalized ducklings was not different from that of the vocal-communal ducklings, whereas the preference of the vocal-communal ducklings for the normal maternal call was more pronounced than all of the other devocalized groups' (unstimulated group, $p = .001$; 2.1/sec group, $p < .001$; 5.8/sec group, $p < .001$).

Discussion

If the ducklings are to show their normal preference for the maternal call at the species-typical repetition rate (4 notes/sec), they must be exposed to their species-typical embryonic contact call at that rate. Exposure to the contact call at other rates fails to maintain this normal preference or to modify it (in the case of exposure to the embryonic call at 2 notes/sec). These results are all the more remarkable because the selective behavioral responsiveness to the maternal call at 4 notes/sec arises in the embryo in advance of hearing its own or maternal vocalizations (Gottlieb, 1979). Thus, in the present instance, the maintenance of seemingly innate postnatal behavioral development is dependent upon a highly specific, normally occurring prior experience; it will not be maintained if only rather general (nonspecific) life-sustaining conditions prevail during ontogeny, as has been assumed in the past (e.g., Lorenz, 1965; Sperry, 1971).

The present results support the view that in the evolution of species-specific perception, natural selection has involved a selection for the entire developmental manifold, including both the organic and normally occurring stimulative features of ontogeny (Gottlieb, 1971, p. 156; 1975b). That view is consonant with the conventionally accepted evolutionary assumption that natural selection operates on behavioral phenotypes and that behavioral phenotypes are the developmental outcomes of individual organism–environment interactions. Just how highly specific such organism–environment interactions might necessarily be in the development and evolution of species-specific perception has not been appreciated. The embryonic developmental pathway of early species-typical adaptive behavior has not been the subject of much analytic experimental investigation, partly because it is technically difficult but mostly because it has been regarded as a theoretically unrewarding enterprise. We have assumed that we already know the unidirectional developmental pathway of "innate" behavior: genetic activity $\rightarrow$ neural maturation $\rightarrow$ species-typical behavior. As I have argued elsewhere in some detail (Gottlieb, 1976a), the newly emerging view of species-typical behavioral development calls for the interpolation of experience as well as the bidirectionality of influences: genetic activity $\leftrightarrows$

Effects of experience
on development of perceptual preference

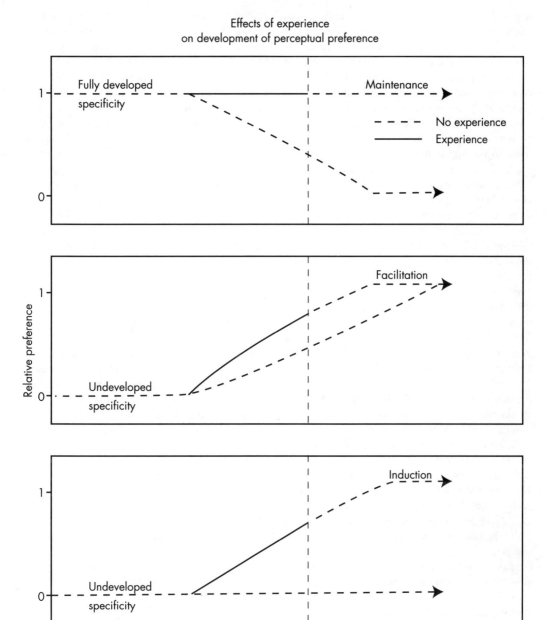

Figure 11.3   Three ways that experience can contribute to the development of species-typical perception. (The present results involve maintenance since the perceptual specificity is developed in advance of experience and is lost in the absence of normal embryonic experience. Facilitation was demonstrated earlier (Gottlieb, 1975c), and induction has yet to be demonstrated.

neural maturation ⇌ experience ⇌ species-typical behavior.

The present results assume greater generality when placed in the context of the other roles that experience plays in the development of species-typical behavior, namely, facilitation and induction (figure 11.3). In a previous study in the present series (Gottlieb, 1975b), it was shown that in order for the duckling to exhibit normal perceptual sensitivity to the higher frequency components of the maternal call at the usual age after hatching, it had to be previously exposed to precisely those frequencies embryonically, and it happens that just those frequencies are present in their own embryonic contact-contentment call (1500–2500 Hz). In that case the specific embryonic auditory experience *facilitates* the appearance of normal high-frequency perceptual sensitivity at 24 hr after hatching, and maintains it at 65 hr after hatching. It remains to determine the specificity of the experimental requirement for the *induction* of a perceptual preference for some feature of the maternal call as has been shown, for example, with early "habitat preferences" in developing amphibia (Wiens, 1970). An opportunity to examine that question will present itself in a later study of this series, one concerning the development of species identification in wood ducklings (*Aix sponsa*).

While we have become accustomed to the high degree of experiential specificity required for the development of visuo-motor coordinations (e.g., Hein and Diamond, 1972), in the present instance such specificity is shown to be necessary for the development of species-typical perception which involves no skilled or highly refined motor component.

Taken together with previous results in this series, the present findings indicate that the development of species-specific auditory perception is a probabilistic phenomenon, in the sense that the threshold, timing, and ultimate normality of such perception are regulated jointly by sensory stimulative as well as organismic factors. In the usual course of development, the manifest changes and improvements in species-specific perception do not represent solely the unfolding of a fixed or predetermined organic substrate independent of normally occurring sensory stimulation. It remains to note that, in lieu of the usual conceptions of learning, the present conception of the various roles of experi-

ence in the development of species-typical behavior (figure 11.3) has been found useful not only in the auditory perception of young birds (e.g., Kerr, Ostapoff, and Rubel, 1979) but in the development of speech perception in human infants (Aslin and Pisoni, 1980), olfactory experience and huddling preferences in rat pups (Brunjes and Alberts, 1979), and the maintenance of emotionality in gerbils (Clark and Galef, 1979), to specify several disparate examples. Traditional learning theory has not been very useful in describing the contributions of experience to the species-typical development of behavior, so it has become necessary to begin to formulate these contributions in a different way. The various contributions of experience (maintenance, facilitation, induction) to behavioral development can, of course, operate postnatally as well as prenatally (Gottlieb, 1976b).

Acknowledgments

I am grateful to Jo Ann Bell, Kathy Bobseine, and Mary Catharine Jackson for their excellent assistance with these experiments. This research was supported by the North Carolina Division of Mental Health and by Research Grant HD-00878 from the National Institute of Child Health and Human Development.

Requests for reprints should be sent to Gilbert Gottlieb, Dorothea Dix Hospital, Raleigh, North Carolina 27611, USA.

References

Aslin, R. N., and Pisoni, D. B. (1980) Some developmental processes in speech perception. In G. H. Yeni-Komshian, J. F. Kavanagh, and C. A. Ferguson (eds), *Child Phonology*, New York: Academic Press.

Bateson, P. P. G. (1976) Specificity and the origins of behavior. In J. S. Rosenblatt, R. A. Hinde, E. Shaw, and C. Beer (eds), *Advances in the Study of Behavior*, Vol. 6, New York: Academic Press.

Brunjes, P. C., and Alberts, J. R. (1979) Olfactory stimulation induces filial preferences for huddling in rat pups, *Journal of Comparative and Physiological Psychology*, 93, 548–55

Clark, M. M., and Galef, B. G., Jr (1979) A sensitive period for the maintenance of emotionality in Mongolian gerbils, *Journal of Comparative and Physiological Psychology*, 93, 200–10.

Gottlieb, G. (1971) *Development of Species Identification in Birds*, Chicago: University of Chicago Press.

Gottlieb, G. (1975a) Development of species identification in ducklings: I Nature of perceptual deficit caused by embryonic auditory deprivation, *Journal of Comparative and Physiological Psychology*, **89**, 387–99.

Gottlieb, G. (1975b) Development of species identification in ducklings: II Experiential prevention of perceptual deficit caused by embryonic auditory deprivation, *Journal of Comparative and Physiological Psychology*, **89**, 675–84.

Gottlieb, G. (1975c) Development of species identification in ducklings: III Maturational rectification of perceptual deficit caused by auditory deprivation, *Journal of Comparative and Physiological Psychology*, **89**, 899–912.

Gottlieb, G. (1976a) Conceptions of prenatal development: Behavioral embryology, *Psychological Review*, **83**, 215–34.

Gottlieb, G. (1976b) The roles of experience in the development of behavior and the nervous system. In G. Gottlieb (ed.), *Neural and Behavioral Specificity*, New York: Academic Press.

Gottlieb, G. (1978) Development of species identification in ducklings: IV Change in species-specific perception caused by auditory deprivation, *Journal of Comparative and Physiological Psychology*, **92**, 375–387.

Gottlieb, G. (1979) Development of species identification in ducklings: V Perceptual differentiation in the embryo, *Journal of Comparative and Physiological Psychology*, **93**, 831–54.

Hein, A., and Diamond, R. M. (1972) Locomotory space as a prerequisite for acquiring visually guided reaching in kittens, *Journal of Comparative and Physiological Psychology*, **81**, 394–8.

Kerr, L. M., Ostapoff, E. M., and Rubel, E. W. (1979) Influence of acoustic experience on the ontogeny of frequency generalization gradients in the chicken, *Journal of Experimental Psychology: Animal Behavior Processes*, **5**, 97–115.

Lorenz, K. (1965) *Evolution and Modification of Behavior*, Chicago: University of Chicago Press.

Miller, D. B., and Gottlieb, G. (1978) Maternal vocalizations of mallard ducks (*Anas platyrhynchos*), *Animal Behaviour*, **26**, 1178–94.

Scoville, R., and Gottlieb, G. (1978) The calculation of repetition rate in avian vocalizations, *Animal Behaviour*, **26**, 962–3.

Sperry, R. W. (1971) How a developing brain gets itself properly wired for adaptive function. In E. Tobach, L. R. Aronson, and E. Shaw (eds), *The Biopsychology of Development*, New York: Academic Press.

Wiens, J. A. (1970) Effects of early experience on substrate pattern selection in *Rana aurora* tadpoles, *Copeia*, No. 3, 543–8.

CHAPTER 12

The Companion in the Bird's World (*excerpt*)

Konrad Lorenz

Imprinting of the Object of Species-specific Instinctive Behaviour Patterns

The *acquired* component of instinct-conditioning intercalation patterns is very often the *object* of the innate behaviour, as I attempted to demonstrate with a number of examples in the paper already quoted. Although the acquisition of this object is generally equivalent to a conditioning process, a basically different process of acquisition takes place with a particular group of innate, instinctive behaviour patterns lacking an innately-determined object. In my opinion, this process cannot be equated with learning – it is the acquisition of the object of *instinctive behaviour patterns oriented towards conspecifics.*

To the uninitiated, it is often surprising (even incredible) that a bird does not recognize conspecifics innately and purely 'instinctively' in all situations and respond accordingly. Very few birds behave in this way, however. *In contrast to all mammals investigated in this respect, isolated, hand-reared individuals of most bird species do not recognize conspecifics as their own kind when introduced to them later*, i.e. behaviour patterns which would normally be elicited by conspecifics are not elicited. On the

From Konrad Lorenz, *Studies in Animal and Human Behaviour* (London: Methuen, 1935/1970), pp. 124–33.

contrary, young birds of most species will direct the instinctive behaviour patterns adapted to conspecifics *towards a human being* if they are reared in human care, isolated from their kind.

This behaviour appears so bizarre – so 'deranged' – to the observer, that any individual observer who encounters this phenomenon when hand-rearing young birds is at first prone to regard it as a *pathological* process, explained as a 'confinement psychosis' or the like. Only when one repeatedly encounters this behaviour even with completely healthy specimens of extremely varied bird species, and observes that it occurs in animals reared in complete freedom, does one gradually realize that a controlled process is involved and that *the object of instinctive behaviour patterns oriented towards conspecifics is not innately determined* in most bird species. Instead, recognition of the object is acquired during the individual's life-time by means of a process which is so peculiar that it merits detailed consideration.

If an egg of the curlew (*Numenius*) or a Godwit (*Limosa*) is hatched in an incubator and the young bird is taken into human care straight after hatching, it will be seen that the bird will not seek contact with human beings as 'foster-parents'. It will flee as soon as it sees a human being, and one will not be able to observe any part of the instinctive behaviour patterns directed towards the parents, except perhaps by using finely-adjusted dummy-experiments.

(Unfortunately, nobody has so far conducted such experiments.) In these two species, as with many nidifugous types (which leave the egg at a very advanced stage of development), these instinctive behaviour patterns can *only* be elicited by conspecific adults. Translated into the terminology of environmentalist studies, this means: The young bird possesses an innate 'schema' of the adult. The image of the adult animal is defined by so many innately-recognized characters that the infantile instinctive behaviour patterns only respond 'species-specifically' to adults of the same species. We can sometimes determine quite accurately how many characters are involved, in cases where *imitation* of these characters successfully elicits infantile instinctive behaviour patterns.

If, instead of taking a curlew, we should take a Greylag gosling into our care, after it has grown for several days in the custody of its parents, we should find the same effect. In this case too, it is impossible for a human being to elicit any infantile instinctive behaviour patterns. *The result is quite different, however, when a Greylag gosling is taken into human care directly after hatching.* Then, all of the instinctive behaviour patterns directed towards the parents are at once elicited by the human foster-parent. In fact, it is necessary to employ specific safety precautions to induce young Greylag goslings which have been *artificially* brooded in an incubator to follow a mother Greylag goose which is leading other goslings. The artificially-hatched goslings *must not be allowed full sight of a human being* between hatching and transfer to the mother goose, since otherwise the following drive will immediately become attached to human beings. Heinroth described this process quite exactly in his work *Beiträge zur Biologie, insbesondere Psychologie und Ethologie der Anatiden*:

> I frequently had to attempt to introduce goslings hatched in an incubator to a pair already leading very young goslings. This involves a number of difficulties, which are in fact quite characteristic of the entire psychological and instinctive behaviour of these birds. If the lid of an incubator is opened after young ducklings have just hatched from the egg and dried out, they will at first crouch quite still and then dash away with lightning speed when the attempt is made to pick them up. In the process, they often jump to the ground and rapidly crawl under nearby objects, so that it is often a difficult

task to catch the tiny things. Young goslings behave quite differently. Without any display of fear, they stare calmly at human beings and do not resist handling. If one spends just a little time with them, it is not so easy to get rid of them afterwards. They pipe piteously if left behind and soon follow reliably. It has happened to me that such a gosling, a few hours after removal from the incubator, was content as long as it could settle under the chair on which I sat. If such a gosling is carried to a goose family accompanied by goslings of the same age, the result is usually the following: The approaching human being is watched suspiciously by the adult male and female, and both attempt to take to the water with their offspring as fast as possible. If one approaches so fast that the goslings do not have sufficient time to flee, the parents naturally angrily turn to defence. One can then rapidly deposit the orphan gosling among them and retreat hastily. Aroused as they are, the parents naturally regard the tiny newcomer as their own offspring at first and will attempt to defend it as soon as they see and hear it in the human hand. But the worst is to come: *The young gosling shows no inclination to regard the two adults as conspecifics*: The gosling runs off, piping, and attaches itself to the first human being that happens to come past; it regards the human being as its parent.

Heinroth continues to explain that a gosling can be successfully foisted onto a goose family if it is placed in a sack straight after removal from the incubator, so that it does not see human beings at all. He rightly expresses the opinion that the freshly-hatched goslings look on the first living thing that they seen in the first light of the world 'with the intention of exactly imprinting this image, since – as has already been mentioned – these delicate woolly things do not appear to recognize their parents as conspecifics in a purely instinctive manner'.

I have described this behaviour of the Greylag gosling because it provides a virtually classic example of the manner in which a *single experience* imprints the relevant object of the infantile instinctive behaviour patterns in a young bird which does *not* recognize this object instinctively. *This object can only be imprinted during a quite definite period in the bird's life.* A further important feature is the fact that the Greylag gosling obviously 'expects' this experience during a receptive period, i.e. *there is an innate drive to fill this gap in the instinctive framework.*

It should also be emphasized that the genus *Anser* represents an extreme, to the extent that so *few* characters of the adult companion are innately determined in the freshly-hatched bird. Apart from an instinctive response to the species-specific alarm-call, no instinctive response to any character present in the parents can be demonstrated. In particular, the instinctive response to the summoning call of the parents evident in so many small nidifugous birds is lacking.

The process of imprinting the object of otherwise innately-determined instinctive behaviour patterns directed at conspecifics is *markedly different from the acquisition of the object of other instinctive behaviour patterns* whose releasing schemata are not innately determined, but acquired like conditioned reflexes. Whereas in the latter case the acquisition process is presumably equivalent to self-conditioning – a learning process – *the process of imprinting of the object of instinctive behaviour patterns oriented towards conspecifics possesses a series of features which are basically different from learning.* There is no equivalent process in the behaviour of any other animals, particularly mammals, but at this point it should be pointed out that there are certain analogies to pathological fixations of the drive object in *human* psychology.

The following factors distinguish the process of imprinting from typical *learning*:

In the first place, the described acquisition of the object of instinctive behaviour patterns can only take place during a narrowly-defined period of time in the individual's life. Thus, the process of imprinting of the object depends upon a *quite definite physiological developmental condition* in the young bird.

Secondly, imprinted recognition of the object of instinctive behaviour patterns directed towards conspecifics, following the *expiration* of the physiological imprinting period determined for the species, has *exactly the same appearance as corresponding innate behaviour – the recognition response cannot be 'forgotten'*! The possibility of 'forgetting' is, as Bühler particularly points out, a *basic feature of all learning processes*. Of course, it is not yet permissible, in the light of the relative novelty of all observations on this process, to make a final statement about the permanence of these acquired objects. The justification for such a pronouncement is based upon the fact, observed in many cases, that birds

which have been hand-reared by a human being and have come to direct their conspecific-oriented instinctive patterns towards the human frame do not alter their behaviour in the slightest, even when kept together with conspecifics and away from human beings for many years. This latter measure is just as unsuccessful in bringing such birds to recognize conspecifics as beings of their own kind as the attempt to induce a bird captured as an adult to recognize a human being as conspecific. (Behaviour directed towards substitute objects, which provides an apparent exception, will be discussed later.)

These two facts, the determination of later behaviour by an external influence (derived from a conspecific) during a specific ontogenetic period and the irreversibility of this determination process, provide a remarkable analogy between the developmental processes of instinctive behavioural systems and processes which have been identified in morphological development.

If, at a certain time in evelopment, cell material is taken from the ectoderm of the posterior abdominal region of a frog embryo – where it would normally form a piece of abdominal skin during further embryonic development – and grafted onto the posterior end of the outer surface of the neural groove, it will form a constituent part of the spinal cord in accordance with its position. The cells are thus influenced by the organizational determinant of the local environment – an effect which Spemann terms 'induction'. The possibility of induction forces us to distinguish between 'prospective potency' and 'prospective significance' of a given cell. The ectoderm cells of the frog embryo transplanted in Spemann's experiment had the prospective significance of a region of abdominal skin; in the absence of experimental manipulation, these cells could *only* have had that fate. At the same time, however, these cells still had the normally latent ability to develop into a region of the spinal cord. Thus, their prospective potency was greater than their prospective significance. If a similar experiment is carried out at a later stage of development, or if the abdominal ectoderm cells (now determined as spinal cord cells) are *transplanted back* to their site of origin, the prospective potency is found to be identical to the prospective significance. When this second transplantation is carried out, those cells which would have otherwise become spinal cord constituents do so even at the

new site, and the transplantation experiment produces a 'monster'. The prospective significance of
the cells is thus 'determined' under the influence of
the local environment, by induction. In other
words, the cell material does not possess inherited
'knowledge' of its fate – this is determined by the
site it occupies. The local environment imprints the
final organ character of the cells. After completion
of this determination process, which takes place at
a particular period in development, the tissue can
no longer 'forget' its determined fate. The pre-
sumptive spinal cord cells transplanted back to
the abdominal epithelium can no longer be 're-
dctermined' to form this type of epithelium! In
some animals, such as the tunicates, even in the
two-cell stage of the developing egg the behaviour
of each of the cells is already completely determined. Here, there is almost no induction. One cell
of an artificially-constricted two-cell stage will liter-
ally develop to form half an organism. Individual
cell-groups in later stages of development, if isolated, will only produce the same organs or organ
components which they would have produced on
combination with neighbouring cells. These cells
are therefore not influenced by the local environment. Each cell has exact inherited 'knowledge'
of its functions and the mosaic of such exactly-
balanced and co-ordinated parts produces a unitary
organism without further influence exerted between the cells. Such embryos are consequently referred to as 'mosaic embryos', in contrast to the
'regulative embryos' described earlier.

The terms 'mosaic' and 'regulative' could well
be applied to instinctive systems, and it would be
quite fitting to use the term *inductive determination*
for instinctive behaviour patterns whose object
is not innately determined in the animal, but
imprinted by the environment (particularly by
conspecifics). The functional plan of the instinctive
system of an animal and the functional morphological plan are in many ways analogous.

When a young jackdaw at about fourteen days of
age directs its infantile instinctive behaviour patterns towards its parents, these patterns have the
prospective significance of direction towards the
parents, towards conspecifics. However, at this time
the species-specific instinctive behaviour patterns
oriented towards conspecifics have a much broader
prospective potency in the choice of object. The
parents, which already function as this object for

the young jackdaw, can still be replaced as such. A
young jackdaw taken from the nest, is at first shy
towards human beings and will crouch in their presence, indicating that the young bird is already
familiar with the sight of the parents. Despite this,
the parental companion – the object of the infantile
instinctive behaviour patterns – can be functionally
replaced in another respect. Within the space of a
few hours, the jackdaw will gape towards a human
being; after about twenty days the young bird has
fledged and will direct its aerial following drive towards human beings and can no longer be functionally re-oriented 'to jackdaw'. A young jackdaw left
with its parents until reaching the same age is no
longer open to imprinting on human beings. The
prospective significance and prospective potency of
the object are now coincident.

We must therefore distinguish between two
phases in the developmental period of instinctive
patterns inherited without an object: an initial, usually very short, phase during which the bird seeks
out the object of the innate behaviour and a second,
longer, phase during which an eliciting object for
the instinctive behaviour has already been found,
but in which 'change of determination' is still possible. In some birds, as in the nidifugous types
already mentioned, where there is determination
through a single impression, the second phase is
extremely short. The entire psychological development which the nidicolous birds undergo during
the long nest-phase is, so to speak, compressed into
the few hours in which a nidifugous bird remains
in the nest. The shortest imprinting phase for infantile instinctive behaviour patterns lacking an innately-determined object (which at the same time
occurs at the shortest interval after hatching from
the egg) is found in nidifugous types from extremely diverse groups, as has already been mentioned. From my own experience, I can verify that
young mallard, pheasant and partridge which have
followed their mothers for only a few hours can
no longer re-orient their following drive to human
beings. Consequently, one can only rear these birds
properly when they are artificially incubated; otherwise, human beings will elicit a flight response
which is so strong that the young birds may stop
feeding and succumb. I regard it as quite possible
that a *single* elicitation of the following response
can bring about complete imprinting to the mother.
I am particularly convinced that this is the case

with the partridge, since I have attempted to rear partridge chicks turned up by farmers whilst reaping. These chicks could not even stand continuously and were forced to squat after each short burst of running. This stage, with which I am well acquainted, lasts for only a few hours after the chicks have dried, and the hen leads the chicks only a few metres during this phase. Nevertheless, the partridge chicks always succumbed, because they persistently fled or crouched immediately they were brought out into the light to feed. They first began to feed after they had become too emaciated to survive. If partridges are artificially incubated, on the other hand, they are at once tame towards the human 'foster-parent' and can be reared without difficulty.

The time of inductive determination, imprinting of the object of instinctive behaviour patterns oriented towards conspecifics, is in most cases not so easy to determine as with the infantile instinctive behaviour of the Greylag goose or the partridge. There are two reasons for this.

In the first place, identification of the imprinting period may be hindered by facilitation of imprinting to the species-specific object by a large number of innately-recognized characters, which serve to prevent false imprinting. The innate positive response of the young bird to these characters has the effect that a juvenile which has previously responded to a species-atypical object can be re-orientated to conspecifics at a time when the reverse process is no longer possible. For instance, the instinctive response of a young Golden Pheasant to the summoning call of the hen (i.e. definite running towards the source of sound) – something which is certainly *not* evident in the Greylag gosling – permits re-orientation of a 'humanized' pheasant at the developmental stage where 'transplantation' from hen pheasant to human being would be unsuccessful. It would be interesting to perform experiments employing people talented with the mimicry of bird-calls – a group to which I most definitely do not belong.

A second obstacle to the exact determination of the time of imprinting is derived from occasional temporal overlap of the time of object-imprinting of one instinctive behaviour pattern with that of another. This remarkable form of behaviour is apparently not uncommon in nidicolous types. Particularly with passerines, I have observed that specimens which are fostered at a relatively late age will still respond to a human being with their infantile instinctive behaviour patterns, and yet will later direct their equally object-less instinctive behaviour patterns towards conspecifics. This struck me most forcibly when I once had several young jackdaws of the same age, three of which had been taken as naked young and six of which were obtained shortly before emergence from the nest. All of these jackdaws were tame towards me whilst they were still gaping for food from me. However, after extinction of the infantile instinctive behaviour patterns the late-reared young rapidly became shy towards me, as if object-imprinting of the sexual instincts had taken place in the jackdaws *before* final determination of the infantile instinctive behaviour patterns. Determination does not seem to be quite final at this time, since I was able to record re-orientation 'to jackdaw' in some cases – something which never happened at a later stage.

Imprinting of different conspecific-oriented functional systems to the relevant object occurs at different points of time in individual ontogeny. This is very important in the present context: It provides the basis for the fact that the different functional systems can be voluntarily or involuntarily imprinted on different objects under conditions of captivity. For instance, I once possessed a young jackdaw reared in complete isolation, in which all behaviour patterns related to conspecifics were imprinted to human beings, with the exception of two behavioural complexes: flying in the company of a flock, and feeding and care of young conspecifics. The former behaviour was imprinted on Hooded Crows at the time of activation of the gregarious drive, these being the first flying Corvids with which the jackdaw became acquainted. This jackdaw even continued to fly persistently with free-living Hooded Crows when the attic which the bird occupied was used as a home-base for a whole flock of other jackdaws, which were not considered as flight-companions. Each morning, after I had liberated the birds, this particular jackdaw would climb high into the air and set off in search of her crow flight-companions, which were always found with great accuracy. At the time of rearing the young, however, this jackdaw abruptly adopted a freshly-fledged young jackdaw, which was guided and fed in a completely species-typical manner. It is in fact obvious that the object of instinctive parental behaviour patterns *must* be innately determined. This object cannot be acquired previously by imprinting, since the jackdaw's own offspring are, of course, the first that it sees. Thus, in this jackdaw's environment, the human being was a parental and sexual companion, the Hooded Crow a flying companion and the young jackdaw an infant companion!

Imprinting which determines the object of instinctive behaviour patterns related to conspecifics in the young bird frequently results through the influence of parents and siblings, yet it must nevertheless determine the behaviour of the young bird to *all* conspecifics. Thus, in the *imprinted* schema of the conspecific, as with the innate equivalent, only *supra-individual* species-characteristic characters may be derived from the image of parents and siblings, to be permanently imprinted. It is amazing enough that this should succeed in normal, species-typical imprinting, but it is astounding that a bird reared by, and imprinted to, a human being should direct its behaviour patterns not towards *one* human but towards the species *Homo sapiens*. A jackdaw for which the human has replaced the parental companion, and which has consequently become completely 'humanized', will thus direct its awakening sexual instincts not specifically towards its former parental companion, but (with the complete unpredictability of falling in love) towards any *one* relatively unfamiliar human being. The sex is unimportant, *but the object will quite definitely be human*. It would seem that the former parental companion is simply not considered as a possible 'mate'. But how does such a bird recognize our conspecifics as 'human beings'? A whole range of extremely interesting questions await solution!

In conclusion we must consider *which* conspecific acts as the source for the stimuli which determine the inductive establishment of the object of an instinctive behavioural chain.

In cases where imprinting of the object occurs long before the appearance of the instinctive behaviour pattern, imprinting must of course be induced by a conspecific which is involved with the imprinted bird in a different functional phase from that for which object-imprinting is induced. For instance, imprinting of the instinctive sexual behaviour patterns in jackdaws is almost certainly determined by the parental companion. At least, young jackdaws will become sexually imprinted on the human being even when reared in the company of several sibling companions, as long as the human foster-parent gives the bird sufficient attention to occupy the rôle of a full parental companion. Many other birds kept by Heinroth similarly showed sexual imprinting on human beings even though reared with several siblings (e.g. owls, ravens, partridges and many more).

On the other hand, there are birds for which the *siblings* determine later sexual behaviour. The mallard ducks which were intensively fostered in my care, proved to be completely normal sexually, whereas a Muscovy drake reared with them was imprinted 'to mallard'. Since this mixed-species company of siblings remained as a group until the next Spring, I am unable to give any answer to the question 'when' regarding imprinting. However, I intend to conduct experiments to investigate this with the easily-reared genera *Cairina* and *Anas* in the near future.

Birds reared in complete isolation from their own kind frequently become imprinted to human beings in all their instinctive behaviour, even where object-imprinting is normally determined by the sibling companion. Since the human being never acts as a sibling companion, the imprinting process does not seem to be unconditionally bound to a particular type of companion.

CHAPTER 13

Development of Perceptual Mechanisms in Birds: Predispositions and Imprinting

JOHAN J. BOLHUIS

Introduction

The development of a social preference of a young animal for its parent has intrigued students of animal behavior ever since Konrad Lorenz's vivid descriptions of avian imprinting (Lorenz, 1935, 1937; see Spalding, 1873, for an early discussion). This chapter is concerned with the development of perceptual mechanisms (Hogan, 1988) involved in such filial behavior in precocial birds. I will briefly describe some general characteristics of the formation of early filial preferences (see Bolhuis, 1991, for a more detailed review), and then discuss the underlying perceptual mechanisms. There is increasing evidence that at least two kinds of perceptual mechanisms play an important role in the development of filial behavior. The first type of perceptual mechanism is essentially a representation or memory of stimuli to which the animal is exposed. The formation of this mechanism is usually known as filial imprinting (Bateson, 1966; Sluckin, 1972; Bolhuis, 1991). The mechanisms of learning in imprinting have been the subject of considerable study (see Hoffman and Ratner, 1973; Bolhuis et al., 1990; Van Kampen, 1993, 1995 for reviews), and will be discussed briefly here.

The second type of perceptual mechanism involved in the development of filial behavior was already indicated by Lorenz (1935), when he pointed out that imprinting is not a universal phenomenon that applies to all species of birds. For example, he noted that newly hatched chicks of the curlew (*Numenius arquata*) could not be made to follow their human keeper, while chicks of the greylag goose (*Anser anser*) could. In Lorenz's terms, the curlew has an "innate perceptory pattern" (Lorenz, 1937, p. 247) of the appropriate "companion" ("Kumpan"), whereas in the greylag goose, the perceptory pattern is formed by experience with a particular object. The latter is equivalent to imprinting, while the former is roughly equivalent to a perceptual mechanism which we have called a predisposition (e.g. Horn and McCabe, 1984). Recent evidence suggests that more generally there is an important role for predispositions in the development of early filial behavior in certain precocial bird species. In this context, predispositions refer to perceptual preferences that develop in young animals without experience with the particular stimuli involved (for reviews, see Gottlieb, 1971; Horn, 1985; Bolhuis, 1991; Johnson and Bolhuis, 1991; Lickliter, 1993; ten Cate, 1994). In this chapter, the nature of these predispositions in the domestic chick (*Gallus gallus domesticus*) will be discussed. In contemporary ethology there is a tendency to avoid the use of Lorenzian concepts such as "Innate Releasing Mechanism." However, as we will see, much of

From C. F. Moss and S. J. Shettleworth (eds), *Neuroethological Studies of Cognitive and Perceptual Processes* (Boulder, CO: Westview Press, 1996), pp. 158–84.

Lorenz's intuition about the development of filial preferences is supported by the evidence that is now available.

The Development of Filial Preferences in Precocial Birds

In research into the formation of social preferences a distinction is made between filial and sexual imprinting. Filial imprinting is involved in the formation, in young animals, of an attachment to, and a preference for the parent, parent-surrogate or siblings. Sexual imprinting is involved in the formation of mating preferences that are expressed in later life; it will not be discussed in detail in this chapter (see ten Cate, 1989b; Bischof, 1994, for recent reviews). The formation of filial preferences has been studied mainly in precocial birds such as ducklings and chicks. These birds can move about shortly after hatching and will approach and follow a conspicuous object to which they are exposed. In a natural situation this object is likely to be the bird's mother or sibling, but in the absence of these, a wide range of inanimate mother-surrogates can also elicit filial behavior (see Bateson, 1966; Sluckin, 1972; Bolhuis, 1991, for reviews). When e.g. a chick is close to an appropriate object it will approach it and attempt to snuggle up to it. When the object is removed the bird becomes restless and emits shrill calls. Initially the young bird approaches a wide range of conspicuous objects to which it is exposed, but after it has had a certain amount of experience with a particular object the bird remains close to it and avoids novel ones. When given a choice between the familiar stimulus and a novel one the bird preferentially approaches the familiar stimulus. Filial imprinting is defined as the process through which social behavior of the young animal becomes limited to a particular object or class of objects, as a result of exposure to an object (Bateson, 1966; Bolhuis, 1991). This contemporary definition actually differs from Lorenz's (1937) original concepts, an issue to which we will return later.

To study imprinting in the laboratory, chicks or ducklings may be hatched and reared in darkness, and exposed to a conspicuous object (see figure 13.1A) when they are about 24 hours old (see Horn, 1985). Chicks may be exposed to a stimulus (training) while they are in individual running wheels, as illustrated in figure 13.1B. The chick can see the imprinting object through the wire mesh floor of the running wheel. After imprinting training the animals are returned to a holding incubator and kept in darkness, until their preferences are measured in a choice test involving sequential or simultaneous exposure to the training stimulus and a novel stimulus. Although other measures have also been used, filial preferences are often expressed as the relative approach (or attempted approach) to the training stimulus, compared with the approach to the training stimulus and a novel stimulus. Bateson (1966) concluded that, in general, the more conspicuous an object is to the human eye, the more effective it will be as an imprinting stimulus. Movement of the object increases its attractiveness (e.g. ten Cate, 1989a) as does the presentation of an auditory stimulus with a visual stimulus (e.g. Van Kampen and Bolhuis, 1993; see below). Imprinting is not an instantaneous process: it takes ≥ 1 hour of exposure for a chick to achieve a significant preference for a simple artificial object, depending on the object. However, a significant preference can be achieved with a considerably shorter period of exposure when the imprinting stimulus is presented with a variable duration/variable interval schedule (Bolhuis and Johnson, 1988).

Learning Mechanisms in Filial Imprinting

Lorenz (1935) initially suggested that the process of acquisition of knowledge about the object to which social behavior becomes directed "has nothing to do with learning": (p. 378: ". . . der mit Lernen nichts zu tun hat"), mainly because it was thought to occur within a sensitive period and to be irreversible. However, in the later English version of his paper he suggested that "Of course, it is a matter of personal opinion how much or how little importance one should attribute to these differences from associative learning" (Lorenz, 1937, p. 266); and we shall see that when the label "imprinting" is removed, Lorenz's views on the learning processes involved appear to be similar to current interpretations. There are two main reasons for this apparent reconciliation of Lorenz's views with contemporary evidence. First, it has become clear that the criteria of a sensitive period and irreversibility are not

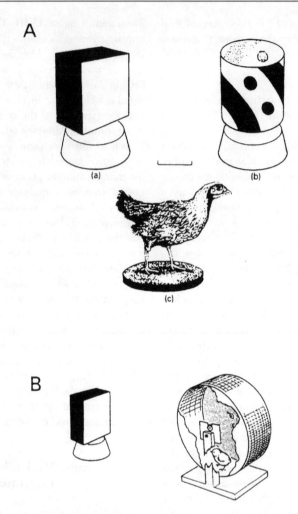

Figure 13.1 (A) Examples of stimuli used in laboratory experiments investigating the development of filial preferences in chicks. All of the stimuli are mounted on motors with a central axle that can rotate. The box (a) and the cylinder (b) are made of perspex. They have colored filters where they are not black, and they are lit from within. Stimulus (c) is a stuffed Burmese red jungle fowl hen (*Gallus gallus spadiceus*). Scale bar is 10 cm. (B) Diagram of a chick in a running wheel. The floor of the running wheel is made of wire mesh, and the sides are made of wood, painted matt black. The diameter of the wheel is 30 cm. For the purposes of illustration one of the opaque sides of the wheel is shown partly removed. In this example the chick can view an imprinting stimulus (in this case a rotating box as in figure 13.1A) through the wire mesh floor. The stimulus is approximately 50 cm away from the center of the running wheel. When attempting to approach the stimulus or to move away, the chick rotates the wheel. In many of the experiments discussed in this chapter the chicks were placed in running wheels such as this one in darkness, without an imprinting stimulus present. (Adapted from Horn, 1985, by permission of the Oxford University Press.)

as strict as Lorenz suggested (see Bateson, 1966; Bolhuis, 1991, for reviews), although they may still play a role (e.g. Cherfas and Scott, 1981; Bolhuis and Bateson, 1990; Cook, 1993; Johnson et al., 1989). Thus, these criteria do not necessarily distinguish imprinting from other forms of learning (Bolhuis et al., 1990). Second, Lorenz (1937, p. 262) actually distinguished between imprinting – which he saw as the acquisition of a "perceptual pattern" of the species – on the one hand, and "an acquiring process, that is . . . conditioning in a broad sense of the word," on the other. Lorenz went on to say that the latter process is "true associative learning which unites the different sets of releasing stimuli emanating from an individual companion" (ibid.). Thus, Lorenz clearly acknowledged that there was a process of acquisition of knowledge of the individual characteristics of stimuli. In fact, it is this process which is called "filial imprinting" by contemporary researchers (e.g. Bateson, 1990; Horn, 1985; Bolhuis, 1991).

The question remains whether filial and sexual imprinting involve the acquisition of a preference for individuals, or for the species (as Lorenz maintained), and whether the latter involves a special process. As regards filial preferences it has been shown that chicks can acquire preferences for individual stuffed fowl (Johnson and Horn, 1987) and ducklings and chicks can learn to prefer maternal calls from particular individuals (Gottlieb, 1988; Van Kampen and Bolhuis, 1991; see Bolhuis and Van Kampen, 1992, for a review). Thus, imprinting is now considered to be concerned with the acquisition of preferences for individuals (cf. Bateson, 1990), as well as for artificial objects (Horn, 1985). Further, birds from a number of precocial species have been shown to have naive preferences or predispositions that appear to be species-specific, both in the auditory (Gottlieb, 1971) and in the visual modality (Lickliter, 1993; Bolhuis and Hampton, 1994). Thus, imprinting is not necessary to achieve a filial preference for the animal's own species. It is often suggested that sexual imprinting involves the acquisition of a preference for the species (e.g. ten Cate, 1989b) although in the sexual context too, birds can acquire preferences for individuals (Bateson, 1982; Bolhuis et al., 1989b), and an apparent preference for the species could be a secondary consequence of a preference for individuals (Bolhuis, 1991).

It has become clear that filial imprinting does not involve simple stimulus-response associations, but that a representation of the training stimulus is formed, that can be used flexibly. For instance, Honey et al. (1993) found that following filial imprinting, chicks showed significantly faster rates of discrimination learning if one of the discriminanda was the imprinting stimulus. This is despite the fact that approach to the imprinting stimulus was not rewarded in the discrimination task. Some indication of the nature of the representation of the imprinting stimulus was provided by Bolhuis and Horn (1992), who demonstrated that there is con-

siderable generalization of learned preferences in imprinting.

Imprinting and Associative Learning

Bolhuis et al. (1990) reviewed some of the evidence for an associative learning account of imprinting, and formulated the requirements for such an interpretation. The most important assumption is that, since filial imprinting proceeds in the absence of a conventional reinforcer, the imprinting object itself must provide the unconditioned stimulus (US). However, the nature of this US is not apparent. Hoffman and his collaborators have formulated a theory of imprinting as Pavlovian conditioning (Hoffman and Ratner, 1973), in which movement is thought to act as the US. During exposure, the bird associates initially neutral aspects of the object (e.g. color and shape) with the US (movement).

Bolhuis et al. (1990) reviewed evidence showing that, if it is assumed that movement of an imprinting object is the US, certain predictions from animal learning theory, such as latent inhibition and extinction, are not confirmed by the data available. Furthermore, several studies have shown that movement of the imprinting object is not necessary for imprinting to occur. Exposure to a conspicuous object (CS) may lead to the occurrence of an internal motivationally significant event, which could serve as a US. Experiments in which presentation of a conspicuous object is used as a US in an operant learning task (e.g. Bateson and Reese, 1968) show that presentation of an imprinting object can be reinforcing it itself. Assuming then that a US occurs at presentation of an imprinting object, certain predictions can be made with regard to the occurrence of associative learning phenomena such as blocking and overshadowing during imprinting. Basically, these involve impairment of learning with one stimulus as a result of simultaneous presentation with another stimulus. Experimental results (de Vos and Bolhuis, 1990; Van Kampen, 1993) are consistent with these predictions, but further research is needed to establish the nature of the underlying mechanisms.

Under natural conditions, the chick is exposed to an object that has both visual and auditory characteristics; the mother hen has a particular size, shape and coloration and emits a specific call. Similarly, during imprinting training in the laboratory the young birds are typically exposed to a visual stimulus accompanied by a recording of the maternal call of a hen. The presence of a call during visual imprinting training can enhance the preference acquired for the visual stimulus. Van Kampen and Bolhuis (1993) exposed chicks either to a visual stimulus together with a maternal call, or to the visual stimulus alone. Subsequently, both groups received a preference test in which the visual training stimulus and a novel visual stimulus were presented without a maternal call. Chicks given the maternal call during training showed a significantly greater preference for the training stimulus than those that were not. In a similar way, the acquisition of a preference for a specific maternal call (Gottlieb, 1988) can be enhanced if that call is accompanied by a visual stimulus during training (Van Kampen and Bolhuis, 1991; see Van Kampen and de Vos, 1991, 1994, for similar results within the visual modality). An interesting interpretation of these findings is that a similar mechanism might underlie the facilitation of imprinting and the potentiation of learning observed when subjects receive conditioning with a simultaneous compound (for a review see LoLordo and Droungas, 1989). For instance, in rats, aversive conditioning of an odor is enhanced when that odor is paired with a taste during the conditioning session. Rescorla and Durlach (1981) have suggested that such potentiation may be a result of within-event learning. That is, during conditioning, associations may form between the representations of the two elements of the compound stimulus. Similarly, during imprinting training with an audio-visual compound, representations of the auditory and visual components of the compound may become associated. The formation of such an association will mean that during a test in which only one of the components is presented there will be two potential sources of preferential responding – that are acquired by the tested component itself and that are due to the associatively-activated representation of the other component of the compound (see Rescorla and Durlach, 1981; Bolhuis and Honey, 1994).

Bolhuis and Honey (1994) tested some of the predictions of such a within-event learning account of potentiation of imprinting. They exposed chicks to a compound stimulus containing an auditory element (a taped maternal call) and a visual element (a moving two-dimensional image). The potentiation

effect was replicated in subsequent preference tests with the training visual stimulus and a novel visual stimulus. That is, chicks that had been exposed to the compound stimulus showed a significantly greater preference for the training (visual) stimulus than chicks that had been exposed to the visual stimulus only. The authors found that additional imprinting training with the call reduced the preference for the visual stimulus, whether exposure to the call occurred after or before exposure to the audio-visual compound. These results are analogous to findings in similar ("sensory preconditioning") paradigms in rats (Rescorla and Durlach, 1981). They support the suggestion that the potentiation of imprinting is a product of within-event learning that is undermined when one element of the compound is presented in isolation.

Configural Representations

Rescorla and Durlach (1981) and Bolhuis and Honey (1994) suggested an alternative interpretation of their respective findings, in which the representation of a compound stimulus is thought to be configurational. That is, under certain circumstances the elements of e.g. an audio-visual compound stimulus might come to address a single or unitary representation, and activity in this representation controls performance. Such an interpretation is accommodated by a neural net model of imprinting and object recognition that was developed by Bateson and Horn (1994; cf. O'Reilly and Johnson, 1994). Figure 13.2 illustrates the simplest version of the model, consisting of three layers, an Analysis, a Recognition and an Executive system, respectively. A basic feature of the network is that links between modules are strengthened when there is simultaneous activity in those modules, and that links are weakened when activity in a Recognition module is not accompanied by activity in an Analysis module. Suppose that the auditory and the visual stimulus activate analysis modules A1 and A2, respectively. If one assumes that the dual input provided by the elements of the compound stimulus enhances the subsequent likelihood for either element to activate a module in the Recognition system, say R1, then compound training would result in a potentiation effect. That is, the links between A1 and R1 and between A2 and R1 become

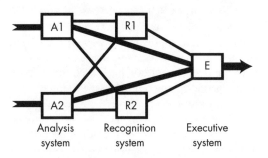

Analysis   Recognition   Executive
system   system   system

Figure 13.2 Flow diagram of the simplest version of the neural net model by Bateson and Horn (1994). The network consists of three systems (Analysis, Recognition and Execution) that contain modules. For simplicity only 2 Analysis modules and 2 Recognition modules are shown. All modules in the Analysis system are linked to all modules in the Recognition system, which, in turn, are linked to all modules in the Executive system. All modules in the Analysis system are also linked directly to the module in the Executive system that controls filial approach behavior. The strength of the links connecting the modules is reflected in the thickness of the lines. (From Bateson and Horn, 1994, by permission of Academic Press.)

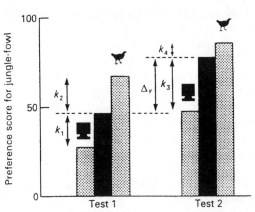

Figure 13.3 Mean preference scores, expressed as a preference for the stuffed fowl, of chicks previously trained by exposure to a rotating stuffed jungle fowl, a rotating red box, or exposed to white light. Preference scores are defined as: activity when attempting to approach the stuffed jungle fowl divided by total approach activity. Preferences were measured in a simultaneous test either 2 hours (Test 1) or 24 hours (Test 2) after the end of training. K_1–K_4 represent the differences between the preferences of the trained chicks and the controls; Δ_Y represents the difference in preference between the control chicks at Test 2 and at Test 1. See text for further explanation. (From Horn, 1985, by permission of the Oxford University Press, after Johnson et al., 1985.)

stronger than they would have been when either of the stimuli had been presented alone. To account for the observation that separate exposure to an element of the compound reduces the potentiation effect (Bolhuis and Honey, 1994) one would need to assume that if activity in R1 is not accompanied by the presentation of one of the elements, then its capacity to activate R1 will be reduced. Given that presentations of the auditory stimulus alone will produce activity in R1 that is unaccompanied by input from the visual stimulus, it is to be expected that input from the visual stimulus will become less able to activate R1.

The results of Bolhuis and Honey (1994), Van Kampen and de Vos (1991, 1993) and those of Van Kampen and Bolhuis (1991, 1993) are remarkably consistent with Lorenz's suggestion, quoted above, concerning the integration of stimulus elements into a unified "perceptual pattern" involved in imprinting on individual stimuli.

Predispositions

As outlined in the Introduction of this chapter, the development of filial behavior in the chick involves two perceptual mechanisms that are neurally and behaviorally dissociable (Horn and McCabe, 1984; Horn, 1985; Johnson et al., 1985, 1992; Bolhuis et al., 1985, 1989a). I have discussed some of the characteristics of the first mechanism, which underlies filial imprinting. Behavioral evidence for the second mechanism, that of a predisposition (Horn and McCabe, 1984), was provided by Johnson et al. (1985). These authors gave day-old dark-reared chicks imprinting training by exposing them either to a rotating red box or to a rotating stuffed jungle fowl hen (*Gallus gallus spadiceus*; see figure 13.1). The approach preferences of the chicks were measured in a subsequent test where the two training stimuli were presented simultaneously. Preferences were tested at either 2 h (Test 1) or 24 h (Test 2) after the end of training (see figure 13.3). At Test 1 the chicks preferred the object to which they had been exposed previously. At Test 2 there was a significantly greater preference for the fowl in both experimental groups. Thus, the preference for the jungle fowl increased from the 2 h to the 24 h test, and did so regardless of the stimulus with which the chicks had been trained. Chicks in a control group that had been placed in the training apparatus with no stimulus except for an overhead light also showed an increasing preference for the jungle fowl with time in preference tests conducted at the same time as in the experimental groups.

Johnson et al. (1985) proposed that the preferences of trained chicks are influenced by at least two different systems. On the one hand, there is an effect of experience with particular stimuli (reflected in the differences K_1–K_4 in figure 13.3), that is, filial imprinting. On the other hand, there is an emerging predisposition to approach stimuli resembling conspecifics (reflected in figure 13.3 as Δ_y for the control group). The existence of these two interacting mechanisms was confirmed in a series of behavioral studies (e.g. Bolhuis and Trooster, 1988; Bolhuis et al., 1989a; Johnson et al., 1992). The results in figure 13.3 suggest that training with a particular stimulus is not necessary for the predisposition to emerge. It was found that the predisposition can in fact emerge in dark-reared chicks, provided that they receive a certain amount of nonspecific stimulation within a certain period in development (e.g. Bolhuis et al., 1985; Johnson et al., 1989; see below).

Induction and Development of a Filial Predisposition

Bolhuis et al. (1985) found that visual experience was not necessary to "trigger" or induce (Gottlieb, 1976) the predisposition. Chicks that were placed in wire mesh running wheels (see figure 13.1B) in total darkness for 2 periods of 1 h preferred the jungle fowl to the red box in a simultaneous choice test 24 h after the end of the period in the wheels. Placement in the running wheels, in darkness, for 2 periods of 1 h (with 1 h in between during which the chicks were kept in a dark incubator) is a standard procedure that is used in many of the experiments discussed here, and that is sufficient to induce a predisposition. However, Bolhuis et al. (1985) found that chicks that had remained in their dark incubator from the time of hatching to the time of testing did not develop a preference. Therefore, some experience associated with being placed in the running wheels is sufficient to trigger the emergence of the preference for the jungle fowl.

In the study by Bolhuis et al. (1985) the period in which the chicks were in the running wheels, in darkness, began approximately 24 h after the birds had hatched. A significant preference for the stuffed jungle fowl was found 24 h, but not 2 h after the end of the period in running wheels. Hampton et al. (1995) investigated whether 24 hours need to pass in order for the underlying mechanisms to develop or to exert their influence on the chicks' behavior. It was found that the predisposition becomes manifest at 10 h and 5 h either after placement in running wheels, or after the chicks had been trained by exposure to a rotating red box. Further, these authors showed that placement in running wheels was not necessary for the predisposition to emerge. Chicks that were taken out of their incubator and handled at the same times that the wheel-treated chicks would normally be, showed a significant preference for the fowl over the red box at 5 h, but not at 2 h after the end of this experience.

Lickliter and his colleagues provided evidence to suggest that in the development of filial preferences in Bobwhite quail (*Colinus virginianus*), the expression of auditory predispositions is affected by visual experience, and *vice versa* (see Lickliter 1993, for a review). Hampton et al. (1995) investigated whether, similarly, auditory stimulation is sufficient for the induction of the visual predisposition in the chick. Exposing 24-hours-old dark-reared chicks to a maternal call of a chicken for 2 h was found to be sufficient to induce the development of a visual predisposition 24 h later. Thus, the evidence from the study by Hampton et al. (1995) suggests that different kinds of experience, in different modalities, are sufficient for the induction of the predisposition.

Hampton et al.'s findings may be similar to those in studies of the development of filial preferences in Bobwhite quail by Lickliter and his colleagues (e.g. Lickliter, 1993). These authors reported that both visual (Lickliter, 1990) and auditory (Lickliter and Stoumbos, 1991) stimulation given before hatching affected the time of expression of a species-specific visual preference. Lickliter and co-workers have reported either a facilitation (Gottlieb, 1976, see below) of, or interference with, perceptual development after auditory or visual stimulation (e.g. Banker and Lickliter, 1993; Lickliter, 1990; Lickliter and Stoumbos, 1991; McBride and Lickliter, 1994). In Bobwhite quail chicks that received standard rearing conditions, without additional auditory or visual experience, a species-specific visual preference developed normally (Banker and Lickliter, 1993). In the studies by Lickliter et al. standard rearing conditions involved placement in social groups immediately after hatching, and visual exposure to siblings in the incubator. Socially reared quail chicks that were visually deprived until testing did not show a species-specific visual preference (Banker and Lickliter, 1993), suggesting that the non-visual experience involved in social rearing is not sufficient to induce a visual predisposition in Bobwhite quail. McBride and Lickliter (1993) found that exposure to the visual features of siblings, but not to those of scaled quail chicks (*Callipepla squamata*), was sufficient for a species-specific visual preference to be expressed. The authors note that Bobwhite quail chicks are marked and colored much like adult Bobwhites. Thus, in this case, very specific visual experience is required for a species-specific preference to be expressed. Hampton et al. (1995) suggested that the Bobwhite quail's preferences may be a result of generalization of learning of the visual characteristics of siblings, rather than of a predisposition, which may develop in the absence of specific experience.

Sensitive Periods

As mentioned earlier in this chapter, Lorenz (1935, 1937) suggested that one of the characteristics that made imprinting unique was that it occurred within a "critical period." Bateson and Hinde (1987) reviewed some of the relevant evidence and suggested that rather than "critical period," which implies a fixed period, the term "sensitive period" should be used. In their words "The sensitive period concept implies a phase of greater susceptibility preceded and followed by lower sensitivity, with relatively gradual transitions" (p. 20). These authors concluded that external experience played an important role in changes in "imprintibility," and that the end of an apparent sensitive period was largely due to the imprinting experience itself (cf. Sluckin and Salzen, 1961), and not so much a consequence of endogenous changes.

In dark-reared chicks there is a sensitive period for the induction of the filial predisposition. Johnson et al. (1989) found that dark-reared chicks

which were placed in the running wheels (for 2 h) at 12 h, 42 h or 48 h after hatching did not show a significant preference in a preference test 24 h later, but chicks that received a 2 h period in the running wheels at 24 h or 36 h after hatching significantly preferred the stuffed jungle fowl to the red box. It was not clear from these results whether the crucial factor was the time at which the chicks were placed in the wheels, or when they were tested. For example, chicks placed in the wheels 48 h after hatching were 72 h old when tested; chicks placed in the wheels 24 h after hatching were 48 h old when tested. The former did not show a preference for the jungle fowl whereas the latter did. To clarify this issue, chicks in a control group were placed in the wheels at 24 h after hatching and given a preference test 72 h after hatching (i.e. at the same time as the chicks in the 48 h wheel placement group). These chicks showed a significant preference for the jungle fowl, demonstrating that the crucial factor is the time at which the chicks are placed in the wheels, not the time of testing. Thus, in dark-reared chicks there is a sensitive period approximately between 20 and 40 hours after hatching during which placement in the wheels may induce the emergence of the predisposition. There is a parallel of this finding in work on auditory predispositions in ducklings. Gottlieb (1985) found that duck embryos needed to be exposed to embryonic calls within a certain period of time to ensure maintenance of species-specific auditory preferences after hatching.

The results of a study by Bolhuis et al. (1989a) were consistent with the existence of a sensitive period for the induction of a predisposition. When chicks were placed in running wheels for 2 × 1 h, in darkness, at approximately 30 h after hatching, exposure to a rotating red box at approximately 70 h after hatching did not result in a significant preference in a simultaneous test with the red box and stuffed jungle fowl. However, when the chicks were placed in the wheels at 45 h after hatching, subsequent box-training at 70 h after hatching resulted in a significant preference for the red box over the stuffed fowl. Thus, in chicks that received non-specific stimulation within the sensitive period, the learned preference had to compete with the effects of the predisposition; when the non-specific experience was given after the end of the sensitive period, when preferences are presumably not influenced by the predisposition, the chicks' preferences were determined by the birds' training experience.

The sensitive period for the induction of the predisposition that was demonstrated in dark-reared chicks (Johnson et al., 1989) is by no means absolute. Visual experience may alter the sensitive period (Hampton, 1995), while manipulation of catecholamine levels in the brain (Davies et al., 1992) or anesthesia (Bolhuis and Horn, 1995) may delay its onset (see below).

Interaction between Perceptual Mechanisms

The results of Johnson et al. (1985) are interpreted as reflecting an interaction between two perceptual mechanisms. The chance-level performance of the box-trained chicks at the second preference test (figure 13.3) is though to result from an interaction between the effects of training to the red box and an emerging predisposition for the stuffed fowl. There are, however, other explanations for these (figure 13.3) results. For example, box-trained chicks may have learned less, or processed the acquired information about the red box less deeply, or have forgotten more quickly, than was the case for chicks exposed to the stuffed fowl. Thus, for one or all of the preceding reasons, by the time the second preference test was given, the red box-trained birds failed to show a preference for the red box, whereas the fowl-trained birds still had a strong preference for their training object. Johnson et al. (1992) addressed this hypothesis in a study where they repeated the training procedure with a red box. However, rather than the preference test consisting of a choice between the red box and a stuffed fowl as before, the chicks were given two choice tests: one between the box to which they had been exposed and a box of a novel color, and one between the familiar box and a novel stuffed fowl. There was a decline in preference for the red box over the fowl from the first to the second test, as before. However, the acquired preference for the red box over a blue box was robust even in the second preference test. Thus, these results replicated previous findings and suggested that they cannot be interpreted in terms of differential forgetting.

Bolhuis et al. (1989a) investigated whether the predisposition served as a filter or "template" (Marler, 1976), restricting the information that the

chick can store in memory, or, alternatively, whether the predisposition acts independently of the effects of learning during development. Dark-reared chicks were allowed to develop the predisposition, manifest as a significant preference for the stuffed fowl over the red box, by placing them in running wheels in darkness for 2 h when they were approximately 24 h old. When the chicks were approximately 50 h old, they were trained by exposing them to the rotating red box. In subsequent preference tests, it was found that these chicks, after the predisposition had developed, were still capable of learning the characteristics of conspicuous objects. These results suggest that the two mechanisms interact at the behavioral level rather than the predisposition constraining the information that can be stored. That is, the activated predisposition will bias the chick's approach response to certain stimuli, and the animal may learn the characteristics of those stimuli; but the chick is still capable of learning the characteristics of other objects.

Stimulus Selection in Filial Predispositions

Baerends and Kruijt (1973) defined stimulus selection as ". . . the phenomenon whereby the various physical stimuli activating the receptors of an organism are not quantitatively equivalent with regard to their controlling effect on a particular behavior pattern" (p. 23). From an extensive series of experiments on the egg-retrieving response of the herring gull (*Larus argentatus*), they concluded that the response to stimulus eggs obeyed the principle of heterogeneous summation, whereby different stimulus characteristics (color, speckling, size) contribute to the induction of the response independently (cf. Baerends et al., 1982; see Baerends, 1993, for similar findings in filial behavior of cichlid fish).

The stimulus characteristics that are important for the filial predisposition to be expressed were first examined by Johnson and Horn (1988). These authors attempted to "titrate" the visual complexity of the stuffed jungle fowl against its "fowl-like" characteristics. To this end, the preferences of dark-reared chicks, which had been placed in running wheels for 2 h when they were approximately 24 h old, were tested either 2 or 24 h later. Stimuli used during the tests were an intact stuffed jungle fowl versus one in a series of increasingly degraded versions of a stuffed jungle fowl. The degraded versions ranged from one where different parts of the model (wings, head, torso, legs) were reassembled in an unnatural way, to one in which the pelt of a jungle fowl had been cut into small pieces that were stuck onto a rotating box. It was found that the intact model was preferred at the second test, when the chicks were approximately 52h old, only when the degraded object possessed no distinguishable jungle fowl features. In addition, Johnson and Horn (1988) demonstrated that chicks did not prefer an intact jungle fowl model over an alternative object that contained only the head and neck of a stuffed fowl. Thus, it seems likely that the head and neck region contains stimuli that are relevant for the predisposition. In subsequent experiments, Johnson and Horn (1988) found that the chicks did not prefer a stuffed jungle fowl hen over a stuffed Gadwall duck (*Anas strepera*) or even a

stuffed polecat (*Mustela putorius*). Thus, the predisposition is not species- or even class specific.

Hampton (1995) provided dark-reared chicks with non-specific stimulation (placement in running wheels) that would induce the emergence of the predisposition, and 24h later their preferences were tested in simultaneous tests involving different pairs of stimuli. One of the test stimuli used was a stuffed jungle fowl hen, of which the eyes had been covered with a patch of color-matched jungle fowl feathers attached to plasticine. Chicks showed an equally strong preference for a stuffed fowl with its eyes covered with patches of feathers and for an intact stuffed fowl, compared with a red box. These findings indicate that areas outside the eyes provide stimulus elements that are sufficient for the predisposition to be expressed. However, in two separate experiments chicks showed a significant preference for an intact stuffed fowl over a stuffed fowl with covered eyes (see

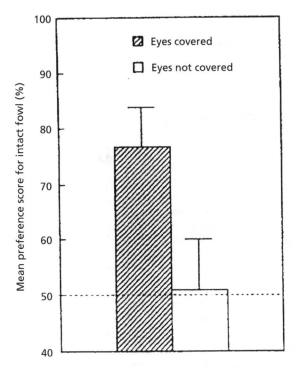

Figure 13.4 Mean preference scores (see figure 13.3) in one of the experiments by Hampton (1995). Dark-reared chicks were allowed to develop a predisposition, then at approximately 50h after hatching approach preferences were examined in a test involving the simultaneous presentation of two stuffed jungle fowls. Scores are expressed as preferences for the intact stuffed jungle fowl over the alternative stuffed jungle fowl. In the case of the "eyes covered" group, the alternative stimulus was another stuffed jungle fowl which had its eyes covered with patches of jungle fowl feathers. In the "eyes not covered" group, the alternative stimulus was another intact stuffed jungle fowl. The results of chicks that were active during the preference test are shown only. See text for further explanation. (Adapted from Hampton, 1995, with permission.)

figure 13.4). These results suggest that eyes are an important stimulus, but that other aspects of the stimulus are also sufficient for the expression of a predisposition.

Thus, it appears that the eyes are not a sign stimulus that is uniquely important for the expression of the predisposition. It may be that stimuli outside the head also play a role in the expression of the predisposition. It is possible that, as in the work of Baerends and collaborators (Baerends and Kruijt, 1973; Baerends et al., 1982; Baerends, 1993), the stimulus selection involved in the predisposition conforms to the rule of heterogeneous summation, with the eyes forming an important stimulus, as well as other stimuli. Alternatively, it is conceivable that the chicks' response is governed by a combination of a configurational stimulus (Tinbergen, 1951), that needs to have a head and neck as well as a body, with added to that certain stimulus elements (such as the eyes) that are separately important. The bird's response is then governed by the rule of heterogeneous summation. This interpretation is consistent with Tinbergen's views, who suggested that configurational sign stimuli may "cooperate according to the rule of heterogeneous summation" (Tinbergen, 1951, p. 101).

Neural Mechanisms of Imprinting and Predispositions

The neural mechanisms of learning and memory processes involved in filial imprinting have been investigated by Horn and his collaborators (Horn, 1985). This work has been reviewed elsewhere (e.g. Horn, 1985, 1992), and will be discussed only briefly here, mainly with regard to the distinction between the mechanisms involved in learning and in predispositions (see also Bolhuis, 1994).

Imprinting is associated with a number of neural changes in a restricted region of the chick forebrain referred to as the intermediate and medial hyperstriatum ventrale (IMHV; see figure 13.5). These changes include an increase in RNA synthesis, an increase in the size of postsynaptic densities of a certain class of synapses, an increase in N-methyl-D-aspartate receptor binding and an increase in phosphorylation of MARCKS protein, a protein kinase C substrate (Horn, 1985, 1992; Sheu et al., 1993). Imprinting also leads to a learning-related

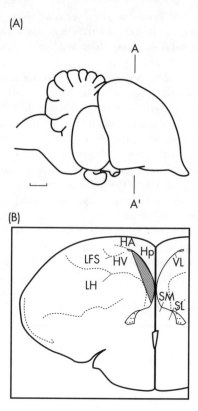

Figure 13.5   Schematic drawing of the brain of the domestic chick. (A) Lateral aspect of the brain. The vertical lines AA' indicate the approximate plane of the coronal section outline of the brain (B). Scale bar: 2 mm. (Adapted from Horn, 1991b.) According to Horn (1991a), the rostro–caudal extent of the IMHV is roughly from A 6.4 to A 9.6 in the stereotaxic atlas by Kuenzel and Masson (1988). (B) Simplified diagram of a coronal section of the chick brain at the level of the IMHV (approximately A 7.6 in the atlas by Kuenzel and Masson, 1988). (Adapted from Ambalavanar et al. (1993).) The extent in the coronal plane of the left IMHV, as removed in biochemical studies (see Horn, 1985), is indicated by the hatched area. (From Bolhuis, 1994, by permission of Cambridge University Press).

increase in immunoreactivity of the immediate early gene product Fos in the IMHV (McCabe and Horn, 1994; cf. Ambalavanar et al., 1993). Bilateral lesions to the chick IMHV impair both acquisition and retention of filial preferences. However, Horn and McCabe (1984) reported that the effects of lesions to the IMHV were dependent on the stimulus used for imprinting training. IMHV lesions greatly impaired filial preferences of chicks trained with a red box, but had a relatively small (but significant) effect on the preferences of chicks trained by exposure to the stuffed fowl. These findings led to the suggestion that the chicks' preferences are influenced not only by learning, but also by a predisposition to approach certain stimuli such as the stuffed fowl.

Although lesion studies led to the original discovery in the chick of the emerging predisposition (Horn and McCabe, 1984), little is known about the underlying neural and physiological mechanisms. Johnson and Horn (1986) found that the development of the predisposition was not affected by early bilateral lesions to the IMHV. Thus, it is likely that the neural substrate involved in the predisposition is located outside the IMHV. However, recent electrophysiological findings (Brown and Horn, 1994; cf. Nicol et al., 1995) suggest that this neural substrate may influence neuronal activity in the IMHV. Brown and Horn (1994) trained dark-reared chicks by exposing them to a rotating red box or a rotating blue cylinder (see figure 13.1). One day after the end of imprinting training, recordings were made from groups of neurons in the left IMHV. There was an effect of training on the response to presentation of a stuffed jungle fowl. A significantly higher proportion of responses to the fowl were excitatory in trained chicks (68%), irrespective of the training object, than in dark-reared chicks (7%). The chicks had received imprinting training with a compound stimulus of the visual imprinting object and the taped call of a hen. It is known that such compound training can lead to potentiation of learning about the elements of the compound (Van Kampen and Bolhuis, 1991; Bolhuis and Honey, 1994). It is also possible that exposure to the call had an inducing effect on predispositions (Bolhuis and Hampton, 1994), thereby influencing the response of neurones in the IMHV to presentation of the fowl during test.

Davies et al. (1992) found that injections of the catecholaminergic neurotoxin DSP4 delayed the onset of the sensitive period for the induction of the predisposition in dark-reared chicks. Chicks were given intraperitoneal injections of DSP4 or vehicle shortly after hatching. The chicks were then placed in running wheels for 2×1 h, in darkness, at a particular time after hatching, and their filial preferences were tested 24 h later. Unlike vehicle-injected controls, DSP4-treated chicks did not show a significant preference for the jungle fowl over the red box when they had been placed in the wheels at 24 h or 36 h after hatching. However, DSP4-treated chicks showed a significant preference for the fowl when they had been placed in the wheels at 42 h or 48 h after hatching, i.e. at times when this wheel placement did not induce a significant preference in the controls. Preliminary results indicate that a similar delay in the onset of the sensitive period is achieved after equithesin anesthesia (Bolhuis and Horn, 1995). After the preference tests, Davies et al. (1992) determined the levels of dopamine and noradrenaline in forebrain samples containing predominantly IMHV. In control chicks there was a significant negative correlation between forebrain dopamine concentration and preference score for the fowl; no such correlation was found for noradrenaline. As the authors note, if dopamine is involved in the expression of the predisposition, it is likely to involve brain regions outside the IMHV, as lesions to this structure do not affect the predisposition (Johnson and Horn, 1986).

It is not known whether catecholamines are involved in the induction of the predisposition. It has been suggested that androgens may have such a role (Bolhuis et al., 1985, 1986; Horn, 1985). Bolhuis et al. (1986) reported that in chicks trained by exposure to a stuffed jungle fowl, there was a significant positive correlation between plasma levels of testosterone and preference score for the stuffed fowl. No such relationship was found in chicks trained by exposure to a rotating red box. Further, subcutaneous injections of a long-lasting testosterone ester shortly after hatching significantly increased the mean preference score of chicks trained on a stuffed fowl, not that of red box-trained chicks. These findings suggest that the preference for the stuffed fowl is limited by the concentration of androgens in the plasma, and they led to the suggestion (Bolhuis et al., 1985; Horn, 1985) that testosterone may be involved in the development of the predisposition. Horn (1985) suggested that increased levels of testosterone or other hormones could render the systems involved in the predisposition operational.

The experience of handling, placement in running wheels, or exposure to a call, might lead to an increase in plasma levels of certain hormones, including testosterone, or catecholamines (Davies et al., 1992). It is known that under certain circumstances, handling leads to an increase in the plasma levels of corticosteroids in laying hens (Beuving and

Vonder, 1978) and androgens in Japanese quail, *Coturnix coturnix japonica* (Ramenofsky, 1985). Within 0.5 min. of being placed into an arena, male Japanese quail showed an increase in plasma testosterone concentration which lasted for approximately 7 min. Further experiments are needed to investigate the role of androgens in the development of the predisposition.

Predispositions, Imprinting, and the Development of Behavior

From a functional perspective, Bolhuis et al. (1985) suggested that a filial predisposition may ensure that the young animal directs its attention to a particular class of objects (i.e. stimuli with a head and neck (Johnson and Horn, 1988) or indeed to conspecifics (Gottlieb, 1971; Lickliter, 1993; Bolhuis and Hampton, 1994). After the predisposition has fully developed, learning the visual and auditory characteristics of a particular object may lead to the recognition of individuals, in filial as well as in sexual imprinting. It is important to realize how the development of filial preferences might proceed in the natural situation. The dynamics of the process as they have been reported may be peculiar to the laboratory conditions that were used (e.g. rearing in visual and tactile isolation, in the absence of maternal vocalizations), and do not necessarily reflect the normal course of development (cf. Rogers, 1995). In this chapter I have reviewed evidence that suggests that the complex visual and auditory experience that the young bird receives before and after hatching would secure a rapid induction and development of a predisposition. For instance, Hampton et al. (1995) demonstrated that in the laboratory, the predisposition in the chick is manifest between 2 and 5 h after the inducing experience. Furthermore, Bolhuis et al. (1985) found that the predisposition is expressed as early as 2 h after complex visual experience. Also, it is likely that in the natural situation, the necessary experience for the induction of the predisposition is available to the young bird at the appropriate time in the "sensitive period," which, as we have seen, is not a strict and absolute constraint.

The terms maintenance, facilitation, and induction that were used earlier, were introduced by Gottlieb (1976, 1980), to distinguish some of the

ways in which experience can affect the development of "species-typical perception." All these three possibilities have been shown to occur in the development of filial preferences (Bolhuis, 1991). Hampton et al. (1995) concluded that, within the time course used in their own and related studies, the effects of experience on the development of the predisposition may be categorized as a case of induction; the predisposition is not expressed initially, and only emerges after non-specific experience. Gottlieb's terms are of course descriptive, and do not elucidate the underlying mechanisms (Hampton et al., 1995). Shettleworth (1994) noted that Gottlieb's classification was introduced as "an alternative to viewing early development in terms of conventional categories of learning" (p. 370). She pointed out the difference between Gottlieb's descriptive concepts and e.g. Rescorla's (1988) theoretical distinctions of learning processes. However, as Shettleworth asserts, Gottlieb's classification may be a useful way of categorizing effects of experience on behavioral development.

The finding that exposure to different kinds of stimuli may lead to the emergence of a predisposition (Hampton et al., 1995) is an example of induction of a perceptual mechanism by non-specific experience (cf. Hogan, 1988, 1994). Similar results have been reported for instance in the development of food recognition in chicks (Hogan, 1977). The work by Lickliter and his colleagues suggests that the same principle applies to the facilitation of the development of perceptual mechanisms. Oetting et al. (1995) provided evidence for maintenance, termed "consolidation" (Kruijt and Meeuwissen, 1991, 1993; Bischof, 1994) or "stabilization" (Bischof and Clayton, 1991; Oetting et al., 1995) of sexual preferences in the zebra finch through non-specific experience (cf. Bischof, 1994; Kruijt and Meeuwissen, 1993). As Hogan's (1988, 1994) reviews of developmental paradigms suggest, the (inducing, maintaining or facilitating) effect of non-specific, seemingly unrelated experience on specific perceptual mechanisms appears to be a fundamental principle of behavioral development.

Acknowledgments

The research of mine reported in this chapter was supported by a Postdoctoral Research Fellowship from the Biotechnology and Biological Sciences Research Council (UK). I am grateful to Gabriel Horn, Sara Shettleworth, Jerry Hogan and Cynthia Moss for their comments on the manuscript.

References

Ambalavanar, R., Van der Zee, E. A., Bolhuis, J. J., McCabe, B. J. and Horn, G. (1993) Co-expression of Fos immunoreactivity in protein kinase (PKCγ)-positive neurons: Quantitative analysis of a brain region involved in learning, *Brain Research*, **606**: 315–18.

Baerends, G. P. (1993) A comparative study of stimulus selection in the filial following response of fry of substrate spawning ciclid fish, *Behaviour*, **125**: 79–155.

Baerends, G. P., Blokzijl, G. J. and Kruijt, J. P. (1982) The processing of heterogenous information of the egg features inducing the retrieval response, *Behaviour*, **82**: 212–14.

Baerends, G. P. and Kruijt, J. P. (1973) Stimulus selection. In R. A. Hinde and J. Stevenson-Hinde (eds), *Constraints on Learning*, New York: McGraw-Hill, pp. 23–50.

Banker, H. and Lickliter, R. (1993) Effects of early and delayed visual experience on intersensory development in bobwhite quail chicks, *Developmental Psychobiology*, **26**: 155–70.

Bateson, P. P. G. (1966) The characteristics and context of imprinting, *Biological Reviews*, **41**: 177–220

Bateson, P. P. G. (1982) Preferences for cousins in Japanese quail, *Nature*, **295**: 236–7.

Bateson, P. (1990) Is imprinting such a special case? *Philosophical Transactions of the Royal Society of London*, Series B, **329**: 125–31.

Bateson, P. and Hinde, R. A. (1987) Developmental changes in sensitivity to experience. In M. H. Bornstein (ed.), *Sensitive Periods in Development*, Hillsdale, NJ.: Lawrence Erlbaum Associates, pp. 19–34.

Bateson, P. and Horn, G. (1994) Imprinting and recognition memory: A neural net model, *Animal Behaviour*, **48**: 695–715.

Bateson, P. P. G. and Reese, E. P. (1968) Reinforcing properties of conspicuous objects before imprinting has occurred, *Psychonomic Science*, **10**: 379–80.

Beuving, G. and Vonder, G. M. A. (1978) Effect of stressing factors on corticosterone levels in the plasma of laying hens, *General and Comparative Endocrinology*, **35**: 153–9.

Bischof, H.-J. (1994) Sexual imprinting as a two-stage process. In J. A. Hogan and J. J. Bolhuis (eds), *Causal Mechanisms of Behavioural Development*, Cambridge: Cambridge University Press, pp. 82–97.

Bischof, H.-J. and Clayton, N. S. (1991) Stabilization of sexual preferences by sexual experience in male zebra finches *Taeniopygia guttata castanotis*, *Behaviour*, **118**: 144–55.

Bolhuis, J. J. (1991) Mechanisms of avian imprinting: A review, *Biological Reviews*, **66**: 303–45.

Bolhuis, J. J. (1994) Neurobiological analyses of behavioural mechanisms in development. In J. A. Hogan and J. J. Bolhuis (eds), *Causal Mechanisms of Behavioral Development*, Cambridge: Cambridge University Press, pp. 16–46.

Bolhuis, J. J. and Bateson, P. P. G. (1990) The importance of being first: A primacy effect in filial imprinting, *Animal Behaviour*, **40**: 472–83.

Bolhuis, J. J., de Vos, G. J. and Kruijt, J. P. (1990) Filial imprinting and associative learning, *Quarterly Journal of Experimental Psychology*, **42B**: 313–29.

Bolhuis, J. J. and Hampton, N. G. (1994) A species-specific predisposition in the domestic chick, *European Journal of Neuroscience*, **7**: 175.

Bolhuis, J. J. and Honey, R. C. (1994) Within-event learning during filial imprinting, *Journal of Experimental Psychology: Animal Behavior Processes*, **20**: 240–8.

Bolhuis, J. J. and Horn, G. (1992) Generalization of learned preferences in filial imprinting, *Animal Behaviour*, **44**: 185–7.

Bolhuis, J. J. and Horn, G. (1995) Effects of anaesthesia on the development of a filial predisposition in the chick. In M. Burrows, T. Matheson, P. L. Newland and H. Schuppe (eds), *Nervous Systems and Behaviour. Proceedings of the 4th International Congress of Neuroethology*, Stuttgart: Georg Thieme Verlag, p. 192.

Bolhuis, J. J. and Johnson, M. H. (1988) Effects of response-contingency and stimulus presentation schedule on imprinting in the chick, *Journal of Comparative Psychology*, **102**: 61–5.

Bolhuis, J. J., Johnson, M. H. and Horn, G. (1985) Effects of early experience on the development of filial preferences in the domestic chick, *Developmental Psychobiology*, **18**: 299–308.

Bolhuis, J. J., Johnson, M. H. and Horn, G. (1989a) Interacting mechanisms during the formation of filial preferences: The development of a predisposition does not prevent learning, *Journal of Experimental Psychology: Animal Behavior Processes*, **15**: 376–82.

Bolhuis, J. J., Johnson, M. H., Horn, G. and Bateson, P. (1989b) Long-lasting effects of IMHV lesions on social preferences in domestic fowl, *Behavioral Neuroscience*, **103**: 438–41.

Bolhuis, J. J., McCabe, B. J. and Horn, G. (1986) Androgens and imprinting: Differential effects of testosterone on filial preference in the domestic chick, *Behavioral Neuroscience*, **100**: 51–6.

Bolhuis, J. J. and Trooster, W. J. (1988) Reversibility revisited: Stimulus-dependent stability of filial preference in the chick, *Animal Behaviour*, **36**: 668–74.

Bolhuis, J. J. and Van Kampen, H. S. (1992) An evaluation of auditory learning in filial imprinting, *Behaviour*, **122**: 195–230.

Brown, M. W. and Horn, G. (1994) Learning-related alterations in the visual responsiveness of neurons in a memory system of the chick brain, *European Journal of Neuroscience*, **6**: 1479–90.

Cherfas, J. and Scott, A. (1981) Impermanent reversal of imprinting, *Animal Behaviour*, **30**: 301.

Cook, S. E. (1993) Retention of primary preferences after secondary filial imprinting, *Animal Behaviour*, **46**: 405–7.

Davies, D. C., Johnson, M. H. and Horn, G. (1992) The effect of the neurotoxin DSP4 on the development of a predisposition in the domestic chick, *Developmental Psychobiology*, **25**: 251–9.

de Vos, G. J. and Bolhuis, J. J. (1990) An investigation into blocking of filial imprinting in chicks during exposure to a compound stimulus, *Quarterly Journal of Experimental Psychology*, **42B**: 289–312.

Gottlieb, G. (1971) *Development of Species Identification in Birds*, Chicago: University of Chicago Press.

Gottlieb, G. (1976) The roles of experience in the development of behavior and the nervous system. In G. Gottlieb (ed.), *Neural and Behavioral Specificity: Studies in the Development of Behavior and the Nervous System*, New York: Academic Press, pp. 237–80.

Gottlieb, G. (1980) Development of species identification in ducklings: VI. Specific embryonic experience required to maintain species-typical perception in Peking ducklings, *Journal of Comparative and Physiological Psychology*, **94**: 579–87.

Gottlieb, G. (1985) Development of species identification in ducklings: XI. Embryonic critical period for species-typical perception in the hatchling, *Animal Behaviour*, **33**: 225–33.

Gottlieb, G. (1988) Development of species identification in ducklings: XV. Individual auditory recognition, *Developmental Psychobiology*, **21**: 509–22.

Hampton, N. G. (1995) *An Investigation of Filial Predispositions in the Domestic Chick*, unpublished dissertation, University of Cambridge.

Hampton, N. G., Bolhuis, J. J. and Horn, G. (1995) Induction and development of a filial predisposition in the chick, *Behaviour*, **132**: 451–77.

Hoffman, H. S. and Ratner, A. M. (1973) A reinforcement model of imprinting: Implications for socialization in monkeys and men, *Psychological Review*, **80**: 527–44.

Hogan, J. A. (1977) The ontogeny of food preferences in chicks and other animals. In L. M. Barker, M. Best and M. Domjan (eds), *Learning Mechanisms in Food Selection*, Waco, Texas: Baylor University Press, pp. 71–97.

Hogan, J. A. (1988) Cause and function in the development of behavior systems. In E. M. Blass (ed.), *Handbook of Behavioral Neurobiology*, vol. 9, New York: Plenum Press, pp. 63–106.

Hogan, J. A. (1994) Development of behavior systems. In J. A. Hogan and J. J. Bolhuis (eds), *Causal Mechanisms of Behavioural Development*, Cambridge: Cambridge University Press, pp. 242–64.

Honey, R. C., Horn, G. and Bateson, P. (1993) Perceptual learning during filial imprinting: Evidence from transfer of training studies, *Quarterly Journal of Experimental Psychology*, **46B**: 253–69.

Horn, G. (1985) *Memory, Imprinting, and the Brain*, Oxford: Clarendon Press.

Horn, G. (1991a) Technique for removing IMHV from the chick brain. In R. J. Andrew (ed.), *Neural and Behavioural Plasticity: The Use of the Domestic Chick as a Model*, Oxford: Oxford University Press, pp. 44–8.

Horn, G. (1991b) Imprinting and recognition memory: A review of neural mechanisms. In R. J. Andrew (ed.), *Neural and Behavioural Plasticity: The Use of the Domestic Chick as a Model*, Oxford: Oxford University Press, pp. 219–61.

Horn, G. (1992) Brain mechanisms of memory and predispositions: Interactive studies of cerebral function and behavior. In M. H. Johnson (ed.), *Brain Development and Cognition: A Reader*, Oxford: Blackwell, pp. 485–513.

Horn, G. and McCabe, B. J. (1984) Predispositions and preferences: Effects on imprinting of lesions to the chick brain, *Animal Behaviour*, **32**: 288–92.

Johnson, M. H. and Bolhuis, J. J. (1991) Imprinting, predispositions and filial preference in the chick. In R. J. Andrew (ed.), *Neural and Behavioural Plasticity*, Oxford: Oxford University Press, pp. 133–56.

Johnson, M. H., Bolhuis, J. J. and Horn, G. (1985) Interaction between acquired preferences and developing predispositions during imprinting, *Animal Behaviour*, **33**: 1000–6.

Johnson, M. H., Bolhuis, J. J. and Horn, G. (1992) Predispositions and learning: Behavioral dissociations in the chick, *Animal Behaviour*, **44**: 943–8.

Johnson, M. H., Davies, D. C. and Horn, G. (1989) A critical period for the development of a predisposition in the chick, *Animal Behaviour*, **37**: 1044–6.

Johnson, M. H. and Horn, G. (1986) Dissociation between recognition memory and associative learning by a restricted lesion to the chick forebrain, *Neuropsychologia*, **24**: 329–40.

Johnson, M. H. and Horn, G. (1987) The role of a restricted region of the chick forebrain in the recognition of conspecifics, *Behavioral Brain Research*, **23**: 269–75.

Johnson, M. H. and Horn, G. (1988) Development of filial preferences in dark-reared chicks, *Animal Behaviour*, **36**: 675–83.

Kruijt, J. P. and Meeuwissen, G. (1991) Sexual preferences of male zebra finches: Effects of early and adult experience, *Animal Behaviour*, **42**: 91–102.

Kruijt, J. P. and Meeuwissen, G. (1993) Consolidation and modification of sexual preferences in adult male zebra finches, *Netherlands Journal of Zoology*, **43**: 68–79.

Kuenzel, W. J. and Masson, M. (1988) *A Stereotaxic Atlas of the Brain of the Chick (Gallus domesticus)*, Baltimore: Johns Hopkins University Press.

Lickliter, R. (1990) Premature visual experience facilitates visual responsiveness in bobwhite quail neonates, *Infant Behavior and Development*, **13**: 487–96.

Lickliter, R. (1993) Timing and the development of perinatal perceptual organization. In G. Turkewitz and D. A. Devenny (eds), *Developmental Time and Timing*, Hillsdale, NJ: Lawrence Erlbaum Associates, pp. 105–23.

Lickliter, R. and Stoumbos, J. (1991) Enhanced prenatal auditory experience facilitates postnatal visual responsiveness in bobwhite quail chicks, *Journal of Comparative Psychology*, **105**: 89–94.

LoLordo, V. M. and Droungas, A. (1989) Selective associations and adaptive specializations: Taste aversion and phobias. In S. B. Klein and R. R. Mowrer (eds), *Contemporary Learning Theories, II: Instrumental Conditioning Theory and the Impact of Biological Constraints on Learning*, Hillsdale, NJ: Lawrence Erlbaum, pp. 145–79.

Lorenz, K. (1935) Der Kumpan in der Umwelt des Vogels, *Journal für Ornithologie*, **83**: 137–213, 289–413.

Lorenz, K. (1937) The companion in the bird's world, *Auk*, **54**: 245–73.

Marler, P. (1976) Sensory templates in species specific behavior. In J. C. Fentress (ed.), *Simpler Networks and Behavior*, Sunderland, Mass.: Sinauer, pp. 314–29.

McBride, T. C. and Lickliter, R. (1993) Social experience with siblings fosters species-specific responsiveness to maternal visual cues in bobwhite quail chicks (*Colinus virginianus*), *Journal of Comparative Psychology*, **107**: 320–7.

McBride, T. and Lickliter, R. (1994) Specific postnatal auditory stimulation interferes with species-typical visual responsiveness in Bobwhite quail chicks, *Developmental Psychobiology*, **27**: 169–83.

McCabe, B. J. and Horn, G. (1994) Learning-related changes in Fos-like immunoreactivity in the chick forebrain after imprinting, *Proceedings of the National Academy of Sciences of the USA*, **91**: 11417–21.

Nicol, A. U., Brown, M. W. and Horn, G. (1995) Neurophysiological investigations of a recognition memory system for imprinting in the domestic chick, *European Journal of Neuroscience*, **7**: 766–76.

Oetting, S., Pröve, E. and Bischof, H.-J. (1995) Sexual imprinting as a two stage process: Mechanisms of information storage and stabilisation, *Animal Behaviour*, **50**: 393–403.

O'Reilly, R. C. and Johnson, M. H. (1994) Object recognition and sensitive periods: A computational analysis of visual imprinting, *Neural Computation*, **6**: 357–89.

Ramenofsky, M. (1985) Acute changes in plasma steroids and agonistic behavior in male Japanese quail, *General and Comparative Endocrinology*, **60**: 116–28.

Rescorla, R. A. (1988) Pavlovian conditioning: It's not what you think it is *American Psychologist*, **43**: 151–60.

Rescorla, R. A., and Durlach, P. J. (1981) Within-event learning in Pavlovian conditioning. In N. E. Spear and R. R. Miller (eds), *Information Processing in Animals: Memory Mechanisms*, Hillsdale, NJ: Lawrence Erlbaum, pp. 81–111.

Rogers, L. J. (1995) *The Development of Brain and Behaviour in the Chicken*, Wallingford: CAB International.

Shettleworth, S. J. (1994) The varieties of learning in development: Toward a common framework. In J. A. Hogan and J. J. Bolhuis (eds), *Causal Mechanisms of Behavioural Development*, Cambridge: Cambridge University Press, pp. 358–76.

Sheu, F.-S., McCabe, B. J., Horn, G. and Routtenberg, A. (1993) Learning selectively increases protein kinase C substrate phosphorylation in specific regions of the chick brain, *Proceedings of the National Academy of Sciences of the USA*, **90**: 2705–9.

Sluckin, W. (1972) *Imprinting and Early Learning*, London: Methuen.

Sluckin, W. and Salzen, E. A. (1961) Imprinting and perceptual learning, *Quarterly Journal of Experimental Psychology*, **8**: 65–77.

Spalding, D. A. (1873) Instinct, with original observations on young animals, *Macmillan's Magazine*, **27**: 282–93. Reprinted in 1954 in: *British Journal of Animal Behaviour*, **2**: 2–11.

ten Cate, C. (1989a) Stimulus movement, hen behaviour and filial imprinting in Japanese quail (*Coturnix coturnix japonica*), *Ethology*, **82**: 287–306.

ten Cate, C. (1989b) Behavioral development: Toward understanding processes. In P. P. G. Bateson and P. Klopfer (eds), *Perspectives in Ethology*, vol. 8, New York: Plenum Press, pp. 243–69.

ten Cate, C. (1994) Perceptual mechanisms in imprinting and song learning. In J. A. Hogan and J. J. Bolhuis (eds), *Causal Mechanisms of Behavioural Development*, Cambridge: Cambridge University Press, pp. 116–46.

Tinbergen, N. (1951) *The Study of Instinct*, Oxford: Oxford University Press.

Van Kampen, H. S. (1993) Filial imprinting and associative learning: Similar mechanisms? *Netherlands Journal of Zoology*, **43**: 143–54.

Van Kampen, H. S. (1996) A framework for the study of filial imprinting and the development of attachment, *Psychonomic Bulletin and Review*, **3**: 3–20.

Van Kampen, H. S. and Bolhuis, J. J. (1991) Auditory learning and filial imprinting in the chick, *Behaviour*, **117**: 303–19.

Van Kampen, H. S. and Bolhuis, J. J. (1993) Interaction between auditory and visual learning during imprinting, *Animal Behaviour*, **45**: 623–5.

Van Kampen, H. S. and de Vos, G. J. (1991) Learning about the shape of an imprinting object varies with its colour, *Animal Behaviour*, **42**: 328–9.

Van Kampen, H. S. and de Vos, G. J. (1994) Potentiation in learning about the visual features of an imprinting stimulus, *Animal Behaviour*, **47**: 1468–70.

CHAPTER 14

Sensory Templates in Species-Specific Behavior

PETER MARLER

Introduction

Insofar as behavioral movements reflect patterns of neuromuscular activity, ultimately owing what specificity they may possess to the particular patterns of physiological activity they are associated with, explanations of behavioral development are ultimately best expressed in physiological terms. Ethological studies can play a valuable role in delineation of the functional properties that are required of the underlying machinery. Inevitably these inferred properties will be defined in general terms. This is a permissible and indeed a productive practice provided the likelihood is recognized that a conceptually similar functional organization of sensory–motor relationships may be underlain by very different physiological mechanisms in different organisms.

I concentrate on the ontogeny of avian vocal behavior in this chapter, because I believe the general principles to be relevant in understanding the development of vocal behavior in other organisms. With specificity as an underlying theme some detail must necessarily be presented to establish that general principles do in fact emerge from the particular cases under study. I shall develop the

From J. C. Fentress (ed.), *Simpler Networks and Behavior* (Sunderland, MA: Sinauer, 1976), pp. 314–29.

argument that sensory templates are significantly involved in the development of birdsongs, in cases where learning plays both major and minor roles, and that the principle has relevance to the development of human speech.

Some of the logically alternative physiological mechanisms for maintaining patterned movements have been outlined by Bullock (1961), Wilson (1964), Konishi (1965b), and most comprehensively by DeLong (1971). As the latter indicates, the basic requirements for the central nervous system to produce coordinated movement are (1) the appropriate muscles must be selected, (2) each participating muscle must be activated or inactivated in proper temporal relationship to the others, and (3) the appropriate amount of excitation and/or inhibition must be exerted on each muscle. This approach is useful, even though imprecision of the terms "appropriate" and "proper," still leaves much to be defined. A classical question has always been: What is the role of sensory stimulation in the development and maintenance of such patterns of muscular activity? At least three possibilities must be considered.

The first is central patterning with automaticity. A typical case is the motor output from the central nervous system of a locust controlling the basic pattern of flight movement, in which patterned activity adequate to maintain the basic locomotor rhythm is instigated and maintained in the absence of any patterned sensory input, though tonic input is necessary (Wilson, 1964).

The second possibility is centrally patterned movement with external triggering. As Bullock (1961) has indicated, many actions come into this category, including reflexive actions, with abundant vertebrate and invertebrate examples. External stimuli are necessary for triggering but not for patterning the internal structure of the movement. An example is swallowing in the dog, studied by Doty (1967), in which a complex sequential coordination that involves 18 different muscles seems to be centrally patterned without any requirement of sensory feedback from one phase to evoke the next. However, the entire sequence requires an external trigger – in this case tactile stimulation in the mouth and pharynx. The purring of cats seems to be a similar case (Remmers and Gautier, 1972).

The third possibility is patterned sensory feedback interacting with central nervous control. In reviewing illustrations of this category, DeLong (1971) notes that

> while the contribution of central patterning is enormous in almost every instance, it is striking how varied is the role of proprioceptive feedback – in some instances exerting only a nonspecific tonic effect (wingbeat-frequency control in the locust flight system), in other cases providing phasic reinforcement of discrete phases of the movement (lobster's swimmerette), and elsewhere providing timing clues for the overall patterning (dogfish swimming).

The care with which conclusions about central patterning and sensory control must be made at the behavioral level in mammals can be seen in the study by Fentress of face grooming in mice (e.g., Fentress, 1972). While sensory feedback resulting from movement can have obvious and powerful influences on actions that follow, especially on their orientation and power, few cases are discussed in which sensory feedback plays a basic role in development of the patterned coordination of a movement. I shall show that the vocal behavior of birds provides an unusually clear and novel demonstration of this type of motor control.

The focus in the present discussion is on problems of behavioral ontogeny. There is a need to distinguish control of development from mature performance. Evidence will be presented which demonstrates that the capacity of certain birds to hear their own voice controls the development of their vocal behavior. However, once mature performance is attained, this dependence of the motor coordination upon auditory feedback is reduced or eliminated. A case in point is the white-crowned sparrow, in which male song is highly abnormal if birds are surgically deafened in youth. However, once singing behavior is fully developed and stable, deafening has little or no immediate effect on the fine structure of the motor coordination (Konishi, 1965b). Only over a period of months is a gradual drift away from the original pattern detectable (figure 14.1). In other bird species auditory feedback seems to retain its importance into maturity, as in the cardinal (Dittus and Lemon, 1970) and the canary (Nottebohm, in press). One could easily be misled in inferring the role that auditory feedback plays in ontogeny from the result of adult deafening on song performance. While there are explicitly ontogenetic studies of the role of sensory feedback in the development of motor skills, such as spatially coordinated hand movements (e.g., Held, 1974), many of the examples in the literature of centrally patterned movement derive from study of adult subjects. The possibility of a more intrusive role for sensory mechanisms in development remains to be explored. It is not hard to imagine that repeated performance of a stable motor coordination gradually reduces reliance on sensory feedback control, leaving a centrally patterned motor outflow in increasing control of the pattern of behavior.

Behavioral Species Specificity and Social Communication

In a review of recent research on the genetic control of acoustic behavior in crickets, Hoy (1974) draws attention to the stereotypy and species specificity of the calling song of his subjects with the remark that these properties make it an ideal preparation for some kinds of physiological and genetic analysis. For communicative behavior to be effective, the participation of at least two individuals is required, often many. Some behavioral rules must be held in common by the participants if the interaction is to

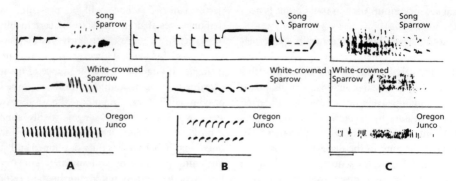

Figure 14.1 Songs of sparrows developed under three conditions: (A) in the wild; (B) after rearing in isolation from conspecific song: hearing intact; (C) after deafening before the onset of singing. The three species illustrated (song sparrow, white-crowned sparrow, and Oregon junco) are close relatives, all members of the subfamily *Emberizinae*. There is a loss of species specificity from (A) to (B) in the white-crowned sparrow and the junco, but not in the song sparrow. All are subject to a further loss of species specificity in (C). (After Konishi, 1964, 1965b; Kroodsma, 1975; Marler, Kreith, and Tamura, 1962; Marler, 1970; Mulligan, 1966.)

be orderly and predictable. Biological constraints on the development of communicative behavior, as manifest in both sender and receiver, are likely to be especially prominent, making such behaviors as the calling song of male crickets, and the responsiveness of female crickets to it especially instructive for study. Avian communication has also provided illuminating illustrations of different strategies involved in the ontogeny of species-specific behavior (Marler, in press).

Ethologists have long emphasized the stereotypy of many of the motor patterns found in the natural behavior of animals, as is embodied in the term "fixed action pattern" (Lorenz, 1935; Tinbergen, 1951). The fixity of some behaviors is indeed remarkable (Schleidt, 1974), as documented in a variety of organisms such as crustaceans (Hazlett, 1972), birds (Wiley, 1973), and mammals (Marler, 1973). In some cases the stereotypy is so marked that one is tempted to postulate special mechanisms detecting and compensating for inevitable perturbations in development that must occur, especially at the behavioral level.

Much of what follows is concerned with such stereotyped motor patterns, which lend themselves to ontogenetic analysis. It should be noted, however, that highly stereotyped actions are probably a special case. Highly variable actions have been described in the signaling behavior of a number of organisms in recent years, and "graded" rather than "discrete" repertoires of motor signaling behaviors

seem to be especially characteristc of species with a complex social organization, particularly primates (e.g., Marler, 1972, 1975; Marler and Tenaza, in press). The ontogeny of such variable motor patterns is harder to analyze and interpret than that of stereotyped behaviors. While more invariant species-specific actions are suitable subjects for broaching the analysis of ontogeny of species-specific behavior, eventually an understanding of the development of variable motor patterns, and how they are responded to, may prove to be of even greater interest.

Given a requirement that members of a population share rules for the production, perception, and mode of response to signaling behaviors, there is a special interest in developmental strategies that might serve to guide both motor and sensory development. Sensory templates, as they have been postulated to explain the process of selective auditory responsiveness and vocal learning in birds, have this dual potential to influence both motor and sensory aspects. A similar point is again illustrated by studies of the development of vocal communication in crickets.

Calling songs of hybrid male crickets were found to be intermediate between those of their parents in a number of respects (Bentley and Hoy, 1970, 1972; Hoy, 1974). Tests of the phonotactic response of hybrid females revealed that their behavior was also intermediate between that of females of the parent species (Hoy and Paul, 1973). While females are normally more attracted to homospecific than to heterospecific song, hybrid females find the calling song of their male siblings more attractive than either parental calling song. Hoy goes on to speculate that, while the coupling of song transmission and song reception might result from two mechanisms evolving in parallel, it would be neurophysiologically economical if both were controlled by a common mechanism.

The demonstration in studies by Walker (1957, 1962) that temperature-dependent variation in properties of male cricket calling songs is paralleled by changes in female responsiveness is consistent with the idea that a common mechanism controls both. The possibility that species-specific song templates might somehow control both male singing and female responsiveness in crickets remains to be studied. The fact that male cricket calling songs develop without the need for auditory experience of song stimulation suggests that direct control of song development by a template mechanism is unlikely, though a proprioceptive channel might still be involved. In birds there is more secure evidence that the shared mechanism underlying both male singing and female responsiveness does involve species-specific sensory templates.

The Ontogeny of Male Birdsong

Extensive studies on the effects of deafening on vertebrate vocal development by Konishi (1963, 1964, 1965a,b) lend support to the hypothesis that species-specific auditory templates are involved in the ontogeny of birdsong. This involvement extends to the imposition of constraints on processes of vocal learning, which underlies the development of song in many bird species, and to the development of female responsiveness to conspecific song. The kind of evidence that implicates a sensory template mechanism is best conveyed by the pattern of song development in one of the best-studied species, the white-crowned sparrow (Marler and Tamura, 1964; Konishi, 1965b; Marler, 1970).

A young male white-crowned sparrow usually begins to sing when a little over 100 days of age, first at irregular intervals, then becoming more continuous until full song emerges, usually after about 200 days of age in *Zonotrichia leucophrys nuttali*. If such a bird is deafened between 40 and 100 days of age,

before singing behavior has developed, he will subsequently begin to sing on a more or less normal schedule, but the structure of the song produced will be very abnormal. The song of such an early deafened male is amorphous and variable in structure, scratchy or buzzy in tone, with components that change rapidly in frequency or even have a click-like quality. An example is illustrated in figure 14.1, together with an example of normal male white-crowned sparrow song. The noisy, amorphous structure of the former is clearly evident.

Figure 14.1 also illustrates normal male songs of two close relatives of the white-crowned sparrow, the song sparrow (top) and the Oregon junco (bottom). Songs of these three species differ in many respects without overlap, as careful descriptive studies have shown (Marler and Tamura, 1962; Marler, Kreith, and Tamura, 1962; Mulligan, 1963; Konishi, 1964). By contrast, the songs produced by males deafened early in life, illustrated in figure 14.1C, have lost the species-specific traits that distinguish them from one another. Only the duration and range of frequencies persist clearly as species-specific qualities (Konishi, 1964, 1965b; Mulligan, 1966). This result demonstrates that audition plays a critical role in the development of species-specific characteristics of sparrow song. Similar gross abnormalities in the song of early-deafened males have been demonstrated in the chaffinch (Nottebohm, 1967, 1968), the cardinal (Dittus and Lemon, 1970), the robin and the black-headed grosbeak (Konishi, 1965a), and the red-winged blackbird (Marler et al., 1972). Further study reveals that the role of audition in development in all these species is a complex one.

If a young male white-crowned sparrow is taken from the nest prior to fledging and raised by hand in isolation from normal conspecific song but able to hear its own voice, some of the abnormalities that characterize the song of early-deafened birds are eliminated. The song now assumes a definite controlled morphology with relatively pure and sustained tones, longer in duration at the beginning than at the end of the song, thus sharing several characteristics with wild white-crowned sparrow singing. As can be seen in figure 14.1, which also presents illustrations of the songs of a male song sparrow and an Oregon junco reared in isolation from normal conspecific song but with hearing intact, in each case and especially in the song sparrow more species-specific traits emerge than in an early-deafened bird. Thus one could arrange the songs of all three species in a series, with the normal song showing the highest degree of species specificity, the song of early-deafened males the least species specificity. The songs of intact but socially isolated males fall somewhere between – closest to normal in the song sparrow and farthest from normal in the white-crowned sparrow. Evidently, audition is involved in the ontogeny of some of the species-specific qualities of birdsong that develop in males reared in auditory isolation from normal conspecific song. The degree of dependence on auditory stimuli varies both with age and with the species investigated.

Further experiments reveal yet another role for audition in the ontogeny of birdsong in males. Not only does it permit the bird to hear its own voice, but it also gives access to patterned stimulation from other birds. This stimulation may have both generalized and highly specific effects on subsequent singing behavior of the subject. The former have been considered elsewhere (e.g., Marler and Mundinger, 1971). Here we are more concerned with cases in which the consequences are specific, as for example in the white-crowned sparrow. Although a male white-crowned sparrow taken as a nestling and reared thenceforth in isolation from normal conspecific song will develop singing with certain normal characteristics, some critical properties of the normal song are still lacking. Figure 14.2 shows the songs of nine male white-crowned sparrows reared together as a group but in isolation from normal conspecific song (Marler, 1970). These particular subjects came from three different areas in California. A typical example of normal white-crowned sparrow song from each of these areas is also illustrated (AN, BN, and CN). A comparison clearly reveals the abnormalities of the songs of intact but isolation-reared males, especially in the second part of the song. There are two significant kinds of abnormality. On the one hand, although the second part of a typical isolate song is broken into a train of separate notes, shorter in duration than the introduction, these notes are never as short in normal song, and lack all the fine detail usually present. In nature, these details have the further property of exhibiting local dialects,

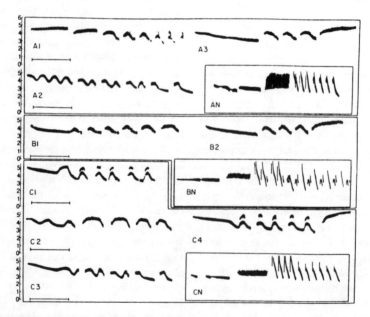

Figure 14.2 Songs of nine male white-crowned sparrows taken as nestlings in three different areas of California and reared as a group in a large soundproof chamber. Illustrations of the three home dialects are given in the boxes (AN, BN, and CN). The songs lack characteristics of the home dialect and some species-specific traits also, especially in the second part of the song. (From Marler, 1970.)

each unique to one area, the second or "trill" portion of the song being especially diagnostic (figure 14.2). In addition to lacking certain species-specific properties, characteristics of the home dialect are also absent from the songs of intact male white-crowned sparrows reared in isolation from normal song.

If a young male white-crowned sparrow taken as a nestling is placed in individual isolation and exposed to 4 minutes of normal white-crowned sparrow song at a rate of six per minute for a period of 3 weeks somewhere between 7 and 50 days of age, his song will subsequently develop normally and will in fact be a copy of the model to which he was exposed. This copy will include the dialect characteristics of the model, though it may differ in some characteristics of the introduction (Marler, 1970).

There is a sensitive period for this learning. Equivalent exposure to a model between 50 and 71 days of age had only minor effects on subsequent singing, and exposure after about 100 days of age has none at all. Sensitive periods have also been demonstrated for song learning in other birds such as the chaffinch (Thorpe, 1958) and the zebra finch (Immelmann, 1969; Amold, 1975a, b). In both these species a male reared without experience of normal song will sing abnormally. Exposure to normal song during the sensitive period not only restores the general characteristics of normal conspecific singing but also results in imitation of specific properties of the model used. In the song of wild chaffinches, dialects are again marked (Marler, 1952).

The learning ability manifest during such sensitive periods has the further significant characteristic that it is selective with regard to which models are acceptable. A male white-crowned sparrow given playback of both conspecific song and that of another related species during the sensitive period will learn only the conspecific song. Young males exposed to alien song and nothing else at this time – the alien model was song sparrow song in this case – develop songs like those of untrained social isolates (Marler, 1970). Although I was surprised at the time to discover how selective song learning is in white-crowns, further reflection on the natural history of this species might have suggested its existence.

In the environment where a young male white-crown spends the early phase of its life, many other bird species are present, all generating sounds to which the young male is exposed. Imitation of these other species rarely occurs in nature. Interspecific learning would be highly dysgenic, for we have shown in other work that females are also responsive to conspecific song, and probably base their initial selection of a mate upon song recognition. Thus a male learning the song of another species would experience both communicative and reproductive difficulties with females and males of his own species. His fitness would surely be reduced as a result. Thus it is not surprising that the evolution of a capacity for song learning has been coupled with genetically based mechanisms that constrain the learning to conspecific models. The song template hypothesis provides a potential explanation for this selectivity.

Constraints on the Song-learning Process: Sensory Templates

Various lines of evidence point to the existence of constraints imposed on the process of song learning. There are constraints in time, such that there are sensitive periods when learning takes place most readily. There are also stimulus constraints in that some acoustical patterns are learned more readily than others. In addition some species exhibit contextual constraints, as will be described later. However, in the white-crowned sparrow and also in the chaffinch (Thorpe, 1958) restrictions on the type of sound that is most readily learned are not attributable to contextual influences, such as the social situation, since they are manifest in a bird making a selection from sounds coming through a loudspeaker. In these cases there must be constraints that are in some sense endogenous to the male bird. We can imagine a wide spectrum of neural and neuromuscular mechanisms that constrain the learning process. One obvious possibility is a limit on what sounds the syrinx can produce.

The structure of the sound-producing equipment of birds – involving the respiratory machinery, the syrinx and its associated membranes, muscles and resonators – clearly imposes restrictions on what sounds can be produced. Recent research has greatly clarified the mode of operation of the avian syrinx (Greenewalt, 1968; Nottebohm, 1971; Gaunt and Wells, 1973; see the review in

Nottebohm, 1975). While the syringes of phylogenetically distant bird species operate in different
ways, those of close relatives seem to be very similar
in both morphology and mode of operation. Indeed,
the structure of the avian syrinx is known to be a
conservative trait that changes only slowly in the
course of evolution. This conservatism has to lead
to extensive use of syringeal structure as a taxonomic character at the higher levels of phylogenetic
classification.

The likelihood that differences in syringeal
structure are responsible for the differences in
learning selectivity that we are considering here is
reduced by demonstrations that species with similar
syringeal structure can produce very different vocalizations. Thus a chaffinch and a bullfinch have
very similar syringes, but a bullfinch, which is a
species in which song learning seems to be guided
only by social constraints, can be trained to imitate
a great variety of unnatural sounds, including musical instruments (Nicolai, 1959; Thorpe, 1955). As a
further point the resemblance that we have already
noted between the songs produced after early deafening by a white-crowned sparrow, a song sparrow,
and a junco suggest that the output of the syringes
of these three species is very similar when freed
from auditory control. Limitations on the sensory
side, such as are invoked by the sensory template
hypothesis, provide a more plausible explanation,
although restrictions on the motor side deserve
more study even in close relatives.

The loss of species specificity in singing behavior that results from auditory deprivation, partial in
the case of isolation from exposure to adult song,
and extreme in the case of early deafening, points to
a sensory mechanism involved in the maintenance
of song species specificity. It is in this context that
the notion of auditory templates has arisen. These
are visualized as lying in the neural pathways for
auditory processing, sensitizing the organism to
certain patterns of stimulation, thus embodying information about the structure of vocal sounds, and
with the capacity to guide motor development. As
such, they are conceived as having a more dominant
influence on vocal development than either the
structure of the sound-producing equipment or the
characteristics of hearing in general, although both
are also involved (Konishi, 1970). According to this
view, as the young male begins to sing he strikes a
progressively closer match between his vocal output

and the dictates of the auditory template. As described in a moment, this is just the impression you
get listening to a young male as he passes through
the stages of subsong, plastic song, and finally full
song.

As indicated in figure 14.3, which diagrams the
pattern of song development in the male white-
crowned sparrow both under normal conditions,
when reared in isolation from normal song, and
when deafened early in life, it can be seen that the
time of song learning, between 10 and 50 days of
age, precedes the onset of singing by several weeks.
The male thus sings from memory. He must be able
to hear his own voice to translate into song this
remembered "engram" of the song, learned earlier
in life. This is implied by Konishi's demonstration
that a male deafened after training but before singing has the same highly abnormal, unspecific song
as a male deafened without training (Konishi,
1965b).

When the male white-crowned sparrow begins
to sing, typically after about 100 days of age in the
nuttalli subspecies we studied, the imitation of the
model experienced earlier does not spring forth
immediately in complete form. Instead the male
goes through a series of vocal transformations such
as one might expect if the task confronting the male
were now to acquire skill in matching its vocal output to the dictates of the auditory template. A bird
that has been exposed to normal song previously
soon manifests syllables in its subsong that resemble
those of the model. However, they are variable, and
jumbled in order. As subsong develops into plastic
song, the form of the syllables becomes more
steretoyped and the matching to the model becomes
clearer. Finally, with the transition from plastic
song to full song, the syllables become properly
ordered, and an accurate imitation of the model
emerges – a model that has not been heard for several weeks.

The temporal separation of the first stage of
auditory song learning from the onset of singing
performance is known in other species, such as the
zebra finch (Immelmann, 1969), but is not universal. In the chaffinch, for example, the two phases
overlap in time. Nevertheless, chaffinch song development has much in common with those in which
the overlap does not occur. By deafening young
males at various stages in the transition from
subsong to full song, Nottebohm (1968) found that,

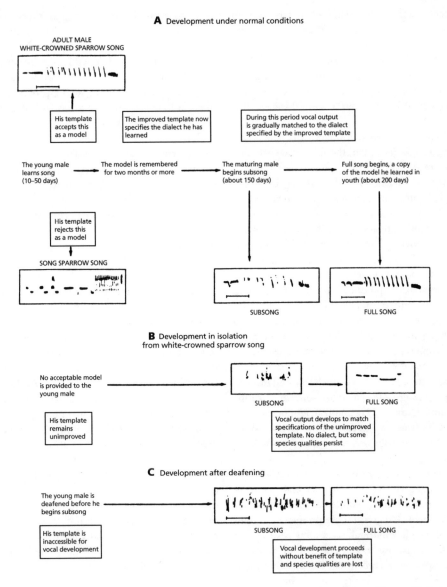

Figure 14.3 Song development of male white-crowned sparrows: (A) under normal conditions; (B) reared in isolation from conspecific song from the early nestling stage; (C) after deafening early in life. (From Marler, 1975.)

while birds deafened early in the sequence reverted to a very simple pattern of singing, after delaying deafening beyond a certain point the bird retained some of the normal characteristics of singing that had been achieved. Finally, a male whose song is fully crystallized shows little deficit after deafening, a result obtained in other species as well (Konishi, 1965b). Thus, while auditory feedback is critical in

the early stages of song development in certain species, it seems to become redundant once song has fully crystallized. This is not the case with others, such as the cardinal and the canary, where song regression occurs after deafening even in adulthood (Dittus and Lemon, 1970; Nottebohm, 1975).

Conceived as sensory mechanisms embodying species-specific information that guide vocal development, auditory templates obviously vary in their competence to generate fully natural song without access to a model from the environment. That of the male white-crowned sparrow is the least competent of the three species displayed in figure 14.1, in the sense that the song of an intact, isolated male is most different from the natural song in this species.

By contrast, an isolated, intact male song sparrow produces songs which, though somewhat variable, are often hard to distinguish from those of wild birds (Mulligan, 1966; Kroodsma, in press). Yet most of these normal song characteristics are lacking from the song of an early-deafened song sparrow, which suggests that a species-specific auditory template is involved in their ontogeny. Unlike that of a white-crowned sparrow, however, which must be extensively modified by environmental learning to produce natural song, a song sparrow template is capable of guiding virtually normal development without any opportunity to learn an environmental model. Correspondingly, learning from other birds seems to play a less intrusive role in the development of song sparrow song. Dialects, though present, are much less well marked than in white-crowned sparrow song as a result (Harris and Lemon, 1972), and neighboring song sparrows show much less conformity in their singing behavior than white-crowned sparrows that live together.

The Oregon junco resembles the song sparrow more than the white-crown, in that dialects in its song are probably either subtle or absent. Also, an intact, isolated Oregon junco produces a song which, although abnormal in several respects, is closer to the natural song than that of a white-crowned sparrow reared in similar circumstances (Marler, Kreith, and Tamura, 1962). Thus the sensory template for song of a naive Oregon junco might be thought of as intermediate between the other two species in its competence to generate normal song. It is modifiable through experience of normal song stimulation, though apparently only in its specifications for overall pattern. Juncos are less prone to slavish imitation of a song model to which they are exposed than are white-crowned sparrows. Instead each male tends to produce individually distinctive morphology of the notes from which the song is constructed, although conforming in overall pattern. It is as though males of this species are prone to improvise individually within rather broad limits set by the auditory template. Thus dependence on a sensory template to guide song development is not incompatible with a significant role for the "invention" of individually distinctive patterns of motor activity. Indeed, such a process has been invoked to explain how new birdsong dialects may arise (Lemon, 1971).

It is clear, then, that species differ in the particular pattern of auditory stimulation specified in the auditory template of a naive individual. It is sometimes sufficient to generate virtually normal song. In other cases it requires more or less extensive learned modification before normal singing can develop, though it still suffices to focus the learning bird's attention upon conspecific song models. Species also seem to differ in the latitude allowed for motor development within the constraints set by the sensory template. In some species, such as the white-crowned sparrow, the constraints are narrow, although even here, with such accurate imitation of the dialect represented by models heard during the sensitive period there is individuality in the introductory part of the song. In species with broader constraints there is less conformity to the models that are heard and correspondingly more latitude for individuality. This is an important point, for most birdsongs have strong individualistic components, and there is evidence that songs mediate individual recognition in several bird species. Further comparative study of the transitions from subsong to full song that accompany song ontogeny is needed if we are to learn more about how the delicate balance between conformity to species-specific properties of song and individuality in other properties of the same song is achieved and maintained in different bird species.

The Significance of Subsong

As already noted in many of the species we have been considering, the male song does not suddenly appear in complete form. It develops over a period of weeks, passing through several distinct stages. The first is known to ornithologists as subsong (Thorpe and Pilcher, 1958; Lanyon, 1960), and differs from full song in a number of respects. It is not as loud as full song, and the components are often given in long irregular sequences. In addition to fragments of song, other sounds from the repertoire are often included. The frequency of its components tends to fluctuate erratically, giving subsong a wider range of sound frequencies than occurs in full song. The variability is such that it is hard to discern with any great precision units that are repeated.

As development proceeds, the subsong becomes louder and in many cases more clearly segmented. Finally, the patterns crystallize into stereotyped themes, thus completing the development of full or primary song.

The significance of subsong is uncertain. On the one hand, it may be regarded as a by-product of increasing androgen levels, without any intrinsic significance. On the other hand, it is conceivable that subsong serves to aid the bird in acquiring skill in the use of its sound-producing equipment as a necessary stage in the accomplishment of full song. There are reasons for thinking that the latter may be true in at least some cases. Male chaffinches and white-crowned sparrows cycling in and out of song in their second or third year of age pass through the stages from subsong to full song more quickly than young males coming into song for the first time. This might be expected after the adult song pattern has been fully established, although it could also be argued that rates of hormone production or sensitivity to hormonal effects might be enhanced in older birds that have already experienced one annual cycle.

A comparison of development in trained and untrained male white-crowned sparrows is illuminating in this regard (Marler, 1970). Males that have been trained with a normal song usually pass through the subsong stage rather quickly. Full song is generally crystallized within a few weeks after the onset of subsong. On the other hand, birds raised in social isolation, or unsuccessfully trianed either with presentation of conspecific song outside the critical period or with exposure to alien song, often remain much longer in this transitional stage of song development. It may take months for full song to become completely crystallized. Thus a bird that is destined to produce abnormal song may persist with variable patterns for a major part of the singing season. If we think of effective training as providing the bird with a clear goal toward which vocal development should then proceed, it is perhaps understandable that the transitional stages of subsong should be passed over more quickly than in a bird which is lacking such specific instruction.

Careful study of the structure of the components of subsong reveals another difference between white-crowns that have and have not heard normal song during a critical period. Although the subsong of the former shares many formal properties with that of untrained birds, the resemblance between the structure of the earliest components produced and those of the training song is apparent. Thus some of the basic acoustical components are established early in the course of song development. Hoever, these fragments are produced in a very disorderly fashion at first, and the complete match with the training song is only achieved gradually as the syllables become organized into the appropriate order and timing.

These results are not inconsistent with the auditory template hypothesis advanced earlier to explain song development. Although a bird trained with normal song during the critical period is assumed to possess a highly specified "template" already, the accomplishment of a perfect match between this template and the vocal output will take time. Novel and complex operations of the sound-producing equipment are required. The sequence of development observed in a trained bird is what one might expect if, by engaging in subsong, it thus acquires more proficiency in matching vocal output to the specified pattern of auditory feedback.

To explain development in a male white-crowned sparrow that has been prevented from hearing normal song during the critical period, we have postulated a cruder template which provides only a rough specification for song development. This will allow considerable latitude, and it might be anticipated that in development guided by this crude template, crystallization of song patterns will take longer than in a trained bird which possesses more highly specified instructions. Untrained birds show every sign of vacillation, sometimes changing major patterns several times in the course of development. It will be recalled that an adult male white-crowned sparrow possesses only one song type. Some untrained males had two song themes at intermediate stages of development, subsequently rejecting one of them. This was never recorded in birds that had been subjected to effective training.

If we carry this line of argument still further, one

might predict that birds deafened early in life, thus deprived of access even to the crude template of an intact untrained bird, would show an even more attenuated and variable sequence of song development. This is precisely what happens. Apart from their abnormal quality and pattern, the most striking characteristic of the songs of male white-crowned sparrows deafened in youth is their instability (Konishi, 1965b). The same is true of other species deafened early in life (Konishi and Nottebohm, 1969). Some deaf birds even pass through their entire first singing season without a stereotyped theme emerging. Many show some degree of crystallization but nevertheless vary much more in successive repetitions of a theme than a normal bird. Even successive units within a single song vary widely. The deaf birds seem to have difficulty in maintaining a steady tone. Many of these traits are reminiscent of an early stage of normal subsong development. These birds behave almost as though deafening arrests their development at this stage, in at least some respects, even though the rhythm of song delivery and the singing posture do continue to develop in the normal fashion. We have already noted that a male chaffinch deafened in youth, but after some subsong experience, develops a more advanced song than a male deafened still aearlier and lacking such experience (Nottebohm, 1968).

It thus seems probable that the subsong of young males does have developmental significance, perhaps providing opportunity both to learn new operations with the sound-producing equipment and to employ trial-and-error learning to match the output with a particular pattern of auditory feedback specified by an auditory template. The recurrence of subsong at the start of each singing seson in adult males remains unexplained.

Sensory Templates and "Innate Release Mechanisms"

An attractive feature of the auditory template hypothesis is its provision of an economical explanation for the initial selectivity of the song-learning process. While the auditory template for song of an untrained male white-crowned sparrow is thought of as only an elementary specification of species-specific song, such as is manifest in the singing of an intact but untrained male, it may nevertheless be sufficient to serve as a kind of filter for external auditory stimuli. In this sense it has much in common with the classical ethological concept of the innate release mechanism, serving to focus the attention of the male on patterns of external stimulation that have assumed a special valence in the course of phylogenetic history of species (Lorenz, 1950; Tinbergen, 1951). The present conception differs in that the sensory template is subsequently involved in motor development (figure 14.4).

An analogous function to that of an innate release mechanism is apparently served by the auditory template of a female. It is known that females are especially responsive to normal male song at the time of sexual pairing (Milligan and Verner, 1971). By injecting females with exogenous testosterone, Konishi derived supporting evidence for the hypothesis that the mechanism underlying responsiveness of females resembles that which guides male song development. Provided she has experienced normal song early in life, such a female will

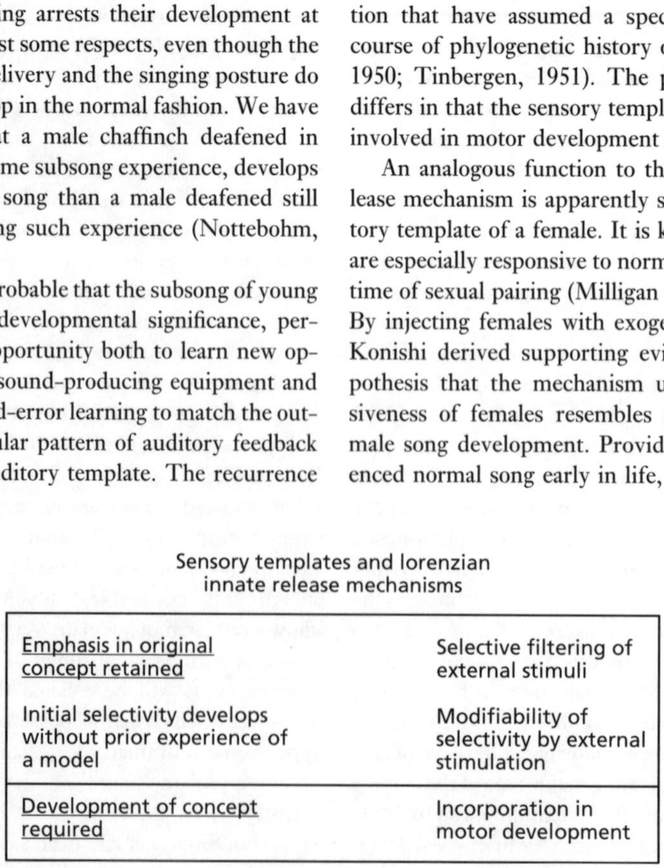

Sensory templates and lorenzian
innate release mechanisms

Emphasis in original concept retained	Selective filtering of external stimuli
Initial selectivity develops without prior experience of a model	Modifiability of selectivity by external stimulation
Development of concept required	Incorporation in motor development

Figure 14.4 Relationships between "innate release mechanisms" and "sensory templates."

not only sing under the influence of testosterone, but will reproduce the particular dialect to which she was exposed earlier, demonstrating that she is in possession of the same information about song as a trained male, though this information is normally manifest in the process of mate selection rather than song development.

Although auditory templates for song development in birds are conceptualized as single functional mechanisms, they may actually involve several physiological components that together serve as filters both for external stimuli and for stimuli derived from the animal's own performance. It might be that components that are modifiable are separate from those which underlie the selective perception of a navie, untrained male. Mechanisms might operate in series or in parallel, with control shifting from one to the other after training. Thus the term should not be taken to imply the existence of single unitary mechanisms. The underlying mechanisms may be several and complex, and may also differ in their nature, number, and mode of coupling from species to species. As with other "feature detectors" and indeed with several mechanisms postulated on the basis of ethological evidence, such as "sign stimuli and releasers" and "innate release mechanisms," one should be prepared for the likelihood that similar behavioral ends are achieved in different organisms by entirely distinct physiological means (Marler and Hamilton, 1966).

Sensory Templates in Human Speech Development

Like such birds as the white-crowned sparrow, human infants are able to discriminate between conspecific, communicative sounds and other sounds at a very early age, probably within a few days after birth (Moffitt, 1971; Morse, 1972; Trehub and Rabinovitch, 1972; Trehub, 1973; Palermo, 1975). There is no evidence that this ability depends upon prior experience of speech sounds by the infant, although careful studies are needed to exclude the possibility of rapid learning after birth, and of intrauterine learning of sounds of the mother or of others. Nonetheless, the point seems well established that speech sounds are recognized as a class prior to the development of speaking.

Another line of research has specified more precisely some of the critical acoustical properties of speech sounds. The results of experiments with synthetic speech sounds, in which continuously varying series of intergradations are presented, show that listeners segmentalize such speech continua at particular boundaries, and find it difficult even to discriminate between sounds that fall on the same side of the normal boundary between two such speech sounds as [ba] and [pa] (Liberman et al., 1957; Liberman et al., 1961; Liberman et al., 1967). While the same is true of recorded sounds of natural speech, the point is made more forcefully with synthetic stimuli in which all parameters are under complete control.

In itself, the demonstration that we are especially sensitive to variations in speech sounds close to critical boundaries is not surprising, and perhaps of more interest to psychologists than to biologists. However, two additional findings draw the phenomenon firmly and irrevocably into the biological realm. Having defined the critical boundaries for some acoustically adjacent speech sounds, Abramson and Lisker, in a long series of comparative studies, have demonstrated recurrence of very similar boundaries in one language after another. This is true, however different the languages may be in other respects, to the extent that one may begin to think of some of these critical boundaries as universals in all human speech (e.g., Abramson and Lisker, 1965, 1970; Lisker and Abramson, 1970). Thus, in addition to the features of grammar that structural linguists and students of early speech development believe to be shared by all languages (e.g., McNeill, 1966; Chomsky, 1967; Lenneberg, 1967; Brown, 1973), some more superficial aspects of the acoustical structure defining categorical boundaries in speech may also be shared by all human speakers. The existence of such species-specific features is an invitation to the biologist to explore the role of genetic factors in their determination.

It appears then that, in either natural or synthetic speech, we perceive the phonemic components of words as discretely different from one another even when they are not. While one may speculate that such features of speech as pitch, intonation, loudness, and tempo, along with other aspects of speech that convey variations in the speaker's mood and intent, are processed in continuous rather than categorical fashion, much of the content of speech is obviously processed segmentally. The work of Eimas and his colleagues (Eimas et al., 1971; Eimas, 1975; Cutting and Eimas, 1975) shows that such segmental processing of speech sounds occurs at normal boundaries in infants as young as 4 months, or even one month, of age, long before they have begun to speak or even to babble. Working with related speech sounds such as [pa] and [ba] or [bae], [dae], and [gae], distinguished by adults according to acoustical criteria that are broadly similar in all languages studied so far, Eimas has found that infants process them in essentially the same way as adults.

The demonstrations rest on a habituation technique. Using sucking as an operant for delivering recorded sounds that catch the infant's attention, habituation with repetitions of one sound pattern to a given criterion is followed by substitution of the sound with another. The extent of revival of the response is used as an index of the degree to which the pre- and posthabituation sounds contrast with one another. Working along series of synthetic speech sounds, Eimas found little or no evidence of contrast between within-category sound pairs until approaching that part of the series where an adult discerns a sharp boundary. In roughly the same area the infant shows a sudden revival of response as the boundary is crossed. Responsiveness to several such boundaries has been demonstrated in infants at ages young enough that it becomes plausible to postulate that certain speech sounds can be processed in the appropriate categorical manner without the need for prior exposure to them. The analogy with innate release mechanisms and with the auditory templates that we have postulated to explain the perception and development of bird song is highly suggestive.

Auditory templates for certain speech sounds could serve a prespeech child well in two respects. First, they would focus an infant's attention on the appropriate class of external stimuli for social responsiveness, much as the auditory templates of some birds are thought to restrict responsiveness to members of their own species when they are living in a community with many others present. Second, auditory templates for certain speech sounds could be of value in providing an orderly frame of reference for the infant's developing responsiveness to speech patterns in the culture in which it grows up, drawing its attention to the particular subset of the myriad, complex properties of speech that retain valence into adulthood (Mattingly, 1972). As postulated for birds such as the white-crowned sparrow, so the templates that a child possesses for guiding some of the initial steps in the perceptual analysis of speech are presumably modified in the process of such analysis. In the human case they would also be multiplied as the infant acquires more competence in the perceptual analysis of additional sounds of the language in which it participates.

One may even take a further step and postulate that an additional function for speech-sound templates might lie in the development of speaking itself. Evidently, the sensory mechanisms for speech perception precede motor development, much as occurs in the white-crowned sparrow (Palermo, 1975). Could it be that some of the early stages of speech development depend upon a process of matching vocal output to sensory templates by auditory feedback? Improvements in a child's babbling, as with a bird's subsong, might reveal a growing skill in achieving this kind of a match. By the time an infant reaches the age at which the first exercises in speech begin, these hypothetical templates for the sounds of speech would now be greatly modified and enriched compared with those of early infancy, as a result of the intervening experience with the speech of adults and siblings. No doubt this elaboration of the perceptual processing of speech sounds interdigitates extensively with the onset of speaking, with the result that in the adult there is extensive and intimate correspondence between the motor performance of speaking and the perception of speech sounds (Liberman et al., 1967).

This interpretation implies that the physiological mechanisms tht underlie the perception of speech sounds are to some extent distinct in their mode of operation from those associated with auditory perception of other kinds of sounds. There is evidence that points to this conclusion from a variety of sources (Liberman et al., 1967; Studdert-Kennedy, 1975). Dichotic listening studies in which competing sounds are presented to the two ears demonstrate that speech sounds are more readily perceived when the sounds arrive at the right ear than the left, whereas the opposite is true for nonspeech sounds (e.g., Kimura, 1961, 1964; Studdert-Kennedy and Shankweiler, 1970). Electrophysiological studies of averaged evoked potentials given in response to speech and non-speech sound stimuli confirm this tendency for separation of the processing of the two classes of sounds in the two hemispheres (Wood, Goff, and Day, 1971; Molfese, 1972). The method also provides an independent demonstration of categorical processing (Dorman, 1974). Molfese (1972) finds stronger responsiveness of the left hemisphere than the right by dichotic testing with speech sounds, even in infants as young as one week of age.

Thus the distinctive attributes of the perceptual processing of speech sounds as compared with other kinds of auditory stimuli seem to include a tendency toward categorical rather than continuous processing, and a tendency for the processing to be associated more with the dominant, left hemisphere of the brain than with the right. The converse tends to be true of nonspeech sounds.

If sensory templates for speech sounds are to be invoked as a factor in the development and operation of speech perception and development, a tendency toward categorical rather than continuous processing is to be expected. The notion is an intriguing one for ethologists, already implicitly accustomed to thinking in terms of categorical modes of perceptual processing whenever innate release mechanisms are invoked. The present tendency for researchers to concentrate on stereotyped species-specific behaviors in developmental studies has already been noted. Yet there also exists an extensive repertoire of highly graded motor actions with signaling significance in many species. It will be a challenge of some magnitude, both theoretical and practical, to achieve some understanding of the perceptual and neurophysiological correlates of communicative stimuli that are graded rather than discrete.

Conclusions

A case has been made, largely on the basis of ethological data, that the concept of a sensory template is heuristically useful in understanding the ontogeny of the vocal behavior of both birds and man. The concept derives from the ethological term "innate release mechanisms" (Lorenz, 1950; Tinbergen, 1951) and seeks to retain the emphasis so implied on species-specific genetic constraints. As applied to avian and human vocal learning, these genetic constraints are viewed as modifiable as a consequence of experience. They impose a general species-specific direction on subsequent behavioral development by sensitizing the young organism to certain classes of external stimuli.

Sensory templates provide a structural framwork for the perceptual analysis of arrays of stimuli that is both plastic and yet constrained. After more or less extensive modification by experience, with their number added to or subjected to attrition, and changed in specification so that their properties may now be both species-specific and also population-, group-, or even individual-specific, they then guide motor development by a process of sensory feedback. Phases of this multistage process may interdigitate in time or they may be temporally separated, proceeding most readily at particular developmental stages or "sensitive periods."

Temporal requirements will vary greatly according to the sociobiology of the species, with such species-specific variables as tendencies for family cohesion or dispersal, seasonal patterns of migration, and community composition, all bearing on the optimal timing for each stage. Since temporal optima may vary even in closely related species, the physiological determinants of sensitive periods for the employment, modification, and motor involvement of sensory templates may prove to vary between species, exploiting opportunistically whatever hormonal, neural, and behavioral events coincide with particular temporal requirements. The same may tend to be true of sensitive periods in other kinds of behavioral development, though the lack of physiological unity so implied need not necessarily undermine the heuristic value of the sensitive period as a concept.

The hypothesis that species-specific, modifiable, sensory templates guide the development of certain kinds of motor behavior has been developed to explain some of the complexities of vocal learning. The sensory equivalence between auditory stimulation from another individual and auditory feedback from one's own voice makes it easier to picture how the process operates in vocal development than in behaviors engaging other sensory modalities. An organism may hear its own voice in somewhat similar terms to those in which it hears another's voice, with opportunities to compare the two in short-term memory and, as suggested here, by reference in long-term memory to a remembered "schema," such as a modified sensory template may provide.

It is harder to imagine a similar process guiding development of visually signaling behavior such as a facial expression, except by use of a mirror. However, one should bear in mind that the feedback loop mediating a template-matching process could be internal to the animal. Even in the present case, bone-conducted sould is surely important in guiding our own vocal development. People are usually surprised when they first hear a sound recording of their own voice.

There is growing evidence that patterned neural commands to motor effectors can be accompanied by collateral patterned inputs to parts of the brain not in the direct line of motor commands (Evarts, 1971). If patterned neural activity of exteroceptive sensory origin converged on the same parts of the brain, an organism might then be able to engage in a matching process with changes in behavior designed to reduce any mismatch, as Holst and Mittelstaedt (1950) visualized in their original formulation of the "re-afference principle." For evidence on such internal channels for matching sensory templates to feedback from motor activity, the ethologist must necessarily turn to the physiologist. Even with external channels such as have been postulated here for the control of vocal learning by modifiable auditory templates, the ethologist is working on the edge of his competence, and must eventually give way to the skills of the neurophysiologist. Hopefully the latter will find the task easier if the ethologist has already defined the problem area, specified its evolutionary context, and made some progress in defining relevant parameters of motor activity and stimulus control.

Acknowledgment

The work reported in this chapter was supported by National Institute of Mental Health grant MH-06686.

References

Abramson, A. S., and Lisker, L. (1965) Voice onset time in stop consonants: Acoustic analysis and synthesis, *Proceedings of the 5th International Congress of Acoustics*, D. E. Commins (ed.), A51, Liège.

Abramson, A. S., and Lisker, L. (1970) Discriminability along the voicing continuum: Cross-language tests, *Proceedings of the 6th International Congress of Phonetic Science, Prague, 1967*, 569–73, Academia, Prague.

Arnold, A. P. (1975a) The effects of castration on song development in zebra finches (*Poephila guttata*), *Journal of Experimental Zoology*, 191, 261–78.

Arnold, A. P. (1975b) The effects of castration and androgen replacement on song, courtship, and aggression in zebra finches (*Poephila guttata*), *Journal of Experimental Zoology*, 191, 309–26.

Bentley, D. R., and Hoy, R. R. (1970) Postembryonic development of adult motor patterns in crickets: A neural analysis, *Science (Wash. D.C.)*, 170, 1409–11.

Bentley, D. R., and Hoy, R. R. (1972) Genetic control of the neuronal network generating cricket song patterns, *Animal Behaviour*, 20, 478–92.

Brown, R. (1973) *A First Language, the Early Stages*, Harvard University Press, Cambridge, Mass.

Bullock, T. H. (1961) The origins of patterned nervous discharge, *Behaviour*, 17, 48–59.

Chomsky, N. (1967) Appendix A: The formal nature of language. In *Biological Foundations of Language*, E. H. Lenneberg (ed.), Wiley, New York.

Cutting, E. J., and Eimas, P. D. (1975) Phonetic feature analyzers and the processing of speech in infants. In *The Role of Speech in Language*, J. F. Kavanagh and J. E. Cutting (eds), MIT Press, Cambridge, Mass.

DeLong, M. (1971) Central patterning of movement, *Neuroscience. Research Programme Bulletin*, 9, 10–30.

Dittus, W. P., and Lemon, R. E. (1970) Auditory feedback in the singing of cardinals, *Ibis*, 112, 544–8.

Dorman, M. F. (1974) Auditory evoked potential correlates of speech and discrimination, *Perception and Psychophysiology*, 15, 215–20.

Doty, R. W. (1967) On butterflies in the brain. In *Electrophysiology of the Central Nervous System*, V. S. Rusinov, (ed.), pp. 96–103, Science Press, Moscow. (Translation available: Plenum, New York, 1970.)

Eimas, P. D. (1975) Speech perception in early infancy. In *Infant Perception*, L. B. Cohen and P. Salapatek (eds). Academic, New York.

Eimas, P. D., Siqueland, E. R., Jusczyk, P., and Vigorito, J. M. (1971) Speech perception in infants, *Science (Wash. D.C.)*, 171, 303–6.

Evarts, E. V. (1971) Feedback and corollary discharge: A merging of the concepts, *Neuroscience Research Programme Bulletin*, 9, 86–112.

Fentress, J. C. (1972) Development and patterning of movement sequences in inbred mice. In *The Biology of Behavior*, J. A. Kiger (ed.), Oregon State University Press, Corvallis, Ore.

Gaunt, A. S., and Wells, M. K. (1973) Models of sytringeal mechanism, *American Zoologist*, 13, 1227–47.

Greenewalt, C. H. (1968) *Birdsong, Acoustics and Physiology*, Smithsonian Institution Press, Washington, D.C.

Harris, M. A., and Lemon, R. E. (1972) Songs of song sparrows (*Melospiza melodia*): Individual variation and dialects, *Canadian Journal of Zoology*, **50**, 301–9.

Hazlett, B. A. (1972) Ritualization in marine crustaceae. In *Behavior of Marine Animals*, B. L. Winn and H. E. Olla (eds), vol. 1, *Invertebrates*, Plenum, New York.

Held, R. (1974) Development of spatially coordinated movements, *Brain Research*, **71**, 347–8.

Holst, E. von, and Mittelstaedt, H. (1950) Das Reafferenzprinzip (Wechselwirkungen zwischen Zentralnervensystem und Peripherie), *Naturwissenschaften*, **37**, 464–76.

Hoy, R. R. (1974) Genetic control of acoustic behavior in crickets, *American Zoologist*, **14**, 1067–80.

Hoy, R. R., and Paul, R. C. (1973) Genetic control of song specificity in crickets, *Science (Wash. D.C.)*, **180**, 82–3.

Immelmann, K. (1969) Song development in the zebra finch and other estrilid finches. In *Bird Vocalizations*, R. Hinde (ed.), Cambridge University Press, London.

Kimura, D. (1961) Cerebral dominance and the perception of verbal stimuli, *Canadian Journal of Psychology*, **15**, 166–71.

Kimura, D. (1964) Left–right differences in the perception of melodies, *Quarterly Journal of Experimental Psychology*, **16**, 355–8.

Konishi, M. (1963) The role of auditory feedback in the vocal behavior of the domestic fowl, *Zeitschrift für Tierpsychologie*, **20**, 349–67.

Konishi, M. (1964) Effects of deafening on song development in two species of juncos, *Condor*, **66**, 85–102.

Konishi, M. (1965a) Effects of deafening on song development in American robins and black-headed grosbeaks, *Zeitschrift für Tierpsychologie*, **22**, 584–99.

Konishi, M. (1965b) The role of auditory feedback in the control of vocalization in the white-crowned sparrow, *Zeitschrift für Tierpsychologie*, **22**, 770–83.

Konishi, M. (1970) Comparative neurophysiological studies of hearing and vocalization in songbirds, *Z. Vgl. Physiol*, **66**, 257–72.

Konishi, M., and Nottebohm, F. (1969) Experimental studies in the ontogeny of avian vocalization. In *Bird Vocalizations: Their Relations to Current Problems in Biology and Psychology*, R. A. Hinde (ed.), Cambridge University Press, Cambridge.

Kroodsma, D. Re-evaluation of song development in the *Junco–Melospiza–Zonotrichia* complex, *Animal Behaviour*. (In press.).

Lanyon, W. E. (1960) The ontogeny of vocalizations in birds. In *Animal Sounds and Communication*, W. E. Lanyon and W. N. Tavolga (eds), American Institute of Biological Sciences, Washington, D.C.

Lemon, R. E. (1971) Differentiation of song dialects in cardinals, *Ibis*, **113**, 373–7.

Lenneberg, E. H. (1967) *Biological Foundations of Language*, Wiley, New York.

Liberman, A. M., Harris, K. S., Hoffman, H. S., and Griffith, B. C. (1957) The discrimination of speech sounds within and across phoneme boundaries, *Journal of Experimental Psychology*, **54**, 358–68.

Liberman, A. M., Harris, K. S., Kinney, J., and Lane, H.

(1961) The discrimination of relative onset time of the components of certain speech and nonspeech patterns, *Journal of Experimental Psychology*, **61**, 379–88.

Liberman, A. M., Cooper, F. S., Shankweiler, D. S., and Studdert-Kennedy, M. (1967) Perception of the speech code, *Psychological Review*, **74**, 431–61.

Lisker, L., and Abramson, A. S. (1970) The voicing dimension: Some experiments in comparative phonetics, Proceedings of the 6th International Congress on Phonetic Sciences, Prague, 563–7, Academia, Prague.

Lorenz, K. Z. (1935) Der Kumpan in der Umwelt des Vogels, *Journal of Ornithology*, **83**, 137–213, 289–413.

Lorenz, K. Z. (1950) The comparative method in studying innate behavior patterns, *Symposium of the Society of Experimental Biology*, **4**, 221–68.

McNeill, D. (1966) Developmental psycholinguistics. In *The Genesis of Language*, F. Smith and G. A. Miller (eds), MIT Press, Cambridge, Mass.

Marler, P. (1952) Variations in the song of the chaffinch, *Fringilla coelebs*, *Ibis*, **94**, 458–72.

Marler, P. (1970) A comparative approach to vocal learning: Song development in white-crowned sparrows, *Journal of Comparative and Physiological Psychology Monographs*, **71**, 1–25.

Marler, P. (1972) Vocalizations of East African monkeys, II: Black and white colobus, *Behaviour*, **42**, 175–97.

Marler, P. (1973) A comparison of vocalizations of red-tailed monkeys and blue monkeys, *Cercopithecus ascanius* and *C. mitis*, in Uganda, *Zeitschrift für Tierpsychologie*, **33**, 223–47.

Marler, P. (1975) On the origin of speech from animal sounds. In *The Role of Speech in Language*, J. F. Kavanagh and J. E. Cutting (eds), MIT Press, Cambridge, Mass.

Marler, P., and Hamilton, W. J., III (1966) *Mechanisms of Animal Behavior*, Wiley, New York.

Marler, P., and Mundinger, P. (1971) Vocal learning in birds. In *Ontogeny of Vertebrate Behavior*, H. Moltz (ed.), Academic, New York.

Marler, P., and Tamura, M. (1962) Song dialects in three populations of white-crowned sparrows, *Condor*, **64**, 368–77.

Marler, P., and Tamura, M. (1964) Culturally transmitted patterns of vocal behavior in sparrows, *Science (Wash. D.C.)*, **146**, 1483–6.

Marler, P., and Tenaza, R. Signalling behavior of wild apes with special reference to vocalization. In *Animal Communication*, T. Sebeok (ed.), 2nd edn, Indiana University Press, Bloomington, Ind. (in press).

Marler, P., Kreith, M., and Tamura, M. (1962) Song development in hand-raised Oregon juncos, *Auk*, **79**, 12–30.

Marler, P., Mundinger, P., Waser, M. S., and Lutjen, A. (1972) Effects of acoustical stimulation and deprivation on song development in red-winged blackbirds (*Agelaius phoeniceus*), *Animal Behaviour*, **20**, 586–606.

Mattingly, I. G. (1972) Speech cues and sign stimuli, *American Science*, **60**, 326–337.

Milligan, M., and Verner, J. (1971) Interpopulation song

dialect discrimination in the white-crowned sparrow, *Condor*, **73**, 208–13.

Moffitt, A. R. (1971) Consonant cue perception by twenty- to twenty-four-week-old infants, *Child Development*, **42**, 717–31.

Molfese, D. L. (1972) Cerebral asymmetry in infants, children and adults: auditory evoked responses to speech and noise stimuli. Ph.D. dissertation, Pennsylvania State University, University Park, Pa.

Morse, P. A. (1972) The discrimination of speech and nonspeech stimuli in early infancy, *Journal of Experimental Child Psychology*, **14**, 477–92.

Mulligan, J. A. (1963) A description of song sparrow song based on instrumental analysis, *Proceedings of the 13th International Ornithological Congress*, **272**–84.

Mulligan, J. A. (1966) Singing behavior and its development in the song sparrow, *Melospiza melodia*, *University of California Publications in Zoology*, **81**, pp. 1–76.

Nicolai, J. (1959) Familientradition in der Gesangsentwicklung des Gimpels (*Pyrrhula pyrrhula* L.), *Journal für Ornithologie*, **100**, 39–46.

Nottebohm, F. (1967) The role of sensory feedback in the development of avian vocalizations, *Proceedings of the 14th International Ornithological Congress*, 265–80.

Nottebohm, F. (1968) Auditory experience and song development in the chaffinch *Fringilla coelebs*, *Ibis*, **110**, 549–68.

Nottebohm, F. (1971) Neural lateralization of vocal control in a passerine bird, I: Song, *Journal of Experimental Zoology*, **177**, 229–61.

Nottebohm, F. (1975) Vocal behavior in birds. In *Avian Biology, 5*, D. Farner, J. R. King and K. C. Parkes (eds), Academic, New York.

Nottebohm, F. (in press) Asymmetries in neural control of vocalization in the canary. In *Lateralization of the Nervous System*, S. Harnad (ed.), Academic, New York.

Palermo, D. S. (1975) Developmental aspects of speech perception: Problems for a motor theory. In *The Role of Speech in Language*, J. F. Kavanagh and J. E. Cutting (eds), MIT Press, Cambridge, Mass.

Remmers, J. E., and Gautier, H. (1972) Neural and mechanical mechanisms of feline purring, *Respiratory Physiology*, **16**, 351–61.

Schleidt, W. M. (1974) How "fixed" is the fixed action pattern? *Zeitschrift für Tierpsychologie*, **36**, 184–211.

Studdert-Kennedy, M. (1975) From continuous signal to discrete message: Syllable to phoneme. In *The Role of Speech in Language*, J. F. Kavanagh and J. E. Cutting (eds), MIT Press, Cambridge, Mass.

Studdert-Kennedy, M., and Shankweiler, D. P. (1970) Hemispheric specialization for speech perception, *Journal of the Acoustics Society of America*, **48**, 579–94.

Thorpe, W. H. (1955) Comments on "The Bird Fancyer's Delight" together with notes on imitation in the subsong of the chaffinch, *Ibis*, **94**, 247–51.

Thorpe, W. H. (1958) The learning of song patterns by birds, with special reference to the song of the chaffinch, *Fringilla coelebs*, *Ibis*, **100**, 535–70.

Thorpe, W. H., and Pilcher, P. M. (1958) The nature and characteristics of subsong, *British Birds*, **51**, 509–14.

Tinbergen, N. (1951) *The Study of Instinct*, Clarendon Press, Oxford.

Trehub, S. E. (1973) Infant's sensitivity to vowel and tonal contrasts, *Developmental Psychology*, **9**, 91–6.

Trehub, S. E., and Rabinovitch, M. S. (1972) Auditory-linguistic sensitivity in early infancy, *Developmental Psychology*, **6**, 74–7.

Walker, T. J. (1957) Specificity in the response of female tree crickets (*Orthoptera, Gryllidae, Oecanthinae*) to calling songs of the males, *Annals of the Entomological Society of America*, **50**, 626–36.

Walker, T. J. (1962) Factors responsible for intra-specific variation in the calling songs of crickets, *Evolution*, **16**, 407–28.

Wiley, R. H. (1973) The strut display of male sage grouse: A "fixed" action pattern, *Behaviour*, **47**, 129–52.

Wilson, D. M. (1964) The origin of the flight-motor command in grasshoppers. In *Neural Theory and Modeling*, R. Reiss (ed.), Stanford University Press, Stanford, Calif.

Wood, C. C., Goff, W. R., and Day, R. S. (1971) Auditory evoked potentials during speech perception, *Science (Wash. D.C.)*, **173**, 1248–51.

CHAPTER 15

Aspects of Learning in the Ontogeny of Bird Song: Where, from Whom, When, How Many, Which, and How Accurately?

Donald E. Kroodsma

A leisurely stroll on a spring day or a casual glance at the literature reveals an overwhelming and bewildering diversity of singing behavior among the songbirds. There are tremendous disparities in song repertoire sizes among birds – males of some species develop a single song (review in Bertram, 1970), some develop 100 songs (Verner, 1975; Kroodsma, 1975), but a brown thrasher (*Toxostoma rufum*) may sing thousands (Kroodsma and Parker, 1977). Continuity or rates of singing vary as does the sequencing of song themes during a song performance. There are musical and nonmusical songsters, superior and inferior singers, and birds that mock and those that don't (Hartshorne, 1973). Mates of some species duet (Thorpe, 1972) while in most species the females do not sing. Males of some species learn exact copies of model songs, but learning plays a minor, and improvisation plays a major, role in song development in other species. Song dialects, a consequence of song learning and dispersal, may be present or absent in congeners (e.g. *Zonotrichia* spp., Marler and Tamura, 1964; Lemon and Harris, 1974). Practically all possible combinations of times for sensitive periods exist: individuals of some species may learn throughout life (Laskey, 1944); some may be capable of adding new

syllables to their repertoire at 18 months (Rice and Thompson, 1968); chaffinches (*Fringilia coelebs*) are sensitive to song learning during their first fall and refine the details in the spring (Thorpe, 1958); cardinals (*Richmondena cardinalis*) and meadowlarks (*Sturnella magna*) stop learning at a year (Lemon and Scott, 1966; Lanyon, 1957); and a number of species terminate their song learning after a couple of months of age (white-crowned sparrow, *Zonotrichia leucophrys*, Marler, 1970; swamp sparrow, *Melospiza georgiana*, Kroodsma, unpublished data).

Selection seems to have run rampant in molding such a diversity of singing behaviors, and it is quite understandable that Marler (1967), in the first serious attempt at a synthesis on understanding the diverse developmental strategies involved, was quite "puzzled." But some progress has been made in the past ten years, and here I review some published and preview several unpublished recent advances in our understanding of the ontogeny of bird song. Since careful analyses of all experimental studies of song development among songbirds have revealed that juveniles must be exposed to normal adult songs in order for song development to proceed in truly normal pathways (Kroodsma, 1977a), the focus of this discussion will be on the various aspects of this song learning process. Specific topics will include where, from whom, when, how many, which, and how accurately songs are learned during song ontogeny.

From G. M. Burghardt and M. Berkoff (eds), *The Development of Behavior* (New York: Garland STPM Press, 1978), pp. 215–30.

Where and from Whom Songs are Learned

Field data on this topic are very meager, with good data on only two species, the Bewick's wren (*Thryomanes bewickii*) and the indigo bird (*Vidua chalybeata*). In the Bewick's wren (Willamette Valley, Oregon), young males disperse from their home territory roughly at the age of five weeks; the birds are resident throughout the year and by 60 days of age juvenile males can establish a territory which will be maintained for the life of the individual. After recording juvenile males, their fathers, and neighboring males where the juvenile established his territory, I concluded that juveniles are probably capable of learning from their father (see also the details of the sensitive period of the long-billed marsh wren, *Cistothorus palustris*, below), but a premium is placed on matching the song types of neighboring males, with whom interactions will occur throughout life; thus, song types of the father may be modified or new ones learned in order to match more closely the songs of neighboring males. So, the songs retained in the repertoire of the juvenile male are those which are acquired from and reinforced by neighboring territorial males where the juvenile is on his own territory (Kroodsma, 1974).

In the indigo bird flexibility to change song types in the repertoire of the individual is apparently maintained throughout life; a premium on song type matching by interacting conspecifics remains, for if a male moves from one area to another, his songs also change to match the songs of the other males at the new display center (Payne, 1975).

Data for several species are available from laboratory experiments, but one must be cautious in relating such data directly to what may be occurring in nature. In the zebra finch (*Poephila guttata*), the social bond with the father appears a strong social constraint on song learning, for songs of natural fathers are learned preferentially to those of conspecifics in the next cage, and songs of foster fathers of other species are learned preferentially to the songs of conspecifics which may be singing nearby. There is a hint, however, of a predisposition to learn songs of conspecifics, since young zebra finches, raised by females under conditions where they could see and hear both conspecific males and males

of other grassfinch species in nearby cages, developed songs consisting only of species-specific elements (Immelmann, 1969). Laboratory data for the bullfinch (*Pyrrhula pyrrhula*) also implicate similar social constraints on song learning (Nicolai, 1959). Vocal learning in a social context also occurs among cardueline finches, where mates tend to converge on similar call notes in their repertoires, and where birds in a cohesive winter flock may also tend to share similarities in their call repertoire (Mundinger, 1970). Finally, it is the social interaction with and song learning from mates which produces the finely synchronized performance among species where mates duet with one another (Thorpe, 1972).

Timing of Song Learning

We have a rough idea of the timing of learning in a number of species. For example, Marler (1970) found that a white-crowned sparrow produced a good copy of a training song if he heard it between 8 and 28 d or between 35 and 56 d of age; exposure before eight days and after 50 d had little effect. Song sparrows (*Melospiza melodia*) have a peak of sensitivity between five and ten weeks of age, when two birds each learned seven song components (Mulligan, 1966). In the zebra finch the juvenile male gradually learns the fine structure of the song elements (through roughly day 66) and develops the proper timing and sequencing of those elements by day 80, when song learning is complete (Immelmann, 1969). The timing of song learning in some species may be hormonally related, for Nottebohm (1969) found that castration of a juvenile chaffinch delayed song learning until exogenous testosterone was administered in the bird's second year; on the other hand, Arnold (1975) demonstrated convincingly that gonadal androgens are not essential for normal song development in zebra finches.

Thus, we know roughly when birds learn their songs, but the very details of the sensitive period are lacking. What is the fine anatomy of this period of learning? Is there a peak, or are there peaks, of sensitivity? Is there a sharp or gradual onset and termination of sensitivity? What are the hormonal and neurophysiological correlates of this sensitive period among different species? Why do species differ? And lastly, how do the fine points of the sensitive period correlate with dependency on parents, dispersal, establishment of the juvenile male's own territory, or other unique features of a given species' exploitation system? Do these fine points vary geographically as these parameters of the population biology vary? In an effort to tackle some of these questions I have begun a study of song learning in the long-billed marsh wren; these insectivorous birds can be hand-reared in the laboratory (though with some difficulties compared with sparrows), and develop large song repertoires, allowing one to glean a great deal of information from a single male.

In a pilot experiment, two males were exposed to nine different song types between the ages of 15 and 65 d, another nine between 65 and 115 d, and still another nine the following spring. Both males learned all nine song types to which they were exposed before 65 d of age, but none of the other 18 songs. In refining this pilot experiment, nine juvenile males were used, but the presentation of tutor songs was refined to such an extent as to allow a very detailed determination of exactly when songs were learned. Over a 72 d period, beginning at ages 6 to 15 d, the males were exposed to a total of 44 different song types. On any given day males heard 1000 repetitions of each of three different song types. However, some song types were presented over nine-day periods (9000 exposures/9 d; $n = 8$), some were presented over six-day periods (6000 exposures/6 d; $n = 12$), while other songs were presented over three-day periods (3000 exposures/3 d; $n = 24$ song types).

The nine long-bill males learned an average of 16 different songs (see figure 15.1), and were adept at learning song types presented over nine-day as well as three-day periods. Song learning occurs roughly between 15 and 60 d of age, and when data for all nine males are graphed together, two peaks of sensitivity appear, one near day 35 and the other near day 53 (figure 15.2). All the birds were housed together and some improvised song types did occur in the repertoires of several of the males; however, several internal controls in the experiment indicate that the influence of males upon each other played a relatively minor role in shaping the sensitive period as depicted in figure 15.2.

In spite of the detail in the picture of the sensitive period, caution must be exercised in attempting

to relate this sensitive period to events occurring in nature. Relating this period of sensitivity to (1) gaining of independence by the juvenile male, (2) dispersal, (3) establishment of territory, (4) the role of hormonal levels, or possibly (5) the postjuvenile molt would be an exciting advance. The clear-cut sensitive period for learning from tutor tapes in the laboratory does provide a nice model for establishing various hormonal and neurophysiological correlates of song learning, but further data on song learning in the long-bill suggest that events in nature may be considerably more complicated than as presented in figure 15.2: (1) In Welter's (1935) study at Ithaca, N.Y., the last peak of hatching occurred after the adult males had stopped singing for the year! Can these juveniles postpone the sensitive period until the following year, possibly by a mechanism similar to that which Nottebohm (1969) simulated through castration of a male chaffinch? (2) Five New York juvenile males learned no songs from nine other New York males to which they were exposed after 120 d of age; however, one Michigan male, under the same conditions, learned five of a possible 15 songs. Population differences in degree or timing of song learning present ideal opportunities for a comparative approach to further our understanding of the selective forces behind different strategies. (3) Finally, two males exposed to tape recorded model songs until day 45, and then exposed to a live tutor, rejected those songs which were heard from the tutor tape and learned the songs from the live bird. Social interactions may play a crucial role in determining exactly where, when, and from whom songs are learned in nature.

How Many Songs are Developed

The number of song types developed varies from species to species (see introduction), but may also vary intraspecifically, both within and between populations. Within a population, for example, three rock wrens (*Salpinctes obsoletus*) had 119, 85, and 69 song types ($n = 1234, 1276,$ and 2262, respectively; Kroodsma, 1975). In Bewick's wrens, the number of song types or song components that a male develops is dependent upon his date of hatching; song learning is completed during the first fall, and birds hatched early in the breeding season develop more songs than birds hatched later

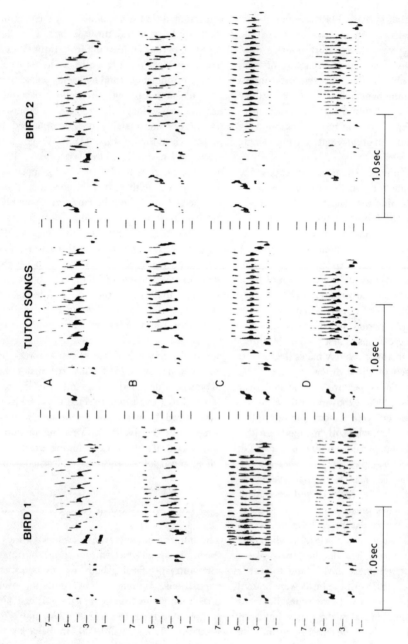

Figure 15.1 Example of songs that two male long–billed marsh wrens learned from the training tapes. The vertical scale on each sonogram is kHz, the horizontal is seconds.

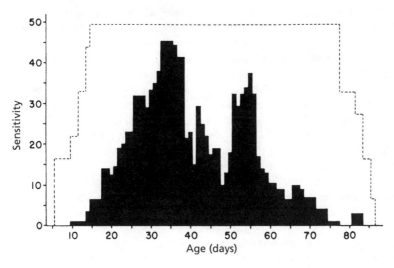

Figure 15.2   The sensitive period for the long-billed marsh wren, a composite of individual graphs from each of nine males.

in the season (Kroodsma, 1972b). In other species where birds can add or modify their vocal repertoire throughout life, repertoire size may continue to increase and be age-correlated. Experiments with canaries (*Serinus canarius*) indicate that females during mate selection are probably attentive to this intraspecific variability in male song (Kroodsma, 1976).

Variation in song repertoire sizes among different populations of a given species may be striking. Long-billed marsh wrens near Seattle, Washington, may have 150 song types, while an Illinois male may have as few as 30 (Verner and Kroodsma, in preparation). Whether such a variation is a consequence of intensified or relaxed selection, or a result of climatic conditions which dictate a resident or migrant status, which could in turn control time available for song development, must await further study.

Those wren species which develop large song-type repertoires deserve further mention, for several population parameters seem well correlated with the repertoire size and singing behaviors of these species. Individual long- and short-billed marsh wrens (*Cistothorus platensis*) and rock wrens have been studied with over 100 song types in their repertoires, but repertoire sizes for house (*Troglodytes aedon*), winter (*T. troglodytes*), Bewick's, Carolina (*Thryothorus ludovicianus*), canyon (*Catherpes mexicanus*), and probably cactus

(*Campylorhynchus brunneicapillus*) wrens do not approach these values. Furthermore, these three species with the larger song repertoires use frequently or exclusively song organizations involving more immediate variety (i.e., ABCABC... MNOMNO..., or ABCDEFGHIJKL...) rather than the more monotonous organization where a given song type is repeated many times in succession before switching to another type (i.e., AAAAAA... BBBBBB...), as occurs in the other 6 wren species. These three wren species occur in higher densities in communities of lower avifaunal diversity, where intraspecific interactions are likely to be more frequent and intense; two of the three are highly polygynous, implicating epigamic selection as possibly playing a role (Kroodsma, 1977b).

In the long-billed marsh wrens of eastern Washington, where males synchronize themselves in long sequences and countersing with like songs, the repertoire sizes of males are surprisingly similar: for 5 males studied the number of song types was 114, 114, 114, 109, and 107 ($n = 1257, 730, 771, 446$, and 461, respectively; Verner 1975)! With a total of only 127 different song types among the 5 males, the intricate communication system of the long-bill seems to place a premium on neighboring males having identical song-type repertoires.

With two captive long-billed marsh wrens, the ontogeny of song matching (or countersinging) was quite evident. Two males, each with identical repertoires of 9 song types, were housed in adjacent cages and allowed to interact freely. Bird 2 lagged behind bird 1 in song development, and remained in plastic song while bird 1 was in full song. Over all, bird 2 matched the song type of bird 1 nearly 1/3 of the time (1/9 expected; see table 15.1), while bird 1 matched the song type of bird 2 no more than expected by chance alone. However, when the songs of bird 2 were amplified over a loudspeaker system, bird 1 matched the songs of bird 2 to a much greater extent (18.5%). Furthermore, during the 14 days that these two birds were studied, there was a gradual reduction in the percent of the time that bird 2 matched the songs of bird 1. It is conceivable that such an ontogeny of song matching and countersinging, coupled with loudness of delivery, could betray the overall vigor or age of a bird, as it seemed to under these experimental conditions, and might even be used by conspecifics in assessing the quality of potential mates or rivals.

Influence on the nature of song dialects

Various constraints on vocal learning often insure that interacting conspecifics will possess like vocalizations. Thus, a male Bewick's wren is probably highly capable of learning from its father before 35 d of age; however, he may reject or modify those paternal song patterns after he disperses (35–100 d; *when*) in order to learn from and match the songs of conspecific adult males (*which* songs and *from*

whom) who hold territories adjacent to the territory which the juvenile male declares (*where*). Close examination of the microgeographical distribution of song patterns or song elements reveals that in the majority of songbirds neighboring males have songs more similar to one another than to more distant males; males usually respond the strongest to songs most like their own (i.e., songs of the same "dialect"), and if they have several different songs in their repertoire, they often countersing with like songs as well.

Yet the nature of the "dialect" in different species may be largely dependent on *how many* different song patterns are in the repertoire of the individual. In the white-crowned sparrow, the great majority of males have a single song type, and in California chapparel, boundaries between different dialects may be very abrupt, even in the absence of habitat barriers, enabling one to map "populations" where all males possess like songs (Baptista, 1975). On the other hand, a Bewick's wren male may have 16 different song types; *each* song type may have a unique microgeographical distribution, often with very sharp boundaries and hybrid songs at contact zones of different song patterns. Emphasis appears to be on neighboring males having like songs, as in the white-crowned sparrow, but in the wren one is not able to map "populations" of birds having identical song repertoires, for the entire system appears as 16–20 *z. l. nuttalli* dialects superimposed on one another.

As more studies emerge, it is becoming increas-

Table 15.1   A summary of the singing behaviors and interactions of two long-billed marsh wren males which were hand-reared and studied in the laboratory

		FOLLOWING EVENT				
		Bird 1		*Bird 2*		*Expected*
PRECEDING EVENT		FREE SINGING		COUNTERSINGING		
	Bird 1	*Matching Self	15.8%	*Match Bird 1	31.1%	11.1%
		*Tutor Sequence	31.8%	*Tutor Sequence	24.6%	12.3%
		COUNTERSINGING		FREE SINGING		
	Bird 2	*Tutor Sequence	22.6%	*Tutor Sequence	25.9%	12.3%
		Match Bird 2	11.4%	*Matching Self	14.6%	11.1%

*Different from expected by random singing; chi-square, $p < 0.001$.

ingly apparent that most songbirds have more than a single song type in their song repertoires, suggesting that something quite unique may be occurring in a species where males have a single, precisely copied song. Instead of the usual question as to "Why do some species develop such large song repertoires?", the opposite question may be appropriate here: "What is unique to the reproductive biology of a species like the white-crowned sparrow that selection has so limited their song repertoires?" Sharp dialect boundaries where all songs in the birds' repertoires change are far more feasible when only one song is involved than when larger numbers of songs are involved (given similar habitat conditions and degree of continuity). Have advantages of sharp dialect boundaries selected for essentially one learned song type in the white-crown?

Baker's (1975) demonstration of genetic differences of birds in neighboring dialect areas is an exciting step; he postulates that dialect areas may have a historical origin, with colonizing individuals establishing new dialect areas. Efforts to determine whether dialect boundaries can actually repel dispersing juveniles is under way (Baker, in preparation).

Selectivity of Song Models

Among mimics such as the mockingbird, much song learning from heterospecifics occurs, but even among other species, the nonmockers, occasional reports do occur of some learning from other species (Kroodsma, 1972a, 1973; Baptista, 1972). Yet, for the most part, species identity in the wild is totally unambiguous, partly because of predispositions to learn only conspecific song.

Two experiments at the Rockefeller University Field Research Center have tested the selectivity in song learning between conspecific pairs, two *Cistothorus* wrens and two *Melospiza* sparrows. For the wrens, a tutor tape with 67 different songs was prepared. On this tutor tape were (1) songs of normal short-billed marsh wrens ($n = 9$), which consist of an introduction of several notes and a trill, (2) songs of normal long-billed marsh wrens ($n = 9$), which consist of an introduction, trill, and several concluding notes, (3) normal songs of Bewick's wrens ($n = 4$), (4) normal swamp sparrow songs ($n = 5$), and (5) all manner of song combinations

with (a) either long- or short-bill introductions, (b) trills of long-bills, short-bills, swamp sparrows, or Bewick's wrens, and (c) presence or absence of a long-bill conclusion ($n = 40$). The short-bills learned nothing from the tapes, whereas the long-bills learned preferentially those songs which contained long-bill trills; this species difference will be explored further below. Interesting here is the fact that the probability that a long-bill would learn a given trill was directly related, exponentially, to the number of long-bill components (0 to 3) that were in the song.

Song and swamp sparrows are closely related members of the genus *Melospiza*. The normal songs of the two species are of similar length but very different temporal organization. The swamp sparrow song is relatively simple, consisting of a phrase of repeated syllables, but the song of the song sparrow is more complex, usually with at least four phrases. As in the *Cistothorus* wrens, the preferred micro-habitats differ, but territories of the two species may abutt or overlap. Data from the laboratory indicate that learning of song models plays an important role in song development in the males of each species. In order to test the selectivity of the song learning process, artificial songs were made from the elements of natural song of the two species. Swamp sparrow features in the training songs included single-phrase songs consisting of sequences of identical syllables delivered at a steady rate, while song sparrow features involved variable rates of syllable delivery (accelerating or decelerating) and a multi-partite song structure (two parts). Natural syllables from each species' song were edited from field recordings and spliced together to make the training songs, 22 of which were presented to each male of the two species.

Eight male swamp sparrows learned twelve syllables from the tutor tapes, and all twelve were of swamp sparrow origin. Four of the learned syllables were from one-phrase songs, while eight were from two-parted songs; five came from phrases of a steady rate, while seven were learned from either accelerated or decelerated syllable series. The swamp sparrow clearly can recognize conspecific syllables regardless of their context in the training songs. The five song sparrows, on the other hand, learned 22 syllables from the training tapes; 11 were of swamp and 11 of song sparrow origin, with no particular preferences exhibited for learning syllables of a given rate of delivery or from one- or two-parted songs (Marler and Peters, 1977).

The evolution of such different ontogenies and song selectivities in the two *Melospiza* sparrows is puzzling. Why is there such a difference, or, to what features of each species' life history are these ontogenies adapted? Evolutionary strategies may become clearer as song development and life history parameters of other closely related species are studied. Such hope is encouraged from studies of the *Cistothorus* wrens, where the differing song ontogenies of the two wren species may be well suited to each species' exploitation system.

Role of Improvisation vs Learning among *Cistothorus* Wrens

The two North American marsh wrens have recently been reclassified as congeneric (*Cistothorus* spp., Thirty-third Supplement to the A. O. U. Checklist, 1976), and are an ideal species pair for a comparative approach to studying vocal ontogenies. The two species are alike in so many ways: (1) males of each species are polygynous (Verner 1965, Welter 1935, Kale 1965; Crawford 1977); (2) the density of breeding pairs is very high compared with all other North American wrens; (3) the preferred habitats, are marshes or wet meadows (essentially monolayers without an appreciable vertical dimension) in which the overall avifaunal diversity of the community is very low, usually making the wren the most abundant species present (Kroodsma, 1977b). To an extent, their singing behaviors are also very similar: males of both species sing a relatively high percentage of the time (30 to 40% singing, 60 to 70% in silence during an actual singing performance), use large song-type repertoires that may number well over 100 in some populations, and continue to sing (presumably for additional mates), often day and night, throughout much of the breeding season.

However, the details of the singing behavior differ markedly. All long-bill males in a population possess nearly identical song-type repertoires (Verner, 1975); in the laboratory, males between the ages of 20 and 80 d readily learn the precise details of songs presented to them over loudspeakers. On the other hand, short-bill males in a natural popula-

tion have very dissimilar song types (except for a stereotyped introduction; see below) and unequal repertoire sizes; they cannot countersing with like songs (though they definitely do influence one another while singing); and males in the laboratory between 15 and 90 d of age demonstrate little to no ability to learn tutor songs presented over loudspeakers. Yet these experimental short-bills are capable of producing sizeable song repertoires which contain, for the most part, songs which are very similar to normal wild-type songs.

In the long-billed marsh wren, juvenile males learn the songs of adults and then, in order to maintain the observed homogeneity of song patterns within a population, must settle to breed nearby and then return yearly to that locality. Juveniles in eastern Washington do disperse a considerable distance from their father's territory ($\bar{x}$ = 1951 m), but fidelity to the site of breeding (and perhaps the site of song learning?) is quite strong: seven of 13 adults returned to the same or adjacent territories in successive years (Verner, 1971). On the other hand, the occurrence of the short-bill from year to year can be very unpredictable; birds may appear on territory or desert their territory in the middle of the normal breeding season. Of ten males banded in Minnesota, none returned to the same locality in the following year (J. Burns, personal communication).

The key to the nomadic-like movements of the short-billed marsh wren, as opposed to the long-bill's, may be found in the habitat stability of preferred breeding sites. The short-bills breed in wet meadows, while the long-bills occur in marshes with more standing water; during periods of insufficient rainfall, the wet meadows are the first to dry up, and even if the two species are breeding in the same vicinity, the short-bills are the first to lose their breeding sites (R. E. Stewart, personal communication). It is probably a direct result of this relative habitat instability and unpredictability that the short-bill demonstrates far less site tenacity than does the long-bill; the fact that no subspecific differentiation has occurred in the short-bill is further suggestive evidence of a relatively high degree of movement within the breeding range of the species.

The song ontogeny in the two species seems nicely correlated with their respective ways of life. The short-bill does not learn precise details of the song, but develops a generalized song (actually a large number of them) which is recognizable as that of the short-billed marsh wren throughout the range of the species in North America. Furthermore, the brief introduction of the song, involving at most four to five different notes, is practically identical among all birds studied, including birds from Michigan, Minnesota, Illinois, North Dakota, and the wintering grounds in Florida; this same introduction did not develop normally in the hand-reared birds, but they did develop introductions in common with one another, suggesting that this very stereotyped introduction is learned. So the short-bill male develops a very stereotyped introduction and a very generalized conclusion to his song, both of which label the species; however, the details offer little clue as to the geographic origin of the bird.

While the song of the long-bill is unmistakable throughout the range of the species, neighboring males tend to have identical songs. Also, considerable geographical variation does exist, and experiments would probably reveal that long-bill males discriminate local versus more distant songs (as has been demonstrated in so many other species where songs are learned and local "dialects" exist). Sub-specific differentiation is extensive among the long-bills, though this occurs predominantly in salt marshes which are outside the geographical range of the short-bill.

Summary

Learning of adult motor patterns plays a role in the song ontogeny of all oscines that have been studied in detail, but there are many different facets to this learning process. (1) Field data reveal that in some species a male learns the songs of adults (*from whom*) at the location where that male will breed (*where*); neighboring males thus can interact with nearly identical songs. (2) In most species, song learning is limited to the first couple months of life (*when*), but within a given species this may vary among populations and is undoubtedly very dependent upon social interactions. (3) Males of some species develop only 1 song pattern per individual, while males of other species may develop more songs (*how many*) and interact in complex ways; the number of songs learned by each male in a population may affect the nature of song dialects. (4) Among *Melospiza* sparrows, the swamp sparrow rejects song sparrow syllables and learns to sing only conspecific song syllables, but the song sparrow will learn song elements of either species with equal facility; selectivity (*which* songs are learned) of song models differs markedly even among closely related species. (5) The *accuracy* of copying models during song learning among *Cistothorus* wrens may have coevolved with the relative stability of the habitats occupied by the two species; short-billed marsh wrens occupy relatively unstable wet meadows, have a generalized song, and populations appear highly mobile, whereas the long-billed marsh wren lives in more stable marshes, has population-specific song patterns and/or sequences, and demonstrates more site tenacity than does the short-bill.

Acknowledgments

Financial support has been provided by the Frank M. Chapman Memorial Fund and by NSF Grant No. BNS76-07704A01. I thank Jared Verner and colleagues at the Rockefeller University Field Research Center for valuable discussion and comment, Roberta Pickert for her unwavering assistance in the research, Cathy Quimby for helping with field work, and Melissa Kroodsma for her unlimited patience, encouragement, and assistance in all phases of these labors.

References

American Ornithologists' Union (1976) Thirty-third supplement to the American Ornithologists' Union Checklist of North American birds, *Auk*, **93**: 875–9.

Arnold, A. P. (1975) The effects of castration on song development in zebra finches (*Poephila guttata*), *Journal of Experimental Zoology*, **191**: 261–77.

Baker, M. C. (1975) Song dialects and genetic differences in white-crowned sparrows (*Zonotrichia leucophrys*), *Evolution*, **29**, 226–41.

Baptista, L. F. (1972) Wild house finch sings white-crowned sparrow song, *Zeitschrift für Tierpsychologie*, **30**: 266–70.

Baptista, L. F. (1975) Song dialects and demes in sedentary populations of the white-crowned sparrow (*Zonotrichia leucophrys nuttalli*), *University of California Publications in Zoology*, **105**: 1–52.

Bertram, B. (1970) The vocal behavior of the Indian hill mynah, *Gracula religiosa*, *Animal Behaviour Monographs*, **3**: 79–192.

Crawford, R. D. (1977) Polygynous breeding of short-billed marsh wrens, *Auk*, **94**: 359–62.

Hartshorne, C. (1973) *Born to Sing. An Interpretation and World Survey of Bird Song*, Bloomington: Indiana University Press.

Immelmann, K. (1969) Song development in the zebra finch and other Estrildid finches. In *Bird vocalizations*, ed. R. A. Hinde, London and New York: Cambridge University Press.

Kale, H. W. II (1965) Ecology and bioenergetics of the long-billed marsh wren (*Telmatodytes palustris griseus* [Brewster]) in Georgia salt marshes, *Publications of the Nuttall Ornithological Club*, No. 5.

Kroodsma, D. E. (1972a) Variation in songs of vesper sparrows in Oregon, *Wilson Bulletin*, **84**: 173–8.

Kroodsma, D. E. (1972b) Singing behavior of the Bewick's wren: Development, dialects, population structure, and geographical variation. Ph.D. dissertation, Oregon State University, Corvallis, Oregon.

Kroodsma, D. E. (1973) Coexistence of Bewick's wrens and house wrens in Oregon, *Auk*, **90**: 341–52.

Kroodsma, D. E. (1974) Song learning, dialects, and dispersal in the Bewick's wren, *Zeitschrift für Tierpsychologie*, **35**: 352–80.

Kroodsma, D. E. (1975) Song patterning in the rock wren, *Condor*, **77**: 294–303.

Kroodsma, D. E. (1976) Reproductive development in a female songbird: Differential stimulation by quality of male song, *Science*, **192**: 574–5.

Kroodsma, D. E. (1977a) Correlates of song organization among North American wrens, *American Naturalist*, **111**: 995–1008.

Kroodsma, D. E. (1977b) A reevaluation of song development in the song sparrow, *Animal Behaviour*, **25**: 390–9.

Kroodsma, D. E., and L. D. Parker (1977) Vocal virtuosity in the brown thrasher, *Auk*, **94**: 783–5.

Lanyon, W. E. (1957) The comparative biology of the meadowlarks (*Sturnella*) in Wisconsin, *Publications of the Nuttall Ornithological Club*, No. 1.

Laskey, A. R. (1944) A mockingbird acquires his song repertory, *Auk*, **61**: 211–19.

Lemon, R. E., and M. Harris (1974) The question of dialects in the songs of white-throated sparrows, *Canadian Journal of Zoology*, **52**: 83–98.

Lemon, R. E., and D. M. Scott (1966) On the development of song in young cardinals, *Canadian Journal of Zoology*, **44**: 191–7.

Marler, P. (1967) Comparative study of song development in sparrows, *Proceedings of the 14th International Ornithological Congress*, 1966: 231–44.

Marler, P. (1970) A comparative approach to vocal development: Song learning in the white-crowned sparrow, *Journal of Comparative and Physiological Psychology*, **71** (2): 1–25.

Marler, P., and S. Peters (1977) Selective vocal learning in a sparrow, *Science*, **198**: 519–21.

Marler, P., and M. Tamura (1964) Culturally transmitted patterns of vocal behavior in sparrows, *Science*, **146**: 1483–6.

Mulligan, J. A. (1966) Singing behavior and its development in the song sparrow *Melospiza melodia*, *University of California Publications in Zoology*, **81**: 1-76.

Mundinger, P. C. (1970) Vocal imitation and individual recognition of finch calls, *Science*, **168**: 480–2.

Nicolai, J. (1959) Familientradition in der gesangsentwicklung des gimpels (*Pyrrhula pyrrhula* L.), *Journal für Ornithologie*, **100**: 39–46.

Nottebohm, F. (1969) The "critical period" for song learning in birds, *Ibis*, **111**: 386–7.

Payne, R. B. (1975) Song dialects and population structure in the indigo birds of Africa, *Proc. Symp. on Dialects in Bird Song*, Media services, St Louis University.

Rice, J. O., and W. L. Thompson (1968) Song development in the indigo bunting, *Animal Behaviour*, **16**: 462–9.

Thorpe, W. H. (1958) The learning of song patterns by birds, with especial reference to the song of the chaffinch, *Fringilla coelebs*, *Ibis*, **100**: 535-70.

Thorpe, W. H. (1972) *Duetting and antiphonal song in birds: Its extent and significance*, Leiden: E. J. Brill.

Verner, J. (1965) Breeding biology of the long-billed marsh wren, *Condor*, **67**: 6–30.

Verner, J. (1971) Survival and dispersal of male long-billed marsh wrens, *Bird-banding*, **42**: 92–8.

Verner, J. (1975) Complex song repertoire of male long-billed marsh wrens in eastern Washington, *Living Bird*, **14**: 263–300.

Welter, W. A. (1935) The natural history of the long-billed marsh wren, *Wilson Bulletin*, **47**: 3–34.

CHAPTER 16

Motor Patterns in Development (*excerpt*)

JOHN C. FENTRESS and PETER J. MCLEOD

Introduction

It is through the production of integrated sequences of movement that animals express rules by which they interact with, and adapt to, their physical, biological, and social environments. The diversity of these motor patterns in the behavior of animals can provide a valuable assay of processes of developmental organization. Our aim in this chapter is to examine motor patterns in development at different levels of organization and from several complementary perspectives.

Preliminary issues

The first issue we address concerns categorizations of motor patterns. To create meaningful taxonomies it is necessary to fractionate processes of movement into basic actions and determine how these actions and their underlying dimensions are combined. Within a developmental context it is important to formulate these taxonomies from explicitly defined criteria that capture both the dynamic and relational properties of observed

From E. M. Blass (ed.), *Handbook of Behavioral Neurobiology*, vol. 8: *Developmental Processes in Psychobiology and Neurobiology* (New York: Plenum Press, 1986), pp. 35–60.

movement sequences. To illustrate this we have placed special emphasis upon the theme of pattern formation in integrated movement.

With appropriate descriptive taxonomies a second issue fundamental to motor patterns in development, the balance between eliciting factors and tendencies toward spontaneous expression, can be examined. This issue has been one of considerable historical debate in ethology, psychology, and neuroscience (see e.g., Bekoff, 1981; Carmichael, 1970; Hamburger, 1977; Hoyle, 1984; Lorenz, 1981; Oppenheim, 1981). As analyses become refined, a third issue arises concerning interactions among different classes of action, both in terms of moment-to-moment expression and over a developmental time frame (see e.g., Bateson, 1981; Fentress, 1984; Hinde, 1982; Moran et al., 1983).

We examine these issues primarily from an ethological perspective. This perspective emphasizes the importance of accurate descriptions in attempts to understand the causal antecedents and functional consequences of behavior (see, e.g., Tinbergen, 1963). Ethologists have also been concerned with problems of the hierarchical *expression* of behavior (Dawkins, 1976; Fentress, 1983a,b; Gallistel, 1980). In keeping with this perspective, we seek themes of motor patterns in development at several levels of organization. We also hope to provide the reader with some sense of the diversity of motor patterns in animal behavior, as only in this way can meaningful generalizations, and their limitations, be brought into clear focus.

Approach taken

In addition to the preceding considerations, we have found it useful to form our review of the literature around two more abstract polarities of motor organization: (1) the relative stability versus change within underlying dimensions and (2) the degree of separation (discontinuity) versus cohesion (continuity) among these dimensions. Each of these conceptual polarities can be applied to different time frames and levels of organization (figure 16.1). By placing appropriate emphasis upon the problem of dynamic relations among movement dimensions, rigid "unit" concepts of motor patterns in development can be avoided, thereby clarifying the operation of underlying processes (Fentress, 1984).

Review of Issues

Basic dimensions of movement

1. Within and between limb coordination
Based upon her observations of chick motor development and a review of related studies, Bekoff (1976, 1981) suggests as a general principle that intrajoint coordination tends to precede interjoint coordination, which, in turn, precedes interlimb coordination (with homologous limbs preceding homolateral limbs). Further, there is evidence for cephalocaudal and proximodistal progressions in

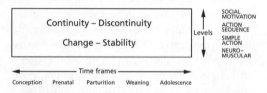

Figure 16.1 Summary of basic organizational polarities relevant to motor patterns in development. Continuity-discontinuity refers to the degree of separation among behavioral phenomena and their underlying processes (mechanisms). Change–stability refers to the extent that properties and processes of behavioral organization remain fixed in time. Each of these two polarities can be examined over a number of levels of organization as well as across complementary time frames. (Adapted from Fentress, 1984.)

movement. While there may be important species differences, and differences among functionally defined classes of behaviour within species (see, e.g., Anokhin, 1964; Carmichael, 1970), similar principles of organization appear to be widespread in the animal kingdom. To cite an invertebrate correlate to Bekoff's chick studies, Bentley and Hoy (1970) demonstrated that interlimb coordination between forewings and hindwings in crickets develops after coordination of muscles within each wing (cf. Altman, 1975; Kutsch, 1971).

In an early study of motor development in fetal rats, Angulo y González (1932) noted that forelimb movements and trunk movements tended to occur together, as did tongue protrusions and movements of the head. Bekoff et al. (1975) found that in 7-day chick embryos alternation of muscle antagonists is imprecise, with partial overlap in some phases. In a study of swimming behavior in postnatal rats, Bekoff and Trainer (1979) report that early independence of limb movements is followed by a progressive coupling within limb pairs. Once the hindlimbs become well coordinated, the forelegs cease paddling movements (cf. Fentress, 1972; 1978).

Bernstein (1967) argued that in the development of human motor patterns there is a trend toward a reduction in the degrees of freedom among movement dimensions. The overall movement endpoints remain more or less constant through increased compensatory responses. A recent study of human marksmanship by Arutyunyun et al. (1981) suggests that during learning of this skill, movements of the wrist and shoulder joints become mutually constrained (cf. Kelso and Tuller, 1984). As shown by Johnston (1980), even young pigtail macaques (*Macaca nemestrina*) are able to compensate for variations in the rigidity of the environmental substrate by varying joint angles. In this way they can maintain an invariance in jumping trajectory.

These references highlight two important issues. First, certain properties of movement may become more finely separated from one another during development, while other movement parameters become mutually constrained. Second, once cohesions among movement dimensions are established, compensatory variation among these dimensions may preserve the functional integrity of the movement as a whole.

2. Skilled actions and locomotion

Bruner (1974) has argued that for human motor development, decompositions and recompositions of individually defined actions are commonplace (cf. Bower, 1979). Collard and Povel (1982) propose that in the development of a variety of skilled actions, rules for overall spatiotemporal structure preserve the integrity of movement when perturbations are applied (cf. Weismer and Fennell, 1983). A study by von Hofsten (1979) on visually guided reaching in human infants provides evidence that the development of postural compensatory mechanisms is an important part of skill acquisition. Such data suggest hierarchically organized motor performance (Connolly, 1977). Moss and Hogg (1983) found that for infants between 12 and 18 months, *increased* variability in movement subunits accompanied improvement in the proficiency of an acquired motor task. This places restrictions on any "brick-by-brick" notions of motor development. As Evarts (1975) and others have noted, relations among abstracted parts of movement provide the important keys for understanding motor patterning.

Such studies in normal developmental contexts can also provide information relevant to a variety of motor disorders. For example, Sherwood (unpublished manuscript) has found that clumsy children tend to recruit fewer motor components in response to experimentally applied perturbations than do normal children of the same age. It is interesting that adults employ an intermediate number of motor components in compensating for the same applied perturbations. This illustrates that it is not just individual components (or dimensions) of movement that we need to examine, but also the rules by which coherent groupings of action are produced.

An increasing number of investigators have looked for developmental changes in movement properties (dimensions) that may transcend motor "acts." Golani (1981) speaks of "attractors" in development to emphasize the changing nodes of relative invariance within which other properties of motor organization vary. In this way both change and stability can be examined together in relative terms.

In her classic study of motor development in macaques, Hines (1942) emphasized that "regression" along certain movement dimensions is prerequisite to "progression" along others. Early fetal reflexes were characterized by briskness and irradiation that involved many muscle groups not activated at later ages. Most of these early movements were "initiated in the proximal muscles and [are] incapable of any variation or rearrangement as it proceeds down the extremity" (p. 157). Independent use of the index finger and thumb was not fully attained until the animals were approximately 1 year of age. Lawrence and Hopkins (1976) have shown that cortical connections to motoneuronal cell groups do not develop until about 6 months in rhesus monkeys. Prior to this time independent finger movements are rarely, if ever, observed (cf. Kuypers, 1981). McGraw (1940) has argued that for human infants, cortical development can lead both to the coordination of previously fragmented actions and to the suppression of previously active pathways. The simple dichotomy of differentiation versus integration cannot be applied to such complex alterations of motor organization (cf. review in Hofer, 1981).

The development of locomotor patterns has been studied thoroughly. Forssberg and Wallberg (1981) examined locomotor patterns in human infants between 5 hr and 6 weeks of age. These infants were held under the arms for support, with their feet on a treadmill. Five infrared diodes were used to feed leg movement data into a computer for analysis. EMG records were also obtained from the tibialis anterior, lateral head of the gastroenemius, medial hamstring, and quadriceps. All infants in the first 6 weeks could perform at least part of a single step, and many performed consecutive leg swings. In comparison with older children, the infant walking patterns were highly irregular, with components that seemed "extreme." In particular, infants differed from older children in the following ways: the swing phase was produced by the hip only, with the result that the foot was lifted to an extreme position; early excessive extensor activity led to a digitigrade rather than the more mature plantigrade walking pattern; EMG records were irregular with high degrees of coactivation and the two limbs often became entangled with one another, demonstrating an imperfect interlimb coordination. Thelen et al. (1983) have shown that interlimb coordination tends to become organized with a tighter coupling between the legs as human infants become older. These studies imply that a wide range of fractionations and exaggerations in early motor performance later give way to more coordinated patterns.

Analogous studies on animals (e.g., rat locomotion; Gruner and Altman, 1980; Gruner et al., 1980) have shown that tracing movement dimensions both separately and in combination provides useful insights. Golani et al. (1981) have demonstrated an ontogenetic sequence from lateral to longitudinal to vertical aspects of locomotory movements for rats. Repeated movements along a single dimension prior to coupling into a coherent multidimensional whole were also observed. Cephalocaudal progressions are also common (see, e.g., Ferron and Lefebvre, 1983, on grooming in squirrels and Richmond and Sachs, 1980, on grooming in rats).

3. Form, orientation, and function

One aspect of movement dimensionality that has received considerable attention is the separation of form versus function and/or orientation. Many actions can be recognized and classified prior to the time that they serve any obvious function. Barraud (1961) and Nice (1943), for example, observed preening movements in passerine birds prior to the time that the feathers had developed. It is as if these early preening movements "anticipate" subsequent function (cf. Anokhin, 1964; Carmichael, 1970). Analogous observations exist for a number of species.

Eibl-Eibesfeldt (1961) has reviewed his own studies on motor development in squirrels (*Sciurus vulgaris*), hamsters (*Cricetus cricetus*), and desert mice (*Meriones persicus*) that suggest the form of many species-characteristic movement patterns develops prior to, and is less dependent upon experience than, the functional orientation of these movement patterns. For example, in the squirrels he studied (Eibl-Eibesfeldt, 1951), gnawing and splitting movements used in opening nuts were at first poorly oriented and gained in precision with practice. Kear (1961) has found, similarly, that the basic movements used in dehusking seeds by finches develop before their effective utilization. Practice, as usually defined, plays a relatively minor role in the initial production of these motor patterns but is much more important in their effective use. To cite a related example, Meaney and Stewart (1981) report that in social development of rats, fighting and mounting patterns are often well coordinated from the perspective of the moving animal

prior to the time that orientation with respect to the partner is perfected. They conclude that the "behavior appears to become more appropriate to the salient stimuli in the environment and especially to stimuli from other animals" (p. 44). Many other ethological examples in a variety of species indicate that proper orientation often occurs after the form of the behavior is well developed, although the full spectrum of interplay among these dimensions deserves further careful study (Fentress, 1984).

Different stimuli may be involved in the elicitation of movement than are involved in its guidance (see, e.g., Hinde, 1970; Wolgin et al., 1980). A common natural history example is that auditory alarms may trigger flight that is directed to the nearest visible cover. The relative importance of various stimuli used in orienting movements may also change during development. The sensory basis for home orientation in kittens and huddling in rats, for example, is initially thermo-tactile, but by the end of the first weeks it is primarily olfactory (Rosenblatt, 1980).

That proper orientation of motor patterns develops after practice does not necessarily imply that learning is primarily responsible. Szechtman and Hall (1980) have found orientational changes in oral behavior elicited by tail pinching of preweanling rats. At 5 days elicited licks were not directed to any object; by 10 days licks were directed at nonfood objects; by 15 days licks were directed at either food or nonfood objects; by days 20–30 licks were directed primarily at food. Concurrently with the increased orientational specificity of tail pinch elicited licks, the required stimulation threshold decreased, giving further indication of maturational changes.

Cruze's (1935) study of the effects of learning and maturation on the development of pecking accuracy in chicks nicely illustrates how these two ontogenetic factors can interact. In Cruze's experiments, chicks were hatched and kept in the dark with no opportunity to peck at food. At 24-hr intervals, groups of chicks were taken out of the dark for the first time and tested for 25 pecks at food daily from then on. The number of errors chicks made on their first exposure to the test situation was inversely related to the amount of time they had been in the dark and therefore their age (figure 16.2). In Cruze's words, "maturation, in the absence of prac-

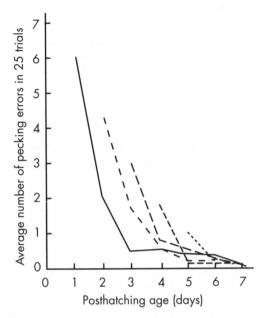

Figure 16.2 Data from Cruze (1935) illustrating the inter-play between maturation and learning in the development of pecking accuracy in chicks. Graphs depict the average number of pecking errors of five groups of chicks kept in the dark for 1–5 days, until the first test day. (Adapted from Cruze, 1935.)

tice, very effectively reduces the number of missing reactions to the point where they are almost elimi-nated" (p. 392). However, when practice was al-lowed, errors decreased in frequency and were eliminated much more quickly. Furthermore, accu-racy improved slightly over the first 25 pecks in groups allowed to peck on the first day. The differ-ential contributions of reinforcers during the estab-lishment of behavioral operants have been reviewed by Hogan and Roper (1978).

Spontaneous and elicited movements

In this section we move further beyond descriptions of motor patterns in development to potential prin-ciples of control. Our concern is with the balance between spontaneous and elicited actions. Three useful introductory perspectives are that (1) ten-dencies toward spontaneity and responsiveness to eliciting stimuli often coexist, (2) different aspects of the same movement can differ in their relative dependence upon central generation versus elicita-tion, and (3) within any given dimension abstracted

for analysis the balance between spontaneity and elicitation can change with time as well as with a variety of contextual factors.

1. Spontaneity
Experimental approaches to the concept of sponta-neity typically involve the removal of inputs that normally impinge upon a defined behavioral or neu-ronal system. If patterns of activity persist it is as-sumed that intrinsic circuitry is sufficient for the production of these patterns (i.e., extrinsic informa-tion sources are not necessary). In practice, most researchers are willing to allow a *permissive* role for extrinsic variables, such as sufficient muscular strength or body support to permit the expression of intrinsic potentialities. Early human locomotor patterns, for example, are studied in this way (Forssberg and Wallberg, 1981; Lagerspetz et al., 1971; Thelen, 1983; Zelazo, 1983).

Spontaneity can often be traced in a develop-mental context (see, e.g., reviews in Bekoff, 1981; Hamburger, 1977; Oppenheim, 1982; Provine, 1983; Szekely, 1976). As summarized by Hamburger (1977), this has led many workers to the "conception of the individual as, primarily a system of action" (as opposed to "reaction"). Historically, an emphasis upon spontaneity has not always pre-dominated. For example, in his studies of fetal movement patterns in man, Windle (1940) accepted the reflex as the basic unit of behavior and con-ducted his experiments accordingly. This was in contrast to the conclusions of Preyer (1885). Based upon analyses of motor patterns in chick embryos, Preyer stressed the "impulsive" nature of early movements. He pointed out that reflexes often could only be elicited after spontaneous movement was observed. Coghill's (1929) many careful obser-vations on behavioral development in the sala-mander *Ambystoma* led to similar conclusions.

A. EARLY EVIDENCE (INVERTEBRATES) Prosser's (1933) study of behavioral and neuromuscular development in embryonic earthworms (*Eisenia foetida*) is an elegant early attempt to come to grips with problems of motor spontaneity. Following the general strategy of Coghill (1929), Prosser sought to correlate changes in early motor expression with changes in underlying anatomy. He traced pro-cesses of differentiation from anterior to posterior, and laterally, in both behavioral and anatomical terms. Prosser noted that motor integration in embryos of *Eisenia* are present from the beginning of behavioral development, with segmental independence appearing later. Most important, Prosser found that these early movement patterns occurred *spontaneously* in the sense that no special experimental manipulations were necessary to elicit them. It was only later that the first responses to tactile stimulation could be elicited.

Wilson (1961) was the first investigator to demonstrate conclusively that motor patterns in invertebrates (in this case locusts) could to a large extent be accounted for by endogenous central pattern oscillators. Wilson, however, did not examine the development of these motor patterns. Bentley and Hoy (1970) found that flight and stridulation motor patterns are not spontaneously active in larval crickets in the strict sense of the term. These motor patterns could, however, be elicited by tonic stimulation (e.g., windstreams and flight), and/or removal of tonic inhibitory circuits (e.g., mushroom bodies and stridulation). As anticipated by Wilson (1961), the detailed patterning of these movements reflects mechanisms that are to a large extent endogenously organized (cf. Ikeda, 1976; Kristan, 1980; Provine, 1983; Wyman, 1976, for useful discussions).

B. RECENT DEVELOPMENTAL EMPHASES Elsner (1981) has recently reviewed a number of studies of motor development in insects. He stresses that electrophysiological techniques can be used to demonstrate motor circuitry that otherwise would not be expressed in overt motor patterns, Elsner is careful to make the important distinction between exogenous influences in the *elicitation* of behavior from possible exogenous *modifications* of the developmental process. He refers to studies by Weber (1972, 1974), who demonstrated that experience can influence the precision of larval flight motor patterns in crickets (as measured through cycle variability). This effect is very temporary (on the order of 10 min). While recognizing that sensory influences may normally contribute both to the functional integration of motor patterns and to that of their developmental precursors. Elsner concludes that many motor patterns in insects are fundamentally autonomous, even in their early stages of development (see also Elsner and Hirth, 1978; Halfmann and Elsner, 1978; and Linberg and Elsner, 1977).

Studies by Provine and his colleagues (see, e.g., Provine, 1976, 1983) on the cockroach (*Periplaneta emericana*) have clarified problems of spontaneity by severing interganglionic connectives and placing individual ganglia into culture. Electrophysiological analyses indicate that the resulting chain cultures show "spontaneous single unit discharges and multiunit bursts" (Provine, 1976, p. 218).

C. "IMPULSIVITY" IN VERTEBRATES As noted previously, Reyer (1885) argued nearly a century ago that "impulsive" behavior is critical to an understanding of motor patterns in vertebrate development. He based his conclusions upon a series of elegant studies of chick motor patterns in which motor responses elicited occurred systematically by external stimuli at a later developmental phase than did the first "spontaneous" actions. Hamburger et al. (1966) have confirmed many of Preyer's earlier insights. These later investigators, also working with chicks, removed the entire dorsal half of the lumbosacral spinal cord at 2–2.5 days of age (which removes all sensory feedback mediated via the dorsal root ganglia) and also performed a transection of the thoracic cord (eliminating descending influences from the brain). Through careful behavioral observations they conclude that "spontaneous" movements continued to develop normally until 15 days of incubation, after which time degeneration of the lateral motor columns appeared to contribute to a deterioration in motor performance. As Bekoff (1981) has summarized, this study "produced unequivocal proof that normal, spontaneous embryonic motility in the chick was centrally generated and, furthermore, that it could develop in the absence of both sensory and descending input" (p. 138) (cf. Bekoff et al., 1975; Corner, 1978; Hollyday, 1980; Landmesser, 1980; Sedlacek, 1978).

There have been numerous other studies on vertebrate species that make a similar point. Szekely (1976) reviews experiments on amphibian species indicating that histological differentiation of the spinal cord commonly occurs at an early embryonic age in spite of severe sensory restrictions. Many of these studies (and studies with chick embryos; see reviews in Bekoff, 1981; Hamburger, 1977; and Oppenheim, 1981) involve cord transplants and lead to the conclusion that within the spinal cord there are central pattern generators with relatively localized and resistant properties. In this sense workers such as Szekely speak of the underlying circuits as being "predetermined."

D. RETROGRADE DEVELOPMENT   In mammals, motor circuits also tend to develop in a "retrograde" fashion. Output pathways are established prior to the time that functioning sources of activation of these pathways become operative. As illustration, kitten forelimb mechanoreceptors develop an effective influence upon cells within the motor cortex at 60 days postnatally while outputs from the motor cortex can be detected by 45 days (Bruce and Tatton, 1980). Before 40 days, movement patterns can be observed, but these are often inefficient and variable. Circuitry within the cortex, cerebellum, and basal ganglia is still immature at this time. Bruce and Tatton conclude that functional outputs emerge prior to activation by afferents.

The retrograde progression in motor system development is of special interest in that it places limits upon the role of experience in the initial formation of output circuitry. Retrograde development also relates to the common occurrence of spontaneous activity prior to the time that reliable patterns of evoked behavior can be observed (see, e.g., review in Bekoff, 1981). Furthermore, a similar retrograde progression is found at many levels of the neuroaxis. In Saito's (1979) in vitro study of reflex development in the rat fetus, evidence for transynaptic evoked discharges in motoneurons of the 14.5-day isolated spinal cord was found, whereas the first reflex discharge via dorsal roots did not appear until prenatal day 15.5.

E. EXAMPLES OF HUMAN "SPONTANEITY"   Wolff (1966) has reviewed evidence that mouthing and other movements in postnatal human infants are common when the infants are drowsy. Particular movements have different periodicities, may (within limits) substitute for one another, and lose their apparent spontaneity of expression when alternative actions are elicited by strong stimuli. Thelen and her co-workers (see, e.g., Thelen, 1981, 1983; Thelen and Fisher, 1983) have demonstrated spontaneity of early kicking movements in human infants, together with evidence that these kicking movements can be affected by the infants' states of "arousal" (cf. Fentress, 1976, for a critical evaluation of this concept). Forssberg and Wallberg

(1981) argue that in the earliest forms of infant locomotion, spinal pattern generations can act "almost spontaneously" (cf. Grillner, 1981). Each of the preceding authors also points out that during later development, higher CNS circuitry may reduce movement spontaneity. The motor patterns become more precisely attached to complex eliciting events (cf. Prechtl, 1981). These conclusions are compatible with the proposition that during development higher CNS functions take on progressively more important roles in movement control (see, e.g., reviews in Doty, 1976; Gallistel, 1980; Teitelbaum, 1982).

F. SYNTHESIS AND REMAINING ISSUES   In sum, these data support the contention of many ethologists that early motor patterns show a high degree of spontaneity (in the sense that they do not depend upon afferent and/or descending pathway activity; see e.g, Hinde, 1982; Hoyle, 1984; Lorenz, 1981). While it is important to qualify the limits of presumed spontaneity, there can be no doubt that early motor rhythms reflect fundamental endogenous tendencies.

Many early motor patterns appear in the absence of causal factors that are of paramount importance at later ages. An example is Kruijt's (1964) ontogenetic study of social behavior in Burmese red junglefowl (Gallus gallus). Socially isolated young junglefowl frequently "attack" their own tails. This illustrates problems associated with concepts of spontaneity. The early attack movements are not associated with social interactions and are in that sense spontaneous (cf. Baerends-van Roon and Baerends, 1979; Leyhausen, 1973; Tooker and Miller, 1980). However, they are associated with proximal moving stimuli provided by the animal's own tail. Motor systems must be studied in their expressive contexts, and these contexts can change with age (cf. Fentress, 1984).

There are numerous cases in which the early expressions of motor patterns "surprise" us in that they are not associated with stimuli that play an important role in alter life and that we might assume to be necessary. For example, in a recent study employing central nervous system stimulation in young rats, Moran et al. (1983) found that motor patterns could be elicited in the absence of sensory cues that later control them (cf. Hall and Williams, 1983; see also preceding examples).

Such evidence does not imply that changes in early sensory events are necessarily without effect. Galef and Henderson (1972), for example, have demonstrated that experiences associated with suckling can have a marked effect upon later food preferences. (For recent reviews also see Galef, 1981, and Hall and Williams, 1983.) During the course of early motor patterns such as suckling, the organism has the opportunity to experience a variety of thermal, tactile, olfactory, and other cues that might contribute to later adaptive functions, including social behavior (Alberts, 1981; Rosenblatt, 1976).

2. Elicited movements

A. REFLEX ACTIONS   Reflexive responses and their development are in many respects more easily studied than are movements that occur "spontaneously" outside of the experimenter's control, and such studies have a long history (see, e.g., Windle, 1944; Hamburger, 1977; Burke, 1981). While the elicitation of isolated reflexes is not our primary concern, reflex elicitation provides a valuable technique for the clarification of a number of issues and principles. Reflexes can be elicited prenatally in a number of animal species. For this to be possible, muscles, motor neurons, and their afferents must be functional. This does not imply that initial reflex patterns are identical to those of later life. Further, as emphasized by Carmichael (1970) and others, many early forms of responsiveness are myogenic in origin; that is, they appear prior to the establishment of sensorimotor connections (cf. Bekoff, 1981; Saito, 1979; and p. 225).

Reflexes tend to develop in cephalocaudal and proximodistal directions. One of the earliest studies to demonstrate this in mammals was Angulo y González's (1932) insightful, albeit qualitative, set of observations on prenatal behavior in rats. These gradients of reflex development were confirmed in a more detailed investigation by Narayanan et al. (1971) and reflect the order of ontogeny of spinal motoneurons (Hollyday, 1980; Landmesser, 1980). Similar developmental gradients are found in many areas of the central nervous system (Cowan, 1978; Jacobson, 1978).

Many early elicited reflexes involve widespread movements that in later development become more localized. For example, Bergstrom et al. (1962) found that stimulation of the trigeminal nerve in fetal guinea pigs initially produced widespread movements of the neck, limbs, and trunk. Later in fetal development this generalized response was replaced by restricted movements of the head. Gatev (1972) has shown, similarly, that both early monosynaptic and polysynaptic reflexes are widespread in children, with subsequent restriction. As emphasized by Hines (1942) in her classic study of motor development in rhesus monkeys, following the period during which elicited motor patterns become restricted there can be a variety of subsequent re-elaborations that may transcend initial reflex dependencies. (See also reviews by Bekoff, 1981; Hamburger, 1977; Oppenheim, 1981; Provine, 1983.)

The degree of "irradiation" for reflexes seen at any given age can also depend in part upon the strength of stimulation (Corner, 1978; Sherrington, 1906). An elegant study of early irradiation and gradual restriction of reflexes is Saito's (1979) in vitro investigation of reflex development in fetal rats. Saito demonstrated that both the development of inhibitory circuits and neuronal cell death sculpt the initially broad reflex excitation. These two processes – (1) inhibitory circuits becoming functional after excitatory circuits and (2) neuronal death – appear frequently in studies of nervous system development (see, e.g., Burke, 1981; Cowan, 1978; Lewis, 1981; Purves and Lichtman, 1980; Wolff, 1981) and undoubtedly contribute to ontogenetic "parcellation" in a number of instances (cf. Ebbesson, 1980). While inhibitory circuits tend to become fully operational after the onset of activity in excitatory circuits, increasingly sophisticated techniques have indicated an earlier onset of inhibitory contributions to patterned movement in various vertebrate species than has often been suspected from earlier studies (Oppenheim and Reitzel, 1975). A recent illustration of developmental segregation is Brown's and Booth's (1983) study on the distribution of motor axons entering the gluteus muscle from segmental roots L4 and L5 in rats. In this study the overlap in distribution at birth was greatly reduced by postnatal day 11 through a process of synapse elimination.

B. EFFECTOR PROPERTIES   Changes in effectors, as well as in neural circuits, contribute importantly to reflex development. In addition to early poly-neuronal and polysnaptic innervation of muscles in development, muscle properties themselves un-dergo marked changes (e.g., differentiation into fast and slow muscle groups; Lewis, 1981; Navarrete and Vrbová, 1983). Fascinating lines of current research show the intimacy of nerve and muscle properties in a number of species. Two especially interesting invertebrate examples are the demon-strations (1) by Lang et al. (1978) that American lobsters housed in smooth-bottomed tanks (without gravel to manipulate) during certain larval stages will grow two cutter claws with predominately fast muscle rather than a single cutter and crusher claw (with slow muscle) and (2) by Mellon and Stevens (1979) that cutting the nerve to the snapper claw in hatchling alpheid shrimp will lead the opposite pincher claw to be transformed into a snapper. Thus changes in peripheral activity can have marked consequences on muscle differentiation on either the same or the opposite side of the body. In chicks it is now clearly established that motoneuron cell death can be modulated by muscle activity. By immobilizing chick embryos, Pittman and Oppenheim (1979) reduced the normal decline of motoneuron numbers in both the brachial and lum-bar motor columns.

There is evidence in mammals that motoneuron activity can control gene expression in muscle fibers, even in adults. Matafora et al. (1980) found marked changes in mRNA sequences of 8-day den-ervated rat gastrocnemius muscles, and Streter et al. (1975) found that cross-innervated fast and slow muscles in rabbits developed changed twitch char-acteristics as well as protein composition. That skeletal properties not only change in development but can be dependent on muscle activity is also well known (see, e.g., Drachman and Coulombre, 1962 – joint development in chicks; Walker and Quarles, 1976 – palate development in mice).

C. CONTROL NETWORKS Changes in reflexes and related processes during development clearly can involve a number of interconnected properties, many of which are just beginning to surface. Because of the richness of potential developmental connections in even relatively simple "elicited movements," elucidation of these processes will have to be sought at a variety of levels, and with an appropriate appreciation for the dynamic matura-tional processes that accompany them (cf. Thelen, 1983, and Zelazo, 1983, for recent related discus-sions with reference to human locomotion).

Certainly, routes of reflex *control* can also change importantly during development, as seen in the transition between vestibular and visual dominance in humans for early righting reflexes (Kuypers, 1981) and in changes in response to nociceptive stimuli in rats (Stelzner, 1971). It is also well estab-lished that the expression of many early reflexes can be suppressed through the subsequent develop-ment of higher CNS regions (see, e.g., DeGroat et al., 1978 – reflexive micturition and defecation in kittens; for additional reviews see Bower, 1979; Doty, 1976; Hofer, 1981; Peiper, 1973).

D. COMPLEXITIES IN ELICITED MOVEMENT Certainly not all forms of early elicited movement qualify as reflexes in the classical sense of the term (Sherrington, 1906). Because of complex patterns of reflex interaction and descending influences, the precise boundary line between reflex and nonreflex in the intact animal is frequently difficult to deter-mine (Berridge and Fentress, in press). There are, for example, a number of documented cases of sen-sorimotor responses in prenatal or larval animals that begin with simple movements only to be fol-lowed by complex sequences involving central pat-tern generators. To cite a recent example, Soffe et al. (1983) have demonstrated that in newt embryos (*Triturus vulgaris*) a tactile stimulus applied to the head produces turning of the head away from the source of the stimulus, followed by a complex pat-tern of swimming movements. That there are cen-trally patterned substrates for these swimming movements can be demonstrated by a variety of means (e.g., through recordings of motoneuron dis-charge in paralyzed animals). In very young animals head turning and subsequent swimming responses are often disassociated.

Measures of prenatal responses to environ-mental stimuli can often be used to demonstrate functional sensorimotor pathways that might not otherwise be anticipated. For example, Armitage et al. (1980) have shown that in sheep, motor activity can be elicited prenatally by auditory stimuli. Motor activity also occurs in third-trimester human fetuses in response to acoustic events (DeCasper and Fifer, 1980), and as early as postnatal day 1, human infants are said to synchronize movements in rhythm with adult speech (Condon and Sander, 1974). That these early responses may, under certain circumstances, affect later behavior is suggested in a study by Vince (1979). She exposed prenatal guinea pigs to mildly aversive acoustic stimuli and found, using measurements of heart rate change, a subsequent reduction in responsiveness to the stimuli. While these changes are almost certainly not focused upon motor pathways per se, Vince's studies establish the need to evaluate measures of motor performance in the intact organism as representing products of complex control networks and previous experience.

Elicited postnatal motor patterns in development often display remarkable degrees of sophistication. Perhaps most dramatic among these are early patterns of imitative movements in human infants. Meltzoff and Moore (1977) have reported that as early as 2 weeks of age infants can articulate recognizable facsimiles of several adult facial expressions. Here we have an instance not only of a considerable degree of control by the infants over their own facial musculature, but also an appropriate responsiveness to stimuli of clear social import.

One interesting laboratory approach to motor and behavioral development in animals is to stimulate central nervous system pathways directly. Gorska and Czarkowska (1973) applied this methodology in an ontogenetic evaluation of motor cortex function in dogs from birth of 12 weeks of age. Their data include observations of comparatively poorly organized somatotopic representation of body parts, incomplete dominance of contralateral movements, limited repertoire, plus short duration and variable movements with a high stimulation threshold in the youngest (birth to 4 weeks) animals. By 12 weeks adult response patterns were found, but still with elevated thresholds compared with adults.

In a recent study, Moran et al. (1983) provided electrical stimulation to the median forebrain bundle at the lateral hypothalamus in 3-, 6-, 10-, and 15-day-old rats. Pups 10 days and younger became behaviorally activated, as expressed through a variety of motor patterns, including mouthing, licking, pawing, gaping, probing, stretching, and even lordosis. As the animals grew older, these motor patterns showed signs of improved organization and often became increasingly dependent upon

the presence of appropriate goal objects. By varying stimulus frequency, differential changes in various forms of motor expression could also be obtained. For example, stretch and lordosis responses "appear to represent 'end behaviors,' occurring at the height of behavioral activation" (p. 13). The importance of central stimulus parameters in eliciting different forms of behavior has also been demonstrated by Beagley (1976) in adult rats.

As animals grow older there is commonly a progressive restriction in the movements elicited by a given stimulus, along with an improvement in their organization. The relatively nonspecific nature of early elicited motor patterns deserves further detailed study. It is likely that developmental restrictions in movement often reflect increased specificity of motivational rather than motor pathways. Further, variation of early elicited motor details may in part depend upon the young animal's current posture (Fentress, 1981a, b, 1983b, d). Mature animals with high-level CNS damage are similar to young animals in that they often become "entrapped" by particular postural and exteroceptive sensory events (see, e.g., Deliagina et al., 1975; Teitelbaum, 1982). Conversely, in the study by Moran et al. (1983), responses of young rats to central nervous system stimulation were *less* dependent upon sensory events in the environment than were responses of older animals. Here motivational control pathways were activated directly in the young rats, which suggests that these pathways may have a high degree of intrinsic organization, and well-established descending connections to motor pathways, prior to the time that they are addressed by sensory events that later play a critical role in their activation.

There are clearly a wide variety of central as well as peripheral sources of behavioral activation. As stressed by Wolgin (1982), both young animals and human infants may fail to express fully their motor capabilities unless they are appropriately "aroused." Once the appropriate circuits are activated, previously hidden competencies in motor performance are often revealed (see also Prechtl, 1981). A recent study by Smiley and Wilbanks (1962) on the effects of noise on the precocial elicitation of play and locomotion in young rats indicates the power of such manipulations within a developmental context. Similarly, experiments by Szechtman and Hall (1980) on the ontogeny of oral behavior in rats indicate that various sources of behavioral activation may be used to clarify underlying developmental (e.g., dopaminergic) circuit properties. Certain of these neurochemically mediated substrates not only alter responses to specified sensory events but also activate motor patterns in development more directly (cf. Tamasy et al., 1981, on dopaminergic and serotonergic pathways in the development of swimming abilities in rats). Thelen (1981) has argued that activation in human infants may trigger previously formed motor stereotypes that are relatively independent of sensory factors in their expression. Movement details, in this case, may be relatively "hard wired" (Thelen and Fisher, 1983) and respond in a characteristic way over a number of activation sources (cf. Turkewitz et al., 1983).

E. SUMMARY   Elicited movements have provided valuable information on motor development. These movements, examined in a variety of invertebrate and vertebrate species, range from relatively simple reflexes to much more complex patterns in which environmental activation and central programming are intimately connected. It is often difficult to localize the critical foci of developmental change in elicited actions due to interactions among sensory, motor, and higher CNS events. However, careful experiments on animals and detailed observations of early human movement patterns have begun to clarify some of the issues.

It is important to emphasize that developmental changes in elicited movements can be examined somewhat separately in terms of movement form, causal antecedents, and functional consequences. The data reviewed in this section also suggest that while some elicited motor patterns in development exhibit progressive improvement, other motor patterns may be perfected early in ontogeny, to be disassembled and perhaps reassembled into novel patterns as development proceeds. These new motor patterns may also come under different systems of control as the functional needs of the organism change. Other early motor patterns may be relatively nonfunctional, yet point unambiguously toward future capabilities. Circuits underlying many motor patterns in development can only be revealed through special experimental techniques.

3. Concluding comments on the distinction between spontaneous and elicited behavior

While we have found it convenient in this section of our review to emphasize the polarities of spontaneous "*versus*" elicited motor patterns in development, we emphasize that the distinction is not absolute. In "elicited" motor patterns, fluctuations of internal state may change the effectiveness of any given stimulus, even in simple reflexes. Concepts of "spontaneity" are necessarily relative in the dual sense that one must always ask, "Spontaneous with respect to what?" and "Spontaneous to what degree?" Central and peripheral events necessarily work in concert. The issue is one of relative (rather than absolute) parcellation.

There is a close conceptual parallel between any forced dichotomy of evoked and spontaneous behavior and inadequacies of the nature versus nurture perspectives on developmental processes. Emphases upon evoked behavior serve merely to stress the importance of *measured* system inputs, while emphases upon spontaneous behavior serve merely to stress the limits of specified system inputs. Demonstrating the importance of one source of control does not negate the importance of another (cf. Hebb, 1955).

Higher-order motor patterns

Basic behavioral and biological functions are often achieved through the simultaneous and sequential articulation of physically distinctive movements. This has led workers in ethology and related disciplines to seek rules by which abstracted actions are joined together. It is "how response units are related" (Hinde and Stevenson, 1969, p. 293) that poses many of the most important problems for developmental analyses.

In this section of our review we examine multiple movements from a perspective that complements the problems of dimensionality in motor behavior already discussed. "Because most natural motor behaviors require complex interactions among multiple movements, conclusions as to the potential contributions of sensorimotor mechanisms based upon unidimensional movement criteria . . . may be premature" (Abbs et al., 1984, p. 196). The importance of examining integrated motor patterns has received growing notice in recent years. Multiple movements may be embedded within a number of higher-order sequences. As summarized by Menn (1981) in the context of human speech, "some motor sequences evidently are easier to coordinate than others, for reasons that we should be starting to study" (p. 132).

1. Integrated sequences and ontogeny

Many motor sequences in young animals are incomplete and appear to be of limited functional utility. As animals get older, new dimensions may be added to the sequence and existing processes may be combined in novel ways. In their study of kitten development, Baerends-van Roon and Baerends (1979) subdivided motor development into three phases characterized by (1) exclusive domination of body musculature, as seen in swaying; (2) legs used, but in a manner secondary to the body; and (3) legs used in a manner relatively independently of gross body movements. "During the first four weeks the behaviour patterns distinguished develop progressively, essentially by the addition of new elements. After this period changing continues, but in our opinion these changes have to be considered as adaptive modifications and combinations of the existing patterns; no essentially new patterns appear" (p. 23). Interruptions within functional motor sequences were also observed frequently in young animals.

A recent study by Etienne et al. (1982) on the ontogeny of hoarding in golden hamsters also illustrates ethological approaches to the development of sequential motor patterns. These authors conducted observations of four litters, beginning on postnatal day 13. Immature forms of pouch filling and emptying were seen first, but actions were not integrated into coherent behavioral sequences. The young animals frequently exhibited evidence of goal-directed actions even though these actions were in themselves imperfectly organized.

Coordinated hoarding trips in the Etienne et al. study were observed from day 21, once motor patterns of inserting and extracting food had gained definitive form. The investigators isolated three ways of inserting food into pouches (one is mature) and five ways of extracting food from the pouches (one is mature). Well-integrated hoarding has four distinct phases that follow each other in a fixed order. The order in which young pups perform constituent acts of hoarding was unpredictable.

Early hoarding patterns were uncoordinated in space and time. For example, inserting and extracting were "randomly" associated. Constituent parts of hoarding were intermingled with other classes of action in the young animals, without the adult temporal groupings of functionally related actions. Increases in the frequency of mature motor patterns accompanied decreases in immature motor patterns.

The decreasing performance of immature actions occurred in a regular sequence, with those motor patterns that were most different from mature movements disappearing first. As the motor patterns became more clearly differentiated, so too did the sequential phases within which these motor patterns were grouped. "The fact that the decrease of immature hoarding components coincides with the reduction of less specific, 'clumsy' activities (such as taking and dropping food), shows that the differentiation of particular motor patterns is accompanied by a general progress in the coordination of movements" (p. 42).

A rich nexus of changes can be traced in the ontogeny of such species-characteristic motor sequences. A possibility that has interested many workers is that the sequential order of movement patterns found in adult animals is paralleled by the ontogenic order in which the movements emerge. Whether or not "integration recapitulates ontogeny" as a general rule is questionable at present (although within limits there often appears to be a formal association in motor sequencing over these two very different time frames). While in most of the hamsters studied by Etienne et al. movements of food insertion developed before those of food extraction, in socially isolated animals mature forms of insertion and extraction appeared more or less simultaneously. The transition to mature hoarding occurred suddenly in these isolated animals.

2. Sequence "pieces" and "relations"

For action properties to be connected they cannot be completely separate. Precisely where the interconnections among otherwise separate motor properties exist and the consequences of these interconnections upon properties that might otherwise be viewed as independent events represent difficult challenges to present research (Fentress, 1984). It is important to determine processes that may transcend abstracted "components" of action (e.g., whether these "components" exhibit regular forms of contextual modification). A number of movement properties, such as the precision of timing, can change during ontogeny and be shared among *sets* of actions. This indicates that the individual actions are either directly influencing one another or share common control processes. Excellent examples are provided by recent studies on speech development of human infants (Cooper, 1977; Kent, 1981). A basic point of these studies is that otherwise individually defined articulatory components change their timing and related properties all together and in this way maintain a relative invariance of overall sequential structure (rather like changing the tempo of an entire melody line in music; Fentress, 1978, 1981b). Kent (1981) compares the articulatory invariances among phonetic attributes in human speech to schema theory in motor learning, where the individual must develop regularities among performance attributes to achieve functionally adequate sequences.

In a wide variety of human motor skills, such as typing (Terzuolo and Viviani, 1980), handwriting (Viviani and Terzuolo, 1980), speech (Tuller et al., 1982; Weismer and Ingrisano, 1979), cycling and piano playing (Whiting, 1980), the *relative timing* of component activities remains invariant even when the overall speed of the sequence changes. This indicates that skilled motor performance is not a simple assemblage of components, but that there are cohesive properties that affect the integrity of the sequence as a whole.

For rapidly performed sequences of movement, anticipatory adjustments can increase the cohesion of elements within the sequence (Bizzi, 1981; Glencross, 1980; Kelso, 1981). Action components are in this sense "coarticulated"; merging together into higher blockings of expression (Liberman and Studdert-Kennedy, 1978). The fragmentation of movement often observed in young organisms reflects an imperfect synthesis of these action components. As Whiting (1980) has summarized, "motor skills . . . do not grow by a simple addition of elements, but by a structural rearrangement – by analysis and synthesis" (p. 543). Even relatively simple motor patterns, such as rodent grooming, are similar in their progressively "coarticulated" expression with age (Fentress, 1983d).

Interesting limitations in sequential motor performance are found in many young mammals, as well as in mammals with various forms of central nervous system disruption. Employing central stimulation in rats, Moran et al. (1983) found that infant animals (1) frequently performed motor sequences in the absence of sensory cues necessary for adults, and (2) showed sequences of movement that cut across functional categories (e.g., lick, probe, gape, lordosis). Vanderwolf (1983) found that decorticate rats would normally show grooming elements but not full sequences as "inappropriate" acts often intervened (such as walking away). "The behavioral deficit in decorticate or decerebrate rats appears to be largely a matter of failing to perform behaviors in the right place at the right time" (p. 85; Vanderwolf, 1983). Similar phenomena are found in many young animals (Fentress, 1984; Teitelbaum, 1982).

In a recent study, Moss and Hogg (1983) rewarded infants 12–18 months of age for successfully manipulating metal rods in sequences involving the lifting of two rods, connecting them together, placing the connected rods in a hole, and moving the rods around a track. Their study was designed explicitly to test the idea that modules of action are sequenced together in invariant form when higher-level skills are perfected. Contrary to the strict modularity view, variation within modules increased with mastery of the sequential task.

It is clear that any full analysis of motor patterns in development must take into account not only the form of the behavior expressed but also the various "strategies" employed with respect to higher-order goals. In many cases it is useful to make a distinction between *how* an organism goes about doing something and its action details defined in isolation. Related to this problem is the logical distinction between capabilities and strategies of action, to which we shall return. Differential roles of experience in the descriptively separable layers of motor performance constitute a related issue.

3. Roles of experience

A common perspective in ethology and related disciplines is that experience during development plays an increasingly important role at higher levels of motor organization (e.g., Eibl-Eibesfeldt, 1956; Lorenz, 1981). Basic motor "components" are viewed as having a strong genetic base, since they take on an invariant form even under diverse developmental conditions (within limits). The *rules of connection* among these "components," as well as the *orientation* of the movement sequences they comprise, are viewed to be more dependent upon particular developmental histories (for an exception see pp. 233–5).

An excellent example of this perspective can be seen in the work by Kruijt (1964) on Burmese red junglefowl noted previously. By rearing animals with different degrees of social experience and by documenting the detailed patterns of their motor behavior, Kruijt was able to conclude that a "lack of social experience has little influence on the motor side of behaviour, but much more so on the way in which the motor patterns are released, orientated and integrated with each other" (p. 170). For example, fighting and mating movements in birds reared in social isolation may appear to be well coordinated in terms of the animal expressing them yet fail to be appropriately coordinated with respect to the birds' social partners. Thus, as we have seen previously in the discussion of eliciting factors in motor development, total motor performance must be judged along a number of dimensions and in explicit association with the contexts that may trigger, guide, and modulate the sequences in question.

Prechtl (1981) reviews evidence suggesting that orientational parameters of movement in mammals, particularly those that involve the coordination of visual information with directed expression, are more sensitive to experiential distortions than are the individual "units" of movement per se. A number of disruptions of normal central nervous system processes also have their most obvious effects upon "higher-order" properties of integrated movement sequences (see, e.g., reviews in Teitelbaum, 1977; Vanderwolf, 1983). Not surprisingly, the brain regions that are viewed to have particularly important effects on "higher-order" aspects of motor performance are those regions that are also considered to be "higher-level" (and later developing).

Sociality integrated motor patterns

Interactive motor patterns in social behavior must be properly oriented with respect to specific social and environmental situations and must occur in the proper context to be functional. For the communicative actions of birds and mammals, contextual variations can alter the interpreted "meaning" of

the signal by the recipient (Green and Marler, 1979; Goosen and Kortmulder, 1979; Gould, 1983; Marler, 1967; Maurus and Pruscha, 1972; Petersen, 1981; Shalter et al., 1977; Smith, 1965). The social contexts in which signals are given have been shown to affect the probabilities of subsequent behavior by the sender (macaques: Goosen and Kortmulder, 1979) and the elicited response in the recipient (mice: Butler, 1980; macaques: Lillehir and Snowdon, 1978; wolf pups: Shalter et al., 1977). Displays by young animals are often less accurate predictors of their own subsequent behavior than are adult displays (Simpson, 1973).

The environment in which social behavior patterns normally develop includes conspecifics. These social agents differ from other components of the physical environment in their greater mobility, decreased predictability, and ability to act upon their surroundings. More importantly, the information processing abilities of these agents make social feedback and mutual influence possible, providing the infant with a wealth of potential stimulation and information (Mason, 1979). Watson (1981) has argued that behavioral development can be influenced directly by such behavior–stimulus contingencies. The ability of human infants to recognize when facial movements are correlated with speech (Kuhl and Meltzoff, 1982) and to imitate both facial and manual gestures (Meltzoff and Moore, 1977) shows that infants are capable of both perceiving and performing contingent behavior.

Although in some sense all social behavior involves communication, for the purposes of the present discussion we find it helpful to treat communication by relatively discrete signals (and human speech as a somewhat special case) separately from behavioral relations among individuals.

1. Communication

The importance of effective communication for survival in a social environment has been recognized since Darwin's (1872) classic work, and many ethological studies have focused on the communication systems used by social animals. In general, the forms of the motor patterns used in social displays of nonhumans have been found to develop with a less appreciable role being played by experiential factors whereas contextual variations in the use of these signals, and the ability to respond properly to the signals of others, is relatively more dependent on experience (Burghardt, 1977; Fox and Cohen, 1977; Green and Marler, 1979). [Some exaggeration of facial expression has been reported in hand-reared monkeys (Bolwig, 1964), and frowning, a display frequently exhibited by rhesus mothers, occurs in mother-raised infants but is not exhibited by terrycloth-surrogate-raised infants (Hansen, 1966), suggesting that the form and expression of these monkey displays are somewhat dependent on environmental conditions.]

Shortly after birth most mammals vocalize. These sounds generally evoke approach or contact by the mother. "Some calls that originate in infancy and appear in the mother–infant context reappear later in life in similar contexts but serve different functions" (Gould, 1983, p. 265). For example, adult female Japanese monkeys use a similar call when sexually soliciting a partner as infants do when soliciting contact from their mothers (Green, 1981). Ontogenetic changes in vocalization and the contexts in which they occur can also differ between the sexes while still sharing some unspecified underlying causal mechanism (Green, 1981).

In some species (e.g., stumptail macaques, Chevalier-Skolnikoff, 1974) the number of different vocal motor patterns increases from the infant to adult with a decrease in vocal activity toward the end of the juvenile stage (Gould, 1983). Specific calls may also undergo some changes in acoustic properties during ontogeny (e.g., Chevalier-Skolnikoff, 1974; Field, 1978, 1979; Lieblich et al., 1980; Newman and Symmes, 1982), generally exhibiting less variability in physical structure (e.g., Field, 1978, 1979; Newman and Symmes, 1982).

Observations that vocalizations usually occur in concomitance with gross head and body movements in neonate kittens (Levine et al., 1980) and wolves (McLeod, personal observation) indicate that these early vocalizations are controlled less independently of general activity than in older animals. Similarly, early facial expressions in human infants involve flashing "fragments of smiles, grimaces, and frowns and these bouts of facial activity tend to occur when the infant's head turns" (Hofer, 1981, p. 105). At the "local" level, these movements appear as fragmented components of adult expression while exhibiting connectivity with general patterns of movement.

A. MONKEY ALARM CALLS In a study by Seyfarth and Cheney (Seyfarth and Cheney, 1980; Seyfarth

et al., 1980a, b; reviewed in Seyfarth and Cheney, 1982), adult vervet monkeys were found to give acoustically distinct alarm calls to leopards, martial eagles, pythons, and baboons. Each type of call elicited different, appropriate responses from conspecifics (e.g., look up and/or run into dense brush in response to eagle alarms). Infants and juveniles, however, gave alarms to a much wider variety of species, though the type of alarm an infant gave in response to a stimulus was not arbitrary (e.g., eagle alarms were given by infants to a variety of birds but not to terrestrial animals).

Although there was no significant difference between age classes in the probability of showing a "wrong" response to broadcast alarm calls, there was a trend toward decreasing errors with age. Infants were more likely to make wrong responses if they were more than 2 m from their mothers and generally responded to all alarm calls by looking at their mothers (Seyfarth and Cheney, 1980). Infants also sometimes emitted different calls when they joined in alarm call "bouts" initiated by other group members, whereas adults and juveniles always called with the same type of alarm (Seyfarth et al., 1980b).

These findings suggest that the association between predatory species and alarm call type sharpens as infants grow older. The stimuli that elicit each of the different signals become more specific as do the developing individuals' responses to the alarms, possibly because of "subtle reinforcement" (Seyfarth and Cheney, 1982). This is consistent with the statement by Newman and Symmes (1982) that the "primary role of learning in the acoustic behavior of primates, including humans, may be gradually to restrict the variability of vocal utterances and behavioral responsiveness with age. By this process, the individual would acquire, at maturity, a considerable degree of communicative predictability" (p. 272).

A similar process of reinforcement by the human infant's social environment has been proposed to account for the emergence of social smiling from the nonspecific smiling that occurs in response to a wide variety of stimuli prior to 3 months of age (Emde et al., 1976).

B. BIRD SONG Studies on the ontogeny of bird song have been most productive in determining the combined contributions of genetic and epigenetic factors in the development of complex communica- tive motor patterns in a variety of species. The neu- roanatomical regions involved in vocal learning, hormonal effects on these areas, and the roles of both auditory and proprioceptive feedback have also been studied in birds (see, e.g., Nottebohm, 1980). We will mention only a few studies that illus- trate issues relevant to the present discussion.

Song development in several bird species starts as an "amorphous, highly variable and unstructured subsong" (Marler and Peters, 1982a, p. 445). As described in detail for swamp sparrows (Marler and Peters, 1982a), syllables then appear in a very rudi- mentary form of unidentifiable sequences. Note sequences, though variable, can then be identified and syllables can start to be repeated. The syllables then become less variable, are produced as trills, and occur in a progressively more stable order. There is a trend that the "acquisition of the smaller acoustic unit [is] accomplished before a complete commitment is made to higher levels of temporal organization" (Marler and Peters, 1981, p. 86). At the same time the variability in song duration is greatly reduced and the number of phrases per song decreases (as does song duration). Subsong also ex- hibits a greater frequency range than crystallized song and tends to be quieter (table 16.1).

During plastic song, swamp sparrows produce four to five times as much song material as is needed for normal adult song (Marler and Peters, 1982a,b). The excess is then subjected to selective attrition (Marler and Peters, 1982b). When young swamp sparrows are exposed to tape recordings of both swamp sparrow syllables and syllables of the closely related song sparrow, they later produce many more conspecific syllables than song sparrow syllables (Marler and Peters, 1982b) in part (at least) because of early perceptual selectivity (Dooling and Searcy, 1980). During crystallization of song production there is also a trend for any song sparrow syllables that might be present to be selectively rejected. Marler and Peters (1982b) suggest that "species- specific motor constraints [possibly] contribute to this 2nd selective phase" (p. 375) as components that fit more comfortably with the "motor predispo- sitions" of the species are selectively retained. Both perceptual and motor constraints may therefore in- fluence the development of motor patterns used in song production. Baptista and Petrinovich (1984), however, have recently argued for the importance of social factors in the development of avian song. They review studies showing that several species will copy whole songs from a live tutor but only limited copying occurs when exposed to tape re- corded songs. Baptista's and Petrinovich's data demonstrate that white-crowned sparrows could learn the alien song of a strawberry finch social tutor even when conspecifics could also be heard but not seen. These authors suggest that social factors can override predispositions to learn species-specific songs.

Other issues in motor pattern development are

Table 16.1   Stages in the song development of swamp sparrows[a]

		Syllables			Songs	
	Stage[b]	*Number*[c]	*Form*	*Repetitions*	*Form*	*Duration*
Crystallized song	I	2.9	Stereotyped	Clear trills	Stable order	Short
	II		Stereotyped	Clear trills	Variable order	Short
Plastic song	III	9.5	Minor variations	Clear trills	Stable order	Longer
	IV		Variable	Clear trills	Variable order ⎤	Long and
	V	12–13	Rudiments	Some	Variable order ⎦	variable
Subplastic song	VI		Rudiments	None	Variable order	Variable
Subsong	VII		None	None	None	Variable

[a] Adapted from Marler and Peters, 1982a.
[b] Stages II and III may represent alternate rather than sequential stages.
[c] Average number of syllables per individual per session.

illustrated by Guttinger's (1981) study of song development in deaf canaries. Canary songs exhibit three main levels of temporal organization but a highly plastic choice in the combination of notes. Briefly, these levels of organization are as follows: (1) Single notes or syllables are the shortest components with individual repertoires of 30–60. (2) "Tours" or trills exhibit a correlation between note duration and repetitions and systematic changes in repetition rate of the tour duration. (3) Phrases or songs exhibit characteristic intervals between syllables, between tours, and between phrases; a restricted number of vocal patterns that can occur after pauses longer than 1.2 sec; and a relation between tour and succeeding interval durations (short tours being followed by longer pauses). Following deafening of juveniles and adults these hierarchical levels of organization were differentially affected. In contrast to the view that sequential organization is in general more susceptible to experiential modifications than the form of motor components (see p. 231), in this case: "The higher orders, the syntactic rules, develop quite normally whereas at the lowest level there is a dramatic reduction not only in repertoire size but also in the diversity of tonal quality" (p. 338). Although auditory monitoring and learning both play important roles in the differentiation of individual notes, Guttinger suggests that the two motor patterns involved (determining the pattern of respiratory movements and the impedance of the syrinx) might be either centrally programmed or monitored by a "proprioceptive template."

Another species that exhibits a complex and variable song structure (as opposed to the relatively simple, stereotyped songs of sparrows), the parasitic widow bird (*Tetraeunura fisheri*) sings both species-specific phrases and vocalizations learned from the host species. In this species, both the species-specific phrases and the syntactic rules controlling switches to learned contraspecific vocalizations are under clear genetic influence and are to a large extent model independent (Nicolai, 1973; cited in Guttinger, 1981). These parallel findings have suggested that in species that exhibit a variable song, in terms of the component syllables, the syntactic rules of connection between syllables may encode species identification (Guttinger, 1981).

C. HUMAN SPEECH   The motor system used in speech is a complex one involving approximately 100 muscles (versus 7 in song birds). Parallels between the ontogenetic development of song in birds and speech in humans, however, have attracted much interest (see, e.g., Marler and Peters, 1981; Studdert-Kennedy, 1981). The issues arising require consideration in any study of motor development.

The first sounds produced by human neonates have been described as discomfort sounds or crying (Cooper, 1977; Emde et al., 1976). Stark (1980) reports that vocalizations recorded in the first 15 weeks of life can be classified as cry, discomfort, vegetative, and comfort sounds. Prior to 15 weeks these vocal categories were highly correlated with nonvocal behavior. After this time the relations to nonvocal behavior decreases as the infant gains control over "reflexive" sound production. As with other developing motor systems, it is important to note that many anatomical and neuromuscular changes in the speech apparatus are occurring during the ontogeny of speech and that these changes may alter the physical constraints acting upon the system (Bosma, 1975; Kent, 1976, 1981).

Between the ages of 16 and 30 weeks, which Stark labels the "vocal play" stage.

> The infant takes apart the elements, of which his utterances are formed, selects simple elements, produces them over and over, prolongs them, elaborates them, and divides the elaborated versions into new segment types by means of glottal stops and silent intervals. The infant then shortens them again and puts the new segment type or new element back in series with others that are of earlier origin or are more highly practiced. . . . This disassembly of parts and their reassembly in new series is an essential characteristic of all subsequent development in speech production [Stark, 1980, p. 86].

By 10 months of age, consonant–vowel transitions are handled efficiently in sequences (Stark, 1980) and the relatively rigid timing characteristics of syllabification that conform to natural language restrictions are apparent. Reduplicated babbling (e.g., "bababa") is common "without communicative intent" (Stark, 1980) or any evidence of a denotative meaning associated with the babble (Oller, 1980). The infant frequently focuses on particular syllables at this stage to the exclusion of others (Oller, 1980). The similarities between babbling and rhythmical stereotypies (cf. Thelen, 1981) in their unidirectionality and functional isolation have been pointed out by Kent and Murray (1982), who also note that both reduplicated babbling and nonspeech stereotyped rhythms peak in frequency at roughly the same age.

Over the longer period during which the child develops his referential speaking abilities, speech is marked by severe restrictions in the range of sounds produced (Cooper, 1977; Locke, 1983). Even after the child's phonetic repertoire is complete, the motor skills of speech appear to continue being perfected (Kent, 1976). These changes in speech production are characterized by diminished variability of segment durations and spectra, a general reduction in segment durations, and increased anticipatory articulation (Kent, 1981). As we have seen in previous sections, a similar separation of articulatory profiles into attributes of relative restrictions, variability, duration, and anticipation can be applied to many forms of animal and human motor performance during development. Potential parallels among these diverse examples during development can lead to the generation of formal rules and hypotheses of control that transcend particular cases (cf. Fentress, 1983c, 1984).

In this spirit, Kent (1981) proposes a motor schema model for speech production involving comparisons between the expected or desired outcomes (phonetic targets) of the speech "motor program" and proprioceptive and auditory feedback.

> Depending on the stage of acquisition and the articulatory requirements of a particular phonetic target, the emerging motor schema must deal with at least three major types of feedback . . . tactile, kinesthetic and auditory. In the early stages of speech acquisition, probably all three types of feedback are closely monitored. But as skill develops (i.e., the motor schemata are well established), the child may lessen dependence on the slow-loop auditory channel and rely to a greater degree on tactile and kinesthetic feedback [pp. 176–7].

Relatively few data are available on the sounds produced by children during the transition from babbling to word acquisition. Although studies such as Stark's (1980) and Oller's (1980) document a developmental progression in sound production from "reflexive" to "nonreduplicated babbling" and "expressive jargon," studies concentrating on

speech produced by children as their lexicon develops (usually with subjects of 10 months of age and older) often conclude that words, and not phonetic elements, are the "units" being manipulated (see, e.g., Labov and Labov, 1978; Leonard et al., 1980; Macken and Ferguson, 1981; Menn, 1981; Menyuk and Menn, 1979). One of the most important developments that occurs during this period is that the child learns that phonological sequences have meanings apart from the contextual situation in which they are usually perceived.

As words are broken into phonetic components, the child discovers or invents rational rules between sounds in different contexts (Macken and Ferguson, 1981). As new words are learned they are often modified so that they will comply with the sound-patterning rules the child has for the existing words in his or her lexicon (Menyuk and Menn, 1979). This overgeneralization of rules may even result in the mispronunciation of words that had previously been articulated properly (cf. Macken and Ferguson, 1981; Menn, 1981; Menyuk and Menn, 1979).

Peters (1977) points out that although it is reasonable to assume that a child's speech is initially simple and gradually becomes "more complex," this progression can occur in either of two ways. The developmental strategy emphasized in most studies involves forming short, clear utterances that are later integrated into long, clear ones. In contrast to this, Peters' (1977) study of the vocalization of one subject indicated that the number of syllables and their intonation (including pitch and amplitude contours) was often more consistent than his articulation of individual segments. This illustrates a second, "gestalt" strategy of speech development whereby longer utterances are first sketchily approximated and later the details are filled in. Individual children vary in the relative degree to which these strategies are employed (Menn, 1981). These strategies therefore should be considered as extremes of a continuum (Peters, 1977).

2. Interindividual behavioral relations

Many ethological studies of development have been directed at accounting for individual variability in the expression of adult behavior patterns. Even minor differences in experience, such as the position of a preferred nipple (Pfeifer, 1980) or slight temporal shifts in physiological development (Cairns,

1976) have been found to correlate with a number of social behavioral differences. (Reite and Short, 1980, however, have tried unsuccessfully to account for individual behavioral differences in pigtailed monkeys by measures of 23 physiological variables.)

After 180 days, "virtually the same experiences have apparently opposite effects on the behavior of cats depending on their early defensive biases" (Adamec et al., 1980). In cichlid fish, social development in one individual may influence the rate of development of the same behavior patterns in other same-aged members of the social group (Fraley and Fernald, 1982). Socially isolated chimps raised in impoverished (less variable) environments developed more highly variable idiosyncratic behaviors than chimps raised in a normal social environment (Rogers, 1973). Social factors can therefore both facilitate and reduce individualization. Social factors have also been found to suppress the expression of adultlike hoarding behavior in hamsters (Etienne et al., 1982) and to decrease the effectiveness of songs developed by male cowbirds in eliciting female receptive posturing (West et al., 1981).

Descriptively, rules of relations between two animals' behavior may be simpler than the component movements of either individual (cf. Fentress, 1981b; Golani, 1976, 1981; Moran and Fentress, 1979; Moran et al., 1981; Simpson, 1973). Most analyses of movement relations in social behavior have, however, focused on interactions between adult animals – for example, "supplanting" (Moran, 1978; Moran et al., 1981) and courtship movements in canids (Golani, 1981; Moran and Fentress, 1979).

References

Abbs, J. H., Gracco, V. L., and Cole, K. J. (1984) Control of multimovement coordinations: Sensorimotor mechanisms in speech motor programming, *Journal of Motor Behavior*, 16: 195–231.

Adamec, R. E., Stark-Adamec, C., and Livingston, K. E. (1980) The development of predatory aggression and defense in the domestic cat (*Felis catus*). II. Development of aggression and defense in the first 164 days of life, *Behavioral and Neural Biology*, 30: 410–34.

Alberts, J. R. (1981) Ontogeny of olfaction: Reciprocal roles of sensation and behavior in the development of perception. In R. N. Aslin, J. R. Alberts, and M. R. Peterson (eds), *Development of Perception: Psychobiological perspectives*. New York: Academic Press, pp. 322–57.

Altman, J. S. (1975) Changes in the flight motor pattern during the development of the Australian plague locust, *Chortoicetes terminifera*, *Journal of Comparative Physiology*, 97: 127–42.

Angulo y González, A. W. (1932) The prenatal development of behavior in the albino rat, *The Journal of Comparative Neurology*, 55: 395–442.

Anokhin, P. K. (1964) Systemogenesis as a general regulator of brain development, *The Developing Brain, Progress in Brain Research*, 9: 54–86.

Armitage, S. E., Baldwin, B. A., and Vince, M. A. (1980) The fetal sound environment of sheep, *Science*, 208: 1173–174.

Arutyunyun, G. H., Gurfinkel, V. S., and Mirsky, M. L. (1981) Investigation of aiming at a target, *Biophysics*, 13: 536–38.

Baerends-van Roon, J. M., and Baerends, G. P. (1979) *The Morphogenesis of the Behavior of the Domestic Cat, with a Special Emphasis on the Development of Prey-catching*, Amsterdam: North-Holland.

Baptista, L. F., and Peorinovich, L. (1984) Social interaction, sensitive phases and the song template hypothesis in the white-crowned sparrow, *Animal Behaviour* 32: 172–81.

Barraud, E. M. (1961) The development of behavior in some young passerines, *Bird Study*, 8: 111–18.

Bateson, P. (1981) Ontogeny of behavior, *British Medical Bulletin*, 37: 159–64.

Beagley, W. K. (1976) Grooming in the rat as an after effect of lateral hypothalamic stimulation, *Journal of Comparative and Physiological Psychology*, 90: 790–8.

Bekoff, A. (1976) Ontogeny of leg motor output in the chick embryo: A neural analysis, *Brain Research*, 106: 271–91.

Bekoff, A. (1981) Embryonic development of the neural circuitry underlying motor coordination. In W. M. Cowan (ed.), *Studies in Developmental Neurobiology*. New York: Oxford University Press, pp. 134–70.

Bekoff, A. (1981) Behavioral embryology of birds and mammals: Neuroembryological studies of the development of motor behavior. In K. Immelmann, G. W. Barlow, L. Petrinovich, and M. Main (eds), *Behavioral Development*. New York: Cambridge University Press, pp. 152–63.

Bekoff, A., and Trainer, W. (1979) The development of interlimb coordination during swimming in postnatal rats, *Journal of Experimental Biology*, 83: 1–11.

Bekoff, A., Stein, P. S. G., and Hamburger, V. (1975) Coordinated motor output in the hindlimb of the 7-day chick embryo, *Proceedings of the National Academy of Sciences*, 72: 1245–8.

Bentley, D. R., and Hoy, R. R. (1970) Postembryonic development of adult motor patterns in crickets: a neural analysis, *Science*, 170: 1409–11.

Bergstrom, R. M., Helvstrom, P. E., and Stenberg, D. (1962) Studies in reflex irradiation in the foetal guinea pig, *Annales Cairvrgiae et Gynaecologiae Fenniae*, 51: 171–8.

Bernstein, N. (1967) *The Coordination and Regulation of Movements*. London: Pergamon Press.

Berridge, K. C., and Fentress, J. C. Contextual control of

trigeminal sensorimotor function, *Journal of Neuroscience*, in press.

Bizzi, E. (1981) Central and peripheral mechanisms in motor control. In G. E. Stelmach and J. Requin (eds), *Tutorials in Motor Behavior*. New York: North Holland, pp. 131–43.

Bolwig, N. (1964) Facial expression in primates with remarks on a parallel development in certain carnivores, *Behaviour*, 22: 167–92.

Bosma, J. F. (1975) Anatomic and physiologic development of the speech apparatus. In D. B. Tower (ed.), *The Nervous System*, vol. 3, *Human Communication and its Disorders*. New York: Raven Press, pp. 469–81.

Bower, T. G. R. (1979) *Human Development*. San Francisco: Freeman.

Brown, M. C., and Booth, C. M. (1983) Segregation of motor nerves on a segmental basis during synapse elimination in neonatal muscle, *Brain Research*, 273: 188–90.

Bruce, I. C., and Tatton, W. C. (1980) Sequential output–input maturation of kitten motor cortex, *Experimental Brain Research*, 39: 411–19.

Bruner, J. S. (1974) The organization of early skilled action. In M. P. M. Richards (ed.), *The Integration of a Child into a Social World*. London: Cambridge University Press.

Burghardt, G. M. (1977) Ontogeny of communication. In Thomas A. Sebeok (ed.), *How Animals Communicate*. Bloomington, Ind.: Indiana University Press, pp. 71–97.

Burke, R. E. (1981) Motor units: Anatomy, physiology, and functional organization. In J. M. Brookhardt and V. B. Mountcastle (eds), *Handbook of Physiology, Section 1*, vol. II. Bethesda, Md.: American Physiological Society, pp. 345–422.

Butler, R. G. (1980) Effects of context on communicatory exchanges in mice: a syntactic analysis. *Behavioral and Neural Biology*, 28(4): 431–41.

Cairns, R. B. (1976) The ontogeny and phylogeny of social interactions. In M. E. Hahn and E. C. Simmel (eds), *Communicative Behavior and Evolution*. New York: Academic Press, pp. 115–39.

Carmichael, L. (1970) The onset and early development of behavior. In P. Mussen (ed.), *Carmichael's Manual of Child Psychology*, vol. 1. New York: Wiley, pp. 447–563.

Chevalier-Skolnikoff, S. (1974) The ontogeny of communication in the stumptail macaque (*Macaca aretoids*), *Contributions of Primatology*, 2: 1–174.

Coghill, G. E. (1929) *Anatomy and the Problem of Behavior*. Cambridge, England: Cambridge University Press.

Collard, E., and Povel, D. J. (1982) Theory of serial pattern production: tree traversals, *Psychological Review*, 89: 693–707.

Condon, W. S., and Sander, L. W. (1974) Neonate movement is synchronized with adult speech: Interactional participation and language acquisition, *Science*, 183: 99–101.

Connolly, K. (1977) The nature of motor skill development, *Journal of Human Movement Studies*, 3: 128–43.

Cooper, W. E. (1977) The development of speech timing, In S. J. Segalowitz and F. A. Gruber (eds), *Language Develop-*

ment and Neurological Theory. New York: Academic Press, pp. 357–73.

Corner, M. (1978) Spontaneous motor rhythms in early life – phenomenological and neurophysiological aspects, *Progress in Brain Research*, 48: 349–66.

Cowan, W. M. (1978) Aspects of neural development, *International Review of Physiology. Neurophysiology III* 17: 149–90.

Cruze, W. W. (1935) Maturation and learning in chicks, *Journal of Comparative Psychology*, 19: 371–409.

Darwin, C. (1872) *The Expression of the Emotions in Man and the Animals*, London: Murray.

Dawkins, R. (1976) Hierarchical organization: a candidate principle for ethology. In P. P. G. Bateson and R. A. Hinde (eds), *Growing Points in Ethology*. Cambridge, England: Cambridge University Press, pp. 7–54.

DeCasper, A. J., and Fifer, W. P. (1980) Of human bonding: Newborns prefer their mother's voices, *Science*, 208: 1174–76.

DeGroat, W. C., Douglas, J. W., Glass, J., Simonds, W., Weimer, B., and Werner, P. (1978) Changes in somatovesical reflexes during postnatal development in the kitten, *Brain Research*, 94: 150–4.

Deliagina, T. G., Feldman, A. G., Gelfand, I. M., and Orlovsky, G. N. (1975) On the role of central program and afferent inflow in the control of scratching movements in the cat, *Brain Research*, 100: 297–313.

Doty, R. W. (1976) The concept of neural centers. In J. C. Fentress (ed.), *Simpler Networks and Behavior*. Sunderland, Mass.: Sinauer Associates, pp. 251–65.

Drachman, D. B., and Coulombre, A. J. (1962) Experimental clubfoot and arthrogryposis multiplex congention, *Lancet*, 2: 523–6.

Ebbesson, S. O. E. (1980) The parcellation theory and its relation to interspecific variability in brain organization, evolutionary and ontogenetic development and neuronal plasticity, *Cell and Tissue Research*, 213: 179–212.

Eibl-Eibesfeldt, I. (1951) Beobachtungen zur Fortpflanzungs biologie und Jugendentwicklung des Eichornchens, *Zeitschrift für Tierpsychologie*, 8: 370–400.

Eibl-Eibesfeldt, I. (1956) Über die ontogenetische Entwicklung der Technik des Nusseöffnens vom Eichhornchen (*Sciurus vulgaris* L.), *Zeitschrift für Säugetierkunde*, 21: 132–4.

Eibl-Eibesfeldt, I. (1961) The interactions of unlearned behaviour patterns and learning in mammals. In D. F. Dclafresnaye (ed.), *Brain Mechanisms and Learning*, CIOMS Symposium. Oxford: Blackwell.

Elsner, N. (1981) Developmental aspects of insect neuroethology. In K. Immelmann, G. W. Barlow, L. Petrinovich, and M. Main (eds), *Behavioral Development*. New York: Cambridge University Press, pp. 474–90.

Elsner, N., and Hirth, C. (1978) Short and long term coordination in a stridulating grasshopper, *Naturwissenchaften*, 63: 160–1.

Emde, R. N., Gaensbauer, T. J., and Harman, R. J. (1976) Emotional expression in infancy: a biobehavioral study,

Psychological issues, vol. 10. Monograph 37. New York: International Universities Press.

Etienne, A. S., Emmanuelli, E., and Zinder, M. (1982) Ontogeny of hoarding in the golden hamster: the development of motor patterns and their sequential coordination, *Developmental Psychobiology*, **15**: 33–45.

Evarts, E. V. (1975) The third Stevenson lecture. Changing concepts of the central control of movement, *Canadian Journal of Physiology and Pharmacology*, **53**: 191–201.

Fentress, J. C. (1972) Development and patterning of movement sequences in inbred mice. In J. Kiger (ed.), *The Biology of Behavior*. Corvallis: Oregon State University Press, pp. 83–132.

Fentress, J. C. (1976) Dynamic boundaries of patterned behavior: Interaction and self-organization. In P. P. G. Bateson and R. A. Hinde (eds), *Growing Points in Ethology*. Cambridge, England: Cambridge University Press, pp. 135–69.

Fentress, J. C. (1978) *Mus musicus*. The developmental orchestration of selected movement patterns in mice. In M. Bekoff and G. Burghardt (eds), *The Development of Behavior: Comparative and Evolutionary Aspects*. New York: Garland, pp. 321–42.

Fentress, J. C. (1981a) Sensorimotor development. In R. N. Aslin, J. R. Alberts, and M. R. Petersen (eds), *The Development of Perception: Psychobiological Perspectives*, vol. 1. New York: Academic Press, pp. 293–317.

Fentress, J. C. (1981b) Order in ontogeny: Relational dynamics. In K. Immelmann, G. Rarlow, M. Main, and L. Petrinovich (eds), *Behavioral Development*. New York: Cambridge University Press, pp. 338–71.

Fentress, J. C. (1983a) Ethological models of hierarchy and patterning of species-specific behavior. In E. Satinoff and P. Teitelbaum (eds), *Handbook of Neurobiology: Motivation*. New York: Plenum Press, pp. 185–234.

Fentress, J. C. (1983b) A view of ontogeny. In J. R. Eisenberg and D. G. Kleiman (eds), *Recent Advances in the Study of Mammalian Behavior*, Special Publication No. 7, The American Society of Mammalogists, pp. 24–64.

Fentress, J. C. (1983c) Hierarchical motor control. In M. Studdert-Kennedy (ed.), *Psychobiology of Language, Neuroscience Research Program*. Cambridge, Mass.: MIT Press, pp. 40–61.

Fentress, J. C. (1983d) The analysis of behavioral networks. In J. P. Ewert, R. R. Capranica, and D. J. Ingle (eds), *Advances in Vertebrate Neutroethology*. New York: Plenum Press, pp. 939–68.

Fentress, J. C. (1984) The development of coordination, *Journal of Motor Behavior*, **16**: 99–134.

Ferron, J., and Lefebvre, L. (1983) Comparative organization of grooming sequences in adult and young Sciurid rodents.

Field, R. (1978) Vocal behavior of wolves (*Canis lupus*): variability in structure, context, annual/diurnal patterns, and ontogeny. PhD thesis, the Johns Hopkins University, Baltimore.

Field, R. (1979) A perspective on syntactics in wolf vocaliza-

tions. In E. Klinghammer (ed.), *The Behavior and Ecology of Wolves*. New York: Garland, pp. 182–205.

Forssberg, H., and Wallberg, H. (1981) Infant locomotion – a preliminary movement and electromyographic study. In K. Berg and B. O. Eriksson (eds), *Children and Exercise*, vol. IX. Baltimore: University Park, pp. 32–40.

Fox, M. W. (1972) *Behavior of Wolves, Dogs, and Related Canids*. New York: Harper and Row.

Fox, M. W., and Cohen, J. A. (1977) Canid communication. In T. A. Sebeok (ed.), *How Animals Communicate*. Bloomington: Indiana University Press, pp. 728–48.

Fraley, N. B., and Fernald, R. D. (1982) Social control of developmental rate in the African cichlid *Haptochromis Burtoni*, *Zeitschrift für Tierpsychologie*, **60**: 66–82.

Galef, B. G., Jr (1981) Development of flavor prefencence in man and animals: the role of social and non-social factors. In R. N. Aslin, J. R. Alberts, and M. R. Petersen (eds), *Development of Perception: Psychobiological Perspectives*. New York: Academic Press, pp. 411–31.

Galef, B. G., Jr., and Henderson, P. W. (1972) Mother's milk: A determinant of the feeding preferences of weaning rat pups, *Journal of Comparative and Physiological Psychology*, **78**: 213–19.

Gallistel, C. R. (1980) *The Organization of Action: A New Synthesis*. Hillsdale, N.J.: Lawrence Erlbaum Associates.

Gatev, V. (1972) Role of inhibition in the development of motor coordination in early childhood, *Developmental Medicine and Child Neurology*, **14**: 336–41.

Glencross, D. J. (1980) Levels and strategies of response organization. In G. E. Stelmach and J. Requin (eds), *Tutorials in Motor Behavior*. New York: North Holland, pp. 551–66.

Golani, I. (1976) Homeostatic motor processes in mammalian interactions: a choreography of display. In P. P. G. Bateson and P. H. Klopfer (eds), *Perspectives in Ethology*, vol. 2. New York: Plenum Press, pp. 69–134.

Golani, I. (1981) The search for invariants in motor behavior. In K. Immelmann, G. W. Barlow, L. Petrinovitch, and M. Main (eds), *Behavioral Development*, New York: Cambridge University Press, pp. 372–92.

Golani, I., Broncht, G., Moualern, D., and Teitelbaum, P. (1981) "Warm-up" along dimensions of movement in the ontogeny of exploratory behaviour in the infant rat and other infant mammals, *Proceedings of the National Academy of Sciences*, **78**: 7226–9.

Goosen, C., and Kortmulder, K. (1979) Relationships between faces and body motor patterns in a group of captive pigtailed macaques (*Macaca nemestrina*), *Primates*, **20**: 221–36.

Gorska, T., and Czarkowska, J. (1973) Motor effects of stimulation of the cerebral cortex in the dog: an ontogenetic study. In N. T. Tankov and D. S. Kosarov (eds), *Motor Control*. New York: Plenum Press, pp. 147–66.

Gould, E. (1983) Mechanisms of mammalian auditory communication. In J. F. Eisenberg, and D. G. Kleiman (eds), *Advances in the Study of Mammalian Behavior*,

Special Publication No. 7. The American Society of Marnmalogists, pp. 265–342.

Green, S., and Marler, P. (1979) The analysis of animal communication. In P. Marler and J. G. Vandenbergh (eds), *Handbook of Behavioral Neurobiology*, vol. 3. *Social Behavior and Communication*. New York: Plenum Press, pp. 73–158.

Grillner, S. (1981) Control of locomotion in bipeds, tetrapods, and fish. In J. M. Brookhart and V. B. Mountcastle (eds), *Handbook of Physiology, Section I*, vol. II. Bethesda, Md.: American Physiological Society, pp. 1179–236.

Gruner, J. A., and Altman, J. (1980) Swimming in the rat: Analysis of locomotor performance in comparison to stepping, *Experimental Brain Research*, 40: 374–82.

Gruner, J. A., Altman, J., and Spivack, N. (1980) Effects of arrested cerebellar development on locomotion in the rat. Cinematographic and electromyographic analysis, *Experimental Brain Research*, 40: 361–73.

Guttinger, H. R. (1981) Self-differentiation of song organization rules by deaf canaries, *Zeitschrift für Tierpsychologie*, 56: 323–40.

Halfmann, K., and Elsner, N. (1978) Larval stridulation in acridid grasshoppers, *Naturwissenschaften*, 65: 265.

Hall, W. G., and Williams, C. L. (1983) Suckling isn't feeding, or is it? A search for developmental continuities, *Advances in the Study of Behavior*, 13: 219–54.

Hamburger, V. (1977) The developmental history of the motor neuron (The F. O. Schmitt Lecture in Neuroscience, 1976), *Neurosciences Research Program Bulletin*, 15 (Supplement): 1–37.

Hamburger, V., Wenger, E., and Oppenheim, R. (1966) Motility in the chick embryo in the absence of sensory input, *Journal of Experimental Zoology*, 162: 133–160.

Hansen, E. W. (1966) The development of maternal and infant behavior in the rhesus monkey, *Behaviour*, 27: 107–49.

Hebb, D. O. (1955) Drives and the CNS (conceptual nervous system), *Psychology Review*, 62: 243–54.

Hinde, R. A. (1970) *Animal Behavior: A Synthesis of Ethology and Comparative Psychology*, 2nd edn, New York: McGraw-Hill.

Hinde, R. A. (1982) *Ethology: Its Nature and Relations with Other Sciences*. New York: Oxford University Press.

Hinde, R. A., and Stevenson, J. G. (1969) Sequences of behavior, *Advances in the Study of Behavior*, 2: 267–96.

Hines, M. (1942) The development and regression of reflexes, postures, and progression in the young macaque, *Contributions to Embryology*, 30: 153–209.

Hofer, M. (1981) *The Roots of Human Behavior*. San Francisco: Freeman.

Hofsten, C., von (1979) Development of visually directed reading: The approach phase, *Journal of Human Movement Studies*, 5: 160–78.

Hogan, J. A., and Roper, T. J. (1978) A comparison of the properties of different reinforcers. In J. S. Rosenblatt, R. A. Hinde, C. Beer, and M. C. Busnel (eds), *Advances in the Study of Behavior*. London: Academic Press.

Hollyday, M. (1980) Montoneuron histogenesis and the development of limb innervation, *Current Topics in Development Biology*, 15: 181–215.

Hoyle, G. (1984) Neuroethology, *The Behavioral and Brain Sciences*, ••: 367–81.

Ikeda, K. (1976) Genetically patterned neural activity. In J. C. Fentress (ed.), *Simpler Networks and Behavior*, Sunderland, Mass. Sináuer Associates, pp. 140–52.

Jacobson, M. (1978) *Developmental Neurobiology*, 2nd edn, New York: Plenum Press.

Johnston, T. D. (1980) Compensation for substrate elasticity in the kinematics of leaping by infant pigtailed macaques (*Macaca nemestrina*), *Brain Research*, 184: 467–80.

Kear, J. (1961) Food selection in finches with special reference to interspecific differences, *Proceedings Zoological Society of London*, 138: 163–204.

Kelso, J. A. S. (1981) Contrasting perspectives on order and regulation in movement. In J. Long and A. Baddeley (eds), *Attention and Performance*, vol. IX. Hillsdale, N.J.: Lawrence Erhlaum Associates, pp. 437–57.

Kelso, J. A. S., and Tuller, B. (1984) A dynamical basis for action systems. In M. S. Gazzaniga (ed.), *Handbook of Cognitive Neuroscience*. New York: Plenum Press, pp. 319–56.

Kent, R. D. (1976) Anatomical and neuromuscular maturation of the speech mechanism: evidence from acoustic studies, *Journal of Speech and Hearing Research*, 19: 421–47.

Kent, R. D. (1981) Sensorimotor aspects of speech development. In R. N. Aslin, J. R. Alberts, and M. R. Petersen (eds), *Development of Perception: Psychobiological Perspectives*, vol. 1. New York: Academic Press, pp. 161–89.

Kent, R. D., and Murray, A. D. (1982) Acoustic features of infant vocalic utterances at 3, 6 and 9 months, *Journal of the Acoustical Society of America*, 72(2): 353–65.

Kristar, W. B., Jr (1980) Generation of rhythmic motor patterns. In H. M. Pinsker and W. D. Willis, Jr (eds), *Information Processing in the Nervous System*. New York: Raven Press, pp. 241–61.

Kruijt, J. P. (1964) Ontogeny of social behaviour in Burmese red junglefowl (*Gallus gallus spadiceus* Bonnaterre), *Behaviour Supplement*, XII.

Kuhl, P. K., and Meltzoff, A. N. (1982) The bimodal perception of speech in infancy, *Science*, 218: 1138–141.

Kutsch, W. (1971) The development of the flight pattern in the desert locust, *Schistocerca gregaria*, *Zeitschrift fuer Vergleichende Physiologie*, 74: 156–68.

Kuypers, H. G. J. M. (1981) Anatomy of the descending pathways. In V. Brooks (eds), *Handbook of Physiology: Motor Control*. Bethesda, Md.: American Physiological Society, pp. 595–666.

Labov, W., and Labov, T. (1978) The phonetics of cat and mama, *Language*, 4:816–52.

Lagerspetz, K., Margaretha, N., and Strandvik, C. (1971) The effects of training in crawling on the motor and mental development of infants, *Scandinavian Journal of Psychology*, **12**: 192–7.

Landmesser, L. T. (1980) The generation of neuromuscular specificity, *Annual Review of Neuroscience*, **3**: 279–302.

Lang, F., Govind, C, K., and Costello, W. J. (1978) Experimental transformation of muscle fiber properties in lobster, *Science*, **201**: 1037–9.

Lawrence, D. G., and Hopkins, D. A. (1976) The development of motor control in the rhesus monkey: evidence concerning the role of corticomotoneuronal connections, *Brain Research*, **99**: 235–54.

Leonard, I. B., Newhoff, M., and Mesalam, L. (1980) Individual differences in early child phonology, *Applied Psycholinguistics*, **1**: 7–30.

Levine, M. S., Hull, C. D., and Buchwald, N. A. (1980) Development of motor activity in kittens, *Developmental Psychobiology*, **13**: 357–71.

Lewis, D. M. (1981) The physiology of motor units in mammalian skeletal muscle. In A. L. Towe and E. S. Luschei (eds), *Handbook of Behavioral Neurobiology*, vol. 5: *Motor Coordination*. New York: Plenum Press, pp. 1–67.

Leyhausen, P. (1973) On the function of the relative hierarchy of moods (as exemplified by the phylogenetic and ontogenetic development of prey-catching in carnivores). In K. Lorenz and P. Leyhausen (eds), *Motivation of Human and Animal Behavior*. New York: Van Nostrand Reinhold, pp. 144–247.

Liberman, A. M., and Studdert-Kennedy, M. (1978) Phonetic perception. In R. Held, H. Leibowitz, and H. L, Teuber (eds), *Handbook of Sensory Physiology*, vol. VIII: *Perception*. Heidelberg: Springer-Verlag, pp. 143–78.

Lieblich, A., Symmes, D., Newman, J., and Shapiro, M. (1980) Development of the isolation peep in laboratory-bred squirrel monkeys, *Animal Behaviour*, **28**: 1–9.

Lillehir, R. A., and Snowdon, C. T. (1978) Individual and situational differences in the vocalization of young stumptail macaques (*Macaca arctoides*), *Behaviour*, **65**: 270–81.

Lindberg, D., and Elsner, N. (1977) Sensory influence upon grasshopper stridulation, *Naturwissenchaften*, **64**: 342–3.

Locke, J. L. (1983) *Phonological Acquisition and Change*. New York: Academic Press.

Lorenz, K. Z. (1981) *The Foundations of Ethology*. New York: Springer-Verlag.

Machlis, L. (1977) An analysis of the temporal patterning of pecking in chicks, *Behaviour*, **63**: 1–70.

Macken, M. A., and Ferguson, C. A. (1981) Phonological universals in language acquisition, *Annals of the New York Academy of Sciences*, **379**: 110–29.

Marler, P. (1967) Animal Communication Signals, *Science*. **157**: 769–74.

Marler, P., and Feters, S. (1981) Birdsong and speech: evidence for special processing. In P. D. Eimas and J. L. Mille (eds), *Perspectives on the Study of Speech*. Hillsdale, N.J.: Lawrence Erlbaum, pp. 75–112.

Marler, P., and Peters, S. (1982a) Structural changes in song

ontogeny in the swamp sparrow (*Melospitza georgiona*), *Auk*, **99**: 446–58.

Marler, P., and Peters, S. (1982b) Developmental overproduction and selective attrition: New processes in the epigenesis of birdsong, *Developmental Psychobiology*, **15**: 369–78.

Mason, W. (1979) Ontogeny of social behavior. In P. Marler and J. G. Vandenbergh (eds), *Handbook of Behavioral Neurobiology*, vol. 3: *Social Behavior and Communication*, New York: Plenum Press, pp. 1–28.

Maurus, M., and Pruscha, H. (1972) Quantitative analysis of behavioral sequences elicited by automated telestimulauon in squirrel monkeys, *Experimental Brain Research*, **14**: 372–94.

McGraw, M. B. (1940) Neuromuscular development of the human infant as exemplified in the achievement of erect locomotion, *The Journal of Pediatrics*, **17**: 747–71.

Mellon, D., and Stevens, P. J. (1979) Experimental arrest of muscle transformation and asymmetry reversal in alpheid shrimp, *Neurosciences Abstracts*, **5**: 254.

Meltzoff, A. N., and Moore, M. K. (1977) Imitation of facial and manual gestures by human neonates, *Science*, **198**: 75–8.

Menn, L. (1981) Theories of phonological development, *Annals of the New York Academy of Sciences*, **379**: 130–7.

Menyuk, P., and Menn, L. (1979) Early strategies for the perception and production of words and sounds. In P. Fletcher and M. Garman (eds), *Language Acquisition*. Cambridge, England: Cambridge University Press, pp. 49–70.

Metafora, S., Felsani, A., Cotrufo, R., Tajana, G. F., Del Rio, A., de Prisco, P. P., Rutigliano, B., and Esposito, V. (1980) Neural control of gene expression in the skeletal muscle fibre: Changes in the muscular mRNA population following denervation, *Proceedings of the Royal Society of London, B*, **209**: 257–73.

Moran, G. (1978) The structure of movement in supplanting interactions in the wolf. Unpublished PhD thesis. Dalhousie University, Halifax, Nova Scotia.

Moran, G., and Fentress, J. C. (1979) A search for order in wolf social behavior. In E. Klinghammer (ed.), *The Behavior and Ecology of Wolves*. New York: Garland Press, pp. 245–83.

Moran, G., Fentress, J. C., and Golani, I. (1981) A description of relational patterns during "ritualized fighting" in wolves, *Animal Behaviour*, **29**: 1146–65.

Moran, T. H., Schwartz, G. J., and Blass, E. M. (1983) Organized behavioral responses to lateral hypothalamic electrical stimulation in infant rats, *The Journal of Neuroscience*, **3**: 10–19.

Moss, S. C., and Hogg, J. (1983) The development and integration of fine motor sequences in 12- to 18-month-old children: a test of the modular theory of motor skill acquisition, *Genetic Psychology Monographs*, **107**: 145–87.

Narayanan, C. H., Fox, M. W., and Hamburger, V. (1971) Prenatal development of spontaneous and evoked activity in the rat (*Rattus norvegicus albinus*), *Behaviour*, **40**: 100–34.

Navarrete, R., and Vrbová, G. (1983) Changes in activity patterns in slow and fast muscles during postnatal development, *Developmental Brain Research*, 8: 11–19.

Newman, J. D., and Symmes, D. (1982) Inheritance and experience in the acquisition of primate acoustic behavior. In C. Snowdon, C. Brown, and M. Petersen (eds), *Primate Communication*. New York: Cambridge University Press, pp. 259–78.

Nice, M. M. (1943) Studies in the life history of the song sparrow, *Transactions of the Linnean Society of New York*, 6: 1–328.

Nicolai, J. (1973) Das lernprogramm in der gesangsausbildung der strohwitwe *Tetraenura fischeri* Reichenow, *Zeitschrift für Tierpsychology*, 32: 113–38.

Nottebohm, F. (1980) Brain pathways for vocal learning in birds: A review of the first 10 years, *Progress in Psychobiology and Physiological Psychology*, 9: 85–124.

Oller, B. K. (1980) The emergence of the sounds of speech in infancy. In G. H. Yeni-Komshian, J. F. Kavanagh, and C. A. Ferguson (eds), *Child phonology*, vol. 1: *Production*, New York: Academic Press, pp. 93–112.

Oppenheim, R. W. (1981) Ontogenetic adaptations and retrogressive processes in the development of the nervous system and behaviour: A neuroembryological perspective. In K. J. Connolly and H. F. R. Prechtl (eds), *Maturation and Development: Biological and Psychological Perspectives*. Philadelphia: Lippincott, pp. 73–109.

Oppenheim, R. W. (1982) The neuroembryological study of behavior: progress, problems and perspectives. In K. K. Hunt (ed.), *Current Topics in Developmental Biology*, vol. 17: *Neural Development*, New York: Academic Press.

Oppenheim, R. W., and Reitzel, J. (1975) Ontogeny of behavioral sensitivity to strychnine in the chick embryo: evidence for the early onset of CNS inhibition, *Brain Behavior and Evolution*, 11: 130–59.

Peiper, A. (1973) *Cerebral Function in Infancy*. New York: Consultants Bureau.

Peters, A. M. (1977) Language learnings strategies: Does the whole equal the sum of the parts? *Language*, 53(3): 560–73.

Petersen, M. R. (1981) Perception of acoustic communication signals by animals: developmental perspectives and implications, *Development of Perception*, 1: 67–109.

Pfeifer, S. (1980) Role of the nursing order in social development of mountain lion kittens, *Developmental Psychobiology*, 13: 47–53.

Pittman, R., and Oppenheim, R. W. (1979) Cell death of motoneurons in the chick embryo spinal cord: IV Evidence that a functional neuromuscular interaction is involved in the regulation of naturally occurring cell death and the stabilization of synapses, *Journal of Comparative Neurology*, 187: 425–46.

Prechtl, H. F. R. (1981) The study of neural development as a perspective of clinical problems. In K. J. Connolly and H. F. R. Prechtl (eds), *Maturation and Development: Biological and Psychological Perspectives*, Philadelphia: Lippincott, pp. 198–215.

Preyer, W. (1885) *Specielle Physiologie des Embryo*, Leipzig: Grieben.

Prosser, G. L. (1933) Correlation between development of behaviour and neuromuscular differentiation in embryos of *Eisonia fostida*, *The Journal of Comparative Neurology*, 58: 603–41.

Provine, R. (1976) Development of function in nerve nets. In J. C. Fentress (ed.), *Simpler Networks and Behavior*, Sunderland, Mass.: Sinauer, pp. 203–20.

Provine, R. R. (1983) Behavioural neuroembryology: motor prespectives. In W. T. Greenough and J. Juraska (eds), *Developmental Psycho/neurobiology*, New York: Academic Press, 1983.

Purves, D., and Lichtman, J. W. (1980) Elimination of synapses in the developing nervous system, *Science*, 210: 153–7.

Reite, M., and Short, R. (1980) A biobehavioural developmental profile (BDP) for the pigtail monkey, *Developmental Psychobiology*, 13: 243–85.

Richmond, G., and Sachs, B. D. (1980) Grooming in Norway rats: The development and adult expression of a complex motor pattern, *Behaviour*, 75: 82–96.

Rogers, C. M. (1973) Implications of a primate early rearing experiment for the concept of culture. In E. W. Menzel, Jr. (ed.), *Precultural Primate Behaviour*, New York: S. Karger, pp. 185–91.

Rosenblatt, J. S. (1976) Stages in the early behavioural development of altricial young of selected species of non-primate mammals. In P. P. G. Bateson and R. A. Hinde (eds), *Growing Points in Ethology*, Cambridge, England: Cambridge University Press, pp. 345–83.

Rosenblatt, J. S. (1980) The sensorimotor and motivational basis of early behavioural development of selected altricial mammals. In N. E. Spear and B. A. Cambell (eds), *Ontogeny of Learning and Memory*, New York: Lawrence Erlbaum, pp. 1–38.

Saito, K. (1979) Development of reflexes in the rat fetus studied *in vitro*, *Journal of Physiology*, 294: 581–94.

Sedlacek, J. (1978) The development of supraspinal control of spontaneous motility in chick embryos, *Progress in Brain Research*, 48: 367–84.

Seyfarth, R. M., and Cheney, D. L. (1980) The ontogeny of vervet monkey alarm calling behaviour: a preliminary report, *Zeitschrift für Tierpsychologie*, 54: 37–56.

Seyfarth, R. M., and Cheney, D. L. (1982) How monkeys see the world: a review of recent research on East African vervet monkeys. In C. T. Snowdon, C. H. Brown, and M. R. Petersen (eds), *Primate Communication*, Cambridge, England: Cambridge University Press, pp. 239–52.

Seyfarth, R. M., Cheney, D. L., and Marler, P. (1980a) Monkey responses to three different alarm calls: Evidence to predator classification and semantic communication, *Science*, 210: 801–3.

Seyfarth, R. M., Cheney, D. L., and Marler, P. (1980b) Vervet monkey alarm calls: semantic communication in a free-ranging primate, *Animal Behaviour*, 28: 1070–94.

Shalter, M. D., Fentress, J. C., and Young, C. W. (1977) Determinants of response of wolf pups to auditory signals, *Behaviour*, 60: 98–114.

Sherrington, C. S. (1906) *The Integrative Action of the Nervous System*. New Haven: Yale University Press.

Simpson, M. J. A. (1973) Social display and the recognition of individuals. In P. P. G. Bateson and P. H. Klopfer (eds), *Perspectives in Ethology*, New York: Plenum Press, pp. 225–79.

Smiley, C., and Wilbanks, W. A. (1962) Effects of noise on early development in the rat, *Bulletin of the Psychonomic Society*, 19: 181–3.

Smith, W. J. (1965) Message, meaning, and context in ethology, *American Naturalist*, 99: 405–9.

Soffe, S. R., Charke, J. D. W., and Roberts, A. (1983) Swimming and other centrally generated motor patterns in newt embryos, *Journal of Comparative Physiology A*, 152: 535–44.

Stark, R. E. (1980) Stages of speech development in the first year of life. In G. H. Yeni-Kormshian, J. F. Kavanagh and C. A. Ferguson (eds), *Child phonology*, vol. 1, New York: Academic Press, pp. 73–92.

Stelzner, D. J. (1971) The normal postnatal development of synaptic end-feet in the lumbosacral spinal cord and of responses in the hind limbs of the albino rat, *Experimental Neurology*, 31: 337–57.

Streter, F. A., Luff, A. R., and Gergely, J. (1975) Effect of cross-reinnervation on physiological parameters and on properties of myosin and sacroplasmic reticulum of fast and slow muscles of the rabbit, *Journal of General Physiology*, 66: 811–21.

Studdert-Kennedy, M. (1981) The beginnings of speech. In K. Immelmann, G. W. Barlow, L. Petrinovich, and M. Main (eds), *Behavioral Development*, New York: Cambridge University Press, pp. 533–61.

Szechtman, H., and Hall, W. G. (1980) Ontogeny of oral behaviour induced by tail pinch and electrical stimulation of the tail of rats, *Journal of Comparative and Physiological Psychology*, 94: 436–45.

Szekely, G. (1976) Developmental aspects of locomotion. In R. M. Herman, S. Grillner, P. S. G. Stein, and D. G. Stuart (eds), *Neural Control of Locomotion*, New York: Plenum Press, pp. 735–57.

Tamasy, V., Koranyi, L., and Phelps, C. P. (1981) The role of dopaminergic and serotonergic mechanisms in the development of swimming ability of young rats, *Developmental Neuroscience*, 4: 389–400.

Teitelbaum, P. (1977) Levels of integration of the operant. In W. K. Honig and J. E. R. Staddon (eds), *Handbook of Operant Behavior*. Englewood Cliffs, N.J.: Prentice-Hall, pp. 7–27.

Teitelbaum, P. (1982) Disconnection and antagonistic interaction of movement subsystems in motivated behavior. In A. R. Morrison, and P. Strick (eds), *Changing Concepts of the Nervous System: Proceedings of the First Institute of Neurological Sciences Symposium in Neurobiology*, New York: Academic Press, pp. 467–98.

Terzuolo, C. A., and Viani, P. (1980) Determinant and characteristics of motor patterns used for typing, *Neuroscience*, 5: 1085–103.

Thelen, E. (1981) Kicking, rocking, and waving: contextual analysis of rhythmical stereotypies in normal human infants, *Animal Behaviour*, 29: 3–11.

Thelen, E. (1981) Rhythmical behavior in infancy: an ethological prespective, *Developmental Psychology*, 17: 237–57.

Thelen, E. (1983) Learning to walk is still an "old" problem: a reply to Zelazo (1983), *Journal of Motor Behavior*, 15: 139–61.

Thelen, E., and Fisher, D. M. (1983) From spontaneous to instrumental behavior: kinematic analysis of movement changes during very early learning, *Child Development*, 54: 129–40.

Thelen, E., Ridley-Johnson, R., and Fisher, D. M. (1983) Shifting patterns of bilateral coordination and lateral dominance in the leg movements of young infants, *Developmental Psychobiology*, 16: 29–46.

Tinbergen, N. (1963) On aims and methods of ethology, *Zeitschrift für Tierpsychologie*, 20: 410–33.

Tooker, C. P., and Miller, R. J. (1980) The ontogeny of agonistic behaviour in the blue gourami, *Trichogaster trichopterus* (Pisces, Anabantoidei), *Animal Behaviour*, 28(4): 973–88.

Tuller, B., Kelso, A. S., and Harris, K. S. (1982) On the kinematics of articulatory control as a function of stress and rate, *Status Report on Speech Research SR-71/72*. New Haven, Conn.: Haskins Laboratories, pp. 81–8.

Turkewitz, G., Lewkowicz, D. J. and Gardner, J. M. (1983) Determinants of infant perception, *Advances in the Study of Behavior*, 13: 39–62.

Vanderwolf, C. H. (1983) The role of the cerebral cortex and ascending activating systems in the control of behavior. In E. Satinoff and P. Teitelbaum (eds), *Handbook of Behavioral Neurobiology*, vol. 6: *Motivation*, New York: Plenum Press, pp. 67–104.

Vince, M. A. (1979) Postnatal effects of prenatal sound stimulation in the guinea pig, *Animal Behaviour*, 27: 908–18.

Viviani, P., and Terzuolo, C. (1980) Space-time invariance in learned motor skills. In G. E. Stelmach and J. Requin (eds), *Tutorials in Motor Behavior*. Amsterdam: North-Holland, pp. 525–33.

Walker, B. E., and Quarles, J. (1976) Palate development in mouse foetuses after tongue removal, *Archives of Oral Biology*, 21: 405–12.

Watson, J. S. (1981) Contingency experience in behavioral development. In K. Immelmann, G. W. Barlow, L. Petrinovich, and M. Main (eds), *Behavioral Development*. New York: Cambridge University Press, pp. 83–9.

Weber, Th. (1972) Stabilisierung des Flugrhythmus durch Erfahrung bei *Gryllus campestris* L. *Naturwissenschaften*, 59: 366.

Weber, Th. (1974) Elektrophysiologische Untersuchungen zur Entwicklung und zum Verlauf von Verhaltensweisen bei *Gryllus campestris* L. Dissertation, University of Cologne.

Weismer, G., and Fennell, A. (1983) Studies of phrase-level speech timing. Invited paper, 105th meeting of the Acoustical Society of America, University of Wisconsin, Madison, pp. 84–142.

Weismer, G., and Ingrisano, D. (1979) Phrase-level timing patterns in English: effects of emphatic stress location and speaking rate, *Journal of Speech and Hearing Research*, **22**: 516–33.

West, M. J., King, D. H., and Eastzer, D. H. (1981) The cowbird: Reflections on development from an unlikely source, *American Scientist*, **69**: 56–66.

Whiting, H. T. A. (1980) Dimensions of control in motor learning. In G. E. Stelmach and J. Requin (eds), *Tutorials in Motor Behavior*. New York: North-Holland, pp. 537–50.

Wilson, D. M. (1961) The central nervous control of flight in a locust, *Experimental Biology*, **38**: 471–90.

Windle, W. F. (1940) *Physiology of the Fetus*. Philadelphia: Saunders.

Windle, W. F. (1944) Genesis of somatic motor function in mammalian embryos: A synthesizing article, *Physiological Zoology*, **17**: 247–60.

Wolff, P. H. (1966) The causes, controls, and organization of behavior in the neonate, *Psychological issues*, vol. 5, no. 1, Monograph 17, New York: International Universities Press.

Wolff, J. R. (1981) Some morphogenetic aspects of the development of the central nervous system. In K. Immelmann, G. W. Barlow, L. Petrinovich, and M. Main (eds), *Behavioral Development*, New York: Cambridge University Press, pp. 164–90.

Wolgin, D. L. (1982) Motivation, activation, and behavioral integration. In R. L. Isaacson and N. E. Spear (eds), *The Expression of Knowledge: Neurobehavioral Transformations of Information into Action*, New York: Plenum Press, pp. 243–90.

Wolgin, D. L., Hein, A., and Teitelbaum, P. (1980) Recovery of forelimb placing after lateral hypothalamic lesions in the cat: parallels and contrasts with development, *Journal of Comparative and Physiological Psychology*, **94**: 795–807.

Wyman, R. J. (1976) A simpler network for the study of neurogenetics. In J. C. Fentress (ed.), *Simpler Networks and Behavior*. Sunderland, Mass.: Sinauer, pp. 153–66.

Zelazo, P. R. (1983) The development of walking: New findings and old assumptions, *Journal of Motor Behavior*, **15**: 99–137.

PART IV

Empirical Paradigms: Development of Behavior Systems

Introduction

The papers collected in Parts III and IV of this book cannot always be neatly separated into the categories that we have used, and few of the papers in Part III on perceptual and motor mechanisms actually limited themselves to those mechanisms. However, we think that the chapters in the final section of the book are sufficiently wide-ranging that they can be said to deal with the development of behavior systems rather than with mainly one of the constituent mechanisms. William Hall and Christina Williams' paper with its memorable title is a classic example of the analysis of the development of a behavior system – or should we say two behavior systems? Their conclusion that in rats, suckling indeed isn't feeding, and their finding that suckling is also not a necessary antecedent for the emergence of feeding, are excellent illustrations of the principle of ontogenetic adaptations that Oppenheim put forward in the paper that is chapter 2 of this Reader. Furthermore, their finding that in rat pups suckling is initially not dependent on the level of food deprivation is a good illustration of the phenomenon of the independence of motor mechanisms and central mechanisms that often occurs early in development, as Hogan suggests in the final chapter of this book (cf. Hogan, 1988). Hogan derived some of his ideas from the work of Jaap P. Kruijt, who proposed that in young animals, the motor components of behavior often function as independent units, and that only later do these motor components become integrated into more complex systems. Kruijt based his proposals on a detailed analysis of the development of social behavior of the Burmese red junglefowl, and we have included some excerpts from his classic monograph.

The next two chapters are concerned with the development of social behavior in monkeys. Harry F. Harlow and Margaret K. Harlow review their pioneering work on the profound effects of social isolation on behavioral development. The paper by Robert Hinde is a review of the work of his group on the effects of short-term mother–infant separation on the development of social behavior. Hinde demonstrates that even relatively brief separation from the mother can have profound effects on the infant's social behavior, effects that last for a very long time. As Hinde indicates in his review, the work on monkeys has had an enormous influence on the psychology and psychiatry of human bonding and emotional development.

The concluding chapter of this section is a more recent exposition of Jerry Hogan's concept of behavior systems in development. These ideas were presented for the first time in detail in Hogan (1988). This chapter also provides a synthesis of much of the empirical work that was discussed in the previous chapters in Part III and Part IV. As such we considered it to be an appropriate final chapter of this book.

Reference

Hogan, J. A. (1988) Cause and function in the development of behavior systems. In E. M. Blass (ed.), *Handbook of Behavioral Neurobiology*, vol. 9, New York: Plenum Press, pp. 63–106.

CHAPTER 17

Suckling Isn't Feeding, or Is It? A Search for Developmental Continuities

William G. Hall and Christina L. Williams

I Introduction: Starting Points for a Developmental Analysis

A strategy in developmental analysis is to observe and manipulate a behavioral system at different stages during its maturation in order to trace how that system is assembled and organized. A critical assumption of this particular developmental approach is one of "continuity," that the system being examined at one stage in development is the same system as that examined at a later stage. Often, in the context of this approach, the system examined in early development is viewed as the infantile behavioral form that is gradually elaborated into the adult pattern.

In recent years, this developmental strategy has been applied to the study of feeding behavior in rats. At first glance, feeding appears to be an excellent system for developmental study. It is one of the few behaviors of mammals that is present at birth and continues throughout life. Moreover, it is a reasonably complex and psychologically interesting system that is subject to both internal and external controls, is associated with basic reward mechanisms, and has been shown to be modifiable by certain forms of early experience. It should be a

From *Advances in the Study of Behavior*, vol. 13 (1983), pp. 219–54.

behavioral system which can be used as a model for the development of motivated behavior in general, and which, if studied in detail developmentally, could reveal much about the specific organization and control of ingestive behavior. Indeed, many current theoretical questions about ingestive behavior may only be resolved by developmental analyses that are able to separate the experiential determinants from the physiological determinants of ingestion.

A problem arises, though, when this type of developmental analysis is used to study ingestion. Suckling, the normally occurring form of early feeding, is not the same behavior that adults use to consume food. This fact raises the fundamental question of whether suckling is the appropriate behavior to utilize as the starting point for analysis of the ontogeny of ingestive systems. While suckling is the primitive ingestive response of the infant and serves to get the infant food, this functional similarity is not in itself confirmation that the suckling system of the infant and the feeding system of the adult are the same system. As we shall argue, suckling and feeding may be quite different in terms of both overt behavior and neural substrates.

In this article, we first describe the suckling behavior of infant rats and some of the recently developed techniques used to study it (Section II). We then discuss the ways in which suckling behavior differs from later ingestive behavior and point out suggestive differences in the physiological controls and neural substrates of suckling and later ingestion (Section III). We go on to show that another ingestive system does exist in rat pups concurrently with suckling, and, while it is not used by the infant during normal development, this system may represent the true forerunner of later ingestive behavior (Section IV). Suckling, in contrast, is a behavioral system well adapted for infants' particular needs, but its influence on and representation in later ingestive behavior remains an open and intriguing question (Section V).

II Suckling in Infant Rats

Our studies have used developing rats, not only because there are considerable data on the feeding behavior of adult rats, but because the altricial rat pup undergoes a remarkable morphological, behavioral, and neural development postnatally. At birth rat pups cannot see or hear, they have no fur, and their behavioral repertoire is limited. In the first 3 weeks of life they grow at a rapid rate: sensory and motor capabilities quickly emerge, and, by 21 days of age, pups resemble small adults. This striking development in behavior and external morphology is paralleled by an equally impressive neuroanatomical, neurophysiological, and neurochemical development. Because these ontogenetic events are compressed into a short 3-week period after birth, a unique opportunity exists for relating neural and behavioral development.

Suckling in the natural setting

The 3 weeks after birth is also the period of suckling in rats. In the first week or so, suckling is virtually the only complex behavior pups exhibit. They can locate and attach to nipples within hours of birth, and this behavior provides their sole source of nutrients and fluid for their first 2 weeks of life (Blass et al., 1979b). At about 2 weeks of age, as pups' sensory and motor capacities mature, they begin to nibble on solid food and drink water, although they still continue to suckle for milk (e.g., Babický et al., 1973). Soon, suckling begins to decline, and between 4 and 5 weeks of age it is completely abandoned, having been inhibited, suppressed, and/or replaced by the adult form of independent ingestion. Galef (1981) has reviewed this literature and provides an interesting perspective on the mother–infant relationship.

Suckling represents a dynamically changing interaction between mother and infant; indeed, several obvious changes occur in pups' suckling interaction. For example, during the early weeks, the mother rat provides the fundamental structure for suckling and controls its occurrence (Rosenblatt, 1965). This relationship changes during the third and fourth weeks of life as pups become more active, mobile, and demanding. They come to initiate and control episodes of suckling while the mother spends less time with her pups, a phenomenon which is seen both in laboratory cages and also in a seminatural environment (Addison and Alberts, 1980).

Getting on the nipple

Since the natural suckling situation is an interactive one, it provides little opportunity to study the developing capabilities and characteristics of pups apart from the mother's contribution to the interaction. To get around this problem, we and other investigators have recently made use of a technique to isolate the pups behavior for analysis. The procedure has been to anesthetize rat mothers and then to study aspects of pup suckling behavior in the absence of any maternal contribution to the situation (figure 17.1). From the very first of these studies it was clear that even poorly developed and motorically immature newborn pups were capable of locating and attaching, unaided, to the nipples of their anesthetized mothers (Hall et al., 1975, 1977). Using this nipple-attachment capability as the basis

Figure 17.1 For many of the experiments described in this article, rat pups' mothers were anesthetized and then placed with their nipple lines exposed, as shown here, so that pups' nipple attachment behavior could be observed.

for assessment it has been possible to describe suckling behavior in some detail.

We now know that the pup accomplishes nipple attachment by a process of searching the mother's ventral surface with sweeping head movements often described as "rooting." When the area of a nipple is located, rooting stops and the pup probes into the ventrum with its snout to establish oral contact with a nipple (Pedersen and Blass, 1972). As contact with the nipple is made by the lips and tongue, the nipple is vigorously brought into the mouth by a process of licking and grasping.

Olfaction provides a primary cue in eliciting nipple attachment (Teicher and Blass, 1976). While the essential odor is usually present on the nipple (Hofer et al., 1976) and normally may be contained in saliva deposited by the mother or other pups (Teicher and Blass, 1976, 1977), it appears that the attachment process can be stimulated by the appropriate odor placed on the mother's ventrum, even if it is not actually on the nipple (Pedersen and Blass, 1981). As might be expected, nipple attachment is also highly dependent on intact perioral sensory input carried by the trigeminal nerve (Hofer et al., 1981). Olfactory cues from the mother appear, therefore, to stimulate pups to search for nipples, and then, when they come near the nipple areas, a complex of olfactory and tactile cues elicits and guides attachment.

Suckling, particularly during the first week, is highly dependent on external controls. In young pups, even though they may have recently suckled, suckling is always quickly initiated when the mother is present (Hall et al., 1977; Lorenz et al., 1982). Depriving pups of suckling (i.e., food as well as oral stimulation) has no effect on the initiation of suckling until after pups are 10 days of age. Moreover, until after 20 days of age, sensory (rather than nutritional) deprivation appears to be the determining factor (Henning et al., 1979; Williams et al., 1980). As well, for the first 2 weeks, pups continue to suckle whether or not they get milk from the nipple (Hall et al., 1977). Five-day-old pups will continue suckling for hours even though they receive no milk. Suckling is thus initially a highly prepotent behavior that is exteroceptively dominated and is not dependent on nutritional state or nutritive consequences. Only after several weeks of age do these factors begin to participate in the control of pups' nipple attachment.

Once a pup attaches to a nipple, it maintains its attachment by exerting a continuous negative pressure on the nipple created by sucking. The frequency and intensity of suckling varies and variations have been classified into several types: bursts, treadles, and rhythmic sucking (Brake et al., 1979, 1982; Williams and Brake, 1982). Rhythmic sucking is of particular interest because its frequency can be altered by physiological and experiential manipulations (considered in more detail below). There are also periods during which no "sucking" occurs, though some negative pressure on the nipple is always maintained by the suckling pup.

Getting milk

In order to explore the process by which pups get milk at the nipple it is necessary to return to the natural situation briefly and to discuss what occurs during normal milk delivery. Much of our understanding of how maternal milk ejections are produced is based on the work of Lincoln and his colleagues (1973; Wakerley and Lincoln, 1971: Wakerley and Drewett, 1975).

In the normal litter situation rat pups suckle for large portions of the day (70–80% in 5-day-olds; e.g., Plaut, 1974), yet during most of the time they receive no milk. Pups do not receive milk in a slow continuous stream (as do some other mammals). Rather, milk is available from the mother only intermittently (at 5 to 20-min intervals) during brief (10 sec) milk ejections (figure 17.2; Lincoln et al., 1973). At each of these ejections, milk is released from the mammary cisterns into the ducts of mammary gland, where the pup can withdraw it. Milk ejection is produced in the mother by pulsatile releases of oxytocin from the pituitary that are stimulated by suckling (Wakerley and Lincoln,

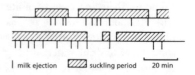

| milk ejection ⬚ suckling period ▬ 20 min

Figure 17.2 Diagram of the distribution of natural milk ejections during periods in which pups are suckling. Note that milk ejections are infrequent and very brief. (Redrawn from Lincoln *et al.*, 1973.)

1971). The systemically released oxytocin stimulates a milk let-down nearly simultaneously at each nipple. After a milk ejection, milk can no longer be withdrawn from the teat (constrictor muscles close the mammary duct), and for the most part, pups become unable to procure milk until the next milk ejection. The amount of milk made available at a milk ejection is limited. Moreover, as will be seen, the amount of this limited volume that pups actually withdraw depends on how vigorously they suck.

Pups show a fascinating response at these brief episodes of milk availability. Just prior to the milk ejection, they tread with their forepaws (Drewett et al., 1974), then, at the beginning of the milk ejection, they immediately extend all limbs (figure 17.3). This response pushes the pups away from their resting position against the mother. Their backs become rigid, their necks arch, their tails often flail, and, though the seal on the nipple is maintained, their jaws open wide. During this "stretch" response, pups make little apparent mouthing movement; they essentially "guzzle" milk from the nipple. The stretch response lasts for the duration of the milk-ejection episode with the pups remaining locked in position, their limbs extended for the entire time. It usually ends with the pups releasing the nipples they were suckling, and shortly afterward searching out and attaching to other nipples.

This process produces a frantic scene in the nest: First, stretch responses occur simultaneously in all pups (since milk is let-down at all nipples at the same time); the mother is often raised off the floor surface, indicating the strength of their response; the pups then leave the nipples they have just been suckling, and each scurries about underneath the dam in search of another nipple. All finally becomes

quiet as pups reattach to nipples and await the next milk ejection.

When rat mothers are anesthetized, their natural milk ejections are blocked. We have taken advantage of this phenomenon in studies of milk intake and pups' milk-getting response (Hall and Rosenblatt, 1977, 1978). To study milk consumption at the nipple in a controlled and observable fashion, thin polyethylene cannulas are installed on the back of pups' tongues (figure 17.4), near the normal position of the tip of the suckled nipple (Martin and Alberts, 1979). Pups will readily attach and suckle from an anesthetized mother with these oral cannulas in position. Using a syringe attached to the cannula with a long piece of tubing, infusions of milk (or other solutions) can be made remotely into pups' mouths.

Pups react to such infusions as if they are receiving a normal milk ejection from the mother. They show the characteristic stretch response, and at the end of the milk delivery come off the nipple they are suckling and attach to another. We found that the stretch response could be triggered by very small infusions of milk (10 µl). On the other hand, if infusions were made for longer durations than the normal 10 sec, pups would remain "stretched" for the duration of the infusion, up to 1 or 2 min. During the stretch response, pups' negative pressure on the nipple is increased by jaw opening and by the draw-

Figure 17.3 Before a milk ejection pups rest quietly at the mother's side (left), but with the onset of milk delivery they engage in a dramatic "stretch" response involving an extension of the whole body (right). Their limbs extend, their backs become rigid, their jaws open wide, and their tails flail.

Figure 17.4 Sagittal section through a young pup's head showing the positioning of a thin polyethylene cannula on the back of the tongue. Infusions of milk can be made through these cannulas at a location in the mouth near where the nipple tip rests during sucking.

ing down of the diaphragm that occurs with the body extension. There is little overt mouthing of the nipple during the response though a shallow high-frequency movement can be detected in electromyographs (Brake et al., 1979).

One of the more instructive findings to come from the studies utilizing simulated milk ejections is that for this unique consummatory response to occur a pup has to be attached to a nipple. If the same milk delivery is made to the same position in a pup's mouth, but the pup is simply lying at its mother's side, off the nipple, no stretch response occurs. The stretch response, as an ingestive pattern for getting milk, appears to be specific to suckling and to being attached to a nipple. Despite some diminution with age (Hall and Rosenblatt, 1971), the stretch remains the technique that pups use to withdraw milk from the nipple throughout the suckling period.

Controls of milk intake

While for young pups it is generally agreed that there is little internal control of nipple attachment (e.g., Lorenz et al., 1982), considerable confusion surrounds the issue of the control of milk intake at the nipple. As will be seen, this issue actually should be a question of "how" and not "whether," and more importantly, what such control of intake "means" with respect to the ontogeny of ingestive systems. Before we elaborate, however, consider a simplified test of intake control in the suckling situation. Using the oral infusion procedures described above, pups, once they have attached, are provided with a milk delivery once every minute rather than after the long intervals that characterize the natural situation. Pups thus have much larger volumes of milk made available to them and can consume the milk without the effort of withdrawing it from the nipple. We are able to assess how much they are willing to consume and how long they were willing to suckle before leaving the nipple in a situation in which we can be certain that they have an unlimited supply of milk.

In such tests, the behavior of 10-day-old and younger pups argued strongly for the absence of any volume control over intake (Hall and Rosenblatt, 1977, 1978). Young pups consumed each infusion, always showing a stretch response, and usually leaving one nipple and reattaching to another before the next infusion. All the while, they became progres-

sively more bloated with milk. At one of their last infusions, as they started to initiate a stretch response, milk would begin to reflux back up their esophagus (due to excessive gastric volumes) and into their mouth and nasal cavity. The pups would become unable to breathe, turn blue, and come struggling off the nipple gasping for air. Five- and 10-day-old pups had to be virtually drowned before they would stop suckling. Even then, if a pup's snout was dried off and its respiration restored, it would usually trundle back to a nipple and attach, and would be willing to undergo further near-drownings, reattaching after each. Thus, in an experimental suckling situation, where milk was frequently available and easy to consume, young pups showed little inclination to control intake by stopping suckling. In contrast, pups older than 2 weeks terminated suckling after consuming modest volumes of milk and appeared to control suckling in a manner related to nutritional state.

The natural suckling situation, though, is more complex because of the intermittent and infrequent milk deliveries, and the fact that pups are required to extract milk from the teat. Natural milk availability is time-bound so that the temporal "window" during which a pup can withdraw milk is limited. In order to withdraw all the milk that is available at any particular milk ejection, pups must be alert to the onset of the milk ejection and respond rapidly with a stretch response. If a pup is late to detect milk ejection, it loses valuable time to withdraw milk. Moreover, a strong negative pressure is required in order to withdraw all the available milk. Therefore, the vigor of suckling may determine how much milk a pup gets at a milk ejection.

These considerations help explain an apparent contradiction in the suckling literature between the lack of intake control seen in pups provided with milk through cannulas and the fact that during normal suckling of a nonanesthetized mother, where natural milk let-down occurs, milk intake *is* influenced by internal factors like deprivation and gastric fill. Lytle et al., (1971) reported this in their seminal study of early ingestion, and it has been replicated many times since (Friedman, 1975; Houpt and Epstein, 1973; Houpt and Houpt, 1975; Blass et al., 1979b; Henning et al., 1979). For example, pups deprived for 8 hr consume more than nondeprived pups when put to suckle with the same mother, and intake in deprived pups is depressed if pups are first stomach loaded by gavage with milk in volumes from 4 to 10% of their body weight (Lorenz et al., 1982). Since we know that pups probably do not control their intake in these situations by whether or not they initiate suckling (see above; recently confirmed for awake mothers by Lorenz et al., 1982), the control of intake by pups sucking from the dam must occur at individual milk let-downs. Such control has in fact been demonstrated (figure 17.5). When deprived and stomach-loaded pups are placed on the nipple and a maternal milk ejection is stimulated with oxytocin, the milk intake of pups in each condition differs without pups leaving the nipples (Blass ct al., 1979b). Deprived pups take more than gastrically loaded pups at the first and each subsequent milk ejection. Thus, there is little doubt that some control of intake can be exercised by pups when they are suckling normally, and that this means that a form of regulation can be achieved by the mother and pups.

These findings do not contradict the data showing an absence of intake control with more freely available milk, but point to a specific component of suckling as the behavioral site at which intake control can occur (one which was of little importance in the cannula studies). That component is the actual "sucking" (or negative pressure) exerted at the time of a milk ejection. Brake's recent studies have shown that 3- to 20-day-old rats do indeed alter the frequency and patterning of their oral sucking movements as a consequence of their nutritional status (Brake et al., 1982). "Rhythmic" patterns of sucking occur more frequently after periods of food deprivation and are depressed by stomach loads of milk. These modulations of ongoing sucking are probably responsible for modulations of intake that occur during normal suckling.

In short, young pups control their intake by how vigorously they suck during the short periods of milk availability, not by whether or not they suckle (i.e., attach or detach from nipples). Only in older pups is the initiation and termination of suckling affected by nutritional state. The control in young pups is effective because of the limited availability of milk and the effort required to extract it, so that pups that are alert and sucking vigorously get more milk than those that are not. Young pups do not terminate suckling, even though they may have received a large amount of milk. More generally, and as an important aside, the mother normally is limited in the amount of milk she can produce and thus provides the ultimate control of intake.

Giving up suckling

At about 15 days of age, the period of weaning begins. At this age, pups have become physiologically competent to digest and absorb foodstuffs other than milk (Henning, 1981). Initially they nibble at solid food; a few days later they take their first drafts of water (Babický et al., 1972, 1973; Galef, 1981). Social interactions facilitate the initiation of feeding and the selection of appropriate foods (Galef, 1982). By 3 weeks of age, pups are consuming a substantial portion of their calories as solid food and by 4–5 weeks of age they have usually stopped suckling altogether. Once suckling has been abandoned, rats differ from many other mammals in that they show no further evidence of suckling or sucking.

As weaning approaches, the prepotency of suckling as a behavior pattern declines. Pups are less likely to spend time suckling unless they are deprived (figure 17.6) and will not remain attached to a nipple for very long unless milk is forthcoming

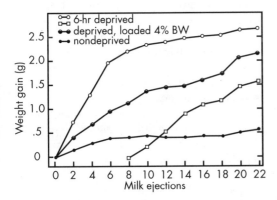

Figure 17.5 Intake (expressed as weight gain) of nondeprived, deprived, and deprived and milk-loaded pups allowed to suckle from a mother whose milk ejections were stimulated by oxytocin injection. Pups were weighed after every two milk ejections and were always observed to have been attached and suckling at the time of the ejection. Each curve is data from an individual pup and indicates that from the first milk ejections there is differential intake based on pup's state. The fourth pup, which was put to suckle after the first six milk ejections, demonstrated that the mother continued to have ample supplies of milk. (From Blass et al., 1979b.)

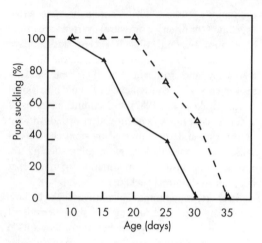

Figure 17.6 The percentage of pups suckling in a 1-hour suckling test with an anesthetized mother, depending on whether pups have been deprived of the mother and food overnight or not deprived. Beginning about 2 weeks of age, deprivation becomes a significant determinant of suckling. (△) Deprived; (▲) nondeprived. (From Williams et al., 1979.)

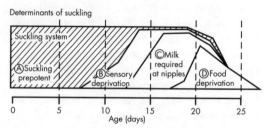

Figure 17.7 Changes in the factors that determine the initiation and maintenance to suckling as pups grow older. (A) Initially suckling is prepotent, and attachment is initiated whenever the appropriate external stimuli are present. (B) By 10 days of age though, the likelihood of suckling initiation is increased if pups have been deprived of sucking (irrespective of whether they are deprived of food). (C) Beginning at 14 days of age there is an onset of control of suckling maintenance; pups will no longer remain attached to a nipple unless they receive milk, instead they will shift from one nipple to another. (D) In the last stages of suckling, pups must also be food deprived for sucking to occur. Finally, after 25–30 days of age, they will not suckle no matter how long they have been deprived.

(Cramer et al., 1980). By 25 days of age, suckling depends on previous food deprivation (Williams et al., 1980). For example, when 20-day-old pups are housed overnight with access to various foods, but deprived of the mother and suckling, they will suckle avidly in subsequent suckling tests (even though they are not nutritionally deprived). Twenty-five-day-old pups given the same overnight food access, but deprived of suckling, are not willing to suckle in subsequent testing. Food deprivation, on the other hand, does reliably stimulate these older pups to suckle. Similarly, Stoloff and Blass (1983), using a Y-maze to examine preference, found that while most food- and suckling-deprived 17-day-old pups prefer the arm of the maze where suckling is permitted, most 28-day-old rats prefer the goal area allowing free feeding. The timing of this transition depends on the type of food and whether social stimuli are present in the food area.

Depicted graphically, the transitions that suckling undergoes might appear as in figure 17.7. In its initial stage (A), suckling is a highly prepotent response of the neonate which is relatively insensitive to any control. As pups mature, suckling becomes dependent on other factors. First, deprivation of suckling per se (B) (independent of nutritional factors) begins to influence whether suckling will oc-

cur. Pups then also begin to attend to whether or not they are provided with milk at the nipple (C). Eventually, pups no longer suckle just for the sake of suckling, but during this period, suckling is maintained only because pups are food deprived and the mother still represents a source of food (D). Finally, suckling is completely abandoned and all feeding occurs independently of suckling. At this time, the mother and other conspecifics still play a role in feeding since they can influence the location where feeding occurs.

The mechanism underlying the transitions in suckling and its eventual disappearance remain a mystery and there are several types of mechanisms that might be involved. For example, some proposed mechanisms involve pups' experiences with changes in the behavior of the mother or characteristics of her milk. Suckling might extinguish if the dam prevented pups' attempts to nurse. In a similar fashion, if the quality of a mother's milk deteriorated, this might discourage pups from suckling. Another type of explanation for the loss of suckling is that it may be a behavior that declines naturally, due to maturing neural substrates, regardless of pups' experience. We (Williams et al., 1980) have found that removing pups from the dam's influence early in the weaning period (15 or 20 days of age) does not prevent the decline in suckling. Pups' willingness or unwillingness to suckle is more dependent upon the age of the pup at the time of testing than on pups' recent experience with suckling. In fact, suckling declines even more rapidly after 20 days of age if the dam is absent and suckling cannot be practiced. Such data suggest that maternal punishment or discouragement is not necessary for weaning and raises the possibility that a maturational change in pups plays a significant role in the eventual disappearance of suckling.

A possible candidate for a role in weaning is the maturation of some component of the serotonergic (5-HT) neurotransmitter system. Pharmacologically blocking 5-HT receptors, presumably deactivating recently developed systems, causes older pups to suckle on a dry nipple in preference to eating (Williams et al., 1979). This suggested that 5-HT maturation may function by altering the salience of oral sensation provided by suckling, since disrupting serotonergic neurotransmission in adult animals increases sensory responsiveness (taste and odor: Brody, 1970; Cicero and Hill, 1970; Lorden and Oltmans, 1978). It may be that blockade of 5-HT receptors in weaning rats reestablishes the oral stimulus characteristics of suckling and in this way induces older rats to attach and suckle. In any event, the maturation of some component of the serotonin system during normal development may be partially responsible for the decline in the importance of perioral sensory stimulation after 20 days of age. Nonetheless, this neural event cannot be totally responsible for the eventual loss of suckling, for 5-HT receptor blockade fails to induce suckling in pups older than 40 days of age.

III Differences between Suckling and Feeding

Our description of suckling is intended to provide a basis for discussion of the relationship between suckling and later ingestive behavior. At the outset, let us note that at least two possible states of affairs could exist. Either the suckling system and later ingestion are continuous and based on the same underlying neural structures and organization, with suckling merely undergoing changes that turn it into the adult ingestive system by the time of weaning (figure 17.8a). Or, the adult ingestive system is

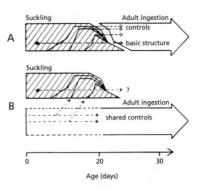

Figure 17.8 Suckling can be viewed as being continuous with later feeding (A), such that it merges into the feeding system at the time of weaning. Or, suckling and later ingestion can be viewed as relatively separate systems (B), sharing only some controls at the time of weaning. In (A), the basic neural structures that subserve suckling would be represented in later ingestion; in (B), there remains a question of what happens to the neural substrates of suckling.

built on a separate ingestive structure (figure 17.8b) and has little in common with that of suckling (though, perhaps overlapping somewhat at the time of weaning). We believe that data from recent studies support the latter notion, and we shall elaborate this position in the following sections. Our major emphasis will be on the distinction between ingestive behavior and the suckling system as it exists in young pups (0–10 days of age), since the differences between ingestion and suckling can be illustrated most straightforwardly at this age.

It cannot be denied that suckling is the means by which infant rats get food and in that sense, suckling is a form of feeding. But this does not mean that suckling and later ingestive behavior represent the same behavioral system or are mediated by the same neural structures. Indeed, in our introduction to suckling behavior, it should have been obvious that there are many aspects of suckling that are unique and distinct from later feeding. These differences contribute to five categories of differences between suckling and later ingestive behavior that we shall discuss: (a) response differences; (b) differences in the external control of behavior; (c) differences in the internal control of behavior; (d) differences in neural substrates; (e) differential experiential determinants. When considered in their totality, these differences argue that suckling in rats is not a system continuous with later ingestion, but is a neurobehavioral system special to infancy. In particular, adult ingestive behavior does not appear to have its origins in suckling behavior.

Response topography

Adult rats lick, lap, mouth, and chew their food. These motor patterns of adult ingestion are a striking contrast to the unique and stereotypic stretch response which rat pups use to get milk during suckling. Unlike the adult, the suckling pup does not use the front of its mouth for ingestion; it guzzles milk at rapid rates without noticeable mouth or tongue movement. Although the stretch response becomes less dramatic as pups grow older, it is still their response to milk delivery at the nipple. Moreover, the stretch response occurs only on the nipple (see Hall, 1979, for the single interesting exception), providing suckling with its own unique consummatory response. Thus, suckling and feeding differ, in that the motor pattern for getting milk from the nipple is very different from the motor pattern for later feeding.

External control of behavior

There appear to be different external determinants of suckling and feeding. A good example reflects the importance of odor cues in stimulating and guiding suckling and their lack of importance for later feeding. Suckling is disrupted by making pups anosmic with $ZnSO_4$ (Singh et al., 1976) or by bulbectomy (Singh and Tobach, 1975), and by removing odor cues from the nipples (Teicher and Blass, 1976). Anosmia has a relatively modest effect on feeding in adult rats (Larue and Le Magnen, 1972). This difference is most obvious when pups are made anosmic around the time of weaning. Suckling is disrupted, but the same pups wean normally to solid food (Alberts, 1976).

Gustatory responsivity may also differ between suckling and feeding. Away from the mother, 20-day-old pups show strong preference for sucrose solutions over milk; on the nipple however, pups will stop suckling if they receive sucrose (Hall and Rosenblatt, 1977). Suckling, but not feeding, is also disrupted by infraorbital nerve section of the trigeminal, which removes orofacial sensory input (Hofer et al., 1981).

The initiation of suckling, as compared to feeding, does not depend on nutritional deprivation. As we have described, suckling is a highly prepotent behavior not sensitive either to young pups' nutritional state or to whether they get milk from the nipple. Early suckling and later feeding can thus be distinguished on the basis of differential dependence on specific sensory cues and nutritional deficit for the initiation of ingestion.

Internal controls of ingestive behavior

In addition to the general absence of control over nipple attachment by nutritional deprivation, there is also no inhibition of attachment by more discrete physiological manipulations. For example, gastric fill produced with either non-nutritive or nutritive gastric preloads (Hall and Rosenblatt, 1978; Williams et al., 1980; Lorenz et al., 1982) does not block nipple attachment, nor does the injection of cholecystokinin (CCK), a putative satiety hormone (Blass et al., 1979a). Even at 2 weeks of age, when nipple attachment first comes to be influenced by separation from the mother, sensory deprivation (figure 17.9) is probably the stimulus for attachment, not nutritive deprivation (Henning et al., 1979; Williams et al., 1980). Thus, internal physiological controls exert little effect on the initiation of suckling until close to the time of weaning at the earliest. This is, of course, in contrast to the distinct physiological control of feeding initiation in adult rats.

When making comparisons between the control of suckling and later ingestion, however, a more appropriate contrast might be between it and the control of intake. Here, though, we are presented with a confusing dilemma, for the usual manner in which food is made available to adults is very different from the way it is made available to the suckling pup. Figure 17.10 depicts the practical differences between the two situations: Pups get intermittent milk deliveries, spaced widely, with a limited volume of milk at each delivery, whereas adults usually have continuous access and unlimited food availability. These differences in how food is offered are so significant that, almost of necessity, if there is control of intake in pups, it could not validly be compared or equated with that of the adult. Even if there were reason to assume that suckling is the precursor to later ingestion, this nonequivalence of feeding situations would cloud all interpretations of

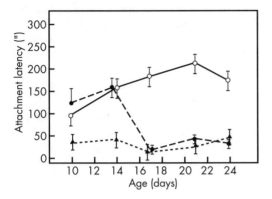

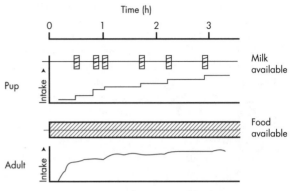

Figure 17.9 Nipple-attachment latencies of pups of different ages and deprivation conditions, showing that until about 2 weeks of age housing pups overnight with a nipple-ligated dam (dashed line) that provides no milk is as effective in reducing attachment latencies as housing pups with a normal mother (solid line). By 18 days of age, though, pups housed with a ligated dam attach as quickly as the totally deprived pups (dotted line); i.e., food is now required to inhibit attachment. (Redrawn from Henning et al., 1979.)

Figure 17.10 Differences between the nature of food availability in the suckling situation and in the typical feeding situation of adult rats. The pups have infrequent opportunities to consume milk and their cumulative intake can only rise gradually over several hours. In contrast, the adult can consume large volumes in a short period of time, and its intake may be controlled by qualitatively different mechanisms.

the ontogeny of intake controls of feeding based on suckling data.

We have reviewed the data demonstrating control of intake at the nipple in the natural suckling situation, and we have shown that the vigor of sucking probably determines how much milk pups get during a milk ejection. As such, "performance" is the major determinant of intake. In contrast, adult animals are usually allowed adequate time to ingest their fill. For adult rats in a typical feeding test, how "good" they are at eating is of little importance. What matters is that, at some point, they stop eating, and so evidence intake control. We have shown that when the suckling situation is made more like the adult feeding situation by providing milk through a cannula, young pups show little control of intake. Thus, although normally there may be some internal control of intake at the nipple, the relationship between this control and that for later ingestion is, at best, unclear.

We should also point out that suckling is probably not "drinking." While Friedman (1975) has shown an increased intake during suckling after a hypovolemic thirst stimulus, Bruno (1979) has more recently found little effect of thirst stimuli on suckling in young pups and an inhibitory effect on both nipple attachment and intake in older pups.

Neural substrates

Results of several pharmacological studies showing differential effects of a drug on the two behaviors suggest that neural systems subserving suckling and feeding are different. An impressive example is the effects of amphetamine treatment: Amphetamine, a catecholamine system excitant, which is known to stimulate activity and depress appetite in adult animals, also increases activity in young rats, whether pups are tested away from the mother (Campbell et al., 1969) or with the mother (increases in approach speed, Raskin and Campbell, 1981; increases in nipple shifting, C. L. Williams, unpublished). However, in suckling rats, amphetamine does not depress intake (Lytle et al., 1971; Raskin and Campbell, 1981), but actually increases the amount of time pups spend rhythmically sucking (Williams and Brake, 1982).

The fact that amphetamine depresses adult ingestion but increases sucking suggests that these two ingestive behaviors are mediated by different pharmacologically reactive neural systems. These data make another point as well: They indicate that a close relationship exists between general motor activity, sucking, and milk intake. When the performance of young pups is enhanced by making them more active, even if this activity is pharmacologically induced, they suck more and as a consequence receive more milk; nutritional needs are secondary.

Other studies support the idea of differences between these two intake systems with respect to catecholamine involvement. Friedman (1974) has shown that when 20-day-old rats are treated with α-methyl-p-tyrosine to inhibit the synthesis of dopamine, their suckling behavior is unaffected, but their ability to wean onto solid food is disrupted. Similar differences with respect to weaning difficulties have been found after chronic catecholamine depletion with 6-hydroxydopamine (Bruno, 1981, also personal communication); such treatment produces slight effects on suckling, but severe disruptions of feeding.

In our own studies (Williams et al., 1979; Williams and Rosenblatt, 1982), we have demonstrated a serotonergic involvement in suckling.

Blockade of 5-HT receptors with drugs such as methysergide or metergoline stimulated nondeprived pups 20–30 days of age to suckle (figure 17.11). Significantly, these antagonists also caused weaning age pups to prefer to suckle rather than eat food, despite the fact that, at this age, even severe food deprivation stimulates little suckling (figure 17.12). The preference for feeding can be reinstated by treatment with a 5-HT receptor agonist. These drug effects appear to be mediated centrally, as 5-HT antagonists injected into the lateral ventricles stimulate weanling rats to suckle in preference to feeding (Schwartz and Williams, 1981). Agonists and releasers of 5-HT completely block suckling, but have only slight depressant effects on feeding in weanlings. In adult rats, pharmacological manipulations of 5-HT neurotransmission do not have dramatic effects on rats' food intake, although there is a suggestion of an inhibitory role for serotonin (Blundell, 1977).

At present, the results from electrolytic brain lesion studies (e.g., of the lateral hypothalamus) do not parallel the pharmacological studies. Most lesions produce similar disruptions of suckling and feeding (for review, see Almli, 1978) and thus do not support the suggested separation of suckling

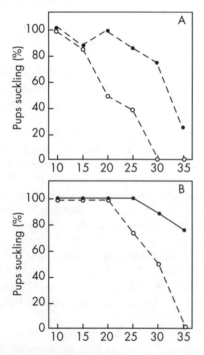

Figure 17.11 Percentage of pups of different ages (from 10 to 35 days) that suckled in a 1-hour test on their anesthetized mother, as a function of deprivation and drug-treatment condition. Methysergide (a 5-HT antagonist) increased the number of pups suckling (and the amount of time spent suckling) in nondeprived (A) and deprived (B) pups. (●) Methysergide; (○) saline. (From Williams et al., 1979.)

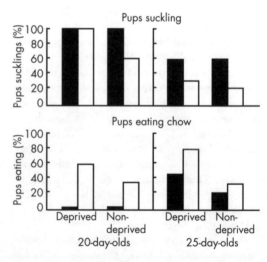

Figure 17.12 When offered a choice between suckling (from an anesthetized mother) and eating chow, methysergide-treated pups (solid bars) at 20 and 25 days of age were more likely to suckle and less likely to eat chow that vehicle-treated pups (pups could do both during these 1-hour tests). (From Williams et al., 1979.)

and feeding systems. However, the multiple and multimodal effects of lesions may allow for the possibility that suckling deficits are caused by different consequences of the lesions than the feeding deficits. We feel that the pharmacological differentiations make a persuasive case for the notion that the neural systems that underlie suckling are not the systems that are of fundamental importance in feeding.

Suckling as an experiential precursor to feeding

Over the years, there have been suggestions that suckling experience may be required for later feeding in rats (e.g., Bash, 1939), or that pups must undergo a weaning process in which they learn about food (Teitelbaum, 1971). Indeed, it has been convincingly demonstrated that suckling experiences can bias later food preferences (e.g., Galef and Henderson, 1972). Nonetheless, pups do not need to experience suckling in order to eat at weaning. If rat pups are artificially reared from shortly after birth to weaning age in the absence of any suckling experience by nourishing them through intragastric cannulas, they will eat and drink normally when first offered solid food (Hall, 1975a). These pups then continue to eat and gain weight at close to normal rates.

This lack of vulnerability of feeding to suckling deprivation can be contrasted to the devastating effect of such deprivation on suckling itself. As early as two days after artificial rearing has started, pups lose the ability or willingness to suckle (Hall, 1975b; Stoloff et al., 1980). Indeed, preventing suckling for just the first 12 hours after birth is sufficient to disrupt suckling behavior (Dollinger et al., 1978). Thus, while suckling is highly vulnerable to disruption by suckling deprivation, feeding is not, and this provides another demonstration of major differences in the systems mediating suckling and feeding.

Another early ingestive system

Using several levels of analysis (from behavioral to neural), we have shown that the suckling behavior of infant rats is different from later ingestive behavior, and is therefore unlikely to be the immature form of the adult ingestive behavior system. Others have argued the same point (e.g., Drewett, 1978) based on some of the same considerations. The best evidence, though, of a difference between suckling and later feeding and drinking would be to demonstrate that there exists during infancy an ingestive system that *is* continuous with later ingestion and is itself distinct from suckling. Such a demonstration would confirm that feeding does not arise out of suckling at weaning, and would rule out the suckling–feeding hypothesis of figure 17.8a. The discovery of just such a system is described in Section IV, and its similarities with adult behavior are explored.

IV   Neonatal Rats Can Feed Away from Their Mother

A difficulty in studying forms of ingestion other than suckling has been that young rats do not feed independently of the mother until after 13 days of age (Babický et al., 1973). Younger pups have been observed to make mouthing movements and occasionally swallow food placed in their mouths, but no significant intake has been observed.

Our own recent studies of early feeding behavior in rats began at the mouth, simply by determining pups' responses to oral infusions of liquid foods (usually milk) made at different ages and under different deprivation conditions (Hall, 1979), an elaboration of a method first used by Wirth and Epstein (1976) in studies on the development of thirst. The infusions were made remotely through fine polyethylene intraoral cannulas so that pups' behavioral responses to milk could be observed. Cannulas similar to those used to study suckling were placed at two locations in pups' mouths (figure 17.13). When infusions were made into the back of the mouth, reliable reflexive swallowing was obtained. In contrast, milk infused into the front of the mouth spilled out unless the pup actively licked, mouthed, and swallowed. Tests, carried out in transparent incubators so that pups' behavior could be observed while they were kept warm, consisted of a 2-min adaptation period followed by a 10-sec infusion of diet every 2 min for 10 min. Infusion rates were standardized in terms of body weight for each age, and, to avoid ceiling effects on intake,

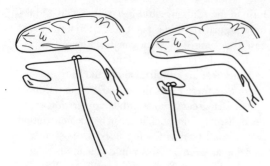

Figure 17.13 Diagram of the two oral cannula positions used for studies of early ingestion. Cannulas were placed either in the back of the mouth (*left*), where infusions would stimulate reflexive swallowing, or in the front of the mouth (*right*), where infusions would spill out unless pups actively licked and swallowed.

were always slightly faster than pups could swallow. Intake volumes were determined by weighing pups before and after testing (in these short tests, weight gain gives an accurate indication of intake). Pups were deprived (of the mother and food) in warm moist incubators.

Behavioral aspects

We were surprised at the beginning of these studies to find that, from 1 day of age, deprived pups actively fed when diet was infused into the front of

their mouths (figure 17.14). They did not utilize the stretch response employed in getting milk during suckling, but instead actively licked and mouthed (like adults) in order to move diet to the back of the mouth for swallowing.

Ingestive responses to oral infusions are not artifacts of the infusion procedure, because we found that pups were capable of an even more independent form of ingestion (Hall and Bryan, 1980). When either milk, sucrose, or wet Purina Chow mash was spread on towels on the floor of test containers, newborn and older pups consumed significant volumes of the diet. To accomplish this, pups probed into the toweling, and lapped the diet off the floor and walls of the test container and from their paws and face (figure 17.15). In short, this ingestion revealed by testing pups away from their mothers appears similar to adult ingestion in many of its motor aspects.

That this ingestive behavior was seen in rat pups where in the past it had not been, is attributable to the fact that pups were tested at warm (33–34°C) temperatures. If pups were tested at room temperature, they rejected milk. This rejection did not depend on body cooling or debilitation because warm pups tested at room temperature rejected milk before body temperature dropped, whereas cool pups fed in a warm incubator immediately ingested diet, even before their body temperature had a chance to rise (Johanson and Hall, 1980).

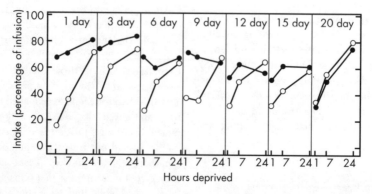

Figure 17.14 Intake (expressed as a percentage of infusion volume, which was scaled to the weight of pups of each age) after various periods of deprivation and at different ages, when infusions were made either into the front or the back of pups' mouths. Intake of infused solutions was highly deprivation dependent for anterior infusions but, with the exception of 20-day-olds, was fairly uniform for the posterior oral infusions where swallowing reflexively protected air passages. (○) Anterior cannula; (●) posterior cannula. (From Hall, 1979.)

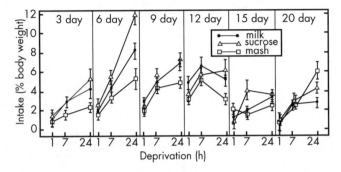

Figure 17.15 Intake (as a percentage of body weight) of test solutions spread on the surface of a test container, for pups of different ages and different deprivation conditions. (From Hall, 1979.)

A second surprise was the behavioral response of deprived pups younger than 9 days of age. In these pups, oral infusions of milk elicited a profound behavioral activation (figure 17.16). Pups not only vigorously mouthed and licked, but they immediately began to crawl, probe, tumble, and climb about their test container, and they continued to do so for the entire 10-min test. They exhibited behaviors that appeared related to suckling and feeding as well as others that were not: It was as if milk infusions elicited all the behavioral fragments in pups' repertoires. Older pups did not display this general activity; rather, their behavior was more directed and specifically ingestive. This overt activity of young pups indicated not only that pups would feed, but also that milk excited them in a manner that was apparent in their affect. This affective component of the response to feeding suggested that more than

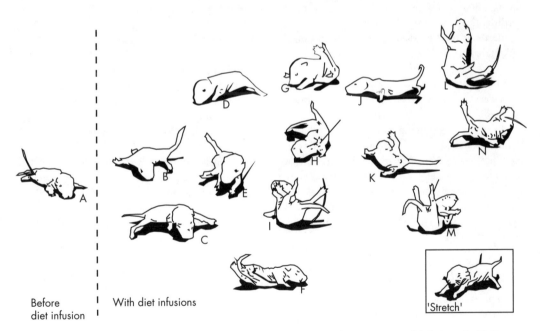

Figure 17.16 Drawings of the behavioral activation shown by deprived pups in response to oral infusions of milk. Pups not only engaged in behaviors that resembled feeding (mouthing, licking, and probing of the floor) and suckling (rooting), but evidenced behavioral fragments of many sorts including vigorous locomotion, rolling, wall climbing, tumbling, grooming, and responses that resembled lordosis and pelvic thrusting. (From Hall, 1979.)

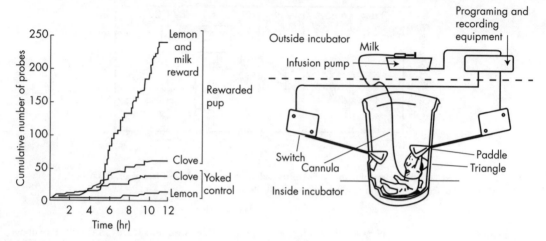

Figure 17.17   Cumulative record (left) of 1-day-old rewarded pup and yoked control in an operant discrimination task (right) with two odor-labeled paddles. Probing up into one paddle (in this case the one with the lemon odor) produced a small oral infusion of milk, while probes into the other paddle has no effect. The yoked control pup received milk infusions when the rewarded pup did, both of its paddles being nonrewarding. (From Johanson and Hall, 1979.)

just reflexive ingestion was being observed; reward and motivational systems were probably already functional.

In fact, in both instrumental and classical learning paradigms, milk delivery was found to be rewarding. One-day-old pups learned to probe into a paddle above their heads for small oral infusions of milk (Johanson and Hall, 1979) and would learn an olfactory discrimination between two paddles, probing into the rewarding rather than a similar nonrewarding paddle several hundred times during the course of a 12-hr test (figure 17.17). Using a classical conditioning procedure, Johanson (Johanson and Hall, 1982; Johanson and Teicher, 1980) has shown that when small milk infusions are paired with a normally aversive odor, pups as young as 3 days of age develop a preference for that odor, and more recently, Johanson et al. (1981) have also reported classical conditioning of mouthing responses to odor cues.

Physiological controls

When pups are eating in the manner described here, away from the dam, both intake volume and ingestive responses were found to be related to the extent of deprivation (e.g., figure 17.14). These results stand in contrast to the lack of (or questionable) intake control exhibited by the same age pups when

they are suckling. Notably, these tests provide food in a manner which is more comparable to an adult ingestion test. Further evidence of internal regulation of food intake similar to that of the adult was obtained in ingestive tests away from the mother when the period of testing was extended to 30 min and oral infusions were made every 2 min throughout. With prolonged tests, deprived pups' ingestion became progressively depressed and activity abated. Mouthing and probing scores also declined in the second half of the test. This pattern of termination of responding resembles the "behavioral sequence of satiety" observed in adult rats (Antin et al., 1975).

The fact that infant rats display behavioral satiety suggests that, along with a deprivation-related initiation of ingestion, certain inhibitory physiological controls are also present soon after birth. We have found that gastric preloads of milk delivered by gavage to 6-day-old pups suppress ingestion (W. G. Hall and J. P. Bruno, in preparation). Similar data, using the same infusion-test procedures, have been presented by Lorenz et al., (1982). These investigators have also shown that vagotomy and cervical sympathectomy eliminate, in an additive fashion, the inhibitory control exerted by gastric preloads.

We can also point out that stimuli which elicit drinking in adult rats (e.g., producing hypo-

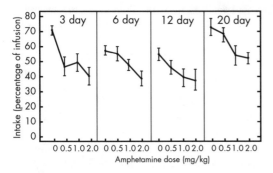

Figure 17.18 Milk intake (during infusion tests) of 24-hour-deprived pups of different ages after amphetamine treatment (n's = 8, $^1/_2$-hr absorption period).

natremia or hypovolemia) will elicit ingestion in pups if they are offered fluids away from the mother (e.g., Bruno, 1981; Wirth and Epstein, 1976). This ingestion is impressive because these stimuli do not enhance suckling.

Neural substrates

Several lines of evidence indicate that catecholamine systems modulate pups' independent ingestion in the same fashion as they modulate adult feeding. For example, when we administered amphetamine to deprived pups tested in either oral infusion tests or "independent" ingestion tests, it suppressed intake in a dose-related fashion in 3-, 6-, 12-, and 20-day-old rats (figure 17.18). Raskin and Campbell (1981) obtained similar data, also using infusion tests, and as already noted, they replicated the earlier studies showing that, when administered to pups suckling at the dam, amphetamine stimulates intake.

Other catecholamine manipulations also alter feeding in infant rats. Ellis and Epstein (1981) found that sated 11-day-old rats ingest infused milk after injections of norepinephrine into the lateral ventricles, whereas control saline-treated pups do not. Norepinephrine does not stimulate pups to ingest water, however. Thus, the noradrenergic system appears to modulate feeding in the young rat as it does in the adult (Davis and Keesey, 1971; Leibowitz, 1976).

Brain lesions, particularly those damaging diencephalic structures thought to participate in ingestive behavior, disrupt ingestion in pups (Almli, 1978; Kornblith and Hall, 1979). Lateral hypotha-

lamic lesions in pups, for example, block ingestive responses to infused milk, though as we pointed out earlier, these lesions also disrupt suckling.

In short, an ingestive system exists in rat pups that is present at birth and is more like the adult system for ingestion than is suckling (i.e., figure 17.8b). This type of ingestion in the pup is similar to adult feeding in several ways: (1) in its motor patterns for consumption, (2) in its ability to support appetitive learning, (3) in its physiological controls, and (4) in at least some of its neural substrates as indicated by response to pharmacological manipulations. This is, of course, in contrast to the suckling behavior of pups younger than 10 days of age, which bears none of these relationships to adult ingestion. In addition, from a purely methodological orientation, the independent feeding procedures represent a situation more analogous to adult feeding situations and so are more appropriate for developmental comparisons. Thus, the infant possesses many of the adult ingestive capabilities, but they are not revealed in suckling behavior. The precursors or origins of the adult behavior appear much better represented by this other ingestive system. It is this system that we believe to be developmentally continuous with the adult behavior and which seems to reflect the common neural substrate for ingestion.

Adaptive significance of the early ingestive system

We do not want to give the impression that the ingestive system we have described is a behavioral system the infant ever uses or one which is of adaptive value to the pup. The only time infants might use their ability to eat independently of the dam would be in the situation where the litter was abandoned or a pup was separated from the litter. In such a situation, the pup is unlikely to be warm (a requirement for feeding away from the mother), and is unlikely to encounter a liquid or semisolid diet. Even if these first two conditions existed, it is even less likely that the pup's new food source would be adequate for growth. Therefore, although infant rats can ingest food independently, and can regulate their intake, they probably could not use these capabilities in nature until weaning.

Pups' independent ingestion is perhaps more usefully conceptualized as a hidden forerunner to later ingestion that will only reveal its presence if tricked in the right manner. This feeding system is not normally suppressed or inhibited in infants, it is just not normally elicited. It provides a good example of the manner in which development "anticipates" function (Anokhin, 1964) and shows that we may be able to tap into some of these anticipatory aspects of developing behavioral systems in order to determine how they are constructed and organized. That is, we have a means of pushing back the time that feeding is first observed so that the functional development of the system can be analyzed.

V   If Suckling Isn't Feeding, What Is It?

If suckling is not the precursor to later feeding, and if it exists in parallel with another ingestive system, how should we view suckling? If it does not represent the primordium for a later developing system, what does it represent?

Suckling as a special adaptation

An informative distinction between suckling and feeding is the difference in the internal control of the two behaviors (i.e., in the relative absence of physiological control over suckling). This difference serves pups well, for it helps ensure that they receive the maximum amount of milk available during the preweaning period of rapid growth. There is little danger that pups will overeat since milk availability is ultimately limited by the mother's ability to produce it. That the mother's milk resources are limited is exemplified by the finding that pups in small litters ingest more milk and grow at more rapid rates than pups in large litters (e.g., Widdowson and Kennedy, 1962). Pups' limited intake control via suckling might best be viewed as an adaptation of infancy which allows pups to take advantage of changing milk availability and maximize growth. In order to do this, the regulatory capabilities the pup already possesses (i.e., control of intake when fed away from the mother) are either irrelevant or are overridden. In a sense, suckling is a behavior that allows pups to avoid feeding and to obviate its intake controls.

Oppenheim (1981) has recently considered a variety of behavioral and morphological structures that appear only at certain developmental stages, conceptualizing them as "transient ontogenetic ad-

aptations." Along with others (e.g., Prechtl, 1981; Galef, 1981), he has emphasized how infants are suited to each developmental stage and how particular forms of early adaptation need not be viewed as steps in the development of adult mechanisms. Suckling is probably a good example of such a transient ontogenetic adaptation. Prechtl notes, as well, that during transitional stages, some primitive response systems may exist simultaneously with those that will replace them, and takes this as an indication of the independence of early and later systems. Such simultaneous existence is exemplified by the coexisting systems for suckling and independent ingestive behavior in infant rats.

Recent work of Martin and Alberts (1979) provides a nice illustration of just how special suckling is for young rat pups. These investigators showed that 10-day-old pups will not learn a conditioned taste aversion if a taste stimulus is presented during suckling and paired with lithium-chloride-induced toxicosis. But, if the same taste stimulus is presented away from the mother and is paired with toxicosis, a robust and lasting aversion is learned. Some aspect of suckling seems to protect young pups from forming any aversion to the cues associated with it. Pups' failure to associate suckling with negative consequences is also clear in the previously described finding that young pups are willing to continue suckling even after they have consumed huge volumes of milk and have severely distended their gastrointestinal tracts. These findings demonstrate that not only is suckling a highly prepotent behavior, but that it is protected from aversive disruption or even aversive association. In this regard, it serves the pup well, maximizing intake from the only potential source and ensuring continual nutritional, thermal, and social interactions with the mother. It is a system unique to the preweaning period and of seemingly great utility. We should not feel compelled to assume that it must be continuous with later ingestive behavior.

Learning in the context of suckling

While suckling may be special to infancy, we are still confronted with the fact that the developing rat spends the majority of its first weeks of life engaged in suckling, and that early formative experiences occur in the context of the nest, siblings, dam, and suckling. It remains possible that infants learn a great deal while suckling and that these experiences carry over into their adult life. The suckling system could be playing a role integrating these experiences into later feeding or into the organization of other behavioral systems, but this remains an open question.

Despite findings showing that experiencing suckling is not necessary for feeding to emerge at weaning, several groups of researchers have shown that experiences associated with suckling can influence later feeding. Galef and co-workers (Galef, 1977; Galef and Clark, 1972; Galef and Henderson, 1972; also Bronstein et al., 1975) found that weanling rats offered a choice between two diets initially tended to choose the diet that their mother had been fed. While such taste preferences were transient, Capretta and Rawls (1974) were able to demonstrate a more lasting preference when the diet was given a distinct odor. Thus, although the artificial-rearing experiments demonstrate that feeding and regulatory ingestive capacities will emerge in the absence of any earlier ingestive experience, it is also clear that taste and odor preferences for certain foods can be influenced by experiences occurring during suckling. Whether these experiences are incorporated into a suckling structure that persists in later behavior, or whether they are incorporated into a more general structure of preference and aversion, is the important question here. The suckling system need not be the mediator of these experiential effects.

Experiences during the suckling period might also influence later behaviors such as olfactory preferences for mates or other conspecifics. On at least a limited basis such suckling-based learning can occur during infancy (Brake, 1981). A recent study (Block et al., 1981) has shown that, in another group of rodents, Mongolian gerbils, saliva-related cues act as chemical signals in all aspects of social development (filial exchanges at weaning, sibling interactions at puberty, and sexual preferences in adulthood). Lee and Ingersol (1979) have shown that saliva is an important chemical cue in the aggressive behavior of mice. Since suckling is partly dependent on saliva-related cues, olfactory experiences with saliva during suckling may have enduring effects on rodents' later social and sexual preferences as well as on their later food choices. In addition, there are numerous opportunities for learning about thermal, olfactory, tactile, and social

relationships as a result of suckling interactions (see Alberts, 1982). Suckling certainly provides the opportunity for the incorporation of innumerable experiences, but the suckling system itself may or may not be important for carrying these effects into adulthood.

Neural representation in later behavior

After suckling disappears from the rats' behavioral repertoire, what happens to the behavior patterns and neural representation of suckling? Are the neural substrates inhibited or suppressed? Do these structures become incorporated as a whole, or in part, into other adult behavioral systems? Answers to these types of questions await the development of techniques that allow us to identify and label a neural system subserving a behavior such as suckling so that it can be traced throughout the animal's ontogeny. In the meantime, we can only speculate on the basis of bits of suggestive data.

The loss of involuntary reflexes as development progresses is a common process among infant mammals (Peiper, 1963). In the human infant, the automatic grasp reflex of the hand and foot, the coordinated stepping pattern, and the rooting and suckling reflexes of the mouth all become increasingly difficult to elicit as the capacity for voluntary reaching, grasping, walking, and eating develop. After brain damage, or with senility, many of these reflexes of infancy reappear. Their neural substrates have not been lost, but merely suppressed by overlying neural structures, or somehow incorporated into more complex adult behavior. The Jacksonian notion of more complex and rostral neural hierarchies being superimposed on primitive caudal systems may be a model for this type of developmental change (e.g., Mabry and Campbell, 1974; Paulson and Gottlieb, 1968).

A similar process of neurobehavioral maturation may also underly the loss of suckling in infant rats. Our research indicates that the maturation of serotonergic neurotransmitter systems plays a role in the disappearance of suckling (Williams et al., 1979), in that, for a time, pharmacological blockage of 5-HT receptors in postweaning rats can reinstate suckling behavior. But something else must also be involved in suppressing or eliminating suckling, since 5-HT receptor blockade does not induce adult rats to suckle.

It is also possible that neural components of portions of suckling are incorporated into ingestive or other behavioral systems of the adult animal. There may be some small degree of overlap between the neural systems for suckling and those for feeding. For example, perioral sensory effects may be represented by the same substrates. At weaning, pups' strong preference for suckling stimulation appears to switch to a preference for licking, biting, and chewing. An oral component is involved in both behaviors, only the manipulated object differs. In this regard, it can be noted that there are repercussions of oral stimulus deprivation for feeding as well as suckling. For example, in adult rats, oral feeding stimulation must accompany nutritional or hydrational repletion in order to terminate the effects of food or fluid deprivation (Antin et al., 1977; Blass and Hall, 1976).

Components of suckling systems could also be represented in later behaviors other than ingestion. That is, a portion of the neural system that underlies suckling may be incorporated into another behavioral system. Experiential effects on suckling might be represented in the later system, though possibly in nonobvious ways or only in ways detectable by a structural analysis (see the recent demonstration by Gottlieb, 1982, of nonobvious effects of experience on later behavior). Freudian notions would fit within the context of this conceptual scheme. Classically, for example, some experience occurring during suckling might affect later social or sexual behavior. There is an interesting but inconclusive body of early experimental animal literature directed to this point (Levy, 1934). The suckling opportunities of puppies were manipulated and later effects on their "personalities" were investigated. More recently, Cramer and Pfister (1981) have shown a relationship between the amount of nipple shifting young pups engage in and later learning performance in a radial-arm (spatial) maze.

These suggestions regarding the eventual disposition of the circuitry underlying suckling illustrate the complexity of, and the current vagueness of, the notion of developmental continuity. They also indicate that the question of continuity during behavioral development might ultimately be reduced to one of neural structure and organization, and not one of function or purpose. The neural representation of suckling may be partially suppressed by more complex neural structures, or may become incorporated into other adult behaviors. Perhaps associations formed through suckling may be utilized in other food-getting, social, or sexual behaviors in adulthood. Not until techniques are developed that will enable us to follow the neural substrates of developing behaviors will we have the information to understand these processes. Then the question may not be whether continuity exists, but in what manner and at what level it occurs.

VI   Conclusion

The morphological ontogeny witnessed by the embryologist reveals a progressive differentiation of tissue, in which later structures can be determined to have originated in or differentiated from earlier structures. A similar process of differentiation is often assumed for the development of behavioral systems, whereby complex behaviors of adult organisms are thought to have had their origins in the simpler behaviors of the infant. Unfortunately, it becomes particularly difficult to confirm the continuity between a behavioral system that exists in early development and a later one that may appear similar. Suckling behavior and later ingestive behavior illustrate this difficulty. Suckling, the early form of feeding, probably has little in common with the adult systems for ingestion. The difficulty of assessing the extent of behavioral continuity or discontinuity is not a small problem, since a great deal of the power of developmental analysis depends on an understanding of the relationship between behaviors observed throughout development. For ingestion, many erroneous conclusions about its emergence, ontogeny, and organization would come from viewing suckling as its point of origin. Such findings for suckling illustrate the general difficulty in determining the relationship between adaptive behaviors of infancy and functionally similar representations in adulthood.

Acknowledgments

Portions of the work reported in this article were supported by grants from the National Science Foundation and the National Institute for Child

Health and Human Development, and by the North Carolina Division of Mental Health. Some of the ideas and themes expressed here date back to stimulating conversations during a visit with J. Alberts and M. Friedman in the summer of 1978.

We are grateful to S. Coyle and I. B. Johanson for comments on an earlier draft of this article.

References

Addison, K. S., and Alberts, J. R. (1980) Patterns of mother–infant interaction in a semi-natural habitat, *Pap., Meet. Int. Soc. Dev. Psychobiol., 1980*, p. 1.

Alberts, J. R. (1976) Olfactory contributions to behavioral development in rodents. In *Mammalian Olfaction, Reproductive Processes, and Behavior*, R. L. Doty (ed.), pp. 67–94, Academic Press, New York.

Alberts, J. R. (1982) Ontogeny of olfaction: Reciprocal roles of sensation and behavior in the development of perception. In *Development of Perception: Psychobiological Perspectives*, R. N. Aslin, J. R. Alberts, and M. R. Peterson (eds), Vol. 1, pp. 322–57, Academic Press, New York.

Almli, C. R. (1978) The ontogeny of feeding and drinking: Effects of early brain damage, *Neurosci. Biobehav. Rev., 2*, 281–300.

Anokhin, P. K. (1964) Systemogenesis as general regulator of brain development, *Prog. Brain Res., 9*, 54–87.

Antin, J., Gibbs, J., Holt, J., Young, R. C., and Smith, G. P. (1975) Cholecystokinin elicits the complete behavioral sequence of satiety in rats, *J. Comp. Physiol. Psychol., 89*, 783–90.

Antin, J., Gibbs, J., and Smith, G. P. (1977) Intestinal satiety requires pregastric food stimulation, *Physiol. Behav., 18*, 421–5.

Babický, A., Pavlík, L., Pařízek, J. Ošťádalová, I., and Kolář, J. (1972) Determination of the onset of spontaneous water intake in infant rats, *Psysiol. Bohemoslov., 21*, 467–71.

Babický, A., Pařízek, J., Ošťádalová, I., and Kolář, J. (1973) Initial solid food intake and growth of young rats in nests of different sizes, *Physiol. Bohemoslov., 22*, 557–66.

Bash, K. W. (1939) Contribution to a theory of the hunger drive, *J. Comp. Psychol., 28*, 137–60.

Blass, E. M., Beardsley, W., and Hall, W. G. (1979a) Age dependent inhibition of suckling by cholecystokinin, *Am. J. Physiol., 236*, e567–e570.

Blass, E. M., and Hall, W. G. (1976) Drinking termination: Interaction of hydrational, orogastric, and behavioral controls in rats, *Psychol. Rev., 83*, 356–74.

Blass, E. M., Hall, W. G., and Teicher, M. H. (1979b) The ontogeny of suckling and ingestive behaviors, *Prog. Psychobiol. Physiol. Psychol., 8*, 243–99.

Block, M. L., Volpe, L. C., and Hayes, M. J. (1981) Saliva as a chemical cue in the development of social behavior, *Science, 211*, 1062–4.

Blundell, J. E. (1977) Is there a role for serotonin (5-hydroxytryptamine) in feeding? *Int. J. Obes., 1*, 15–42.

Brake, S. L. (1981) Suckling infant rats learn a preference for a novel olfactory stimulus paired with milk delivery, *Science, 211*, 506–8.

Brake, S. L., Wolfson, V., and Hofer, M. A. (1979) Electromyographic patterns associated with nonnutritive suckling in 11–13 day old rat pups, *J. Comp. Physiol. Psychol., 93*, 760–70.

Brake, S. L., Sager, D. J., Sullivan, R., and Hofer, M. A. (1982) The role of intra-oral and gastrointestinal cues in the control of sucking and milk consumption in rat pups, *Dev. Psychobiol.* (in press).

Brody, J. F. (1970) Behavioral effects of serotonin in depletion and of p-chlorophenylalanine (a serotonin depletor) in rats, *Psychopharmacology, 17*, 14–33.

Bronstein, P. M., Levine, M. J., and Marcus, M. (1975) A rat's first bite: The nongenetic, cross-generational transfer of information, *J. Comp. Physiol. Psychol., 89*, 295–8.

Bruno, J. P. (1979) The ontogeny of thirst systems in rats. Doctoral dissertation, Johns Hopkins University, Baltimore. Maryland (unpublished).

Bruno, J. P. (1981) Development of drinking behavior in preweaning rats, *J. Comp. Physiol. Psychol., 95*, 1016–27.

Campbell, B. A., Lytle, L. D., and Fibiger, H. C. (1969) Ontogeny of adrenergic arousal and cholinergic inhibitory mechanisms in the rat, *Science, 166*, 635–7.

Capretta, P. J., and Rawls, L. H. (1974) Establishment of a flavor preference in rats: Importance of nursing and weaning experience, *J. Comp. Physiol. Psychol., 86*, 670–3.

Cicero, T. J., and Hill, S. Y. (1970) Ethanol self-selection in rats: A distinction between absolute and 95% ethanol, *Physiol. Behav., 5*, 787–91.

Cramer, C. P., and Pfister, J. F. (1981) Learning to forage in the nest: Nipple-shifting and later spatial learning, *Pap., Meet. Int. Soc. Dev. Psychobiol., 1981*, p. 9.

Cramer, C. P., Blass, E. M., and Hall, W. G. (1980) The ontogeny of nipple shifting behavior in albino rats: Mechanisms of control and possible significance, *Dev. Psychobiol., 13*, 165–80.

Davis, J. K., and Keesey, R. E. (1971) Norepinephrine-induced eating – Its hypothalamic locus and an alternative interpretation of action, *J. Comp. Physiol. Psychol., 77*, 394–402.

Dollinger, M. J., Holloway, W. R., and Denneberg, V. H. (1978) Nipple attachment in rats during the first 24 hours of life, *J. Comp. Physiol. Psychol., 92*, 619–26.

Drewett, R. F. (1978) The development of motivational systems, *Prog. Brain Res., 48*, 407–17.

Drewett, R. F., Statham, C., and Wakerley, J. B. (1974) A quantitative analysis of the feeding behavior of suckling rats, *Anim. Behav., 22*, 907–13.

Ellis, S. B., and Epstein, A. N. (1981) Norepinephrine-induced feeding in the suckling rat, *Pap., East. Psychol. Assoc. Meet., 1981*.

Friedman, M. (1974) Ontogeny of feeding and drinking: Catecholamine involvement in the weaning process, *Pap., East. Psychol. Assoc. Meet., 1974.*

Friedman, M. I. (1975) Some determinants of milk ingestion in suckling rats, *J. Comp. Physiol. Psychol.,* **89,** 636–47.

Galef, B. G. (1977) Mechanismms for the social transmission of acquired food preferences from adult to weanling rats. In *Learning Mechanisms in Food Selection,* L. M. Barker, M. Best, and M. Domjan (eds), pp. 123–50, Baylor University Press, Waco, Texas.

Galef, B. G. (1981) The ecology of weaning: Parasitism and the achievement of independene by altricial mammals. In *Parental Care in Mammals,* D. J. Gubernick and P. H. Klopfer (eds), pp. 211–241, Plenum, New York.

Galef, B. G. (1982) The development of flavor preferences in man and animals: The role of social and nonsocial factors. In *Development of Perception: Psychobiological Perspectives,* R. N. Aslin, J. R. Alberts, and M. R. Peterson (eds), Vol. 1, pp. 411–31, Academic Press, New York.

Galef, B. G., and Clark, M. M. (1972) Mother's milk and adult presence: Two factors determining initial dietary selection by weanling rats, *J. Comp. Physiol. Psychol.,* **78,** 220–5.

Galef, B. G., and Henderson, P. W. (1972) Mother's milk: A determinant of the feeding preferences of weanling rat pups, *J. Comp. Physiol. Psychol.,* **78,** 213–19.

Gottlieb, G. (1982) Roles of early experience in species-specific perceptual development. In *Development of Perception: Psychobiological Perspectives,* R. N. Aslin, J. R. Alberts, and M. R. Peterson (eds), Vol. 1, pp. 5–44, Academic Press, New York.

Hall, W. G. (1975a) Weaning and growth of artificially reared rats, *Science,* **190,** 1313–15.

Hall, W. G. (1975b) The ontogeny of ingestive behavior in rats. Doctoral dissertation, Johns Hopkins University, Baltimore, Maryland (unpublished).

Hall, W. G. (1979) The ontogeny of feeding in rats, I: Ingestive and behavioral responses to oral infusions, *J. Comp. Physiol. Psychol.,* **93,** 977–1000.

Hall, W. G., and Bruno, J. P. (1982) The ontogeny of feeding in rats, VI: Inhibition of ingestion by gastric preloads (in preparation).

Hall, W. G., and Bryan, T. E. (1980) The ontogeny of feeding in rats, II: Independent ingestive behavior, *J. Comp. Physiol. Psychol.,* **94,** 746–56.

Hall, W. G., Cramer, C. P., and Blass, E. M. (1975) Developmental changes in suckling of rat pups, *Nature* (London), **258,** 318–20.

Hall, W. G., and Rosenblatt, J. S. (1977) Suckling behavior and intake control in the developing rat pup, *J. Comp. Physiol. Psychol.,* **91,** 1232–47.

Hall, W. G., and Rosenblatt, J. S. (1978) Development of nutritional controls of food intake in suckling rat pups, *Behav. Biol.,* **24,** 412–27.

Hall, W. G., Cramer, C. P., and Blass, E. M. (1977) Ontogeny of suckling in rats: Transitions toward adult ingestion, *J. Comp. Physiol. Psychol.,* **91,** 1141–55.

Henning, J. S. (1981) Postnatal development: Coordination of feeding, digestion, and metabolism, *Am. J. Physiol.,* **241,** G199–G214.

Henning, J. S., Chang, S. S. P., and Gisel, E. G. (1979) Ontogeny of feeding controls in suckling and weanling rats, *Am. J. Physiol.,* **237,** R187–R191.

Hofer, M. A., Shair, H., and Singh, P. (1976) Evidence that maternal ventral skin substances promote suckling in infant rats, *Physiol. Behav.,* **17,** 131–6.

Hofer, M. A., Fisher, A., and Shair, H. (1981) Effects of infraorbital nerve section on survival, growth, and suckling behaviors of developing rats, *J. Comp. Physiol. Psychol.,* **95,** 123–33.

Houpt, K. A., and Epstein, A. N. (1973) Ontogeny of controls of food intake in the rat: GI fill and glucoprivation, *Am. J. Physiol.,* **225,** 58–66.

Houpt, K. A., and Houpt, R. T. (1975) Effects of gastric loads and food deprivation on subsequent food intake in suckling rats, *J. Comp. Physiol. Psychol.,* **88,** 764–72.

Johanson, I. B., and Hall, W. G. (1979) Appetitive learning in 1-day-old rat pups, *Science,* **205,** 419–21.

Johanson, I. B., and Hall, W. G. (1980) The ontogeny of feeding in rats, III: Thermal determinants of early ingestive responding, *J. Comp. Physiol. Psychol.,* **94,** 977–92.

Johanson, I. B., and Hall, W. G. (1982) Appetitive conditioning in neonatal rats: Conditioned orientation to a novel odor, *Dev. Psychobiol.,* **15,** 379–97.

Johanson, I. B., and Teicher, M. H. (1980) Classical conditioning of an odor preference in 3-day-old rats, *Behav. Neural Biol.,* **29,** 132–6.

Johanson, I. B., Polefrone, J. M., and Hall, W. G. (1981) Classically conditioned activation in neonatal rats, *Pap., Meet. Int. Soc. Dev. Psychobiol., 1981,* p. 24.

Kornblith, C. L., and Hall, W. G. (1979) Brain transections selectively alter ingestion and behavioral activation in neonatal rats, *J. Comp. Physiol. Psychol.,* **93,** 1109–17.

Larue, C. G., and Le Magnen, J. (1972) The olfactory control of meal pattern in rats, *Physiol. Behav.,* **9,** 817–21.

Lee, C. T., and Ingersoll, P. W. (1979) Salivary cues in the mouse: A preliminary study, *Horm. Behav.,* **12,** 20–9.

Leibowitz, S. F. (1976) Brain catecholaminergic mechanisms for control of hunger. In *Hunger: Basic Mechanisms and Clinical Implications,* D. Novin, W. Wyrwicka, and G. Bray (eds), pp. 1–18, Raven Press, New York.

Levy, D. (1934) Experiments on the sucking reflex and social behavior of dogs, *Am. J. Orthopsychiatry,* **4,** 203–44.

Lincoln, D. W., Hill, A., and Wakerley, J. B. (1973) The milk-ejection reflex of the rat: An intermittant function not abolished by surgical levels of anesthesia, *J. Endocrinol.,* **57,** 459–76.

Lorden, J. F., and Oltmans, G. A. (1978) Alteration of the characteristics of learned taste aversion by manipulation of serotonin levels in the rat, *Pharmacol., Biochem. Behav.,* **8,** 13–18.

Lorenz, D. N., Ellis, S. B., and Epstein, A. N. (1982) Differential effects of upper gastrointestinal fill on milk ingestion and nipple attachment in the suckling rat, *Dev. Psychobiol.*, 15, 309–30.

Lytle, L. D., Moorecroft, W. H., and Campbell, B. A. (1971) Ontogeny of amphetamine anorexia and insulin hyperphagia in the rat, *J. Comp. Physiol. Psychol.*, 77, 388–93.

Mabry, P. D., and Campbell, B. A. (1974) Ontogeny of serotonergic inhibition of behavioral arousal in the rat, *J. Comp. Physiol. Psychol.*, 86, 193–201.

Martin, L. T., and Alberts, J. R. (1979) Taste aversions to mother's milk: The age-related role of nursing in acquisition and expression of a learned association, *J. Comp. Physiol. Psychol.*, 93, 430–55.

Oppenheim, R. W. (1981) Ontogenetic adaptations and retrogressive processes in the development of the nervous system and behavior: A neuroembryological perspective. In *Maturation and Development: Biological and Psychological Perspectives*, K. J. Connolly and H. F. R. Prechtl (eds), pp. 73–109, Lippincott, Philadelphia.

Paulson, G., and Gottlieb, G. (1968) Developmental reflexes: The reappearance of fetal and neonatal reflexes in age patients, *Brain*, 93, 37–52.

Pedersen, P. E., and Blass, E. M. (1982) Olfactory control over suckling in albino rats. In *Development of Perception: Psychobiological Perspectives*, R. N. Aslin, J. R. Alberts, and M. R. Peterson (eds), Vol. 1, pp. 359–81, Academic Press, New York.

Peiper, A. (1963) *Cerebral Function in Infancy*, Consultants Bureau, New York.

Plaut, S. M. (1974) Adult–litter relations in rats reared in single and dual-chambered cages, *Dev. Psychobiol.*, 7, 111–20.

Prechtl, H. F. R. (1981) The study of neural development as a perspective of clinical problems. In *Maturation and Development: Biological and Psychological Perspectives*, K. J. Connolly and H. F. R. Prechtl (eds), pp. 198–215, Lippincott, Philadelphia.

Raskin, L. A., and Campbell, B. A. (1981) The ontogeny of amphetamine anorexia: A behavioral analysis, *J. Comp. Physiol. Psychol.*, 95, 425–35.

Rosenblatt, J. S. (1965) The basis of synchrony in the behavioral interaction between mother and her offspring in the laboratory rat. In *Determinants of Infant Behavior*, B. M. Foss (ed.), Vol. 3, pp. 3–43, Methuen, London.

Schwartz, G. J., and Williams, C. L. (1981) Serotonin agonists and antagonists administered intraventricularly alter suckling of weanling rats, *Pap., East. Psychol. Assoc., 1981.*

Singh, P. J., and Tobach, E. (1975) Olfactory bulbectomy and nursing behavior in rat pups, *Dev. Psychobiol.*, 8, 151–64.

Singh, P. J., Tucker, A. M., and Hofer, M. A. (1976) Effects of nasal ZnSO$_4$ irrigation and olfactory bulbectomy on rat pups, *Physiol. Behav.*, 17, 373–82.

Stoloff, M. L., and Blass, E. M. (1983) Changes in appetitive behavior in weanling age rats: Transitions from suckling to feeding behavior, *Dev. Psychobiol.* (in press).

Stoloff, M. L., Kenny, J. T., Blass, E. M., and Hall, W. G. (1980) The role of experience in suckling maintenance in albino rats, *J. Comp. Physiol. Psychol.*, 94, 847–56.

Teicher, M. H., and Blass, E. M. (1976) Suckling in newborn rats: Eliminated by nipple lavage, reinstated by pup saliva, *Science*, 193, 422–4.

Teicher, M. H., and Blass, E. M. (1977) First suckling response of the newborn albino rat: The roles of olfaction and amniotic fluid, *Science*, 198, 635–6.

Teitelbaum, P. (1971) The encephalization of hunger, *Prog. Physiol. Psychol.*, 4, 319–50.

Wakerley, J. B., and Drewett, R. F. (1975) The pattern of sucking in the infant rat during spontaneous milk ejection, *Physiol. Behav.*, 15, 227–81.

Wakerley, J. B., and Lincoln, D. W. (1971) Intermittent release of oxytocin during suckling in the rat, *Nature* (London), 233, 180–1.

Widdowson, E. M., and Kennedy, G. C. (1962) Rate of growth, mature weight, and life-span, *Proc. R. Soc. London, Ser. B*, 156, 96–108.

Williams, C. L., and Rosenblatt, J. S. (1982) (In preparation).

Williams, C. L., and Brake, S. E. (1982) Drug effects on EMG-recorded sucking responses in 20-day-old rats (in preparation).

Williams, C. L., Rosenblatt, J. S., and Hall, W. G. (1979) Inhibition of suckling in weaning-age rats: A possible serotonergic mechanism, *J. Comp. Physiol. Psychol.*, 93, 414–49.

Williams, C. L., Hall, W. G., and Rosenblatt, J. S. (1980) Changing oral cues in suckling of weaning-age rats: Possible contributions to weaning, *J. Comp. Physiol. Psychol.*, 94, 472–83.

Wirth, J. B., and Epstein, A. N. (1976) The ontogeny of thirst in the infant rat, *Am. J. Physiol.*, 230, 188–98.

CHAPTER 18

Ontogeny of Social Behaviour in Burmese Red Junglefowl (*Gallus gallus spadiceus*) (*excerpt*)

JAAP P. KRUIJT

Ontogeny of Behaviour

In *The Study of Instinct* (1951), Tinbergen stated clearly that causal explanations of the ontogeny of species-specific behaviour should be sought. He stressed our ignorance in this respect, but discussed a number of facts bearing on the problem. He gave examples illustrating that at the level of locomotion, growth of the nervous system plays a role, and discussed the influence of hormones. He suggested that descriptions of the ontogenetic appearance of more complex behaviour are urgently needed. Following Lorenz, Tinbergen phrased some of the other ontogenetic problems in terms of a superposition of learned on innate components.

The latter approach has been criticized by Beach, Hebb, Lehrman and Schneirla. These authors pointed out that the dichotomy of innate and learned does not work. They advanced the view that in reality the ontogeny of behaviour is, like all biological phenomena, due to a complete interaction between genetical and environmental factors. In consequence, it is impossible to isolate components due to the genetical complex of factors from components due to the environmental complex.

From J. P. Kruijt, 'Ontogeny of Social Behaviour in Burmese Red Junglefowl (*Gallus gallus spadiceus*)', *Behaviour*, Supplement 9 (1964), pp. 2–5, 172–5, 177–9.

Although ethologists were very much aware of the interactions between organism and environment, they had not completely realized to what extent the ways in which the term innate was used prevented the recognition of certain problems. Accordingly, some ethologists have modified their use of the term innate. Other ethologists have maintained the original use of the term, so that it is clear that the controversy continues to exist. It thus seems necessary to briefly indicate my opinion about the dichotomy in so far it has to do with ontogenetic problems.

Lorenz has recently once more defended the usefulness of the dichotomy and has shown how these terms can be applied to a behaviour pattern. He emphasizes that when he speaks of behaviour and its problems, he implies adapted behaviour and the problems of adaptation.

First, he stresses that if behaviour is adapted, information about the environment must somehow have entered the organism. Unless one believes in preformation, such a process can only take place in one of two ways: during the life of the individual, or during evolution. Second, he emphasizes that it is of the utmost importance to find out which of the two processes has taken place. Third, he discusses the method that can be used to distinguish the two ways. The only thing that is necessary is to isolate the individual during the ontogeny from those aspects of the environment with respect to which the animal shows adapted behaviour. If the animal shows adapted behaviour when it is exposed to these aspects, then this proves that the adapted feature is innate. Innate thus means: adaptedness acquired during evolution, stored in the genoma, and developed in the individual regardless of the circumstances with respect to which the property under study is adapted.

It seems to me that Lorenz correctly emphasizes the importance of studying to what extent adaptedness is determined by evolutionary factors, and not directly dependent on environmental factors during the ontogeny. In my opinion, the method Lorenz proposes is valid, if cautiously applied. However, it also follows from Lorenz' definition that the term innate is not concerned with the problem of which processes underlie the ontogeny of innate behaviour. Yet, it is clear that if an adapted feature of behaviour develops in an animal deprived of even all external factors except those minimally required to stay alive, *another* causal question still remains: how does this behaviour pattern develop ontogenetically? Surely, something must have happened inside the organism between the moment that the egg started to develop and the moment that the behaviour is produced. The ontogenetic problem is not only concerned with verifying that the animal possesses certain potentialities, but also with the problem how these potentialities become realities during the life of the individual. The concept innate as defined by Lorenz does not help with regard to the latter problem, since it does not consider this question. The deprivation experiment, as recommended by Lorenz, is also not designed to answer this question. It is true that in this experiment the animal is deprived of circumstances which matter from the point of view of adaptation, but it is equally true that the animal is not deprived of the circumstances which matter from an ontogenetic point of view. Whether or not the environment has contributed in an indirect way to the structure of an adapted feature during the ontogeny can simply not be deduced from such a deprivation experiment.

It seems to me that the controversy need not exist if evolutionary and ontogenetic problems are recognized as equally important. One way to approach the analysis of behaviour is to ask how behaviour has arisen in the species during evolution. Lorenz has, by insisting on the rigidity and

adaptedness of fixed patterns and by stressing the necessity of phyletic comparison, greatly furthered this approach. As said before, this problem is only indirectly considered in this paper.

Another approach, equally legitimate, is to ask how behaviour arises in the development of the individual. This question should be stated for innate behaviour in Lorenz' sense as well, just as much as it has been stated by experimental embryologists for the ontogeny of structures. There is much that students of behaviour can learn from the framework of experimental embryology.

To mention one example: a structure like the amphibian eye has many of the properties of instinctive behaviour. The eye is constant in form and characteristic of the species. Further, the eye develops in individuals which are raised in isolation of others and also, in individuals which are prevented from using it. Finally, there is no doubt that the eye, like instinctive behaviour, possesses adaptedness which is determined by evolutionary factors. Yet, experimental embryologists have shown that the eye develops in an orderly and predictable manner and that it is possible to study the causal factors of the ontogenetic development in a meaningful way. This has led to a fascinating picture, which implies that 'the normal development of the eye is based on an interplay of inductions, whereby each part influences the development of all others, and also, reacts to the influences of all others, all parts having acquired the necessary reactivity in their previous chemodifferentiation' [C. P. Raven (1954), *An Outline of Developmental Physiology* (London), p. 135].

I consider this result as a challenge to students of behaviour; it is time that we start to tackle the problems of ontogeny in the spirit of experimental embryology. Undoubtedly, many processes in ontogeny follow rigid canals, leading often to an unmodifiable end-result, such as instinctive behaviour. However, the fact that these processes are canalized does not relieve us of the task to trace them. On the contrary, just because of the fact that they are canalized, we are enabled to study them.

Despite the fact that many people have concerned themselves with species-specific behaviour of juvenile animals, the problem of ontogeny of complete inventories of species-specific behaviour can scarcely be said to have been studied in this form. There is little doubt in my opinion that this is partly due to the fact that the term innate does not invite one to ask causal questions about the ontogeny to its final consequences. For this reason I have avoided the use of this term in this paper.

The idea to apply the method of experimental embryology to the ontogeny of behaviour is not new. It has been stated explicitly by Beach, Baerends, Tinbergen and possibly by others. It has also been implied by the criticisms by Lehrman and others of ethology and by their approach to the ontogeny of behaviour. If misunderstandings have arisen between some comparative psychologists and some ethologists, then this was perhaps due to the fact that some of the former were more interested in ontogenetic problems, whereas some of the latter were more interested in evolutionary problems. The difficulties disappear as soon as one recognizes that *both* problems exist and need explanation.

.   .   .

Concluding Remarks

Trends in the course of development

The development of social behaviour in groups of Junglefowl chicks occurs according to regular and predictable lines. The main course of this development can be roughly described as follows.

The first indication of social behaviour after hatching is the strong tendency of chicks to follow nearby moving objects. This soon leads to the development of attachments to other chicks (and to the mother-hen). Escape behaviour is also present soon after hatching, but does not yet occur in response to social companions.

At the age of one week, aggressive behaviour starts to develop. This behaviour has very little autonomy at first. Rather, the elements of which it is composed – locomotion, attraction to other chicks, and pecking – are at first relatively independent of each other and have their own causal factors. These elements gradually combine to form what later is called aggressive behaviour. The probability that these elements will occur together is low at first; consequently, early fighting occurs infrequently and is incomplete. Another consequence is that fighting is easily inhibited when incompatible behaviour which has developed earlier, such as escape, is activated. Thus, aggression and escape oc-

cur largely in isolation of each other. The factors underlying fighting gradually become stronger: fighting occurs more frequently and is more complete. As a result, escape is often activated during fighting. Initially this leads to inhibition of fighting; but soon fighting and escape start to occur in rapid alternation. Furthermore, aggression and escape are now often simultaneously activated and interact with each other; this follows from the fact that new behaviour starts to occur during fighting which is controlled by both systems. The development of interactions between aggression and escape takes place in two stages. During the first stage, the interactions take place during actual fighting only. During the second stage, both systems interact before and after fighting; this can be concluded from the fact that conflicts between approach and withdrawal start to occur in the context of fighting.

The new patterns which become associated with fighting as a result of the interactions between aggression and escape are of several types. First, some of the patterns appear to be combinations of components of aggressive and escape behaviour (ambivalent and redirected patterns). In other words this type is due to an interaction process in which aggression and escape are integrated with each other. Second, the form of some of the patterns suggests that they are functionally irrelevant. This type may be due to an interaction process between aggression and escape, which leads to the activation of other extraneous systems. The nature of these interactions has not been analysed in detail, but it seems very likely that some of the new patterns are caused by both types of interaction processes simultaneously.

Two trends stand out in the development of aggressive behaviour: it becomes more and more difficult for earlier developed behaviour to inhibit aggression, and aggression starts to exert control over other behaviour in increasingly complex ways. These changes can perhaps best be expressed by saying that aggressive behaviour becomes more and more a relatively autonomous system.

Further evidence for the developing autonomy of aggressive behaviour is provided by the fact that its occurrence becomes increasingly linked to specific external stimuli. At first aggressive components appear to be mainly under internal control. Later, external stimuli begin to control the orientation; and still later, external stimuli begin to control both the initiation and the orientation of aggressive behaviour in an increasingly specific way: appearance of, familiarity with, and proximity of, another bird begin to play a role. At the same time, aggressive behaviour becomes less and less dependent on some of the conditions which initially determine its occurrence, such as the activation of strong general locomotory activity.

In many respects the development of male copulatory behaviour follows a similar course. Some of the underlying mechanisms appear to be determined by as yet unidentified long-term processes which are linked with the occurrence of early social behaviour. The underlying causal factors of copulatory behaviour are initially weak; this is deduced from the fact that it occurs infrequently and incompletely. Activation of earlier developed behaviour readily suppresses the occurrence of compulatory behaviour. Only if other factors are not activated or inhibit each other mutually can copulatory behaviour occur. During later stages copulatory behaviour start to occur more frequently and becomes more complete. Mutual conflicts with earlier developed patterns start to occur, especially with agonistic behaviour. This again leads to the occurrence of new patterns, which are produced by the interactions of the three systems, which now can all be activated simultaneously. The form of most of the patterns suggests that integration at a still more complex level is taking place.

Male copulatory behaviour is linked with a specific external situation at first: the presence of a sitting bird. The fact that it does not occur with respect to standing and moving birds can be interpreted as being due to a stronger activating effect of these other postures on agonistic behaviour. This is another indication of its initial dependence on earlier behaviour. At later ages the releasing situation becomes at first less specific. Still later, after the male has had experience in contact with males and females, the releasing situation becomes highly specific. Copulatory behaviour is then only elicited by females and only completed after the male has adopted an appropriate position on her back.

Thus, both aggressive and copulatory behaviour are initially strongly dependent on factors underlying earlier developed behaviour. Further, both develop increasing autonomy during later stages. This latter conclusion is supported by the following facts:

(a) increasing independence of some of the factors which played a role in the initial occurrence,

(b) increasing specificity of external factors which release the behaviour in the final stage,

(c) increasing resistance to inhibition of the behaviour by other behaviour systems, and

(d) increasing inhibitory influence on other behaviour systems, as a result of which the expression of several systems may be transformed, and new, integrated patterns start to occur.

The foregoing remarks imply the general conclusion that behaviour systems develop through increasing interaction and integration of causal factors which are initially active in relative isolation of each other. It remains to be seen to what extent these trends are also applicable to other systems than aggressive and male copulatory behaviour, which were emphasized in this paper.

An extensive study on principles underlying the course of the development of behaviour has been made by Kortlandt. He stresses two principles which he derives from his own observations of Cormorants and from the work of Freud and others. The first principle is that of isolated development of newly appearing instincts; the second that of ascending integration of instincts which mature independently at first. Although there are many differences in detail, these principles appear to be similar in some respects to the ideas presented here. A precise comparison is difficult however because Kortlandt has approached the problems of development in a different theoretical framework.

It may be noted that some of the differences which exist between juvenile and adult behaviour of Junglefowl run parallel with what has been described as differences between play and serious behaviour. Thus, for example, fighting behaviour of young chicks is neither complete, nor elicited in the same way as adult fighting, nor are the activities grouped in the way which is usual for adult birds. The approach which is followed in this paper shows that one can analyse the causation of play-like activities. Similarly one can analyse their function in order to find out to what extent play contributes to the characteristics of adult behaviour. In this way differences between play and serious behaviour become understandable as being due to developing changes in the underlying organization of behaviour. The term play does not help in understanding these differences and therefore becomes superfluous. It is to be expected that many aspects of juvenile behaviour, which are now sometimes classified as play, can be analysed in a similar way, even in mammals.

. . .

Factors underlying the development of social behaviour

The question of which factors underlie the development of social behaviour in Junglefowl is still practically unexplored, but it will now become possible, on the basis of the descriptions given in the previous chapters, to tackle these problems.

As mentioned at several places in this paper, deprivation of normal social experience during early life does not affect many aspects of the development of social behaviour, notably on the motor side. This fully confirms Lorenz' conclusion that many aspects of the ontogeny of behaviour are rigidly canalized. There is no doubt therefore that evolutionary factors are of tremendous importance in determining the adult form and organization of adult behaviour. Nevertheless this behaviour is not present in fill-fledged form when the animal starts to live. Each animal gradually unfolds the received potentialities during its own individual life, necessarily in interaction with the environment. In this sense, each individual has to develop its own behaviour however much is determined by evolutionary factors and present from the beginning in potential form. To find out where the environment is necessary and where not, how it acts, and which processes take place inside the developing animal is therefore an important field of study.

Although deprivation of normal social experience appears to have little effect on the development of many motor patterns, these patterns are sometimes released in abnormal ways in birds raised in isolation. It appears that the interactions between the factors underlying them is sometimes also deficient. It is significant in this connection that cornering in Junglefowl, which appears to be due to very complex interactions, is only very rarely shown by males which were raised in isolation. A precise

understanding of the causes of these abnormalities is still lacking.

As has been pointed out by Schneirla and Lehrman, the fact that deprivation of social experience does not affect certain aspects, does not mean that the general experiences to which the animal has been exposed have had no influence at all. It is probable that early experiences often act in a diffuse and subtle manner and that the effects will not become noticeable until later stages. Several of the abnormalities in behaviour of partially isolated males could be studied from this point of view. For example, why do these males start to attack their own tail? Does this mean that the male always develops aggressive behaviour toward nearby moving objects to which it has been exposed for a long time? It would be interesting to know what happens if a partially isolated male is not allowed to grow tail-feathers: will aggression develop toward other parts of the body, or toward moving or motionless objects in the immediate environment? A further question is whether exposure to general environmental disturbances is necessary in order that self-directed aggression develops in isolated males and if so, which experiences are necessary and at what age. Similar questions can be raised with regard to the development of escape and copulatory behaviour.

For example, the fact that one of the partially isolated males developed copulatory behaviour with a feather, whereas the others did not, raises the questions as to which experiences the bird must be exposed, and at what age, in order for this behaviour to develop. Further, to what extent does this behaviour depend on prior development of agonistic behaviour? It is to be expected that in this way, systematic manipulation of the experiences to which the animal is exposed, will throw light on the processes underlying the development of the social behaviour patterns, as well as on the interactions between the underlying causal factors.

It will further be necessary to study the internal processes which are going on while the animal is growing up, a problem which will in many respects be much more difficult to tackle. As a first step, the influence of hormonal factors (in interaction with experiential factors) is likely to give further insight in the development of behaviour. In this respect, Lehrman has pointed the way to a whole field of problems which is waiting for further study.

CHAPTER 19

Social Deprivation in Monkeys

Harry F. Harlow and Margaret K. Harlow

In *An Outline of Psychoanalysis*, published posthumously in 1940, Sigmund Freud was able to refer to "the common assertion that the child is psychologically the father of the man and that the events of his first years are of paramount importance for his whole subsequent life." It was, of course, Freud's own historic investigations, begun a half-century before, that first elucidated the role of infantile experiences in the development of the personality and its disorders. The "central experience of this period of childhood," he found, is the infant's relation to his mother. Freud's ideas have now shaped the thinking of two generations of psychologists, psychiatrists and psychoanalysts. Much evidence in support of his deep insights has been accumulated, particularly from clinical studies of the mentally ill. Contemporary writers stress inadequate or inconsistent mothering as a basic cause of later disorders such as withdrawal, hostility, anxiety, sexual maladjustment, alcoholism and, significantly, inadequate maternal behavior!

The evidence from clinical studies for this or any other view of human personality development is qualified, however, by an inherent defect. These studies are necessarily retrospective: they start with the disorder and work backward in time, retracing the experiences of the individual as he and his relatives and associates recall them. Inevitably details are lost or distorted, and the story is often so confounded as to require a generous exercise of intuition on the part of the investigator. Nor does evidence obtained in this manner exclude other possible causes of personality disorder. Against arguments in favor of a biochemical or neurological causation of mental illness, for example, there is no way to show that the patient began life with full potentiality for normal development. Given the decisive influence ascribed to the mother–infant relation, there may be a tendency in the reconstruction of the past to overlook or suppress evidence for the influence of other significant early relations, such as the bonds of interaction with other children. Little attention has been given, in fact, to child-to-child relations in the study of personality development. Yet it can be supposed that these play a significant part in determining the peer relations and the sexual role of the adult. Plainly there is a need to study the development of personality forward in time from infancy. Ideally the study should be conducted under controlled laboratory conditions so that the effects of single variables or combinations of variables can be traced.

Reprinted from *Scientific American*, 207(5), November 1962, pp. 136–46. Copyright © 1962 by Scientific American, Inc. All rights reserved.

. . .

Acceding to the moral and physical impossibility of conducting such an investigation with human subjects, we have been observing the development of social behavior in large numbers of rhesus monkeys at the Primate Laboratory of the University of Wisconsin. Apart from this primate's kinship to man, it offers a reasonable experimental substitute because it undergoes a relatively long period of development analogous to that of the human child and involving intimate attachment to its mother and social interaction with its age-mates. With these animals we have been able to observe the consequences of the deprivation of all social contact for various lengths of time. We have also raised them without mothers but in the company of age-mates and with mothers but without age-mates.

We have thereby been able to make some estimate of the contribution of each of these primary affectional systems to the integrated adult personality. Our observations sustain the significance of the maternal relation, particularly in facilitating the interaction of the infant with other infants. But at the same time we have found compelling evidence that opportunity for infant–infant interaction under optimal conditions may fully compensate for lack of mothering, at least in so far as infant–infant social and heterosexual relations are concerned. It seems possible – even likely – that the infant–mother affectional system is dispensable, whereas the infant–infant system is the *sine qua non* for later adjustment in all spheres of monkey life. In line with the "paramount importance" that Freud assigned to experience in the first years of life, our experiments indicate that there is a critical period somewhere between the third and sixth months of life during which social deprivation, particularly deprivation of the company of its peers, irreversibly blights the animal's capacity for social adjustment.

Our investigations of the emotional development of our subjects grew out of the effort to produce and maintain a colony of sturdy, disease-free young animals for use in various research programs. By separating them from their mothers a few hours after birth and placing them in a more fully controlled regimen of nurture and physical care we were able both to achieve a higher rate of survival and to remove the animals for testing without maternal protest. Only later did we realize that our monkeys were emotionally disturbed as well as sturdy and disease-free. Some of our researches are

therefore retrospective. Others are in part exploratory, representing attempts to set up new experimental situations or to find new techniques for measurement. Most are incomplete because investigations of social and behavioral development are long-term. In a sense, they can never end, because the problems of one generation must be traced into the next.

Having separated the infant from its mother, our procedure was to keep it alone in a bare wire cage in a large room with other infants so housed. Thus each little monkey could see and hear others of its kind, although it could not make direct physical contact with them. The 56 animals raised in this manner now range in age from five to eight years. As a group they exhibit abnormalities of behavior rarely seen in animals born in the wild and brought to the laboratory as preadolescents or adolescents, even after the latter have been housed in individual cages for many years. The laboratory-born monkeys sit in their cages and stare fixedly into space, circle their cages in a repetitive stereotyped manner and clasp their heads in their hands or arms and rock for long periods of time. They often develop compulsive habits, such as pinching precisely the same patch of skin on the chest between the same fingers hundreds of times a day; occasionally such behavior may become punitive and the animal may chew and tear at its body until it bleeds. Often the approach of a human being becomes the stimulus to self-aggression. This behavior constitutes a complete breakdown and reversal of the normal defensive response; a monkey born in the wild will direct such threats and aggression at the approaching person, not at itself. Similar symptoms of emotional pathology are observed in deprived children in orphanages and in withdrawn adolescents and adults in mental hospitals.

.   .   .

William A. Mason, now at the Yerkes Laboratories of Primate Biology, compared the behavior of six of these animals, which were then two years old and had been housed all their lives in individual cages, with a matched group of rhesus monkeys that had been captured in the wild during their first year of life and housed together in captivity for a while before being individually housed in the laboratory. The most striking difference was that all the animals that had been born in the wild – and not one of the laboratory-born animals – displayed normal sex behavior. That the laboratory-born animals were not lacking in sex drive was indicated by the fact that the males frequently approached the females and the females displayed part of the pattern of sexual presentation. But they did not orient themselves correctly and they did not succeed in mating. Moreover, the monkeys born in the wild had apparently learned to live with others in a stable hierarchy of dominance, or "pecking order"'; consequently in the pairing test they fought one another less and engaged more often in social grooming. They would also release a companion from a locked cage more frequently than did the laboratory-born animals, which usually ignored their caged partner's plight.

The severity of the affliction that grips these monkeys raised in the partial isolation of individual wire cages has become more apparent as they have grown older. They pay little or no attention to animals in neighboring cages; those caged with companions sit in opposite corners with only rare interaction. No heterosexual behavior has ever been observed between male and female cage-mates, even between those that have lived together for as long as seven years. When efforts have been made to bring about matings, by pairing animals during the female's estrus, they have sometimes fought so viciously that they have had to be parted. Attempts to mate the socially deprived animals with sexually adequate and experienced monkeys from the breeding colony have been similarly frustrated.

In the summer of 1960 we undertook to devise a group-psychotherapy situation for 19 of these animals – nine males and 10 females – by using them to stock the monkey island in the municipal zoo in Madison, Wisconsin. This was their first experience outside the laboratory, and they had much to learn in order to survive. They had to learn to drink water from an open trough instead of from a tube in the wall of a cage, to compete for food in a communal feeding situation, to huddle together or find shelter from inclement weather, to climb rocks and avoid the water surrounding the island. Most difficult of all, they had to learn to live together. Within the first few days they made all the necessary physical adjustments. The three casualties – a male that drowned and two females that were injured and had to be returned to the laboratory –

resulted from the stress of social adjustment. Fighting was severe at first; it decreased as effective dominance relations were established and friendship pairs formed. Grooming appeared in normal style and with almost normal frequency. A limited amount of sex behavior was observed, but it was infantile in form, with inadequate posturing by both females and males. In the hope of promoting therapy along this line we introduced our largest, strongest and most effective breeding-colony male to the island around the middle of summer. He immediately established himself at the head of the dominance order. But in spite of his considerable persistence and patience he did not succeed in starting a single pregnancy.

Back in the laboratory these animals ceased to groom and fought more frequently. In pairings with breeding-colony monkeys, not one male has achieved a normal mount or intromission and only one female has become pregnant. After two years we have had to conclude that the island experience was of no lasting value.

As the effects of the separation of these monkeys from their mothers in infancy were first becoming apparent in 1957 we were prompted to undertake a study of the mother–infant affectional bond. To each of one group of four animals separated from their mothers at birth we furnished a surrogate mother: a welded wire cylindrical form with the nipple of the feeding bottle protruding from its "breast" and with a wooden head surmounting it. The majority of the animals, 60 in all, were raised with cozier surrogate mothers covered by terry cloth. In connection with certain experiments some of these individuals have had both a bare-wire and a cloth-covered mother. The infants developed a strong attachment to the cloth mothers and little or none to the wire mothers, regardless of which one provided milk. In fright-inducing situations the infants showed that they derived a strong sense of security from the presence of their cloth mothers [see "Love in Infant Monkeys," by Harry F. Harlow, *Scientific American*, June, 1959]. Even after two years of separation they exhibit a persistent attachment to the effigies.

In almost all other respects, however, the behavior of these monkeys at ages ranging from three to five years is indistinguishable from that of monkeys raised in bare wire cages with no source of contact comfort other than a gauze diaper pad. They are

Experimental condition	Present age	Behavior					
		None	Low	Almost normal	Probably normal	Normal	
Raised in isolation							
TOTAL — Cage-raised for 2 years	4 years	■□					
Cage-raised for 6 monts	14 months	□	■				
Cage-raised for 80 days	10½ months			■□■			
PARTIAL — Cage-raised for 6 months	5 to 8 years	■	■	□			
Surrogate-raised for 6 months	3 to 5 years	■	■	□			
Raised with mother							
Normal mother: no play with peers	1 year	■				□	
Motherless mother: play in playpen	14 months			□	■	■	
Normal mother: play in playpen	2 years					■□■	
Raised with peers							
Four raised in one cage: play in Playroom	1 year				■	□■	
Surrogate-raised: play in playpen	2 years				■	■□	
Surrogate-raised: play in playroom	21 months					■□■	

■ Play
□ Defense
■ Sex

Figure 19.1 Summary of results of experiments. The monkey's capacity to develop normally appears to be determined by the seventh month of life. Animals isolated for six months are aberrant in every respect. Play with peers seems even more necessary than mothering to the development of effective social relations.

without question socially and sexually aberrant. No normal sex behavior has been observed in the living cages of any of the animals that have been housed with a companion of the opposite sex. In exposure to monkeys from the breeding colony not one male and only one female has shown normal mating behavior and only four females have been successfully impregnated. Compared with the cage-raised monkeys, the surrogate-raised animals seem to be less aggressive, whether toward themselves or other monkeys. But they are also younger on the average, and their better dispositions can be attributed to their lesser age.

Thus the nourishment and contact comfort provided by the nursing cloth-covered mother in infancy does not produce a normal adolescent or adult. The surrogate cannot cradle the baby or communicate monkey sounds and gestures. It cannot punish for misbehavior or attempt to break the infant's bodily attachment before it becomes a fixation. The entire group of animals separated from their mothers at birth and raised in individual wire cages, with or without surrogate, must be written off as potential breeding stock. Apparently their early social deprivation permanently impairs their ability to form effective relations with other monkeys, whether the opportunity was offered to them in the second six months of life or in the second to the fifth year of life.

One may correctly assume that total social isolation, compared with the partial isolation in which these subjects were reared, would produce even more devastating effects on later personality development. Such disastrous effects have been reported in the rare cases of children who have been liberated after months or years of lonely confinement in a darkened room. We have submitted a few monkeys to total isolation. Our purpose was to establish the maximum of social deprivation that would allow survival and also to determine whether or not there is a critical period in which social deprivation may have irreversible effects.

. . .

In our first study a male and a female were housed alone from birth for a period of two years, each one in its own cubicle with solid walls. Their behavior could be observed through one-way vision screens and tested by remote control. The animals adapted to solid food slowly, but they had normal weight and good coats when they were removed from the isolation boxes at the end of two years. Throughout this period neither animal had seen any living being other than itself.

They responded to their liberation by the crouching posture with which monkeys typically react to extreme threat. When placed together, each one crouched and made no further response to the other. Paired with younger monkeys from the group raised in partial isolation, they froze or fled when approached and made no effort to defend themselves from aggressive assaults. After another two years, in which they were kept together in a single large cage in the colony room, they showed the same abnormal fear of the sight or sound of other monkeys.

We are now engaged in studying the effects of six months of total social isolation. The first pair of monkeys, both males, has been out of isolation for eight months. They are housed, each monkey in its own cage, in racks with other monkeys of their age that were raised in the partial isolation of individual wire cages. For 20 minutes a day, five days a week, they are tested with a pair of these monkeys in the "playroom" of the laboratory. This room we designed to stimulate the young monkeys to a maximum of activity. It was not until the 12th and 27th week respectively that the two totally deprived monkeys began to move and climb about. They now circulate freely but not as actively as the control animals. Although frequently attacked by the controls, neither one has attempted to defend itself or fight back; they either accept abuse or flee. One must be characterized as extremely disturbed and almost devoid of social behavior. The other re-

sembles a normal two-month-old rhesus infant in its play and social behavior, and the indications are that it will never be able to make mature contacts with its peers.

A considerably more hopeful prognosis is indicated for two groups of four monkeys raised in total isolation for the much shorter period of 80 days. In their cubicles these animals had the contact comfort of a cloth-covered surrogate. They were deficient in social behavior during the first test periods in the playroom. But they made rapid gains; now, eight months later, we rate them as "almost normal" in play, defense and sex behavior. At least seven of the eight seem to bear no permanent scars as the result of early isolation.

Our first few experiments in the total isolation of these animals would thus appear to have bracketed what may be the critical period of development during which social experience is necessary for normal behavior in later life. We have additional experiments in progress, involving a second pair that will have been isolated for six months and a first pair that will have been isolated for a full year. The indications are that six months of isolation will render the animals permanently inadequate. Since the rhesus monkey is more mature than the human infant at birth and grows four times more rapidly, this is equivalent to two or three years for the human child. On the other hand, there is reason to believe that the effects of shorter periods of early isolation, perhaps 60 to 90 days or even more, are clearly reversible. This would be equivalent to about six months in the development of the human infant. The time probably varies with the individual and with the experiences to which it is exposed once it is removed from isolation. Beyond a brief period of neonatal grace, however, the evidence suggests that every additional week or month of social deprivation increasingly imperils social development in the rhesus monkey. Case studies of children reared in impersonal institutions or in homes with indifferent mothers or nurses show a frightening comparability. The child may remain relatively unharmed through the first six months of life. But from this time on the damage is progressive and cumulative. By one year of age he may sustain enduring emotional scars and by two years many children have reached the point of no return.

. . .

In all of these experiments in partial and total isolation, whether unwitting or deliberate, our animals were deprived of the company of their peers as well as of their mothers. We accordingly undertook a series of experiments designed to distinguish and compare the roles of mother–infant and infant–infant relations in the maturation of rhesus monkey behavior. Our most privileged subjects are two groups of four monkeys each, now two years old, that were raised with their mothers during the first 18 and 21 months respectively and with peers from the first weeks. Each mother–infant pair occupied a large cage that gave the infant access to one cell of a four-unit playpen. By removing the screens between the playpens we enabled the infants to play together in pairs or as foursomes during scheduled observation periods each day. In parallel with these two groups we raised another group of four in a playpen setup without their mothers but with a terrycloth surrogate in each home cage.

From the time the mothers let them leave their home cages, after 20 or 30 days, the mothered infants entered into more lively and consistent relations with one another than did the four motherless ones. Their behavior evolved more rapidly through the sequence of increasingly complex play patterns that reflects the maturation and learning of the infant monkey and is observed in a community of normal infants. The older they grew and the more complex the play patterns became, the greater became the observable difference between the mothered and the motherless monkeys. Now, at the end of the second year, the 12 animals are living together in one playpen setup, with each original group occupying one living cage and its adjoining playpen. All are observed in daily interaction without the dividing panels. The early differences between them have all but disappeared. Seven of the eight mothered animals engage in normal sexual activity and assume correct posture. The deviant is a male, and this animal was the social reject in its all-male group of four. Of the two motherless males, one has recently achieved full adult sexual posture and the other is approaching it. The two motherless females appear normal, but it remains to be seen whether or not their maternal behavior will reflect their lack of mothering.

Observation of infants with their mothers suggests reasons for the differences in the early social and sexual behavior of these playpen groups. From early in life on, the infant monkey shows a strong tendency to imitate its mother; this responding to another monkey's behavior carries over to interaction with its peers. It is apparent also that sexual activity is stimulated by the mother's grooming of the infant. Finally, as the mother begins occasionally to reject its offspring in the third or fourth month, the infant is propelled into closer relations with its peers. These observations underlie the self-evident fact that the mother–infant relation plays a positive role in the normal development of the infant–infant and heterosexual relations of the young monkey.

That the mother–infant relation can also play a disruptive role was demonstrated in another experiment. Four females that had been raised in the partial isolation of individual wire cages – and successfully impregnated in spite of the inadequacy of their sexual behavior – delivered infants within three weeks of one another. This made it possible to set up a playpen group composed of these "motherless" mothers and their infants. The maternal behavior of all four mothers was completely abnormal, ranging from indifference to outright abuse. Whereas it usually requires more than one person to separate an infant from its mother, these mothers paid no attention when their infants were removed from the cages for the hand-feeding necessitated by the mothers' refusal to nurse. Two of the mothers did eventually permit fairly frequent nursing, but their apparently closer maternal relations were accompanied by more violent abuse. The infants were persistent in seeking contact with their mothers and climbed on their backs when they were repulsed at the breast. In play with one another during the first six months, the infants were close to the normally mothered animals in maturity of play, but they played less. In sexual activity, however, they were far more precocious. During the eight months since they have been separated from their mothers, they have exhibited more aggression and day-to-day variability in their behavior than have the members of other playpen groups. The two male offspring of the most abusive mothers have become disinterested in the female and occupy the subordinate position in all activities.

More study of more babies from motherless mothers is needed to determine whether or not the interrelations that characterize this pilot group will characterize others of the same composition. There is no question about the motherless mothers themselves. The aberration of their maternal behavior would have ensured the early demise of their infants outside the laboratory. As for the infants, the extremes of sexuality and aggressiveness observed in their behavior evoke all too vivid parallels in the behavior of disturbed human children and adolescents in psychiatric clinics and institutions for delinquents.

Another pilot experiment has shown that even normal mothering is not enough to produce socially adequate offspring. We isolated two infants in the exclusive company of their mothers to the age of seven months and then brought the mother–infant pairs together in a playpen unit. The female infant took full advantage of the play apparatus provided, but in three months the male was never seen to leave its home cage, and its mother would not permit the female to come within arm's reach. Social interaction of the infants was limited to an occasional exchange of tentative threats. For the past two months they have been separated from their mothers, housed in individual cages and brought together in the playroom for 15 minutes each day. In this normally stimulating environment they have so far shown no disposition to play together. Next to the infants that have been raised in total isolation, these are the most retarded of the infants tested in the playroom.

It is to the play-exciting stimulus of the playroom that we owe the unexpected outcome of our most suggestive experiment. The room is a relatively spacious one, with an eight-foot ceiling and 40 square feet of floor space. It is equipped with movable and stationary toys and a wealth of climbing devices, including an artificial tree, a ladder and a burlap-covered climbing ramp that leads to a platform. Our purpose in constructing the playroom was to provide the monkeys with opportunities to move about in the three-dimensional world to which, as arboreal animals, they are much more highly adapted than man. To assess the effects of different histories of early social experience we customarily turn the animals loose in the room in groups of four for regularly scheduled periods of observation each day.

The opportunities afforded by the playroom were most fully exploited by two groups of four infants that otherwise spent their days housed alone in their cages with a cloth surrogate. In terms of "mothering," therefore, these monkeys were most closely comparable to the four that were raised with surrogates in the playpen situation. These animals were released in the playroom for 20 minutes a day from the first month of life through the 11th, in the case of one group, and through the second year in the case of the other. In contrast with all the other groups observed in the playroom, therefore, they did their "growing up" in this environment. Even though their exposure to the room and to one another was limited to 20 minutes a day, they enacted with great spirit the entire growth pattern of rhesus-monkey play behavior.

They began by exploring the room and each other. Gradually over the next two or three months they developed a game of rough-and-tumble play, with jumping, scuffling, wrestling, hair-pulling and a little nipping, but with no real damage, and then an associated game of flight and pursuit in which the participants are alternately the threateners and the threatened. While these group activities evolved, so did the capacity for individual play exploits, with the animals running, leaping, swinging and climbing, heedless of one another and apparently caught up in the sheer joy of action. As their skill and strength grew, their social play involved shorter but brisker episodes of free-for-all action, with longer chases between bouts. Subsequently they developed an even more complex pattern of violent activity, performed with blinding speed and integrating all objects, animate and inanimate, in the room. Along with social play, and possibly as a result or by-product, they began to exhibit sexual posturing – immature and fleeting in the first six months and more frequent and adult in form by the end of the year. The differences in play activity that distinguish males and females became evident in the first two or three months, with the females threatening and initiating rough contact far less frequently than the males and withdrawing from threats and approaches far more frequently.

Thus in spite of the relatively limited opportunity for contact afforded by their daily schedule, all the individuals in these two groups developed effective infant–infant play relations. Those observed into the second year have shown the full repertory of adult sexual behavior. At the same chronological age these motherless monkeys have attained as full a maturity in these respects as the infants raised with their mothers in the playpen.

Another group of four motherless animals raised together in a single large cage from the age of two weeks is yielding similar evidence of the effectiveness of the infant–infant affectional bond. During their first two months these animals spent much of their time clinging together, each animal clutching the back of the one just ahead of it in "choo-choo" fashion. They moved about as a group of three or four; when one of them broke away, it was soon clutched by another to form the nucleus of a new line. In the playroom the choo-choo linkage gave way to individual exploratory expeditions. During periods of observation, whether in their home cage or in the playroom, these animals have consistently scored lower in play activity than the most playful groups. We think this is explained, however, by the fact that they are able to spread their play over a 24-hour period. At the age of one year they live amicably together. In sex behavior they are more mature than the mother-raised playpen babies. No member of the group shows any sign of damage by mother-deprivation.

. . .

Our observations of the three groups of motherless infants raised in close association with one another therefore indicate that opportunity for optimal infant–infant interaction may compensate for lack of mothering. This is true at least in so far as infant–infant and sexual relations are concerned. Whether or not maternal behavior or later social adjustment will be affected remains to be seen.

Of course research on nonhuman animals, even monkeys, will never resolve the baffling complex roles of various kinds of early experience in the development of human personality. It is clear, however, that important theoretical and practical questions in this realm of interest can be resolved by the use of monkeys. The close behavioral resemblance of our disturbed infants to disturbed human beings gives us the confidence that we are working with significant variables and the hope that we can point the way to reducing the toll of psychosocial trauma in human society.

References

Affectional Responses in the Infant Monkey. Harry F. Harlow and Robert R. Zimmermann, in *Science*, vol. 130, no. 3373, pp. 421–32; August 21, 1959.

Determinants of Infant Behaviour. Edited by B. M. Foss, London: Methuen, 1961.

The Development of Learning in the Rhesus Monkey. Harry F. Harlow, in *Science in Progress: Twelfth Series*, edited by Wallace R. Brode, pp. 239–69. Yale University Press, 1962.

The Heterosexual Affectional System in Monkeys. Harry F. Harlow, in *American Psychologist*, vol. 17, no. 1, pp. 1–9; January 1962.

Love in Infant Monkeys. Harry F. Harlow, in *Scientific American*, vol. 200, no. 6, pp. 68–74; June 1959.

CHAPTER 20

Mother–Infant Separation and the Nature of Inter-Individual Relationships: Experiments with Rhesus Monkeys

ROBERT A. HINDE

Introduction

During the late fifties the extent to which a period of separation from the mother-figure could have adverse effects on the development of a human child was a matter of some dispute. While some psychiatrists and paediatricians held that the consequences could be severe (see for example, Bowlby, 1951, 1958; Ainsworth, 1962), their views were based largely on clinical and retrospective evidence, and conflicted with established medical and social practice. Since controlled experiments with human subjects were out of the question on ethical grounds, we decided to see what progress could be made with rhesus monkeys. It was apparent from the start that the consequences of a separation experience could not be studied in isolation – it was, for instance, necessary for us to do some initial work on processes of intraspecific communication in rhesus monkeys, and on how the mother–infant relationship develops. Some of this work was reviewed previously (Hinde and Spencer-Booth, 1968). As the work progressed it became apparent (*a*) that the consequences of a separation experience vary with the nature of the mother–infant relationship, and (*b*) that the nature of the mother–infant relationship, and (*b*) that the nature of the mother–infant relationship

relationship varies with the social situation. Furthermore, a number of conceptual issues arose in the course of the work, such as precisely what one means by a 'relationship', and how the important but somewhat intangible 'natures' or 'qualities' of relationships could be assessed and compared in a hard-headed manner. The aim of this paper is not to review the current state of the evidence bearing on any one of these problems, but rather to demonstrate, from the work of one laboratory, how the various problems are inter-related.

Materials and Methods

The work discussed here was carried out with rhesus monkeys nearly all of which were obtained from zoos or other sources in this country, or were bred in the colony.

The monkeys live in small groups each consisting of a male, three to four females and their young. Each group lives in an outdoor cage (548 cm × 243 cm × 246 cm) communicating with an inside room (185 cm × 133 cm × 239 cm). This situation provides the monkeys with a moderately complex social situation, though one much simpler than that of a natural troop, and at the same time permits a moderate degree of experimental control and moderately precise recording. Until recently, all records were made on check sheets using half-minute time

From *Proceedings of the Royal Society of London B*, **196** (1977), pp. 29–50.

intervals (Hinde, 1973). More recently a keyboard event recorder system has been used (White, 1971); each of the keys on the 39-key keyboard is assigned to a particular aspect of behaviour, and the observer depresses the appropriate keys as he watches. The record is stored initially on magnetic tape and can subsequently be computer analysed and stored on computer magnetic tape.

All the data were collected between 09h00 and 13h00, except that some watches during separation were continued until 14h30 local time.

Development of the Mother–Infant Relationship

At birth, the infant monkey has a limited repertoire of movement patterns which are elicited appropriately by stimuli from the mother. With some help from the latter he clings to her ventrum and is able to find a nipple with his mouth. The subsequent development of the mother–infant relationship involves an ongoing interaction between mother and infant, in which the behaviour of each partner affects that of the other and thus the subsequent course of the relationship. The complexity of this constantly changing relationship can hardly be over-emphasized: the infant's perceptual and motor skills develop, its several responses become directed appropriately and preferentially to the mother, and she likewise comes to respond individually to him. The infant explores his mother and his physical environment, and his cognitive development proceeds as he does so. His mother gradually permits and promotes his independence (see, for example,

Harlow and Harlow, 1965; Hinde, 1974). It will be apparent that, to unravel this complex interaction, it is necessary to establish reliable measures of the behaviour of the participants. Only some of those now used can be mentioned here, but it is convenient to introduce five which show how the mother–infant relationship develops over the first few months of life (figure 20.1).

Time off (TT off).   The proportion of half-minutes in which the infant was recorded off its mother.

Relative frequency of rejections ($R/Mk_I + Mk_M + R$).   The ratio of the number of occasions on which the infant attempted to make ventro–ventral contact with its mother and was rejected by her, to the total number of occasions it was accepted by her (i.e. contact made on the infant's initiative, Mk_I), picked up by the mother (contact made on mother's initiative, Mk_M), or rejected.

Infant's rôle in ventro–ventral contact (% Mk_I − % Bk_I).   The difference between the percentage of the occasions on which ventro–ventral contact was made that were due to the infant (Mk_I $100/(Mk_I + Mk_M) = \% Mk_I$) minus the percentage of breaks due to the infant (% Bk_I).

Time at a distance from mother (> 60 cm).   The number of half-minutes in which the infant was recorded more than 60 cm from its mother, i.e. out of her reach.

Infant's rôle in maintenance of proximity (% Ap_I − % L_I).   The difference between the percentage of approaches (distance between mother and infant decreases from more than 60 cm to less) that were due to movement by the infant and the percentage

Figure 20.1   The course of mother–infant interaction in small captive groups of rhesus monkeys. **Top left**: total time off mother (number of half-minutes in which infant was off mother as proportion of number watched). **Top right**: time out of arm's reach of mother (number of half-minutes in which infant was more than 60 cm from mother as proportion of number for which it was off her). **Centre**: relative frequency of rejections (ratio of number of occasions on which infant attempted to gain ventro–ventral contact and was rejected by mother (R) to number of occasions on which it made contact on mother's initiative (Mk_M), made contact on its own initiative (Mk_I), or attempted unsuccessfully to gain contact (R). **Bottom left**: infant's rôle in ventro–ventral contacts (number of contacts made on infant's initiative, as a percentage of total number made, minus number of contacts broken by infant, as a percentage of total number broken). **Bottom right**: infant's rôle in maintenance of proximity (number of approaches, i.e. distance decreases from >60 cm to <60 cm, made by infant, as percentage of total number made, minus number of leavings made by infant, as percentage of total number made). Each point is based on data from 14 to 20 mother–infant pairs. Observations were made between 09h00 and 13h00 over the first 30 weeks of life. Medians and inter-quartile ranges are shown.

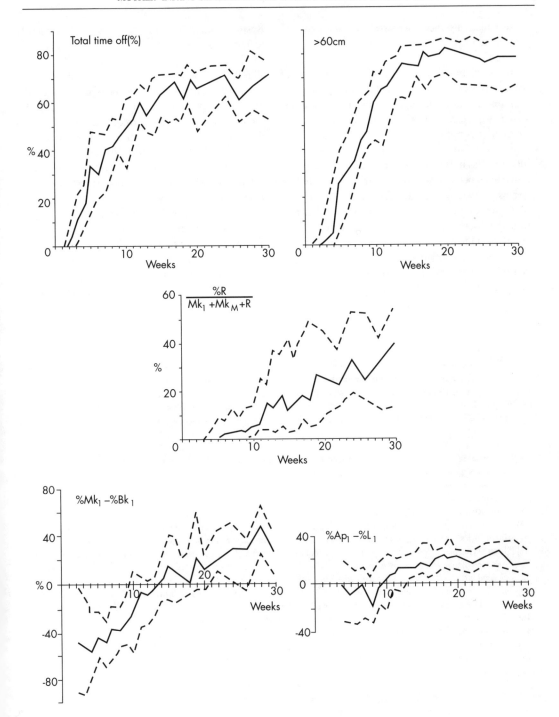

Figure 20.1

of leavings (distance increases similarly) due to movement of the infant.

It will be noted that Time off and Time out of reach, measured in terms of number of half-minutes *in which* the infant was in the conditions stated, will slightly over-estimate the actual times (see, for example, Altmann, 1974; Simpson and Simpson, 1976). The status of the measures of the infant's rôles in ventro–ventral contact and in proximity have been considered elsewhere (Hinde and Atkinson, 1970; Hinde and White, 1974).

Figure 20.1 shows that time off the mother and time at a distance from the mother increase with age of infant. During the early weeks the mother seldom rejects the infant's attempts to gain ventro–ventral contact and is primarily responsible for ventro–ventral contact (% Mk_I − % Bk_I negative).

Responsibility for proximity is also primarily maternal or shared (% Ap_I − % L_I near zero). As the infant develops it becomes primarily responsible for nipple contacts (*c.* week 14) and the proportion of ventro–ventral contacts initiated by the mother diminishes to near zero (*c.* week 20). Although rejections become frequent, the infant continues to spend *c.* 30% of the morning hours on its mother until nearly the end of the first year, though he may be obtaining little milk. Infants are capable of feeding themselves if the mother is removed from week 20 or earlier.

While from this brief account it might appear that, with the increasing frequency of rejections and the appearance of tantrums, the age changes in the relationship involve increasing tension between mother and infant, this is only part of the story. Infant and mother also become progressively more

Figure 20.2 Diagrammatic representation of the relations between interactions, relationships and social structure. Interactions, relationships and social structure are shown as rectangles on three levels, with successive stages of abstraction from left to right. The discontinuous circles represent independent or intervening variables operating at each level. Institutions, having a dual rôle, are shown in both a rectangle and a circle. In the specific instance of a non human primate, the rectangles might represent:

(1) Instances of grooming interactions between a mother *A* and her infant *B*.
(2) Instances of nursing interactions between *A* and *B*.
(3) Instances of play between *A* and *B*.
(4) Instances of grooming between female *A* and male *C*.
(5) Instances of copulation between *A* and C.
(6) First stage abstraction – schematic grooming interactions between *A* and *B*. Abstractions of between other mother–infant pairs are shown behind, but the specific instances from which they were abstracted are not shown.
(7) First stage abstraction – schematic nursing interactions between *A* and *B*. Abstractions of nursing interactions of other mother–infant pairs are shown behind.
(8) Second stage abstraction – schematic grooming interactions between all mother–infant pairs in troop.
(9) Mother–infant relationship between *A* and *B*. Mother–infant relationships of other mother–infant pairs are shown behind (but connections to grooming, nursing, etc., interactions are not shown).
(10) Consort relationship between *A* and C. Other consort relationships are shown behind.
(11) Specific relationship of another type (e.g. peer–peer).
(12), (13), (14) Abstraction of mother–infant, consort and peer–peer relationships. These may depend on abstractions of the contributing interactions.
(15) Surface structures of troop containing *A*, *B*, *C*, etc.
(16), (17) Surface structures of other troops (contributing relationships not shown).
(18) Abstraction of structure of troops including that containing *A*, *B*, *C*, etc. This may depend on abstractions of mother–infant, etc., relationships.
(19) Abstraction of structure of a different set of troops (from another environment, species, etc.)

Rectangles labelled MI_I refer to behaviour of dyad female *A* and her infant *B*. Rectangles labelled $\male\female_I$ refer to consort pair female *A* and male *C*. Rectangles labelled MIs, $\male\female$ refer to generalizations about behaviour of mother–infant dyads and consort pairs respectively (after Hinde, 1976a).

attuned to each other, learning to respond to each other's signals and to align their behaviour with that of the other. For example, in the early weeks a mother is more likely to terminate bouts of ventro–ventral contact initiated by the infant than bouts she had initiated herself, and an infant is more likely to terminate a bout initiated by the mother than a bout he had initiated. This implies that mothers are prone to initiate bouts when the infants are not ready, and the infants when the mothers are not ready. Later the difference disappears, implying that the behaviour of mothers and infants comes to mesh better as the infant develops. Similar generalizations apply to bouts out of ventro–ventral contact (Hinde and White, 1974).

This quality of 'meshing' is only one aspect of the mother–infant relationship that requires detailed study. We shall return to this issue shortly.

Interactions, Relationships and Social Structure

At this point it is necessary to digress briefly. What exactly does one mean by an inter-individual relationship? How can one set about studying the nature of relationships? Such questions demand a conceptual scheme which will underpin the empirical investigations. Such a scheme is presented in figure 20.2 (Hinde, 1976a). It involves three levels.

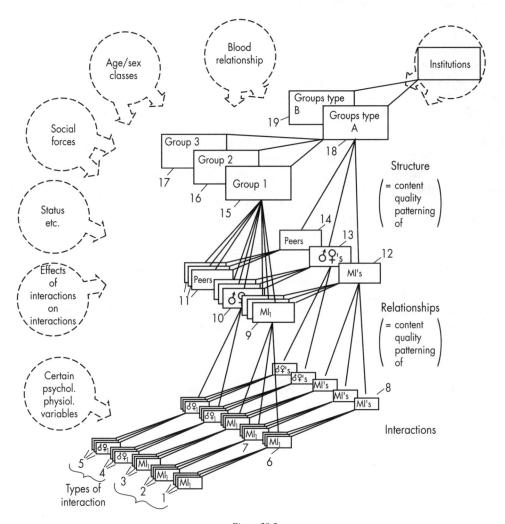

Figure 20.2

Interactions are seen as the atoms of social structure. No precise definition of an interaction has been formulated, but the category is intended to include all incidents that can be described in such terms as '*A* does *X* to *B*' or '*A* does *X* to *B* and *B* responds with *Y*'. To describe an interaction, it is necessary to state both what *A* and *B* did together, and how they did it – i.e. the quality of their interaction. For example, *A* might hit *B* gently or forcefully, and *A* might hold *B*'s hand in a restraining or an affectionate manner.

At the molecular level, *relationships* arise when one individual interacts with a known other on a number of occasions. So far as behaviour is concerned, their relationship *is* the nature, quality and patterning of the interactions between them. This is discussed briefly later. Finally *social structure* is seen as the nature, quality and patterning of relationships.

At each of these levels, the investigator must seek for generalizations in two directions. First, from data about the actual interactions that he observes he must abstract generalizations valid over a wider range of instances, contexts or participants. These are indicated in figure 20.2 by successive blocks of rectangles from left to right. Relationships always involve a degree of abstraction, but further generalizations (necessarily involving greater remoteness from actual data) will be required. The same is true of social structure. Here the pattern of relationships actually observed in a particular instance may be referred to as the 'surface structure', 'structure' being reserved for abstractions of greater generality. In each case the abstractions or generalizations will be in the data language – that is, they will employ the same words as were used to describe the basic phenomena originally.

The second direction involves a search for 'organizational principles' which serve to explain the patterning of the data. These are represented by the discontinuous circles in figure 20.2. They need not be in the data language, and may employ concepts not necessary for the original collection of the data. At the interaction level, these principles will be concerned with the patterning of responses within an interaction and will be primarily physiological, or perhaps psychological, in nature. At the level of the relationship they will be concerned with the patterning of interactions within a relationship: organizational principles concerned with status (including dominance/subordinance), with the effects of interactions on subsequent interactions, and with social forces from outside the relationship, have so far proved valuable. And for the patterning of relationships within the social structure organizational principles concerned with blood relationships, relationships within and between age/sex categories, and with status, have proven relevance for non-human primates. It is important to emphasize that these principles will never be expressed in empirical instances in pure form: we shall thus always be concerned with the ways in which they interact.

In the human case a further set of principles operates – those concerned with institutions. The term 'institution' is used here to refer to sets of one or more recognized positions in a society which constrain the behaviour of the incumbents, and thus covers unique positions (e.g. the king), recognized relationships (e.g. marriage) and large-scale systems (e.g. the National Health Service). In that the common feature is one or more positions with recognized rights and duties, it is linked to the concept of rôle.

In fact institutions appear to play a dual rôle in much of the literature of the social sciences. In so far as they constitute goals, patterns of relationships which the incumbents of positions in society strive to achieve, they have the status of organizational principles, and can be used to explain the phenomena observed. But they also appear as abstractions from the data – the best description that an anthropologist can give of, say, the organization of three villages may involve reference to an idealized village council which does not actually exist in any one of them. Institutions are thus shown by both symbols in figure 20.2.

This conceptual scheme represents perhaps somewhat of a digression from the main theme of this paper, and will not be pursued further here (see Hinde, 1976a).

The Social Nexus

At each level in this scheme new properties emerge. Relationships are more than the sum of the interactions of which they are composed, in part because the various types of interaction within a relationship may affect each other, and in part because new properties arise which depend on how the interactions are patterned. Similarly, at the level of social structure, each dyadic relationship within a group is affected by the other relationships within that group. Two examples of the latter from our rhesus monkey groups may be mentioned.

1 The mother–infant relationship and social companions   The extent to which a mother permits or promotes the independence of her infant is affected by the presence of social companions. Infants of isolated mother–infant pairs spend more time off their mothers and more of that time at a distance from their mothers, than do infants of group-living mothers. This is correlated with a greater frequency of rejections on the part of their mothers and an increased rôle of the infants in maintaining proximity to their mothers while off her (Hinde and Spencer-Booth, 1967). These correlations suggest that the differences in the relationship are due primarily to differences between mothers (see below).

2 The infant's social nexus   Figure 20.3 is a qualitative representation of the types of relationship which affect an infant, the thickness of the continuous lines indicating the 'strength' of its relationships with its various social companions and of their relationships with each other. The discontinuous lines represent the effects of one relationship on another. For instance, adolescent females are prone to attempt to cuddle, carry and groom young in-

fants, but the extent to which they are permitted to do so by the mother depends on the nature of the relationship between the infant's mother and the adolescent. That relationship in its turn may be affected by the male's relationship with the adolescent; if she is his favourite, he may intervene on her behalf in a dispute with the infant's mother. While figure 20.2 is to be interpreted in purely qualitative terms, each of the lines drawn is based on quantitative data, and it does represent the complexity of the effects of relationships upon relationships within even a small group.

The Effects of Brief Periods of Mother–Infant Separation

We are now in a position to consider data derived from experiments involving brief periods of separation between mother and infant. These experiments were conducted when the infants were between 21 and 32 weeks old, and thus quite able to feed themselves. The earlier experiments involved the removal of the mother from the pen for 6 or 13 days, at the end of which time she was returned to the group (Hinde and Spencer-Booth, 1971a, and references cited therein). The procedures and measures used are explained in the figure legends.

We may consider first the general nature of the infant's response (see figures 20.4, 20.5 and 20.6, data labelled M/R). When the mother is removed there is a great increase in 'whoo' distress calling. This calling decreases after the first day, but is likely to remain higher than before separation for some weeks after reunion. The infant frequently sits in a hunched depressed posture, and at the same time its locomotor activity falls. Upon reunion, some, but not all, infants spend a great deal of time on their mothers for the first few days. At this time tantrums are frequent. During the weeks after reunion there is often a complex interaction between mother and infant, with the infant being very demanding of its mother's attentions, the mother at first yielding to its demands, then becoming intolerant, and so on until a more stable relationship is again established.

Although the course of events always followed this general pattern, there were marked individual differences in the extent and severity of the effects. In searching for factors related to these individual

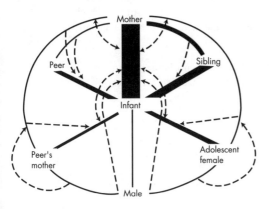

Figure 20.3   First order zone for a rhesus infant. Continuous lines represent inter-individual relationships, their thickness roughly indicating the importance of the bond. The discontinuous lines show ways in which the relationship has been shown to affect another relationship.

differences, we used primarily the four measures of infant behaviour when off its mother – locomotor activity in terms of number of sections of cage entered, activity when active (a measure of the proportion of the period in which the infant was active at all in which it was hyperactive), sitting still and adoption of the hunched posture, and whoo-calling. However, since some infants tended to be affected in one way and others in another, we also calculated an overall rank based on the sum of the inverse rank of locomotor activity and the actual ranks on sitting hunched and whoo-calling. This 'distress index' provided only a crude overall measure of the behaviour exhibited, but was useful in this context.

First, the length of the separation period proved to be an important variable. Infants which had been separated for 13 days showed a greater and more prolonged depression of locomotor activity, and a higher rate of distress calling, than did those which had been separated for one or two periods of 6 days.

Of other factors that could affect the response to separation, we found that the age of the infant (within the range studied) and the extent to which the infant was taken on by other group companions during its mother's absence, were at most of minor importance in our groups. Since nearly all mothers were multiparous and most infants had peers present in the cage, the influences of these factors could not be assessed. There were, however, some differences related to the sex of the infant: during separation and after reunion male infants whoo-called more than did females.

A more important issue was the relationship between individual differences before and after separation. Although the median scores for locomotion fell, and for sitting hunched and for whoo-calling rose, as a result of separation, the rank order correlation coefficients between pre- and post-separation scores were mostly significantly positive. Thus the effects of the mother's removal can be seen as an accentuation of pre-existing trends.

However, an even more crucial issue turned out to be the nature of the mother–infant relationship. Table 20.1 shows the rank order correlation coefficients between the distress index and four measures of the mother–infant relationship before separation. There was little relationship with the time that the infant had spent on or near the mother, but those infants that were most distressed in the two later post-reunion periods tended to be those that had been rejected most by their mothers and that had had to play the greatest relative rôle in staying near them, when off them. The distress index during these post-reunion periods was related also to contemporaneous values of these measures of the mother–infant relationship: examination of Kendall tau partial correlation coefficients showed that the relationship of the distress index to the pre-separation measures of the mother relationship was strongest at reunion and wanes with time, while that to the post-reunion measures of the relationship increased with time.

Thus the experiments up to this point demonstrated that a separation experience could produce symptoms in rhesus monkeys which are at least comparable with those seen in man, that the re-

Table 20.1 Spearman rank order correlation coefficients between distress index in three post-separation periods and pre-separation measures of mother–infant relationship

Measures of mother–infant relationship	(Day 10 was the day of reunion) Correlation coefficient		
	Day 10	Days 11–16	Days 23–7
time off	+0.02	−0.07	−0.13
$R/(Mk_I + Mk_M + R)$	+0.41	+0.59*	+0.43*
>60 cm	−0.26	−0.28	−0.18
% Ap_I − %L_I	+0.30	+0.64**	+0.41

*$P < 0.05$, **$P < 0.01$.

sponse can in part be regarded as an exacerbation of pre-existing tendencies, and that it is closely related to the nature of the mother–infant relationship. The next problem that concerned us was, what is it precisely about a separation experience that produces these effects? Is it separation from the mother *per se*; or the associated emotional deprivation (Howells, 1970); or the stresses that almost inevitably accompany a separation experience (Robertson and Robertson, 1971), or the long-term disruption of the ongoing mother–infant relationship, or what? In attempts to make some progress with these problems, the separation procedure was varied. Whereas in the experiments discussed so far the mother was removed from the home pen, the infant staying in the physical and social environment to which it was accustomed, in later experiments either the infant, or both infant and mother, were removed from the pen: in the latter case infant and mother were either confined together or separated. Since all separations lasted thirteen days, the data can be compared with those from the 13 day separations mentioned above. The groups concerned are shown in table 20.2. Some of these experiments were conducted by Linda McGinnis (1975; Hinde and Davies, 1972; Hinde and McGinnis, 1976).

There were no significant intergroup differences in measures of the mother–infant relationship before separation, though infants in the groups in which only the mother or only the infant were removed from the home pen scored more highly on activity measures before separation.

In considering the data on the effects of separation, three points must be borne in mind.

(i) Activity scores during the separation period for groups in which the infant was removed from the home pen and confined in a small cage are not comparable with those in which the mother was removed and the infant remained in the $5\frac{1}{2}$-m long home pen.

(ii) In any case activity scores are interpretable only in relation to other measures, for a high activity score can result from relaxed play and exploration, or from frantic searching for an absent mother.

(iii) As will become apparent later, a crucial issue in determining the post-reunion behaviour of the infants was the mother's preoccupation with re-establishing relationships with her group companions.

Considering first the behaviour of the infants during the separation period (figure 20.4), those infants who remained in their home pens (M/R) showed moderate locomotor activity and high distress calling on the day of separation, but soon became depressed, with locomotor activity falling to a low level. Their rate of whoo-calling was initially high but soon fell. The proportion of time sitting hunched, though falling a little, remained at a fairly high level.

Turning to the groups in which the infants were moved to a strange pen, the infants which remained with their mothers ((MI)/R) showed on the first day a marked decrease in locomotor activity which recovered quickly to levels comparable with those shown in the larger pens before separation, but remained much lower than either of the other infant-removed groups. The infants were in fact relatively little disturbed.

Data on the other two infant-removed groups (I/R and M–I/R) for the separation experience can be considered together since, in both cases, the infant was separated from its mother and placed in a strange cage. There was, however, a procedural dif-

Table 20.2 Four separation procedures used to study effects of temporary separation of infant from mother rhesus monkey

(Separation and/or removal occurred on day 4 and reunion on day 17)				
	N	Mother's pen	Infant's pen	Separation
M/R	6	strange	home	yes
I/R	6	home	strange	yes
M–I/R	7	strange	strange	yes
(MI)/R	7	strange	strange	no

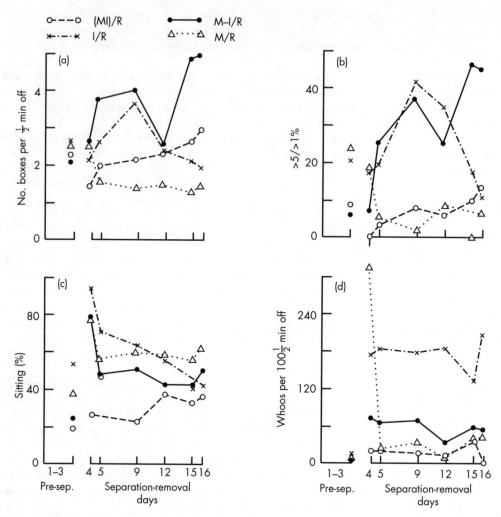

Figure 20.4 Behaviour of infants before and during separation/removal days – group medians. Separation and/or removal started on day 4, and reunion was on day 17. No. of boxes per half a minute off is a measure of locomotor activity. >5/ > 1% is a measure of how active the infants were when they were active – specifically, the number of half-minutes in which they entered more than 5 of the 16 boxes, into which the pen was divided, divided by the number of half-minutes in which they entered more than one. Sitting %: number of half-minutes in which they sat in the hunched depressed posture; Whoos per $100\frac{1}{2}$ min off is a measure of the actual frequency of distress calls.

ference in the way that the data were collected: with the group in which the mothers were left in the home pen the observer was in sight of the infants, while with the group in which the mothers were also removed and placed elsewhere the observer was in a hide behind one-way glass. Since the infants were well habituated to observers, we do not believe that the procedure adopted in the first case made much difference to their behaviour.

In both these infant-removed and separated groups the infants showed high activity levels, with the separation means even higher than the levels for the day of separation. (Two males in the M–I/R group were almost immobile with fear on the first day, and this partially accounts for the difference between the day of separation and the rest of the separation period.) Their activity consisted in part of bouts of frantic pacing, as indicated by their high

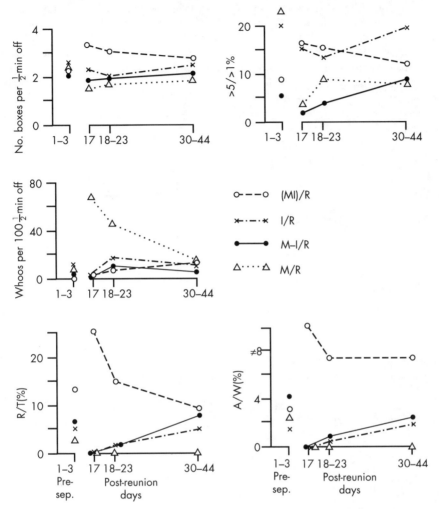

Figure 20.5 Behaviour of infants before separation/removal and after reunion – group medians. R/T (%) and A/W (%) are measures of the frequency of rough-and-tumble play and approach/withdrawal play respectively. Other measures as in figure 20.4.

scores on activity when active (> 5/ > 1, figures 20.4, 20.5). Between such bouts they sat immobile, but depression was less evident in these groups than amongst the separated infants who remained in their home pens. The rate of whoo-calling in both infant-removed-and-separated groups (I/R and M–I/R) was high during the separation period.

From these data we can conclude that the response to separation runs a different course according to whether the infant is kept in a strange small cage or the familiar home pen during the separation period. In the latter case symptoms which can be

likened to those of depression set in fairly soon after separation, whereas if the infant is in a strange small cage 'searching' behaviour persists for longer. Furthermore infants removed to a strange small cage but accompanied by their mothers show relatively little disturbance. Separation from the mother is thus a crucial issue.

We may now consider infant behaviour after reunion ((MI)/R) (figure 20.5). The group in which mother and infant were not separated showed an increase in activity on reunion: this activity consisted in large part of play with their peers, which continued at a high level for several weeks. These infants showed at first little whoo-calling, though this did increase to moderate levels later. By and large these infants were little disturbed.

With the infants whose mothers were moved (M/R), the depression-like symptoms which set in early in the separation period persisted after reunion: for some weeks activity levels remained lower, and sitting and whoo-calling levels higher,

than before separation. In these respects they differed from the infants who were separated by removal to a strange pen (I/R and M–I/R): in these the median activity levels approached more closely their pre-separation values, and sitting hunched and whoo-calling were lower, than with the mother-removed infants.

These differences can be related to the mother–infant relationship on reunion (figure 20.6).

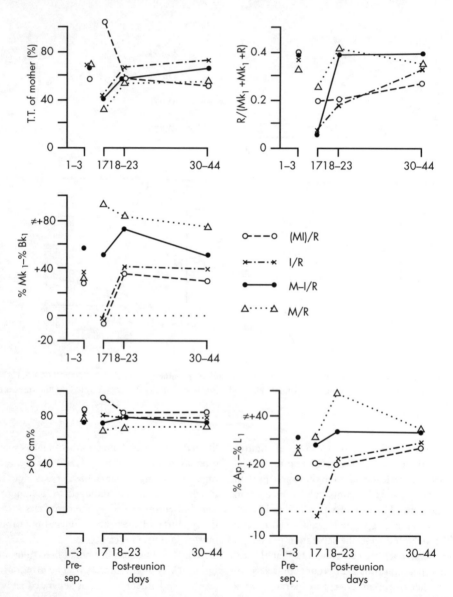

Figure 20.6 Measures of mother–infant relationships before separation/removal and after reunion – group medians. The measures used are described in figure 20.1.

Consider first the infant removed (I/R) and mother-removed (M/R) groups. Within the latter, the frequency of rejections and the infant's rôle in ventro–ventral contact were high on reunion. With the infant-removed group, the reverse was the case. Thus the greater distress shown by the mother-removed group can be understood as a consequence of the less adequate maternal care they received on reunion. We believe that these differences arose because mothers removed and then re-introduced to the pen were preoccupied with re-establishing relationships with their group companions, and were therefore less attentive to their infants. Some data on this were analysed extensively by L. McGinnis, and showed that the effect was especially marked with the less sociable, low-ranking mothers. By contrast, in the group in which only the infants were removed, the mothers staying with their group companions in the home pen, the mothers could devote all their energies on the day of reunion towards meeting the demands of their infants.

We may now consider the group in which infants and mothers were removed and separated from each other (M–I/R). These mothers also had to re-establish their relationships with their group companions. The frequency of rèjections, and the relative rôles of infants in contact and proximity, were again high. However, unlike the infants of the M/R group, these M–I/R infants showed little sign of depression. Their activity levels were little below pre-separation levels, and their play behaviour showed considerable recovery. It was probably for this reason that their level of distress calling was much lower than that of the M/R group.

Mothers of the non-separated (MI)/R group also had to re-establish their relationships with their group companions, but here no separation had occurred. In this group, the frequency of rejections, and the infants' rôle in contact and proximity, were all relatively low. Presumably the more receptive behaviour of the mothers in this case was related to the fact that the mother–infant relationships had not been interrupted.

In summarizing these findings, four issues may be emphasized.

(1) Infants who remain in their home pen while their mothers are removed become depressed and remain so after reunion. The persistence of the depression could be due to a persisting physiological state or to conditioning to the environment in which separation occurred, or both.

(2) Mothers which are removed from the home pen must re-establish their relationships with their group companions on return, and thus have less to spare for their infants.

(3) Depressed infants are less effective in eliciting maternal care than are non-depressed infants.

(4) If the mother–infant relationship is interrupted by separation, mothers are less prone to be adequately maternal on reunion, than they would be if they had been continuously together.

Thus in the M/R group the infants remained depressed; although they called frequently they did not pursue their mothers, the mothers were distracted by their other group companions, and the infants were not sufficiently persistent to direct their mother's attentions to themselves.

In the M–I/R group the situation was similar but, since the infants had not been in the home pen, they were not so depressed and were more persistent in pursuing their mothers. The high activity levels shown by this group can be partially understood in these terms.

Infants of the infant-removed group were not only not depressed, but also had fully responsive mothers. They were thus less affected than infants in the other separated groups.

In the group where both mother and infant were removed and not separated the infants were again not depressed, and the mothers were responsive to them presumably because their relationship had been unbroken. On reunion both mothers and infants were concerned with re-establishing relationships with group companions and the infants at first spent much time off their mothers, while keeping visual contact with them.

One last aspect of these separation experiments must be discussed. So far we have been concerned only with the consequences of the separation experience in the immediately ensuing weeks. While these can be profound, it remains possible that in the longer term all effects of the separation experience are erased.

Some of our previously separated animals have become old enough to assess this. We have gathered data on their behaviour when 1 year, 18 months and $2\frac{1}{2}$ years of age. So far data are available only for infants subjected to one or two 6 day separation experiences.

In brief we could detect no clear differences between these infants and non-separated controls when we observed them in their home pens. When tested with strange objects in their home pens, some suggestive differences emerged. But when tested with strange objects in a strange environment clear differences appeared: these differences can be summarized by saying that the previously separated infants were less able to cope with slightly alarming situations (Spencer-Booth and Hinde, 1971).

The Nature of the Mother–Infant Relationship

These experiments have produced clear evidence that the consequences of a separation experience are related to the nature of the mother–infant relationship. They indicated that, in the conditions of these experiments and within the range exhibited by our subjects, the amount of time that infant and mother spent in contact with or near each other were of at most minor importance. But certain measures which can be described as measures of tension in the mother–infant relationship – namely the relative frequency of rejections and the infant's rôle in the maintenance of mutual proximity–are correlated with the effects of the separation experience on the infant.

This of course raises questions about the development of the mother–infant relationship. What determines the individual characteristics of each mother–infant relationship?

We have recently completed an analysis of 63 mother–infant pairs, in an attempt to obtain some information on this issue. When divided according to sex of infant, availability of peers, and dominance status, parity and source of mother, relatively few subjects fell into each subgroup. However, it was possible to make a number of comparisons for each of the factors considered (e.g. male versus female infant; dominant versus subordinate mother). These showed that although all the variables studied, except perhaps maternal parity, affected the relationship, none produced effects that were wholly consistent over all comparisons. Interactions

were thus ubiquitous, and we must await even more extensive data before the various factors involved can be disentangled (White and Hinde, 1975).

The experiments reviewed above show also that the consequences of a separation experience depend in part on the extent to which the relationship is disturbed as a consequence of the separation. Further progress here demands more basic knowledge about the nature and dynamics of inter-individual relationships than is at present available. At present, much of what is known depends either on case history studies, with general principles relatively inaccessible, or on investigations, many excellent in themselves, but designed to illustrate particular points of view (Swenson, 1973). Although the nature and dynamics of human interpersonal relationships pose problems even more complex than those with which biologists usually deal, it seems possible that biology can make some contribution, for two reasons.

First, if there is to be a science of interpersonal relationships, it must surely rest on a descriptive base. Biologists, whose science depends on the work of generations of taxonomists and systematists, may be able to contribute towards providing this. As a start, certain dimensions along which interpersonal relationships differ, and which may be important for understanding their dynamics, have been specified (Hinde, 1976b). But it is crucial to be able to specify the qualities of interpersonal relationships in reasonably objective terms. Here the biologist may contribute by using relatively simple animal cases to work out methods. Consider for example, the extent to which the behaviour of each partner in the relationship is directed with respect to the ongoing goals of the other. We have already seen that this 'meshing' as assessed in one way, increases with age. Using a slightly different measure, M. J. A. Simpson has shown that at any one age rhesus monkey mother–infant pairs differ in the extent to which the behaviour of each partner 'meshes' with that of the other. Figure 20.7 contains data on two dyads. It shows the probability that each partner will leave the other in successive time intervals after a particular reference event – namely an approach by the infant to the mother. In one dyad the probabilities that mother and infant will leave run closely parallel, whilst in the other they bear little relationship to each other. In the former the mother is likely to leave when the infant is likely to leave,

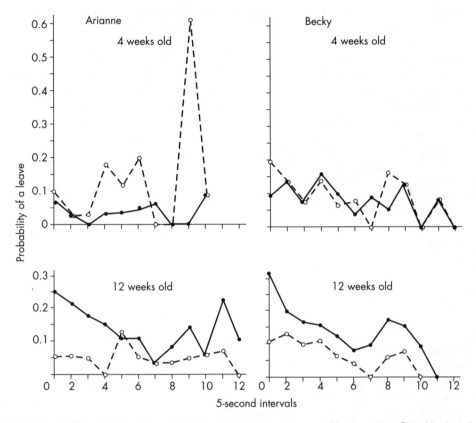

Figure 20.7 Probabilities of visits to the mother initiated by the infants being ended by the mother (○) and by the infant (●) when the visits had lasted between 0 and 5 s, 5 and 10 s, 10 and 15 s, and so on (from Hinde and Simpson 1975.)

and vice versa: we could describe them as, by this criterion, a 'well-meshed' pair (Hinde and Simpson, 1975); and it is at least possible that 'meshing' is a property akin to 'intersubjectivity' (Asch, 1952).

The second way in which biologists may contribute also stems from the relative simplicity of animal inter-individual relationships. It has become apparent that, in studying relationships, it is extremely difficult to obtain measures of the behaviour or of the behavioural propensities of either partner within the relationship that are independent of the behaviour of the other. For instance, how quickly a mother responds to her baby's cry, which might seem to be a measure of maternal behaviour, must surely reflect also how often the baby has cried recently, itself in turn perhaps dependent on maternal responsiveness. For this reason, the contributions of the two partners to the

nature of the relationship at any one time, to changes in its nature with time, or to differences between relationships, are difficult to disentangle. However, studies of rhesus monkeys have shown that some progress can be made by using correlations between measures. The method has been discussed elsewhere (see, for example, Hinde, 1969, 1975; Hinde and Herrmann, 1976) and one example will suffice. Suppose one infant spends more time off its mother than another, is the difference primarily due to a difference between mothers or to a difference between infants? If attempts by the former infant to make contact are more frequently rejected than attempts by the latter, the difference in time off must be due primarily to a difference between the mothers, but if it is off more even though it is rejected less, the difference must be primarily between the infants. Similarly if, for a number of dyads, rank order on time off is positively correlated with rank order on frequency of rejections at a particular age, inter-mother differences are primarily responsible for inter-dyad differences in time off. This method, basically very simple, can be used to answer questions of the types posed above and thereby to tease apart the dynamics of the relationship. Further progress must of course depend on the specification of principles that will provide understanding of the dynamics of interindividual relationships – that is of how interactions affect subsequent interactions, and of how relationships may change their properties with time, yet preserve their integrity in spite of changes in the nature of the individuals concerned and the vicissitudes of their respective social worlds (see, for example, figure 20.2 and accompanying discussion). Some of the issues involved have been discussed elsewhere (Hinde and Stevenson-Hinde, 1976) but two points arising from these separation experiments may be mentioned here.

1 Continuous or threshold effects? The finding that any particular factor affects the course of a relationship proves neither that the presence of that factor *in any degree* is of importance, nor that there is a straight line relationship between the extent to which it is present and its effects. For example, these experiments show that length of separation is an important issue. However, common sense indicates that very short separation experiences will have no or negligible consequences. Furthermore, while marked differences between the effects of 1 and 20 day separation experiences are to be expected, effects of 30 and 50 day separations might be quite similar. In other words we must expect a threshold region, below which a separation experience has at most minor consequences, and above which they are major. Of course the threshold need not be sharply defined.

2 Regulation versus positive feedback That relatively minor perturbations produce negligible long-term effects on the course of the mother–infant relationship implies that it has considerable capacity for regulation (cf. Dunn, 1976). Where marked diversions do occur, they can sometimes be understood in terms of positive feedback, the consequences of a minor deviation becoming magnified and over-riding the regulatory mechanisms. An example is perhaps provided by the infants left in the home pen while their mothers were removed (M/R): after reunion their continued high level of distress calling was a consequence of two factors, the mothers' social distractions (present also in the M–I/R group) and the infants' depression, the former exacerbating the latter and leading to a more permanent distortion of the relationship which was not fully corrected, at least in the weeks following reunion.

Conclusion

These experiments were started with reference to a particular controversy – can a period of separation from the mother affect the personality development of the human infant? The evidence that a brief period of separation can have long-term effects in monkeys adds force to the evidence, now itself considerable, that long-term effects *can* occur in man (see, for example, Bowlby, 1969, 1973; Rutter, 1972; Douglas, 1975). Evidence comes not only from the experiments reviewed here, but also from those conducted in a number of other laboratories (see Suomi, 1974; Kaufman, 1970). The monkey data also provide evidence about what sort of individuals are most likely to be most affected, and how the effects can best be ameliorated – evidence whose relevance to the human case is certainly worth assessing. But this material also opens up questions of even more far-reaching importance – questions concerning the nature and dynamics of interindividual relationships. Of course monkeys are different from people, and of course human personal relationships are infinitely more complex than relationships between monkeys. But just because monkeys are *relatively* simple, their study may the more readily be used to harden up concepts, to generate principles and to suggest methods which are worth trying out in the human case.

References

Ainsworth, M. D. (1962) The effects of maternal deprivation: A review of findings and controversy in the context of research strategy. In *Deprivation of maternal care: A reassessment of its effects*, Geneva: World Health Organization.
Altmann, J. (1974) Observational study of behaviour: Sampling methods, *Behaviour*, 49, 227–67.
Asch, S. E. (1952) *Social psychology*, New York: Prentice-Hall.

Bowlby, J. (1951) *Maternal care and mental health*, Geneva: World Health Organization.

Bowlby, J. (1958) *Can I leave my baby?* National Association for Mental Health.

Bowlby, J. (1969) *Attachment and loss*, vol. 1: *Attachment*, London: Hogarth Press.

Bowlby, J. (1973) *Attachment and loss*, vol. 2: *Separation: Anxiety and anger*, London: Hogarth Press.

Douglas, J. W. B. (1975) Early hospital admissions and later disturbances of behaviour and learning, *Developmental medicine and child neurology*, vol. 17, 456–80.

Dunn, J. (1976) How far do early differences in mother–child relations affect later development? In *Growing points in ethology*, eds P. P. G. Bateson and R. A. Hinde, Cambridge: Cambridge University Press.

Harlow, H. F. and Harlow, M. K. (1965) The affectional systems. In *Behavior of nonhuman primates*, vol. 2, eds A. M. Schrier, H. F. Harlow and F. Stollnitz, New York and London: Academic.

Hinde, R. A. (1969) Analysing the roles of the partners in a behavioural interaction – mother–infant relations in rhesus macaques, *Annals of the New York Academy of Science*, 159, 651–67.

Hinde, R. A. (1973) On the design of check-sheets, *Primates*, 14 (4), 393–406.

Hinde, R. A. (1974) *Biological bases of human social behaviour*, New York and London: McGraw-Hill.

Hinde, R. A. (1975) Mothers' and infants' roles: Distinguishing the questions to be asked, *Parent–infant interaction*, Ciba Foundation Symposium 33, pp. 5–16, Elsevier.

Hinde, R. A. (1976a) Interactions, relationships and social structure, *Man*, 11, 1–17.

Hinde, R. A. (1976b) On describing relationships, *Journal of Child Psychology and Psychiatry*, 17, 1–19.

Hinde, R. A. and Atkinson, S. (1970) Assessing the roles of social partners in maintaining mutual proximity, as exemplified by mother/infant relations in monkeys, *Animal Behaviour*, 18, 169–76.

Hinde, R. A. and Davies, L. (1972) Removing infant rhesus from mother for 13 days compared with removing mother from infant, *Journal of Child Psychology and Psychiatry*, 13, 227–37.

Hinde, R. A. and Herrmann, J. (1976) Frequencies, durations, derived measures and their correlations in studying dyadic and triadic relationships. In *Studies in mother–infant interaction*, *Loch Lomond Symposium*, ed. H. R. Schaffer (in the press).

Hinde, R. A. and McGinnis, L. (1976) Some factors influencing the effects of temporary mother–infant separation – some experiments with rhesus monkeys, *Psychology and Medicine* (in the press).

Hinde, R. A. and Simpson, M. J. A. (1975) Qualities of mother–infant relationships in monkeys. In *Parent–infant interaction*: Ciba Foundation Symposium 33, pp. 39–67, Elsevier.

Hinde, R. A. and Spencer-Booth, Y. (1967) The effect of social companions on mother–infant relations in rhesus monkeys. In *Primate ethology*, ed. D. Morris, London: Weidenfeld and Nicolson.

Hinde, R. A. and Spencer-Booth, Y. (1968) The study of mother–infant interaction in captive group-living rhesus monkeys, *Proceedings of the Royal Society of London*, 169, 177–201.

Hinde, R. A. and Spencer-Booth, Y. (1971) Effects of brief separation from mother on rhesus monkeys, *Science, N.Y.*, 173, 111–18.

Hinde, R. A. and Stevenson-Hinde, J. (1976) Towards understanding relationships: Dynamic stability. In *Growing points in ethology*, eds P. P. G. Bateson and R. A. Hinde, Cambridge: Cambridge University Press.

Hinde, R. A. and White, L. E. (1974) Dynamics of a relationship: Rhesus mother–infant ventro–ventral contact, *Journal of Comparative and Physiological Psychology*, 86, 8–23.

Howells, J. (1970) Fallacies in child care, I: That 'separation' is synonymous with 'deprivation', *Acta Paedopsychiatrical*, 37, 3–14.

Kaufman, I. C. (1970) Mother/infant relations in monkeys and humans: A reply to Professor Hinde. In *Ethology and psychiatry*, ed. N. F. White, pp. 47–68, Toronto and Buffalo: University of Toronto Press.

McGinnis, L. M. (1975) *Analysis of the factors involved in mother–infant separations in rhesus monkeys*. Ph.D. Thesis, University of Cambridge.

Robertson, J. and Robertson, J. (1971) Young children in brief separation: A fresh look, *Psychoanalytical Study of Children*, 26, 264–315.

Rutter, M. (1972) *Maternal deprivation: reassessed*, Harmondsworth: Penguin Books.

Simpson, M. J. A. and Simpson, A. E. (1976) One-zero and scan methods for sampling behaviour, *Animal Behaviour* (in the press).

Spencer-Booth, Y. and Hinde, R. A. (1971) Effects of brief separations from mothers during infancy on behaviour of rhesus monkeys 6–24 months later, *Journal of Child Psychology and Psychiatry*, 12, 157–72.

Suomi, S. J. (1974) Factors affecting responses to social separation in rhesus monkeys. In *Animal models in human psychobiology*, eds G. Serban and A. Kling, New York and London: Plenum Press.

Swenson, C. H., Jr (1973) *Introduction to interpersonal relations*, Glenview, Illinois, and Brighton, England: Scott, Foresman and Co.

White, R. E. C. (1971) WRATS: a computer compatible system for automatically recording and transcribing behavioural data, *Behaviour*, 40, 135–61.

White, L. E. and Hinde, R. A. (1975) Some factors affecting mother–infant relations in rhesus monkeys, *Animal Behaviour*, 23, 527–42.

CHAPTER 21

Structure and Development of Behavior Systems

JERRY A. HOGAN

The postulation of behavior systems is one attempt to reduce the complexity of naturally occurring behavior. In this paper, I will first define what I mean by a behavior system, and then provide some examples of how such systems develop. I will use the dustbathing and feeding systems of the fowl as my primary examples, but will also briefly discuss the aggressive and sexual systems. These systems are considered to be typical of behavior systems in other species (see Hogan, 1988). Finally, I will discuss whether it is possible to extract some general principles from the data. One such principle is that learning, as studied by experimental psychologists, is but one aspect of the processes underlying behavioral development.

What is a Behavior System?

I have proposed motor, central, and perceptual mechanisms as the basic units of behavior (Hogan, 1988). These entities are viewed as corresponding to structures within the central nervous system. They are conceived of as consisting of some arrangement of neurons (not necessarily localized) that acts independently of other such mechanisms.

Previously published in *Psychonomic Bulletin and Review*, 1, 4 (1994), pp. 439–50. Copyright © 1994 Psychonomic Society, Inc.

They are called behavior mechanisms because their activation results in an event of behavioral interest: a specific motor pattern, an identifiable internal state, or a particular perception. Behavior mechanisms are cognitive structures, and thus, this conception can also include entities such as ideas, thoughts, and memories. It should be noted that although I define behavior mechanisms as structures in the nervous system, this definition does not imply that the study of behavior involves neurophysiology. The study of behavior is the study of the functioning of the nervous system and must be carried out at the behavioral level, by using behavioral concepts: our major concern is the *output* of the nervous system, manifested as perceptions, thoughts, and actions (see Hogan, 1994a).

Behavior mechanisms can be connected with one another to form larger units called behavior systems, which correspond to the level of complexity indicated by terms such as feeding, sexual, and aggressive behavior (Baerends, 1976; Hogan, 1988). The organization of the connections among the behavior mechanisms determines the nature of the behavior system. Thus, a behavior system can be considered a description of the structure of behavior. It can be defined as any organization of perceptual, central, and motor mechanisms that acts as a unit in some situations (Hogan, 1971; Hogan and Roper, 1978). A pictorial representation of this definition is shown in figure 21.1. It can be noted that

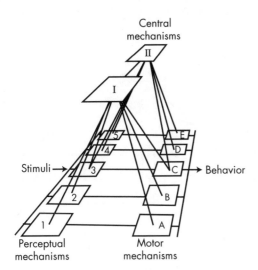

Figure 21.1 Conception of behavior system. Stimuli from the external world (including stimuli produced by the behavior) are analyzed by perceptual mechanisms. Output from the perceptual mechanisms can be integrated by central mechanisms and/or channeled directly to motor mechanisms. The output of the motor mechanisms results in behavior. In this diagram, Central Mechanism I, Perceptual Mechanisms 1, 2 and 3, and Motor Mechanisms A, B, and C form one behavior system; Central Mechanism II, Perceptual Mechanisms 3, 4, and 5, and Motor Mechanisms C, D, and E form a second behavior system. 1-A, 2-B, and so on can also be considered less complex behavior systems. (From "Cause and Function in the Development of Behavior Systems," by J. A. Hogan, in *Handbook of Behavioral Neurobiology*, vol. 9, p. 66, ed. by E. M. Blass, 1988, New York: Plenum Press. Copyright 1988 by Plenum Publishing Corp. Reproduced by permission.)

this definition is quite similar to Tinbergen's definition of an instinct: "a hierarchically organized nervous mechanism" (1951, p. 112). The activation of an instinct produces instinctive behavior, and the activation of a behavior system produces behavior. In both cases, behavior is the expression of the activity of structures in the nervous system. This definition is also similar in many respects to McDougall's (1928) conception of an instinct. McDougall, however, insisted that the essence of an instinct is its goal (1928, p. 119), which raises a number of problems that are beyond the scope of this paper; one of these problems, however, is discussed in the next paragraph.

In the context of this sysmposium, I should point out that my definition of a behavior system in

terms of its structure is different from Timberlake's (1983, 1994) definition. Timberlake defines a behavior system in terms of its functional characteristics. There may often be a close correspondence between systems defined in structural and functional terms, but this is by no means always the case; and it is very easy for confusion to arise. For example, a structural definition of sexual behavior would include a description of the perceptual mechanisms that analyze stimuli and activate a central sexual coordinating mechanism plus a description of the motor patterns that occur when the central mechanism is activated. A functional definition of sexual behavior would emphasize reproduction – that is, those behaviors that lead to successful propagation of the species. It should be clear that many animals, including humans, engage in sexual behavior by the structural definition when that behavior definitely will have no reproductive function. Further, courtship behaviors in many species are necessary for successful reproduction, even though the courtship behaviors themselves can be considered to belong to nonsexual behavior systems such as fear and aggression (Baerends, 1975; Tinbergen, 1952). This distinction between structure and function will continue to be an issue throughout this paper.

Development of Behavior Systems

Development implies changes in the structure of behavior. The study of development comprises (1) describing the changes in the organization of the behavior mechanisms themselves as well as changes in the connections among the behavior mechanisms, and (2) investigating the causes of those changes (Hogan, 1988). This view of development is a generalization of a proposal by Kruijt (1964), who suggested that the motor components of behavior often function as independent units in young animals, and that only later, after specific experience, do these motor components become integrated into more complex systems, such as hunger, aggression, and sex. In looking for the causal basis of developmental changes, I have found it convenient to make use of the concept of *prefunctional* (Hogan, 1988; Schiller, 1949/1957). If a behavior mechanism develops prefunctionally, this means that functional experience (or practice) is not necessary for normal development to occur. It should be stated that there is no implication about the role of other kinds of experience. I make this distinction because most people assume that experience means functional experience and that cause and function go hand in hand. As mentioned above, however, this is not always the case.

Dustbathing

Dustbathing in the adult fowl (and many other bird species) consists of a sequence of coordinated movements of the wings, feet, head, and body that serve to spread dust through the feathers. It occurs regularly, and bouts of dustbathing last about half an hour (Vestergaard, 1982). When dust is available, dustbathing functions to remove excess lipids from the feathers and to maintain good feather condition (van Liere and Bokma, 1987).

The sequence of behaviors in a dustbathing bout begins with the bird pecking and raking the substrate with its bill and scratching with its feet. These movements continue as the bird squats down and comes into a sitting position. From time to time, the bird tosses the dusty substrate into its feathers with vertical movements of its wings and also rubs its head in the substrate. It then rolls on its side and rubs the dust thoroughly through its feathers. These sequences of movements may be repeated several times. Finally, the bird stands up, shakes its body vigorously, and then switches to other behavior.

Dustbathing can also be described as a behavior system, as shown in figure 21.2. A perceptual mechanism analyzes stimuli from the substrate; a central mechanism integrates information from the perceptual mechanism with various internal factors and controls the timing and duration of dustbathing; and motor mechanisms coordinate the individual behavior patterns. This figure depicts the structure of the dustbathing system in the adult fowl. However, dustbathing does not appear fully formed in the young animal. Rather, individual elements of the system appear independently, and only gradually do these elements become fixed in the normal adult form. Pecking is seen on the day of hatching, but the other motor components appear gradually over the first 10 or 12 days posthatch. We have carried out a number of experiments to determine what causal factors are necessary for this be-

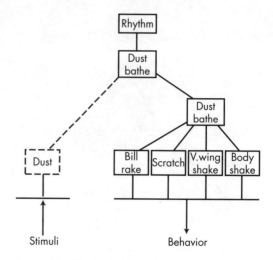

Figure 21.2 The dustbathing behavior system of a young chick. Boxes represent putative cognitive (neural) mechanisms: a perceptual mechanism responsible for recognizing dust, a central dustbathing mechanism responsible for integrating input from the perceptual mechanism and other internal influences as well as for coordinating output to the motor mechanisms, and several motor mechanisms responsible for the various motor patterns constituting dustbathing. Solid lines indicate mechanisms and connections among them that develop prefunctionally. Dashed lines indicate mechanisms and connections that develop as the result of specific functional experience. (From "The Development of a Behavior System: Dustbathing in the Burmese Red Junglefowl: I. The Influence of the Rearing Environment on the Organization of Dustbathing," by K. Vestergaard, J. A. Hogan, and J. P. Kruijt, 1990, *Behaviour*, *112*, p. 100. Copyright © 1990 by E. J. Brill. Reproduced by permission.)

havior to develop. We have looked at the development of the motor mechanisms and their coordination, the central mechanisms, and the perceptual mechanism for the recognition of dust.

According to Kruijt (1964), most of the dustbathing "movements are, at their first occurrence after hatching, immediately shown in their characteristic form, even though the chick has not had any opportunity to practice their function" (p. 23). Vestergaard, Hogan, and Kruijt (1990) asked whether the rearing environment influenced the organization of the motor components. They observed small groups of chicks that were raised either in a normal environment containing sand and grass sod or in a poor environment in which the floor was covered with wire mesh. A comparison of the dustbathing motor patterns of 2-month-old birds raised in the two environments showed surprisingly few differences. The form and frequency of the individual behavior patterns as well as the temporal organization of the elements during extended bouts of dustbathing developed almost identically in both groups (see figure 21.3). There were some differences in the microstructure of the bouts that could

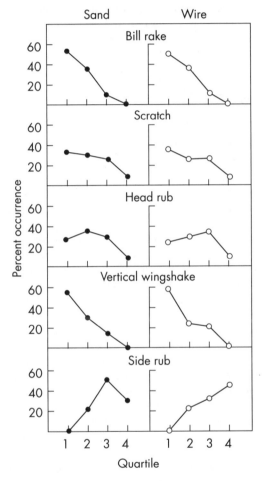

Figure 21.3 Percent of total occurrence of each of five components of dustbathing during successive quarters of a bout on a sand substrate or a wire mesh substrate. A bout was defined as beginning with the first vertical wingshake and ending with body shaking. All subjects were raised in the environment in which they were tested. (From "The Development of a Behavior System: Dustbathing in the Burmese Red Junglefowl: I. The Influence of the Rearing Environment on the Organization of Dustbathing," by K. Vestergaard, J. A. Hogan, and J. P. Kruijt, 1990, *Behaviour*, *112*, p. 108. Copyright © 1990 by E. J. Brill. Reproduced by permission.)

be related to the presence or absence of specific feedback (see also van Liere, 1992; van Liere, Kooijman, and Wiepkema, 1990), but the motor mechanisms and their coordination developed essentially normally in chicks raised in a dustless environment. Clearly, the experience of sand in the feathers removing lipids or improving feather quality is not necessary for the integration of the motor components of dustbathing into a normal coordinated sequence.

In adult fowl, the occurrence of dustbathing varies directly with the length of time a bird has been deprived of the opportunity to dustbathe; it also occurs primarily in the middle of the day (Vestergaard, 1982). In young chicks, as soon as dustbathing behavior is seen, at about 1 week of age, it is controlled by the effects of dust deprivation. Hogan, Honrado, and Vestergaard (1991) found that deprivation effects could be demonstrated at as early as 8 days of age and that they did not change over at least a 4-week period (see figure 21.4). (It should be noted that once a chick has experience at dustbathing in sand, longer periods of dust deprivation are necessary before it will show "vacuum" or "sham" dustbathing on wire mesh.) No specific experience seemed to be necessary for the motivational factors associated with dust deprivation to gain control of dustbathing, which suggests that the central mechanism and the connections between it and the motor mechanisms develop prefunctionally.

Similarly, Hogan and van Boxel (1993) found that a daily rhythm, with most dustbathing occurring in the middle of the day, was seen in chicks at least as young as 14 days of age (see figure 21.5). The occurrence of dustbathing, however, was not as strongly restricted to the middle of the day as in adults, and the length of dustbathing bouts was also shorter in the young birds. This study was not designed to test whether the daily rhythm controlled dustbathing prefunctionally, but the results are consistent with such an interpretation.

Functional experience does play an essential role in the development of the perceptual mechanism for recognizing dust and the connection between it and the central mechanism. Young chicks can be seen engaging in dustbathing movements on almost any surface that is available, ranging from hard ground and stones to sand and dust. In fact, Kruijt (1964) found that making the external situation as

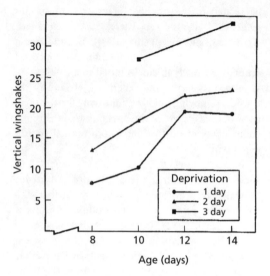

Figure 21.4 The amount of dustbathing (mean number of vertical wingshakes per chick) seen during a 1-h test on sand as a function of age and length of dust deprivation (chicks were held on wire mesh between tests). Each line represents data from a separate group of chicks. Chicks in the 1-day deprivation group were exposed to dust for 1 h on odd-numbered days, but their behavior was not recorded on those days. (From "Development of a Behavior System: Dustbathing in the Burmese Red Junglefowl (*Gallus gallus spadiceus*): II. Internal factors," by J. A. Hogan, G. I. Honrado, and K. Vestergaard, 1991, *Journal of Comparative Psychology*, *105*, pp. 271. Copyright © 1991 by the American Psychological Association. Reproduced by permission.)

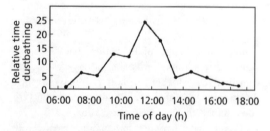

Figure 21.5 Percent of total daily dustbathing per hour for chicks with continuous access to dust during the 3rd week after hatching. Chicks were kept on a 12:12-h light:dark cycle. (From "Causal Factors Controlling Dustbathing in Burmese Red Junglefowl: Some Results and a Model," by J. Hogan and F. van Boxel, 1993, *Animal Behaviour*, *46*, p. 631. Copyright © 1993 by Academic Press. Adapted by permission.)

favorable as possible for dustbathing was insufficient for releasing the behavior. This result implies that early dustbathing may be controlled exclusively by the internal factors mentioned above. With respect to the behavior system model of dustbathing (figure 21.2), it implies that the connection between the dust-recognition perceptual mechanism and the central mechanism is not formed until well after the motor and central mechanisms are functional.

Some evidence is available for how the dust-recognition mechanism itself develops. The stimulus properties of a substrate constitute one important factor. For example, Vestergaard and Hogan (1992) found fine black coal dust to be much preferred to white sand, and Petherick and Duncan (1989) and van Liere (1992) found dark peat to be much preferred to sand and wood shavings. In the case of peat, the preference developed gradually, which implies that some aspect of the experience during dustbathing was crucial. It remains to be determined whether removal of lipids, the sensory feedback from the substrate in the feathers, or facilitation of the dustbathing behavior itself is the crucial factor. Other evidence from the same studies shows that early experience can lead to stable preferences for normally nonpreferred stimuli. As an extreme example, Vestergaard and Hogan (1992) raised birds on wire mesh but gave them regular experience on a substrate covered with coal dust, white sand, or a skin of junglefowl feathers. In choice tests given at 1 month of age, some of the birds that had had experience with junglefowl feathers were found to have developed a stable preference for dustbathing on the feathers. This example is important because it shows how a system can develop abnormally. It also suggests that the pecking associated with dustbathing may be a cause for "feather pecking," a common pathological condition in which some hens pull out the feathers of their cage mates, which is seen in many commercial groups of fowl (Vestergaard, Kruijt, and Hogan, 1993).

Overall, a general conclusion from all these studies is that particular classes of stimuli are more efficacious than others for the development of the perceptual mechanism for the recognition of dust. This conclusion is similar to that reached in studies of the development of perceptual mechanisms for the recognition of conspecific song in some species of song birds (e.g., DeVoogd, 1994; Marler, 1987) and perceptual mechanisms for the recognition of conspecifics in imprinting studies in various avian species (Bischof, 1994; Bolhuis, 1991; ten Cate, 1994).

Hunger

The hunger system of an adult chicken consists of various perceptual mechanisms that serve a food-recognition function, motor mechanisms that function to locate and ingest food, and a central mechanism that integrates signals from the physiological mechanisms concerned with nutrition and modulates signals from the perceptual mechanisms and to the motor mechanisms. A diagram of the hunger system of a young chick is shown in figure 21.6.

As with dustbathing, both the individual motor mechanisms of the system (pecking, ground scratching, walking) and the integration of these mechanisms into effective foraging behavior appear prefunctionally. Unlike with dustbathing, however, the integration of the motor mechanisms disintegrates in the absence of effective functional experience (Hogan, 1971). Hogan (1988) suggested that new connections were formed between the central hunger mechanism and individual motor mechanisms on the basis of the specific experience of the individual chick, and that these new connections effectively blocked the expression of the original prefunctional connections (see figure 21.6).

Another difference between the dustbathing and hunger systems is that the central mechanism for hunger does not immediately control the motor mechanisms of the system. A chick begins pecking within a few hours of hatching, but its nutritional state does not influence pecking until about 3 days of age (Hogan, 1971). Early experiments showed that some kind of pecking experience is necessary for this change in control to occur (Hogan, 1973a), and further experiments led to the hypothesis that it is the experience of pecking followed by swallowing that causes the connection between the central hunger mechanism and the pecking mechanism to be

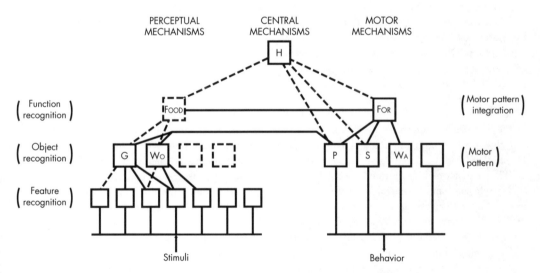

Figure 21.6 The hunger system of a young chick. Perceptual mechanisms include various feature recognition mechanisms (such as of color, shape, size, and movement), object recognition mechanisms (such as of grainlike objects [G], wormlike objects [Wo], and possibly others), and a function recognition mechanism (Food). Motor mechanisms include those underlying specific behavior patterns (such as pecking [P], ground scratching [S], walking [Wa], and possibly others) and an integrative motor mechanism that could be called foraging (For). There is also a central hunger mechanism (H). Solid lines indicate mechanisms and connections among them that develop prefunctionally. Dashed lines indicate mechanisms and connections that develop as the result of specific functional experience. (From "Cause and Function in the Development of Behavior Systems," by J. A. Hogan, in *Handbook of Behavioral Neurobiology*, vol. 9, p. 83, ed. by E. M. Blass, 1988, New York: Plenum Press. Copyright © 1988 by Plenum Publishing Corp. Reproduced by permission.)

formed (Hogan, 1977). In other words, it appears that a chick must learn that pecking is the action that leads to ingestion; once this association has been formed, nutritional factors can directly affect pecking (see figure 21.6). Subsequent experiments have shown that the association of pecking with ingestion is, indeed, the necessary and sufficient condition for pecking to become integrated into the hunger system (Hogan, 1984).

The development of the perceptual mechanism for recognizing food and of the connection between the food-recognition mechanism and the central hunger mechanism requires functional experience, and is similar to the development of the corresponding structures of the dustbathing system in this way. The putative food-recognition mechanism in newly hatched chicks must be largely unspecified because of the very wide range of stimuli that are characteristic of items that chicks will come to accept as food. Although certain taste and tactile stimuli are more acceptable than others, these stimuli can be effective only after the chick has the stimulus in its mouth. Chicks learn to associate the visual characteristics of an object with its taste and tactile characteristics as early as 1 day of age, and they treat such objects as food or nonfood before nutritive factors gain control of pecking on Day 3 (see Hogan, 1973b, for review). This means that the food-recognition mechanism is independent of the central mechanism of the developing hunger system. Other evidence shows that the long-term effects of ingestion can also affect the development of the food-recognition mechanism, but only after the chicks are 3 days old (Hogan-Warburg and Hogan, 1981).

The existence of a connection between a perceptual mechanism and a central mechanism can be inferred by demonstrating the existence of "priming" or "incentive" effects (Hogan and Roper, 1978, pp. 231–2). For example, presentation of food may make an animal hungrier, or presentation of a sexual stimulus may increase its sexual appetite. There is evidence in young chicks that food particles develop incentive value between 3 and 5 days posthatch based on the long-term effects of ingestion (Hogan, 1971; Hogan-Warburg and Hogan, 1981). This would then be the time when the connection between the food-recognition and central hunger mechanisms develops (see figure 21.6). Hogan (1988) has discussed in detail the evidence on which

these conclusions are based and has reviewed similar evidence for the development of a hunger system in rat pups and kittens (see also Baerends-van Roon and Baerends, 1979; Blass, Hall, and Teicher, 1979; Hall and Williams, 1983).

Aggression and sex

The aggression system of an adult chicken consists of perceptual mechanisms that serve an "opponent" recognition function, various motor mechanisms that are used in fighting (including those that control threat display, leaping, wing flapping, kicking, and pecking), and a central mechanism that is sensitive to internal motivational factors (such as testosterone) and that coordinates the activation of the motor mechanisms. Kruijt (1964) showed that fighting develops out of hopping, which is a locomotory pattern that is not initially released by or directed toward other chicks. While hopping, chicks sometimes bump into each other by accident, and in the course of several days, hopping gradually becomes directed toward other chicks. Frontal threatening then starts to occur, and by the age of 3 weeks, pecking and kicking are added to aggressive interactions. Normal, well-coordinated fights are not seen until 2–3 months.

The sex system of a normal adult rooster consists of perceptual mechanisms that serve a "partner" recognition function; motor mechanisms for locomotion, copulation (which includes mounting, sitting, treading, pecking, and tail lowering), and various courtship displays, such as waltzing, wing flapping, tidbitting, and cornering; and a central mechanism that is sensitive to internal motivational factors such as testosterone and that coordinates the activation of the motor mechanisms. In small groups of junglefowl, Kruijt (1964) saw mounting and copulatory trampling (treading) on a model in a sitting position as early as 3–4 days, but such behavior was not common until weeks later. Full copulation with living partners did not occur before the males were 4 months old.

As in the dustbathing and hunger systems, the motor mechanisms and their coordination in the aggression and sex systems develop essentially normally even in animals that have been raised in social isolation. Several lines of evidence suggest that the neural circuits for the motor mechanisms in both systems are organized at least as early as 2 or 3 days after hatching and that the expression of aggressive and sexual behavior requires only the proper motivational state (Andrew, 1966; Evans, 1968; Hogan, 1988). Under normal circumstances, a sufficient level of external and internal causal factors is not reached until weeks or months after hatching.

Connections between the central coordinating mechanism for aggression and the motor mechanisms for aggressive behavior patterns develop prefunctionally. Although some aspects of the development of fighting under normal social conditions would allow a role for operant conditioning, Kruijt (1964) also found that junglefowl chicks raised in social isolation showed full-fledged fighting when confronted with each other at 1 week of age – that is, 2–4 weeks earlier than fighting is seen in group–raised chicks. Social experience thus seems to inhibit the expression of aggressive behavior. The situation for the sex system is somewhat different. The copulatory motor patterns seem to be connected to the central mechanism prefunctionally, but the courtship displays of waltzing and tidbitting are seen first in other contexts, and only gradually come to be controlled by the sex system as a result of specifically sexual experience. Here an operant conditioning model fits the data well (Hogan, 1988; Kruijt, 1964).

Finally, the perceptual mechanisms for recognizing the "opponent" or the "partner" develop to a certain extent prefunctionally, although both are also influenced by functional experience. For example, the chicks mentioned above that were raised in social isolation for a week recognized other chicks as "opponents" prefunctionally. Nonetheless, isolated chicks of the same age can also direct aggressive behavior toward a light bulb hanging in the cage; and older isolated cockerels are often seen to direct aggressive behavior toward their own tails (Kruijt, 1964). Development of the perceptual mechanism for "partner" recognition seems to be even more dependent on functional experience. For example, junglefowl chicks become sexually dimorphic at about 1 month of age. By about 2 months, young males begin to show incomplete sexual behavior toward conspecifics, but such behavior is directed equally often toward males and toward females. Only gradually, as a result of specifically sexual experience, does sexual behavior become directed exclusively toward females (Kruijt, 1964). The development of the partner recognition me-

chanism has also been intensively studied for many years in the context of filial and sexual imprinting, and there is extensive evidence documenting the influence of both prefunctional and functional factors (Bischof, 1994; Bolhuis, 1991; Lorenz, 1935/1970). Some of these studies are discussed below.

Some Principles of Development

Development of the nervous system

Changes in neural structure and/or connections between neurons must be the cause of behavioral development. It is therefore useful to consider what is happening at the neural level during development. Those processes can give us some insight into corresponding changes in behavior. Brown, Hopkins, and Keynes (1991) have divided brain development, at the cellular level, into four major stages: (1) genesis of nerve cells (proliferation, specification, and migration); (2) establishing connections (axon and dendritic growth, and synapse formation); (3) modifying connections (nerve cell death and reorganization of initial inputs); and (4) adult plasticity (learning and nerve growth after injury). Stages 3 and 4 are the most relevant to our question.

During fetal development, many more nerve cells are formed than will be found in the adult brain. These nerve cells all send out axons and establish connections with target cells (other neurons and muscle cells), but a large proportion of them die before the synapses become functional. The mechanism underlying this process involves electrical activity in the nerve cells and their targets, but it is still not fully understood (see Oppenheim, 1991). It is thought that neuronal death may serve to eliminate errors in the initial pattern of connections. The axons of the cells that remain are often found to have more extensive branches and to contact more post-synaptic cells than they will in the adult. The mechanisms that bring about axonal remodeling – that is, the elimination and reorganization of these terminal branches – also involve activity in the neurons. In brief it has been shown that specific spatial and temporal patterns of electrical activity in both the nerve cells and their target cells are necessary for functional connections to form between them:

"cells that fire together wire together" (Shatz, 1992, p. 64).

The process of axonal remodeling occurs both pre- and postnatally, but it is essentially irreversible. Once the axons have established functional connections with other neurons or muscles, those connections appear to be a permanent part of neural organization. The mechanisms that are responsible for adult plasticity involve facilitation or inhibition of synaptic transmission and the growth of dendritic spines, which presumably correlates with the formation of new synapses (Bolhuis, 1994; Brown et al., 1991; see also DeVoogd, 1994, for a discussion of neurogenesis in adult birds). Whether these changes are reversible remains a matter of conjecture.

The work of Hubel and Wiesel established that visual stimulation plays a vital role in the development of the mammalian visual system (see Blakemore, 1973, and Wiesel, 1982, for reviews). They showed, for example, that normal development of the connections between cells of the lateral geniculate nucleus and the visual cortex in the cat requires binocular visual stimulation soon after the kitten's eyes open. Allowing a kitten to see with only one eye at a time during the critical period results in most cortical cells' being responsive to stimulation from one eye only, whereas binocular stimulation results in most cortical cells' being responsive to stimulation from both eyes. These results were interpreted in terms of the eyes' competing for control of cells in the cortex and are an example of axonal remodeling. They were important because they showed that the organization of a sensory system was actually driven by stimulation from the environment. They also provided a model for how the perceptual mechanisms underlying bird song learning and filial and sexual imprinting might develop (see Bischof, 1994; Bolhuis, 1994; DeVoogd, 1994).

The neural activity responsible for axonal remodeling in the visual cortex is triggered by stimuli originating in the environment after the kitten is born and has opened its eyes. More recently, other investigators have asked whether neural activity is also necessary for neural connections to form in utero, and, if so, how this activity is instigated. Shatz (1992) and her collaborators, for example, have looked at axonal remodeling in the lateral geniculate nucleus of the cat, which occurs before

birth. They found that the same kind of action-potential activity is necessary for developing normal connections from the retina to the lateral geniculate as is later necessary for normal connections to form in the cortex. Rather than being instigated by stimulation from the external world, however, the neural activity was caused by patterns of spontaneous neural firing. How these waves of activity are generated remains to be discovered.

These two cases of axonal remodeling illustrate the difference between development based on functional experience (organization of the visual cortex) and development that occurs prefunctionally (organization of the lateral geniculate nucleus). What is important in the present context, however, is that the mechanisms for synaptic change are the same before and after birth, and it is irrelevant for the connection being formed whether the neural activity arises from exogenous or endogenous sources. In fact, the same connection can be formed in either way. Some behavioral examples will be used to illustrate this point in the next section.

Critical periods, irreversibility, and the concept of prefunctional

Groothuis (1992, 1994) found that the oblique posture in the black-headed gull developed normally when a gull was reared either in social isolation or in large social groups, but that it sometimes developed abnormally when a gull was raised with only two or three peers. One can suppose that under circumstances of social isolation, endogenously produced patterns of neural firing provide the information necessary to develop the normal connections in the motor mechanism responsible for the form of the display, prefunctionally. When peers are present, functional social experience provides the information. Performance of precursors of the display often leads to reactions by the other gulls. These reactions, in turn, provide additional neural stimulation which could interfere with endogenously produced patterns and thus lead to different (abnormal) connections' being formed in the motor mechanism. If these connections require repeated stimulation to form, the probability that the average experience will be "correct" is greater in a large group than in a small group, where the effects of the behavior of one abnormal individual companion would be relatively greater. This line of reasoning suggests that functional and prefunctional "experience" provide alternative routes for the control of behavior system development, a suggestion that can also account for some of the results for the development of the aggression system in chickens reviewed above.

Individuals of most species of song birds require exposure to the species' song when young in order to be able to develop the species-typical song when adult. The early phase involves development of a perceptual mechanism, often called a template, and the later phase involves development of the motor mechanism responsible for the production of the song (DeVoogd, 1994; Marler, 1976). One of the interesting aspects of the perceptual phase of song learning is the very large differences among species with respect to what kind of experience is needed for an adequate template to develop. At one extreme, a male cowbird, raised in social isolation, will develop a normal species' song (King and West, 1977), whereas a chaffinch or white-crowned sparrow, raised similarly, will develop a song that at best contains only a few species-specific elements (Marler, 1976; Thorpe, 1961). On the other hand, the time at which hearing the species' song is effective for learning is much more restricted in the white-crowned sparrow than it is in the chaffinch. Likewise, if socially isolated males are played variants of the typical species' song, or indeed songs of other species, or even pure tones, some species are able to learn only the song of their own species, whereas other species are able to learn a much wider range of sound patterns. Similar species differences are also characteristic of the range of stimuli to which young birds will imprint and the time at which these stimuli are effective (Lorenz, 1935/1970). In all cases, however, a perceptual mechanism develops that serves a species-recognition function.

One way to understand how so many apparently different ways can lead to a similar functional outcome is to suppose that once certain kinds of structural change have occurred in the development of a perceptual mechanism, further change is no longer possible (crystalization, consolidation, irreversibility). It then follows that the timing of triggering events becomes crucial in determining which events will affect development. In a particular species of songbird, for example, one can imagine that, if genetically triggered events occur in the percep-

tual mechanism for song recognition before the young bird can hear, then the perceptual mechanism is fixed, prefunctionally, in that species, and posthatching experience can no longer have an effect. If the triggering events are delayed, however, the posthatching experience of the bird can provide the trigger. In this way, the same type of perceptual mechanism can be used for either "innate" or "learned" song recognition.

The timing of events that trigger irreversible changes in developing behavior mechanisms can also explain some apparent differences between perceptual and motor mechanisms. It is noteworthy that, without exception, the motor mechanisms of the behavior systems discussed above all develop prefunctionally, whereas all the perceptual mechanisms require at least some functional experience in order to achieve the normal adult form. This fact might suggest that there are some fundamental differences in the causal factors responsible for the development of perceptual and motor mechanisms. Such a conclusion is unlikely to be true because, in both cases, the organization of neural or neuromotor connections depends on particular spatiotemporal patterns of neural activity that can be generated either endogenously or exogenously. Prior to birth, most of the causal factors would be endogenous, although external stimulation may play a role in some cases (e.g., the auditory system in ducks: Gottlieb, 1978). After birth, both internal and external factors could be important. The fact that most of the motor mechanisms we have considered develop prefunctionally very likely reflects the fact that motor mechanisms generally become organized earlier in development than perceptual mechanisms (Hogan, 1994b).

It is tempting to speculate that development of behavior mechanisms that involves the elimination and reorganization of terminal axon branches (axonal remodeling) is essentially irreversible. The critical period then becomes the time at which the axonal remodeling occurs; it would depend on all the factors that can affect the timing of the remodeling. The production of new synapses continues to occur throughout life and could modulate the structure of behavior mechanisms after the critical period has passed. (Some readers will note that these ideas have some similarities to a proposal by Greenough, Black, and Wallace (1987) that different neural mechanisms have evolved for brain systems that serve different functions. They distinguish between experience-expectant and experience-dependent neural systems. However, as I have discussed in detail elsewhere (Hogan, 1994b), their view proposes a functional explanation for a causal phenomenon (see also Bolhuis, 1994). My proposal is considerably broader and is congruent with the putative neural mechanisms underlying it.)

Finally, it must be clear that I use the word *prefunctional* in many places where others would say *innate*. It is logically consistent to talk about behavior development that is prefunctional (or innate) versus behavior development that is learned when the criterion is the absence or presence of functional experience. (I prefer the word *prefunctional* because *innate* has too many additional meanings.) I think it is important to show how behavior that can be classified as prefunctional still presents interesting developmental problems that can be investigated in a causal framework. Nonetheless, it should be emphasized that any particular structural change could be triggered by genes or by the experience of reinforcement. The change itself cannot be classified as innate or learned because it could have been triggered either way, and it does not matter which way actually occurred.

Learning and development

The changes in the structure of behavior that occur as the individual goes from a fertilized egg, to birth, to maturity, and finally death, are brought about by the complex effects of genes and the environment on the developing organism. Learning, as studied by experimental psychologists, is one of the processes that cause changes in behavioral structure, but there is no generally accepted conception of how learning differs from other developmental processes (see Balsam and Silver, 1994; Shettleworth, 1994). We have seen above that the biochemical processes responsible for synapse strengthening are basically the same for all aspects of development ("cells that fire together, wire together"), and that these processes are all determined by "experience" that can originate either internally or externally. Thus, events at the cellular level provide no theoretical basis for separating learning from other developmental processes.

Nonetheless, as discussed in the previous section, most examples of what the majority of people (including psychologists) would consider learning fall into the category of changes in the structure of behavior due to *functional* experience. In this context, the phrase *functional experience* means all experience directly relevant to the change in behavior being considered. It thus includes habituation, sensitization, and Pavlovian conditioning, as well as instrumental, goal-directed learning.

If we accept this definition, we can go one step further and ask whether the structures that are changing might not provide a good basis for classifying different types of learning. That is what I will do in this last section. The structures that change as the animal develops are the perceptual, central, and motor mechanisms and the connections between them. I will first consider the perceptual mechanisms, then the motor mechanisms, and finally various connections among the behavior mechanisms.

Development of perceptual mechanisms has been studied most intensively in the ethological literature with respect to imprinting and song learning. In both cases, exposure *per se* to an appropriate stimulus leads to the formation of a "schema" (Lorenz, 1935/1970), or a "template" (DeVoogd, 1994; Marler, 1976), respectively. There is evidence that external factors such as social interaction can influence what is learned (see Clayton, 1994, ten Cate, 1994), but de Vos and van Kampen (1993) have suggested that social interaction is a special case of directing the attention of an animal toward particular stimuli. In the psychological literature, it has been suggested that exposure to a stimulus (situation) can lead to the formation of "cognitive maps" (Tolman, 1948), "cell assemblies" (Hebb, 1949), and "neuronal models" (Sokolov, 1960). All these perceptual mechanisms are supposed to form because different aspects of the stimulus always have the same relationship to each other, and repeated experience of these relationships leads to the formation of a neural representation (e.g., Hebb, 1949). A modern "connectionist" model of how such representations could form has been proposed by McLaren, Kaye, and Mackintosh (1989; see also McLaren, 1994). This conception can also be applied to the formation of "memories" and "ideas," which are also examples of perceptual mechanisms.

Development of motor mechanisms proceeds somewhat differently. In one of the best studied examples, song learning, the bird learns to adjust its motor output to match the image (template) it has previously formed. Auditory feedback is essential for this adjustment, because deafened birds never learn to produce any song that approaches normal song (Konishi, 1965). Hinde (1970) suggested that sounds produced by the bird that matched the image would be reinforced, whereas other sounds would extinguish. In this way, a normal song could develop in much the same way as an experimenter originally "shapes" a rat to press a lever (Skinner, 1953). It seems likely that the learning of skilled movements proceeds similarly, with the feedback from the instructor providing the reinforcement. It should be noted that in these cases reinforcement selects out bits of motor behavior, but that the actual formation of the motor mechanism requires repeated experience of sequences of those bits: Practice makes perfect.

Most cases of operant conditioning do not involve the shaping of a response (formation of a motor mechanism). Rather, motor mechanisms that already exist become attached to specific central mechanisms. For example, reinforcing a keypeck with food leads to a connection of the motor mechanism for pecking with the hunger system, while reinforcing with water leads to a connection with the thirst system. Schiller (1949/1957) reported the results of studies of problem solving by chimps. He noted that many of the behavior patterns used by his chimps to procure food that was placed out of reach were the same manipulative patterns that had first appeared spontaneously and prefunctionally. He suggested that these patterns could be considered operant responses that were used to solve the problem, and that they were reinforced when the chimp was successful. In the terminology used here, we could say that the originally independent motor mechanisms responsible for the various observed behavior patterns became connected to the hunger system as a result of operant reinforcement. The function of the reinforcer in all these cases is to activate the central mechanism so that it and the motor mechanism are active at the same time; under these conditions, a connection between the central and motor mechanisms can form.

Classical conditioning generally involves the development of a connection between a perceptual and a central mechanism. There are numerous examples of complex, species-typical behaviors that become released by previously neutral stimuli that develop their effectiveness by means of a classical conditioning procedure. For instance, Adler and

Hogan (1963) paired the presentation of a weak electric shock with a mirror to a male Siamese fighting fish and showed that full aggressive display could be conditioned to the shock. In a similar way, Farris (1967) conditioned the courtship behavior of Japanese quail to a red light; this situation has now been examined much more extensively by Domjan (1994). These and many other cases exemplify the development of a connection between a perceptual mechanism and a set of behaviors as a result of a classical conditioning procedure. They do not, however, distinguish between a connection between a perceptual mechanism and a central mechanism or directly between a perceptual mechanism and a complex motor mechanism.

There are some cases in which a connection between a perceptual mechanism and a central mechanism is directly implicated. For example, Wasserman (1973) looked at the behavior of young chicks tested in a cool environment. The chicks were trained by being exposed to a lighted key for several seconds and then to presentation of heat from a heat lamp. After several pairings of the light and the heat, the chicks began to approach the key when it lighted up and showed pecking and snuggling movements to it. These behaviors were never shown to the heat lamp itself (which was suspended above the chicks, out of reach). Pecking and snuggling movements are behaviors that belong to the filial system of a young chick, and are shown when the chick solicits brooding from a mother hen (Hogan, 1974). Wasserman's results thus imply that the perceptual mechanism for the lighted key became connected to the filial system in the young chick, and that the presentation of this stimulus to a cold chick elicited brooding solicitation movements. Other similar examples are discussed by Hogan (1988).

Modern accounts of association learning posit that certain temporal relationships between two events lead to an association between the two events (Dickinson, 1980). One event is usually the occurrence of a neutral stimulus, while the other event is the occurrence of some salient stimulus. The salient stimulus is generally salient because it is already connected to some central mechanism. Although it is generally assumed that it is the representations of the two events that become associated, it is also possible that the representation of the neutral event becomes associated with (attached to) the central mechanism that makes the second event salient.

Which connection is formed may lead to different predictions of experimental outcomes. For example, van Kampen (1993) has presented data on filial imprinting suggesting that the formation of the object-recognition perceptual mechanism depends on simple exposure to the stimulus. The perceptual mechanism can become attached to the central filial mechanism only when the filial mechanism is active (i.e., when the chick is in the motivational state for imprinting). His results suggest that blocking and overshadowing, two phenomena typical of association learning, are seen in the formation of the perceptual-central connection, but not in the formation of the perceptual mechanism itself. It seems quite possible that typical association learning phenomena are in general seen only in perceptual-central connections, and that other phenomena may be typical of other types of connections.

In conclusion, I would maintain that an understanding of the phenomena of learning can be reached only when the type of structures involved in the learning are specified. Traditionally, distinctions between types of learning have been made in terms of the experimental procedures used rather than the structures and processes that actually control performance. Recent accounts of instrumental learning, however, posit specific behavioral structures (representations) and interpret results in terms of connections (associations) formed between these structures (e.g., Colwill and Rescorla, 1986; Dickinson and Balleine, 1994; Rescorla, 1994). Although some of these ideas date back to Tolman (1949a, 1949b), it is only recently that they have been incorporated into contemporary learning theory. Most of these behavioral structures have direct counterparts with the structures depicted in figure 21.6 in this paper, and I have made some suggestions for the interpretation of certain learning phenomena in my terms. Further exploration of the mutual implications of these various formulations should prove highly fruitful, and could lead to a much more comprehensive theory of changes in behavior due to specific experience.

Acknowledgment

Preparation of this article and the research from my laboratory reported herein were supported by an operating grant from the Natural Sciences and Engineering Research Council of Canada. Correspondence should be addressed to J. A. Hogan, Department of Psychology, University of Toronto, Toronto, ON, Canada M5S 1A1.

References

Adler, N. T., and Hogan, J. A. (1963) Classical conditioning and punishment of an instinctive response in *Betta splendens*, *Animal Behaviour*, 11, 351–4.

Andrew, R. J. (1966) Precocious adult behaviour in the young chick, *Animal Behaviour*, 14, 485–500.

Baerends, G. P. (1975) An evaluation of the conflict hypothesis as an explanatory principle for the evolution of displays. In G. P. Baerends, C. Beer, and A. Manning (eds), *Function and Evolution in Behaviour* (pp. 187–227), Oxford: Oxford University Press.

Baerends, G. P. (1976) The functional organisation of behaviour, *Animal Behaviour*, 24, 726–38.

Baerends-van Roon, J. M., and Baerends, G. P. (1979) The morphogenesis of the behaviour of the domestic cat, with a special emphasis on the development of prey-catching. *Verhandelingen der Koninklijke Nederlandse Akademie van Wetenschappen: Afd. Natuurkunde* (Tweede Reeks) [*Proceedings of the Royal Netherlands Academy of Sciences: Physics Section* (Second Series)], Part 72.

Balsam, P. D., and Silver, R. (1994) Behavioral change as a result of experience: Toward principles of learning and development. In J. A. Hogan and J. J. Bolhuis (eds), *Causal Mechanisms of Behavioural Development* (pp. 327–57), Cambridge: Cambridge University Press.

Bischof, H.-J. (1994) Sexual imprinting as a two-stage process. In J. A. Hogan and J. J. Bolhuis (eds), *Causal Mechanisms of Behavioural Development* (pp. 82–97), Cambridge: Cambridge University Press.

Blakemore, C. (1973) Environmental constraints on development in the visual system. In R. A. Hinde and J. Stevenson-Hinde (eds), *Constraints on Learning* (pp. 51–73), London: Academic Press.

Blass, E. M., Hall, W. G., and Teicher, M. H. (1979) The ontogeny of suckling and ingestive behaviors, *Progress in Psychobiology & Physiological Psychology*, 8, 243–99.

Bolhuis, J. J. (1991) Mechanisms of avian imprinting: A review, *Biological Reviews*, 66, 303–45.

Bolhuis, J. J. (1994) Neurobiological analyses of behavioural mechanisms in development. In J. A. Hogan and J. J. Bolhuis (eds), *Causal Mechanisms of Behavioural Development* (pp. 16–46), Cambridge: Cambridge University Press.

Brown, M. C., Hopkins, W. G., and Keynes, R. J. (1991) *Essentials of Neural Development*, Cambridge: Cambridge University Press.

Clayton, N. S. (1994) The influence of social interactions on the development of song and sexual preferences in birds. In

J. A. Hogan and J. J. Bolhuis (eds), *Causal Mechanisms of Behavioural Development* (pp. 98–115), Cambridge: Cambridge University Press.

Colwill, R. C., and Rescorla, R. A. (1986) Associative structures in instrumental learning. In G. H. Bower (ed.), *The Psychology of Learning and Motivation*, Vol. 20 (pp. 55–104), New York: Academic Press.

DeVoogd, T. (1994) The neural basis for the acquisition and production of bird song. In J. A. Hogan and J. J. Bolhuis (eds), *Causal Mechanisms of Behavioural Development* (pp. 49–81), Cambridge: Cambridge University Press.

de Vos, G. J., and van Kampen, H. S. (1993) Effects of primary imprinting on the subsequent development of secondary filial attachments in the chick, *Behaviour*, 125, 245–63.

Dickinson, A. (1980) *Contemporary Animal Learning Theory*, Cambridge: Cambridge University Press.

Dickinson, A., and Balleine, B. (1994) Motivational control of goal-directed action, *Animal Learning & Behavior*, 22, 1–18.

Domjan, M. (1994) Formulation of a behavior system for sexual conditioning, *Psychonomic Bulletin & Review*, 1, 421–8.

Evans, R. M. (1968) Early aggressive responses in domestic chicks, *Animal Behaviour*, 16, 24–8.

Farris, H. E. (1967) Classical conditioning of courting behavior in the Japanese quail (*Coturnix c. japonica*), *Journal of the Experimental Analysis of Behavior*, 10, 213–17.

Gottlieb, G. (1978) Development of species identification in ducklings: IV. Change in species-specific perception caused by auditory deprivation, *Journal of Comparative & Physiological Psychology*, 92, 375–87.

Greenough, W. T., Black, J. E., and Wallace, C. S. (1987) Experince and brain development, *Child Development*, 58, 539–59.

Groothuis, T. G. G. (1992) The influence of social experience on the development and fixation of the form of displays in the black-headed gull, *Animal Behaviour*, 43, 1–14.

Groothuis, T. G. G. (1994) The ontogeny of social displays: Interplay between motor development, development of motivational systems and social experience. In J. A. Hogan and J. J. Bolhuis (eds), *Causal Mechanisms of Behavioural Development* (pp. 183–211), Cambridge: Cambridge University Press.

Hall, W. G., and Williams, C. L. (1983) Suckling isn't feeding, or is it? A search for developmental continuities, *Advances in the Study of Behavior*, 13, 219–54.

Hebb, D. O. (1949) *The Organization of Behavior*, New York: Wiley.

Hinde, R. A. (1970) *Animal Behaviour: A Synthesis of Ethology and Comparative Psychology*, New York: McGraw-Hill.

Hogan, J. A. (1971) The development of a hunger system in young chicks, *Behaviour*, 39, 128–201.

Hogan, J. A. (1973a) Development of food recognition in young chicks: I. Maturation and nutrition, *Journal of Comparative & Physiological Psychology*, 83, 355–66.

Hogan, J. A. (1973b) How young chicks learn to recognize food. In R. A. Hinde and J. G. Stevenson-Hinde (eds), *Constraints on Learning* (pp. 119–39), London: Academic Press.

Hogan, J. A. (1974) Responses in Pavlovian conditioning studies, *Science*, 186, 156–7.

Hogan, J. A. (1977) The ontogeny of food preferences in chicks and other animals. In L. M. Barker, M. Best, and M. Domjan (eds), *Learning Mechanisms in Food Selection* (pp. 71–97), Waco, TX: Baylor University Press.

Hogan, J. A. (1984) Pecking and feeding in chicks, *Learning & Motivation*, 15, 360–76.

Hogan, J. A. (1988) Cause and function in the development of behavior systems. In E. M. Blass (ed.), *Handbook of Behavioral Neurobiology*, Vol. 9 (pp. 63–106), New York: Plenum.

Hogan, J. A. (1994a) The concept of cause in the study of behavior. In J. A. Hogan and J. J. Bolhuis (eds), *Causal Mechanisms of Behavioural Development* (pp. 3–15), Cambridge: Cambridge University Press.

Hogan, J. A. (1994b) Development of behavior systems. In J. A. Hogan and J. J. Bolhuis (eds), *Causal Mechanisms of Behavioural Development* (pp. 242–64), Cambridge: Cambridge University Press.

Hogan, J. A., Honrado, G. I., and Vestergaard, K. (1991) Development of a behavior system: Dustbathing in the Burmese red junglefowl (*Gallus gallus spadiceus*): II. Internal factors, *Journal of Comparative Psychology*, 105, 269–73.

Hogan, J. A., and Roper, T. J. (1978) A comparison of the properties of different reinforcers, *Advances in the Study of Behavior*, 8, 155–255.

Hogan, J. A., and van Boxel, F. (1993) Causal factors controlling dustbathing in Burmese red junglefowl: Some results and a model, *Animal Behaviour*, 46, 627–35.

Hogan-Warburg, A. J., and Hogan, J. A. (1981) Feeding strategies in the development of food recognition in young chicks, *Animal Behaviour*, 29, 143–54.

King, A. P., and West, M. J. (1977) Species identification in the North American cowbird: Appropriate responses to abnormal song, *Science*, 195, 1002–4.

Konishi, M. (1965) The role of auditory feedback in the control of vocalizations in the white-crowned sparrow, *Zeitschrift für Tierpsychologie*, 22, 770–83.

Kruijt, J. P. (1964) Ontogeny of social behaviour in Burmese red junglefowl (*Gallus gallus spadiceus*), *Behaviour* (Suppl. 9), pp. 1–201.

Lorenz, K. (1970) Companions as factors in the bird's environment. In R. Martin (tr.), *Studies in Animal and Human Behaviour*, Vol. 1 (pp. 101–258), London: Methuen. (Original work published 1935.)

Marler, P. (1976) Sensory templates in species-specific behavior. In J. Fentress (ed.), *Simpler Networks and Behavior* (pp. 314–29), Sunderland, MA: Sinauer.

Marler, P. (1987) Sensitive periods and the roles of specific and general sensory stimulation in birdsong learning. In

J. P. Rauschecker and P. Marler (eds), *Imprinting and Cortical Plasticity* (pp. 99–135), New York: Wiley.

McDougall, W. (1928) *An Outline of Psychology*, London: Methuen.

McLaren, I. P. L. (1994) Representation development in associative systems. In J. A. Hogan and J. J. Bolhuis (eds), *Causal Mechanisms of Behavioural Development* (pp. 377–402), Cambridge: Cambridge University Press.

McLaren, I. P. L., Kaye, H., and Mackintosh, N. J. (1989) An associative theory of the representation of stimuli: Applications to perceptual learning and latent inhibition. In R. G. M. Morris (ed.), *Parallel Distributed Processing – Implications for Psychology and Neurobiology* (pp. 102–30), Oxford: Oxford University Press.

Oppenheim, R. W. (1991) Cell death during development of the nervous system, *Annual Review of Neuroscience*, **14**, 453–501.

Petherick, J. C., and Duncan, I. J. H. (1989) Behaviour of young domestic fowl directed towards different substrates, *British Poultry Science*, **30**, 229–38.

Rescorla, R. A. (1994) Transfer of instrumental control mediated by a devalued outcome, *Animal Learning & Behavior*, **22**, 27–33.

Schiller, P. H. (1957) Manipulative patterns in the chimpanzee. In C. H. Schiller (ed.), *Instinctive Behavior* (pp. 264–87), New York: International Universities Press. (Originally published in 1949.)

Shatz, C. J. (1992, September) The developing brain, *Scientific American*, **267** (3), 60–7.

Shettleworth, S. J. (1994) The varieties of learning in development: Toward a common framework. In J. A. Hogan and J. J. Bolhuis (eds), *Causal Mechanisms in Behavioural Development* (pp. 358–76), Cambridge: Cambridge University Press.

Skinner, B. F. (1953) *Science and Human Behavior*, New York: Macmillan.

Sokolov, E. N. (1960) Neuronal models and the orienting reflex. In M. A. B. Brazier (ed.), *The Central Nervous System and Behavior* (pp. 187–276), New York: Josiah Macy Foundation.

ten Cate, C. (1994) Perceptual mechanisms in imprinting and song learning. In J. A. Hogan and J. J. Bolhuis (eds), *Causal Mechanisms of Behavioural Development* (pp. 116–46), Cambridge: Cambridge University Press.

Thorpe, W. (1961) *Bird Song*, Cambridge: Cambridge University Press.

Timberlake, W. (1983) The functional organization of appetitive behavior: Behavior systems and learning. In M. D. Zeiler and P. Harzem (eds), *Advances in Analysis of Behaviour, Vol. 3: Biological Factors in Learing* (pp. 177–221), New York: Wiley.

Timberlake, W. (1994) Behavior systems, associationism, and Pavlovian conditioning, *Psychonomic Bulletin & Review*, **1**, 405–20.

Tinbergen, N. (1951) *The Study of Instinct*, London: Oxford University Press.

Tinbergen, N. (1952) Derived activities: Their causation, biological significance, origin and emancipation during evolution, *Quarterly Review of Biology*, **27**, 1–32.

Tolman, E. C. (1948) Cognitive maps in rats and men, *Psychological Review*, **55**, 189–208.

Tolman, E. C. (1949a) There is more than one kind of learning, *Psychological Review*, **56**, 144–55.

Tolman, E. C. (1949b) The nature and function of wants, *Psychological Review*, **56**, 357–69.

van Kampen, H. S. (1993) *An Analysis of the Learning Process Underlying Filial Imprinting*. Unpublished doctoral dissertation, University of Groningen, The Netherlands.

van Liere, D. W. (1992) The significance of fowls' bathing in dust, *Animal Welfare*, **1**, 187–202.

van Liere, D. W., and Bokma, S. (1987) Short-term feather maintenance as a function of dust-bathing in laying hens, *Applied Animal Behaviour Science*, **18**, 197–204.

van Liere, D. W., Kooijman, J., and Wiepkema, P. R. (1990) Dustbathing behaviour of laying hens as related to quality of dustbathing material, *Applied Animal Behaviour Science*, **26**, 127–41.

Vestergaard, K. (1982) Dust-bathing in the domestic fowl – diurnal rhythm and dust deprivation, *Applied Animal Ethology*, **8**, 487–95.

Vestergaard, K., and Hogan J. A. (1992) The development of a behavior system: Dustbathing in the Burmese red junglefowl: III. Effects of experience on stimulus preference, *Behaviour*, **121**, 215–30.

Vestergaard, K., Hogan, J. A., and Kruijt, J. P. (1990) The development of a behavior system: Dustbathing in the Burmese red junglefowl: I. The influence of the rearing environment on the organization of dustbathing, *Behaviour*, **112**, 99–116.

Vestergaard, K., Kruijt, J. P., and Hogan, J. A. (1993) Feather pecking and chronic fear in groups of red junglefowl: Its relations to dustbathing, rearing environment and social status, *Animal Behaviour*, **45**, 1127–40.

Wasserman, E. A. (1973) Pavlovian conditioning with heat reinforcement produces stimulus-directed pecking in chicks, *Science*, **181**, 875–7.

Wiesel, T. N. (1982) Postnatal development of the visual cortex and the influence of the environment, *Nature*, **299**, 583–91.

Author Index

Subject Index